People's History and Socialist Theory

History Workshop Series

General Editor
Raphael Samuel, *Ruskin College, Oxford*

Already published
Village Life and Labour edited by Raphael Samuel
Miners, Quarrymen and Saltworkers edited by Raphael Samuel
*Rothschild Buildings: Life in an East End Tenement Block
1887–1920* Jerry White
East End Underworld: Chapters in the Life of Arthur Harding
Raphael Samuel

ROUTLEDGE & KEGAN PAUL
London, Boston and Henley

edited by

Raphael Samuel

Tutor in Social History and Sociology
Ruskin College, Oxford

People's History and Socialist Theory

First published in 1981
by Routledge & Kegan Paul Ltd
39 Store Street, London WC1E 7DD,
9 Park Street, Boston, Mass. 02108, USA, and
Broadway House, Newtown Road,
Henley-on-Thames, Oxon RG9 1EN
Printed in Great Britain by
Lowe & Brydone Ltd.

British Library Cataloguing in Publication Data

People's history and socialist theory. - (History
workshop series).
1. History - Philosophy
I. Samuel, Raphael   II. Series
901   D16.9   80-41391

ISBN 0 7100 0765 5
ISBN 0 7100 0652 7 Pbk

Contents

viii *Contents*

Britain's most distinct contribution to Marxist and socialist
thought is arguably in the field of history, and recent years
have seen a very large expansion of work in this field, as
can be seen by the wide readership for the work of such
historians as Christopher Hill, Eric Hobsbawm, E.P, Thompson
and Shiela Rowbotham; by the publication of outstanding and
innovatory work by a large number of younger historians;
by the vitality of the social history journals - *Past and
Present*, *History Workshop*, *Oral History* and *Social History*;
by the flourishing state of the regional labour history
societies, notably those in Lancashire, Sheffield and South
Wales; by the large amount of historical material appearing
in the form of cultural studies and by the extensive coverage
of historical work in the pages of the labour and socialist
press.

One of the striking features of this work is how much of
it is being nurtured outside the universities and polytechnics,
or on their extra-mural fringes: in WEA groups, such as the
'People's autobiography of Hackney' whose work is discussed
in this volume, in community arts projects, in women's
studies groups, and in the work of independent worker-
historians - one might instance John Gorman's *Banner Bright*,
a pioneering exploration of popular art, Malcolm Pitt's
The World on Our Backs (a history of the Kent miners by one
of them), and the work of A.L. Lloyd and Ewan MacColl on
the history of folk song. Retrieval projects have also taken
inspiration from this source, as in the Labour History Museum
in Limehouse, the Miners' Library in Swansea, and Eddie and
Ruth Frow's 'Working Class Movements Library' in Manchester,
a remarkable collection of nineteenth- and twentieth-century
source materials collected, as a labour of love, by a retired
engineer and a school teacher. Some of the most ambitious
historical work in recent years - e.g. Ronald Fraser's
Blood of Spain, a massive oral history of the Spanish Civil
War written by a novelist turned historian - has been produced
in proud independence of the academy, challenging both the
form of academic historical production and its content; while
within the universities one can see determined attempts to
escape from institutionally defined lines of specialisation and
sub-specialism. In another sphere one could point to the
importance of history in socialist work in the arts: plays such
as Red Ladder's *Taking our Time*; films such as Kevin

Brownlow's *Winstanley*, and television productions such as
Garnett and Loach's *Days of Hope* have probably done as much
to popularise a socialist interrogation of history as all the work
undertaken in more traditional historical modes; while John
Arden and Margaretta D'Arcy's *Non Stop Connolly Show*, a
twelve-part cycle of plays, set in the years of the Second
International, represents a notably ambitious attempt, through
theatre, to extend an understanding of the dialectics of
socialist politics.

It is both a weakness and a strength of this work that it is
being fragmented into entirely separate discourses, with, at
one extreme, the global synthesis of Perry Anderson's
Lineages of the Absolutist State, or Hindess and Hirst's
Pre-Capitalist Modes of Production, and, at the other, a
materialist analysis of the *lumpenproletariat* in a single London
street (Jerry White's recent 'Campbell Bunk', *History Workshop
Journal* No 7, November 1979). Feminist history groups,
community-based publishing projects, local history workshops,
regional labour history societies, oral history groups,
independent writers and specialist scholars, each pursue
their particular projects, sometimes with outstanding results –
but with little reference to each other; while in another sphere
entirely, a ferocious discussion is going on among socialists
about the philosophical foundations of historical enquiry. This
book is an attempt to bring these different kinds of work into
dialogue with one another; to take stock of work undertaken
in the recent period; to explore, or at any rate indicate, some
of the main new lines which an oppositional history needs to
pursue; and to look at the political and idealogical circumstances
shaping the direction of historical work, both in the past and
in the present. In all there are fifty-two pieces, covering a
wide range of both problems and perspectives. They are
drawn from a History Workshop held in December 1969 at
Ruskin College, Oxford, and attended by some 1,000 people,
where many of these issues were rehearsed. The papers have
been extended in the light of the discussion and criticism
directed at them, and bibliographies added to make the book
serviceable to those who will use it as an introduction to the
work of British socialist historians.

A feature of the book – as of the Workshop – is its
internationality, as can be seen from the strong contributions
on African history; the grouping of pieces on fascism and
anti-fascism; the contributions on French labour history and
feminist history in the United States; and the articles by
Hans Medick on the transition from feudalism to capitalism,
and Alf Lüdtke on the Prussian state. Another feature of the
book is the contribution of feminism, and its attention to some
of the leading questions raised, for socialist historians, by
the women's movement. Finally one might mention that the
contributions to the book, like those which appear in *History
Workshop Journal*, are in no sense confined to the ranks of

professional historians. At the same time - again like the
Workshop - the book draws on, and speaks to, the full
resources of scholarship. We hope it will indicate some of
the richness and variety of work being undertaken within,
or close to, the Marxist and socialist tradition; that it can
introduce this work to students and first-time readers; and
that it can encourage others to take part in the task of
constructing a history which speaks to the condition of our
time.

ACKNOWLEDGMENTS

Thanks are due to Tim Mason and Jane Caplan for proof-
reading; to Mary Kuper, for help in design; to Miranda
Chayfor, Glynis Cousins and Andrew Lincoln for translation;
and to Liz Fidlon and Carol Gardiner of Routledge for help
and support in getting this volume through at speed. The
woodcuts illustrating this book are from the veteran
American artist Lynd Ward and are taken from the collection
Storyteller Without Words, New York, 197 . The poem
'Questions of a studious working man', Svendborger Gedichte,
copyright 1939 by Malik-Verlag, London is reproduced by
permission of Eyre Methuen Ltd. London and Methuen and
Co. Ltd. New York. The translation from German is by
Michael Hamburger and is taken from the volume *Bertolt
Brecht Poems, 1913-1956*, edited by John Willett and Ralph
Manheim. Royalties for this book are being paid to *History
Workshop Journal*.

Editorial prefaces

People's history

Raphael Samuel

The term 'people's history' has had a long career, and covers
an ensemble of different writings. Some of them have been
informed by the idea of progress, some by cultural pessimism,
some by technological humanism, as in those histories of
'everyday things' which were so popular in 1930s Britain. The
subject matter of 'people's history' varies too, even if the
effort is always that of 'bringing the boundaries of history
closer to those of people's lives'. In some cases the focus is
on tools and technology, in others on social movements, in
yet others on family life. 'People's history' has gone under a
variety of different names - 'industrial history' in the 1900s
and the years of the Plebs League, 'natural history' in those
comparative ethnologies which arose in the wake of Darwin
(Marx called Volume 1 of *Capital* a 'natural history' of
capitalist production); 'Kulturgeschichte' (cultural history) in
those late-nineteenth-century studies of folkways to whose
themes the 'new' social history has recently been returning.
Today 'people's history' usually entails a subordination of the
political to the cultural and the social. But in one of its
earliest versions, splendidly represented in this country by
John Baxter's *New and Impartial History of England* (1796) -
the 830-page work of a radical Shoreditch artisan, dedicated
to his friends in jail - it was concerned rather with the
struggle for constitutional rights.

The term 'people's history' is one which could be applied,
in the present day, to a whole series of cultural initiatives
which are to be found mainly, though not exclusively, outside
the institutions of higher education, or on their extra-mural
fringes. It has been enthusiastically adopted by such
community based publishing projects as the 'People's autobiography of Hackney', whose work is discussed in these
pages by Ken Worpole, Jerry White and Stephen Yeo. Here
the emphasis - as in the History Workshop - has been on
democratising the act of historical production, enlarging the
constituency of historical writers, and bringing the experience
of the present to bear upon the interpretation of the past.
A good deal of oral history work falls within the same ambit.
'People's history' is also a term which might be retrospectively
applied to those various attempts to write an archive-based
'history from below' which have played such a large part in
the recent revival of English social history. As a movement,

this began outside the universities. One of the key texts -
The Making of the English Working Class (1963) - was
generated in the WEA classes of the West Riding. 'History on
the ground', the movement immediately preceding 'history from
below' - represented by such fine books as Maurice Beresford's
Lost Villages of England (1954) and Hoskin's *Making of the
English Landscape* (1955) - found its natural constituency
among those who were termed, in the 1950s, 'amateur
historians'; much the same is true of that kindred recent
enthusiasm, industrial archaeology. Nevertheless 'history from
below' has found an increasing resonance in the research
seminars, and one may note a gravitational shift in scholarly
interest from the national to the local or regional study, from
public institutions to domestic life, from the study of statecraft
to that of popular culture. Parallel shifts of attention appear to
be occurring in other countries in Europe, as a number of
papers in the present volume suggest. In France, where there
is a long-standing reading public for 'vie privée' and 'vie
quotidienne' (i.e. the history of everyday things), and where
social history has long enjoyed a far greater intellectual
prestige than it does in England, the change is less apparent.
Yet one may note, in the wake of the student revolt of 1968,
a shift in the *Annales* school from a 'history without people' -
a history built on the impersonal determinants of climate, soil,
and centuries-long cycles of change - to the kind of
ethno-history, dealing with individual experience at a particular
time and place, represented by Le Roy Ladurie's *Montaillou* and
Carnival; a new attention to outcast social groups (the
'marginal' and 'deviant'); and latterly (as Paul Thompson
reports in the present volume), a strong, if somewhat belated,
recognition of the claims of oral history.

People's history always represents some sort of attempt to
broaden the basis of history, to enlarge its subject matter,
make use of new raw materials and offer new maps of knowledge. Implicitly or explicitly it is oppositional, an alternative
to 'dry as dust' scholarship, and history as taught in the
schools. But the terms of that opposition are necessarily
different in different epochs and for different modes of work.
For J.R. Green, writing in the 1870s, the main enemy was what
he called 'drum and trumpet' history - i.e. the preoccupation
with wars and conquest. Against these his *Short History of the
English People* (1877) opposed the history of English civilisa-
tions, a history of society rather than of the state. As he
wrote in his famous preface:

> The aim of the following work is defined by its title;
> it is a history not of English kings or English conquests,
> but of the English People. . . . I have preferred to pass
> lightly and briefly over the details of foreign wars and
> diplomacies, the personal adventures of kings and nobles,
> the pomp of courts, or the intrigues of favourites, and to
> dwell at length on the incidents of that constitutional,

intellectual, and social advance, in which we read the
history of the nation itself. It is with this purpose
that I have devoted more space to Chaucer than to
Cressy, to Caxton than to the petty strife of Yorkist
and Lancastrian, to the Poor Law of Elizabeth than to
her victory at Cadiz, to the Methodist revival than to
the escape of the Young Pretender.

For Paul Lacombe (1839-1919), one of the intellectual forefathers of the *Annales* school, the chief enemy was the notion
of historical contingency, and the preoccupation of historians
with individual personalities and events. As against this -
'histoire événementielle' as the *Annales* historians were to call
it - he wanted history to be placed on a scientific footing and
to occupy itself with causal uniformities; even when studying
a particular subject - as in his own work on the family in
ancient Rome - the historian had to devote the major effort
to showing its place in an overall scheme of development.
Thierry, writing in the 1820s, was no less opposed to the
ruling historical orthodoxies of his day, but it was their
abstract reasoning which he reproached them with, the
'calculated dryness' of their philosophy. The alternative which
he pursued (much influenced by the novels and poems of Sir
Walter Scott) was that of immersing himself in medieval
ballads and ransacking the documents for concrete, pictorial
detail. He was, in fact, an early practitioner of what a recent
writer, in another context, has witheringly labelled 'resurrect-
ionism': i.e. attempting to bring the past to life again by
listening to the voices of the dead.

   People's history today is charactistically used to denote a
history which is local in scale, taking as its subject the region,
the township or the parish: in the case of the city, the
morphology of the individual quarter or suburb, or even of the
individual house and street. In the past, however, it was more
concerned with the broad lines of national development.
'Whatever value this book may have', writes A.L. Morton in
his preface to *The People's History of England* - a Marxist
work, first published by the Left Book Club in 1938 - 'must
be rather in the interpretation than in the novelty of the facts
it presents. . . . It sets out to give the reader a general
idea of the main lines of the movement of our history.' Much
the same might be said of J.R. Green's *Short History* which
takes its start from the 'peasant commonwealth's of Anglo-Saxon
times, and moves in measured sweep across the centuries.
Similarly Michelet, in his populist histories as in the profiles
he wrote of his time (*Tableau de France* and *Le Peuple*) was
concerned with the great collective forces shaping the destiny
of the French nation. He was interested in events as
illustrations of underlying social processes, in individuals as
representatives of movements and groups. His whole notion of
society was that of an organic historically derived unity, and
he saw the task of people's history as that of covering all

departments of human activity, following (as he wrote) industry and religion, law and art, as interrelated threads.
   The practitioners of what was called in Germany 'Kultur-geschichte' (cultural history), and in other countries historical anthropology, cultural sociology, or the history of 'civilisation', worked on an even longer time-span. Their subject matter was nothing less than universal history, whether in the sphere of material culture, mass psychology or popular religion. They were concerned to seek out a linear path of development, delving into the recesses of pre-history, and tracing the evolution of humanity through savagery and barbarism to civilisation. This was the version of people's history that was most highly regarded in the Plebs League, as can be seen from the Ruskin student paper on 'Worker-historians in the 1920s'. It offered a captivating sense of totality - 'not a partial history of facts . . . but an attempt . . . to understand how history worked'. Müller-Lyer's *History of Social Development* (translated into English in 1920) was a favourite text, the work of a disciple of Lamprecht. He believed that everything, from the evolution of tools to the rise of romantic love, could be reduced to world-wide uniformities: divergences were largely accidental or of a purely local character. The worker-historians of the 1910s and 1920s followed suit, and their histories - 'outline' histories such as Mark Starr's *A Worker Looks at History* - were global in scale and universal in their time-span, following the trajectory indicated by Engels, and exploring the origins of family, class and state.
   The main thrust of people's history in recent years has been towards the recovery of subjective experience. One might note, in oral history, the overwhelming interest in reconstituting the small details of everyday life; in local history, the shift from 'places' to 'faces', from topographical peculiarities to the quality of life; in labour history, the preoccupation with the more spontaneous forms of resistance. More generally one could note the enormous research ingenuity which has gone into attempting to capture the voice of the past - the cadences of vernacular speech, the tell-tale turns of phrase which can be gleaned from court records or anonymous letters. As in hermeneutics, the major effort is to present historical issues as they appeared to the actors at the time; to personalise the workings of large historical forces; to draw on contemporary vocabularies; to identify the faces in the crowd. Seventy or eighty years ago, by contrast, the whole attention of people's history was turned on the working of *impersonal* historical forces, located by some in climate and geography, by others in tools and technology, by yet others in biological necessity. Its leading feature was a kind of multi-layered determinism, in which contingency could be disregarded while necessity ruled in its stead. History was conceived of as an orderly, logical development, an inevitable

passage from lower to higher stages. In a conspectus like this, there was little patience for the small details of everyday life. As a Welsh miner told the Ruskin students: 'We weren't interested in whether so-and-so had sugar in his coffee or not. What interested us was how and why societies change.' This version of people's history invoked the authority of Marx, but it borrowed freely from the positivist sociology of Spencer and Comte as also, in another direction, from Darwinian biology. Folk-life studies in this period were conducted in the same spirit using the comparative method to situate myths in an evolutionary grid. The deterministic vision is no less apparent in the 'folk psychology' of Wundt - a kind of historical ethnography of mental characteristics and in those various theories of mass behaviour which make the individual a compulsive creature of instinct. The most deterministic history of all was that of human geography, which explained the character of peoples by reference to geography, climate and soil. In France it was influentially represented by Vidal de la Blache, in Britain by H.T. Buckle, whose *Civilisation in England* figures alongside the works of Marx, Engels, Darwin and Dietzgen in the standard book-lists of the Plebs League.

As a literary mode, people's history bears the enduring marks of both the aesthetic of realism and the romantic movement in literature. The 'discovery of the people' in late-eighteenth-century Europe - i.e. the discovery of popular ballads, and the use of folk-life materials to reconstitute the ancient past - was in the first place, as Peter Burke has argued in *Popular Culture in Early Modern Europe*, the work of literary scholars and poets, seeking in peasant culture an escape from the artificialities of the salons and the courts. Later, the emergence of people's history in France is part of a very much wider movement of literary sensibility to which the label of 'social remanticism' has been attached. Many of the early writers of people's history were self-conscious literary artists. Some wrote their history as epics, like Motley in his *Rise of the Dutch Republic*. Others found their poetry in the symbolical use of circumstantial detail, as Thierry put it, 'constantly filling the senses with the sharp detail of sight and sound'. E.P. Thompson's work shares both these characteristics, and his philippics against the abstractions of structuralism echo Thierry's thunderbolts against the 'calculated dryness' of the philosophers. Above all, the conceptual importance which Thompson and others give to 'experience' - the central point at issue in the debates around *The Poverty of Theory* - is clearly derived from the fundamental opposition which the Romantics made between reason and passion, imagination and mechanical science. The social realism of people's history may also be derived from the Romantic movement in poetry and art, especially from the ways'in which it was developed in 1830s and 1840s France. Michelet's *Le Peuple* (1846) - radical and democratic in its purposes,

realistic in its mode – is, on this view, absolutely at one with
the social realism of Victor Hugo's novels, or the peasant
paintings of Gustave Courbet: a tireless search for authenticity. In today's people's history it is not difficult to see
affinities to the documentary realism of the cinema, or the
social realism of television drama; while in a more symbolic
mode – what Isaac Deutscher has called 'Marxist realism' – an
aesthetic of the socially typical, and symbolic, is no less
apparent in such classics of socialist history as Marx's
Capital, Trotsky's *History of the Russian Revolution,* or the
work of Deutscher himself.

In a very different lineage, people's history may be seen
as one of the oldest forms of social science. It traces one of
its origins to the eighteenth-century Enlightenment, and in
particular to Vico, whose *Scienza Nuova* (1725) introduced
the whole notion of stages of historical development which
was to be so central for Michelet and for Marx. It was Vico,
too, who, in his portrait of the 'heroic states' of antiquity,
first set out a paradigm of class struggle:

> The whole life of these heroic states centres in the
> conflict between patricians and plebeians . . . the
> plebeians wishing always to change the state, the
> nobles to preserve it as it was. The patricians were
> better organized; they owned the land; they had the
> arms and the military discipline; they had a monopoly
> of public office and knowledge of law; they alone
> knew how to ascertain the will and win the favour of
> the gods; the solemn rites of marriage and burial were
> theirs alone; and they were bound by oath to keep the
> plebs in subjection. But it was inevitable that the plebs
> should press successively for land tenure, legal marriage,
> legitimate children, testamentary succession, citizenship,
> eligibility to office, and the sharing of the auspices, the
> key to all the rest. And it was inevitable that the ruling
> class should be compelled to admit the plebs to one after
> another of the rights which it had at first so jealously
> guarded.

People's history, whatever its particular subject matter, is
shaped in the crucible of politics, and penetrated by the
influence of ideology on all sides. In one version it is allied
with Marxism, in another with democratic liberalism, in yet
another with cultural nationalism, and it is difficult to dismiss
these couplings as illegitimate even where they may be mutually
exclusive. The main thrust of people's history has usually been
radical, yet the Left can make no proprietorial claim to it. In our
own time one might note the almost simultaneous appearance of
E.P. Thompson's *Making of the English Working Class* (1963) and
Peter Laslett's *World We Have Lost* (1965), the one a celebration
of popular insurrection, the other a Betjamenesque lament for the
vanished patriarchal family of old. Each, in its own way,
represents a revolt from 'dry as dust' scholarship and an

attempt to return history to its roots, yet the implicit politics in them could hardly be more opposed.

The 'people' of people's history have as many different shades of meaning as the term has usages. They are always majoritarian, but the connotations vary according to whether the pole of comparison is that of kings and commons (as it is in J.R. Green), rich and poor; or the 'educated' and those whom Michelet called the 'simples'. In one version of people's history – radical-democratic or Marxist – the people are constituted by relations of exploitation, in another (that of the folklorists) by cultural antinomies, in a third by political rule. The term also takes on quite different meanings within particular national traditions. In France, the nineteenth-century idea of the people was indelibly marked by the rhetoric of the Revolution, the term was inescapably associated with notions of class power. In England, with its long inheritance of popular constitutionalism, it was rather associated with the defence of political and social rights. In Germany, where folk-life studies ('Volkskunde') provided the chief idiom for people's history, in both its radical and conservative versions, the people were defined in terms of externality, as a folk community subject to alien influences and rule. For the folklorists 'the people' is fundamentally a peasantry, for sociologists it is the working class, while in democratic or cultural nationalism, it is coextensive with an ethnic stock.

The right-wing version of people's history is characteristically a history with the politics left out – as in Trevelyan's *English Social History* – a history devoid of struggle, devoid of ideas, but with a very strong sense of religion and of values. It is apt to idealise the family – 'a circle of loved, familiar faces' – and to interpret social relationships as reciprocal rather than exploitative. Class antagonisms may be admitted, but they are contained within a larger whole, and softened by cross-cutting ties. The characteristic location of right-wing people's history is in the 'organic' community of the past – the recent past in the case of Ronald Blythe's *Akenfield*, early modern England in Laslett's *World We Have Lost*, the free German peasants before the Carolingian conquest in Riehl's *Natural History of German Life*. The ideology is determinedly anti-modern, with urban life and capitalism as alien intrusions on the body politic, splintering the age-old solidarities of 'traditional' life. In the case of Riehl, the father of German ethnology, and the founder of 'Volkskunde' as an empirical science, the conservative implications are quite explicit. Writing in the aftermath of the failed revolution of 1848, he advocated decentralisation, a return to the system of feudal estates, and a revival of the traditional family 'in which the key virtues were authority, piety and simplicity'. G.K. Chesterton – a liberal populist turned Catholic – is more ambiguous: he had a keen sense of the dignity of the poor, and his *Short History of England* (1917) retains an anti-plutocratic edge: medieval England 'possessed many democratic ideals . . . it . . . was

. . . moving towards a more really democratic progress'. But
there is no doubt that he regarded 'Protestantism', 'Rationalism'
and the 'Modern World' as enemies; he yearned for a return to
the 'lovable localisms' of the past, and in his enthusiasm for it,
he was apt to idealise medieval kingship - Edward I 'was never
more truly representative . . . than in the fact that he expelled
the Jews'; Richard II championed the cause of the peasants.

Despite their obvious differences, the left- and right-wing
versions of people's history overlap at an uncomfortable number
of points. Both may be said to share a common heritage of
romantic primitivism, celebrating the natural, the naive and the
spontaneous. Both share a common yearning for the vanished
solidarities of the past, and a belief that modern life is inimical
to them; but whereas for socialists the alienating force is
capitalism, in the right-wing version of people's history it is
characteristically such a-social forces as 'individualism',
'industrialism' or 'mass society'. There is a certain traffic of
ideas between the right- and left-wing views. G.K. Chesterton's
interpretation of medieval England leans heavily on Cobbett's
History of the Reformation (1827), a proclaimedly radical work
which anticipates some of the leading themes later developed, in
a more socialist direction, by R.H. Tawney and Christopher
Hill. Conversely, one could point to the indebtedness of
contemporary Marxist and left-wing studies of 'mentalités
collectives', to the anti-class sociology of Durkheim, the right-
wing crowd theories of Le Bon, and even to such sinister
inventions of turn-of-the-century social theory as the notion of
the racial soul.

The liberal version of people's history is characteristically
much more optimistic than either the socialist or the conservative,
treating material progress as fundamentally benevolent in its
effects. Capitalism, whether in the form of the growth of towns,
the extension of commerce, or the rise of individualism, is very
far from being a destructive force, but appears rather as the
harbinger of moral and social advance, 'laying the foundations of
that glorious and growing system which is destined, ere long, to
sweep from the face of the land the last vestiges of feudal
tyranny'. Modernisation is synonymous with the march of mind,
the progress of civil liberty, and the extension of religious
toleration. The people, far from representing the forces of
traditionalism, may rather be seen as the subterranean source of
change, 'a slow but always progressive influence upon the social
life of the country'. Medievalism, by contrast, is equated with
superstition and warfare. One of the major themes of liberal
nineteenth-century history is the struggle of the medieval
municipalities to achieve self-government (the subject of a
massive appendix in Thierry's *Rise of the Third Estate*).
Another is the emancipation of the peasantry from serfdom. While
in the battle of ideas between science and religion, liberal history
places itself firmly on the side of heresy and experimentalism
against the sacerdotal authority of the church. The idea of

nationality is pursued in a similar spirit – as a progressive
assertion of liberty on the part of subject peoples.

These were some of the grand themes taken up by the French
liberal historians of the Restoration – Guizot, Mignet and Thierry
– using the platform of history to vindicate the principles of
1789, and combat the mystifications of a resurgent Bourbon
monarchy. Guizot and Mignet were moderate constitutionalists,
championing the cause of the Third Estate by showing the
inevitability of the bourgeois triumph. Thierry went a good deal
further. He had started life as a disciple of Rousseau, and
served as a secretary to the socialist Saint-Simon before
becoming a historian. He was distinctly an innovator, using
ballad literature and folk tradition to give him access to the
mental world of the past, and insisting that the study of history
should be based exclusively on the use of primary sources.
Thierry regarded the common people – he calls them 'the masses'
– as both the victims of history and its ultimate arbiters. He had
a keenly developed sense of pathos (a childhood reading of
Chateaubriand's *Les Martyrs* seems to have converted him to the
study of history), and in the most radical and productive period
of his life – the 1820s – his whole sympathy was engaged by the
historically defeated and oppressed. In his *Conquête d'Angleterre*
(1826) he adopted the theory of the Norman Yoke, starting from
the free Anglo-Saxons and then mapping the contours of their
subsequent degradation. In his *Histoire de Jacques Bonhomme*
(1820) – a typification of the Third Estate through the medium of
an imaginary peasant – he tells the story of a relentless series of
travails.

Victim of Romans, Franks, the absolute rule of republicans
and then the Empire, and finally five years of laws of
exception under the Charter, Jacques Bonhomme had led a
long life of servitude. In recounting these trials, Thierry
made Jacques' feelings strikingly vivid; his overwhelming
sadness on experiencing the Frankish invasion; his resigned
fatigue as he toiled for his master; his shame as he was
himself confounded with real property; his furious outrage
in the fourteenth century rebellion. Always he loved liberty;
and always he suffered under conquerors.

This was a note which was to be powerfully amplified in the
'romantic realism' of the 1830s and 1840s. It was a leitmotif in
Michelet's work, and it was to be given powerful fictional
representation in the novels of Victor Hugo and Eugène Sue
(Sue's *Mysteries of the People*, subtitled 'the history of a
proletarian family across the ages', starts as an exact imitation
of *Jacques Bonhomme*, but carries the story up to the revolution
of 1848). The people's history of the 1830s and 1840s moved far
beyond the moderate constitutionalism of Guizot and Mignet. It
was definitely republican in its sympathies, anti-clerical, or
even – in the case of Michelet – anti-Christian, and by no means
uncritical of the bourgeoisie. Buchez and Roux set about the
rehabilitation of Robespierre in their *Histoire Parlementaire de la*

Révolution Française; Buonarroti that of Babeuf, while works such
as Michelet's *The People* (1846), Louis Blanc's *Histoire des Dix
Ans* (1841-4) and Lamartine's *Girondins* are widely credited
with having prepared the way for the outbreak of revolution in
February 1848. In short, the liberal history of these years moved
as far in the democratic direction as the Jacobinism which it
celebrated. These were the years which saw the republican Left
making full use of the so-called 'Celtic' myth (i.e. the notion of a
Free Gaul, subjugated by Roman and Frankish invaders), and
they also saw the rather belated French 'discovery' of folklore.
Above all there was the work of Michelet, who combined scholarly
audacity with lifelong loyalty to his plebeian childhood, growing
up, 'like a blade of grass' between the Paris cobblestones. His
work prefigures some of the favoured subjects of social history
today - as in his writings on language, on sexuality, and on
witchcraft; and the human geography and regionalist themes
which his *Tableau de France* explored may be said to have
determined some of the main lines of subsequent French social
history. Michelet translated his democratic sympathies into a
populist methodology, using folk ballads as his access to the
categories of ancient law, studying folk magic for the origins of
science, and using oral history as his faithful companion when
exploring the recent past.

The remote origins of people's history in England are lost in
that no-man's land of ballad tradition where myth and historicity
cross, though it is clear from such studies as that of Rosamund
Faith printed in this volume that the notion of 'lost rights'
figured prominently among them. Better documented, in a fine
early study by Christopher Hill, is the notion of the Norman
Yoke, a kind of plebeian equivalent to that idea of the 'ancient
constitution' which has recently been preoccupying the historian
of ideas. Hill calls it an 'elementary class theory of politics' and
traces its influence first in the writings of the seventeenth-
century constitutional lawyers, then in the pamphlets and
addresses of the Levellers and Diggers; finally - and perhaps
most influentially - in the reborn radicalism of the 1780s. The
notion of the free Anglo-Saxons, with their democratic forms of
self-government and people's militia, was one which sustained
the English Jacobins of the 1790s, when they went on trial for
their ideas. It was largely elaborated in the pamphlet literature
of the time, proving the historicity of democracy and showing
that it was a birthright of which the English people had been
robbed. (It appears in the lengthy passages on tythings and
shire moots in Baxter's *New and Impartial History*.) The English
Civil War was another great touchstone for popular radicals,
yielding encouraging examples of how tyrants met their doom;
while in another kind of discourse, pioneered by Cobbett in his
History of the Reformation, and taken up by the English
socialists of the 1880s, a second golden age of self-government
was discovered in the Middle Ages.

People's history surfaces, as a self-conscious literary and
intellectual practice, in the 1860s and 1870s, when it is

represented by Goldwin Smith, J.R. Green and Thorold Rogers.
Politically it was associated with the Liberal Party, especially its
more advanced and radical wing. These were the years which
saw the passage of the Second Reform Bill, and the first hesitant
alliance between the Liberal Party and the trade unions; they
were also marked, on the Liberal side, by a growing attack on
the landed interest and a deliberate appeal to the 'masses'
against the 'classes' (i.e. the common people versus
aristocratic vested interests). These were also, educationally,
the first years of 'extension' classes, i.e. of university-based
adult education; of the popular publications of the classics
(Stopford Brooke's Primers; Sir John Lubbock's Hundred Best
Books; Morley's Universal Library); and of the coming of
universal elementary education. Amongst the Liberal
intelligentsia one sees a very mild (and very English) version of
Russian populism, with liberal academics 'going to the people' (as
extra-mural lecturers), appearing on public platforms with such
unorthodox figures as Cobden and Bright, and in one famous
case – that of the historian Thorold Rogers – allegedly taking
part in a riot. Goldwin Smith, Regius Professor of History at
Oxford, took up the cause of the artisan 'against the united
phalanx of employers', C.G. Brodrick in *The Domesday of
Enclosures* exposed the cupidity of the landowners. J.R. Green
was the most widely-read of the liberal-radical historians of this
epoch, and his *Short History* came to enjoy the same kind of
esteem which an earlier generation of readers had bestowed on
Macaulay.

The liberal-democratic impulse can also be seen in the local
newspapers of these years. They devoted a vast amount of space
to local history, both in the form of regular 'Notes and Queries',
and also, if more occasionally, by serialising autobiographies of
local life (Joseph Lawson's recently reprinted *Progress in
Pudsey*, a celebration of nineteenth-century social change,
looking back to the hard times of the 1830s and 1840s, is a
representative example). Another symptomatic publication of the
period is the civic histories of the manufacturing towns of the
Midlands and the North. In the large towns these histories are
apt to be taken up with the story of municipal progress, and
they may be said to reflect, in some sort, the newly formed civic
consciousness of the local bourgeoisie. But in the smaller
industrial towns one finds a species of what might be called
'democratic antiquarianism': books, often written by liberal
worthies or radical journalists, which leaned on oral tradition,
and placed a high valuation on the more plebeian elements in
local life (Frank Peel's *Spen Valley, Past and Present* is a fine
example). Democratic antiquarianism can also be seen, in two
other characteristic developments of the time – the publication of
county and regional glossaries (the English Dialect Society was
founded in 1873); and the starting of the *Folklore Record* in
1878. (The Folklore Society, which was led by enthusiastic
Darwinians, represents another important strand in the

advanced liberalism of the day: militant free thought and
agnosticism.)

The grand theme of this liberal version of people's history is
that of democratic self-government. It is this which accounts for
the utterly arbitrary but brilliantly chosen starting point of
J.R. Green's *Short History* - the lyrical evocation of a 'Merry
England' when three-fourths of the population were landowners,
and unemployed beggars were unknown; and it also provided him
with a uniting thread for his subsequent chapters: the 'real life'
of the English people lay in their 'ceaseless, sober struggle with
oppression, their steady, unwearied battle for self-government'.
This is also the focal point of his widow, Alice Stopford Green,
in her splendid *Town Life in Fifteenth Century England* - a
'picture', as she wrote in the preface, 'inspired by ardent
sympathy' which showed a time when the English boroughs lived
in a republican spirit of independence, 'a free self-governing
community, a state within a state, boasting of rights derived from
immemorial customs'. A similar inspiration may occasionally be
encountered among the folklorists. Laurence Gomme, one of the
founding fathers of the Folklore Society, editor of the
Archaeological Review, and in his professional life, a clerk at the
London County Council, found his democratic ideals realised by
the open-air assemblies of the ancient Britons. His *Primitive
Folk Moots* (1880) leaves little doubt about where his sympathies
lay: 'These researches tell us that Englishmen of the nineteenth
century are connected by innumerable ties to Englishmen of
preceding centuries, before Cromwell had broken . . . the
fetters of feudal monarchy, before William had fastened these
fetters, before Alfred. . . .'

A more controversial contribution to 'people's history' in this
period is that of Thorold Rogers. Rogers was a thoroughgoing
radical, who stood with Joseph Arch, the farm-workers' leader,
during the strikes of 1872, and whose anti-Tory opinions were so
pronounced that in 1868 he was run out of his professorship at
Oxford. Rogers set out a programme for 'people's history' in the
preface to his monumental *History of Agriculture and Prices*,
published in seven volumes between 1864 and 1902. Here,
rejecting a history of 'constitutional antiquities', he turns
instead to what he calls sometimes 'social' and sometimes
'economical' history. Despite its daunting title, Rogers's book is
in fact an immense treatise on social and domestic economy. He
tells us that he began his work by collecting prices, 'but soon
widened my research and included . . . everything which would
inform me as to the social condition of England six centuries ago
and onwards'. Rogers was a tireless scholar who worked with
zest in the archives, and brought a splendid wealth of
documentation to his cause (he seems to have been the first
English historian to appreciate the value of Domesday book). He
was incapable of touching a document - even the remotest
statistic in a medieval building account - without it coming alive;
and he also engaged in various types of 'action' research -

tramping through Hampshire to track the ancient distribution of land, measuring, by his own walks, the medieval cost of transporting a sack of flour from Oxford to Eynsham. Doctrinally, Rogers never moved beyond advanced liberalism. Temperamentally, though, he was more intransigent, and his book, like Marx's *Capital*, is a tremendous historical indictment of the English ruling class. It breathes a spirit of indignation against oppression, and it is perhaps this - the felt and sustained sense of injustice - which explains why, in its abridged version as *Six Centuries of Work and Wages*, it was regarded as a fundamental text in the education classes of the early socialist movement.

The early socialists took up a different class standpoint from that of the advanced liberals, proclaiming capitalists rather than landlords as the main enemy, and identifying the people, first and foremost, with the industrial working class. But they took over the liberal-radical version of 'people's history' almost intact. Land served them - as it did the liberal-radicals - as the chief idiom for class oppression, and in their historical work they devoted far more attention to peasant risings than they did to industrial strikes. Enclosure rather than the factory system served them as the historical symbol of injustice - the great act which had robbed the English people of their birthright; while the fifteenth century is the 'Golden Age' of the artisan and peasant - for H.M. Hyndman, Belfort Bax and William Morris, as for Thorold Rogers and Mrs J.R. Green. Another common link was the historical taking of sides in the English Civil War, while in Belfort Bax's three-volume *Social Side of the German Reformation* (1894-1903) it is not difficult to discern an unarticulated Protestant view of history very much akin to that of the liberal-radicals. There was also a shared commitment to the cause of Ireland, and it is no accident that James Connolly in his *Labour in Irish History* (1910) pays especial tribute to Mrs Green's *Making of Ireland and its Undoing*. In France, the indebtedness of the early socialists to their liberal-radical forbears is even more apparent, both in the centrality accorded to the French Revolution, and in a common loyalty to Jacobinism which has continued to mark the 'Marxist' interpretation of the Revolution down to the present day. Jaurès declared that he owed as much to the mysticism of Michelet as he did to the materialism of Marx, and in compiling his *Histoire Socialiste de la Révolution Française* (1890) he displayed some of Michelet's finer qualities - the appetite for new archives, the strong sense of region, the belief in the creative power of the masses, the importance attached to popular art.

The notion of 'people's history' is not one which Marxists find themselves at ease with, even though in Britain they make up a large part of its present-day practitioners. As the previous pages have indicated, it has in the past been appropriated by the Right as well as by the Left, while its philosophic roots are pre-Marxist. People's history is very often backward-looking

while socialism, in principle, is futurist, seeking - in the spirit
of Tom Paine - to throw off the dead hand of tradition, and make
the world anew. Again, the spirit of Marxism is critical, while
that of people's history is characteristically affirmative,
celebrating the creative power of the masses while ignoring (so
it is alleged) the imperatives under which they labour. Marxism
is concerned with the totality of social experience, whereas
'people's history' (so its critics argue) takes as its optic only
one point of view, 'privileging' the people as the bearers of
change, while ignoring the wider determinations at work. The
term 'people' is also one which many present-day British
Marxists view with discomfort. It belongs, they feel, to an alien
vocabulary - at its best, that of bourgeois democracy, at its
worst that of the capitalist press. It is a unifying notion
whereas Marxists (so the argument runs) should be concerned
with identifying points of division. When applied to history it is
mystificatory, lumping together artisans and tradesmen,
proletarians and peasants. It can show the people as a
community, but hardly as a class. People's history is also
suspected of 'naive' realism, and it is certainly true, as I have
tried to indicate, that its fortunes have often been tied to a
realist movement in literature, and the documentary movement
in the arts. This realism, it is argued, subverts the Marxist
enterprise, substituting description for explanation and
privileging the visible at the expense of the invisible forces at
work. The gain in immediacy is purchased by the loss of that
necessary moment of abstraction which is the essence of a
Marxian analysis. These strictures are sometimes amplified by
derogatory references to 'populism' which in the contemporary
Marxian Dunciad seems to occupy a place of dishonour somewhat
akin to that of the 'labour fakirs' of old.
    These difficulties are not, on the face of it, easily
surmountable, but they rest in part on a false opposition
between Marxism and the bourgeois-democratic currents of
thought which preceded it. Marx himself was less frightened of
contamination than some of his latter-day followers, and many of
his political concepts are borrowed or transposed from his
bourgeois-democratic predecessors. Lenin - notwithstanding his
polemics in that field - was positively insistent in
acknowledging the populist heritage, and in 1917, on the eve of
revolution, he acclaimed Jacobinism as 'the greatest expression
of an oppressed class in its struggle for liberation'. It is true
that Marx spoke not of 'the people' but of 'the proletariat', but
in his writing the term is used in a convertible sense, and its
specifically industrial component is apt to be subsumed in a wider
if more indeterminate constituency, that of the propertyless and
the poor. Marx may not have used a populist vocabulary, but
the working class, as it appears in his thought, is always, by
definition, *majoritarian*, and in embryo indeed a universal class -
one that in abolishing its own conditions of existence will
emancipate humanity as a whole. Socialism, for Marx as for his

followers, was a realisation of the democratic idea. The populist strain in Marxist thought became far more pronounced when - in the twentieth century - socialists and communists found themselves at the head of mass movements. In Europe, in the epoch of the October Revolution and the Third International, Communist appeals were characteristically directed at 'the broad masses' or 'the toiling millions'; while in the more moderate years which have followed the turn to the Popular Front (1935-6) Communists (in common with Social Democrats) have preferred the term 'working people' to the stricter terminology of *The Communist Manifesto*; often, as in present-day campaigns of 'the people' against 'the monopolists', they have taken on a populist vocabulary unchanged. In Italy Gramsci's notion of the national-popular is one of the historic bases of Italian communism. In Chinese communism and the Third World Liberation movements of recent years, Marxists have necessarily adopted the idiom of nationalism, in which the people are addressed as a whole.

The relationship of Marxism to people's history may be an uneasy one, but they are tied to one another as by an umbilical cord. It should be evident that Marxist historians, whether they are aware of it or not, have drawn heavily on the work of their radical-democratic forbears, as one can see from the shaping influence of the Hammonds on the work of E.P. Thompson, of Tawney on Christopher Hill, of Frazer and Jane Harrison on George Thomson, of Riegel on Antal and Klingender. Marx himself certainly practised a species of people's history, and the debt to his predecessors in this respect - Vico, the Scottish historical school of the eighteenth century, the French liberal historians of the Restoration, the German folklorists and peasant historians - has hardly been explored. His whole account of *Capital* might be described, under one optic, as a history of below - the history of a development seen through the eyes of its victims; and his chapters on 'Primitive Accumulation' in that book are very far from displaying that Olympian spirit of detachment which some of his latter-day epigones seem to regard as the quintessence of 'method'. Marx derives his concept of the 'bourgeois revolution' from Thierry and Guizot, who applied it both to the English Revolution of 1640 and to the French Revolution of 1789; and it is arguable that the 'two great camps' which confront each other in the opening passages of the *Communist Manifesto* - bourgeois and proletarians - are modelled on, or transposed from, those which confronted each other at the States-General in 1789: the privileged on one side, the productive on the other. Certainly Marx's notion of proletarian revolution - that day of reckoning for which generations of socialists were to look - seems to come less from his study of capitalist industry than from the Jacqueries of the medieval peasantry, and the plebeian uprisings in ancient Rome, while the universalist claim for the proletariat, at a time when, in every country but Britain, the industrial working class was

comparatively insignificant in numbers, surely takes its
paradigm from that age-old contrast of patricians and plebeians
which provided people's history - and the 'discovery of the
people' generally - with its very groundwork.
   For Marxists, to reject people's history would be, in Britain,
to reject the major heritage of socialist historical work. The
whole movement of 'history from below', and therefore, if only
indirectly, the present flourishing state of English social history,
was incubated in the Communist Party Historians' Group of the
late 1940s and early 1950s, during the dark days of the Cold
War. It was there - as Hans Medick indicates in his paper - that
some of its major themes were rehearsed; that its most creative
practitioners - Christopher Hill, Eric Hobsbawm and E.P.
Thompson - did their early work; and that its most prestigious
journal, *Past and Present*, was conceived, as also, if more
obliquely, the Society for the Study of Labour History. In the
case of the second folk song revival, and the 'discovery' of
industrial song, the whole movement, from the Hootenannies of the
early 1950s to the folk clubs of today, owes its inspiration (and
much of its historical scholarship) to two Communist scholar-
singers, A.L. Lloyd and Ewan MacColl. Socialists have also been
very much to the fore in the recovery of popular art: one need
only mention the pioneering role of the Marxist art critic Francis
Klingender, whose *Art and the Industrial Revolution* (1947) was
undertaken in collaboration with the Amalgamated Engineering
Union, of John Gorman's *Banner Bright*, the work of a printer-
historian who was making banners for the labour movement
before he came to research them, or of Victor Neuberg and Louis
James in the 'discovery' of popular literature. Community-based
publications projects - such as Centerprise in Hackney,
Queenspark in Brighton, Strong Words in Durham - usually turn
out to have a nucleus of strongly committed socialists among
both the writers and the co-ordinators. Women's history in
Britain is to a striking extent in the hands of, or strongly
influenced by, Marxist-feminists, and Sheila Rowbotham's work
has given some of its themes a mass readership. It is right that
such work should be submitted to theoretical interrogation, but
to reject it on the grounds that it was tainted with populism or
epistemologically impure, would leave us with little but such
histoire raisonnée as Hindess and Hirst's *Pre-Capitalist Modes of
Production* - a thin fare to offer the labour movement, and
hardly the brightest ornament of either literary art or Marxist
historical scholarship.
   The notion of 'real life experience' is certainly in need of
critical scrutiny; but whatever its ambiguities it is certainly not
one which Marxists can afford to despise at a time when
questions of subjectivity are so insistently on the socialist
agenda. The attempt to recover the texture of everyday life may
be associated with a 'neo-Romantic intellectual enterprise' - one
of the charges levelled against it; but it is perfectly compatible
- if that is to be the test of scientificity - with elaborate day-

charts and passionless prose. Among Marxist and feminist
historians it has arisen from a radical discontent with the use of
categories which remain wholly external to the object they
purport to account for. For the women's movement it is plainly
a political decision; not a question of investigating trivia, but a
way of challenging centuries of silence. It is unclear why
a preoccupation with the material practices of everyday life
- or for that matter the structure of popular belief - is either
Utopian or undesirable from a Marxist point of view. Nor is there
any reason to counterpose the personal and the familial with
global, overall views. In most of the periods with which
historians deal, the home has been the principal site of
production, the family the vector of property and inheritance,
the locality a universe of class. Hans Medick, in his work on
'proto-capitalism', has shown that it is only by reconstructing
the life cycle of domestic workers, and the material deprivations
under which they worked, that one can understand the base, in
production, of primitive capitalist accumulation; and it seems
possible that the work of Marxist-feminist historians, centring on
the inter-relationship of family, work and home, will have a
comparably radical effect on our understanding of class
formation and class consciousness. It is of course possible for a
preoccupation with the everyday to degenerate into a catalogue
of inanimate objects. But work such as Ronald Fraser's *Blood of
Spain*, or Luisa Passerini's article on Turin workers under fascism shows that, ambitiously handled, an understanding of subjective experience and everyday social relationships can be used
to pose major questions in theory.

British Marxism is certainly in need of the kind of
nourishment - or dialectical tension - which an encounter with
people's history could provide. Too often, in theory as in
political practice, its propositions have been impoverished by
the fact that they have remained locked in their own conceptual
world, as though designed to keep reality at bay rather than to
engage with it. A history of capitalism 'from the bottom up'
might give us many more clues as to the sources of its
continuing vitality than debates on the law of value, necessary
and illuminating though these may be; a discussion of lordship
or chivalry in the Middle Ages or of, say, the peasant roots of
individualism might do more for our theoretical understanding of
ideology and consciousness than any number of further
'interpellations' on the theme of 'relative autonomy'; and indeed
it is unlikely that we shall ever be able effectively to combat
bourgeois ideology until we can see how it arises in ourselves,
until we explore the needs and desires it satisfies, and the
whole substratum of fears on which it draws. Our
understanding of socialism too might be less abstract, if we
were to explore it historically 'from the bottom up', looking at
its secret languages, its unarticulated passions, its cognitive
unconscious and dissonances. Above all, the questions
posed by feminism leave no category of Marxist historical

analysis unscathed, and it is one of the strengths of people's
history that it is proving a far more hospitable terrain for
asking them than more abstract analytic planes. People's history
also has the merit of raising a crucial question for both
theoretical and political work – that of the production of
knowledge, both the sources on which it draws and its ultimate
point of address. It questions the existing intellectual division
of labour and implicitly challenges the professionalised
monopolies of knowledge. It makes democratic practice one of
the yardsticks by which socialist thought is judged, and thus
might encourage us not only to interpret the world, but to see
how our work could change it.

On the other side of the coin, it is also true that people's
history needs, or at any rate would benefit from, a more
sustained encounter with Marxism. If it is to achieve the aim
implicit in its title – that of creating an alternative, or
oppositional history – then it has to link the particular to the
general, the part to the whole, the individual moment to the
longue durée. To write a history of the oppressed – one of its
abiding inspirations – needs an understanding of the totality of
social relations, while that of marginal social groups, one of its
more recent preoccupations (e.g. bandits, outcasts, heretics),
can only be understood in terms of centre-periphery
relationships. Working lives – one of the major subjects of
community-based people's history – need to be situated within
the wider social and sexual division of labour and the ideologies
clustering around the notions of (say) skill and masculinity;
family reconstitution, if it is to do more than computerise nuclear
households, must address itself to those questions of power,
patriarchy and property relationships which Marxist-feminists
have so insistently raised. Popular culture, if it is not to be cut
up by students of 'leisure' and 'recreation', needs to be
discussed in relation to those questions of symbolic order and
non-verbal communication which structural linguistics have
raised, as well as to that changing balance of the 'public' and
the 'private' spheres which, in this volume, Catherine Hall
discusses in relation to notions of femininity. Again, if we are
to learn from life histories, whether in the form of oral history
or written autobiography, we need a theoretically informed
discussion of both language and oral tradition if we are to
avoid misconstruing the words that we record. That is, that we
have to ask ourselves theoretical questions about popular memory
and historical consciousness, to take into account the double
character of the spoken word – what it conceals as well as what
it expresses – and to build our understanding from such
dualities.

Left to itself, people's history can enclose itself in a locally
defined totality where no alien forces intrude. It can serve as a
kind of escapism, a flight from the uncertainties of the present
to the apparent stabilities of the past. But it can also suggest
a strenuous programme of work, an attempt to change our

understanding of history as a whole. One major element of it is
suggested by Brecht, in a poem which interestingly explains
why Marxism and people's history - for all the theoretical
differences between them - have so often had occasion to
converge:

> Who built Thebes of the Seven Gates?
> In the books stand the names of Kings.
> Did they then drag up the rock-slabs?
> And Babylon, so often destroyed,
> Who kept rebuilding it?
> In which houses did the builders live
> In gold-glittering Lima?
> Where did the bricklayers go
> The evening the Great Wall of China was finished?
> Great Rome is full of triumphal arches.
> Over whom did the Caesars triumph?
> Were there only palaces for the inhabitants of much-sung
>   Byzantium?

> Even in legendary Atlantis
> Didn't the drowning shout for their slaves
> As the ocean engulfed it?
> The young Alexander conquered India.
> He alone?
> Caesar beat the Gauls.
> Without even a cook?
> Philip of Spain wept when his fleet went down.
> Did no one else weep besides?
> Frederick the Great won the Seven Years' War.
> Who won it with him?

> A victory on every page
> Who cooked the victory feast?
> A great man every ten years.
> Who paid the costs?

> So many reports.
> So many questions.

FURTHER READING

General
An attractive, if now unfashionable, introduction to some of the
themes discussed in this essay will be found in Edmund Wilson,
To the Finland Station, a book written in the shadow of the
author's 1930s engagement with Marxism. It traces the
development of the revolutionary idea through the medium of
history, and has the merit of discussing Marx and Michelet,
Lenin and Vico, within a single cover. Three almost unreadable

books by Harry Elmer Barnes nevertheless contain interesting
snippets of information about now forgotten historians: *The
New History* (New York 1925); *History of Sociology* (Chicago
1961)'; *A History of Historical Writing* (New York 1963). G.P.
Gooch, *History and Historians in the Nineteenth Century*
(London 1913) is more reflective but has little to say about those
currents of work which might be claimed as 'people's history'.
L. Poliakov, *The Aryan Myth* (London 1974), for the underworld
of sociological theory; Marvin Harris, *The Rise of
Anthropological Theory* (London 1968) and John Burrow,
Evolution and Society (Cambridge 1966), are excellent
introductions to evolutionary social science; Wilhelm Wundt,
Elements of Folk Psychology (London 1916), and Friedrich
Ratzel, *The History of Mankind* (London 1896), represent two
of its more curious and interesting phases. On changing
meanings of the term 'people', Raymond Williams, *Keywords*
(Fontana 1979), is helpful, original and precise. For England see
Asa Briggs's pioneering article 'The Language of "class" in early
nineteenth century England' in Briggs and Saville (eds),
Essays in Labour History (London 1960); also the same writer's
more recent 'The Language of "mass" and "masses" in 19th
century England', in D. Martin and D. Rubinstein (eds),
Ideology and the Labour Movement (London 1979). For France,
two helpful books are the collection of essays *Images du Peuple
au dix-huitième siècle* (Paris 1973), and Regine Robin, *Histoire
et Linguistique* (Paris 1973); also Robin and others, *Langage
et Idéologies* (Paris 1973). On social romanticism, V.G. Kiernan
'Wordsworth and the People', in John Saville (ed.), *Democracy
and the Labour Movement* (London 1954); David Owen Evans,
Social Romanticism in France 1830-1848 (Oxford 1951),
excellently conveys the warmth and enthusiasm of its subject,
and is a surprising book to have come out of Cold War Britain.
Leon Rosenthal, *Du Romantisme au Réalisme* (Paris 1914), covers
the strange and interesting passage from anti-Enlightenment
reaction to the left-wing humanitarianism of the 1840s. Two
splendid books by Tim Clark, *The Absolute Bourgeois, Artists
and Politics in France 1848-51*, and *Image of the People, Gustave
Courbet and the 1848 Revolution* (both published 1973), break
new ground in art history as well as being an excellent
introduction to the political mentality of the period.

On right-wing people's history, apart from the titles mentioned
in the text, one could add H.D. Traill's six-volume *Social
England* (London 1893-7), Storm Jameson, *The Decline of Merry
England* (London 1930), and, for the less inviting side of inter-
war Catholic reaction, Hilaire Belloc, *The Jews* (London 1922).
Wolfgang Emmerich, *Germanistische Volkstumideologie* (Tubingen
1968), traces the sad line from the eighteenth-century discovery
of folklore to its appropriation by the Nazis, which can also be
followed in John E. Farquarson, *The Plough and the Swastika*
(New York 1976). For a very intelligent Marxist discussion of

right-wing populism, Ernesto Laclaw, *Politics and Ideology in Marxist Theory* (London 1977).

On people's history in England, I can think of no secondary work except for Christopher Hill's always rewarding 'Norman Yoke' essay (reprinted in *Puritans and Revolutionaries*, London 1958). Green's *Short History* is currently available in Everyman Library. Thorold Rogers's *Six Centuries of Work and Wages*, his *Industrial and Commercial History of England* (1892), and *The Economic Interpretation of History* (1888), turn up quite frequently on the second-hand bookstalls. Cobbett's *History of the Reformation* (1827) unfortunately does not. For the folklorists, R. Dorson, *The British Folklorists, A History* (Chicago 1968), contains a lot of biographical information and is written by an enthusiast, but he seems quite incurious about the ideological and political dimensions of his subject, which hopefully somebody will one day take up. Until then Edwin Clodd's *Memoirs* and his various polemical writings give one some idea of the place of folklore in the battle of ideas. For the Communist Party Historians Group, there is a memoir by Eric Hobsbawm in M. Cornforth (ed.), *Rebels and Their Cause* (London 1978), and a series of articles by the present writer currently appearing in *New Left Review*: 'British Marxist historians, 1880-1980'. Richard Johnson, 'Culture and the historians', in John Clarke *et al.* (eds) *Working Class Culture* (London 1979), valuably connects recent work in labour and social history with that in cultural studies and sociology: it also has an interesting critique of the work of G.D.H. Cole.

Sources and Methods
Among the more attractive and accessible of recent books, Paul Thompson, *The Voice of the Past: Oral History* (Oxford paperback, 1978); Victor E. Neuberg, *Popular Literature, a History and Guide* (Penguin 1977); W.G. Hoskins, *Local History in England* (London 1972); Alan Rogers, *This Was Their World, approaches to local history* (London 1972); R.W. Brunskill, *Illustrated handbook of vernacular architecture* (London 1970); W.E. Tate, *The Parish Chest* (Cambridge 1946); A.L. Lloyd, *Folk Song in England* (London 1967; 1975).

For some interesting approaches to a 'people's history' of art: Louis James, *Print and the People 1819-1851* (London 1976); F.D. Klingender, *Art and the Industrial Revolution* (Paladin paperback); John Gorman, *Banner Bright* (London 1973); John Barell, *The Dark Side of the Landscape, The rural poor in English painting, 1730-1840* (Cambridge 1980); David Kunzle, *The Early Comic Strip* (Berkeley, Calif., 1973).

On demography: Alan Macfarlane, *Reconstructing Historical Communities* (Cambridge 1977); E.A. Wrigley, *Nineteenth Century Society, Essays in the use of quantitative methods*

(Cambridge 1972); Peter Laslett (ed.), *Household and Family
in Past Time* (but see, for a criticism of this approach, Miranda
Chaytor, 'Household and Kinship', *History Workshop Journal*
10, November 1980).

On people's history in France: C. Rearik, *Beyond the
Enlightenment* (Indiana 1974), though primarily concerned with
the development of folklore, is an excellent discussion of the
historical imagination in the period 1815-50, and altogether to be
preferred to Stanley Mellon, *The Political Uses of History, A
study of Historians of the French Restoration* (Stanford, Calif.,
1958), which in the manner of too many doctoral dissertations
manages to make an interesting subject dull. Alice Gerard, *La
Révolution Française, mythes et interprétations* (Paris 1970),
gives a systematic treatment to one long-lasting strand, and
M. Touchard, *La Gauche Française* (Paris 1974), is excellent on
the political uses of it. P. Viallaneix, *La Voie Royal. Essai sur
l'Idée du peuple dans l'oeuvre de Michelet* (Paris 1959), is
massive and informative, but curiously uncritical, as though the
writer had constituted himself Michelet's mouthpiece. For *Annales*
history, Peter Burke, *A New Kind of History* (London 1973);
T. Stoianovic, *French Historical Method* (Cornell 1976), and
Luciano Allegra and Angelo Torre, *La Nascita de la Storia
Sociale in Francia* (Turin 1977). For a present (or near-present)
statement of *Annales*-type thinking, usefully arranged in the
form of an extended dictionary, and with bibliographies
attached, Jacques Le Goff (ed.), *La Nouvelle Histoire* (Paris
1978).

On people's history in Germany, on which, for reasons of space,
I have omitted a section, there is an excellent introduction to its
early left-wing phase, in John G. Gagliardo, *From Pariah to
Patriot, The Changing Image of the German Peasant* (Lexington,
Ky, 1969).

On people's history in America: Richard Hofstadter, *The
Progressive Historians*, is a thin treatment of a subject which
ought to be complex and exciting.

Journals
History Workshop Journal publishes two book-length issues a
year (subscriptions from PO Box 69, Oxford); *Oral History*,
twice-yearly journal of the Oral History Society (subscription
from Department of Sociology, University of Essex, Colchester);
Bulletin of the Society for the Study of Labour History
(subscriptions from John Field, Northern College, Wentworth
Castle, Barnsley, Yorks); *Past and Present* (subscriptions from
the business manager, *Past and Present*, Corpus Christi
College, Oxford); *Social History* (subscriptions from Methuen
and Co., Fetter Lane, London EC4); *The Local Historian*
(subscriptions from National Council for Social Service, Bedford

Square, London WC1). In addition one might mention *Llafur*,
the excellent journal of the Welsh Labour History Society,
subscriptions from The Miners Library, Sketty Road, Swansea;
Le Mouvement Social, the journal of French labour history
(subscriptions from Les Editions Ouvrières, 12 avenue Soeur-
Rosalie, 75621 Paris, France); *Radical History Review*, sister
journal of *History Workshop* in the United States (from The
Radical Historians' Organisation, John Jay College, 445 West
59th Street, New York, NY 10019, U.S.A.). For anyone who
reads Italian, there are three excellent social history journals,
Movimento operaoi e socialista (subscriptions from piazza
Campetto 8a, 16123 Genoa, Italy); *Quaderni Storici* (subscriptions
from Editrici il Mulino, Via Santo Stefano 6, 40125 Bologna,
Italy), and *Studi Storici*; *Feminist Review* (subscriptions from
65 Manor Road, London N16); *Feminist Studies* (subscriptions
from Women's Studies Program, University of Maryland, College
Park, Maryland 20742, USA).

Labour History
The vast amount of material published in the last 20 years defies
abbreviated epitome. For Great Britain there is now a comprehensive bibliography, Harold Smith, *The British Labour Movement
to 1970* (London 1980). This covers, in some 4,000 entries, books,
pamphlets and periodical articles published in the English
language between 1945 and 1970. A further volume, in preparation,
will cover the 1970s. Ruth Frow, Eddie Frow and Michael Katanka,
The History of British Trade Unionism, a select bibliography
(Historical Association, 1969) is a helpful introduction. Ian
MacDougall, *A Catalogue of some Labour Records in Scotland*.
(Edinburgh 1978) gives a magnificent coverage of original sources.
J.F.C. Harrison and Dorothy Thompson, *Bibliography of the
Chartist Movement, 1837-1976* (Hassocks 1978); Royden Harrison
ed., *The Warwick Guide to British Labour Periodicals, 1790-1970*
(Hassocks 1977).

Factory History
A crucial potential meeting point of people's history, labour history
and the history of capitalism which has hardly been explored. Some
indication of its potential can be found in Alfred Williams, *Life in a
Railway Factory* (London 1915); Peter Fieldander, *The Emergence
of a UAW Local, 1936-1939*, (Pittsburgh 1975); Liliana Lanzardo,
Classe Operaie e Partito Communista all Fiat, 1945-1968 (Turin
1971); Patrick Fridenson, *Les Usines Renault* (Paris 1972); Huw
Beynon, *Working for Fords* (Harmondsworth 1973); Tony Lane and
Kenneth Roberts, *Strike at Pilkingtons* (London 1972); Arthur
Exell, 'Morris Motors in the 1930s and 1940s', *History Workshop
Journal* nos 6,7,9; A.E. Grigg, *The History of the Bletchley
Branch of the National Union of Railwaymen* (privately printed
1978) is a vast, lavishly illustrated book by a worker-historian,
informed by a sharp political sense and enlivened by flashes of a

melancholy wit. An interesting example of what labour history
might be if more of it were written by workers, as also the Arthur
Exell articles referred to above.

Material Culture
C.S. and C.S. Orwin, *The Open Fields* (Oxford 1938) is a pioneering work to which the present movement in industrial archeology
owes much. W.G. Hoskins, *The Making of the English Landscape*
(1955) is reprinted in Penguin. Fernand Braudel, *The Mediter-
ranean* shows the far greater ambition of French work in this
field, and the magnificent scholarship which supports it. Cf.
also the same author's *Capitalism and Material Life, 1400-1800*
(Fontana 1973). Robert Forster and Orest' Ranum, eds. *Food and
Drink in History* (Baltimore 1979) translates and reproduces some
essays from the *Annales*. Pierre Bourdieu, *Outline of a Theory of
Practice* (Cambridge 1977), informed by an anthropological study
of the domestic interior, raises the discussion of material culture
to a new level. Kenneth Hudson's various books, *Industrial
Archaeology* (London 1976); *Food, Clothes and Shelter* (London
1978); *Street Furniture* (London 1979); and *A Social History of
Museums* (London 1975) are helpful introductions to conservation
work in this field and some of the historical subject-matter it
opens up.

Family History
Phillipe Aries, *Centuries of Childhood* (Penguin 1973); Robert
Forster and Oreste Ranum, eds. *Family and Society, Selections
from Annales E.S.C.* (Baltimore 1976); John Demos, *A Little
Commonwealth. Family Life in Plymouth Colony* (New York 1970);
Christopher Hill, *Society and Puritanism in Pre-Revolutionary
England* (London 1964); Peter Laslett, *Family Life and Illicit Love
in Earlier Generations*; Jean-Louis Flandrin, *Families in Former
Times* (Cambridge 1979); Hans Medick, 'The Photo-Industrial
Family Economy', *Social History* 1, no.3, October 1976; Rayna
Rapp, Ellen Ross and Renate Bridenthal, 'Examining Family
History', *Feminist Studies* V, no.1 Spring 1979; Lutz K. Berkner,
'The Stem Family and the Developmental Cycle of the Peasant
Household', *American Historical Review*, 77, no.2, April 1972;
Oral History 111, no.2, 'Family History' issue; Paul Thompson,
The Edwardians (London 1977).

Marginals, migrants, outcast groups
J.J. Jusserand, *English Wayfaring Life in the Middle Ages*;
Bronislaw Geremek, *Les Marginaux Parisens aux XIV et XV
siècles* (Paris 1976); Eric Hobsbawm, *Bandits* (Penguin 1972);
Peter Clark 'Migration in England during the late Seventeenth and
early Eighteenth Century', *Past and Present* 83, May 1979;
Raphael Samuel 'Comers and Goers' in ed. H.J. Dyos and M. Wolff,
The Victorian City (London 1973); Charles van Onselen, '"The
Regiment of the Hills". South Africa 's Lumpenroletarian Army,
1890-1920', *Past and Present* 80, August 1978; Jerry White,

'Campbell Bunk', *History Workshop Journal* 8, Autumn 1979;
Olwen Hufton, *The Poor in Eighteenth-Century France, 1750-1789*
(Oxford 1974); Gareth Stedman Jones, *Outcast London* (Oxford
1971); A.L. Beier 'Vagrants and the Social Order in Elizabethan
England', *Past and Present* no.64 August 1974; Judith Walkowitz,
Prostitution and Victorian Society (Cambridge 1980).

History and theory

Raphael Samuel*

Historians are not given, at least in public, to introspection
about their work, and except on ceremonial occasions, such as
inaugural lectures, eschew general statements of their aims. Nor
do they attempt to theorise their inquiries. They are suspicious of
orthodoxy, dislike abstractions, and are never so happy as when
questioning received opinions, or multiplying exceptions to the
rule. When faced with conceptual difficulties, they instinctively
reach for the 'facts', and, rather than waste time in
philosophical speculation, prefer to get on with the job. They
see themselves, first and foremost, as researchers, attentive
listeners and close observers, guided by an imaginative
sympathy with the past and an intuitive feel for its manuscript
and material remains. Enquiry is framed in terms of the evidence
available rather than of the phenomenon to be explained, and the
argument then proceeds by inference and illustrations.
Interpretation, so far as possible, is embodied in the 'findings'
– i.e. the selection and interpretation of the facts. The facts
themselves are regarded as relatively unproblematical: provided
the researcher is diligent enough in collecting them, what
'really' happened will eventually emerge. Problems of
historiography – i.e. of the construction of historical knowledge
– are by and large left for the philosophers to deal with, while
historians advance their cause, as the founders of *Annales* put
it, 'not by means of methodological articles and theoretical
dissertation, but by example and fact'. Behind this conceptual
reticence will sometimes be found remnants of that complacent
assumption that there exists an agreed body of knowledge which
can be expected to accumulate with the passage of time – what
Professor Elton, with bluff disregard for the mutability of the
subject, calls 'just ordinary sound history'.
 The hostility to theory, which has of course an ancient
lineage, was probably at its height in the years of the Cold War,
when historians, along with British intellectuals as a whole, went
into battle against international Communism under the war-cry of
'methodological individualism'. Theory was equated with
'continental Marxism' and dismissed as either metaphysical
rubbish, or an arbitrary imposition of 'pre-conceived' ideas. A
whole number of revisionist works were published with the more

---

*Raphael Samuel is an editor of *History Workshop Journal*, and
has been a tutor at Ruskin College, Oxford, since 1964.

or less explicit intention of undermining Marxist, or neo-Marxist, interpretations of history - notably in the field of seventeenth-century studies, and the industrial revolution - while on a higher plane historians lined up enthusiastically behind Isaiah Berlin and Karl Popper in stigmatising the very idea of 'laws of development' as being incipiently totalitarian. Cold War themes were blended with an increasingly militant professionalism, which resented the intrusion of extra-curricular concerns. Not only Marxists but also scholar-radicals, such as Tawney and the Hammonds, came under increasingly vehement attack. 'Historicism' was condemned as unprofessional as well as being cast in the role of a Trojan Horse for the would-be Soviet invader, and those who practised it were accused of having betrayed the historian's vocation. 'Disproved by all intellectual tests', wrote Professor Trevor-Roper in 1956, 'the Marxist interpretation of history is sustained and irrationally justified by Soviet power alone.' Marxist historians for their part, subject to the witch-hunt, and fighting for the right to be heard, tried to legitimise their work by removing theoretical prolegomena, softening Marxist terminology, and embodying their work in the empirical form expected of scholarly monographs.

The first major challenge to this confident, if self-enclosed, empiricism, came from sociology, which began to make its influence felt in British universities from the late 1950s. In historical work, it was energetically propagated by the *Past and Present* conferences of the early 1960s on such themes as 'leisure' and 'social mobility', by the spread of inter-disciplinary seminar courses, and by the various attempts to modernise the curriculum which followed the proliferation of new universities and polys. In the context of a narrowly political and constitutional historiography, largely devoted to statecraft, sociology appeared as a progressive and even a subversive force, opening up new subject areas for historical enquiry - family, community, popular culture - and directing the historian's gaze at hitherto untravelled terrain. It encouraged historians to engage in the use of comparative method, and instead of prohibiting reference to the present day (in the 1950s, many history courses still stopped sternly short at 1914), positively encouraged them to modernise their footnotage, and bring their work into line with more contemporary sociological or anthropological findings. But though, under such influences as these, the subject matter of history was generously enlarged, the basic mode of historical enquiry was in many ways unchanged. Sociology provided the empty theoretical boxes: it was for the historians to fill them with facts.

The challenge posed by 'structuralism' - the issue at stake in the debates around E.P. Thompson's *Poverty of Theory* - is both more recent and more radical. It is concerned not with this or that subject matter, but with the construction of knowledge itself - i.e. epistemology. Structuralism has been developed outside historiography and is indeed associated with

a definite attempt to expel history from the realm of social
theory, and to substitute 'synchronic' for 'diachronic'
explanation - i.e. to study phenomena at a given point in time
rather than in their historical evolution. Nevertheless it poses
important questions which historians ought to face. First and
foremost it challenges induction (i.e. the derivation of
arguments and concepts from facts), which is conventionally
what historians believe themselves to be doing when engaged in
researching or writing up their work. Second, it attacks
reflection theory - i.e. the notion that the mind is a neutral
medium on which some pre-existing reality imprints itself. It
argues that it is language, rather than reality, which structures
thought, and thought which 'signifies' - i.e. gives meaning to -
reality. There is no 'real' world independent of our perceptions
of it - only a self-contained circuit of 'signs'. Third, it attacks
what it defines as 'historicism' - i.e. the notion that historical
structures can be explained by their genesis. It argues that
such attempts are necessarily flawed by teleological modes of
reasoning, i.e. the notion of ineluctable cause and effect implicit
in the Marxist version of 'stages' of historical development, and
in such older evolutionary schemes as the Whig interpretation of
history. Beyond this, it attempts to sever theoretical categories
from any notion of historical time. It makes a sharp distinction
between the ways in which concepts are formed and the empirical
study of phenomena: history does not contain its own methods of
explanation within itself, nor its own logic of enquiry; causality
is not generated by the evidence, but by the conceptual understanding that is brought to bear on it. Finally, it 'de-centres'
the human subject: history is not the study of Man but of the
subliminal languages and codes of which men and women are the
compulsive 'bearers'.

Broadly speaking, one could say that structuralism, as it was
developed particularly in France in the 1960s, and latterly in
Britain, represents a mainly left-wing response to the collapse,
or questioning, of evolutionary and humanist notions of progress.
Like the philosophically very different schools of Marxism which
are to be found in West Germany and the United States, it is
marked by a certain tone of cultural pessimism, a preoccupation
with structures of domination, and an emphasis on men and
women as the victims and prisoners of social process rather than,
potentially at least, free agents of change. One is dealing here
not with a single school of thought, but with a major intellectual
current which has been influential in a variety of contexts -
linguistics, literary criticism, anthropology, cinema and art.
Those Marxists who have been most influenced by variants of a
structuralist approach (e.g. Louis Althusser in France) take
their categories and their political commitment from Marxism, but
their unifying concepts, their metaphorical vision are borrowed
- or rather transported - from psychoanalysis, structural
linguistics and anti-evolutionary theories of science. The debt to
and influence of Freud is evident and acknowledged: the

preoccupation with the hidden elements in the social order, the emphasis on dream-like and self-deluding character of ideological representations, and the opaque character of the social formations, arguably provides the fundamental social vision on which structuralism builds, and is evidently derived from Freud's notion of the unconscious. While a psychoanalytic concept of language – an insistence on the repressed dialogue going on beneath the surface discourse – may be seen in the central importance attached to the 'symptomatic' reading of texts, i.e. reading the texts against the grain of their surface volubility for gaps, silences and guilty absences.

British Marxist structuralism, a rapid growth in recent years, is in many ways a contradictory phenomenon. On the one hand, by treating Marxism as 'unfinished' – i.e. as a continuous and cumulative mode of understanding the world rather than as an unquestioning set of dogmas – it has undoubtedly released an enormous amount of theoretical energy on the Left, and helped to produce both a greater diffusion of the basic Marxist texts, and a greater readiness to use them, quite explicitly, in current intellectual work. On the other hand, it has created a climate of anxiety around the very notion of theory, and has had the effect, however unintended, of suggesting that it was the close preserve of an esoteric sect of initiates. However fruitful the questions, the discourse itself is imprisoning. Much of the recent work which has proceeded under the influence of structuralism is disfigured by a mannered prose, a talismanic use of reference, and by a defensive recourse to a limited number of well-thumbed, mostly recent texts – almost all of them French. Like other academic fashions (and there is undoubtedly an element of modishness about the spread of structuralism on the radical fringes of British universities and polys) it involves a good deal of posturing, and insofar as it has a discernible political purpose it is that of keeping an uncomfortable world at bay. The justified attack on the empiricist theory of knowledge (i.e. the notion that the mind is a blank page on which the facts imprint themselves) slides into a lofty dismissal of empirical work itself. At its most naive and unreflective – as in Hindess and Hirst's *Pre-Capitalist Modes of Production* – it exalts theoretical practice to the point where it becomes an end in itself, arriving at formularistically irreproachable conceptual categories which are empty of usable content.

Nevertheless structuralism is addressed to a real area of problems about which historians have no reason to feel complacent, above all the intractable relationships between ideology and consciousness and economic and social phenomena. By drawing attention to the means of representation, it necessarily shifts our attention from the real world of objects to the categories of language and thought through which they are perceived – i.e. to the imaginary, the subjective, and the sub-conscious. Despite the novelty of some of the language employed, the questions raised by structuralism have to do with some of the oldest and most intractable problems in European philosophy. They are certainly relevant to any form of historical enquiry. By focussing on the forms of knowledge, and the ways in which meanings are mediated, structuralism necessarily makes us more aware of the contingent nature of historical representations, and forces us to consider them as ideological constructions rather than as the empirical record of past events. By insisting on the primacy of theory, structuralism may force us to consider not only the political implications of our work – something which will scarcely be news to socialist historians – but also, something more rarely a subject for consideration, its conceptual basis. By stating the case against history in the most extreme way, it has the negative virtue of forcing historians to justify explicitly what they are doing. It asks us, in common with other intellectual workers, to question the unarticulated assumptions on which our work is based – to look again at the ways in which the subject matter of history is constituted, questions framed, evidence assembled, inferences drawn. It questions the status assigned to the documents as reflections of the 'facts' and asks us to consider the artifices we employ to give them context and shape. Any historical work (structuralism alleges) imposes a false unity on its subject in the very processes by which the subject is defined. The themes, whether descriptive or analytical, are necessarily selected by the historian, and so too are the selectivities and exclusions. Periodisation, however convincing, is always arbitrary; detail, however 'immediate', is necessarily partial; while the choice of problematic is trimmed, in greater or lesser degree, to what the frame of reference will accommodate. The documents do not only corroborate; they also falsify, substituting for structure and process a while series of separated fragments, and introducing us not to the real world of the past, but only to its system of representations. Transparency, however much the historian may strive for it, is evidently impossible when so many displacements intervene. As in a still-life picture, some objects will have been blown up out of all proportion, others reduced in scale, while the great majority will have been crowded out of the frame entirely. It is the historian, not the documents, which have produced it. However elegant the explanation, or easy the narrative flow, the totality is nevertheless, in the final analysis, constructed, the product of conceptual premeditation – or perceptual blindness – rather than a spontaneous response to the material. Historians thus do not reflect the past – they signify and construct it: meaning is in the eye of the beholder.

It by no means follows from this that historians are inevitably the victims of their own perceptions, or that the empirical evidence of the past is so irretrievably contaminated that the attempt to order it becomes a labour of Sisyphus, piling up facts 'Pelian upon Ossa' while meaning recedes into twilight. It is one thing to point to the displacements which take place in any process of thought, and to emphasise the mediations which separate representation and reality. It is quite another to resolve the problem by abolishing one of its terms entirely, by jettisoning the notion of

the real. Indeed in doing so structuralism may be said to subvert
its own enterprise - the exploration of the cognitive and cultural
unconscious - by abolishing the dialectical tension on which any
notion of symbolic order ultimately rests.

Nor is it possible to accept the suggestion that historians
simply constitute the past according to their own preconceptions.
It may be, as Barbara Taylor and Sally Alexander argue in this
volume, that 'History only answers questions which are put to it'.
But it by no means follows that we get the answers we expect.
When you go to the evidence you don't just find one thing - the
instance or illustration you were looking for - but also half a
dozen which catch you unawares. A text may prove - or seem to
prove - what you want it to prove, but, disconcertingly, it may
simultaneously suggest alternative readings, subtly at variance
with the one you have chosen, and you will have to have an amour-
plated confidence in the adequacy of your concepts if you leave
them unexplored. Nor is the evidence simply constituted by the
historian. It has a pre-existing reality, determined by literary
form or archival protocol, so that for the most part we are having
to extract meaning against the grain of the documentation
however much it may appear to be obedient to our will.

It is true that our knowledge of the past is crucially shaped by
the preoccupations we bring to bear on it, and that we can only
interpret the evidence within the limits of an imaginative vision
which is itself historically conditioned. But this is by no means
as unilaterally disabling as it may appear. Our own experience
may blunt our perceptions in certain directions, but it will
certainly sharpen them in others, giving us access to meanings
which were not available to the historical actors at the time, and
allowing us to counter their 'representations' with our own. It
will also spotlight whole orders of phenomena to which even our
immediate predecessors were blind. An obvious case in point
would be the discovery (or rediscovery) of women's history in
the last ten years. It has not only opened up vast new fields of
research - in law, medicine and political economy, no less than in
such newly-constituted subject matter as marriage, childhood and
family life - but has also put in question some of the leading
conceptual categories on which historians have relied. Only
twenty years ago a fine social historian could write that 'class
happens, when some men, as a result of common experience
(inherited or shared), feel and articulate the identity of interests
as between themselves, and as against other men whose interests
are different from (and usually opposed to) theirs'. Such a statement would be difficult to defend in the light of the new knowledge
of the past which the women's movement has brought, and the
new questions posed by it. An earlier example would be the
discovery of economic history in the 1880s and 1890s, which
permanently altered the map of knowledge and the compasses
used to read it. Meaning is only made manifest retrospectively,
and this is not only a matter of knowing what happened - the
historian's peculiar, if sometimes ambiguous, advantage of

hindsight - but also of being able to offer new interrogations of
the past on the basis of present-day preoccupations and
experience. To say this is not to subscribe to a Whig view of
knowledge as a progressive development. It is possible for
understanding to be lost as well as gained - as happened, for
instance, to the first women's history, and to the centrality
given to the family in late nineteenth-century European social
thought. It is also possible for the field of knowledge to be
narrowed, for more and more to be learned about less and less -
the fate arguably, of the second and third generation of economic
history in Britain, and certainly one against which the 'new'
social history has to guard. Nevertheless, even if knowledge is
not, in any simple sense, cumulative (the present is continually
subverting our understanding of the past), the gains of previous
generations do provide us with the invisible premises from which
present-day inquiry starts, and the hinterland of thought in
which we move.

What of that other crucial mediation on which structuralism
focusses attention - the radical imperfection of our documents?
By questioning the 'naive' reading of texts, and arguing that
language camouflages more than it reveals, structuralism
necessarily puts into question the status we assign to our
documents as reflections, or guides, to the facts: there is no
'real' world of the past, only an infinite regress of disguises.
It is true that what we have in the documents is not the past,
but only its fugitive remains, flashing up at us, as the German
Marxist Walter Benjamin put it, 'at a moment of danger'. Nothing
can compensate for the long silences and the huge absences, and
it is true that we can be so mesmerised by the palpable reality of
the documents which come before us that we can mistake them for
reality itself. But the historian is not necessarily dazzled by the
surface appearance of the texts, and in fact it is often by juxta-
posing them against each other that it is possible to reveal
something of the interstices in which they existed. Nor is the
historian necessarily at the mercy of the past's representation
of itself.

Historians don't only work from what structuralists call 'texts'.
A good deal of their work has to do with artefacts and material
remains. Numismatics may provide the critical evidence for the
historian of Roman trade routes, burial hoards for the historian
of Viking settlement. Ridge and furrow, manifesting their original
shape after centuries of tillage, have been vital evidence for
historians of medieval agriculture, while the lost villages of that
time were identified, in many cases, by field research and aerial
photography. Our written texts can only be treated as 'representations' if the term is used metaphorically, and it is quite
reductionist to treat them as all of a kind. A bishop's sermon has
a different evidential status from, say, the entries in a baptismal
register, and allows a quite different interpretative range. Each
may be allowed to have its ideological 'conditions of existence',
yet they occupy quite separate spheres even if, formally, both

could be assigned to the 'discourse' of church government. The
first may be construed in terms of its rhetorical codes: the
second allows the historical demographer to draw out long-run
projections of fertility. Doré's phantasmagoric representations
of 1870s London may tell us more about the mind of the artist,
or the pictorial ideology of the time, than they do about the slums
of East London, but the same could not be said of those contem-
poraneous Ordnance Survey maps which yield the uttermost
detail about the physical topography of streets, and the strategic
sitings of pubs, wood-yards and schools.

It is true, as structuralism argues, that there is no such thing
as an innocent text, and it is right that we should be asked to
consider the ideological context in which our documents are
produced – the notions of family which underpin, say, a household listing; the visual codes which lithographs such as Doré's
obey. But it does not follow from this that the whole of the
historian's subject matter can be dissolved into 'interpellations'
of 'discourse'. Learning the code – the categories of thought
within which the documents are produced – may be essential if
we are to situate them, and to identify their selectivities and
silences. But there is no reason why that should usurp our whole
attention. A will, for example, may be of great interest for the
'discourse' about death, and this is how wills have been used by
Michel Vovelle in his work on dechristianisation in eighteenth-
century Provence. But there are quite other kinds of information
which a study of wills may yield – in peasant wills, the relative
salience, say, of household posessions and stock, the 'grid of
inheritance' (as Edward Thompson has called it), the mechanisms
and incidence of debt. Again – to take another example – the
manuscript census returns of nineteenth-century England can be
shown to falsify certain kinds of evidence, and to be blind to
others (for instance, women's work), but it would be absurd, on
these grounds, to think that the only legitimate use we could make
of them was to reconstitute 'discourse' of the enumerators.

A large part of the historian's work consists in subverting – or
escaping from – the categories of thought in which the documents
are conceived. Thus defamation cases, as they appear before the
consistory courts of the sixteenth and seventeenth centuries,
can tell us a great deal about the language of insults, and the
'discourse' of honour and shame. But they also – like police court
cases in the nineteenth century – provide us with a vast amount
of incidental information, in no sense an effect of that discourse,
nor intended by those who drew up the text, about the economy
of family life: who is and who is not at home at particular times of
the day, on particular days of the week, or in particular seasons
of the year; who sits down to meals and when and where; child-
minding arrangements; fuel-gathering or fuel-saving strategies;
patterns of neighbouring and visiting; sexual divisions in work
and play. Again, a murder case can be used – as Foucault has
used it in *I, Pierre Riviere, having slaughtered my mother, my
sister, and my brother* – to reconstitute ideas of sanity and guilt,

and to distinguish the moral codes of judges, doctors and
parishioners. But it may, like the Euston Square tragedy of
1877, be more valuable for what it tells us about the vicissitudes
of domestic service in a third-floor back, or the standards of
shabby-genteel domestic comfort. A more difficult case is that
of autobiographies, which historians are certainly in the habit
of using as though they constituted an unmediated, spontaneous
testimony. It is valuable that we should be asked to consider them
as exercises in memory, and to inquire into the invisible conventions they obey. But it does not follow from this - as is sometimes
argued - that this is the only use to which they can be put, and
that historians should not have access to them for the sake of
quite other contexts: the reconstruction of a narrative sequence,
say, or the corroboration, in subjective experience, of some
generalised statement about class relations, family life, or
domestic economy.

Some classes of document do give a more direct encounter with
the past than others, either because they are more impromptu -
unmediated by after-thought or formality - or because of the
order of phenomena to which they relate. Household inventories,
such as those used by Professor Hoskins to chart the changing
fortunes of the sixteenth-century yeoman, are indisputable
evidence about the level of material culture; the consistory court
records of the same period amply testify to the occasions of
neighbourly quarrels. Neither of these classes of document will,
of themselves, allow a picture of, say, the rise of capitalist
farming to appear, still less explain it, but an account of class
formation in sixteenth-century England which ignored them would
be gratuitously impoverished. Again, there are certain documents
which enable us to enter - or at any rate approach - the mental
landscape of the past by giving us access to the spoken word.
A striking example is the use of the Inquisition records by Carlo
Ginzburg in *I Benandanti* or (more recently) by Le Roy Ladurie
in *Montaillou*. An older one might be Sir Charles Firth's discovery
of the transcripts taken down during the Putney debates, when
Cromwell and Ireton debated 'Puritanism and liberty' with the
rank-and-file army agitators. In a more shadowy domain one might
instance the poems of François Villon, reproducing the argot of
the Paris streets and restoring identity to those underworld
bands, like the Coquillards, who would otherwise remain mere
names on the police registers.

The starting point of the structuralist critique, that theoretical
propositions can't be derived from empirical evidence, is a correct
one. But it by no means follows that the inverse of this is true,
i.e. that the construction of new theoretical concepts can proceed
by a purely deductive process of reasoning without reference to
empirical work. For Marxists, theoretical work has always generated propositions designed to explain and understand the real
world, and to interpret concrete situations even if they cannot be
verified by reference to empirical enquiry alone. Theory-building
cannot be an alternative to the attempt to explain real phenomena,

but is, rather, a way of self-consciously defining the field of enquiry, clarifying and exposing to self-criticism the explanatory concepts used, and marking the limits of empirical investigation. It is right and proper that we should be warned against mistaking the historian's patterning of the representations of the past for the reality of the past itself. But it would be absurd, on these same grounds, to urge the abandonment of the study of history. If theory persuaded socialist historians to give up the ambition to comprehend the real world on the ground that the effort was epistemologically disreputable, the only effect will be to leave the terrain to the undisputed possession of those with no such qualms, and allow 'just ordinary sound history' to regain its former mastery.

Theory-building cannot claim a privileged immunity from empirically-grounded critiques. If it chooses a point of historical and social reference, as in the case of Marxist theory it is bound to do, it cannot simply constitute its own evidence by declaring that its real object is the refinement of theoretical concepts. In any historical enquiry the ways in which the evidence is read matter quite as much as the ways theory is built, and the two are necessarily interdependent, even if they occupy different plans of abstraction. Historians necessarily deal with particular cases - not just with, say, the capitalist mode of production, but with specific forms and epochs of its development: the slave trade and the plantation economy in the ante-Bellum South, for instance, enclosure and labour supply in the Industrial Revolution, fascism and the war economy in the Third Reich. Similarly, in dealing with labour history, historians are not just dealing with some hypostasised 'workers' movement', or even with such generalities as 'labourism' or 'social democracy', but with such very specific manifestations of it as, say, the socialism of the Second International, or the struggle for the Eight Hour Day. In the light of such work we shall have continually to re-make our theoretical categories, since it is precisely the reality which they have to build from and answer to.

In history, there are limits to how far you can go on the basis of synthesis or abstract reasoning. Events have to be situated in their original context; the language of the sources decoded; the lines of association re-drawn. The historian has constantly to deal with ambiguous meanings, or with phenomena that are too ephemeral to be subjected to the regularities of testable hypothesis or the construction of ideal types. Narrative and description - however lowly their status in a theory of knowledge - are an inescapable part of the historian's repertory. They may not, in themselves, constitute explanation, but they are a necessary component of proof; and they will also perform the crucial negative function of making certain kinds of hypothesis (e.g. that Chartism was a result of family 'disturbance') untenable. Criticism of the sources - i.e. weighing up the worth of different kinds of evidence - is also an inevitable part of the historian's repertory if he or she is not to fall victim to precisely those illusions of 'realism' with which structuralism is concerned. In short, problems of method in history are inseparable from the complexities of data-gathering, and even if they are assigned to different domains, there will be a continual traffic between them.

To say this is not to deny the need for conceptual self-awareness, nor to suggest that questions of method can be resolved by reference to problems of research technique. Nor is to subscribe to professor Hexter's common sense notion of a 'reality' rule, in which the historian plumps for the most likely story that the relevant evidence will sustain. Nor is it to support the idea, inviting though it may be, that historians are protected by some immanent procedural technique - what E.P. Thompson calls 'the logic of the discipline' - from outside philosophical criticism. It is only too easy, when you are immersed in a particular line of inquiry, to inflate its relative significance; to mistake the part for the whole; and even, by your very success in penetrating the reticence of the documents, to succumb to the illusion that the past has come alive. Historians, even Marxist historians who are more exposed to criticism than most, are only too apt to take their premises for granted, and to treat their procedures as unproblematic and pre-given. It is right and proper that such reticence should be challenged, and that we should be called upon to say what we are doing, as well as to explain - or to question - the ways in which we are doing it. A socialist history isn't, or shouldn't be - simply a question of a different subject matter, but rather of a different way of looking at a society as a whole. It needs to be theoretically informed if it is to resist the scholastic fragmentation of the subject matter, and to escape those territorial sub-divisions which corral historical inquiry within professionally-defined fiefs. It needs theory if it is to help bring about the reunification of history with other forms of knowledge; if it is to engage in comparative inquiry; and if it is to bring the interpretation of the past and the understanding of the present into dialogue with one another. It also needs theory for studies in depth. Theoretical work may be undertaken for the purposes of putting things together, and connecting seemingly fragmented orders of historical phenomena - say, culture and politics, or crime and family order. Equally it may be used to deconstruct reality, and focus on its subterranean determinants. It is necessarily central in any attempt to achieve an overall synthesis, but it may be no less serviceable in fragmenting the historian's symmetries and exposing them to critical gaze.

But theory is not something ready-made, waiting for us to adopt in the form of 'hypotheses', 'models' or protocol. Like any other intellectual artefact, it has its material and ideological conditions of existence. This can obviously be seen in the case of such major revolutions in thought as those associated with the names of Marx, Darwin and Freud, but it also needs to be borne in mind when confronting more recent conceptual innovations. Theoretical currents only become important because they respond, or seem to respond, to some pre-existing silence or unease. The emergence of structuralism, for instance, clearly needs to be related to those political phenomena which have undermined rationalistic and optimistic views of the universe; just as the current popularity of the notion of 'hegemony' is evidently related to the visibly growing powers of the state. Again, the emergence in recent years of the women's movement has put into question the whole mental landscape of socialist thought: sexuality and patriarchy cannot, in any simple way, be derived from property relationships; nor can modes of production – or notions of class consciousness – any longer be divorced from the crucial mediations of the home. Theoretical advances, in short, will often emerge not from conceptual refinement, but from the difficulties and unsolved questions thrown up by political practice. The relationship between history and theory, if it is to be fruitful, must be a two-way affair. It only becomes worthwhile if we engage in theoretical work ourselves, taking nothing on trust, but bringing a historical understanding to bear on the questions with which we are faced. The theoretical issues which are now common currency on the radical fringes of British universities and polytechnics are properly the philosophic heritage of the socialist movement as a whole. Many of the key categories now being bandied back and forth are in the first place, at least for Marxists, historically defined, and the historian is likely to bring as much understanding to bear on them as the economist 'reconceptualising' Marx so as to expel the labour theory of value, or the sociologist reducing the notion of class struggle to the status of an interesting 'heuristic' device.

A theoretically informed approach ought not to be identified with any particular way of writing and it is in no sense dependent upon canonical texts or heraldic verbal devices. The theoretical worth of a project is not to be gauged by the manner of its expression, but by the complexity of the relationships it explores. It is compatible with a great variety of analytic and literary modes – compare Marx's discussion of ideology in *The Eighteenth Brumaire of Louis Napoleon* with that in *Capital* – with different modes of reasoning and different fields of study. Within Marxism, it certainly doesn't involve the implication that certain types of subject matter are inherently more legitimate than others – mode of production, say, but not culture or family life: in principle, the lyrical poetry of Baudelaire, or the musical language of the Blues, are just as susceptible to materialist analysis as such more obvious candidates for Marxist analysis as the New Poor Law or the Anti Corn Law League. Nor is it right to associate 'theory' with any particular school of thought, however imperialist its claims. In this book we attempt to show that there are major theoretical issues in every field of historical work – in the local history of Hackney no less than in that of African slavery, in the history of the home no less than in that of state formation or capitalist development. We also focus on the forms of historical knowledge, the conditions in which it is produced and the ways in which it is appropriated. In short, the book has taken the occasion of the current debate on theory to ask historians to consider the conditions of existence of their work, and the possibilities of a different kind of knowledge.

FURTHER READING

Any reading list on so vast a theme is arbitrary. Here what I have tried to do is to group some of the recent developments in theory, and then to look at some of those points where they bear most obviously on the subject matter of 'people's history'. I have tried not to duplicate the bibliographies attached to the various sub-sections of this book; so, readers in search of references to, say, 'primitive accumulation' are referred to the articles by Hans Medick and Michael Ignatieff.

The debate on empiricism
E.H/ Carr's *What is History* (1961, reprinted by Penguin books 1977) represented, in its time, a brave stand against the ortho-doxies of the Cold War, and it has rightly been established, for two decades, as the most radical and accessible critique of the assumptions underlying orthodox historical practice. It is a rare blend of old-fashioned elegance and commitment to revolutionary change. Gareth Stedman Jones, 'History: the Poverty of Empiricism', in ed. Robin Blackburn, *Ideology in Social Science* (Fontana 1972) is a fiercer essay in a similar vein, informed by a fine wit and somewhat influenced by French Marxist structuralism. Barry Hindess and Paul Q. Hirst, *Pre-Capitalist Modes of Produc-tion* (London 1975), in spite of a leaden, incantatory style, a meretricious use of historical sources and an inability to acknow-ledge intellectual or fraternal debts, is nevertheless a valuable provocation to anyone who feels complacent about the adequacy of historical practice (see especially pp. 308 ff). Richard Johnson, 'Thompson, Genovese, and Socialist-Humanist History', *History Workshop Journal* 6, Autumn 1978 is a much better-mannered - as well as more historically-informed - critique, and a principled attempt to build bridges between theoreticism and empiricism. The same writer's essays in ed. John Clarke and others, *Working-Class Culture* (London 1979) represent a considerable elaboration of his themes. Jean Chesneaux, *Pasts and Futures, or What is History For?* (London 1978) is an impassioned attack on profes-sionalism by a French *gauchiste* and apostate professor of history. Well worth reading.

Sociology and social history
Neil Smelser, *Social Change in the Industrial Revolution* (London 1959) is the most systematic attempt to submit historical evidence to sociological protocols, and attempts to explain the social movements of the early nineteenth century in terms of family

disturbance. It is discussed polemically in E.P. Thompson, *The Making of the English Working Class* (London 1963) and in a more historiographic context by Arthur L. Stinchcombe, *Theoretical Methods in Social History* (London 1980). In spite of its much-ridiculed boxes, it raises fundamental interpretative problems to which feminist historians, from a very different perspective, are now returning. Keith Thomas, 'History and Anthropology', *Past and Present* no.24, 1963, was a seminal advocacy of a position whose force can be measured in the same writer's *Religion and the Decline of Magic* (Penguin 1978). E. Le Roy Ladurie, *Le Territoire de l'Historien* (Paris 1973) demonstrates some of the ways in which history and social science are combined in the *Annales*. For some more critical approaches to both sociology and the 'new' social history, E.J. Hobsbawm, 'From Social History to the History of Society', *Daedalus* 100, 1971; E.P. Thompson, 'Anthropology and the Discipline of Historical Context', *Midland History* 1, no.3, Spring 1972; Gareth Stedman Jones, 'From Historical Sociology to Theoretic History', *British Journal of Sociology*, XXVII, no.3, September 1976; Elizabeth Fox-Genovese and Eugene D. Genovese, 'The Political Crisis of Social History: a Marxian Perspective', *Journal of Social History* X, no.2, Winter 1976; Tony Judt, 'A Clown in Regal Purple', *History Workshop Journal* 7, Spring 1979. Peter Burke's forthcoming *History and Sociology* is likely to provide a synoptic survey of the impact of social science on history in the last twenty years.

Historical materialism
Etienne Balibar, *Cinq Études du Matérialisme Historique* (Paris 1974) develops the structuralist perspectives first essayed in the author's contribution to *Reading Capital* (London 1970). Pierre Vilar, 'Marxist History', *New Left Review* 80, July-August 1973 is the moderate critique of an eminent French Marxist historian. G.A. Cohen, *Karl Marx's Theory of History: A Defence* (Oxford 1978) upholds, with philosophic sophistication and scrupulous attention to the texts, a 'strict' version of Marxism, in which the productive forces provide the dynamic of historical change. The issues of 'base' and 'superstructure' are debated with passion in E.P. Thompson, *The Poverty of Theory* (London 1978) and Perry Anderson *Arguments within English Marxism* (London 1980). Raymond Williams, *Marxism and Literature* (Oxford 1977) is a wide-ranging and compelling argument, very relevant to the present debate among historians.

Structuralism
The writings of Lévi-Strauss, Barthes, Althusser, Lacan, Foucault and Derrida are available in English translation, and they have inspired a vast Anglo-Saxon commentary. Since structuralism deliberately sets out to complicate and fracture meaning, the reading of it is not easy. Ino Rossi, ed. *The Unconscious in Culture: the Structuralism of Claude Lévi-Strauss*

in Perspective (New York 1974) shows some of its potential
relevance to historians. John Sturrock, ed., *Structuralism and
Since* (Oxford 1979) is a reasonably accessible introduction from
the point of view of literary studies. Two Marxist works, Fredric
Jameson, *The Prison-house of Language* (Princeton 1972), and
Sebastiano Timpanaro, 'Structuralism and its Successors' in *On
Materialism* (London 1975) have the merit of bringing a wide
literary and political culture to bear on their exposition, as well
as situating it in a historical context. For the application of
'discourse analysis' to historical material, Michel Foucault,
Discipline and Punish. The Birth of the Prison (London 1977) and
The History of Sexuality (London 1979); Jacques Donzelot, *The
Policing of Families* (London 1980) is the work of a French
disciple, notable for its thin documentation and surrealist method,
but discussing an important historical question. Michael Ignatieff,
*A Just Measure of Pain: the Penitentiary in the Industrial
Revolution 1750-1850* (London 1978) is a moving book which
attempts to set discourse analysis in a more recognisably materialist framework; Keith Tribe, *Land, Labour and Economic Discourse*
(London 1978) in spite of an abrasive presentation has a fine
sense of the interplay of language, economy and thought.

Popular memory, folklore, oral tradition
This is a field to which oral history, Marxism and structuralism
all address themselves, and it is to be hoped that the discussion
can be joined since it points to one of those questions about which
we are almost wholly ignorant - the nature of historical consciousness itself. Michel Foucault, *Language, Counter-Memory, Practice*
(Oxford 1977) gives some idea of a structuralist perspective, as
do numerous articles in the neo-Marxist film journal *Screen*. From
a more classical Marxist position, George Thomson, *Marxism and
Poetry* (London 1945); Walter Benjamin 'The Storyteller' in
Illuminations (Fontana 1977); Antonio Gramsci, *Letteratura e
Rivoluzione* (Turin 1973). Maurice Halbwachs, *La Mémoire
Collective* (Paris 1950) is an important work, in the tradition of
Durkheimian sociology, which would be well worth translating.
Francis Yates, *The Art of Memory* discusses some memory banks
of the sixteenth and seventeenth centuries. Jan Vansina, *Oral
Tradition* (Penguine 1973) discusses problems of method from the
point of view of field work in anthropology. Luisa Passerini,
'Conoscenza Storica e Storia Orale' in ed. Passerini, *Storia Orale*
(Turin 1978) reviews some of the theoretical and historical
difficulties in oral history, as also does her 'Work, Ideology and
Concensus under Italian Fascism', *History Workshop Journal* 8
Autumn 1979. Critical discussions of the limits of oral history by
Yves Léquin and F. Raphael will be found in *Annales* 35, Jan-Feb.
1980, and B. Bernardi, C. Poni and A. Truilzi, *Fonti Orali*
(Bologna 1978). Ronald J. Grele, ed., *Envelopes of Sound*
Chicago 1975) seems to be a victim of the British Museum's
economy cuts - I have not yet been able to get hold of a copy.
Philippe Joutard, *La Legende des Camisards* (Paris 1977) is a

splendid demonstration of the possibility of reconstituting the
oral tradition of the past. Gerald M. Sider, 'Christmas Mumming
and the New Year in Outport Newfoundland', *Past and Present*
71, May 1976, is a fine Marxist contribution to the historical use
of folklore as are also the various studies of E.P. Thompson to
be collected in his forthcoming *Customs in Common*. Gwyn
Williams,'Dic Penderyn', in *Llafur* 1978 is an eloquent testimony
to the mutations of historical memory in Merthyr Tydfil and his
Madoc, The 'Making of a Myth' (London 1979) combines scholarship and high comedy with a Gramscian understanding of the
'national-popular' tradition. Nathan Wachtel, *The Vision of the
Vanquished: the Spanish Conquest of Peru through Indian eyes,
1530-1570* (Hassocks 1977) demonstrates the subversive power of
this kind of inquiry for the history of colonialism.

Sexual identity
The women's movement and the Gay Liberation movement have
inspired a vast literature on gender roles and the social construction of sexual identity. Much of it is historical in character and
serves to question the descriptive and analytic categories commonly in use among historians. Among many accessible works, Sheila
Rowbotham, *Women's Consciousness, Man's World* (Penguin
1973); Joan Scott and Louise Tilly, *Women, Work and Family*
(New York 1978); Gayle Rubin, 'The Traffic in Women: Notes on
the "Political Economy" of Sex' in ed. Rayna R. Reiter, *Towards
an Anthropology of Women* (New York 1975); Ellen Ross and Rayna
Rapp, 'Sex and Society: a research note from social history and
anthropology' in a forthcoming issue of *Signs*; Catherine Hall,
'The Early Formation of victorian Domestic Ideology' in ed. Sandra
Burman, *Fit Work for Women* (London 1979); Leonore Davidoff,
'Mastered for Life: Servant and Wife in Victorian and Edwardian
England', *Journal of Social History* 1974; Anna Davin, 'Imperialism
and Motherhood', *History Workshop Journal* 5 Spring 1978;
Jeffrey Weeks, *Coming Out, Homosexual Politics in Britain, from
the Nineteenth Century to the Present* (London 1977) and the
same writer's 'Movements of Affirmation: Sexual Meanings and
Homosexual Identities', *Radical History Review* no.20, Spring/
Summer 1979; Lutz Neithammer, 'Male Fantasies', *History Workshop
Journal* 7, Spring 1979, discusses the connection between anti-
feminism and the rise of Nazism.

Class formation
This has proved one of the most rewarding fields in recent
Marxist historical work; any choice involves multiple exclusions -
e.g. the splendid work of Maurice Agulhon on peasant radicalism
in Provence. Here I simply take some of the books bearing on
this theme in late eighteenth and early nineteenth century
England. Douglas Hay, 'Property, Authority and the Criminal Law'
in ed. D. Hay and others, *Albion's Fatal Tree* (London 1975) is
an exemplary study in the political dimension of social relations,
making a pioneering use of symbolic analysis; Iorwerth Prothero,

Artisans and Politics in early Nineteenth-Century London
(Folkestone 1979); John Foster, *Class Struggle and the Industrial
Revolution* (London 1974); David Jones, *Before Rebecca, Popular
Protest in Wales 1793-1835* (London 1973); ed. Royden Harrison,
*Independent Collier: the Coal Miner as Archetypal Proletarian
Reconsidered* (Hassocks 1978); and Patrick Joyce, *Work, Society
and Politics: the Culture of the Factory in later Victorian
England* (Brighton 1980) are finely-wrought works of committed
scholarship.

Ideology and consciousness
Theoretical work in this field is, to an extraordinary degree,
self-enclosed and self-referring, and the work undertaken in
recent years by Marxist historians might be a better basis for
renewing understanding and confronting some of the more
baffling phenomena of our time. Amidst much work one might
mention, E.J. Hobsbawm, 'Class Consciousness in History' in ed.
I. Meszaros, *Aspects of History and Class Consciousness*
(Hassocks 1971) and the same writer's 'Labour Traditions' in
Labouring Men (London 1964); Herbert Gutman, 'Work, Culture
and Society in Industrializing America', *American Historical
Review* 78, June 1973; Gareth Stedman Jones, 'Working-Class
Culture and Working-Class Politics in London 1870-1900', *Journal
of Social History* VII no.4, Summer 1974; Stephen Yeo, 'The
Religion of Socialism', *History Workshop Journal* 4, Autumn 1977;
Carlo Ginzburg, *The Worm and the Cheese*, London 1980, and the
same writer's 'Clues' (*History Workshop Journal* 9, Spring 1980)
and 'High and Low: The Theme of Forbidden Knowledge in the
Sixteenth and Seventeenth Centuries' (*Past and Present* 73,
November 1976). Christopher Hill, 'The Norman Yoke' in ed.
John Saville, *Democracy and the Labour Movement* (London 1955)
is always worth revisiting, as is his *Society and Puritanism in
pre-Revolutionary England* (London 1964).

Papers

People's history

1 PEOPLE'S HISTORY OR TOTAL HISTORY

Peter Burke*

In the short space I have at my disposal I want to say three
kinds of thing. The first will be historiographical - when did
people's history begin? The second will be an attempt to assess
the achievement of people's history in the late eighteenth and
early nineteenth centuries. The third will be a similar
assessment of people's history as it is practised today.

The idea of people's history goes back to the later
eighteenth century. In the classical tradition of Greece and
Rome, which was revived at the Renaissance, history was
regarded as a 'noble' literary genre, like epic and tragedy.
Epic, tragedy and history were all supposed to be concerned
with the great deeds of great men. To mention ordinary people
was generally considered to be beneath what was called the
'dignity of history'. An example of what this view meant in
practice is the following: the Roman emperor Vitellius was
deserted in his last moments by everybody except his cook.
When the Roman patrician Tacitus came to write about this
episode in his history, he could not bring himself to write the
word 'cook'. He referred rather more vaguely to 'one of the
meanest' in the emperor's household. Given this idea of what
was 'dignified', people's history, and social history in general,
simply could not develop.

It's true that classical historians, notably Herodotus, and
Renaissance historians, too, were interested in what they
called the 'manners' or customs of different peoples. They were
aware that the way in which (say) the Scythians behaved was
different from the way in which the Greeks behaved, and so on.
But they did not realise that these customs changed over time.
They were aware that law and language changed over time, that
new laws were made and that new words came into use, but they
were not aware of changes in what we would call 'society'. I say
'what we would call society', because, until the middle of the
eighteenth century, the word 'society' in its modern sense did
not exist in any European language, and without the word it is
very difficult to have any conception of that network of
relationships which we call 'society' or 'the social structure'. It
was only in the middle of the eighteenth century that a few
writers, notably in Britain and in France, began to discuss

---

*Peter Burke teaches at Emmanuel College, Cambridge. Author of
Popular Culture in Early Modern Europe, London 1978; *Venice
and Amsterdam: A study of seventeenth-century elites*, London
1974; *History and Sociology*, London 1980. An associate editor of
History Workshop Journal.

changes in manners, changes in customs, and changes from one
type of society to another.

Voltaire's *Essay on Manners*, for example, is concerned with
changes in the European way of life from Charlemagne's day to
his own. Voltaire was interested in chivalry, trade, costume and
so on and he finds a place in his essay for the introduction of
table linen. He was descriptive rather than analytical, but what
was lacking in Voltaire in this respect was to be found in other
writers of the time, such as Turgot, Adam Smith and William
Robertson, who all distinguished four stages in the history of
mankind according to the dominant 'mode of subsistence',
hunting, pastoral, agricultural and commercial. (Marx's debt
to these eighteenth-century thinkers will be clear enough.) In
Scotland in particular, a group of intellectuals were concerned
with what they called 'the history of civil society' or 'the civil
history of mankind', in other words, social history. The phrase
that they coined at this time, 'feudal system', shows their
awareness of the interconnections between the economic,
political and military organisations of the Middle Ages, and the
leading ideas of the time, such as chivalry.

At much the same time (and this was surely no coincidence),
came the discovery of popular culture by a group of German
intellectuals, the most famous of whom were J.G. Herder, who
coined the term 'popular culture', and the brothers Grimm,
who were assiduous collectors of folktales. Middle-class
enthusiasm for popular culture, for what came to be called
'folksongs', 'folktales', and all forms of 'folklore', spread
rapidly across Europe in the late eighteenth century.

In the early nineteenth century we find the first histories
with the word 'people' in their titles. One of the first was the
History of the Swedish people by E.G. Geijer, another was the
History of the Czech People by Palacký. These books were
obviously part of the early nineteenth-century movements of
national self-discovery. It is interesting to find that both
Geijer and Palacký, when they were students, had gone round
their respective countries collecting folksongs. There is a link
between that kind of cultural interest and their ambition to
write a history which would not be just a history of the
government but a history of the whole people. In Germany
there was Zimmermann, who wrote about the German Peasant
War (see Bob Scribner's contribution, below, p. 242). In
Russia, the poet Pushkin planned to write a history of
Pugachev, the leader of a peasant revolt of the seventeenth
century. (The Tsar's comment on this scheme is notorious:
'Such a man has no history.') In France there was Michelet.
In England there was Macaulay; the famous third chapter of the
History of England he published in 1848 is an early English
example of people's history, and of course later on J.R. Green
wrote his *Short History of the English People*. But the English
were a little backward in this respect compared to the Swedes
and the Czechs.

So much for a brief, schematic and oversimplified account of the early history of people's history. How successful was it? The writers I have mentioned were pioneers; voyagers in uncharted historical waters. It isn't surprising that the history they wrote was not entirely satisfactory. From Voltaire onwards, they tended to begin with a manifesto saying that history was not concerned with war and politics alone, but with the daily lives of the whole people. In practice, however, all these historians tended to devote much of their space to a conventional narrative of political and military events, and only every now and then did they include a chapter about 'the state of the people'. They did not make very much effort to relate these state-of-the-people chapters to the narrative chapters. I don't think anyone before Marx and Engels had a very acute awareness of the need to relate structures and events to one another.

Another weakness in this group of historians was the ambiguity in the term 'people', as they used it. Who are the people? Sometimes the term is used to refer to the whole population, but not always. Sometimes the aristocracy is excluded from the people, and sometimes the inhabitants of the towns. For Herder, who coined the term 'popular culture', the people (*Das Volk*), did not include what he called the urban 'mob'. For Herder and his friends, the people *par excellence* were the peasants, because they were untainted with foreign ways and lived close to nature. The concept 'people' had nationalist and sometimes even racist overtones. In Bohemia, Germans and Jews lived among the Czechs, but Palacký and others saw them as foreign to the history of 'the Czech people', defined by the use of the Czech language. In other words, the Romantic nationalist historians had a tendency to treat the people as a kind of club, a club to which not everyone was admitted. *We* are the people. *They* are not.

In the work of these early nineteenth-century historians, as in the work of Thucydides and Livy, the historical epic rode again. This time, however, the hero was collective; not Pericles or Scipio, but 'the people'. The people were seen in an idealistic light, whether they were collectively creating folksongs, or enduring or resisting oppression by 'Them' - the foreigners, the aristocracy, or whoever. The counterpart of the idealised people was the villainous non-people. And so, like the *Annals* and *Histories* of Tacitus, written by a Roman patrician for Roman patricians, or the *Chronicle* of Matthew Paris, written by a monk for monks, this Romantic people's history is obviously time-bound. It belongs quite clearly to an era of wars of national liberation (the Greek revolt, the Serb revolt, the Polish insurrection, etc.), and also to an era of an alliance between bourgeoisie and workers against common enemies (think of the 1830 revolution in France, and the struggle for the Reform Bill in England). The term 'people' was a useful one for papering over the cracks in that alliance. It expressed an ideology.

In short, despite its many merits, the people's history of Geijer and Palacký and the other writers of the early nineteenth century suffered from serious limitations. It may be contrasted with what has been called 'total history', a term which was coined a few years ago by the great French historian Fernand Braudel. In a sense total history is an impossibility. All historians have to select from the evidence surviving from the past before they can write, and they make their selection according to what they consider important, in other words according to their values, the values of the group to which they belong. Braudel would not deny this. He uses the phrase 'total history' to express an ideal. He believes - I am translating him rather freely - that we should be trying to write a history which deals with all the activities of all sorts of people, not a history restricted either to one kind of human activity, such as politics, or to the activities of one social group, such as middle-class adult males. Because life is short we have to tolerate some degree of specialisation, a division of historical labour by which different people study different fragments of the past, but this is only a temporary expedient, and we should not lose sight of our ultimate aim of fitting the pieces into a whole.

Judged by these standards, I fear that the people's history practised today suffers from serious limitations, no less than Romantic people's history. It is of course quite different in some respects from Romantic people's history. It is much more concerned with the relationship between events and structures. It no longer idealises the bourgeoisie. But it has inherited ideas and assumptions from Romantic people's history, ideas and assumptions which are, to put it mildly, counter-productive. The term 'people' remains ambiguous. It is often exclusive. When I call it exclusive I mean that in people's history as it is practised today, some people are considered as more 'people' than others; the proletariat, perhaps, or the 'democratic classes' (a somewhat misleading term), or people with radical views. This exclusiveness is an invitation to confusion, to assuming that everyone (the people in one sense of the term) shares the views of a particular group, large or small (the people in another sense). It's possible to find this kind of confusion in some of the very best people's history written in Britain today. To quote only two examples, and to take examples only from works which in other respects I admire intensely, works by Edward Thompson and Christopher Hill. Edward Thompson's *Making of the English Working Class* comes quite close to excluding working-class Tories from the people. As for *The World Turned Upside Down*, it deals alternately with radical ideas and with the ideas of ordinary people, so that an incautious reader may very well be led to equate the two. However, in seventeenth-century England, not all ordinary people were radicals and not all radicals were ordinary people.

The epic approach to people's history still survives. The

work of Edward Thompson, Christopher Hill and Raphael Samuel
has this epic quality, a quality which is one of their great
virtues. They and others have restored human dignity to
ordinary people in the past. At the same time, this epic approach
involves some very grave dangers. It's terribly easy to slide
into a view of history as essentially a struggle between virtue
and vice; a Whig or Romantic view of history. The signs have
now been reversed, and the bourgeoisie, once the hero of the
epic, has become the villain of the piece, but the basic
structure of interpretation is the same.

I should like to conclude by suggesting that whatever group
you take as the hero of your epic – bourgeoisie or proletariat,
or the blacks, or womanhood – the result is always mystification.
A history constructed round heroes and villains makes it
impossible to understand how the past happened as it did. The
value of the study of history is surely that it reminds us of
awkward truths, such as the truth that not everyone on our
side – whatever that side is – is necessarily good or intelligent,
and that not everyone on the other side is necessarily bad or
stupid. We need to place ourselves in historical context, just as
we need to place the Romantic historians and Tacitus in historical
context. That means that we ought to spend some time looking
at our own prejudices.

To end on a personal and a controversial note, I should like
to say that (although I consider myself a socialist and a
historian), I'm not a socialist historian; that is, I don't believe
in socialist history. I believe that to use history as a weapon in
political struggle is counter-productive. One comes to believe
one's own propaganda, to overdramatise the past, and hence to
forget the real complexity of the issues at any time. One comes
to idealise one's own side, and to divide human beings into Us
and Them. I don't believe in idealising any group, whether it
is as small as the fellows of my college or as large as the
proletariat. And so I should like to give two cheers for people's
history; the first for showing us the social structures underlying
political events, and the second for giving ordinary people back
their human dignity. My third cheer is reserved for total history,
a history in which the distinction between Us and Them is at
last obliterated.

FURTHER READING

Burke, Peter, 'The Discovery of the People' in *Popular Culture
   in Early Modern Europe*, London 1978.

On Herder
Pascal, Roy, *The German Sturm und Drang*, Manchester 1953.

On folklore
Dorson, R. *The British Folklorists*, London 1968.

Cocchiaro, G., *Populo e Letteratura in Italia*, Turin 1959.

On *Annales* history
Braudel, Fernand, *Capitalism and Material Culture*, London 1973.
Le Roy Ladurie, E., *The Territory of the Historian*, Hassocks 1979.
Burke, Peter, *A New Kind of History*, London 1973.
The Review, 1, nos 3-4, winter-spring 1978, special issue on Braudel.

2   THE CHANGING IMAGE OF THE SCOTTISH PEASANTRY, 1745-1980

Ian Carter*

Until the end of the eighteenth century ruling class attitudes to the Scots peasantry were universally hostile. Peasants were sub-human, mere beasts of burden who produced rents upon which a gentleman might live in comfort. When, under the influence of the Scottish Enlightenment's brief efflorescence, ideas of scientific agriculture began to circulate in genteel circles, then the peasantry moved from being simply irrelevant to being positively awkward. With their unaccountable preference for doing things in time-hallowed ways, they represented a major obstacle to the rational – and, for landlords and proto-capitalist farmers, highly profitable – reorganisation of agriculture. This attitude clings on in some historians' work, as we shall see.

Two events complicated this simple picture of class prejudice. The first was, in the literary sense, cultural: the romanticisation first of the highlands and then, by extension, of all rural Scotland. The key figure here was Scotland's last novelist of European stature: the high Tory Sir Walter Scott (1771-1832). In *Rob Roy* the outlawed cattle thief, hitherto regarded as a murdering robber who should be strung up from the highest gibbet, became a romantic bandit. The highland mountains and glens, hitherto gloomy and dangerous obstacles to the establishment of safe communications and profitable trade,

*Ian Carter teaches sociology at the University of Aberdeen and works in peasant studies. Author of *Farm Life in Northeast Scotland 1840-1914*, Edinburgh 1979. An associate editor of *History Workshop Journal*.

became picturesque. The trappings of the highland culture proscribed after Culloden became, under Scott's influence, immensely chic. Highland estate owners – educated in England and domiciled in Edinburgh – trawled up and down the New Town's streets dressed in full kilt and sporran to attend the elegant meetings of the (aristocratic) Edinburgh Highland Society. More and more tourists visited the highlands to see not only the picturesque scenery but the picturesque natives as well.

The second complicating factor was the Disruption of the Church of Scotland. A conflict between evangelical and conservative wings within the national (presbyterian) Kirk had rumbled through the eighteenth century, occasionally sputtering into minor schism and then dying down. The 1843 Disruption was something different. Carefully prepared beforehand, the dramatic secession of a large number of the kirk's most intelligent and socially aware ministers and laymen to form the Free Church of Scotland forms perhaps the most significant single event in the social history of Scotland in the nineteenth century. Its importance lies in the fact that the Free Church, seeking a social base, eagerly entered all the contentious areas of social life. Crucially, for us, they identified the rump of the Auld Kirk with the interests of landlords and capitalist farmers, while presenting themselves as the natural defenders and representatives of both lowland and highland peasants. This gave a doctrinal base on which to pursue political campaigns; a respectable foundation for class action which was most important in nineteenth-century Scotland with its relatively badly developed class institutions.

With this background information we now can turn to the substantive concern of this paper; the changes in the way in which peasant life was viewed in literature and history between 1745 and 1979. We will take literature first.

LITERATURE

I argued earlier that Scott is the key figure in transforming ruling-class perceptions of the Scottish countryside. As far as perceptions of the peasantry are concerned, however, there is a more interesting starting point. Robert Burns (1759-96) is remembered today for the sentimental lyrics of Ayrshire peasant and artisan life with which he beguiled the Edinbourgeoisie. But alongside these couthy poems he wrote bitter social satire, pillorying lairds and ministers from a relentlessly democratic stance. In Burns' work we see two attitudes to the lowland peasantry, one sentimentally patronising and the other democratically supportive. Subsequent literary accounts of that peasantry take their lead from Burns, mixing these two elements in different proportions. Scott's attitude, in *The Heart of Midlothian* for example, is wholly sentimental: the Lothian peasant

Deans family bears quintessentially Scottish virtues which are
on the point of extinction - steadfastness, independence - and
which can only be saved through aristocratic patronage from a
disinterested, philanthropic grandee like the Duke of Argyll.
But move forward half a century to the finest nineteenth-century
Scottish peasant novel, and the attitude is almost wholly
democratic. William Alexander's *Johnny Gibb of Gushetneuk*
(1869) is the one important novel about the 1843 Disruption. But
while the leaders of the Free Church, of which Alexander was a
leading Aberdeen layman, used peasant resistance to
engrossment as a means to attack the Auld Kirk, Alexander
used conflict over church government as a stick with which to
attack landlords and capitalist farmers in his lifelong defence of
that middle peasantry from which he sprang. Alexander's defence
was still possible in the 1860s; the northeast peasantry had not
yet broken. The difficulties of the last three decades of the
century, however, and the failure of the attempt - in which
Alexander took a leading part - to get legislative protection for
the lowland peasantry in the 1880s meant that this peasantry
was doomed. In the 1890s one finds the literary response to this
perception; kailyard. Noxiously sentimental and wistfully
nostalgic, the novels of kailyard writers like Ian Maclaren and
S.R. Crockett eulogised a peasantry that both the novelists and
their audience recognised to be in its death-throes. The middle
peasantry, as with Scott, was seen to exemplify all that was
essentially Scottish, and - in a characteristically populist touch
- to be internally harmonious. Dad might make all the decisions,
but this did not mean that other family workers were exploited.
    The reaction against kailyard took two forms. On the one
hand the overwhelmingly sentimental image of the Scottish
countryside was inverted in George Douglas Brown's gloomy
masterpiece about Ayrshire small burgh life, *The House with
the Green Shutters* (1901). In this novel the democratic
attitude to the lowland peasantry darkened into sardonic
cynicism. The worst possible motives were ascribed to any action
as a comfortable and self-satisfied merchant was humbled
through external pressure and the collapse of his family's
internal stratification. The novel ends with patricide and a
welter of gore that is positively Wagnerian: and the antithesis
of kailyard attitudes. The second reaction against kailyard takes
a form comparable with contemporary literary events in Ireland
- Synge's *Playboy of the Western World* is a good example.
Novels of the lowland peasantry begin to appear that emphasise
not the harmony of the farm family but its internal stratification.
In the first part of James Bryce's *The Story of a Ploughboy*
(1912) the hero rejects this tyrannous patriarchalism and moves
on, in later sections, to argue for rural anarchism; the first
evidence that I know of a Scottish rural novelist pushing beyond
the advanced Liberalism of a man like Alexander to socialist or
quasi-socialist ideas. Finally, in the early 1930s one gets a
clutch of novels that looked backwards to the final collapse of

the lowland Scots peasantry - dated to the First World War - and
identified the reasons for that collapse: the relentless advance of
capitalist agriculture, and the internal disintegration of the
peasantry as peasant children no longer accepted the family
farm's internal stratification. One of these novels - Ian
Macpherson's *Shepherd's Calendar* (1931) - provided the model
(to put it kindly) for the much better known novel that still
occupies an honoured place in British socialist iconography,
Lewis Grassic Gibbon's *Sunset Song* (1932). In Gibbon's work a
socialist line becomes explicit; *Sunset Song* is an attempt (only
partly successful in my view) at a dialectical novel that will
synthesise the sentimental and democratic/sardonic attitudes to
the lowland peasantry, and provide the basis for the birth of a
new, socialist Scotland in the lived experience of the mass of
Scots - many the descendants of evicted peasants - in the great
industrial cities from Glasgow to Dundee.

With Gibbon the line of novels about the lowland countryside
runs into the sand. For reasons which are quite unclear - but
worth speculation - a major theme in Scots literature simply
disappears. It is not as if the issues have gone - the lowland
peasantry may be dead but there are still thousands of small
farmers facing great, and write-aboutable difficulties - but
their plight no longer stirs the Scottish muse.

If we move from the lowland to the highland peasantry, then
for someone who does not have access to Gaelic novels -
unstudied but, in the opinion of competent judges, eminently
worth socio-historical investigation - novels about the highland
peasantry appear to devote an almost exclusive attention to the
nineteenth-century clearances; Neil Gunn's *Butcher's Broom*
(1934), Fionn MacColla's *And the Cock Crew* (1945), Iain
Crichton Smith's *Consider the Lilies* (1968). If we except
contemptible productions like the effusions of Lillian Beckwith
then we are left with little serious fiction about the highland
peasantry since the clearances: some of Neil Gunn's novels
(notably *The Keys of the Chest*, 1945) and, marginally,
MacColla's *The Albannach* (1932). Once again modern Scottish
writers seem to be unable to find suitable subjects in
contemporary highland rural class relations.

HISTORY

Much the same point can be made about historical work on the
highlands. If we exclude the 'prince in the heather' school of
sentimental historical obfuscation, and professional Scottish
historians' continuing obsession with minutely boring political
and diplomatic history, then historical work on the highlands
largely comes back, once again, to the old sore of the
clearances.

But the history of the clearances is contested. As the
evictions proceeded in the nineteenth century so comment

divided sharply. One group of commentators took the lairds'
part, asserting the inevitability of clearance. A second group
took the tenants' part, arguing that clearance was a scandalous
abrogation of the customary rights of highland society. Initially
this second attitude drew its inspiration from the romanticisation
of highland life that was institutionalised in bodies like the
Highland Society. Thus, much of the critical contemporary and
near contemporary comment on clearance came from men deeply
involved in Gaelic revivalism; J.S. Blackie is a good example.
But comment soon became more radical (even if, as in Marx's
account of the Sutherland clearances in *Capital* I, ch. 27,
notions drawn from the romantics lead the analysis astray). The
crofters' struggle for legislative protection - largely won in the
1886 Crofters Holdings Act but pursued further thereafter -
threw up work like the *Forward* essays of G.B. Clark, Crofters'
Party MP for Caithness, in which a radical historiography of the
highlands was fused with socialist beliefs - Clark joined the ILP
- and with strong nationalist elements derived from Ireland.
These nationalist elements would soon sink and not surface again
until Scottish socialists tried to make sense of the resurgent
SNP in the 1970s, but the link forged between a critical line on
the highland clearances and socialist commitment - however
antithetical the essentially populist aims of the crofters might be
in comparison with Clydeside Marxism — was to endure.
In Tom Johnston's *History of the Working Classes in Scotland*
(1920), for instance, one finds a detailed account of the
clearances. Crofters had been granted honorary proletarian
status.

  Later historians reproduced this bifurcated history of the
highland peasantry. Most modern economic historians, working
from estate papers, take the clearances to have been inevitable;
examples are P. Gaskell's *Morvern Transformed* (1968), R.J.
Adam's edited *Papers on Sutherland Estate Management
1802-1816* (1972) and the summary account of the highland
economy in T.C. Smout's *A History of the Scottish People
1560-1830* (1969). Against these pro-laird accounts one could,
until recently, range no serious modern historical work that
took the crofters' part. J. Prebble's *The Highland Clearances*
(1963) is interesting in its major thesis that the British state's
later techniques of colonial conquest and oppression were test-
run in the highlands, but it takes too many myths for fact to
stand as good history. We had to wait for J. Hunter's *The
Making of the Crofting Community* (1976) for a competent
account of the clearances from the crofters' viewpoint:
amazingly, Hunter's is the first modern history of the
clearances by a historian who could read Gaelic. This fact,
together with his study's underlying class analysis (and the
way in which, for the first time, it chronicles the crofters'
fight back up to the First World War) makes Hunter's book
central to any future attempt to write socialist history about the
Scottish highlands.

When we move from the highland to the lowland peasantry
then we find not a contested history but scarcely any history at
all. Bourgeois economic historians, blinded by nineteenth-
century Improvers' propaganda, typically paid no attention to
changes in class structure brought about by the shift to
capitalist production in the lowland countryside or, as with
Smout's book listed above, simply assumed that the peasantry
withered as capitalism became the dominant mode of production.
Socialist writers did no better; Johnston's book pays almost no
attention to the lowland countryside after 1830. We have only
one socialist study of class relations in the lowland countryside
– I. Carter's *Farm Life in Northeast Scotland 1840-1914* (1979).
Indeed, this is the only book-length agricultural history that
we have for any lowland region, from whatever standpoint.
Important farming regions like the southwest, with its major
dairying industry, await any significant social historical work.

WHAT IS TO BE DONE?

The opportunities for doing social historical work in Scotland are
immense. The extremely narrow conceptions of their task held
by professional Scottish historians over recent generations means
that we have scarcely any competent social history of any aspects
of Scottish life. Even the effect of the 1843 Disruption, the hinge
upon which so much nineteenth-century controversy turns, has
been investigated only in one city (A.A. Maclaren, *Religion and
Social Class: the Disruption Years in Aberdeen*, 1973), though
Hunter demonstrates the vital part played by highland sections
of the Free Church in liberating crofters from ideological
dependence on lairds. Thus we need a comprehensive
investigation of the class consequences of the Disruption in
rural areas of both highlands and lowlands. We also need
investigation in the scandalously neglected field of lowland class
relations; initially this will have to take the form of local studies,
since until we have a number of case studies from different areas
we will be unable to make any generalisation about the lowlands
as a whole. We need more investigation of highland class
relations by competent historians who can understand Gaelic;
the academic history of the highlands currently is much like the
histories of west Africa that district commissioners used to write
in their spare time. As far as literary work is concerned, there
is plenty of room to follow up David Craig's pioneering attempts
to do socialist literary criticism on Scottish material (see, for
example, D. Craig, 'The Radical Literary Tradition' in G.
Brown (ed.), *The Red Paper on Scotland*, 1975). Gaelic
literature is an obvious though far from simple candidate for
socialist investigation. But the general point about Scottish
social history – and, more widely, about people's history in
Scotland – is that they are so underdeveloped that important
opportunities can be found in areas that have been worked over

very heavily in England. The difficulty lies not in identifying a
topic for investigation, but in deciding which of several dozen
ideas for research should be done first.

FURTHER READING

Carter, I., *Farm Life in Northeast Scotland 1840–1914*,
  Edinburgh 1979.
Craig, D., *Scottish Literature and the Scottish People,
  1680–1830*, London 1961.
Hunter, J., *The Making of the Crofting Community*, Edinburgh
  1976.
Levitt, I. and Smout, T.C., *The State of the Scottish Working
  Class in 1843*, Edinburgh 1979.
Smout, T.C., *A History of the Scottish People, 1560–1830*,
  London 1969.

3 WORKER-HISTORIANS IN THE 1920s

Ruskin History Workshop Students Collective

This project was an attempt to compare the way in which history
was presented in the working-class movement of the 1920s, with
the history which is being written and read by socialists today.
In doing so we examined in a small and preliminary way the
history that was taught in the 'Plebs' movement, both at the
Central Labour College in London and at the local classes
organised under the National Council of Labour Colleges. We
also hoped to gauge its impact on the labour movement by
interviewing some of the worker students who studied then. Our
material, and our interviews, are taken from the South Wales
coalfield, where the Plebs movement was particularly strong. We
have consulted some of the materials at the South Wales Miners'
Library, and in the miners' collection in the archives of Swansea
University, and we are grateful to Hywel Francis, librarian of
the Miners' Library, for his suggestions and comradely help.
    The main feature of the history inside the Central Labour
College was its 'totality'. History was seen as an explanation of
the political, social and economic conditions of mankind at that
time. But, it was thought, only Marxism could do this
satisfactorily. History was seen somewhat as a Natural Science
with the Materialist Concept of History (MCH as it was called) as
the secret formula. George Thomas, a student at the Central
Labour College, in 1928, told us:

The point was, of course, we had the bourgeois textbooks on history but we knew how to handle them, how to approach them. It was this drilling we had in Marxism really that put us on our feet, also Marxist philosophy, they did a lot with Dietzgen in those days, Joseph Dietzgen, *The Science of Understanding*, as an introduction to dialectical materialism. So when I left the Labour College I was equipped. I knew what I was doing and why I was doing it as I was.

As a science, history had no room for personalities, only theories of development and evolution. Detail was overlooked in the quest to explain the overall movement of social change. For example, in 1923-4 the 'Industrial History of England' syllabus comprised ten lectures, starting with 'Primitive Communism' and 'Germs of Property' and ending with 'the Industrial Revolution' and 'Capitalism Today'. No room here for social cameos. Indeed, the whole attitude towards detail in history was summed up by Dai Davies, an eighty-year-old ex-miner and student in 1920, who told us that 'we weren't interested in whether so-and-so had sugar in his coffee or not. What interested us was how and why societies change.'

From the college notes of D.J. Williams (c. 1920-1), George Thomas (1928-9), and the preliminary synopsis of Glyn Evans (1923-4) - miners who studied at the Central Labour College - it is clear that what was available to students at the Labour College was not a history of facts, dates and standards of living, but an attempt to understand the *totality* of history, that is to understand how history worked in the larger formations of society. That is what they meant by the Materialist Conception of History.

A considerable portion of study-time was concerned not only with labour history and economics, but also with the way in which these subjects could be thought about by Marxists with, that is, a theory of knowledge. The name of Dietzgen recurs with the same, if not greater, frequency as Marx. Some students even were to rebel against this prominence in the later history of the Labour College. His works regarding the theories of knowledge were used to complement historical study. *How* history was studied was considered to be just as important as *what* was actually studied. The gaining of knowledge by the working class was seen not as an appropriation of bourgeois knowledge, but as a complete rethinking of the form and use of knowledge. The working class had to be self-conscious in seeking its knowledge. Here lies the importance of Dietzgen. In a section on the position of Dietzgen in relation to Karl Marx and Engels from lecture 4 of the series 'Science of Understanding' D.J. Williams took the following note: 'Marx and Engels showed how history produces new ideas. Dietzgen demonstrates the role of the mind in the process.'

Knowledge was seen as a *totality*, and a cluster of thinkers were used to reinforce this belief. 'Knowledge is essentially a whole' D.J. Williams wrote in his notes on lecture 1 in the series on The Science of Understanding. This was Dietzgen's central message. He linked Darwin and Hegel together as thinkers who had raised the 'monistic conception' of the world to a height hitherto unknown and strengthened it with positive discoveries. That is, Hegel and Darwin could see the world as one and total. God could be excluded from it. Dietzgen committed man to a *total* knowledge of the world and the world included the working of the *mind* who sees the world.

The interplay of evolution and revolution, the unconscious and the conscious in history, can be seen throughout the lecture notes and class essays. Evolution is the *unconscious* development of nature. Revolution is the *conscious* extension of it for the purposes of mankind as a whole. The evolutionary view is fundamental to the Labour College's favoured philosophers. Hegel, for instance, talked of the development of the individual to self-knowledge in the world. Darwin traced the development of the species from the evidence of fossil remains. Dietzgen had linked Hegel and Darwin in his *Excursions into the Domain of Epistemology* (p. 315). Similar themes can be seen in the Labour College correspondence course on 'The Rise of Scientific Socialism.' Talking of Hegel, Craik says:

> He proclaimed the ceaseless movement of all things, that is to say, universal evolution. He thus teaches the theory of evolution prior to Darwin, although of course he had not considered the details of evolution in the special field of organic nature.

The history courses of the NCLC were also informed by evolutionism. Mark Starr, writing on 'The History of History and its Uses' in the April 1926 issue of *Plebs*, lists what is necessary to reorientate history for the workers. Much of what he says is predictable, e.g., 'less about kings and more about the peoples'. But note:

> More about the wonderful story of human control over nature and less about battles.
> More about the steady progress of humanity and the succeeding social systems and less about the rise and fall of empires.

Starr's history has behind it an evolutionary view. There is a 'steady progress' of humanity. The new Soviet state is the end of a chain of 'succeeding social systems'. His notes on the 'steady progress of humanity' betrays the conviction that behind specific events of history, in which the working class or its class representatives can intervene in a revolutionary manner, there is an evolutionary and unconscious process.

We append samples of history courses of the Central Labour
College which, we hope, will give a clearer idea of the kind of
history being taught then.

D.J. Williams collection 1920-1

European history
Lectures included: The French Revolution, The State of Europe i
1789, Main movements of the century, National movements
1830-48, Years of revolution and reaction.

History of philosophy
Lectures included: The pre-Platonic philosophers, Plato and
Aristotle, The problem of knowledge in modern times. Books
included: Lewes *History of Philosophy*; Benn *Ancient
Philosophy - Modern Philosophy*.

History of the family
Books included: Müller-Leyer *History of Social Development*;
Engels *Origins of the Family*; Morgan *Ancient Society*; Mason
Women's Share in Primitive Society; Bebel *Women under
Socialism*; Gilman *Women and Economy*.

History of British socialism
Lectures included: Thomas More, Medieval church and the
papacy, Humanism, The utopian economy, The utopian family.

Origins of Christianity
Lectures included: The pagan source, The rise of Christianity,
Christianity and slavery, MCH and the downfall of slavery.

The nature of the state (notes incomplete)
Lectures included: Society and Roman empire, The state and
trade.

Ireland
Lectures included: Early history, The nineteenth century, The
twentieth century.

There were also courses on The science of understanding, and
Marxism and the racial question.

Glyn Evans collection 1923-4

History of socialism
Lectures included: Heretical communism in general, Heretical
movements in Southern Europe (conditions were right for the
rise of the heretical movement at the beginning of the
fourteenth century - the French monarchy was powerful and
the papacy was the tool of France), Thomas More and his
Utopia - economic and political, Chartism, trade unionism and

revolutionary trade unionism.

Industrial history of England
Lectures included: Primitive communism, Germs of property,
Slavery, Feudal unit, The church, Trade, Guilds of the Middle
Ages, Magna Carta and the Peasants' Revolt, Industrial
Revolution, Capitalism today.

Historical materialism
Lectures included: What it is not and what it is, Science and
inventions, HM and law, HM and politics, HM and ethics (a)
the lower, HM and ethics (b) the higher, HM and religion
pre-modern and modern, HM and aesthetics.
There were also courses on Economic geography, Economics and
What the worker should know about capitalism. Books included:
Labriola *Essays on the MCH*; Pannekoek *Marxism and Darwinism*;
Kautsky *Ethics and History*; Dietzgen *Philosophical Essays*
(section on Religion and Social Democracy); Engels *Landmarks
of Scientific Socialism* (section on Morality); Lafargue
Philosophical Studies; Müller-Leyer *History of Social
Development*.

General history
Books included: De Gibbins *Industrial History of England*; Ault
Ancient Britain; Wells *Outline of History*.

Synopsis of a lecture by C.L.C. Principal, W.W. Craik

1   History of socialism Lecture 7:
    Heretical communism in general

The role of the church in the Middle Ages − natural that those
who had the interests of the propertyless at heart should turn
against it. The church also made itself the enemy of other
exploiters. But as long as the conditions for a new social
order were not given the papacy could not only hold its own,
but exploit every misfortune and every rebellion for its own
advantage.
    The social structure favourable for communist propaganda
but not for a specific class struggle of the propertyless.
Comparison with France 1830-48.
    Distinction between rich and poor in the Middle Ages not
so great as to-day but more openly displayed.
    Communism in the Middle Ages like that of early
Christianity a communism in the means of consumption. The
ascetic and mystical character of this communism.
    Mysticism. The ignorance of the masses and reasons for
the same. The promotion of knowledge the task and interest
of rising social classes. With the rise of commodity production
and trade, the ground was prepared for a revival of the

mysticism characteristic of the declining ancient world and among the corresponding layers of society. The future was not yet possible or therefore visible to the proletariat. The greater the longing, then, for the mystical. Example: Thomas Münzer. A mysticism that produced heroes and martyrs and, therefore, unlike modern bourgeois mysticism.

Asceticism. The undeveloped state of production - refined enjoyment not possible for the masses - reaction of the communists against all luxury as sinful. Münzer and the Anabaptists.

Internationalism and the Revolutionary Spirit. The local communism of Plato - the international character of Christian communism - the inter-local character of the merchant - the inter-local feeling of proletariat. The merchant can count upon the protection of his government. The proletarian cannot and the less so, the more he is disposed to communism. Peasant narrow-mindedness a great impediment in the Middle Ages to conjoint revolutionary movements. The centralising activities of the communist wandering preacher, e.g., in England in 1381.

The revolutionary spirit of heretical communism and its appeal to militant portions of the Old and New Testament. Books:

Kautsky: *Communism in Central Europe in the Time of the Reformation* - Ch. 1.
Robinson: *Medieval and Modern Times* - Ch. X.
Green: *Short History of the English People* - Ch. 5, Sections 3-4.
Trevelyan: *Wycliffe and his Time*.

FURTHER READING

Barton, A., *A World History for the Workers*, London 1922.
Craik, W.W., *A Short History of the Modern British Working-Class Movement*, London 1919.
Craik, W.W., *The Central Labour College, 1909-1929*, London 1964.
Millar, J.P.M., *The Labour College Movement*, London 1979.
Paul, Eden, *Proletcult*, London 1921.
Starr, Mark, *A Worker Looks at History*, London 1918.
Paul, Willie, *The State, its origin and Function*, Glasgow 1917.

Local history

4 A GHOSTLY PAVEMENT: THE POLITICAL IMPLICATIONS OF LOCAL WORKING-CLASS HISTORY

Ken Worpole*

> It comes back to the question we have already emphasised:
> is it sufficient for a philosophical movement to devote itself
> to the development of a specialised culture for restricted
> groups of intellectuals, or must it, in elaborating a thought
> which is superior to common sense and scientifically
> coherent, never forget to remain in contact with the
> 'people' and, moreover, find in this contact the source of
> its problems to be studied and solved?
>
> (Antonio Gramsci, *The Study of Philosophy*)

In 1908 a group of radical working-class students at Ruskin
College, increasingly alarmed at the direction in which the college
was being guided by its management, launched the 'Plebs
League', a discussion group to argue the case for an independent
system of working-class adult education, funded wholly by the
labour movement. A year later, in 1909, following a student
strike at the college, many of these same students left to set up
the Central Labour College and promote their new journal, *The
Plebs Magazine*. From that year until 1964, when the National
Council of Labour Colleges agreed to dissolve itself and enter
into the general educational apparatus of the TUC Education
Committee, the Labour College movement had been an unstinting
provider of Marxist education for the organised working-class
movement. It had its own full-time college, it ran numerous
correspondence courses, published many books and pamphlets,
organised weekend and summer schools, and retained to an
extraordinary degree its consciously chosen educational
constituency: working-class trades unionists.

Throughout its long and frequently stormy life, it had
encouraged the study of history as an essential part of the
wider education towards class consciousness. In fact of the first
three books published by the Plebs League, two were historical
works: W.W. Craik's *Outlines of the History of the Modern
British Working Class Movement*, and Mark Starr's *A Worker*

*Ken Worpole is a former teacher who has worked for some ten
years at Centerprise bookshop and community publications
centre, Hackney. He is co-ordinator of the People's
Autobiography of Hackney.

Thanks to Philip Corrigan, Jane Mace, and Eileen and Stephen
Yeo for discussions. Thanks also to Jerry White for his reply to
this, which helped me clarify the concluding section.

Looks at History. The Plebs League books had initial print runs
of between 5,000 and 10,000 copies and were constantly being
reprinted. One of the former organisers of the NCLC, Andrew
Boyd, recently described in *Tribune* what happened in 1964
when the TUC finally incorporated the NCLC programme into
its own educational work: 'Immediately after rationalisation, the
education department of the TUC instructed its regional
education officers not to have classes on such subjects as public
speaking or the history of the British working class' (*Tribune*,
29 June 1979).

The full political implications of this TUC proscription ought
now to be openly discussed and challenged. We have to ask
ourselves why there was no effective labour movement resistance
to this seemingly irrational act of self-mutilation.

It is obvious to anyone that the last two decades have
produced an outstanding growth in the range of work done in the
field of Labour studies and the more informal modes of working-
class self-organisation and forms of cultural identity. Social
history has been probably the fastest growing sector of academic
study within the universities for some years now. There has been
a proliferation of research papers, published essays and full-
length books emerging from this powerful intellectual current.
Yet despite all this activity, I seriously wonder whether we could
with any confidence suggest that we have a more historically
conscious labour movement now than we have done at previous
periods of crisis in the past. I would think not.

Clearly the reasons for this major discrepancy, by which an
embarrassment of historical riches have been accrued in one
section of the culture at the expense of the larger constituency,
are complex and difficult to disentangle. But two observable
trends have presented themselves openly and consistently. The
first has been the so far irreversible tendency for all historical
projects to find themselves a home within the ambivalent
political world of higher education, and then turn naturally to
that same world for their validation and legitimation. The move,
as it were, from draughty Co-op halls and Trades Halls to
modern Polytechnic lecture rooms was more than a change of
venue.

The second and related trend has been that the publication
and dissemination of the work produced has been, for the most
part, unproblematically offered into the hands of the commercial
publishing houses, and consequently distributed to a
readership chosen by the market priorities of capital
investment. Expensive hardbacks for the higher education
libraries, rather than pocketbooks for the people, has been the
general trend.

The tragic result of the increasing separation of the academic
world of social history from the pressing day-to-day concerns of
working-class and socialist politics, is that neither is exercising
any interventionist influence on the other. Much historical work
within the academic world has become obsessive about the minutiae

of social history, so that its exponents have become self-parodying, like the fossil collectors and butterfly hunters of 1950s' children's fiction. There seems to be an unspoken assumption that if, somehow, every detail of the past could be described and understood, then the immanent meaning of history would reveal itself, no longer through a glass darkly, but truly face to face.

There is a story by Arthur C. Clark, *The Billion Names of God*, in which he tells of a Tibetan monastery founded in the sixteenth century whose purpose was, using prayer wheels, to spell out every one of the billion names of God as indicated by divine prophecy. When this has been accomplished the world would end. A younger acolyte is elevated to the most senior position in the monastery and promptly orders an IBM computer to complete the divine project. The computer is shipped and delivered to the remote monastery and installed by an American technician who calculates that only four days is needed to complete the billion names. On his way back down the mountain he becomes disturbed that the prophecy might in fact be true. Still journeying towards the seaport to go home, he calculates the exact moment when the computer's work will be completed. That moment arrives, and looking up into the night sky he sees the stars begin to disappear, one by one.

There's a sense in which there is a theory about history similar to the Tibetan prophecy, the socialist version being that once every moment of past working-class experience has been noted and analysed, then all the forms and structures of capitalist relationships will powder and disintegrate leaving at last, pure, unmediated working-class authentic being. It is more important to make history than understand it, though of course we should try to do both.

A further source of evidence of the isolation of much contemporary labour history from its originating constituency, is its more recent obsession with its own theoretical status. Like Bishop Berkeley, many socialist historians have become seized with terror at the lack of any positive proof that they and their subject really do exist. That debate, which is now beginning to dominate the *History Workshop Journal*, has become so abstract that it is now impenetrable to anyone other than full-time academic historians. The retreat into a closed epistemology curiously comes at a time when contemporary class conflict is more pronounced than it has been for many years. Surely the first responsibility of socialist historians is to promote as widely as possible the discussion of the accumulated historical experiences of the working-class and socialist movement, and help re-create a strong sense of the history which brought people to the positions inherent in contemporary political struggles. Otherwise many people will come to cynically regard the new socialist history in the same terms as Milton regarded the libertarian rhetoric of his period: 'a fugitive and cloistered virtue, unexercised and unbreathed, that never sallies out and sees her adversary.'

The new socialist history might well be in danger of becoming nothing more than a textual movement in which nothing is self-explanatory in itself, but always rests on assumptions made elsewhere by other historians in other texts. One of the results of this kind of development is that people coming to the new texts of socialist history from outside the universities are actually made to feel more ignorant after reading them, rather than more enlightened. And we must remember something Jack Common wrote in the 1930s, 'Socialism will not be built book by book.'

To return to the potentially subversive nature of historical knowledge, which the TUC Education Committee seemed to fear so much, we ought to ask ourselves what kind of historical consciousness fulfils this attribution? It is certainly rooted in people's understanding that our lives are connected with the lives, struggles and understandings of previous generations of working-class people. It is certainly to know and feel that we live our lives and take much of the meaning of our lives from within the sometimes continuous, sometimes discontinuous, flow of time, conscious action and achieved change. History is an integral part of the cultural ecology in which we live, and to which we contribute. It should also include an awareness that there is a common moral responsibility inherent in the historical process, both backwards to our parents' and grandparents' generations, and forwards to our children and those who come after them.

This is why a socialist historical consciousness is quite different from, and much more important than, a received sociological consciousness. Sociology tends too often to find social institutions ever-present and all-pervasive: a historical consciousness knows that all institutions, social, psychological and material, are susceptible to mutability and change. It was Marx who deflated the comfortable bourgeois notion of progress when he characterised it thus: 'Thus there has been history, but there is no longer any.' Conventional wisdom always assumes that the present represents the final point of arrival of all social relationships and institutions. A socialist historical consciousness realises that, in Jack Lawson's words in his autobiography, *A Man's Life*, 'our institutions have not arrived yet'.

People associated with radical politics have at different times written about what such a consciousness feels like. It is wonderfully described by M.K. Ashby in her biography of her father, *Joseph Ashby of Tysoe*:

But Joseph was interested now in the district he was seeing. Three things came to him in this period; some idea of how events elsewhere affected his own home and village; some knowledge that other communities produced other manners and other men; and then the sense, to describe it as best I can, that under the wide acreage of grass and corn and

woods which he saw daily there was a ghostly, ancient
tessellated pavement made of the events and thoughts and
associations of other times. This historical sense he shared
with many of the men he met about his work. Their strong
memory for the past was unimpaired by much reading or
novelty of experience, and yet their interest had been
sharpened by the sense of rapid change.
Such a consciousness is well understood by Len Doherty in his
novel of Yorkshire pit life, *The Man Beneath*:
This book [a history of the miners] made an exciting thing of
the life he was used to: it made of the past a splendid
struggle that fired his imagination. He asked himself how and
why such low-born and illiterate men could fight so constantly
for a better life for their children. How had they come
through defeat after defeat without giving up? What gave
them the patience to wait and gather strength and try again?
   He read his answers out of every page. . . . On the
following day, while he was working at the coal-face, he
paused to look about him with new interest. On either side
stretched away the long, black wall of glinting coal. Between
the props, his mates' cap-lamps flashed and beamed as they
chopped and shovelled. He thought of the book he had read
while he looked at their naked, glistening bodies, rolling
shoulders and sinewy arms. They were part of that history;
they were the present guardians of the old traditions.
   It might be answered that the above two extracts come from
somehow more 'authentic' working-class occupations, and that
today they would be irrelevant. But both, irrespective of
particularities of time and place, provide powerful examples of a
'way of seeing' that is transferable to other conditions and other
moments. This quality of consciousness, I suspect, is actually
very weak at present within the traditionally defined labour
movement. This should not be said, for example of the
contemporary women's movement where the study of women's
history, and the history of patriarchal attitudes, has been given
an important place in the work of consciousness-raising.
Similarly many black and other ethnic political groups treat the
history of colonialism and transmigration very seriously indeed
as part of their own political education. It is now in the most
traditional institutions of the working-class movement, in the
trades unions and in the Labour Party particularly, that the
crucial historical sense of past and present causes is virtually
non-existent. The academic social history momentum of recent
years has had very little effect within this constituency. To
have characterised much contemporary popular consciousness –
or popular memory – as worryingly unhistorical may seem
paradoxical given the current popularity of social history themes
in the popular culture of television drama and paperback
publishing. This paradox needs examination. For it is obviously
true that social history themes on television have been very much
in evidence in the past few years. *When the Boat Comes In*, a

serialised drama set in the Tyneside docks and shipyard communities in the 1920s and onwards, has been repeated on three occasions in the past six years. The series was very much concerned with the militant left-wing political attitudes of many of the Tyneside workers in that period. *Days of Hope* was a four-part, and excellent, series built around the political fortunes of a working-class family between 1910 and the defeat of the 1926 General Strike. This series was totally sympathetic with the militant working-class politics of that period. Lewis Grassic Gibbon's, *A Scots Quair*, was also recently dramatised for television, as was Mervyn Jones' fine novel, *Holding On*, based on trade union and community solidarity in the East End of London.

This popularity is even more in evidence if one looks at contemporary publishing. Commercial publishers have been quite eager to publish detailed working-class autobiographies, or social histories of specific rural or urban communities. There is almost a small industry devoted to West of Ireland peasant reminiscences. Hutchinson have published perhaps six volumes in paperback of Fred Archer's accounts of his Vale of Evesham village childhood. Flora Thompson's classic *Lark Rise to Candleford* is permanently in print now. Two working-class women from the East End of London, Grace Foakes and Dolly Scannell, have both had several volumes of personal autobiography commercially published. Winifred Foley's marvellous *Child of the Forest* was originally serialised on BBC Radio and then published in hardback and paperback. Robert Roberts' two excellently written books about his Salford childhood, *The Classic Slum* and *A Ragged Schooling*, sell consistently. Well-documented accounts of popular civilian struggles during the Second World War have become mainstream bookshop stock. And even left publishers are now busy publishing, or re-printing, classic works of labour movement propaganda, or autobiographies of known and unknown militants. In the last eighteen months, for example, Lawrence & Wishart have republished Phil Piratin's, *Our Flag Stays Red*, Harry Pollitt's *Serving My Time*, Willy Gallacher's *Revolt on the Clyde* and Lewis Jones' two documentary novels *Cwmardy* and *We Live*. Self-published and independently published Labour movement autobiographies are quietly finding the light in many different towns and cities. Feminist publishing houses are involved in serious work of autobiographical discovery and retrieval. The autobiographical mode is in the ascendancy.

All this surely adds up to something important - it ought to. Yet I'm not sure it does. The crucial element lacking in the chemistry by which such rich works might help shape popular class consciousness is any kind of social context for their reception. They are watched, if they are television programmes, or read, if they are books, as discrete products of self-contained historical reconstruction. The naturalism of the television series or the anecdotal autobiography is to a large extent self-sealing.

Television companies and commercial publishing firms produce
these programmes or books as though they had been found
buried in polythene beneath the foundations of the welfare state
to be rediscovered at a later date as representative, but
disconnected, texts of a previous culture. The continuity of
experience is not an ideology widely promulgated within the
capitalist mode of cultural production.

This is why the preclusion of history from the TUC education
programme, and its decline in significance, until recently, as a
subject within the WEA tradition is so critical. And this is why
the new local people's history movement is so important, possibly
central, to the project of reviving the historical component of
an affirmative class consciousness. This is why it is a matter of
priority that the relationship between the growing number of
autonomous local history projects, nearly all of whom have
attached themselves to the flourishing Federation of Worker
Writers and Community Publishers, and the movement associated
with the Ruskin History Workshop and the *History Workshop
Journal*, is subject to a new discussion of common aims and
modes of activity.

The relationship to date has been an uneasy one, if anything
growing more distant. Yet there is no doubt that many of the
community history projects were directly inspired by attendance
at one or more of the Ruskin Workshops. It was at the Workshop
on Childhood in May 1972 that many political activists, but
non-historians, were inspired to see the political importance of
the new history movement. Producing shareable and common
history from the spoken reminiscences of working-class people
seemed a positive and important activity to integrate with various
other new forms of 'community' politics. This development
coincided with many activists' involvement in some kind of
alternative newspaper or printing resources centre which
provided the material and productive basis for local publishing.
And at first there was some very important practical and
political encouragement given to the first groups started, by
Ruskin History Workshop activists.

But on the whole, parental interest waned rather quickly.
Many Ruskin students, it seems, on leaving the college, went
into the academic sphere rather than returning to the local
history initiatives which seemed to be being promoted as the way
forward in 1972. 'Dig where you stand' was the motto of the day,
but some had already left the site and were down the road before
the first morning tea-break, leaving the rest to carry on with
blunt and inappropriate instruments – and no architect's
drawings either. Later on one heard the occasional charge of
'populist' levelled at the community-based history groups, to
which the counter-charge was 'academic'. Neither observation
was either useful or constructive. Visits back to the family home
at Ruskin became less frequent, conversations more perfunctory
and superficial. The local groups were one part of a wider
movement which formed the co-ordinating FWWCP in 1976, which

became also, but not very satisfactorily, the theoretical discussion place of the local history projects. The Ruskin movement co-ordinated local and regional enthusiasts around the *History Workshop Journal*, also significantly founded in 1976. Two separate directions were formalised in these two bodies, which since then have not had any serious relationship at all. The position must clearly be remedied. Both movements have much to learn from each other and therefore joint discussions should begin to take place in the near future.

I would like here to point out some of the particular and important strengths of the local projects in terms of building a much wider co-ordinated working-class constituency for the workers' history movement. To begin with, in Bristol, Hackney, Peckham, Rochdale, Southwark and Tottenham, for certain, local history projects have been run in conjunction with the Workers' Educational Association as continuing evening classes. It has been the community-based groups, ironically, who have been important in helping revitalise the WEA and radicalise it as a workers' education body. This has created open and accessible meeting places for working-class people to meet each other around the theme of making the history of their lives. Often there have been genuine political difficulties, in that for many people there seems to be no link between past experiences of struggle, hardship and oppression, and contemporary attitudes towards socialist and trade union politics. But these difficulties must be faced and talked through. And for many elderly people in areas such as those mentioned above where this local history work is being carried on, it is colour not class which seems to be the self-evident reason for the continuing inadequacies of housing, health facilities and secure employment. If the historical continuity of working-class exploitation is something which we know to be true, it is therefore something which we should argue in as many places as possible. Local history work is an ideal place in which to discuss these contradictory appearances and realities. Apparently it is the local working-class history section of the Liverpool University 'Second Chance' course which has been the most politically revealing to the working-class students on that course.

Second, many of the local history projects are based in known local 'alternative' and self-produced institutions: Bristol Broadsides, which publishes the work of the WEA history projects, with the Full Marks Bookshop; Brighton with the Queenspark newspaper, publishing project and shop; Aberdeen with the Aberdeen People's Press; Hackney with the Centerprise bookshop and community centre; Stepney with the THAP bookshop and publishing project; Peckham with the Peckham Bookplace. All of these centres have known socialist colourings and therefore the local history work is clearly seen as being part of a partisan cultural and political strategy/presence/formation. I think that in these areas it is now commonly accepted that it is active socialists who have helped provide the energies and time

to promote the interest in, recording and publishing of local
working-class experience. This helps explain why, for example,
there was a genuine and widespread local outrage when the
Centerprise project was set on fire one night by the neo-fascist
'11th Hour Brigade'. Through, to an important degree, its local
history commitment and its local publishing work it had earned a
widely shared agreement to its being an important institution in
the cultural fabric of Hackney working-class life. It is now, for
many people in Hackney, the first place to bring old
photographs, old letters, the notebooks of recently deceased
relatives, partly written or completed autobiographies, as well,
of course, as people's own poetry and other writings.

Locating history work in these local institutions provides the
structure for a large degree of local accountability for the
accuracy and sympathy of the work done. The working-class
movement needs these kind of self-organising institutions if it is
to appear to be part of a long-term project towards socialism.
Permanent institutions are essential, otherwise socialist activity
is restricted to occasional moments of struggle, occasional,
discontinuous political and cultural happenings. It is significant,
too, that quite a few of the people who initially came along to a
WEA class or project at Centerprise stayed to become involved in
other aspects of the work of the total project.

It is the study circle, discussion group, evening class - call it
what you like - which best provides the context in which the
study of history, local and national, can be socialised and
politicised. The substantial account of a WEA history class
organised by Edmund Conway in Blackburn, and described in
History Workshop Journal No. 3, is the kind of reporting back
we need much more of. It is significant that in the index to the
first six volumes of the *Journal*, which appeared in No. 7, under
the headings 'Local History', 'Report Back', 'Work in Progress',
or 'Workers' Education', there is no reference to any of the
activities or achievements of the local history projects associated
with the FWWCP.

Nearly all of these local projects have proved to be in
important positions from which to intervene in and influence
history teaching in local schools. And it is in schools where
intervention is rather crucial. Valerie Chancellor in her book on
the history of school history quotes a Mr John Baker Hopkins
writing in the *School Board Chronicle* in 1872: 'Very few men
forsake the religious creed they are taught in childhood; and it
is not less usual for men to cleave to the political creed they
learn from histories.'

All of the projects mentioned have won support from local
teachers and many of the locally published books are now
extensively used in schools, with projects lasting from a few
days to a whole term built around particular local history
publications. In some schools CSE syllabuses are being re-drawn
to include local working-class autobiographies and local histories.
Queenspark in Brighton recently organised a well-attended day

conference for local teachers and librarians simply to talk about how the Queenspark books were used in schools, and how this usage could be developed and extended elsewhere. Primary schools as well use the books, and invite the authors into schools to talk about their lives.

One of the most significant effects of this kind of local publishing, particularly the publishing of characteristic working-class autobiographies, has been that for the first time perhaps, a book used in school is picked up by the parents at home and becomes the basis for a real discussion between parents and children, in which the parents' own experiences are both significant and important to the school syllabus. It is now a commonplace that in many schools it is such local autobiographies which get taken home in connection with 'homework' and never get returned to school again. Parents pick them up, read them and often inadvertently keep them, and in many cases begin to talk to their children about past memories and experiences which connect to the themes and occasions mentioned in the locally published autobiography. That breakthrough, in which it is possible for young people to begin to see their own parents as historical figures, is critically important, and we ought to know more about it.

The people's history projects I have written about here contribute very importantly to socialist politics in their commitment to trying to carry through the socialism of production. They struggle on, with perhaps long periods of unevenness, but then occasional bursts of speed, with the whole process of recovering history and making history books, taking turns in taping, transcribing, typing, pasting-up, selling, book-keeping, public speaking and convening and organising in mutual and associated ways. Through active membership of these local history projects, many people have gained important experiences in being producers and organisers of cultural material production. And further, through the national co-ordinating work of the Federation, many people are, for the first time in their experience, travelling regularly across the country to other towns and cities to take part in management and editorial meetings of the national body. We attach great importance to the politics of access to high speed Inter-City travel. For too long the shiny yellow 125 trains have remained in the hands of the managerial class.

Much of the criticism of the political weakness of the local history projects comes from those whose socialism seems to be largely based on the socialism of distribution, which is characterised by a preoccupation with end products and the 'correct socialist consciousness' of the final texts. The books are not read in their own right, but as texts which can be sifted for particular nuggets, which can then be added to other nuggets sifted from other books to make yet more texts. There is nothing intrinsically wrong with this process, but one mode of socialist

history is the mode of the long revolution, and the other of the
short revolution.

The autobiographical mode, widely espoused by the local
history projects, is the mode of the long revolution, slower,
acknowledging difficulty, mixing occasional insights into the
prime causes and determinants of life – homelessness,
redundancy – with experiences of sudden bereavement, a loving
relationship, mental breakdown in the family, the party that
lasted for three days, the failed attempt to emigrate. And who is
to say that the latter experiences do not help us clarify the
complexity of the revolution we have ahead of us? A passage
from Stuart Hood's autobiography, *Pebbles from my Skull*, has
helped many local groups to understand why the autobiographical
mode is so important.

> We may record the past for various reasons: because we find
> it interesting; because by setting it down we can deal with it
> more easily; because we wish to escape from the individual
> prison where we face our individual problems, wrestle with
> our particular temptations, triumph in solitude and in
> solitude accept defeat and death. Autobiography is an
> attempted jail-break. The reader tunnels through the same
> dark.

The problem is not the long revolution or the short revolution;
history probably expects both. But which is best fought first,
given the political formlessness and difficulties of our times?

FURTHER READING

Publications of the people's autobiography of Hackney, available
from Centerprise, Kingsland High Street, London E9:
Dot Starn, *When I was a Child*.
Arthur Newton, *Years of Change*.
Ron Barnes, *Licence to Live*.
Ron Barnes, *Coronation Cups and Jam Jars*.
Doris Knight, *Millfield Memories*.
Rose Lowe, *Daddy Burtt's for Dinner*.
The Threepenny Doctor.
Hackney Camera.
A Second Look.
Barry Burke, *Rebels with a Cause*, a History of Hackney Trades
    Council.
Harry Harris, *Under Oars* (jointly with Stepney Books).
Ken Worpole, *Local Publishing and Local Culture*.

5   BEYOND AUTOBIOGRAPHY

Jerry White*

Ken Worpole's article on the political implications of local
working-class history is a passionate defence of the development
in community-based local history over the past ten years; and
rightly so, for there's much to admire in this radical departure
from the traditional antiquarian concerns of almost all local
history written before it. The major unanswered question,
though - taken for granted, I think, in Ken's paper - is *what
sort* of local working-class history should we be producing? The
response, for all of us here, must be a *socialist* local history.
But what do we mean by this? And having decided what we
mean, are the recent developments going to take us there, if
they go on as their current tendencies promise?
    This article suggests that the recent developments of what
Ken calls 'the new local oral history movement', though in their
time beneficial and corrective, need a new radical change of
direction (building on the movement, throwing nothing away) if
they are to give us a socialist local history. First, though, we
should try to assess just why we want a socialist local history at
all, and why it's worth putting energy and commitment into
producing it. Second, and in a comradely way, we need to ask
what's wrong with much of the new people's history. Arising
out of the answers to these questions should come some indication
of what the tasks for a socialist local history might be at the
present time. And lastly, there are some proposals for
strengthening the practice of a socialist local history. Both the
first and last sections will build on issues already raised by
Ken.

WHY DO WE NEED A SOCIALIST LOCAL HISTORY?

We believe that history is a source of inspiration and
understanding, furnishing not only the means of interpreting
the past but also the best critical vantage point from which
to view the present. So we believe that history should
become common property, capable of shaping people's

---

*Jerry White works as a housing officer for Islington Borough
Council. He is an editor of *History Workshop Journal* and author
of *Rothschild Buildings, Life in an East End Tenement Block,
1887-1920*, London 1980; and "Campbell Bunk", A lumpen
Community between the wars', *History Workshop Journal* 7,
November 1979.

understanding of themselves and the society in which they
live. (Editorial, *History Workshop Journal*, 1, Spring 1976)
Nowhere is this potentially more true than in the production of
local history. There are many other areas of a socialist history
which can bear on people's life experiences in a direct way –
political history and the history of the labour movement, social
history in all its many recent varieties – but none so completely
as the history of a locality and its people. For it is within the
totality of local experience that historical consciousness for most
of us is actually made.

Consciousness of the past is a living experience at the local
level in a way that it rarely is in any other sphere. It is forced
on us every day of our lives by the physical change in
neighbourhoods – streets and buildings that were there one,
five, ten years ago, but are now gone; by the changing
functions of buildings and places – the street market now a car
park, the cinema now a warehouse, the factory now a wasteland;
by the change in the people around us, the coming and going of
our neighbours and our families and our friends. Change has no
meaning without comparison with what used to be, and those
comparisons in things near at hand are a part of the daily
thought processes of all of us in recognising just where we are.

This recognition, this way in which we construct our
consciousness of what we see around us by comparing it with
what we used to see, is generally a *superficial* process. We see
what *is* around us and we remember what *was*. Depending on its
effects on our aesthetic sensibilities or our personal convenience
or our social conscience, we will decide whether the change has
been good, bad, or neither, or whether it's been good or bad
for other people even if it doesn't affect us. It is a superficial
consciousness because we do not know how or why the change
has come about if, as usual, we ourselves have not been the
agency of that change. It is superficial, too, because it appears
that change began from what we knew: what we remember
becomes the starting point, rather than itself the result of prior
change. Our everyday experience at the local level gives us a
consciousness of history which is placed within the continual
movement of which we are part. Everything appears to be moving
and changing so that the existence of continuity is denied or
ignored because less apparent; or continuity is itself seen in
terms of change, for example as in 'history repeats itself'.

The process of change which our local historical
consciousness recognises is laden with significance for us. It is
a source of unending interest. At its sharpest, it expresses
itself in the passion for learning about the history of our own
locality – local history is an intensely working-class concern.
But all of us, healthily obsessed or not, make judgments
every day on the meaning of local change for both present and
past. There is a constant and contradictory struggle within us
about the place of the past in our understanding of the present:
it was a golden age when things were better and since when things

have gone steadily downhill; or, and often in one and the same
breath; it was a bad time, when things were hard, since when
there's been a time of progress so that we've all got it easy now.
    Constructing in this way our own view of the past is
something we all do now, without 'history' of any kind, so that
we can make sense of the present for ourselves. This blending of
past and present is most smooth, even at the local level, for that
is the world in which recognition of change is most active. The
role of a socialist local history is to give understanding to that
local process of change. That understanding is an integral and
essential part of a socialist understanding of the present. The
struggle for such an understanding has never been more
worthwhile.

PEOPLE'S HISTORY AND THE INVISIBILITY OF CAPITALISM

> The social structure and the state are continually evolving
> out of the life-process of individuals, but of individuals,
> not as they may appear in their own or other people's
> imagination, but as they *really* are; i.e. as they operate,
> produce materially, and hence as they work under definite
> material limits, presuppositions and conditions independent
> of their will. (Marx and Engels, *The German Ideology*, 1846)

We are back with the question of *levels of reality* which I hinted
at when talking about the superficial historical consciousness
largely produced by local experience. In my view, the dominant
tendencies within the production of people's history by the
'new local oral history movement' do little to break through this
superficial historical consciousness: indeed, often they reinforce
it.
    The assumption underpinning virtually all of this work is that
for working people to speak for themselves, about their own
history, is somehow a political act in itself, inherently socialist.
It is seen as a way of making people conscious of their past, and
so it is - up to a point. But the dominant mode of production of
this sort of history does not set out to change that
consciousness of the past which we all make for ourselves
anyway: it states, through memory and anecdote, it does not
try to analyse. And because it is locked in an autobiographical
mode - with absolute and inviolable primacy given to what people
say about themselves - it does little, if anything, to capture
those levels and layers of reality outside individual experience.
    Let's look at a few ways in which the autobiographical mode
reinforces a superficial historical consciousness and by doing so
actually distorts reality. First, and at a commonsense
philosophical level, we are rarely objective about ourselves -
perhaps, indeed, it's impossible to be so. We hide or ignore or
justify our faults, our secret lives, our embarassing or tragic
mistakes. It is not, necessarily, that we tell lies about ourselves
or that what we say can never be true - it has a validity within

its own terms. It is that at all times we should treat
autobiography as one particularly rich type of historical
understanding, but one with immanent biases and distortions.
It can never be complete in itself.

Second, and more important, it can tell us little beyond the
world in which the individual who is writing actually lived. Even
in our own world, within our own narrow sphere of existence –
family, street, school, workplace, political party – our contacts
are limited and never comprehensive. The events we see might
look quite different even to a close neighbour who has other
relationships in the same world. This is even more evident when
we step outside the narrow world the chronicler actually occupied
– a world which might well have ended at the street next door.
Perhaps this might be overcome by somehow selecting
'representative' individuals from all the worlds that make up our
chosen locality so that they eventually merge into a totality: an
'Islington Childhood' is not enough – we need 'A Highbury
Childhood', 'A Mildmay Childhood', 'A Canonbury Childhood',
et cetera *ad infinitum*.

Perhaps. But even the (I'm sure illusory) search for
'representative autobiographies' will not overcome the third, and
even more important still, objection. For individual experience
can tell us little about the forces which shape our lives – make
us what we are and where we live what it is. There is a huge
reality outside the boundaries of individual consciousness. It is
the *critical understanding* of that reality, of the relations of
capitalist society and our historical place within them, which must
be the object of an actively socialist local history.

This critical consciousness of capitalism is missing from the
new local history (as it is from much local and political life). It is
not that people's reminiscences are necessarily quietist or
uncritical: indeed, many of them are fired by a fine anger. But
this is criticism without understanding; it lapses into mere
sloganising. Without a socialist understanding, criticism is always
in danger of latching onto any apparent 'explanation' that
happens along: 'colour not class', as Ken says, or (and just as
much) 'the council', 'the government', 'the unions' and whoever
and whatever people blame for getting us where we are now.

At its worst, and few local oral history publications are free
from this, autobiography can reinforce capitalist values so that
the whole tone (notwithstanding the angry bits) is politically
bland and negative and unprovocative. They give us moving
insights which enrich the brotherhood of man and boost the
self-confidence of working people, but it all appears to take
place in a social vacuum. I'll give just one example here. Work is
treated very much as if it were a thing complete in itself, instead
of being one part of a social relationship: we do it because we
do it. The dignity of labour, stressed by many of the local oral
histories which focus on work, disguises what work is for – who
owns what we produce, where profits come from, why we are
deprived of work, how new jobs are made, the social

consequences of the things we do, and so on. We should thus be made to question the function of what, after all, amounts to nearly half the product of our waking lives: unthinking pride in a job well done is just what the capitalist ordered.

WHAT IS TO BE DONE?

> The socialist historian has the privilege of keeping the record of resistance to oppression, but also the duty of analysing the enemy's campaign, and showing how men and women become accomplices in their own subjection. (Raphael Samuel, *Village Life and Labour*, 1975)

We need a socialist local history which maintains the immediacy and sympathy of autobiography (working people speaking directly to one another) *and* which leads to a critical re-evaluation, a fresh understanding of our place in capitalist relations in a sphere which is relevant to us all – the places and people we see around us. Capitalism and its critique must be brought up front. How?

There are no easy answers at all. Indeed, what is needed is more *hard* thinking and work at the local level. One task, certainly, is to raid the academic historians' treasure trove and take back what they've appropriated for their own narrow ends. We should use all the information we can get our hands on, not just the spoken word, and turn it to our own account. We should fight against a social division of labour which leaves books and papers to the intellectuals and leaves us, like noble savages, with just an oral tradition – we are, after all, creating a new written tradition ourselves. We should learn from and build on the best ideas and techniques of social and urban history, as well as oral history.

This will undoubtedly result in a second task – the creation of new forms of expression away from an unvarnished autobiographical mode. There are probably several ways of making interventions with the material gathered from elsewhere, either into a straightforward autobiography or into the collective memory, so that we are led to re-assess our own life experiences. Groups will have to find the form which best suits their own working and political practice, and will learn from the examples of others: the collective work of which this will be an important function will be explored in a little more detail in the next section.

A third task is to develop new ways of seeing, looking for the hidden realities and relationships which underpin what we see around us. For example, seeing population changes (the growth of a town, immigration from country districts or the colonies, the moving away of the young) in terms of the needs of capital and the amassing of a labour force in response to those needs. Seeing school in terms of the purpose it serves in the relations between classes, the values it transmits and its role of educating for industrial requirements; and in terms of the contradictions inherent in the ideals of education and their practical reality in school and labour process. Seeing housing, for example, not as a *thing* again, but as the product of a social relationship between classes and fractions within classes, in terms of the needs of factory owners and the needs of their workers; the profits of builders, rents of landlords, and the standard of living of tenants; the ideology of owner-occupation; the struggle between classes within which housing is one issue, as it takes place in street and council chamber. Looking at poverty in relative rather than absolute terms to destroy the illusion held by many that poverty doesn't exist any more (I've not been able to check this, but there's probably more official poverty in places like Hackney and Tottenham, where local groups are active, now than there was in the depression). Seeing pauperism and dependency on state aid as a permanent and inevitable feature of capitalism, and relating change in the treatment of those without work to the struggle between classes. Looking at work from the point of view of all those in the relationship - ourselves and the people who buy our labour-power (we know what people's wages were, but we can also find out what the shareholders took home as well). Listening to and challenging myths about the past where misunderstanding could be politically dangerous: that poor housing, juvenile crime, street violence are new phenomena, instead of in reality permanent but explicable features of a competitive capitalist society. Seeing community life and its perceived deterioration not in terms of a general moral decline, but in terms of those tendencies within capitalism which have indeed damaged collective life outside the workplace in the last fifty years. And so on.

Lastly, a whole new area of tasks must be taken up, too. That is the relationship of the local with the world outside - the non-local aspects of local history. The locality is impinged on by its social environment at every level. The links stretch not only across borough boundaries, but beyond cities and even countries, and they affect directly, but often in subterranean ways, individual life-experiences. We must help develop a wider consciousness than the local alone can provide - we live in a national and international capitalist society; we belong to a national and international working class. (Contrary to all appearances, Hoxton really doesn't end at Old Street!)

None of this asks for a reversal of anything that has been achieved within local oral history over the past ten years. Indeed, those achievements form the only foundation on which this new work can be built. The life histories of working people, in their own words, will remain the basis of production of a socialist local history, but in a way which enables the meaning of those lives, and our own, to be seen in a new way.

THE PRACTICE OF A SOCIALIST LOCAL HISTORY

> This study is necessarily incomplete. As I realised when
> half way through the work, such a task really needs a whole
> group of people working on different aspects of the problem.
> But perhaps this attempt may encourage some Left Book Club
> groups to start on a study of their own. Much precious
> working-class history is waiting to be studied. (Ellen
> Wilkinson, *The Town that was Murdered: the life-story of
> Jarrow*, 1939)

There are many benefits of collective work in the sort of
enterprise I'm advocating, apart from those which are already
experienced by local groups and which are elaborated by Ken.
The new type of local history project will, by its ambitious scope
and size, actually need more people to share the work and ideas:
working in libraries on newspapers, MOH reports, poor law and
school records; finding and interviewing people and transcribing
tapes and so on. In any group, some people are happiest when
using their talents in certain ways, and this extended project,
not confining itself to either interviewing or reading and note-
taking, allows group members to find their own niche and still
play a full part.

But, and again as Ken points out, the work needs to be
collective in the widest sense. Local history workshop groups or
people's history groups need to meet and talk over mutual
problems and new ideas. How often, even just in London, have
scattered individuals working in their own groups in Southwark
or Tottenham or Hackney said that we must get together
sometime? And although one or two groups can meet together,
how much better this would be if their experience could be
shared as widely as possible. This sharing of experience must
not be uncritical. The new local history is well enough
established to bear comradely criticism without charges of
rocking the boat, or of intellectual elitism.

One way ahead might be to hold an annual workshop
specifically for local people's history groups to discuss problems
and achievements. That is why we are setting up a Federation
of History Workshops and why we hope to have a major workshop on the relationship between local history and urban
history. That will at least be a start, but we need as many
ways of talking to one another as we can.

Ken has raised the role of the *History Workshop Journal* in
spreading the word about new developments in local history. The
original commitment to local people's history projects remains as
strong as it was in the beginning, and 'Noticeboard' has grown
into as complete a directory of what's going on in this field as
you'll find anywhere. I think that the lack of reporting that
Ken complains of is due in some part to an unarticulated feeling
that people's history has stagnated over the past couple of
years; and to a reluctance to criticise the admittedly outstanding
achievements of the best-established local groups. This will

change as new developments take off, and no one will be able to complain that the next number of the *Journal* (issue 8) is short on matters of interest to socialist local historians.

The problem at this time is to create the climate for a new way forward. The time is right for a critical re-examination of what has been achieved at the local level over the past few years and just where it's taking us. And there's no doubt that the local workshop movement, and the *Journal* within it, will play a crucial role in that self-criticism and new growth.

POSTSCRIPT

In the light of Stephen Yeo's reply to my original paper, I wanted to give the reasons for having arrived at the position I outlined there, and at the workshop I said something on the following lines.

I was sucked into people's history by accident and by an obsession, sometime in 1973. I set out to describe all aspects of life in an East London tenement block, using primarily oral sources. Motives in a venture of this kind are always mixed, but among mine two stood out: the need to understand, make sense of, the material for myself; and the wish to explore class relations and oppressions, and to get across messages about those things. My aims were at once auto-didactic and propagandist; at once individualist and collectivist.

At first, the project shaped itself into a kind of collective biography, with me matching and contrasting remembered life experience. But it was the needs of the second objective which forced me more and more to *intervene* in the material, mainly by looking for other evidence outside the conscious, remembered experience which I was collecting. I needed to go over to the other side, to look at what others were saying about and doing to the people I was interested in, the ways in which these outsiders were intervening in their families' lives: landlords, employers, poor law officers, school teachers and so on.

Self-satisfaction with my own methods gave me a vague dissatisfaction with the work of the People's Autobiography of Hackney, although I felt/feel very close to the group, both spiritually and geographically. (Indeed, it was difficult and traumatic for me to put down these *un*satisfactions in the position paper - some five or six years after knowing their work.)

In the summer of 1977 I was asked by the WEA to tutor a group which had formed itself in Tottenham (2-3 miles down the road from the Hackney group) and which wanted to write a people's history of the area. The group were Labour Party-based at first, although its constituency widened when the WEA advertised the course publicly. When the group began meeting, and to my surprise, I found that the unease I'd felt about the autobiographical project was to some extent mirrored in the attitudes of some of the members. It revolved around three areas: (i) mistrust of memory, wanting to check 'facts' - a concern for 'accuracy'; (ii) the need for a 'context' in which to place the individual (context is a weak and undialectical word but it does express awareness of other levels of reality, raised in the paper); (iii) that the past should bear explicit relation to the present and that it should be 'political' in a broadly socialist (but non-sectarian) way - to move readers to see the present differently. This third unease was perhaps only felt by a couple of us, but was held strongly, none the less.

In the weeks running up to the Workshop (and after writing the paper) I was struck by some passages in Peter Townsend's magnificent *Poverty in the United Kingdom* (1979); they sharpened for me the view I'd held for some time that one of the dangers in the oral history/ autobiography project is not so much the romanticisation of the past, but the romanticisation of the *present*. History (and not only history from above) can be used and *is* used to legitimate the present. For example, Townsend shows (pp. 239, 429-30) that some of today's poor deny the existence of poverty, and use the past as their direct reference point; this is just one of the internalised legitimations behind the confusion felt by large numbers of the poor about their situation:

[although many of the poor recognise they are relatively deprived, these feelings are] largely sealed off from more general or abstract perceptions of society. Some of the poor have come to conclude that poverty does not exist. Many of those who recognise that it exists have come to conclude that it is individually caused, attributed to a mixture of ill-luck, indolence and mismanagement, and is not a collective condition determined principally by institutionalised forces, particularly government and industry. In this they share the perceptions of the better-off. Divided, they blame individual behaviour and motivation and unwittingly lend support to the existing institutional order.

In the light of feelings like this I would argue for the right to take issue with and confront the way people understand their own oppressions, to be more heavily consciousness-raising than the autobiographical mode *usually* allows for.

So what's the way ahead? I'm not arguing for a new self-referring orthodoxy, rather for a variety of voices (the Tottenham group has been working on autobiography, as well as publications which use oral history to develop themes). I don't want to take up the position, invited by Stephen's polemic, at one end of a polarity of 'people speaking for themselves/ academicist interference'. I want not an either/or, but a new synthesis. In exploring the space around individual experience (and locating it within class relations and the capitalist economy) we are able to see that individual experience in a new light. We enter the tensions between individual consciousness/ other levels of reality: people making their own lives/having their lives shaped for them, which were at the very core of History Workshop 13

A People's History which focuses on only one side of these tensions will be incomplete by itself.

FURTHER READING

There are many examples of local people's history in the auto-biographical mode – those of the 'People's autobiography of Hackney' are listed at the end of Ken Worpole's article. Urban history, which gained great strength in the 1960s through Jim Dyos and the work centred on the University of Leicester, is often of much interest in charting the forces which shape our local environment. Dyos's *Victorian Suburb* (London 1961) is a pioneering study of the built environment; *The Study of Urban History* (ed. H.J. Dyos, London 1968) discusses some of the issues in the first decade of urban history work, and subsequent progress can be followed in *The Urban History Yearbook* which also provides massive bibliographies. For a brief critique of some aspects of this work, especially its detachment from the study of social relationships, see the editorial 'Urban History and Local History' in *History Workshop Journal* no. 8, autumn 1979. Some locally-produced studies have gone beyond autobiography to bring together collective experience. A couple of local produc-tions come to mind, Neil Griffiths' *Shops Book*, published by Queenspark Books, Brighton, and *The Island* produced by the People's Autobiography of Hackney. Some similar, more extensive work, is being done by Tottenham History Workshop, and other groups in London are working in the same direction. Any group doing this work will want to take note of the various Community Development Project reports published during the 1970s: some, particularly from Benwell and Canning Town, give excellent historically-informed studies of local economies. Two attempts at a synthesis of oral testimony and manuscript and printed materials in a community-based study, are Raphael Samuel's 'Quarry Roughs' (in R. Samuel, ed., *Village Life and Labour*, London 1975); and my own 'Campbell Bunk', *History Workshop Journal* no. 8, autumn 1979; and *Rothschild Buildings: Life in an East End Tenement Block, 1887-1920*, London 1980.

6   THE POLITICS OF COMMUNITY PUBLICATIONS

Stephen Yeo*

When I read that 'critical consciousness of capitalism is missing from the new local history' I wonder if I have been reading the same texts, or working with the same people, as Jerry White.

'Criticism without understanding', 'lapses into mere
sloganising', 'the whole tone (notwithstanding the angry bits) is
politically bland and negative and unprovocative', 'moving
insights which enrich the brotherhood of man and boost the self-
confidence of working people, but it all appears to take place in
a social vacuum', 'people's history has stagnated over the past
couple of years'. . . . This is not where I live, and not the way
to start (much-needed) criticism or appreciation of achieved
practices and products. I am sure Jerry does not think like this,
but when he calls for 'a radical new change of direction' and
speaks of a change of 'level' to a 'socialist local history' I think
there is a bit of party/class thinking in his contribution: there
has been a lot of 'spontaneous', semi-conscious activity, now
what we need and what *we* can contribute is - socialism.
    The experience of the last few years has been more dense
than Jerry's phrases suggest. There have been more constraints
- things you do because of what has happened, what is
knocking at the door, rather than because of any free-floating
choice to 'go socialist'. I am sure the same is true of the
production of the *History Workshop Journal*. Things get
published for lots of reasons, including personal ones. There are
obligations to people already in association with the group,
there are texts which people not only like but are prepared to
work hard on, and so on. The process is not at all like designing
in the head a 'socialist local history' and then executing it
through dividing the labour of research. Precisely for that
reason it has some of the ingredients of associated production
by, with and for labour. By no means all of the people involved
would want to use the word 'socialist' about themselves.
    The products of groups like those in the Federation of Worker
Writers and Community Publishers:
(a) Are not simply 'local'. The word is a subtracting one which
I dislike. What activity is *not* local? Where do *you* live and work?
Is the ruling class not located?
(b) Cannot simply be annexed to the history industry, left,
right or centre. They are seen by many historians as being good
'raw material' for that industry, as being 'useful', 'on that
level'. They are criticised by some historians who know what a
history 'complete in itself', a 'totality', a 'comprehensive'
account would look like; or who have access to 'those levels and
layers of reality outside individual experience'. I don't. They
insist on escaping from, in order to extend, the category
'history' as she is practised, even by socialists.

---

*Stephen Yeo is a long-standing socialist working with Queen's
Park community action and publications group; teaches history
at Sussex University. Author of 'The Religion of Socialism',
History Workshop Journal 4, November 1977, *Religion and
Voluntary Organisation in Crisis*, London 1976. Associate editor
of *History Workshop Journal*.

(c) They are more than history in obvious ways, e.g. that they
are also poems, 'literature' of a very exciting kind identifiably
un-bourgeois, stories, mixed forms; that they appear as part of
street newspapers as well as in 'books'; that they are sometimes
designed explicitly as propaganda-for-change; and so on. The
excitement of the *writing*, creativity, cultural *production*
(unpredictability) of some of the works can only be conveyed
through reading and quoting at length. Such excitement is very
rare indeed in history as she is currently done: it is
correspondingly golden.

(d) They constitute a quite different practice, not perfect, not
always practised, but there all the same. Here are some of its
more obvious characteristics:

cheap price, accessible format;

close relationship with schools rather than with higher education,
with adult literacy rather than with the literati;

sales and new ideas/manuscripts through person-to-person
contact, including that of the author, or through quite
distinct places, e.g. Peckham Book Place, with a relationship
rather different from the 'customer-shop' or 'subscriber-
mailing list' relationship;

a very close relationship with the 'private', working all the time
on the private/public borderline (which John Berger has
explored recently in reference to photography) - this may be
the richest seam of all to mine in this half of the twentieth
century;

substantial effect on authors' lives, whether in terms of
something to do, in terms of providing a mirror of a
collective/cultural kind where none had been before, altering
relations with children, providing a platform, or whatever -
think of the analogies or contrasts with history as done by
historians in these regards;

close relationship, where there is a Writers' Workshop, with
performance;

work which arises through direct emulation, one work leads
explicitly to another, one author thinks another has got it
wrong so does something new rather than destroying the
original polemic - emulation, not competition, as the old
trade union banners put it;

work which returns experience to the places where it has already
been nurtured so that it and other experience can be
transformed and developed *in those places*, rather than being
exported for manufacture into finished goods miles away and
never coming back - against the commodity form, 'local
accountability';

collective, or rather associated work which really does make
products which are not directed from a single head, and
which are different from what any of the individuals alone
could do - critique of authorial autonomy;

use of technology - tape recorders, video, offset litho, for
labour rather than capital;

large sales, by which I mean intensive sales specific to areas,
   rather than similar numbers extensively, but thinly,
   distributed;
demystification of the production processes themselves - paste-
   up, etc.;
vision of the authorship of all readers - and an attack on
   divisions between writing and reading, consumption and
   production, teaching and learning, the cultured and the
   masses, etc.;
close attention to *forms* and context, as in Ken Worpole's
   argument;
emphasis on labour, the human toil behind everything - who
   planted the trees on Brighton level? From whose work did
   families survive?
emphasis, but not exclusively so, on the autobiographical mode -
   here I would disagree head-on with Jerry, but there is no
   space to argue it here (Stuart Hood, *Pebbles from my Skull*;
   Malcolm X; *Roots*; St Augustine; etc., etc.) - the strengths
   and capacity for development (even collectivisation) of this
   mode need emphasis, in my view, much more than its
   weaknesses. *History Workshop Journal*, still more history in
   general, needs adequate autobiographical work much more
   than community publishing needs to proceed beyond it.
   Worker writing and community publishing has a lot to teach
historians, particularly, perhaps, socialist ones. This is partly a
matter of detail in which a particular historian, e.g. me, might
be interested (like the extraordinary diffused presence of
provided voluntary association, e.g. the penumbra of churches
and chapels, or like the role of class struggle for instance
between different types of shopkeepers in shaping the place
where we live way beyond the points of production). Such details
may be used as 'raw material' and may be used/exploited
elsewhere. But it is more a matter of texture than of detail: the
texture of lives and the complications and contradictions of
consciousness: the struggles within as well as between people:
the existence of quite different consciousnesses within one
person. They can also make *theoretical* contributions of a large
kind: e.g. Les Moss on the environment as an educator, seen as
much more than 'economic'; and, if I could add the marvellous
work of Arthur Exell for a moment (*History Workshop Journal*
nos 6, 7 and 9), Arthur Exell on the relations between community
struggle and factory struggle. Many working militants simply do
not have, and have not found it necessary, to get themselves
into the theoretical straitjackets of some of us. We must be
very careful not to see work like Arthur Exell's as 'document'
rather than history/theory.
   Beyond detail or texture, however, they challenge history
itself. The web is, of course, not seamless at all: it is full of
the tears and tatters of struggle, struggle which can, perhaps,
certainly from the point of view of changing the world, best be
articulated in class terms. What does a seriously held view of

class and struggle do to history? It breaks it up, it stops it
being an 'it', it turns it into histories, rival ways of seeing
put forward for antagonistic purposes, battles over words,
experiences, over the meanings and implications of 'change',
'society', 'history' themselves. I don't think we have in our
heads (the 'ours' here referring to people who spend a lot of
their time or are paid, to teach, edit, write, publish history) a
known version of 'socialist history' (local or otherwise) to which
we can seek to assimilate the practices and products of local/
peoples/community groups. I am not sure that we even know too
clearly what it would look like if we did have it. It is all
to-be-made, to-be-known, to be discovered and produced in
association. I am not sure whether we have grasped the extent
of cultural revolution from above, the extent of long cultural
imperialism in the Heart of the Empire itself, and the implications
this has for the difficulty and nature of class expression, class
history with, by and for labour.

Yes, Jerry, the assumption underpinning virtually all of this
work IS that for working people to speak for themselves, about
their own history, IS somehow a political act in itself. Whether
such self-utterance is 'inherently socialist' is socialism's
problem, and, hopefully, will never become here, as it has done
in Eastern Europe, working people's problem. Socialism
which does not grow from the achievements, the consciousness
(including pride in work, which is never uncomplicated), the
human aspirations and complexities of working people *even in
capitalism*, will wilt. We have to try, in the first instance, to
learn from these histories, not to teach them what correct
socialist theory is. This is, I know, a slow and detailed business.
And there may not be time, given capital's nuclear gambling with
all our futures: but does anyone know of a way to dash
effectively for the tape? History looks different, IS different
from different points of view, different locations, different class
positions. Any reports of length, depth and authenticity from
the position of those to whom the world sometimes seems upside-
down (it's a topsy-turvy world) – any faltering steps towards
'finding a dictionary for the language of the voiceless' – however
disconcerting, are correspondingly golden. A sense of time,
place and connection *is* revolutionary.

Disconcerting, 'unsocialist', incorrect, the work may often be.
But what are the current credentials of the concerted, correct,
socialist ones amongst us? Who speaks from a position of
strength? Who has forged the broken links of the chain
connecting 'politics' to people? There are lots of people around
on the left who aspire to do so, including me. There are even
some who have announced for years now that they have already
done so: join the party. But do we believe them? We can try to
be party to what is going on and to what could be: but, in my
view, the movement has not crystallised into an Organisation,
Party, Formula, Way Forward, Socialism to which recruitment
can be urged in a simple manner. In which case close

attentiveness, the politics of minute particulars, activity as
complex as any semiotics, the courage to move in directions
which open up but which do not seem 'correct', may all be at a
high premium. There *are* formidable obstacles to any working-
class-for-itself association, expression, language, culture,
history: they have grown no less formidable through centuries
of discontinuous cultural revolution, cultural imperialism from
above. In the face of such obstacles, which necessitate us
moving through (realising rather than abolishing) contradiction,
all kinds of allies, all kinds of messages of hope, all kinds of
things which quicken the spirit, may be welcomed. It is indeed
Federation that we need, rather than The Party.

And it's not all gloomy, either. Even if it does sometimes feel
as if we (socialist historians) are fish who would like to swim but
haven't got a sea to do it in, it's not quite like that - as History
Workshop 13 and the Workshop Movement and *History Workshop
Journal* have already helped us to feel. Through our own
histories, workshops and community books we can begin to get
a smell of the waves. One of the strong messages I get from
many of these writings is how little the authors, whatever their
'level of consciousness' or 'position' may be, have bought of
the present system. In the face of all the long cultural
revolution from above, it is remarkable how 'unsocialised' we
remain, how little of our humanity we have collapsed into our
social roles, how little we have invested of ourselves in the
bubbles supplied to us at work, at home and so on. There is
a lot of space for creative production and politics to work within.
Even the nostalgia, 'those were the days' - given the sharp
characterisation of the starvations, etc. of those days - is, in
my view, a rejection of these days, or at least a quite specific
critique of Now, running through a channel of Then.

Finally, these writings have educated me. They have helped
me to understand, with more than my head, what phrases like
'the materiality of cultural production' actually mean. There
have obviously been other powerful influences, notably the
magnificently sustained work of Raymond Williams and Edward
Thompson. But without seeing, in a more rooted way, the
possibility (not, of course, the *achievement* - I am not boasting
of that) of practices which may disappear tomorrow, but which
represent the associated production of different ideas,
counter-rationalities, alternative histories, mere statements of
ideas would not have had so much bite. I can now see many
varieties of Marxist thought (base-superstructure dichotomy,
material being equated with economic, culture being seen as
derivative/reflective/secondary, determination meaning
inevitability, the revolution being like 1789, working-class
consciousness being a known 'it', etc., etc.) as being ideology:
ideology which reinforces head-hand divisions, rationalises
exile, distance from struggle, advisory rather than
participatory relations to production, and so on. Moreover, such
Marxisms have a peculiar attractiveness to people in my social

48   *Local history*

position (university lecturer). We need help to be prised free
from them. Part of that help has come from FWWCP publications,
and the whole movement of which the Workshops and *Journal*
are such a central part. Cultural work-people have specific
responsibilities, which should not be confined to telling
everyone else how difficult/impossible it all is.

Oral tradition

7 THE CLASS STRUGGLE IN FOURTEENTH-CENTURY ENGLAND

Rosamond Faith*

The study of the peasantry of thirteenth- and fourteenth-century England may seem remote from the concerns of peasant studies today, but I believe it has a relevance which earlier contributions have emphasised. Many of the themes that I touch on will be familiar ones: the struggle over rent, for communal rights, for free access to woods and game. Moreover, the important question raised about peasant ideology is one which concerns the medieval as much as the modern historian: how far were peasant aspirations and programmes conservative, aimed simply at establishing good lordship, rather than putting an end to lordship altogether? One is struck, in studying the revolt of 1381, by the revolutionary and fundamental nature of the ideals of the leaders of the movement and the preachers associated with it, who called for 'an end to villeinage in England', proposed to set up 'a king in every county', and who questioned the whole basis of social inequality with 'When Adam delved and Eve span, who was then the gentleman?' But it is equally striking, on those rare occasions when we can find out what demands groups of peasants made when they actually, though briefly, achieved power, to see how seemingly local and limited their demands were; access to this or that wood or common, rights to hunt and fish, and so on. Why is this? Is it because they were an essentially conservative class, unable to see beyond the boundaries of their own fields and villages, beset by what has been called a naive monarchism?

My own feeling is that there is, certainly, a strong element of conservatism in peasant ideology, but that it is what we might call a radical conservatism. By this I mean that in claiming ancient rights and keeping alive the idea of ancient liberties whether real or fabricated, people were, in fact, making a radical plea for social justice in the terms that seemed most

---

*Ros Faith is employed as a research assistant on the medieval volumes of the History of the University of Oxford. She has worked on the English peasant land-market in the later middle ages. Her current research interests are: the origins of the idea of villeinage, the peasants' revolt of 1381 in Hertfordshire, medieval marriage-fines, 'droit de seigneur', and medieval horses. The following paper makes no scholarly claims, but was intended to interest a group of non-medievalists in the kind of information that can be extracted from medieval records about peasant struggles, both day-to-day and in such major episodes as that of 1381.

appropriate to them. Moreover, in studying rural class struggle in its most day-to-day manifestations, as well as in revolutionary clashes such as 1381, we can see traditions of resistance developing in village communities which must have been an important element in forming peasant class consciousness. This is what this brief paper is about.

The village community in question is the small Hertfordshire manor of Park, just south of St Albans. In the period of which I am writing, the mid-thirteenth to the late fourteenth century, it was the property of the Benedictine abbey of St Albans, and it is from the records of the courts which the abbey's representative, the cellarer, held for the tenants there that most of my information is drawn.

I

The payment of compulsory labour rent is perhaps the most distinctive feature of the relationship of medieval peasants and their manorial lords. Labour-rent was not particularly high on the St Albans manors: the most important aspect was the obligation to work on the Abbey lands at the most labour-intensive times of the year; at haymaking and harvest. The tenant of a virgate holding of 20 to 30 acres had to provide four men (members of his family or perhaps his under-tenants) at haymaking, and four men on every day of a 'book-work' - times when the lord could call on the labour-supply of all his unfree tenants.

It is not always easy to tell, from court records, how much trouble the lord had in exacting these services. The absence of references to refusals of labour-rent can be very misleading, and has more than once induced historians of manorial economy to assume a social peace that may not have existed. On some manors, of course, the labour-rent system may have worked without friction. On others, it may be that only when demands for labour-rent met concerted or large-scale refusal did the compiler of the court record make a record of it. Constant, day-to-day resistance may have been common and remained unrecorded. At Park, there seem to have been periods at which resistance to performing labour-services reached the level of what looks like a series of strikes, interspersed by long periods when there was little sign of resistance. What I have called strikes- nonperformance of labour-services by groups of (named) tenants- seem to have taken place in 1246, 1265 and the 1270s. (The court records for the manor begin in 1237.) There was a much more prolonged and consistent series in the crisis years of the early fourteenth century, when harvest failures and stock disease meant disaster for many peasant families. There were extensive refusals of labour-services, or failure to do them, in 1309 and then in every year from 1318 to 1327. As will appear later, these years were also critical ones in the protracted

struggle of the townspeople of St Albans against the Abbey, and
it may well be that this outbreak of strikes had as much to do
with the political as the economic climate of the time. After the
1320s there is little sign of labour service refusals, and services
were largely replaced by money rents after the Black Death.
What extent of conscious, concerted and organised action lies
behind the terse statements of the court book that 'Gilbert
Schad, Richard de Smaleford Peter de Slape . . . withheld two
men each from the lord's haymaking . . .' and so on? Can we
really call such action 'strikes'? There are several difficulties in
the way of such an interpretation: one can't tell from the
evidence whether or not there was any attempt to involve the
whole tenant work-force, or to achieve any particular objective.
It is more realistic to imagine tenants simply not turning up to
take their places in the line of reapers or mowers, than downing
tools and walking off the job. Moreover, we have to guard
against interpreting such evidence too crudely as showing the
poor peasant's struggle against seigneurial demands. Many of
the people involved may have been nearer to yeomen in status;
some very likely had tenants of their own. Some may not have
been living in the village at all, but have left the holdings to
find land or work elsewhere. Nor is there much sign that the
Abbey's tenants were particularly heavily burdened as far as
labour-services were concerned compared to those elsewhere;
though the administration was extremely authoritarian in other
ways, as will appear.

What is very notable about the labour-service cases at Park
is the fact that the same names keep cropping up year after
year. Of the twelve men presented to the court in 1265, for
instance, six were to be involved in similar successive cases in
the 1270s. In the almost continuous labour disputes of the 1320s
about a third of the names (14 out of 45) occur in more than one
year, and several in two or three years. In several cases we can
be fairly sure that the *sons* of men who withdrew their labour on
one or more occasion would act in the same way when they in
their turn took over the family holding. Alexander Wikyng,
presented to the court in 1357, was the son or more probably the
grandson of Thomas Wikyng, presented for the same offence in
1272. Richard Wikyng, who appeared in the courts for not doing
labour services in 1318, 1319, 1321 and 1322 was succeeded by
his son John, who appeared on similar charges in 1326. More
research would, I feel sure, reveal more such family connections
and perhaps identify for us a number of tenants – I'm not sure
how far one should think of them as a group consciously acting
together – who were consistently withholding labour rent. Such
research, which would focus on the peasant as someone who
could and did take independent action against the lord or his
representative, would to my mind be more productive, as well as
more interesting, than the rather arid social and economic
analyses which seek merely to define his place in the social scale
in terms of land-holding, office-holding and so on.

I turn now to two other issues which were to come to the fore in 1381, but which had been important in the village for many years before that. The first is the long series of prosecutions for poaching in, and taking timber from, the Abbot's woodland. (The Abbey had rights of 'free warren' over extensive areas in its liberty of St Albans, then a heavily wooded district, which gave it a monopoly of game and timber there.) I should say that I consider poaching to be an absolutely basic source of conflict in English rural life wherever there is private landlordism. From the landlord's point of view ownership of land has always implied ownership of the game on it; from the peasants' point of view there is an unassailable common right to what the land naturally provides. The issue is a fundamental enough one, for all that our evidence consists simply of a string of individual court entries, year after year that 'Fulk de Spitalstrate set snares to catch hares in the warren', 'John Hendegome and his brother frequently put snares and nets and catch partridges, hares and rabbits', 'John Smith, John Howe, and Henry Prat and John the beadle catch fish with their nets in the lord's private waters', 'Roger le Boteler set snares and other devices in the warren' and so on. This kind of hunting was silent, secret, and probably generally undetected; I would think that it was more often a matter for individual enterprise than for co-operation, though there are occasional cases of tenants hunting with hounds, which may have involved a larger group of people.

Illegally felling timber, and lopping trees, taking wood and brushwood, and hedge-breaking round the lord's enclosed fields, all increased dramatically after the Peasants Revolt, when seigneurial prohibitions on this type of offence seem virtually to have broken down for a time.

Not having analysed these cases in terms of the individuals involved I cannot yet say whether there were individual regular poachers in medieval Park as there are in many English villages today, but I think it is fair to say that there was a *tradition* of poaching and taking wood there in the Middle Ages which must have been a regular feature of life in the village.

To turn, finally, to the dispute over hand-mills is to come to the most striking, and certainly the best-documented, aspect of peasant protest at St Albans. It figures in most of the major accounts of the revolt and obviously caught the attention of the Abbey's chronicler, Thomas Walsingham, whose account of the Abbey's relations with its tenants, and with the townspeople of St Albans sometimes reads like an account of this issue alone. Its symbolic as well as its actual importance was as clear to him as it was to the people involved in the dispute. The fact that townspeople as well as peasants were involved, and made common cause over the matter, makes it of particular interest and importance.

The basic issues in the conflict were simple. The Abbot's villein tenants 'owed suit' to the Abbot's own mills: that is to say that they had to take their own grain there to be ground,

and their cloth to his fulling-mills for fulling. A proportion of
the grain had to be paid to the Abbot. The system was expensive
and a nuisance; the tenants naturally preferring to grind their
grain at home in hand-mills. (These were probably not querns,
properly speaking, but two round millstones.) The Abbey's
eagerness to enforce suit to its own mills is understandable in
the light of the considerable profits that could be made from
milling and of the fact that it had made a heavy capital
investment in its mills and their machinery - over £100 had been
spent on a horse-mill. The Abbey mills were large, modern and
expensive; the peasants' hand-mills were small basic and cheap:
in part it is a conflict over technology. Of course, the dispute
over mills was only part of a wider and protracted struggle on
the part of the townsmen of St Albans to achieve borough
status.

This struggle was by no means simply one of an urban
proletariat alone, but involved, and was probably led by, a
self-confident and politically sophisticated urban ruling class.
It is very hard to tell to what extent the interests of this ruling
group actually coincided with those of the urban working class
and the peasantry. One can tell from the chronicler's account
though, that at times these disparate groups felt themselves to
have a common purpose. He emphasises the solidarity of the
crowd, recounts how they swore oaths for their mutual support
and established a common chest for the expenses of furthering
their cause. They had a common seal - a fact which emphasises
the similarity of the movement to the urban commune movements
of France. The element of *confederacy* in the St Albans crowd,
in fact, is something that particularly shocked the chronicler.
The leadership of the urban movement was not always in the
hands of the urban patriciate, however, in spite of the fact that
the aim it professed - the recognition of the town's borough
status - was of particular appeal to this group. The sheer
weight of popular support could shift the balance of power: in
1327, when the 'lesser people' (*inferiores*) bound themselves in
a confederacy by oath, 'Their numbers grew in three days to
such an extent that they compelled all the greater people of the
town to follow them in public, who would have preferred to
support them secretly.'

Briefly, the trouble over mills - both hand-mills and small-
scale fulling-mills - began in 1274 when

the whole congregation of our monastery of St Albans groaned
under a heavy load of troubles. The men of that town, rising
up against us like wild people, began to propose a great
outrage against us; to no little damage to our church they
fulled their cloths and ground their own corn to please their
own wishes and also - just as if they were allowed to do so -
ventured to erect hand-mills in their own houses.

The Abbot reacted sharply, sending his steward and a
party of sixteen men to the houses of two of his tenants, Michael,
son of Richard Bryd, and Henry de Porta to distrain on their

goods. They seized 'the upper stone of a hand mill' and 30
shillings' worth of cloth found there and imprisoned Michael
and Henry. This was the first round in a battle which lasted
for at least a hundred years. In fact the story may well go
back earlier than 1274, and it is reasonable to suppose that it
does, for communal reaction in that year to the Abbot's action
was swift and determined, as if the townsmen were well aware
of the issues involved and of how they should act:

> they arouse others, bring about dissensions, and set in
> motion a long-lasting dispute . . . they pledge themselves to
> be ready for anything to achieve their ends . . . our enemies
> met together more often, all the more powerful men of that
> town, as if glorying in their strength . . . who extorted
> from the great and the lesser . . . much money, putting it
> into a common chest for the purpose of sustaining law suits
> *as if for a holy and pious work*.

This is not the last time Walsingham points to an almost
sacramental air about the townsmen's actions.

It is not possible to do more than outline the main events in
the disputes with the abbey before 1381. The highlights to bear
in mind are *the seige of 1327* in which the monastery, fortified
by the Abbott with a contingent of 200 armed men, was besieged
by the townspeople. They put forward a list of demands, partly
political, for borough status and parlimentary representation
and so on, among which are embedded demands for common
rights in 'lands, woods, waters, fisheries, and other commodities
as are contained in Domesday Book as they used to have' and
that 'they shall be allowed to have hand-mills as they used to
do'. Negotiations between the two sides, the town represented
by 'six of the greater men of the town and certain people of the
neighbourhood' began in London. Back in St Albans the siege
continued, with the townsmen attacking the Abbey with missiles.
(Walsingham uses the word *tola* which can mean darts but also,
interestingly enough, a weaver's beam.) The London
negotiations produced first an appeal to Domesday Book, in
which the town's claim to borough status was clearly vindicated,
and then a virtual capitulation on the part of the Abbey. A
document was issued meeting most of the demands but,
significantly, stating that it did not prejudice the Abbey's claims
over mills or its right to remove illegal hand-mills. The granting
of this charter was greeted none the less as a popular victory
by the townspeople. In a celebration which seems to involve as
much an assertion of popular rights as the formal
acknowledgment of political victory they

> rushing in a crowd like madmen, breaking down the branches
> from the beech trees in the name of seisin, carried them
> round the town *cum clamore pomposo* [with great uproar].
> They pulled down the hedges and [destroyed] the ditches
> round Barnetwood and Frithwood and Eywodemede for their
> common, and from then on fished in the Abbott's waters at
> will and for the following five years hunted both hares and

rabbits in the warren. They set up hand-mills to the number of 80 round the town.

This victory was a temporary one. A tough and determined Abbot, Richard of Wallingford, succeeded Abbot Hugh. He purged the monastery of monks who came from local families and might be sympathetic to the townsmen's cause and set about winning back the ground lost by his predecessors. The charter that Abbot Hugh had issued was given up, the townsmen's seal was broken up and the metal used to repair the shrine of St Alban in the Abbey Church. The three keys of the common chest were surrendered 'and the chest itself, lest they should ever entertain any hope of having a *communitas*' – a word best translated as 'commune' I think. The record of the Abbot's concessions was erased from the records of the central government. Lastly, the people 'surrendered their millstones in the Church as a sign of the absolute renunciation of their right to mill'. The millstones, in a gesture which was surely made in full consciousness of the symbolism involved, were cemented into the floor of the Abbot's parlour.

To turn back to the village of Park we can see that disputes about hand-mills there go back almost as far as the Court Book itself, to 1237, and continued throughout the fourteenth century. The entries do not alter much in form: a typical one running 'Margaret Newman fined sixpence because she used another mill than the lord's mill'. It seems to me that one can say two things about these milling disputes. Firstly, although seemingly of small importance, the issue seemed of crucial importance to people at the time. Secondly, though hand-milling, like poaching, was necessarily a private rather than a communal offence, the need for secrecy must have meant that a certain amount of communal solidarity was shown to conceal the existence of hand-mills from the eye of beadle or bailiff. As with many types of offence that recur in manorial court rolls year after year and are punished only by small fines, we have to ask whether these fines are in effect licences for permission to continue committing the offence rather than a serious attempt at deterrence. There may be an element of this in the milling cases at St Albans but I don't think it is the whole explanation. As we have seen, the Abbot's monopoly was fiercely defended, and a substantial source of seigneurial income was involved. The occasional seigneurial ordinances against hand-mills, with increased penalties, show that the Abbey was not prepared to let the matter go by default.

I now turn to the actual events of 1381 in St Albans, or rather to a handful of aspects of those events which seem to me to put the rather scrappy picture of conflict given by the Court Books into a clearer perspective. I believe that it is only when we bear in mind the long history of conflict in the town and on the Abbey's manors that what people did in 1381 really makes sense.

II

One of the most striking things, to my mind, about the revolt in St Albans - and it would be interesting to know how typical this is of peasant revolt in general - is its sense of tradition and history. I think this is a very important theme in the 1381 revolt as a whole and has not been very well understood because the radical nature of the revolt, the attacks on important officers of state, and the revolutionary nature of the programme and philosophy attributed to its leaders have tended to obscure it. (Aspects of that philosophy remain obscure. Historians have not been able to make much sense of such reported slogans as 'there shall be no law but the law of Winchester', for instance.)

Some strange ideas were going about in St Albans in 1381. The crowd assembled at the Abbey gate demanded to be given 'a certain charter of King Offa with letters of alternately blue and silver by which King Offa had granted their liberty to the people of St Albans - the common people, masons and workmen - as a reward for their help in building the town.' Now King Offa, who founded the monastery of St Albans in the eighth century, almost certainly never granted such a charter. The chronicler Walsingham has an educated man's joke at the expense of the gullible townsmen over the idea that such a thing could exist. There are charters of liberties granted by Offa to the monastery and there are, incidentally, many charters which have alternately coloured lists of names at the foot. There is no extant charter, as far as I know, that fits the townsmen's description, and Walsingham was probably right to say that no such document ever existed. The point is that the people passionately believed in Offa's charter and, when the Abbot said he couldn't find it, sent him back to the monastery again and again to look for it until he eventually offered to write out a new charter at their direction.

One of the interesting things about Offa is that he was a figure of popular local legend. His story was probably as familiar to local people as that of the local dragon, whose lair had been discovered nearby. We know he was popular, because the compiler of the hagiographical *Lives of the Two Offas* gathered information about him in the thirteenth century from local people. Even more interesting is the fact that, according to Walsingham, certain men in St Albans had been leading the young people of the town astray by telling them tales of Offa and his charter. One of these men was Bernard Spichfat whose family, and perhaps himself, had been involved in disputes with the Abbey for over 50 years. We are seeing here a live, popular, political tradition at work, with its own folklore.

It is significant, I think, that the townsmen demanded a *charter of rights*. With due respect to Edward Thompson, who, in an inspiring paper on Blake, has brought out the central idea of charters as defining privileges for an exclusive group, I think the popular reverence for charters in the Middle Ages was filled with a different spirit. Rights really depended, and were coming to depend more and more, on the written word. The St Albans Chronicle is scattered with stories of forged charters, some most ingeniously done. (A Barnet man, for instance, fabricated a charter and hung it in the smoke of his fire to give it an authentically antique appearance.) The court books themselves, which originally functioned as an instrument of seigneurial policy, came eventually to be valued as a register of land tenures. On the other hand, seigneurial documents did record seigneurial privilege: the burning of many such documents during the revolt is witness to this fact. In demanding Offa's charter, the people of St Albans were in effect going back to an idea of ancient liberties. The fact that they thought those liberties must have been embodied in a document is characteristic of the political folklore of the medieval crowd. The 'greater men' had appealed to both Domesday Book and Magna Carta without much lasting success; this was a much less sophisticated, more grass-roots ideology at work.

Appeals to tradition, and a tradition which had its roots in local folklore: what else is significant, in the context of our discussion of class struggle in the countryside? I can only deal with a very small aspect of the revolt: the beginning. This is how things went.

The local leaders, William Gryndecobbe and William Cadyndone, who had been in touch with Tyler in London and received his promise of support, announced to the 'great rout' of townsmen and villeins and serfs at St Albans - a group of whom have themselves been to London and made contact with the rebels there - that all would go well, that they would in future be not serfs but lords and that great and wonderful things would be done against the Abbey.

The next day there is a kind of procession 'with great pomp' to Faunton Wood of an armed crowd from the town, some under threats, where they destroy the enclosures and gates erected by the Abbey. They return to St Albans and are joined by a great crowd of 2,000 or more commons and peasants from the Abbey's lands. Joining their right hands, all swear an oath to be faithful to one another. They take branches from the trees and give seisin of the warren and common of woods and fields. Then they take a live rabbit which some of the crowd had caught in the open field and fix it on a pole on the pillory in the town as a sign of the free warren they have won. (Later, when the revolt had failed, some of these offenders against the Church's property were drawn through the same fields and hanged on a scaffold cut from these same woods.) To break down a few fences to string up a live rabbit, to hand round branches of trees: these will only seem trivial actions to us if we forget that these men and women and their parents and grandparents, too, very likely, had through trespass, poaching and taking wood effectively been claiming rights of common and warren for over a hundred years.

On into the town, the crowd open the Abbot's prison and free all the prisoners but one, whom they execute, shouting slogans which they had learned in London. They fix his head to the pillory 'so that all should see that they could enjoy new laws and could claim new privileges'.

From this point on the St Albans events follow a much more conventional political pattern of mass meetings, negotiations, demands, concessions and so on. There is one further event, however, which has the same almost ritualistic and symbolic character as these early demonstrations. I think that the following passage from Walsingham is a moving witness to the spirit of an occasion which must have had something about it of an exuberant and triumphant occupation of enemy territory, but something also, of a solemn rite to which over a 100 years of struggle had given weight and significance:

some ribald people, breaking their way into the Abbey cloisters, took up from the floor of the parlour doorway the millstones which had been put there in the time of Abbott Richard as a remembrance and memorial of the ancient dispute between the Abbey and the townsmen. They took the stones outside and handed them over to the commons, breaking them into little pieces and giving a piece to each person, just as the consecrated bread used to be broken and distributed on Sundays in the parish churches, so that the people, seeing these pieces, would know themselves avenged against the Abbey in that cause.

FURTHER READING

This paper arose from some fairly detailed work on manorial records rather than from any knowledge of the wider subject of medieval oral tradition or popular culture, so I do not feel competent to give a very helpful list for further reading. Such a list, in any case, would have to be either very long, for the subject enters tangentially into so many works on medieval life and literature, or very short, because there does not seem to be very much written specifically on it. However, from a personal point of view, the book which best conveys the 'feel' of pre-Reformation popular thought – despite the later focus indicated by its sub-title [*Studies in Popular Beliefs in Sixteenth and Seventeenth Century England*], is K.V. Thomas, *Religion and the Decline of Magic* (London, 1971), especially ch. 2., 'The magic of the medieval church' and ch. 13, 'Ancient Prophesies'. The book has wonderfully rich notes and bibliographies. On the medieval English peasantry generally, H.S. Bennett, *Life on the English Manor: a Study of Peasant Conditions 1150-1400* (Cambridge, 1956), and G.C. Homans, *English Villagers of the Thirteenth Century* (Cambridge, Mass., 1941) are much less rigidly economic than most more recent work on manorial history. On popular religion, G.R. Owst,

Literature and Pulpit in Medieval England (Oxford, 1933) has a
mass of references to popular stories and beliefs. For traditions
of protest and social criticism, much of which centred on
historical or semi-historical figures; M. Keen, *The Outlaws of
Medieval Legend* (London, 1961) (Appendix II lists collections
of ballads, etc.). R.H. Hilton, *Bond Men Made Free* (London,
1973), and his 'Peasant movements in England before 1381',
Econ. H.R., 2nd. series, vol. 2 ii (1949-50), and C.C. Dyer,
'A re-distribution of incomes in fifteenth-century England?',
Past and Present, no. 39 (April 1968) deal specifically with
peasant resistance and revolt, the first in a European context,
the other two locally. A. Reville, *Le Soulèvement des
Travailleurs d'Angleterre en 1381* (Paris, 1898) and the relevant
sections of Hilton, *Bond Men Made Free* are the best accounts,
both analytic and narrative, of the revolt of 1381; R.B. Dobson,
The Peasants' Revolt of 1381 (London, 1970) is a very useful
collection of extracts, mostly from contemporary sources.

There must be a large number of works on oral traditions
with which I am not familiar, but I found A.B. Lord, *The Singer
of Tales* (Cambridge, Mass., 1960) fascinating because it shows
what a living ballad tradition is like at work; Lord deals mainly
with twentieth-century Yugoslavia, but refers back to Homer
and *Beowulf*. C.E. Wright, *The Cultivation of Saga in Anglo-
Saxon England* (London, 1939), in spite of its rather forbidding
scholarship, shows interestingly how early literary forms, such
as hagiography, drew on contemporary oral culture.

Lastly, important work by M.T. Clanchy: 'Remembering the
Past and the Good Old Law', *History*, IV (1970), pp. 165-176,
and *From Memory to Written Record: England 1066-1307* (London,
1979), describes how medieval England moved from a mainly oral
to a mainly written culture. Clanchy is mainly concerned with
the documentation of law and administration, but emphasises
the great shift in attitudes this involved, and reflected, and the
accompanying growth of literacy. His is a new, and seemingly
immensely productive way of looking at conventional historical
sources.

8   'WORMS OF THE EARTH': THE MINERS' OWN STORY

Dave Douglass*

It's been said that in the Durham and Northumberland coalfield, when you're a kid in a pit village you don't get Goldilocks and the Three Bears or Little Red Riding Hood as a bedtime story. You get Churchill and the '26 strike and the betrayal of Thomas and the railwaymen and things like that. And it's this interpretation of miners' history that I want to focus on, because it's this manner of carrying history, of awakening a deep curiosity in it, setting the starting-blocks of learning, which is truly the miners' history. It was, after all, the way we the miners carried our history in recent years before we could read or write. We carried our own history to each other in this fashion for a great many years longer than we've done it by any other fashion. Miners writing their own history, for themselves, about themselves, are still, even in these days of super-media exposure, a rarity.

What I'm talking about is the wealth of oral miners' history; history as carried in stories, in memories, in old arguments, revisited over the bevvie, like: 'That's Harry Carson. He scabbed during the '26 strike'. That kind of history.

The miners, particularly those of Durham, Northumberland, Scotland and Wales, have an interest and a passion for history which is almost devotional. It is an element of the pitman's character which at once forces itself upon those who would study the miners. Many a would-be researcher has sat down with a bunch of lads to discover the strike patterns of the 1950s only to be steered time and again to the 1930s. The miners themselves, in their own minds, have already embossed the crucial areas which need to be mentioned. This was a phenomenon experienced very strongly by the comrades in Cinema Action when they were struggling to make *The Miners' Film*. This film was to feature, in bold celluloid, the '72 and '74 strikes. However, at every turn, and in every interview, and in

---

*Dave Douglass is a working miner, at Hatfield Main colliery, Doncaster. Student at Ruskin 1971-3. Author of 'Pit Life in County Durham' and 'Pit Talk in County Durham', History Workshop pamphlets reprinted in *Miners, Quarrymen and Saltworkers*, ed. by R. Samuel (London 1977). An active revolutionary since he joined the Young Communist League at the age of 16, he has been variously an anarchist, syndicalist, Trotskyist. He is also both a singer and collector of traditional songs; and an active member of the National Union of Mineworkers.

almost every take, the miners swung the focus time and again to 1926. The impact of that strike was such that it held a central stage around which other events had to take a secondary place, at least in description. It became clear that to many '72 was a continuation of the '26 conflict. It was round two of a battle that had taken on almost a religious profundity in mining families. The shutting of those gates at Saltley was greeted by an intense feeling of satisfaction among many an old lad who lived hundreds of miles away from that place at the time.

Twenty years ago, perhaps even fifteen years ago, a kid could learn almost every important feature of the miners' history at a very early age and without ever opening a book. Year after year at the Durham gala since babyhood you watched the epic stages of our history parade by on magnificent banners. Each scene was explained as the banner came up, and then again as it did the rounds of the big field, then again as the banner marched away – and this every year from the shoulders of your dad through to adolescence, year after year this kind of thing was reinforced.

Here was a walking museum – a history book so vividly illustrated that you were left with a perfect chronology of struggle and conciliation (because of course many of the banners portrayed conciliation rather than struggle). It's sad, to me at least, that W.A. Moy's *The Banner Book* carries the kind of commentary it does. In an attempt to knock any sort of revolutionary intention or clear class militancy, he objects that militant banners such as the Wardley one I reproduced in *Pit Life in County Durham* – with its hammer-and-sickle, and portraits of Marx, Lenin and James Connolly – were comparative rarities. The fact that they were rarities meant that they were all the more watched for, and their notoriety made the knowledge of those characters portrayed there more likely. Not simply this, but as these selfsame faces towered over you as you walked along from childhood they also became a symbol of security. For example, once a lodge reached a meeting place, the mams picked a corner of the field which was theirs, and picnics were begun, and throughout the day it was a rally point for the dads coming back drunk from the pubs and committee men strolling back from their speeches. Many a little lad, ice cream dripping on his bag of chips as he fought his way back through the crowds thinking himself lost, has seen over the milling thousands the face of A.J. COOK and it's been like a welcome lighthouse. A.J. Cook isn't just something on a page then, it's an absolute personal connection, it's the way you find your way back over the field.

Great events and characters passed through childhood memories by proxy, by the proxy of those who'd experienced them directly, either informally by front-room conversations of the adults or else at sports days and suchlike where formal speeches are made. I've already written a bit about Geordie Harvey, the great Geordie Bolshevik in 'Pit Life in County

Durham', and I think I mentioned in that how we grew up with him; even though he was absent we grew up with his presence. People had always been talking about him and the deeds of his time, so much so that by the time it was my turn to go underground, I felt quite able to join in the conversations of the older men as if I'd known him myself intimately.

Of course, people like Lady Astor and Churchill were constant targets for vilification. Churchill's record *vis-à-vis* the miners was, as I've said, passed on from the knee. Astor, equally hated, was credited with almost every bizarre and nonsensical idea in relation to the miners and work, particularly during the war. Ideas like the miners should have their beds sent down the pits so they wouldn't come home and they could get more production out, and stuff like that.

The hostility of the ruling class was remembered and is currently remembered in bitter recollection of things said at the time of '26, like when A.J. Cook said: 'We'll let the grass grow on those pulley wheels before we submit to tyranny.'
And Churchill said: 'And I'll make you eat it.'
And choice phrases he had like, 'The worms of the earth' and 'Drive them back down their holes like rats'. They're reflections of history which not only convey events; they convey the bitterness and the class hatred not found in more academic things.

Of course, there comes a whole bevy of folktales which, if they're lacking in provable facts, at least convey ongoing attitudes. It's still quite common today for people to tell stories about Winston Churchill knocking Lady Astor off and Lady Astor saying:
'And tell me, do the miners do this?'
'Well, I suppose so.'
'It's far too bloody good for them - have it stopped.'
It's true!

I should mention songs as a way of transporting and appreciating history, but I'm not going to illustrate any so you can rest easy on that. But songs, particularly the old ones, are a unique and highly accurate way of understanding old methods, work systems and conditions. Both the serious ones and the humorous ones really roll back the years and give a living picture of life gone by: songs like *The Waggoner*, *Follow the Horses*, and *The Row Between the Cages*. Like the banners, somewhat musty to New Wave ears, are a vision of dynamism compared to a vast majority of books on mining: while one gives appreciation and inspiration, the other, if you are lucky, gives you cold information.

An old, now retired, cutterman called Ginna Dawson carried a history of coal work as old as time in his bones. He was an ex-Lancashire miner working his last years in Yorkshire on the most modern coal-cutting machinery. He'd graduated through every type of mechanical and explosive coal-getting device there was. One day, when the face was stood and everything had

broken down, he gave us all a demonstration of how they used to
fell coal with a mallet and wooden wedges when he first started in
the pits in Lancashire. This method is probably the oldest ever
used; and yet here we were from mallet to sophisticated multi-
drum coal-cutters - our history is absorbed and advanced almost
in the same action. The use of the old skills diminishes with the
introduction of new machines, but the knowledge of them, and
often even the dexterity at them, doesn't. For example, if you
have falls of ground, it's wooden timber that we use in the holes
- props, boards, tree-trunks, planks, etc. They're knocked into
position with hammers and wedges - patterns of support learned
through centuries of understanding strata and weight.

One of the things I consciously associate with the dawning of
a consciousness of history, and one I suppose experienced by
generations of North Durham miners, was going on walks with
my dad along the river banks. These walks were illustrated at
almost every yard by descriptions and stories of this ruined
building or that wooden structure, or a mound of earth from
centuries ago, and by the sites of old disused collieries. I was
literally to encounter much of this in *Sketches of the Coal Mines
in Northumberland and Durham* by T.E. Hair (1817). Here I was
able to fill out the memory gaps and actually see the scenes
observable by pitmen before my dad was born. But impressive
above all was the walk taken twice a week past Jarrow Slake -
that scene of degradation to the miners. A miner had in the
1830s been executed, covered in pitch, and dragged through the
villages, the route being determined by the optimum number of
villages remotely near. The body was guarded by the army and it
was a demonstration to us of the cost of struggle. Not simply
death, but vilification, as the body swung in the gibbet, black
and eyeless, up to the knees at high tide, and quite clearly
visible to every collier on his way to work, and the kids at play.
That was the justice that we learned to expect from the state.

The pitmen to me *are* history, the struggle today a
continuation of the last one, generation to generation. But the
pits themselves, as tributes to the toil, labours and endeavours
of decades of workers from ancient times to the present are a
source of wonder and fascination among old miners, of constant
debate and hours of walking to find where such a legendary pit
was supposed to have been. The pits aren't inanimate, not in the
way we normally mean by that term. In a trade so ancient it's
perhaps inevitable that myths and yarns and legends abound.
For example, an old Geordie collier working in Doncaster told me
that as a boy he worked in a shallow pit in Northumberland,
and during this time he came upon the strange evidence of
earlier coal working; it took the form of a perfectly tubular
tunnel about two-and-a-half feet in diameter, of undeterminable
length. The weirdest thing was that it seemed to come from
nowhere, and go nowhere.

Of course, the pitman in the ancient fields used to find masses
of monks' mines and their abandoned tools and shovels and picks

and that. Another man told me of how he and his marra broke into an old working and caught the glimpse of a horse standing upright in the darkness before the inrush of air rendered it to powder. The more common discovery on hitting those old workings is that of ancient chalk messages left on the roof and walls. It's a strange sensation, and one I couldn't touch on in a word nor explain, but to stand there as a pitman and read those messages, and by so doing provide a link through time between reader and writer, is a gut feeling of miners' history.

The old songs are not only still sung and very often in the original settings for which they were written but also there are notable modern writers today. Some of them, like Eddie Pickford, sons and grandsons of miners if not pitmen themselves, capture the old pit poeties' style and feelings.

We have, I suppose, a kind of collective memory in which the historical event or process once absorbed is passed on through generations. The old men talking of experiences with ponies, the middle-aged ones, or even myself, can add two penn'orth to this collective experience. Young lads who've never seen a gallowa (pony) thus absorb a whole period and will have 'memories' about them long after the last pony-driver is dead, even if it's by proxy. For example, if I sing *The Collier's Rant* - as I often do, to modern miners, after 300 years of its history, it's still clearly understandable and relatable to us, particularly because of the process of history through yarn that I'm speaking of. I was taught at the age of about twelve how to trim a candle to test for gas. An old pitman was showing me how his father had done it when he first went down. The lesson, of course, was in an outhouse and not down the pit. He told me of explosive gas in the roof and taking the candle down slowly to the floor so as neither to put it out nor blow the place sky-high by a sudden movement.

Now, how does this rendering of miners' history stand in relation to the countless written histories? Not well, I think. I can't mention here, in the time left, all the books, and I've not read all of them by any means. But the books about the mines themselves, for the reasons I've said, are often far more interesting to us than the ones that purport to be about us. There are realms of wonder in John Bell Simpson's *Coalmining by the Monks*. One can push the village coal trade back to the ninth and tenth centuries with it. And don't think these monks' mines means a few old lads working in a hole somewhere. I mean, we're talking about real pit work. The sites of the ancient collieries are well illustrated and I can tell you that the facts are still debated by the old miners at Felling, in The Bluebell, or at Wardley in the Ex-Servicemen's Club, or at the Black Bull, about the old collieries. With a bit of luck you can follow the old maps, and I've scarcely stood on any place in Geordieland, be it Bill Quay, Bamburgh Castle or Holy Island, and not reflected on the mining done there in years gone by, nor yet sat at peace an hour on the beach without taking off, looking for the abandoned pits. I did it in Antrim, too, by the way, and I was able to do that because the old books on mining itself can add air to the fuel of enquiry.

J.U. Neff, *Rise of the Coal Industry* (1930), Litchefield's *Our Coal and Our Coal Pits* (1853), Archer's *Sketch of the Coal Trade in Northumberland and Durham*, sketch-maps of places on the Tyne-and-Wear where coals were being worked in 1700, Galloway's big history *Annals of Coalmining* (1904) - boring? No, not boring. These technical histories of coal work, these archaeological tracts, become the fibre on the skeletons of native-told stories, they become evidence of things said for generations, and I've never met a pitman not fascinated by them.

The same, usually, is true of pit autobiographies. Why is there such a contrast between formal histories and these? Is it because the majority of the pit autobiographies are written by miners, as opposed to the other writers of formal histories? It seems to follow, because television dramatisations like *The Camerons*, *Days of Hope*, the first series of *When the Boat Comes In*, *The Price of Coal*, etc., were spot-on, to my mind anyway. And now again, Radio Hallam, Radio Sheffield station, is doing a dramatisation of the life of Dick Kelly, the longest-serving miners' MP, and a Geordie DeLeonist in the pits, and it's brilliant. In the television programmes you can see the banners wave and the old pits talk, and not just because it's on vision, but because they capture the body of history.

Books like McCutcheon's *Troubled Seams*, Jack Lawson's *Peter Lee*, Joseph Halliday *Just Ordinary* (1969), Jack Lawson's *A Man's Life*, *The Life of Herbert Smith*, George Hitchin's *Pit Yakker* (1962=, to name a few novels and biographies or autobiographies, all of which give you a keen insight into the miners themselves. I just can't understand why the heel when it comes to laboured, self-designated official histories of the miners you get such flat and squelchy, undigestible, boring monologues like that - you know, I just don's see why the contrast is like that. Mind, I don't say this is true of them all. Reactionary and downright conciliatory leaders of the miners, ex-miners themselves, have still made better readinf than the work of bourgeois historians. Burt is a bloody interesting writer, even though if I'd been alive at the time I'd have probably put a bullet through his head.

Obviously I'm not going to go on talking about the books - that's for the discussion. But if I was to end on a positive theme, and as a Trotskyist of course it's a critical one, I would take Fyne's book *The Miners of Northumberland and Durham* (1873) as perhaps the only formal history worth lending to my mates. His detail with antiquity is, to us, at once riveting. His moralising is annoying, but the sympathy of that writer is moving and although his theme is reformist - perhaps it's reformist, you've got to see it in its time I suppose - it's undoubtedly about us, there's no question of that. Some of the parts in it, particularly dealing with people like Tommy Hepburn,

are very very well done - never been done since in that way. I
don't think I can say that for any other writers. Even Page
Arnot, whose heart is in the right place, relates a set of
histories which in many ways are abstracted from the miners
themselves. Very few histories are about the miners themselves,
their working life, etc. They are for the most part bureaucratic
works in which the miner is treated as synonymous with his
union and the union itself identified with the activities of the
area officials. Others, like Machin's book, begin with good
intentions but eventually bury themselves in endless lists of
detail the very weight of which render the book unreadable.
if, as it is said, most working people learn their socialist theory
from *The Ragged-trousered Philthropists*, a novel, and not from
the dusty texts of economic theory, perhaps it is similarly true
that novels and screen plays by and about miners impart more
of the living reality of history than the mighty volumes of formal
miners' histories.

9   THE NEW ORAL HISTORY IN FRANCE

Paul Thompson*

Oral history in France has a distinguished ancestry, as one might
indeed expect from a country which has for so long maintained
an exceptionally high level of both popular and intellectual
concern for history. And in the last three years a number of
steps have been taken which are likely to ensure French oral
history a significant future. October 1977 saw the first national
conference on oral sources at the community museum or
'écomusée' of the old metal industry town of Le Creusot near
Lyon. A year later *Ethnologie française* published a survey and
discussion by Rolande Bonnain and Fanch Elegoet (1978, VIII, 4,
pp. 337-55) on oral history work in progress, chiefly in
universities but including some other centres: altogether fifty-
six projects were listed, and well over half of these had been
launched in the previous two years. Subsequently Philippe
Joutard, one of the editors of an impressive (and beautifully
produced) new popular historical monthly, *L'histoire*, provided a

*Paul Thompson is editor of *Oral History* and an associate editor
of *History Workshop Journal*. This article first appeared in *Oral
History*, VIII, 1, April 1980, and has been slightly abbreviated.

second critical survey ('Historiens, à vos micros!', 12 (mai 1979), pp. 106-12); and one of the editorial aims of the journal is to include regular oral history contributions. The possibilities of starting new projects have since been improved by a government decision - ironically inspired partly by conservative hostility to the social sciences - to set up a special centre for research in contemporary French history, 'l'histoire de nos temps', headed by a historian of London familiar to many British urban historians, François Bédarida. Lastly, perhaps the most certain sign of all: the world-famous historical journal *Annales*, which has been one of the major inspirations of professional Anglo-American social history, and a pioneer of new ways, has published a special issue devoted to oral history, including contributions from three or four of the historians mentioned here. Thus while the pattern is still far from set, and in certain ways remains perplexing, especially to an outsider, it seems increasingly clear that in France oral history is likely to evolve in an interesting and distinctive way. It seems a good moment to look at the emerging scene.

French oral history can draw on special strengths. One is in its own antecedents. Among the major European historians of the last century, Jules Michelet stands out for his understanding of the potential of *both* documentary and oral sources. The leading professional of his day, professor at the Sorbonne and chief curator of the National Archives, he was also a great popular historian; a man who came from an artisan Parisian background and always at heart a populist. Both for his *History of the French Revolution*, and for his remarkable contemporary essay on the social impact of mechanisation, *Le Peuple*, he drew systematically on oral evidence, and his reflections on the experience are still telling. Contemporary oral history in France can thus be seen as recovering an approach which goes back to the founding fathers of the historical profession: and indeed, well beyond Michelet, to Voltaire himself (who used interviews with members of the upper class as one of his historical sources) - and still further back to the medieval chroniclers which he so despised. In between are many lesser known figures who are beginning to be rediscovered: observant travellers, local clergy and bureaucrats, early collectors of folklore and ethnography. The result is that French historians today can make use of a wealth of previously recorded oral sources. The most startling example is provided by Emmanuel Le Roy Ladurie's best-seller *Montaillou* (1975). This reconstructs in extraordinary detail, from interviews procured by an inquisition against the Cathar heresy in 1318-25, and kept in the Vatican library (because the inquisitor later became Pope Benedict XII), the intimacies of family life in a tiny hamlet in the Pyrenean foothills: the intrigues of the parish priest and the lord's wife, the common caring for children, the freedom of the bachelor shepherds, the subordination of women, the mutual pleasures of love-making and flea-picking.

For us, however, the experience of Philippe Joutard has an
equal significance. He began his research in 1967 after returning
to the south from Paris, where he had first trained as a
historian. He had known from childhood the mountain valleys of
the Cévennes which border Provence to the west, and have
remained for more than three centuries one of the very few
strongholds of French Protestantism. Although the mountain
economy is now changing rapidly and many of the small
'temples', reminiscent of Methodist chapels, are closing for lack
of pastors, there are still many pockets of Protestantism in the
valleys, clusters of small peasant families with a strong pride in
the part played by family ancestors in resisting the unsuccessful
attempt of Louis XIV to exterminate them in the war of the
Camisards, and a continuing tradition of left-wing individualism
- expressed, for example, by their part in providing refuges
for French Jews during the Second World War. Joutard was
aware of some of the local potential of oral evidence from his own
family; and although not starting with this intention, his work
gradually became a systematic historiographical comparison of
oral and documentary sources, leading to his important recent
book, *La Légende des Camisards* (1977). In this process a vital
moment was the discovery of a set of manuscript interviews,
recorded from the 1730s for his *Histoire des troubles des
Cévennes ou de la guerre des Camisars* (1760) by Antoine Court,
and including oral traditions which Joutard also was able to
collect in his own fieldwork, preserved in an archive in the old
Calvinist capital of Geneva.

Nor has there been a complete gap between such distant
precedents and the more conscious 'oral history' of today. One
can cite amateur historians like the Poitou country schoolmaster
Roger Thabault, whose history of a hundred years of change in
his village published in 1945 as *Mon Village, ses hommes, ses
routes, son école* drew heavily on old people's memories; or the
professional research begun in 1962 by Jacques Ozouf on French
teachers before 1914 for his book, *Nous, les maîtres d'écoles*
(1967), substantially based on the written life stories which came
to him as the unexpected outcome of a large-scale postal survey
inquiry. In the field of popular traditions there has been
vigorous activity since the founding of local amateur folklore
societies in the nineteenth century, although their collecting was
unfortunately too often marred by belief in a timeless past
peasant culture, and hence a neglect of precise dating and social
documentation. Their fieldwork has been succeeded by that of
university departments of ethnology, with the Musée des Arts et
Traditions Populaires in Paris providing a national centre with a
substantial archive as well as publishing the review,
Ethnologie Française. Paris also has the national record library
(Phonothéque Nationale) and sound archives with material,
chiefly musical or political, going back to the 1900s; and a
national association of French sound archives has recently been
formed, including some leading oral historians, based on this

national archive. Lastly, there has been the widespread
collecting of testimonies of the experience of German occupation
and resistance in 1940-4, suffering perhaps in value from a
misleading retrospective myth of heroic unity and togetherness,
but thoroughly organised with a journal (*Revue d'Histoire de la
Seconde Guerre Mondiale*), regional representatives and central
committee, which has now moved under the umbrella of the new
national centre for contemporary history.

A second great advantage for the future of French oral
history is a long-standing but in recent years much extended
enthusiasm for autobiography. A growing number of publishers
have launched series under banners such as *Témoignages*,
Vécu, or *Biographies*, and altogether perhaps as many as 400
individual titles have been issued if one includes local
publications. No doubt many of these again suffer from a
characteristic weakness, for they tend to play to the taste of the
French middle-class reading public, in the present period of
rapid social transformation, for a comforting myth of a 'merry
old France', of a good old peasant and artisanal past.
Nevertheless, there can be no doubt that some of these books
have been enormously popular and the best of them at the same
time perceptive and even provocative. The notable successes
include *La Mémoire du Village* (1977), the story of a peasant
family recorded by its journalist son Maxime Chaleil; Serge
Grafteaux's *Memé Santerre* (1975); the memories of an Alpine
village collected by a former teacher, Emilie Carles, which
under the title *La Soupe aux herbes sauvages* (1978) has topped
600,000 copies; and best-known of all, now past a million, *Le
Cheval d'Orgueil* by Pierre Jakez Hélias - first published in 1975
by Plon in the *Terre Humaine* ethnographical and biographical
series which has owed so much to the shrewd editorial hand of
Jean Malaurie (and now also available in English as *The Horse
of Pride*, Yale University Press, 1978).

Hélias is one of those rare people able to write, through his
own autobiography, the story of an entire community in a
lifetime of devastating change. Brought up among fishermen and
peasants on the far south-west coast of Brittany, himself the son
of a landless farmworker, he can draw not only on the direct
memory of early life, but also on his later wider experience as a
Breton nationalist, broadcaster, academic folklorist and collector
of life histories. The bulk of the book is a richly descriptive
account of his own childhood and youth and the society about
him, vividly conveying experiences of his first jobs minding
cows, in the bean factory (with the women), and threshing (his
initiation to manhood); the miseries of illness, and the wet and
cold of winter; the pleasures of the harvest feast; or the
conflicts between farmers and fishermen. But the peculiarly
compelling quality of the book lies I think in the way in which
Hélias draws out both the matter and the spirit of a particular
Breton experience in the present century. He does this partly
through a type of intensely detailed material description (an

interesting parallel to the earlier History Workshop writing in
Britain, or further back to the almost passionate detailing of
share-cropper's lives by James Agee). The book opens, for
example, with his parents' marriage day; but what Hélias chooses
first to discuss is the pile of twenty-four hemp shirts which his
father carried on his head that day - what they were meant for,
the labour and the material which had gone into them, and how
they were never worn, because other new kinds of shirt had
come into use. Cumulatively, he builds up a sense of the sheer
weight of material concern in a society which possessed very
little, and nothing won without incessant effort. Yet at the same
time he interweaves with this, in equally specific detail, the
Breton way of thinking, the myths and ideals seized on to make
sense of the struggle to survive: 'la Chienne du Monde', the
haunting misfortune which could excuse those driven so far into
despair by poverty that they chose to take away their own lives;
and 'le cheval d'orgueil', the proud self-reliance of a man with
no means other than his head and hands, which makes Alain le
Goff, grandfather of Hélias, the true hero of his book. Later
come the times of the tourists, the flight from the land, and
mass consumption; while Hélias himself rises as a scholarship
boy; and the last part of his book is a reflection on how far,
amid this material ending of the old peasant Brittany and the
commercialisation of its culture for visitors, some special Breton
spirit might yet survive. It is this which makes *Le Cheval
d'Orgueil* so powerful: for here is an authentic, thoroughly local
voice from the provinces of France who at the same time conveys
both the intimate texture of a hidden and fascinating culture,
but can also speak for a much more universal experience, the
sense of loss of past community in the western world today.

There is, in short, clearly a groundswell on which oral
history in France could readily go forward. But a second look
suggests that the situation is not quite as simple as that. For
none of the recent books which have so far been mentioned
concern the urban and industrial experience which is basic to
twentieth-century French history; and they deal with the
peripheries of the country, the mountains, Brittany and the
south, rather than with its central heartland. Nor - with some
exceptions - have most of their authors been professional
historians. Although this latter point is less surprising, it
connects with the former. For the truth is that French
professional history, for all the undoubted distinction of its
advances in social history in recent decades, remains in a
peculiar sense socially isolated. That isolation does not produce
an atmosphere favourable to the development of oral history;
and it is probably most marked in Paris, where academic power
in France is above all concentrated.

There are both intellectual and organisational reasons for
this. There is, first of all, the lack of a sufficiently strong
intellectual bridge, in terms either of method or subject, between
past and present. As Alain Cottereau has pointed out in a recent

paper presented to History Workshop 13, while French social historians have enlarged the themes of history to take in 'everyday life and mentalities', they have not developed the fieldwork method which through contact with living experience would help to test out their theories. They have been prepared to borrow themes and theories and quantification from the social sciences, but have not seen either the interview or participant observation as relevant. There is thus 'frequently an absence of any systematic movement between theory and verification'. This is partly explained by a tendency at least until recently to concentrate reseach on earlier periods, from the Middle Ages up to the era of the French Revolution. But even now, despite a lively development in recent years of historical debate about working-class organisations from the nineteenth century onwards, the full history of the French working class remains to be written. As Cottereau puts it:

no systematic study of working class life, of its experiences and the social relations within the workplace, is available. After the works of Levasseur, published in the nineteenth century, we have only a few isolated studies (the best known are Louis Chevalier, *Classes laborieuses et classes dangereuses* (1958; English translation Routledge, 1973) and G. Duveau, *La vie ouvrière en France sous le Second Empire* (1946)). These works have been criticised in terms of their ideology. But, in my opinion, their principal lacuna is rather the following: they do nothing but resume the investigations and the philanthropic vision of condition of the working class in the nineteenth century. Thus they simply present us with the bourgeois perception of working-class life and in no way actually talk about the latter.

This is not so much through any lack of historians writing from an alternative socialist perspective, as from the absence of any strong contact with either the workers' movement or working-class life today. There is no equivalent not only to an admittedly exceptional individual historian like Edward Thompson, but also to group activities like History Workshop or Centreprise, or the regional British activities in labour history. French labour history started relatively late, and although its principal journal, *Le Mouvement social*, has succeeded in winning academic recognition, it has done so at the price of dropping its initial links with the working class movements. Paradoxically, this seems in part to be because any attempt to address itself to questions which are politically relevant and therefore divisive today would threaten the co-operation of the different currents of the left represented among the editors. Conversely, both trade unions and left-wing political parties have been reluctant to see the opening up of potentially explosive historical debates on recent history. Thus though trade-union backed adult education comparable to Ruskin College exists, its historical content is safely stilted; while the political parties still wield a powerful influence in discouraging any internal challenge to the comfortable myths of the recent past which help to justify their current standpoints. In other words, because of the professional isolation of history from everyday life, the very political commitment of historians has made for a less politicised practice of history.

To all this must be added the impact of centralisation of power in academic life so characteristic of French education in general. The high road to academic prestige, to power and money, lies through Paris. Here, gathered around the politicians, are the chief administrators of the disciplines who command the purse-strings of research, the most prestigious teaching chairs in the country, and the largest clusters of full-time research workers. There is thus by British standards an extraordinary concentration of French intellectual talent and authority in the single capital city - just where distance and difficulty of contact between the social classes is likely to be most severe. This is still more true of the social sciences than of history, for the Parish research centres must house the majority of better-known sociologists in the whole of France. And this very concentration not only aggravates the inevitable isolation of research activity from the wider world, but seems even to intensify individualistic rivalry between researchers. Perhaps the concentrated power of patronage here is the clue: as if the old monarchy, though decapitated, stalked on behind the spirit of the modern republic, academics now jostling for their place in the sun with courtesy and wit, watching each other, acutely conscious of prestige and status, prepared to struggle for the possession not only of ideas but of words themselves. For in France, the right to give a word a certain meaning is one form of academic power; and between Paris sociologists, a dispute over such rights may sometimes be fought out in a public debate at one of the research centres. The sheer resources behind such hot-house glass boxes of scholarship means that in any new major development of history, Paris takes a leading role: and as we shall see, this has been again true of oral history. But equally, the very nature of the research context in Paris also implies that full development will also depend on how it grows in the distinctly different social atmosphere of the peripheral provinces.

In surveying the projects now in progress, let us begin then with Paris. At the primary centre, the Ecole des Hautes Etudes en Sciences Sociales (or EHESS, as hereafter) the first steps were taken by sociologists. Cottereau's research on Parisian working-class culture - especially clothing and metal workers - in the last hundred years, begun in 1967, combines documentary and oral sources and also participant observation. Daniel Bertaux's study of Parisian artisan bakeries was started in 1970, partly because of an increasing dissatisfaction with statistical research, since strongly voiced in his book on social mobility, *Destins personnels et structure de classe*. He has become the leader of a growing number of French sociologists turning from the quantitative survey to the life history approach, and is currently editing a collection of sociological essays on the method under the title, *Biography and Society*. His object in the bakery research was to turn from the abstractions of figures to an investigation of the making a basic daily product, bread: and hence to the problem of the survival in France of the small family bakery. The initial suspicion of these husband-and-wife business couples was in fact only broken when the research developed into a joint project with Isabelle Bertaux-Wiame; and her thesis on bakery apprenticeship in the 1920s and 1930s under the historian Michelle Perrot, subtitled 'une enquête d'histoire orale' (1976), was thus probably the first French oral history project as such to be completed. Subsequently she has gone on to study migration into Paris between the wars, taking a particular interest in what can be learnt from the different ways in which women and men tell their life stories (see her article in *Oral History*, 7, 1). Here – and perhaps less directly in some of the oral history work in the south of France – one can see the influence of Foucault and the debates on language in current French Marxism.

Nevertheless, it is not until we have turned our backs on the capital that we can gain a true sense of the potential within French oral history. We can return first briefly to Brittany, the land of *Le Cheval d'Orgueil*, for Hélias is not alone here as a scholar with roots. There is also the university sociologist Fanch Elegoet who teaches at Rennes and Brest, but has only moved a few doors from the family farm in the hamlet near the north coast where he was born, and still lends a hand in its local youth club. He too is equally concerned with salvaging Breton culture from the collapse of peasant agriculture in the present generation. He has been working with his students collecting life histories from Bretons of all kinds – men and women, peasants and fishers, priests and artisans – and has begun publishing the material collected in local booklets. The first was the autobiography of a Léon peasant published in Breton in 1975, and subsequently in French as *Nous ne savions que le breton et il fallait parler français*. As the title suggests, one of Elegoet's main points is to show the way in which state pressure and economic modernisation have forced Bretons even to abandoning their mother language. And in 1979 he was able to launch a new review, *Tud Ha Bro, sociétés bretonnes* (B.P. 25, 29232 Plougerneau), publishing life stories in a cheap form, mostly sold in local bookshops and cultural associations. The first number focusses on the sea, and opens with a remarkable account by a woman seaweed-gatherer who, like many others on this densely-populated coast, would spend much of her year on a desolate islet far out to sea towards Ushant, sleeping on hammocks in huts, her only contact with home a fortnightly sailboat bringing linen and pancakes. The second number is on the rural world and the third will be on women in the village. The venture has no university backing, and depends entirely on local support. And a similar success has also been achieved in

the small industrial town of Fougères on the Breton-Norman
border, where a group of schoolteachers led by Jacques Soteras
have been publishing for the last three years a small illustrated
bimonthly on the traditions, history and economy of the local
environment, *Le pays de fougères* (86 avenue de la Verrerie,
35300 Fougères). This combines articles and oral tradition with
life histories of, for example, a quilter or a granite worker.

One finds again more encouraging signs of a community-based
approach to oral history work in the south. Here there are two
clusters of projects. The first is around Lyon. At the
university's centre for economic and social history here, a strong
group led by Yves Lequin have been collecting oral history
material on the working class of the city and its region, and
particularly on the metal workers of Givors (Carmen Gan and
Jean Metral). They have also maintained close links with the
nearby Le Creusot museum, which from the Château de la
Verrerie, the great former mansion of the Schneider family, the
town's ironmasters, runs a very active community programme of
meetings and exhibitions, collecting documents of all kinds
including life histories, combining this with an international
Centre for Research into Industrial Civilization. Also within the
Lyon region is the industrial town of St Etienne, where an
especially interesting project resulted recently from the
takeover of a local metal turbine factory by an international
Belgian company, which decided on a reorganisation leading to
the redundancy of half the workforce. A local doctor, worried
by the signs of shock and illness which this sudden economic
catastrophe brought to the men and women he saw in his own
practice, succeeded in drawing in Chombart de Lauwe, one of
France's most creative urban anthropologists who is well-known
for his earlier writing on housing and the family. Rather than
study the problem as an external 'expert', he organised the
redundant workers and their families in a series of group
discussions on their situation. The results have been published
in two books, *Nous travailleurs licensiés* and *Le Mur de Silence*
(UGE 10/18 paperbacks). The first is about their lives, work
and families, and the second about work relations in the factory
as they saw them. Although not strictly oral history, it is clearly
close to it, and points towards interesting possibilities: a project
which is less the collection of life histories, than the
encouragement of collective reflection on a community way of
life in the moment of its loss.

Lastly, there is France's far south, from the Pyrenees to the
Alps. (Corsica we shall omit.) Here perhaps has emerged the
most distinctive type of project in the whole country, the
collaboration between historians, ethnographers and linguists in
oral history work on local communities, focussing on what are
called 'ethno-textes'. This co-operation originated from the
recognition of linguists and specialists in dialect, who were
mapping out the country in the *Atlas linguistiques* of France,
that they needed to place their research in a social and historical

context: and the use of the term 'ethno-texte' has been adopted
by these collaborative projects to indicate that they are
prepared to use written documents of all kinds - including
letters, books, broadsheets and so on - as well as direct oral
evidence. The overall aim is to recapture how a community
speaks about its own past and present; and one principal means
is through recording a substantial number of life stories within
a few relatively small chosen localities.

There are at present three main centres. In the south-west,
in Toulouse and Carcassonne respectively, are Xavier-Ravier,
and Daniel Fabre, who (with Jacques Lacroix) has written two
notable books on southern culture and traditions: one on oral
tradition in story-telling (*La tradition orale du conte occitan*)
and the other - drawing on both documents and oral evidence -
on the daily life and family and community customs of the
peasantry in the last century (*La vie quotidienne des paysans
du Languedoc au XIXe siecle*, 1973). Then in the Alpine region,
at Grenoble, there is an active programme at the Musée
Dauphinois under Charles Joisten, collecting and publishing in a
regular review material on the folklore, social life and economy
of the region, such as its glove-makers and its pedlars.
Alongside him at the university are the linguist Gaston Tuaillon
and the historian Henri Broue, working on the oral traditions
of rural communities and life histories of trade unions
respectively. In the high alps too there has been the rather
special independent development of memoir-writing by
former great mountain guides, like Luc Tournier's *Il était une
fois la montagne*. And finally, there is the work in Provence
and Marseilles. Here again there are regional museums with
oral history programmes, like the Ecomusée du Camargue at
Mas Roustry near Arles. But the chief thrust comes from the
group at the university at Aix-en-Provence, led by the linguist
Jean-Claude Bouvier, and Philippe Joutard, whose historical
work on the Cévennes we have already noticed.

This varied work is held together by two assumptions. One is
that oral sources should be seen essentially as a means of
understanding a society and its culture *from within*. The second
is that it is possible to combine rigorous academic standards with
strong commitment to the region to which the groups belong and
a sharing of the results of their research with the communities
among whom the work is carried out. Already, for example,
Anne Roche and her students have held a joint day meeting
with Marseilles workers combining papers and direct testimonies.
In the Cévennes Philippe Joutard and his wife Geneviève (who is
a Marseilles teacher) organised a local village exhibition on the
traditions of Protestantism and the Camisards, for which families
loaned old documents, photographs, even a sixteenth-century
book by Calvin - and which in turn stimulated further valuable
memories. The group is also producing local pamphlets, like one
on songs from the Ardèche, along with a companion cassette
recording. And it is a policy of the group that as its work goes

forward, results should always be published in a double form, one academic and the other for the local community. It is an ambitious aim; and if fulfilled, will set a social and intellectual standard in French oral history which surely any of us would be glad to emulate.

Peasant studies

10 VILLAGE ECONOMIES

Peter Worsley*

One might think that the study of the peasantry would not be of
much importance, and therefore interest, to people in Britain,
where only 2.8 per cent of the workforce are engaged in
agriculture. Moreover, as a proportion of the world's population,
peasants are declining. In fact, we are at a watershed in history:
within the lifetime of most people, if not mine, there will be more
people living in towns and cities than in the countryside for the
first time in human history.

Nevertheless, in absolute terms, the peasantry is actually
growing and in individual countries, some as massive as India or
China (with its 800 million people), the peasantry constitute 85
per cent of the population or even more.

An understanding of the nature of the peasantry, therefore,
remains extremely important, and needs to be clarified, for
concepts used in respect of the peasantry are multiple, and
contradictory. It is thus common in English to talk simply about
'the' peasantry, or in Spanish of the *campesinos*, to refer to
people who work and live in the countryside, including many
who do not necessarily work in agriculture. Within agriculture
itself, however, I would want to distinguish, at least as ideal
type, between the smallholder-producers and the rural
proletarians, the landless workers who work for wages for
someone else.

If we take one classic definition of the peasantry, as, e.g.
given by Teodor Shanin,[1] there are four basic characteristics.
The first is that the peasant economy is based on a particular
kind of unit of social organisation: the household (the 'domestic'
mode of production, it has been called by Marshall Sahlins[2] for
primitive society). The household, in this model, is an economic
unit oriented only in part to exchange in the market, because it
also produces its own subsistence. Second - and this may seem
obvious - they are engaged primarily in agriculture. But the
point is not that obvious, since the concept 'urban peasantry'
has been applied not only to rural craftsmen - or to the rural
peasants who engage in handicrafts and other ancillary activities
during the winter season (and may move even to the towns) -

---

*Peter Worsley is professor of sociology at Manchester University
A former editor of *The New Reasoner* and *New Left Review*.
Author of *The Trumpet Shall Sound* (1954), a study of cargo
cults in Melanesia.

but also to those people who live and work as part of the urban poor in Third World cities, and who use family-labour rather than wage-labour in ways that involve gross *self*-exploitation.

The classic capitalist model of a contractual relationship, mediated by the cash-nexus and entailing the performance of a specified number of hours of work in return for a certain wage, does not apply to such households. One does not pay one's wife for her labour, nor are there any statutory hours when the crop needs harvesting.

Third, as anthropologists always emphasise, the peasant family is not simply a production unit. It is also a unit of consumption, ownership, residence and descent. It is multiplex both in terms of its functions, and in terms of its composition, which is commonly wider than the nuclear family, at least in certain stages of the domestic cycle. It is also 'eternal' or 'timeless': it reproduces itself as a unit from generation to generation in a cyclic way. The land, therefore, is the basic focus of survival, and is quasi-sacred, held by a corporation, whose contemporary members are merely a link in a chain that extends from the ancestors to the future, the head of the corporation being more of a 'manager' operating a transgenerational trust, rather than an absolute owner. All are bound by customary norms, and their job is to hand on the land in good heart to future generations. Land is not a commodity to be bought and sold. Fourth, these households are part of a wider community composed of similar units, whether concentrated villages or dispersed hamlets. These are linked to one another through 'multiplex' networks of marriage, economic interdependence, ritual connections and so forth, all of which are shaped by the norms of a common culture which even has a place for customary inequalities in its moral economy. And finally, at the highest level, all these peasant households and villages taken as a whole constitute a segment of a wider society. Peasant society, Redfield said,[3] was a *part*-society; and most peasantries today, Wolf argues,[4] are only 'secondary' peasantries. But even where they constitute the majority – the 'primary' peasant societies – peasants are not the people who take the important economic or political decisions at the societal level. It is the non-peasant part which dominates the peasant part, including the landlords, with their big estates (or, now, agri-businesses), the merchants and moneylenders, the urban bourgeoisie, and the state, which is usually under the control of some combination of these classes in capitalist society (though not in state socialist societies). The agencies of the state: the police, tax-collectors, the army recruiters, etc., are there to keep the peasant majority docile and at the service of the privileged minority.

Precisely because the peasant sector as a whole is incorporated within the wider society and dominated by it, there are those who argue that you really cannot generalise about peasants at all. They do not exist conceptually. Shanin has referred to some of the general consequences of the 'partness' of peasant society: that they rarely think or act in class terms, but exhibit, rather, high 'massness'; when they do act violently to defend their interests, they tend to generate jacqueries rather than revolutions, and so on. Wolf argues that they only become a revolutionary class when organised from outside. Despite this emphasis in Shanin, Wolf or Redfield upon the external relations of the peasantry, writers in the Chayanovist tradition generally tend to focus not upon these 'external' relationships at all, but upon the internal dynamics of the peasant household and village community, and in particular upon its 'purely' economic activities (production and consumption, selling and buying) as if peasants chose freely for themselves without reference to the power, economic and political, of outsiders to regulate what peasants do.

The four characteristics mentioned can be grouped into two sets: the 'inward' and the 'outward' dimensions of the peasantry. It is the first of these that is usually emphasised by Chayanovists: the way agriculture is done; the role of the household in production; the organisation of the household; the constraints set upon it by changing kinship and age composition. These constitute what he calls the production 'machine'. (Marxists generally tend to talk of the 'labour process' when analysing how agriculture gets done, what kinds of people co-operate in what ways in producing crops, etc.) The second dimension, the relationship of the peasantry to the wider society, entails something quite different: looking at the sectoral relationships of the peasantry as a collectivity, of part to whole.

Now, Chayanov[5] emphasised that the peasant economy operated on quite different principles from capitalist farming: that it was characterised by a non-capitalist logic. Hence all kinds of weird things happened that wouldn't occur in purely capitalist ('rational') production or in the market-oriented enterprise. Higher prices led to lower production, for example, or poor people often invested more heavily than rich in high-priced land, and so on. He explained most of this in terms of the demands of the household economy and in terms of fixed wants. In his discussion of the domestic mode of production, Sahlins developed this theme: production was not necessarily limited by technical considerations, or even by non-availability of land. Surpluses were quite common in 'Stone Age' economies (and even 'affluence' in hunting-and-collecting societies). But surpluses could not be readily translated into other kinds of 'goods', particularly when the surpluses were perishable vegetables. They could, however, be translated into 'immaterial' goods, such as social or religious status. Commoners would give their political support to chiefs who were able to distribute income from tribute to them when they were in need. Excess production could also be redistributed 'horizontally', in the form of mutual aid or reciprocity, so that when one's own turn came for calamity to strike, moral (and practical) credit could be cashed in. Expansion and contraction of production could occur, as when, for instance, yams were exchanged for pots, but they changed hands at customary prices. With fixed prices and inelastic output, more goods could only be acquired by trading with more trading-partners, but always at the traditional exchange-rates. Hence, price did not respond to demand and supply.

For these reasons, the 'substantivist' anthropologists tended to side with Chayanov, though his model, based overwhelmingly on the Russian peasantry, was not overly convincing because, in large parts of Russia, land was readily available and therefore did not constitute a major constraint on production, as it does in other parts of the world. But even for Russia, he noted that the bulk of certain cash-crops (notably flax, the key export) were produced by peasants, which seems to suggest that they were much more involved in the market, on capitalist terms, than his model allows for. But 'substantivist' anthropologists have tended to follow Chayanov in arguing that the peasant economy is not organised on capitalist principles, and that 'the economy', in any case, cannot be abstracted from its total social and cultural integument. These ideas naturally aroused the fury of those Marxists and socialist critics who argued from much more economistic assumptions. Lenin, in particular, in his famous analysis,[6] insisted that the peasantry were indeed being penetrated by capitalist relationships, and rapidly; and that the crucial scarce factor was the principal means of production, land; whereas Chayanov had stressed labour as the crucial determinant of the peasant economy, which was in its turn conditioned by the family cycle. Such analytical differences were, of course, crucial for understanding the direction of Russian society as a whole, and in consequence for political programmes. In Chayanov's model, class struggle was not inevitable. As children grew up in the peasant household, they provided more labour, so the household moved from rags to - well, at least blouses - until the children left home, when the labour-force, and therefore output, sank once more: back to rags again. Others emphasised fixed levels of peasant wants, determined by cultural value-systems, a form of argument that scarcely accorded with the abundant empirical evidence that peasant production often exhibits amazing bursts of innovation and output. But where demographic explosion occurred, virtual revolutions in output might still result in 'involution': the static living-standards of Geertz's Javanese peasantry.[7]

Lenin, however, was looking for class differentiation, and, of course, it was there: kulaks were emerging, polarisation was taking place, and the concentration of land in the hands of ever fewer, with landlessness at the opposite pole. For the landless, the alternatives were to become proletarians in the countryside, or to migrate to the cities or abroad and become urban proletarians there. Or they might die, in famines. Today, from Melanesia to Peru, land is scarce and has been for a long time, both because of changes in death-control and because of the concentration of property. There is scarcely a peasant, even in the Amazon and New Guinea, who is unaffected by the world capitalist market for his production, the goods he consumes, or the demand for his labour.

But there is still an element of considerable utility in the Chayanov model, for the capacity of peasants to produce their own means of subsistence means that they are not totally dependent upon the capitalist market for their survival. At the same time, 'survival', defined in terms of calorific minima, becomes ever less acceptable to them as a goal in life, exposed as they are, like all of us, to the massive machinery of want-manufacture. But to the extent that there does remain the possibility of survival, for all the attacks on 'dualism', those peasants who have not gone over to 100 per cent cash-crop production, who have one foot in the capitalist market but the other firmly planted in the soil of subsistence, are not entirely at the mercy of that market.

One of the less valuable consequences of the Chayanovist approach is its relative neglect of the world outside the village: the societal and sectoral levels of institutionalised power. Macfarlane's stimulating onslaught on the notion of an English 'peasantry' before capitalism,[8] for instance, is based upon a conception of the peasantry in terms of the internal 'machine', particularly of hereditary tenure and sale as alternative means of transferring farms, and domestic or hired labour as alternative ways of working them. Land, he shows us, was widely bought and sold; labour commonly hired. And people neglected their duties to support their relatives in their drive to maximise their own economic opportunities. This attack helps demolish the notion of an English peasantry only if that peasantry is conceived of à la Chayanov. What Marx, Weber, Vinogradoff, Kosminsky and all the other 'discredited' authorities were writing about, however, was not the English *peasantry* so much as English *feudalism*, i.e., a societal system of political economy, in which land, whether inherited or purchased, carried with it obligations, usually termed 'extra-economic', to pay *rent* to a lord, whether in the form of produce, services or money. To use a model which focuses upon the family/household smallholding as its major conceptual building-block leads, I would suggest, to the underplaying of those rights and duties attaching to land which are determined neither by the market nor by the logic of production, but by the overall political structure of the feudal social order - similarly, users of this kind of model studying contemporary society have kept too close to the minutiae of 'on-farm' organisation, whilst the grand encompassing structures and changes of land reform, migration, harassment by landlord thugs, the role of peasant production in the national economy, or the 'rationalisation' of agri-business are inadequately attended to.

NOTES

1 Teodor Shanin, *Peasants and Peasant Societies*,
   Harmondsworth 1971.
2 Marshall Sahlins, 'The Domestic Mode of Production', in
   Stone Age Economics, Chicago 1972, pp. 41–148.
3 Robert Redfield, *The Little Community* and *Peasant Society
   and Culture*, Chicago 1965.
4 Eric Wolf, *Peasants*, Englewood Cliffs, New Jersey, 1966.
5 A.V. Chayanov, *The Theory of Peasant Economy*, eds
   Daniel Thorner, Basile Kerblay, and R.E. Smith, Homewood,
   Illinois, 1966.
6 V.I. Lenin, 'Theory of the Agrarian Question', in *Selected
   Works*, vol. 12, London 1939.
7 Clifford Geertz, *Agricultural Involution: The processes of
   ecological change in Indonesia*, Berkeley 1963.
8 Alan Macfarlane, *The Origins of English Individualism: The
   Family, property and social transition*, Oxford 1978.

11 THE SCOTTISH PEASANTRY

Ian Carter*

I teach sociology at the University of Aberdeen. For the last ten
or twelve years I've done odd bits of research on class relations
in the north of Scotland. I started that work because not many
other people seemed to be doing decent social historical or
sociological work on this area. To a large extent that is still
true.

   I became increasingly interested in the question of whether
one could use 'peasant studies' in examining rural class relations
in northern Scotland. Little assistance was to be gained in
answering this, or related questions, from the published social
science literature. In this context I must note that the article
on the changing image of the Socttish peasantry is largely background material; it was simply an attempt to describe the way in
which peasants have been viewed in Scottish literature and

*Ian Carter teaches sociology at the university of Aberdeen and
works in peasant studies. Author of *Farm Life in Northeast
Scotland 1840-1914*, Edinburgh 1979. An associate editor of
History Workshop Journal.

Scottish history over the last couple of centuries. This article
does not refer specifically to the previous one. Instead, it draws
out some of the more interesting, and rather more abstract,
consequences of looking at nineteenth-century northeast Scotland
through the spectacles of 'peasant studies'.

There was very little help in understanding rural class
relations to be gained by looking at the literature because
published work by socialist academics, and by their bourgeois
counterparts, assumed that there was no problem about a
peasantry in northern Scotland because there was no peasantry
– outside the highlands, which were seen to be a rather special
case. This is true even of a fine book like Hobsbawm's *Industry
and Empire*, which merits our close attention. This is a welcome
book for someone north of the Border, because Hobsbawm does
recognise special features in Scotland, Wales and Ireland. They
may merit only one chapter out of twenty as 'The Other Britain',
but these cases are there in a vestigial form.[1] Hobsbawm
recognises that things in the periphery were different from how
they were in the heartland of southern England; thus he argues
that while in England the peasantry effectively was dead by
1780, penetrated by the inexorable development of capitalist
agriculture, a peasantry or peasantries continued to exist in
Ireland, in the Scottish highlands and in Wales – for particular
historical reasons.

If one asks where Hobsbawm's account of the decline of the
English peasantry comes from, then it soon becomes clear that
it comes from *Capital*: from Marx's analysis of primitive
accumulation which, you will recall, is based on English
evidence. In a famous passage Marx talks of 'the expropriation
of the agricultural producer, of the peasant, from the soil' as
'the basis of the whole process' of primitive accumulation. The
mode of expropriation will vary from case to case but, Marx tells
us, 'only in England, which we therefore take as our example,
has it the classic form'.[2] It is now becoming clear that Marx's
classic form refers not to England as a whole but to the corn
belt of the midlands and the southeast; if one goes to parts of
England outside this very restricted region (with the British
Museum Reading Room at its centre), then Marx's account of
the separation of the English peasant from his land is not at all
as accurate as he would have us believe.

Hobsbawm takes from Marx, then, the belief that in England
you had the complete penetration of the peasantry, the
dissolution of a graded agrarian structure into a rural
proletariat and a class of big capitalist farmers. Scottish
historians, both bourgeois and socialist, extended Marx's
analysis of England to lowland Scotland. For non-socialists like
Christopher Smout and Bruce Lenman the agricultural revolution
swept through lowland Scotland, destroying the peasantry and
creating a yawning gulf between rural proletarians and capitalist
farmers.[3] One sees much the same thing in socialist agrarian
history, to the extent that one has such a thing for Scotland.

Perhaps the best example is Tom Johnston's *History of the Working Classes in Scotland*.[4] In discussing the countryside Johnston describes in minute detail the legal changes facilitating the expropriation of the highland and lowland peasantry up to 1830: *Capital I* is the clear model for this analysis. For the period after 1830 we get the statutory chapter on the Highland Clearances and seven pages on hired farm workers' attempts to build a union. Nothing more; and, in particular, no analysis of rural class relations in the lowlands. The cash nexus is assumed to mediate the relationship between a proletarianised farm labour-force and capitalist farmers.

Yet if one takes the trouble to examine class relations in the nineteenth-century rural lowlands, then one quickly finds that things were not that simple. From the 1885 Scottish agricultural census figures one can calculate that only some one farmer in six in the northeast was a capitalist in that his farm was of a size that would require most of the permanent labour-squad to be hired in the feeing market. The other five-sixths were farmers working smaller holdings: either middle peasants (small farmers) who had to balance their household's labour supply against the farm's labour needs, or poor peasants (crofters) who had to sell a proportion of the household's labour power on the market in order to achieve an adequate subsistence level. Thus, in the nineteenth-century northeast we have a situation in which capitalist farmers were dominant in that they cultivated more than half the tilled land – and the best land in any district, at that – but they formed islands set in a sea of peasant farmers. The numerical dominance of peasant farmers, set against the economic dominance of capitalist farmers, gave a particular colour to social relations of agricultural production. It is a colour that cannot be analysed through the assumption of Johnston and Smout that capitalism completely penetrated the northeast countryside in the early nineteenth century, destroying the peasantry in the process. The peasantry was not destroyed: still very powerful numerically, it tried to transform numbers into political power at one point, as we shall see.

To understand the survival of the northeast Scottish peasantry we must turn away from work like that of Johnston and Smout, rooted in Marx's analysis of primitive accumulation in southern England, and turn towards the post-Marxist work on peasants that, for a British audience, is most closely associated with the *Journal of Peasant Studies*. We have to examine the articulation of capitalist and pre-capitalist modes of production in the countryside. To put it crudely, we have to ask why a capitalist agricultural sector, where capitalism had been the dominant mode of production since the end of the eighteenth century, allowed peasant farmers to continue to exist. What was the point? What benefits did the peasant sector provide for capitalist farmers or other powerful classes?

Asking these kinds of questions not only allows us to get a new grasp on the history of class formation in the countryside,

but also allows us to make sense of things which usually are
seen to be completely separate; the province of completely
different specialists. It allows us to tie cultural elements back to
social relations of agricultural production. In the case of
northeast Scotland that means that we can make sense of a
unique body of folksong called the bothy ballads.[5] These songs
were generated in one generation - between 1830 and 1860. They
were found only in one segment of northeast Scotland;
Aberdeenshire, Banffshire and north Kincardine. Folksong
scholars have asked a range of questions about these songs - is
the music Irish, are the words based on English models, and so
on. Through peasant studies we can ask other questions: why
do these realistic songs of farm life, giving a precise description
of conditions on a particular farm at a particular date, appear
only in one area and in one generation? By asking questions
about the articulation of modes of production we can study the
class conditions that generated this novel cultural form,
together with other cultural phenomena that appear at the same
time like the witchcraft-based primitive trade union called the
Society of the Horseman's Word which seems to have been
centred in northeast Scotland.[6]

The bothy ballads and the Society of the Horseman's Word
were peasant defensive tactics, levelling strategies, which were
used by a still vital and reproducible middle and poor peasantry
attempting to inhibit the full development of capitalist productive
relations in the countryside. This was an attempt to maintain a
view of appropriate social relations based not simply on the cash
nexus, but on what is called in the northeast 'kindly relations';
relations which ought to contain some quasi-family element,
which ought to rest on conceptions of morally admirable rather
than simply expedient behaviour. At the deepest level the bothy
ballads tell us that a big farmer is to be admired only if he
treats his hired workers in a morally admirable fashion. If he
tries to screw too much work out of them, or if he feeds them
badly, then hit the bastard: and hit him where it hurts by
proclaiming his vices in a song to be sung in the feeing market
where the farmer will have to recruit new servants.

One can only take bothy ballads, or the Society of the
Horseman's Word, to be peasant defensive tactics if the
peasantry was strong enough to mount an effective defence
against an economically dominant capitalist agriculture. That
requires that we examine the connections between capitalist and
peasant production. By doing that we come to see the northeast
peasantry not as a backward sector inhibiting the full
development of capitalist agriculture - the usual bourgeois
economic historical view - but as moulded by capitalist
production to a shape that maximised the profitability of the
capitalist sector. Thus we return to the question that I posed
earlier; what benefits did dominant classes in northeast Scotland
derive from having a multitude of peasant farmers in the region?

We can identify three important benefits. First, we find that most northeast districts still had a considerable reservoir of unimproved land in 1800. Much of this land could be made to bear arable crops; but it would not pay landowners or capitalist tenant farmers to bear the costs of reclamation themselves. In 1780 wage costs for reclaiming boulder-strewn moorland around Aberdeen city were running at the level of £20 sterling per acre - an enormous cost at contemporary values. These wage costs could be borne around the city because high rents could be charged for grazing the market gardening land. Away from Aberdeen potential rents were lower and the full wage costs of reclamation could not be paid. Landlords had to find another way to reclaim land. They found it in the improving lease. A peasant family was given a lease on a barren patch of moorland, usually for nineteen years. The lease conditions encouraged the family to reclaim the land as quickly as possible; generally the unbelievably hard work of spade-trenching, draining bags and clearing earth-fast boulders was completed within ten years, leaving nine years for the farm family to reap what proportion of the household's subsistence they could from the holding. At the end of the lease the laird received back arable land that two decades before had been worthless waste land. He could re-let the holding to the former tenant - often at an enhanced rent - or he could engross the new land in an existing larger farm or create a new large farm from the ruins of several peasant holdings. The most spectacular example I know of this latter procedure concerns an Aberdeenshire farm - Cultercullen, Foveran - which swallowed twenty-two peasant farms in sixty years. The peasant family had been given nineteen years lease on land on which they could grow subsistence crops: in return the landlord had been spared the full cost of producing arable land by cutting it from waste beyond the margin of cultivation.

The other two benefits of a large peasant population accrued to capitalist farmers rather than landlords. 'Muckle farmers' needed two essential inputs. The first was hired labour power - the basis of their mode of production. The second was high quality lean cattle for fattening; particularly important after 1840, when improvements in communications had allowed capitalist farmers to specialise in the very profitable cattle-feeding business for the London meat market. They got both inputs from the peasantry. Hired farm workers were drawn from peasant children whose parental holdings were in labour surplus. A loon was trained to farmwork on his father's small farm or croft, then left for farm service in his early teens. Twenty years later he would probably have given up farm service to go to the towns, the colonies or, for many men, back to peasant farming by taking over his father's lease or taking a lease on an existing holding or an improving lease. Thus, labour power circulated from the huge reservoir of the peasantry into wage work and out again. The capitalist farmer bought the labour of peasant children at the peak of skill and physical strength, but was spared the cost of reproducing that labour power. He also bought the peasants' cattle; peasant farmers could not follow capitalists into systematic cattle feeding - their land often was not good enough, and the high investment/high return strategy of the feeder meshed badly with the peasants' overriding concern to assure the household's subsistence - so they continued to raise young cattle which could be sold to get money to pay the rent. This meant that capitalist farmers had an assured supply of high-quality, lean cattle for feeding off; again the peasantry bore the cost of producing one of the capitalist farmer's essential means of production, while the capitalist took a quick - and often large - profit from the value added by intensive feeding.

It remains to explain why, by 1914, the northeast peasantry effectively was finished as a class. The short answer is that they lost their indispensability for dominant classes. As landlords found difficulty in letting large farms in 'the great depression' after 1875, so they lost interest in extending their estates' tilled acreage. The importation of lean cattle from Ireland, and sometimes from as far away as Canada, meant that the northeast Scottish capitalist farmer had alternative sources for one essential input. He still needed hired labour power, of course; though the amount that he needed was reduced steadily through the introduction of machinery on big farms. He continued to draw some labour from children in the rapidly decaying peasant sector, but after 1870 one finds cottar houses being built in large numbers on northeast capitalist farms, and the hired labour-force becomes steadily more proletarian in nature. The cultural consequence is the collapse of the cultural forms that had been grounded in the peasantry. No more bothy ballads. The Society of the Horseman's Word degenerated from primitive trade union to what Hamish Henderson calls 'the fun and games committee of the countryside'.[7]

One serious attempt was made to mount a political defence of peasant interests. Between 1881 and 1886 land agitation gripped the whole of northern Scotland. In the west highlands this agitation led to the establishment of a class-conscious peasant party - the Highland Land Law Reform Association. In the northeast it was channelled into the Scottish Farmers' Alliance; an organisation with mass peasant support but led by capitalist farmers. It is not too difficult to predict the outcome. In 1886, the high point of nineteenth-century land agitation in Britain, highland peasants got legislative protection under the Crofters' Holdings Act. Northeast peasants got nothing; the achievement of heritability and security of tenure for peasant farmers - what highland peasants achieved - would have threatened the class interest of capitalist tenants. Why, then, did northeast peasants put their faith in the SFA? The answer takes us back, for the last time, to articulated modes of production. In west-highland crofting areas peasant farmers faced large capitalist sheep farmers in mutual hatred. Crofters knew that sheep grazed where the crofters' ancestors had grown their subsistence crops. Big sheep farmers did not need to hire crofters' labour on any extensive scale and feared that their prize ewes might end up in the crofter's cauldron in hard years, or be inseminated by the crofter's weedy tup that had staggered off the common grazing with a randy gleam in its eye. The lack of articulation between crofters and capitalist farmers allowed crofters to see themselves as a class with a distinct class interest – and with particular class enemies. This allowed them to build a peasant political party that could trade with an enfeebled Liberal administration for the 1886 Act. Northeast peasants did not have that opportunity. Intricately interlinked with capitalist farmers through labour and commodity markets, they failed to recognise that they had a distinct class interest. Instead of a peasant party they built the SFA – a Liberal pressure group that asserted that all tenant farmers shared a single interest. That allowed capitalist tenants to pursue, and achieve, their sectional objectives – compensation for tenants' improvements, the right to shoot ground game – and then ditch the peasantry when policies were proposed that would threaten capitalist interests. It's an old story, and one that is not limited to the social history of northeast Scottish agriculture; the bourgeoisie finds it much easier to develop class consciousness than does the working class or quasi-working classes like the peasantry.

NOTES

1   E. Hobsbawm, *Industry and Empire*, Penguin 1969, p. 96.
2   K. Marx, *Capital Vol. I*, ed. by E. Mandel, Penguin 1976, p. 876.
3   T.C. Smout, *A History of the Scottish People, 1560–1830*, London 1969, p. 347; B. Lenman, *An Economic History of Modern Scotland, 1660–1976*, London 1977, pp. 195–6.
4   T. Johnston, *The History of the Working Classes in Scotland*, Glasgow 1920.
5   R. Munro, 'The bothy ballads: the social context and meaning of the farm servants' songs of north-eastern Scotland', *History Workshop Journal*, 3, 1977, pp. 184–94.
6   G.E. Evans, *The Horse in the Furrow*, London 1960.
7   H. Henderson, 'A slight case of devil worship', *New Statesman*, 14 June 1952; 'The oral tradition', *Scottish International*, November 1973.

FURTHER READING

Alexander, W., *Johnny Gibb of Gushetneuk*, Turriff 1979.
Allan, J.R., *North-East Lowlands of Scotland*, London 1974.
Carter, I., *Farm Life in Northeast Scotland, 1840–1914*, Edinburgh 1979.

Toulmin, D., *Hard Shining Corn*, Aberdeen 1972.
Whyte, B., *The Yellow on the Broom: The Early Years of a Traveller Woman*, Edinburgh 1979.

12 A MUSEUM OF PEASANT LIFE IN EMILIA

Alessandro Triulzi*

It all started in 1964 when Ivano Trigari, a former peasant then employed in the agricultural co-operative of Castelmaggiore (near Bologna, in central Italy), found outside a friend's house, half-covered by earth, an old farming tool locally known as a *stadura*. The *stadura* is a round iron bar, fifty or sixty centimetres long, which was used in old Bolognese ox-carts both as a brake and as an ornament. The top of the bar was usually embellished with a cross or other decorations, and it had one or more iron rings which gave each cart when moving its own characteristic sound.

The first *stadura*, all polished and brought back to life after lying idle for many years, was taken by Ivano Trigari to the Castelmaggiore co-operative where he worked, and there put on show. Nobody knew then that this long disused iron bar was to be the first item in a self-made peasant museum, the beginning of a new and far-reaching cultural experience in the area. A second *stadura* was soon produced (from an old granary), partly because the first was found to be wanting in aesthetic merit, and it was placed side by side with the first. In Trigari's own words:

> The fever for *stadure* among the peasants of Castelmaggiore dates from that day. News of other discoveries and offers of tools came from every corner: school children passing in front of the cooperative brought me specimens of *stadure*, rolled in paper, which their fathers had given them for the display. In a few days I had amassed some twenty of them. The most beautiful were on show in front of the shop. The others were piled in a corner inside. Old retired peasants came from the People's House and from the nearby bar. They stood in front of the shop, looking and commenting, at times so many that the traffic in the *piazza* was blocked.

---

*Alessandro Triulzi is an anthropologist teaching at the University of Naples. This article first appeared in *History Workshop Journal* 1, May 1976.

The comments varied: some cursed the tools which reminded them how hard they had worked in the past; others were excited, reminded of their youth. They said that times were better now, and started exchanging memories of the past, of times when they had to rise at two in the morning to go ploughing; of how they had to take their ox-carts to the rice fields to collect forage and the rice-straw which was used then as litter for the animals. . . . And again of when they used to take all the hemp to their landlord's mansion or how they carried the huge grape baskets on their heads; or of the great bundles of firewood which were carried to the baker; or finally, of when, with the best cart and oxen, the *stadura* all shining, the bridegroom went to the bride's house to take her dowry.

I listened with great interest to these memories, and often I challenged them so that the peasants would tell me details I did not know. Out of it came a general fresco of an epoch which had disappeared already, or was soon to disappear.

After the *stadura* other tools started coming in: old looms, hemp tools, yokes of all sorts, hoes and ploughs, parts of carts, and so on. And out of this grew up the idea of systematically collecting old working implements among the peasants of Castelmaggiore and its vicinity. The idea was first broached and enthusiastically accepted among the peasants, who started hunting up old tools in their houses and in disused depots, and rapidly persuaded their friends to do the same. Before long several hundred old agricultural tools had been recovered, shaped up, and brought to life. This gave the movement further impetus, and it gradually spread to nearby villages and peasant communities.

A *festa della stadura*, or 'stadura day', was organised, which has become an annual event, and this provided an occasion to spread the idea among peasants from the surrounding area who came for the celebration. Old traditions were thus revived together with the memories of old customs and usages, and the enthusiasm for reconstructing their history by means of their own museum grew as a natural result. In 1968, after the peasants had formalised their project by setting up an association called the *Gruppo della stadura* (*stadura* group), a selection from the collection was organised into a travelling exhibition. An ancient cart drawn by an old tractor carried samples of the tools from village to village and put them on show during carnival and fair times, or the celebrations of local saints' days. There was no need for explanatory panels or illustrations: these were the same tools old peasants had used throughout their lives. A man with a megaphone would explain the purpose of the initiative and the aims of the group. Peasants would listen, and often contributed on the spot tools, money, advice, and suggestions where further material could be found.

The very success of the project and the flood of tools created the first administrative problem, that of storage. To begin with the incoming objects were stored in peasants' houses and in scattered depots round the district. But the need was soon felt for an adequate public space for the hundreds of implements, some of them of considerable size, which were enriching the museum's collection. A big sign was made for the cart with the mobile display, during the Carnival of Castelmaggiore in the late 1960s, which said in big letters: Museum of Agrarian Culture Looking for a Shelter. The search was to last until 1973, when the provincial administration of Bologna gave the museum – now with some 4,000 pieces – a home, the eighteenth-century Villa Smeraldi, and its spacious surrounding park *all'inglese* (English-style), in the small nearby town of San Marino di Bentivoglio.

The granting of Villa Smeraldi marked the end of the pioneering first phase of the peasants' initiative. A series of linked exhibitions on peasant life and labour were successfully held there in 1973, and a permanent exhibition on Emilian agrarian society and labour conditions has enlivened San Marino ever since, drawing thousands of visitors, and especially schoolchildren from local (mostly peasant) communities who come with their teachers to learn history there. Thanks to the continuing efforts of the Castelmaggiore peasants gathered around the *Gruppo della stadura*, of the provincial administration of Bologna, and of a group of university students and researchers gathered around Carlo Poni, professor of Economic History at Bologna's State University, the Museum is now a living reality, a self-made proletarian archive unique in central Italy and perhaps elsewhere.

The problems the peasants had to face at the beginning were enormous. They were overcome through a collective effort that involved almost everybody in the community; it was based on an unfailing faith and pride in their own sense of history and on the will to re-appropriate for themselves a cultural experience consistently denied them by official textbook history. Today the problems the Museum is facing are still greater. The almost 4,000 objects need to be preserved, safeguarded, catalogued and codified. New collections are being formed and are going to enrich the peasants' archive at San Marino in the near future. These include labour contracts, the archives of co-operatives, of peasant leagues and associations, estate papers, pictures and other iconographic material. The Museum is to be assigned by the Region a specialised library on agrarian history, and is to act in the future as a centre for research in agrarian history and for the training of local researchers and animators of similar initiatives in the rest of the Region and outside it.

In spite of this official recognition, the very existence and running of the peasants' museum confronts its sponsors with hard-to-solve institutional and administrative problems. How can a spontaneous proletarian initiative become an institution without losing the initial enthusiasm and shared sense of purpose that mobilised hundreds of peasants and gave them a new pride in their culture and past? Will the struggle for cultural

re-appropriation which animated the peasants' initiative during
the past ten years not lose its impetus if the museum is to be
formalised as an official show-ground with visiting hours, entry
tickets, postcards, directors, and the usual anonymous
paraphernalia of all official shows? Can the perspective of an
alternative (subordinate) culture resist indefinitely the
voracious institutionalising capacity of the official (dominant)
culture?

The answer to these questions lies not just in museography.
The role of subordinate classes and their so far neglected
contribution to history, and the need to find alternative sources
as basic data for this important historical reconstruction, are
both part of the same problem; the breaking of Benedetto
Croce's distinction 'between men who are active and men who
are passive in history, between men who belong to history and
men who belong to nature (*Naturvölker*)', the distinction in
other words between little history and Great History. The man
who works in a factory, or who ploughs in the fields, has been
mainly considered by traditional historians as a 'folkloric man'
(in G. Bosio's definition), a man, that is, whose systems of
values and modes of living and working have been ignored as
representing merely 'chronicle not history, the far off
shouting of drunkards and strikers, the unseemly screams of
those who mourn their dead, not art.'

The debate in Italy around this central historiographical
problem has been very lively in the past 15 years. It was
revived by Antonio Gramsci in his critical *Observations on
Folklore*, drafted while in prison; and since the early 1960s it
has given rise to several class-history works and publications.
The *Avanti* press publications, the important researches on
peasant and proletarian culture organised through the 'Istituto
De Martino' or the 'Nuovo Canzoniere Italiano' in Milan, the
growing number of works on the resistance period, and a series
of important reviews like *Movimento Operaio*, *Classe*, or *Primo
Maggio* have animated this debate among socialist-oriented
historians and anthropologists in Italy.

The rise of a peasant-created museum is the workers' own
answer to the cultural expropriation they have been subjected to
by the dominant classes, and is a further incentive for the
long-term work of cultural re-appropriation of values and
contributions that have long been ignored or trivialised and
distorted by the state official culture. The Castelmaggiore
peasants' project has in fact not only attracted people to the
Museum but has given rise to a series of similar undertakings
that are involving groups of workers, peasants, and young
administrators in the region. Quite in harmony with the original
idea of creating a local museum born from, and geared to, the
local community, some fifteen new agrarian museums are being
created in Emilia alone, while the idea is spreading in other
provinces. Parallel to this, a series of cultural initiatives have
come out of the Museum at San Marino, from seminars on peasant

modes of production and Emilian agrarian society in the past, to school children writing their own term papers using the Museum material, and producing their own 'textbooks' on local history and society based on interviews in their communities.

At the university level, the working association of students and peasants around the Museum has pushed several university students to undertake research on peasantry and agrarian history; and special courses and seminars geared to local history have been offered at the University of Bologna. Two economic history students at this university, Pier Paolo Bastia and Marco Melega, have just finished a doctoral dissertation on 'Oral sources and written sources: History and methodology of a research on Bolognese peasants', the first thesis to have come out of the Museum's experience. In the course of their research the two students have interviewed several peasant-historians one of whom at least needs to be mentioned here. This is Giuseppe Barbieri of S. Giovanni in Persiceto, a small town in the vicinity of Bologna.

Aged 78, Giuseppe Barbieri, now a retired peasant, has a poor scholastic record (he didn't get beyond third grade) but a considerable record as local historian. His first work, a 300-page manuscript titled 'My memories in war and in peace. Some family remembrances', was written in 1936. In it the then 39-year-old peasant described at length his war experience, the peasants' working conditions in pre-First World War Emilia, the agrarian struggle of 1919-20, and peasant reactions to national events, like the rise of fascism, or to local tragedies, like the earthquake of 1929. Written in ungrammatical Italian (almost a foreign language to him since, like most peasants in the area, he speaks the local dialect both at home and at work), his exercise book manuscript lay idle in his house until 1975, when news of the peasant museum spread in the region and publicity was given to it in local newspapers.

Giuseppe Barbieri decided to take up pen again and, inspired by the new interest in local history the Museum had produced in the region, has started composing a second book on rural traditional structure and daily labour. In a letter he wrote to the provincial deputy for cultural affairs, included in the two students' theses, the peasant-historian told him that he was starting this new book 'and would like to continue it quickly, while my memory is still good, since I have passed my 77th year already and I feel proud to express our past'.

Thus, from a small village of central Italy, the literary effort of Giuseppe Barbieri joins the peasant movement for cultural re-appropriation centred around the Museum of Peasant Civilisation, and provides a working man's answer to the scholars' false dichotomy between the little history of daily life and labour and the Great History of official textbooks.

The state

13 THE STATE AND SOCIAL DOMINATION IN EIGHTEENTH- AND NINETEENTH-CENTURY PRUSSIA

Alf Lüdtke*

I

For most Marxist historians dealing with the genesis of the capitalist mode of production, the emergence of the modern i.e. centralised, bureaucratic state, seems to be an annoying 'second order' question. Our interest, therefore, is aroused when, in *The Lineages of the Absolute State*, Perry Anderson makes the state the focus of an encompassing and, above all, comparative study of global economic and social formations. He contrasts the West European (or 'genuine') development with an East European 'displacement' of politico-legal coercion 'upwards towards a centralized, militarized summit - the absolutist state'.[1]

So far as Western Europe is concerned, Anderson adopts the traditional Marxist view that the absolutist state was a function of - or more precisely a reaction against - the dissolution of feudal ties of exploitation. In this picture, intensified commercial exchange sustained by an urban bourgeoisie and regionally centred primitive accumulation of manufacturing capital seemed to threaten the feudal system. The absolutist state sought to maintain noble domination over the rural masses, although ambiguities of its policies worked in favour of the bourgeoisie too.

On the other hand, in the *eastern* (estate-based) socio-economic system - according to Anderson - this new form of feudal domination was not caused by a dissolution of serfdom, but stimulated by external threat (from the commercialising and militarised West). In Prussia or Russia the erection of bureaucratic and military organisation therefore was a sheer 'device' useful for preserving and strengthening the 'second serfdom' of the dependent peasants.

This seems to be a helpful analytic differentiation. But nothing follows from it - that is to say, Anderson remains with the feudal lords and kings, with bureaucratic apparatuses and military organisation, with aspects of the international system (although missing the problem of a developing international division of labour, already under the conditions of the feudal mode of production; he simply denies the possibility; but see

---

*Alf Lüdtke researches on eighteenth- and nineteenth-century German history (in particular the history of the police) at the Max Planck Institute, Göttingen.

Wallerstein[2]). In the end one gets nothing from him but a
renewal of the approach of certain Prussian court
historiographers, who like Otto Hintze, treat history primarily
as one of institutions and of dominant cliques, with an attitude
of dull but solid arrogance.

In Anderson's analysis then, two crucial perspectives are
missing.
(1) The internal socio-economic dynamic of the societies
generating this system of domination. An argument important
here is that of the French Marxist medievalist Guy Bois.[3] He
stresses the case of Normandy and argues about the
impossibility of compensating for a decreasing rate of feudal
extraction by further extension of agrarian production in
the late fourteenth century, because of a shortage of land;
therefore the extra-economic exploitative forces had to be
strengthened by the lords and princes.
(2) More important, his categories do not enable him to deal
seriously with the dominated people suffering permanently and
cyclically from exploitative seigneurs and lords and also (or
even more so) from tax collection, violent police enforcement,
military billeting and coercive recruitment. Anderson only
repeats quite abstract and outworn stereotypes when he refers
to the *Kadavergehorsam* within the Prussian army and
bureaucracy (p. 227) or the 'extreme militarization of the State'
as a structural characteristic of Prussian as well as of Russian
absolutism (p. 216). Whether or not these labels are appropriate
in terms of the 'immediate producers' and the dominated people
remains as an undiscussed assumption.

In Anderson's book we have history of the *dominant classes*
and of their *institutions*. What it lacks is a systematic approach
to grasp the *practice* of their domination – and the
complementary *'costs'* for the dominated masses.

II

It is the intention of my paper[4] to analyse forms of political
control and domination or, to use the German term which seems
more encompassing and therefore perhaps more accurate,
Herrschaft. The context for this examination has been Prussia
during the process of capitalisation – particularly the
capitalisation of agrarian production in the east-Elbian
Gutswirtschaft from the eighteenth century onwards; the
development and crisis, in the 1830s and 1840s, of regionally
centred 'proto-industry'; and the growth of factory production
which developed regionally, especially from the 1830s.

I am concerned to see how the *Herrschafts*-apparatus actually
functioned and to get a sense of the 'costs' of *Herrschaft* for the
dominated; I am not concerned with questions of organisation or
with institutions, but with the standards of perception and
behaviour, and the resulting day-to-day practice, especially on

the lower levels of the civil administration. Put simply, my
conclusion suggests that changes within the practice of
Herrschaft took place, but that these changes deviated in crucial
ways from those within other Western European societies involved
in the process of capitalisation. For the period under
observation, there was no shift to 'internal controls'. Instead,
one can observe throughout the nineteenth century, especially
between 1815-48, a revitalisation of 'external control'; that is to
say, of physically violent practices and standards of *Herrschaft*.
These methods of *Herrschaft* had evolved in the context of the
pre-capitalist Ancien Régime during most of the eighteenth
century, but were 'officially' abolished in the course of the
administrative state reforms, or 'revolution from above', around
1810-15.

The point I am trying to make is that the Prussian case
illustrates that the processes of commercialisation and
capitalisation did not effect parallel changes from 'extra-
economic' forms of exploitation and control to 'economic' ones. In
this sense, I find Marx's thesis of the growing importance of
'silent constraints' instead of violent force and its 'bloody
discipline' inadequate. At the same time, I can't agree with
congruent arguments of Weberians and Parsonians which
underscore the preponderance of internal or attitudinal control
as a consequence of rationalisation and modernisation, or with
the argument of those Marxists who, influenced by Gramsci,
stress the ideological elements of 'internal control' (hegemony,
but also legitimation strategies and manipulation) as inherent in
the process of capitalisation.

III

(a) The dispositions of the state administration in Prussia were
profoundly influenced by the daily experience of civilian officials
in dealing with situations of perceived 'danger' (threats to the
law, to the *bürgerliche* order and to the state in general). The
officials often felt themselves to be powerless in dealing with the
rapidly growing numbers of 'vagrants', who could be industrial
or agricultural day-labourers, pauperised proto-industrial
producers, or professional beggars. They often felt themselves
impotent against the 'impudent stubbornness' of these lower
orders, especially their increasingly mobile segment as well as
against dissolute 'mobs' who provoked riots. The officials could
throw them in prison, beat them or fine them. But the next day,
or several months later (because in many cases suspects could
be detained on the responsibility of the police), they were
behaving in the same way - with an insubordination that
manifested indifference or even open resistance to the
authorities.

(b) Entangled in daily troubles and unease, the lower officials
had only unclear or imprecise regulations upon which to rely.

These regulations drew upon *general Klauseln* in the laws (cf. *Allgemeines Landrecht*, II/17, § 10; Regulation of Dec. 26th 1808; Oct. 23rd 1817). The daily police administration was thus confirmed with the very comprehensive charge (as the legal commentary Rönne/Simon, put it in 1840) of being concerned with the 'public security and welfare in regard to daily needs'.

The umbrella of the law was continuously expanded from the 1750s, in order to guarantee traditional 'rights' as private property, and to make them exchangeable on the market. But simultaneously in all matters of 'order and security' the developing *Rechtsstaat* remained so loosely defined that it afforded the authorities an extremely broad privilege of interpreting misconduct and illegal behaviour. Arbitrary actions against the dominated, especially against those who had the smell of being 'suspect', were legitimated. But at the same time, the lower officials, who actually did the work on the streets and in the inns, had to be aware of the traps built into the regulations and legal rules: these only very rarely hinted concretely at specific methods of treating suspects or at precise criteria to measure the success of one's efforts.

Realising, by the late 1830s, the relative ineffectiveness of the use of force, the lower officials often may have considered moderation in law enforcement to be the easiest means by which they could control riots or brawls. But simultaneously they had to contend with the fact that the unstated assumption of the higher officials, shaped by the demands of the local agents for the immediate use of force a decade earlier, intensified by perceptions of subversive activities growing after crowd actions and riots in 1830, and strengthened by officially disseminated conspiratorial theories according to which every vagrant was a potential revolutionary, was that the full application of force was required. This assumption of the superiors that the law should be enforced most fully and in its harshest dimensions thus paradoxically often rendered the law enforcement of local officials less effective. Caught in a conflict between the actual demands of their local situations and the standards of their superiors, the lower officials were constantly risking criticism and negative sanctions from those above because of ineffective, especially 'non-vigorous' performance of their 'duties'. This situation 'at the police front' caused the lower officials once again in the 1840s to draw immediately upon those means of physical violence which could make short shrift with insubordinate people or crowds – the military troops usually were at hand, especially in the towns where they were garrisoned.

(c) At these garrison towns, more than 200 of which were scattered over the country, so that they contained 53 per cent of all town inhabitants and 14 per cent of the total population in 1840, the officials had no choice. The military was permanently on stage, especially in the twenty-six fortresses (including the large cities and commercial-industrial centres such as Cologne,

Berlin or Breslau), and the military troops actually did the bulk of the daily police work, this despite the fact that the officers believed it unprestigious and an impediment to training activities. On the other hand, the legal omnipresence of the troops (cf. orders from 1788, 1793, renewed in 1817, 1819), and their 'superarbitrium' in case of danger (order of 1820), offered them a chance to demonstrate not only the real power relations but the real arrogance of power as well.

(d) Except for these garrison towns, however, the ambiguous regulations laid all the responsibility for quiet streets - as a symbol of a well-policed state - on the shoulders of badly, though regularly, paid and ill-equipped 'police servants', recruited from the *Invaliden*, the old and ill soldiers. They rarely obtained advice or substantial assistance from civilian officials if they were confronted with a brawl or a riot; normally, the two or three gendarmes (who also actually belonged to the military, but were under the direction of the civilian *Landrat*)who were assigned to a district of about 6000 km^2, were on duty twenty or thirty kilometres away. Therefore, from the lower levels of the bureaucracy, there emerged in the 1820s to the mid-1830s, and again in the mid-1840s, a massive pressure for a prophylactic use of military force or, at least, for the re-adoption of military standards in assessing and handling dangerous or difficult situations. These standards had been common during the eighteenth century. They were part of the 'military co-government in all matters of police' (as Max Lehmann, a bourgeois-liberal historian, put it in 1887). The problems generated by social changes accompanying the growth of capitalism in the countryside as well as the towns, thus stimulated inclinations toward the 'military way' of perceiving social reality and dealing with the visible social problems. Moreover the process of socialisation in their offices taught newcomers to all ranks of the civil service that 'external control' - physically violent methods of treating suspect people or crowds - was not only legitimate, but advisable and effective.

(e) The latter seems to be a paradox, because those who actually had 'to police' the people outside their offices quickly realised how ineffective their treatment of 'suspects' proved to be. They therefore faced the dilemma of either performing a kind of Sisyphean labour or, more commonly, of adapting to the expectations of their superiors and reporting, in the knowledge that it could not be checked, measures stronger than those which they had really undertaken. For those in higher positions in the administration this produced the impression that 'accidents' and other disruptive incidents were taking place, but that, except for some riots that could be quelled by the military, nothing was happening to pose a serious threat to the civil order or to the state. The monitoring of the rapidly increasing numbers of the people under police surveillance (which rose in Berlin between 1838 and 1847 from 7,800 to 13,200) or the

increasing number of police offences in the late 1830s in the
Rhine Province stimulated some memoranda and renewals of
orders for harsh law enforcement, as well as some charitable
activities. Most regulations were restrictive; for example, laws
were issued (31 December 1843/6 January 1843) to obstruct the
influx of migrants and 'vagrants' into the great cities and into
the rural centres of industrial production (e.g. Bergisches
Land and districts on the left bank of the Rhine). These,
however, were effective only in the imagination of the
ministerial officials: the immediate economic pressures and
constraints of the demographic 'explosion' on the east-Elbian
estates (i.e. the sharp increase of unemployed day-labourers
since the last third of the eighteenth century), the structural
crisis of household production since the 1820s, which was
intensified since the 1840s, the parallel growing need for a
mobile industrial workforce – these processes sharply raised the
rate of migration of pauperised and proletarianised immediate
producers and propertyless. State institutions of physical
violence had to fulfil a double-sided function: to guarantee
private property and simultaneously to protect 'public order'
against potential threats of these migrant and vagrant 'masses'.
In performing these 'duties' the officials increasingly clashed
with urgent claims of some members of the propertied classes
– demanding 'free play' for accumulation, including the 'free'
disposal over 'their' workforce.
    These quarrels of (at least some) capitalists symbolised and
expressed the transformation of the mode of production: the
police activities were primarily congruent with the interest of
'petty' property and of an agrarian aristocracy just becoming
involved in capitalist production. The socio-economic position of
these traditional proprietors was based not only on the disposal
of their means of production (in hand), but also on the command
over a dependent workforce. The capitalists instead relied on
the disposal of mobile capital reducing all connections between
men to 'cruel bare payment' ('cruel cash nexus', Marx/Engels).
    These discrepancies were never openly discussed within the
state-machine. But, for petty proprietors as well as for
capitalist entrepreneurs, the discipline and immediate obedience
of the 'lower orders' remained a central common interest.
Therefore, by enforcing calmness on streets and public places
in their daily practice, the police officials usually could
satisfy the demands of their superiors and of the local
well-to-do-people simultaneously.

IV

The Prussian case seems to be characterised by a *symbiosis* of
the classes and class-specific modes of *Herrschaft*. Classes
participating in capitalist production and circulation – Junkers
as well as commercial capitalists or industrial entrepreneurs –

had parallel interests in quiet streets and disciplined lower orders who could provide workers for the profit and prestige of the proprietors. And here they came very close to the interests of the 'relatively autonomous' branches of *Herrschaft*: the civil administration and the military. The latter especially was and remained closely tied to the Junker class.

A positive esteem of military force and violence penetrated the standards and practices of civilian officials and shaped the manner in which civilian authorities intervened in various 'dangerous' situations, not only in riots. By their daily routine work the officials were trained in a set of standards and rules which could be labeled as *Festungspraxis* ('citadel practice'). It reflected the military police practice built on the model of a fortress or citadel in a state of siege. One of the crucial facets of this 'citadel practice' was its inclination to physical force and violence. In consequence the differences between the modes of force diminished in the daily routine of the police. Physically brutal treatment of suspects or vagrants by beating or whipping easily could be switched over to the use of fire-arms, which meant the calling-in of the military guard or even the garrison. (Note: corporal punishment, as it was practised by the police in the towns and in the rural districts of the west, was the traditional means of physical domination on the east-Elbian estates.) Legal changes, as the prohibition of corporal punishment in 1848, only stimulated more camouflage on the part of police officials. On the level of legal prescriptions the inclination of the officials 'on the spot' towards physical and especially military violence could not be mitigated. And it does not seem to be a case singular to the 1840s, when in 1846 even the Minister of the Interior encouraged one of his county magistrates (*Landrat*) in Upper-Silesia not to take a fine too seriously (the *Landrat* was sentenced for brutal whipping of three suspect young men). An 'excess of competence because of zeal is by no means dishonourable', the minister declared in an official letter.

The legal umbrella of the presumed *Rechtsstaat* should be kept in function to mask the practice of physical violence by state officials, which was partly illegal even before 1848. In the long run, *Festungspraxis* penetrated all spheres of administrative behaviour throughout the whole of the nineteenth century. Or, as a professor of administrative law summarised it in the 1880s:

> The consequence is, on the one hand, that the welfare activities of the administrative institutions appear to be police activities and, on the other hand, that those procedures which require coercion, and which should really be reserved for extreme situations, are often employed in areas which should only need welfare treatment.

V

In the end, the Prussian case points to a more general feature of capitalist society, which seems to be widely masked in other capitalist societies 'in the making'. Perhaps those pitfalls of positivism into which even critical analysts such as Marx (and Weber) may, at times, have fallen are only becoming visible in the present stage of advanced capitalism. That is to say, the analyses of Marx and Weber underrated one basic dimension of societal regulation – the permanent use and threat of *physical violence 'from above'*, executed by state officials, as a necessary condition not only for the establishment, but also for the *continuation* of exploitation, unequal exchange and institutionalised reproduction. In other words: during the process of capitalisation external political control is not substituted, but completed by means of internal control.

State violence not only stimulated but triggered off learning processes that, first of all, constituted the 'belief in legality' which was claimed as one of the 'conditioning foundations of legitimate order' (Weber). Those directly concerned experienced the overwhelming power of the state, suspending any question of legitimation; other subjects learned that they belonged to those potentially concerned. From this point of view *violence douce* (Bourdieu) and *violence ouverte* are related to one another, in the sense that the different forms of symbolic violence for the dominated always include the experience as well as anticipation of physical violence 'from above'. So *violence douce*, which masks itself in the way it works, should not be perceived as the more modern or rational opposite of physical force; on the contrary it works only by the permanent presence of *violence brute* which it symbolises.

NOTES

1 Perry Anderson, *Lineages of the Absolutist State*, London 1974, p. 19.
2 I. Wallerstein, *The Capitalist World Economy*, Cambridge, Paris 1978.
3 Guy Bois, *Crise du Féodalisme*, Paris 1976.
4 Cf. for the argument and the empirical evidence an article on this topic in *Social History* 4, 1979, pp. 175 ff.

14 STATE AND PEASANTRY IN COLONIAL AFRICA

John Lonsdale*

African historiography is, I think, only now beginning to square
up to the implications of what for historians of India has long
been a truism, that native peasant production was the bedrock
of alien domination. This was so much the case in India, as I
understand it, that when the needs and purposes of British rule
outran the capacity of the land revenue to pay, the Raj was
obliged to make those financial and political shifts which were,
by reason of their growing complexities and contradictions, the
first dread harbingers of its own collapse. For too long in
African history peasant and proconsul have inhabited two
worlds, not so much different (as of course they were) but
entirely separate. This is partly due to the heritage of dualist
models of economics, themselves based on faulty perceptions of
the peasant world; partly to the essentially moral legacy of the
best of British colonial historiography; partly to the unthinking
ease with which the 'Africanist' insistence on Africans' initiative
in making their own recent history has been transferred from
politician to cultivator - while at the same time the politician is
increasingly portrayed as the willing dupe of external forces.
The consequence of this historiographical separation has been
the reduction of the relationship between 'state' and 'peasant' to
all the subtleties of a Punch and Judy show.
   Three models of the state have been recently or are still
current. The earliest was the administrative model of the state as
an ideological apparatus, calling all the messy complexities of the
colonial situation to order in the minds of its prefects; it
allowed a long run to a discussion of the distinctions between
Direct and Indirect Rule. Except, so far as I know, for
discussion by Wrigley and Low on the importance of 'the
discovery of the peasant'[1] for Uganda's reforms to chiefs' rights
in labour and rent, the debate was remarkably innocent of any
concept of exploitation, save in the entirely characteristic sense
of exploitation by educated elites of Western ideas or peasant
trust. That the debate was nevertheless not too unfaithful to
those whose governance it sought to interpret is given
backhanded corroboration by Polly Hill's discovery that the high
noon of Indirect Rule in Northern Nigeria was really a chaos of
non-rule, with the Hausa themselves describing a programme of
political reorganisation designed to create organic links between

---

*John Lonsdale is a university lecturer in history at Cambridge;
national service in Kenya led to a major interest in African
history.

village and Emirate as, rather, *yayyaga*, or 'tearing asunder'.[2]
It is sobering to conceive of British administration presiding
over a degree of social dislocation which might, in another
language, be described as *mfecane*.[3] But then, on the other
side of the continent too, Tanganyikan villagers had in the
same period to be on their guard against *wazimu wa mzungu*,
the 'white man's madness' which drove each new district
commissioner to impose his own pet ideas of improvement, often
at the expense of those idiosyncrasies of subservience which
the population had just learned to offer to his predecessor.[4] The
apparent separation of the state apparatus from the society over
which it ruled which one finds in these examples may, as I have
implied, grant a certain validity to the study of Indirect Rule as
a branch of political theory. But it does also raise genuinely
awkward questions about the 'statishness' of the colonial state
to which I hope to return in my conclusions.

A second model of the state which, I judge, now holds the
field as an explanatory device for the historical development of
white supremacy in southern Africa is that of 'an ideal collective
capitalist'.[5] The state, in South Africa in particular, has, it is
argued, acted to guarantee the process of accumulation by
capital, whether national (in farming and in manufacture) or
international (mainly in mining) by pursuing a conscious policy
of primitive accumulation at the expense of the African
peasantry. These have largely lost their independent access to
the means of production, but not entirely, so that they become
the cheapest of labour forces, able to reproduce much of their
labour power in the homelands outside the capitalist circuit, yet
constrained also to sell their labour to white employers.[6] I do
wonder, however, whether the model of the state which is
employed is not, for all its complexities, in fact too simple. It is
shown to serve capital's need to produce surplus value, by
means of labour repression. But capital needs, equally, to be
able to realise this surplus value, through social peace and
effective demand – a major contradiction within the capitalist
mode of production to which South Africa's 'liberal' historians
have perhaps paid more attention than its 'Marxists'.

If, in South Africa, therefore, the state seems to have
disposed of the peasantry, in the Gold Coast the British
administration – now in the guise of guarantor of metropolitan
capital – appears to have gone in abject fear of the Gold Coast
cocoa farmer, whose enterprise both competed with British
capital for labour and resources and threatened to dissolve the
bonds of civil society.[7] While there may be real doubt whether
the rural capitalists of the cocoa belt come within the definition
of peasantry,[8] it is none the less curious to find the Gold
Coast's feeble little administration confronting a much higher
proportion of its civil society than was the case even in South
Africa.

All three models of the colonial state in Africa, therefore,
however different in their theoretical origins, share the quality

of separation from society, especially peasant society. The
administrative state tore asunder when it was seeking to put
together; the collective capitalist state destroyed its peasantry;
the guardian of metropolitan capital sought by all means to
suppress the energies of its local wealth-creators. It may be of
course that this is because they were *colonial* states, necessarily
subjecting their peoples to 'a trial, a kind of test . . ., a crude
sociological experiment', as Balandier puts it.[9] But were they
not also capitalist states? And if they were, what does this
imply for new lines of enquiry? I think two recent trends in
historiography here may perhaps give a new sense of direction.

First, historians of the industrial world are working more
and more on the assumption that the economic history of modern
capitalism is incomplete without enquiry into the managerial
roles played by the apparatuses of the nation states.
Conversely, the political and administrative ramification of the
modern state, it is increasingly realised, can scarcely be
adequately explained unless seen in some part as a continual
process of response to the social disorders and economic crises
of capitalism. The 'state' is very much on the historiographical
agenda of the European world. Second, this same interest in the
historical formation of the state has been taken up in the study
of the non-European world. It arises from a sense of
dissatisfaction with the explanatory power of the earlier
statements of the 'underdevelopment' approach to the problems
of poverty, oppression and disorder in the Third World, not
least in Africa. These, it is now clear, were too exclusively
preoccupied with the allegedly determinant status of colonial
and neo-colonial 'dependency' upon the capitalist world market,
with its cumulative inequalities. The first attempts to add the
concept of the state to the analysis carried the
underdevelopment perspective to its paradoxical but logical
conclusion, that the post-colonial state structures of the Third
World were 'overdeveloped'; they were not so much related to
the development of internal social forces as indeed imposed
upon them by those who dominate their external markets, the
metropolitan bourgeoisies of the Western world.[10] Something
of these assumptions can be seen in the three models of the
state which I have outlined. But modern capitalism is a mode of
production rather than exchange; its fortunes are governed as
much by local social relations as by global markets, and subject
as much to the uncertainties of social conflict as to the
operation of impersonal laws. It follows that one must be more
alert to the constraints on economic development which were
imposed by the conflicts within and contradictions between the
different forms of production, non-capitalist and capitalist,
within the formerly colonial lands. These threatened social order
and the rate of accumulation; they called for counter-measures
to be undertaken by the state. The colonial state must therefore
be seen as a local growth as much as a foreign import.

This revision of paleo-underdevelopment theory does not

entail going back to so much as beyond the 'sociology of development'[11] or 'modernisation theory' which held sway in the optimistic heyday of behavioural social science in the 1960s, and to which underdevelopment theory was initially too faithful a mirror-image. This development theory had placed the blame for Third World poverty upon the suffocating grip of traditional societies which resisted 'modernisation'. It was a diffusionist theory, blessed with 'trickle down effects'. It echoed colonialism's own self-justifying ideology. Capitalism was seen not as a mode of production (although the 'dual economy' lurked in the background) but as a set of normative values; these were destined, so it was thought, to liberate traditional man for innovation by 'penetrating' his social relations. But capitalism *is* a social relation; it does not penetrate, it transforms all others into new hierarchies of exploitation and gain.

From this rather obvious point it follows that one's problem is how to relate the structures and purposes of the colonial state to the conflicts and contradictions within its political economy. The problem is quite different to those conceived by either modernisation or underdevelopment theory. By contrast with the first, the question is not one of identifying obstacles to modernisation within traditional society; it is how to analyse the competition within and between all levels of colonial society for a firm footing in the slippery process of growing social and economic differentiation. Our subject matter is the historical relationship between ever-changing indigenous and immigrant societies, their forms of production and conditions of reproduction, their hierarchies of authority, between all these and the colonial state, with its equally shifting strategies for the pursuit of capitalist dominance and social cohesion. In contradiction to the starker claims of underdevelopment theory therefore the purpose of the colonial state was not, I would argue, the subordination of all indigenous social classes or pre-capitalist social formations[12] in order to fulfil its role as the instrument of the metropolitan bourgeoisie (which I like to think of, at least as seen by the underdevelopmentalists, as the metrobogey). It was at once more complicated and less costly than that. Briefly, it was the contradictory purpose of accumulation, both local and metropolitan, but within a framework of local control. It demanded the creation of a local political system. This evolved in a kaleidoscopic rather than single-minded hierarchy of bureaucratic relations with local social forces, governed not simply by the 'needs of capitalism' but, rather, by crisis-driven efforts to contain the social conflicts which were generated by them.

None of the models of the state which I have adduced for colonial Africa seem to be very well fitted to cope with these contradictions.[13] The administrative 'Indirect Rule' model of the state had little by way of an economic dynamic. The South African 'ideal collective capitalist' model seems to me to be too omniscient and omnicompetent, meeting the needs of capital at

all phases of its development rather than coping with the
unpredictability of class struggle. It may be the case that the
combination of South Africa's status as a *late* industrialiser
requiring, like Wilhelmine Germany or Stalinist Russia, a
continuing degree of labour repression, and the fact that the
surplus value of mining, still the dominant sector, is realised
on the external rather than internal market[14] *does* make the
black peasantry irrelevant to analysis of class struggle after
1913,[15] though I have my doubts.[16] If that is nevertheless the
case, if the decisive conflict is, rather, between white capital
and a white proletariat determined not to have its labour power
valued at kaffir standards, then the South African experience
ought to be held *sui generis*, and not in any way generalised
into Central Africa. Nor, lastly, does the 'guarantor of
metropolitan capital' model seem to do justice to the complexities
of the colonial Gold Coast. The administration did not 'confront'
civil society,[17] rather, it took sides in the internal African
struggles over economic differentiation. The big cocoa farmers,
and especially the land speculators, were also often the props
of colonial rule, the chiefs of whom it was said, in matrilineal
society, that 'cocoa makes them kill their uncles'.[18]
Government was thus itself a resource in the conflicts of social
dislocation, not somehow lifted above that process. And the
state intervened with considerable vigour in the allocation of
Ghanaian resources, thanks to the way in which its revenue
crisis in the 1930s prompted the development of Native
Treasuries, something on which Kay has nothing to say.[19]

If one's understanding of the ambiguities of the state, as both
guarantor of accumulation and of social cohesion, is thus
impoverished by its analytical separation from society, such
criticism is still more valid when one considers the peasantry.
For when one adds to this separation the academic historian's
ignorance of the physical conditions of peasant agriculture – as
distinct from a theoretical approach to peasant societies – one is
only too likely to produce a morality play featuring heroic
peasant versus malignant state. Inattention to the very real
costs of adding cash crop production to subsistence
agriculture[20] has meant that the elasticity of the peasant supply
reponse has in some instances acquired all the incantatory
power lately enjoyed by its antithesis, modernization theory.
Such a perspective, which fits in well with underdevelopment
theory, requires that any collapse of peasant economy be
explained by the state's extra-economic manipulation of market
forces in favour of capitalist agriculture or mining. But it is
increasingly clear that the image of the profit-maximising
peasant, based on uncritical generalisations of 'vent for surplus'
theory, is misleadingly simple.[21]

To obtain an historical engagement between African peasantry
and colonial state one must, I think, concentrate more on the
conditions of reproduction for both. While the state needed, so
far as possible, to provide for its own political legitimacy and a

secure taxable base - and both would be ruined by continuous recourse to coercion - peasants struggled to maintain the conditions of their own social reproduction. It is rash to attempt to define peasantry in a sentence or two, but perhaps it is most useful in the present context to see it as that part of agrarian society in which the factors of production, land and labour especially, are provided outside market relations - but in which the maintenance of the social and political ties controlling these factors entails an increasing sale of produce (or, if needs be, labour) on to the market, to pay for the funds of ceremonial and rent or tax.[22] But the reproduction of the household production and consumption unit also depends, vitally, on defending from the risks of market fluctuation those technical and social arrangements which, so experience shows, are needed to safeguard one's subsistence.[23] In Africa, as in southeast Asia, one often finds a sectoral division in the peasant economy: between cash and food crops, between husbands' and wives' fields, between the use of hired and communal labour, between agricultural income and savings in livestock and, of particular importance in the Africa of the savannahs, in the competition between industrial crops (e.g., cotton) and food grains for first planting in the rains or in first use of newly cleared land.

From all this it follows that peasant societies are societies in turmoil. They are subject to a deep conflict between survival and citizenship. For it is those whose subsistence is more secure, or those to whom their wider social networks give superior information over markets, who set the pace in agricultural investment and social inflation. It is here that peasant society and colonial state were most fully engaged with each other. Time and again, those who enjoyed the margin of security needed for risk-avoidance in innovation were to be found among the ranks of official chiefs, mission teachers, government clerks, the agents of immigrant business houses. Conversely, the colonial politics of collaboration were so often built upon the peasant marketing chain. And they were inevitably volatile. They were subject not only to the periodic ecological crises of subsistence, droughts and pests; not only to the cyclical market crises of citizenship, but also to the continual erosion of the peasant's moral economy by the temptations offered to his society's patrons to become private accumulators.

But however immoral the patron, the peasant was condemned to dependence on the leader of his 'peasant coalition' (Eric Wolf's term), for access to land and markets. It was a dependence which governed peasant mentalities, identities, politics.[24] Peoples became tribes, no longer merely exploiting a particular ecological niche so much as occupying a level in a productive and marketing hierarchy threaded to rail-heads and ports, producing cash-crops, or food surpluses, or exporting their male labour.[25] 'Tribe' became the most inclusive of peasant coalitions, now defined by its officially recognised patrons, the chiefs, now created by alternative elites (farmers, traders, teachers) as a solidarity against them. [26] So the peasant marketing chain, once the base for the politics of collaboration, became available in the crucible of local conflict to the politics of nationalism.

Two examples of crisis in Kenya, a colony I sometimes think I understand, may help to clarify the processes of engagement between peasant economy and the reproduction of the state. To understand both one has first to grasp that peasant reproduction in Kenya - and perhaps everywhere in savannah Africa - depended on a *cycle* of accumulation. The surpluses of household commodity production, largely but not entirely the product of female labour, were invested in trade with pastoral neighbours. The livestock thus acquired was in turn invested in female labour power, through bride-wealth, and in family formation which, finally, guaranteed continued access to land for cultivation. [27] In colonial times this cycle was diversified but not supplanted by investing the earnings of migrant labour, especially the labour of the educated.

The first crisis came in the aftermath of the First World War. It was a crisis of habitability (to adopt Ali Mazrui's phrase, *The Listener*, 9 November 1979). It was also a crisis of peasant differentiation. Taken as a whole, Kenya's peasantries were drained of manpower by wartime conscription and influenza, drained of livestock and maize surpluses for rationing the forces, and dangerously dependent upon the repeated cultivation of the same fields by women without their men. But some had done well out of the war, those influential enough to resist conscription and sell foodstuffs on the rising market, and those demobilised military porters fortunate enough to return with fat gratuities; some Africans became employers. [28] Peasant economy required a huge investment of labour, for survival of the many, for the profit of the few. But so did the white settlers; they demanded, and got, from the state a policy of scarcely veiled labour coercion. There was a row, not only from the House of Lords, but also from the chiefs, whose positions of patronage could stand so much traffic in the relations of exploitation and no more. Further, the state itself was bankrupt. Settlers could produce little in the post-war slump, and pay even less in tax. Peasants could. The crisis was resolved with the first, but brief, central government spending on African agriculture and the regularisation of the politics of African collaboration through chiefs-in-councils. Peasant economy and peasant politics had edged a little further into the structure of the state.

The 1930s brought the second crisis. It involved fiscal crisis, again, for the state, and a crisis of involution for the peasantry, as the modest agricultural prosperity of the 1920s was invested increasingly in the unrewarding wealth of livestock, for lack of opportunity to invest in such land-saving income-earners as coffee or tobacco growing. The state intervened in peasant farming to resolve both issues. It attempted to cull surplus cattle, it began to require peasants to work on measures of soil conservation. The state also hitched the peasant cultivation of new crops, even coffee, long the settlers' monopoly, to exclusive buying and processing licences for immigrant capital, too wary of risk-taking to enter the African reserves without the hand-hold of the state. Marketing boards followed, and compulsory co-operatives (or coercitives) for growers of designated crops. Peasant economy was lifted still further into the state; and the state took into itself the contradictions within peasant economy, the contradictions between peasants and settlers, the contradictions between producers and the trading houses.[29] The monopoly structures characteristic of colonial (and neo-colonial) economies were born out of the double crisis of the Depression which had threatened the reproduction of both producers and states.

If this sort of analysis has little to offer to the study of South Africa, then surely it does for the Gold Coast.

By way of conclusion I want to return to the question of the statishness of the colonial state in Africa. One can perhaps get as good an insight as any by looking at its festivals. All over the Empire there were celebrations on 6 May 1935, the silver jubilee of King George V, even in little Kakamega, a district headquarters in the hills of western Kenya, complete with Indian and Somali bazaar, government primary school, police lines and prison, a few bars and hardware dealers to meet the needs of indigent settlers-turned-gold prospectors. The *power* of the state was on view with a parade of police (but how many besides the district commissioner knew that they were unable to fire their annual musketry practice for want of a suitable rifle range?). The *majesty* of rule was invoked with a speech from the governor, read by the district commissioner, who observed that King George was present, even to the meanest of his subjects, in his image on their coins, on the medals of their chiefs. He was 'a very great ruler and dearly loves his people and sees that they are ruled justly. He has always shown a very deep personal concern in your welfare' - and the schoolmaster-leaders of peasant opinion were even then acting on the principles of peasant legitimism by by-passing the king's servants and petitioning his House of Commons for redress of grievances occasioned by the recent discovery of gold. The royal family was still further linked to the material *improvement* in peasant citizenship. In Queen Victoria's day 'very few people had any clothes except skins and blankets and hardly any knew how to read. Now you have railways and roads, schools and hospitals, towns and trading centres, which give you the opportunity for development which civilization and good government bring in their train.' Colonial improvement was linked to peasant *recreation*. The day's proceedings included a display by the local boy scout troop under the care of Jeremia

Segero, trained in Nairobi at the Jeanes School as a community teacher (but who also, as the district commissioner well knew but to which he dared not object, had hidden away behind a banana patch a well-tended stand of coffee trees). The rulers sought their subjects' affection in carnival, almost indeed in *saturnalia*. There were games for Africans only, the slippery pole, a tug-of-war, blindfold football biffing; but there was inter-racial sport too, a bicycle race, a donkey derby, even a fancy-dress soccer match between Europeans and Indians for the natives to gawp at. Peasant *economy* was co-opted too; there was an egg, cent and flour race, there was also a women's bottle race, in which presumably the women showed off their skill in carrying on their heads the bottles which contained the kerosene with which they fuelled their lamps. Peasant *culture* was used too; the day started with church services. Europeans attended the 'high culture' of an Anglican service; to Africans was left the 'low culture' of a Catholic celebration. Can one see in all this the indigenisation of the state, the peasantisation of its subjects?[30]

If so, it was in many respects a feeble state, with an appalling memory, and its peasants proved fully equal to defending their subsistence requirements against its demands. In 1958 Professor Sir Joseph Hutchinson, the Empire's cotton expert, revealed that experiments in Nyanza with 'early' sowings in the June of 1950 had given far better yields than the normal peasant practice of September sowings. Then in 1955, sowing in March and April, at the start of the long rains, had given yields better still.[31] But this had been discovered half a century earlier, by the first agricultural instructor posted to the province (and at that time its best cricketer), the West Indian Harry Holder.[32] The Luyia and Luo peasants doubtless knew it well enough too, but their grains and oil-seeds were a much more important call on their labour in the critical planting season.

Nevertheless, Kenya was perhaps in a deeper sense a peasant state, a coalition of peasant coalitions, a segmentary state, whose character has only been permitted full development since independence. It is true that its mechanisms of *extraction* are impersonal, almost invisible, through the crop levies taken off by marketing boards, and by indirect taxation: direct rural taxation was abolished for the majority of the population in 1969. But the mechanisms of resource *allocation* could scarcely be more personal and direct, through the reciprocal transactions between peasant voters and their elected representatives to the centre, whose failure to bring to their locality the goods of roads, schools, jobs and hospitals brings retribution at the polls.[33] It is therefore possible to analyse politics in Kenya, as in Orissa, as one of choice between at least two systems, the clientilist and the administrative, and the choices were there, if rather suppressed, in colonial times.[34] If this is the mark of a low degree of statishness, it is none the less salutary to note

that it is also the mark of a high degree of economic success,
even perhaps of equity, in post-colonial Africa, where the
non-mineral economies of Kenya and the Ivory Coast stand out
not only by reason of their peasant prosperity but also for their
segmentary politics of patronage.

NOTES

1 C.C. Wrigley, *Crops and Wealth in Uganda*, Kampala 1959;
   D.A. Low, *Buganda in Modern History*, London 1971,
   chapter 5.
2 Polly Hill, *Population, prosperity and poverty: rural Kano
   1900 and 1970*, Cambridge 1977, p. 48.
3 'The time of troubles', 'the crushing', from which emerged
   Shaka Zulu's flawed despotism.
4 J.G. Liebenow, *Colonial Rule and Political Development in
   Tanzania: the Case of the Makonde*, Evanston 1971, p. 143.
5 Bob Jessop, 'Recent theories of the capitalist state',
   Cambridge Journal of Economics, 1, 1977, esp. pp. 361-4.
6 The literature on the subject is large and growing. Two
   recent and influential books are R. Palmer and N. Parsons,
   eds, *The Roots of Rural Poverty in Central and Southern
   Africa*, London 1977; and Colin Bundy, *The Rise and Fall
   of the South African Peasantry*, London 1979. Something of
   their perspective is to be found in E.A. Brett, *Colonialism
   and Underdevelopment in East Africa: the Politics of
   Economic Change 1919-1939*, London 1973.
7 G.B. Kay, *The Political Economy of Colonialism in Ghana*,
   Cambridge 1972. The nadir of official confidence must have
   been reached in 1944 when the Governor forwarded the
   Colony's development plan to London with these defeatist
   sentiments (p. 45): 'So little can be *counted on* with
   confidence in the future that I put forward with some
   diffidence proposals which must inevitably cover a number of
   years. We do not know, for instance, what will be the future
   of Gold mining or cocoa . . . nor can we be *sure* of the
   response which the people of the Colony themselves will make
   to *any* plans formulated by Government' (emphases added).
8 Polly Hill, *Migrant Cocoa Farmers of Southern Ghana*,
   Cambridge 1963, would exclude them from the peasantry;
   Sara S. Berry, *Cocoa, Custom and Socio-Economic Change in
   Rural Western Nigeria*, Oxford 1975, would include them,
   largely on the score of their 'imperfect' factor markets, with
   so many farm inputs being supplied by social rather than
   market means.
9 G. Balandier, 'La situation coloniale: approche théorique', as
   translated in *Social Change, the Colonial Situation*, ed. by
   I. Wallerstein, New York 1966, p. 38.
10 H. Alavi, 'The state in post-colonial societies: Pakistan and
    Bangladesh', *New Left Review*, 74, 1972.

11 Cf., I. Oxaal, T. Barnett and D. Booth, eds, *Beyond the Sociology of Development*, London 1975.
12 Alavi, *op. cit.*, p. 61; John Saul, 'The state in post-colonial societies: Tanzania', in *The Socialist Register 1974*, ed. by R. Miliband and J. Saville, London 1974, p. 353.
13 J. Lonsdale and B. Berman, 'Coping with the contradictions: the development of the colonial state in Kenya, 1895-1914', *Journal of African History* 20, no. 4, 1979, attempts to adumbrate a more flexible model. This present paper is a continuation of the attempt and owes much to the ideas of Bruce Berman, although it may in some respects depart from his.
14 S. Trapido, 'South Africa in a comparative study of industrialization', *Journal of Development Studies*, 7, no. 3, 1971.
15 1913, the year of the Native Land Act, is according to Bundy, the date at which the 'curtains swish shut' on the peasantry (*South African Peasantry*, p. 246). And the subsequent irrelevance of the peasantry has been argued in a 1978 Witwatersrand conference paper by Glen Moss, as cited in Terence Ranger, 'Growing from the roots: Reflections on peasant research in Central and Southern Africa', *Journal of Southern African Studies*, 5, no. 1, 1978, p. 127.
16 Prompted by M.L. Morris, 'The development of capitalism in southern Africa: Class struggle in the countryside', *Economy and Society*, 5, 1976 – from which it appears that African farm tenants' resistance to proletarianism was still vigorous in the 1930s.
17 Kay, *op. cit.*, p. 9.
18 T.J. Johnson, 'Protest: Tradition and Change. An analysis of southern Gold Coast cocoa riots 1899-1920', *Economy and Society*, 1, no. 2, 1972, p. 179.
19 R.L. Stone, 'Rural politics in south-central Ghana, 1919-1945', Cambridge seminar paper, 1973.
20 A concept which must embrace production not only of the 'normal surplus' insurance against a bad harvest but also of surpluses sufficient to buy the specialisations of local artisans and ecological neighbours, and to contribute to however modest a 'ceremonial fund', as defined by Eric Wolf, *Peasants*, Englewood Cliffs 1966, pp. 7ff.
21 Ranger, *op. cit.*, 116f; J. Iliffe, *A Modern History of Tanganyika*, London 1979, ch. 9; and, in a definitive treatment, J. Tosh, 'The cash crop revolution in tropical Africa: An agricultural reappraisal', forthcoming in *African Affairs* (1980).
22 Harriet Friedmann, 'Peasants and petty commodity producers: Analytical distinctions', London University seminar paper, May 1979, is most helpful here.
23 J.C. Scott, *The Moral Economy of the Peasant: Rebellion and Subsistence in Southeast Asia*, London 1976, and, more

succinctly, in M. Lipton, 'The theory of the optimising peasant', *Journal of Development Studies*, 4, no. 3, 1968; and J. Weeks, 'Uncertainty, Risk and Wealth and Income Distribution in Peasant Agriculture', *Journal of Development Studies*, 7, no. 1, 1970.

24 K. Post, 'Peasantization and rural political movements in West Africa', *Archives européennes de sociologie*, xiii, 1972.

25 J. Iliffe, *Agricultural Change in Modern Tanganyika*, Nairobi 1971; *A Modern History*, ch. 10.

26 One of the few insights perhaps still valid in J. Lonsdale, 'Some origins of nationalism in East Africa', *Journal of African History*, ix, no. 1, 1968 – in its discussion of 'paramount chief' movements.

27 This summary is derived from Judith Butterman, 'Women's work in South Nyanza, Kenya, in a changing context, 1800-1945', (American) African Studies Association conference paper, Nov. 1978; but it would apply very widely.

28 D. Feldman, 'Christians and politics: the origins of the Kikuyu Central Association in northern Murang'a', Cambridge PhD thesis 1979, ch. 4; M.P. Cowen and F. Murage, 'Notes on agricultural wage labour', in *Developmental Trends in Kenya*, Centre of African Studies, Edinburgh 1972.

29 Compare David Washbrook, 'State, law and society in colonial India, 1860-1947', Cambridge seminar paper, Feb. 1978.

30 Appendix, *North Nyanza District Annual Report*, 1935 (Kenya National Archives).

31 J.B. Hutchinson, 'Cotton in East and Central Africa', in *Rhodesia and East Africa*, ed. by F.S. Joelson, London 1958, p. 370.

32 *Kenya Agricultural Department Annual Report 1907/08*, 35.

33 C. Leys, 'Politics in Kenya: The development of peasant society', *British Journal of Political Studies*, 1, no. 3, 1971.

34 F.G. Bailey, *Tribe, Caste and Nation*, Manchester 1960, pp. 10ff. If Orissa is a rather unrepresentative, peripheral case of centre-periphery relations in India, it could be much more usefully generalised for Africa.

Capitalism

Hans Medick*

The recent renewal of the seminal controversy of the 1950s on
the 'Transition from Feudalism to Capitalism' has so far provoked
relatively little resonance from Marxist historians in Britain.

Originally it was otherwise. The debate was started by the
publication of Maurice Dobb's *Studies in the Development of
Capitalism* in 1946. Besides Paul Sweezy and the Japanese
historian Takahashi it was above all British Marxist historians
who contributed to the subsequent controversy, which appeared
in book form in 1955 under the title *The Transition from
Feudalism to Capitalism.*

The initiative to reopen the debate came from two American
historians Immanuel Wallerstein[1] and Robert Brenner[2] in 1974
and 1976 respectively. In Britain, Rodney Hilton published his
introduction to the new edition of the *Transition* as Essay 1 in
No. 1 of *History Workshop Journal.*[3] Clearly this was meant as
an encouragement for further discussion. But if the very
placement of Hilton's article indicated a programmatic intention
on the part of the *History Workshop* editorial collective, it did
not have any consequences. In the debate on history and theory
which has since then begun to rage in the pages and columns of
History Workshop Journal the strengths of the Anglo-Marxist
tradition before 1956 do not seem to be remembered very well,
in particular Dobb's attempt to develop 'material theories' out
of the practice of historical research, and his concern to
abolish the frontier 'between what it is fashionable to label as
"economic factors" and as "social factors".'[4]

In the beginning things looked different. The issues raised
by Dobb in his *Studies* were formative for the genesis of
Marxist history in Britain. They were indeed central to the
discussion of the Communist Party Historians Group before it
broke up in 1956, as Eric Hobsbawm testified in a recent essay.[5]
But the influence of Dobb's book and of the ensuing debate
went much further. Through its publication in *Science and
Society* and other journals it may be regarded as the first
successful effort to internationalise the discussion of British
Marxist historians.

---

*Hans Medick researches at the Max Planck Institute,
Göttingen. His *Industrialisation before Industrialisation* is due to
be published by Cambridge University Press in 1980. His first
research was on classical political economy in eighteenth-century
Britain.

A very specific impact of this discussion is evident from the minutes of the Historians' Group Summer School on The Development of British Capitalism at Netherwood in July 1954. According to Hobsbawm this school witnessed 'the most ambitious effort', which the Group ever undertook, namely the planning of a volume of studies, which in the end was never completed. It was to be entitled 'Some Marxist Contributions to the Study of British Capitalist Society'. 'In a sense it was a systematic attempt to see where we had got in eight years of work and where Marxist history ought to go next.'[6]

Dobb's *Studies* and copies of the then recent contributions to the transition debate in *Science and Society* were recommended as the basic reading for the School besides the classics: Marx *Capital* vol I and III and Lenin's *Development of Capitalism in Russia*. The conference minutes themselves witness the direct influence of Dobb who contributed the 'Note on Some Questions Concerning Capitalism and its Development'. What seems to be most remarkable in this paper is Dobb's insistence that

the *essential* role in the rise of capitalist production was played by social differentiation within the petty mode of production as soon as this had secured a measure of freedom for emancipation from feudal bonds and feudal exploitation. In the degree that this petty mode of production prospered, and was able to retain within itself a substantial share of its surplus product, a class of petty capitalists emerged (putting-out clothiers and improving farmers) from the ranks of the producers themselves.

The results of the Netherwood School can by no means be seen as a mere acceptance of Dobb's argument. The 'Concluding Report' by 'E.J.H.' - I suppose it is Eric Hobsbawm - indicates a lively and partly controversial debate among the participants whose main points were summarized by 'E.J.H.' as follows:

there is a growing convergence of ideas, *but*:
We agree more about the superstructure than the basis.
More discussion on culture is needed.
We need to improve our knowledge of the common people determining and shaping history.
Many of us . . . tend to overspecialize.

It is interesting to note that this *contemporary* indication of the weak spots of the conference's debate stands in a certain contrast to those points which Hobsbawm mentions himself in *retrospect* in his recent essay. Though he used the same source as I did - and some others in addition - he mentions only one - rather specific - point of his own original concluding report - if it is his - and passes over the other - fundamental - ones, which I quoted above, in silence. In 1978 his abbreviated view of what was thought of as weaknesses and consequently future tasks in 1954 looks like this: 'As we concluded from this and from other experiences we were particularly weak on the history of empire and colonial exploitation, Scottish, Welsh and Irish history and the "role of women in economic life".'[7] It is clear

from the final summary statement that this memorable conference
has to be understood not just as a listing of empirical deficits.
It has to be seen as a declaration of future intent to write the
history of British Capitalism as a 'History of Society', as an
economic, social and cultural history from the point of view of
the 'common people determining and shaping history'.

These far-reaching aims were only partly fulfilled in the
specialised division of labour which British Marxist historians
entered into after 1956. What was visualised as a great
co-operative project in 1954 divided itself into several parts.
This holds true for the economic historians as well as for those
who from then on developed so fruitfully the history of
working-class life, culture and politics. The two discourses
which had come together under the presidency of the
'benevolent abbess' Dona Torr and in the good spirit of Maurice
Dobb's 'historical political economy', now went their separate
ways. Historically this has - even today - to be considered as a
loss. From then on until the 1970s there was relatively little
mutual questioning of fundamental categorical assumptions and
until quite recently little effort at a synthetic 'history of
society'.

Viewed against this background of unfulfilled potentialities
and great projects which only partly came to be realised, the
recent renewal of the 'Transition Debate' can only in some
respects be seen as a true continuation of this comprehensive
discourse.

But before we pursue this let us return to Dobb and Sweezy
first: Dobb interprets the development and crisis of the feudal
system as a consequence of the inner dynamic and contradictions
of its social and productive relations. Periodic 'overexploitation'
of peasant labour in a system in which the immediate producer
controlled production and in which an increase of surplus for
the lord could therefore only be gained by an increased
application of direct force on the peasant was for Dobb an
essential feature of the feudal relations of production. At one
and the same time this 'overexploitation' was the cause of the
stagnating productivity of the feudal system and the 'prime
mover' of its dissolution. For Sweezy, on the contrary, feudalism
did not contain the seeds of its dissolution within itself.
External elements were necessary to develop it beyond itself.

Sweezy located this 'creative potential' not in relations of
production and of direct exploitation, but in the sphere of
'commodity circulation'. The 'market-creating' forces of
merchant and trading capital in his view were the decisive cause,
making for the dissolution of feudalism and the transition to
capitalism.

In his controversy with Sweezy Dobb by no means underrated
the importance of the urban economy and the exchange-relations
between town and country in the development and crisis of
feudalism. He did not, however, believe in their final dissolving
effect. The urban economy, trade and the circulation of

commodities for him were not factors *external* to the feudal
system, necessarily making for the transition to capitalism, they
were on the contrary decisively determined and limited through
it.

Dobb's explanation of the origins of capitalism can only
indirectly be traced to his analysis of the contradictions within
the feudal system. In a characteristic way, however, his
explanation mirrors his view of the limited growth potential of
agrarian and craft-industrial production under the feudal
system. The development of capitalist relations of production –
at least for the case which Dobb calls the 'classical' one, that
of England – is described as a largely self-generating process.
It takes place – so to speak – in a social void, in the interstices
of the feudal system and is seen as the quasi-autonomous 'birth
of a capitalist class from the ranks of production itself'.

Capitalism thus originates for Dobb as a genuine process of
proto-capitalist development. Its essential features are seen in
the 'accumulation of capital within the petty mode of production
itself and hence . . . the start of a process of class
differentiation within that economy of small producers.'[8] In
tracing this process of accumulation and class differentiation
Dobb's emphasis is primarily on the activities of the small
entrepreneur. The peasant-kulaks and the middle-scale
craftsmen turned capitalists are for him the true representatives
of the 'revolutionary' transition towards capitalism, which is
however not sufficiently analysed as a process of transition.
Landlords, merchant-capitalists and large entrepreneurs of the
'Sombartian' type do not generally stand against development,
but as representatives of the feudal system, as proponents of
the 'non-revolutionary' way.

Dobb's 'historical political economy' at this point does not
seem to be free from the dangers of an analysis, which is written
from the standpoint of a 'history from below', but works with
paradigms of a 'history from above'. His emphasis is quite
clearly not on analysing the 'broad social basis' of this process
of proto-capitalist accumulation and class-formation. This has to
be searched for in the history of the rural and urban property-
poor and propertyless classes of dependant labourers, small
peasants and paupers, whose role as 'common people shaping
and determining history' does not first date from the origins of
proto-capitalism. As Guy Bois and Catherina Lis and Hugo
Soly[9] have recently shown in their very interesting and
impressive books, these propertied poor and propertyless classes
have to be seen as an essential force in the production and
reproduction of the feudal system, and, in economic terms too,
as the 'broad basis' from which proto-capitalism could originate.
'Primitive accumulation' is seen by Dobb too much in the light of
a process of 'original accumulation', whose main characteristic
is that it is 'previous' to industrial capitalism. That other form
of 'previous accumulation' which occurred as a discontinuous
and intermittent process in the feudal system and lately has been

analysed by Guy Bois, does not enter his analysis of the origins of capitalism.

What is called for then is an approach which integrates the analysis of proto-capitalism more closely into the investigation of the dissolution of feudal society. Here there may be some relevance in recent and current work on rural industrialisation in which I am interested together with several friends and colleagues. This work originated from the observation that the mass-manufacture of craft-industrial commodities for supra-regional and international markets between the sixteenth and early nineteenth century to a large extent was a rural phenomenon. First beginning in the late Middle Ages, industrial commodity production, especially in textiles and metalwares, increasingly left the towns to be organised as a household industry in the countryside by peasant-kulaks and merchant-capitalist-putters-out alike. An essential pre-condition for this process was the growing class differentiation and polarisation of the rural population which, however, cannot necessarily be seen as the consequence of a previous dispossession of a majority of the peasantry through primitive accumulation.

At least in its origins it was an integral feature of the development of feudal-agrarian society. Moreover the increase in numbers of the propertyless and propertied poor often did not deprive them entirely of their agrarian base or their claims to common rights. At the level of safeguarding their accustomed subsistence through these rights they often fought a very successful class struggle both against feudal appropriation and parts of the village bourgeoisie. In the end this did not always prevent capitalist accumulation in the village as has been maintained by Robert Brenner.[10] It may on the contrary be said that it made accumulation possible. On the one hand day-labouring and/or industrial bye-employments at low wages were very often the means for these underemployed rural poor to retain their family-economy-way-of-life under conditions of increasing misery which would not have allowed them a subsistence from agricultural work on their own plots and the use of common rights alone. On the other hand the extra profits to be derived by exploiting this marginal situation of life and work of the small producers in the countryside were one of the central features of the growth of capitalism in the countryside in many regions of Europe. The marginal situation of 'zero opportunities' often enforced a measure of self-exploitation for mere survival upon these small familial producers which made them produce and reproduce below their labour costs. This same situation on the other side enabled the capitalist putter-out to gain a specific 'differential profit' which lay above the profit which could be realised in manufactures.

Taking up the perspective of the Dobb-Sweezy controversy again, this process of proto-capitalist development through rural industrialisation may well be described as belonging to the second phase in the dissolution of feudalism and probably was

its primum movens. Whereas the first phase in the dissolution
of feudalism began in the high Middle Ages with the origins of a
division of labour between town and country and the generation
of merchant-capital through a form of 'urban colonialism', the
second phase is characterised by the reversal of this division
of labour and the increasing recourse of merchant capital to
organising rural industry in the countryside on a regional
basis. It remains to be seen, however, how far and whether
rural industrialisation may be considered as a moving force in
the second phase of the dissolution of the feudal system.

A NOTE ON BRENNER AND WALLERSTEIN

The relationship and interactions between the 'outer' and the
'inner' spheres - that is, the dynamics of exchange and trading
relationships - and the transformation of modes and relations of
production in town and country, was the essential legacy of
the Dobb-Sweezy debate. It comes as no surprise, then, that
this problem is paramount for the two authors to whom we owe
most in the resumption of the 'transition' debate - Robert
Brenner and Immanuel Wallerstein.

Robert Brenner's work shows him clearly to be a supporter
of Dobb and an opponent of Sweezy,[11] even where he differs
from Dobb on a number of important points. On the one hand,
he falls behind Dobb, taking as the main factor for economic
development 'class constellation' and 'class conflict'. But he
treats this too much from a legal-institutional point of view and
in terms of peripheral political effects. He ignores the specific
economic contradictions of the feudal mode of production, which
also include as an integral moment population development and
the market relations through which exchange rates, price
trends, real wages and feudal rents were constituted.

On the other hand, Brenner goes beyond Dobb. He does not
share the general view that capitalist relations of production
arose in the sphere of small production. Instead, he
differentiates between the various legal-political and socio-
economic conditions in early modern Europe, seeing only one
case, that of England, as an example of a 'successful' transition
to capitalism. Here the 'short-circuiting of the emergence of
small peasant property'[12] and the retention of widespread
landlord control over country property, even after abolition of
serfdom, made, he argues, the decisive condition for the growth
of a 'productive' relationship between landlord and capitalist
farmer. In England, the growth of capitalism required the
expropriation of the small agrarian producers and their
reduction to the status of wage labourers. On this foundation
the antagonism between farmers and feudal labourers could make
way for the 'co-operation' of farmer and aristocrat (by means of
agricultural improvements, investments and innovations), and,
starting from the sixteenth century, the introduction of an

agrarian-capitalist development based on capital investment and increased productivity. This, says Brenner, was the 'key to England's uniquely successful overall economic development'.[13]

Brenner contrasts England with other European societies and regions – e.g. France or the Central European area – in which the outcome of class conflict between landlord and peasant and the abolition of serfdom led to a *strengthening* of peasant rights of ownership. Here the 'agrarian basis' was lacking for an all-round economic development to capitalism. Both the 'self-reproductive' dynamics of a peasant economy and the strong fiscal 'skimming off' of the peasant surplus by the absolutist state impeded a development of landlord-peasant relations. In consequence, a process of continuously expanding reproduction and accumulation, based on capital investment and continual increases in productivity, was blocked.[14] Even where, as for example in viniculture, horticulture and dairy-farming – or through the introduction of new crops such as flax – a considerable rise in incomes was achieved on the basis of small peasant farming economy, this still, according to Brenner, created no basis for the development of capitalist production relations either in the agrarian or manufacturing-industrial sector:

> this sort of agriculture generally brought about increased yields through the intensification of labour rather than through greater efficiency of a given unit of labour input. It did not, therefore, produce 'development', except in a restricted, indeed misleading use of the term.[15]

Brenner's fixation on the English model prevents him from asking the question about a 'peasant way to capitalism', a question raised by Dobb and recently re-introduced into the discussion by J. de Vries and Eric Hobsbawm.[16] He pays little attention to development possibilities and limitations in peasant 'micro-capitalism' (Braudel) and the basis of the latter in the peculiar logic of peasant 'micro-accumulation' (not least in the form of indebtedness, through marriage and inheritance). Nor does he concern himself with one of its basic conditions: the strengthening of class differentiation among the agricultural producers themselves that already existed under feudal relations of production and led to forms of wage dependency or quasi-wage dependency. These problems of the 'peasant way' are largely unresearched, and yet should be crucial for the Central European areas, particularly in the countryside surrounding the city centres; for the Netherlands; and for France too from the sixteenth to the nineteenth centuries.[17]

Brenner's more ambitious thesis – that successful peasant resistance to super-exploitation inside the feudal system prevented not only the breakthrough of capitalism on the land, but also in the economy as a whole – leaves out of consideration the questions Wallerstein begins with. Wallerstein's argument is contained in his richly documented, secondary analysis *The Modern World System. Capitalist Agriculture and the Origins of*

the European World Economy in the Sixteenth Century and in
some rewarding smaller, mainly conceptual, studies and critiques
to be put alongside it.[18]

For Wallerstein as for Brenner it is the uneven economic
development of the societies of early modern Europe, which form
the starting-point. But he does not see these developments as
the result of multiple and diverse indigenous transitions from
feudalism to capitalism – with England as a pioneer, running
ahead. He sees them as the consequence of a unified world-
economic relationship in which division of labour and commodity
exchange increasingly mould the relationship of the economic
units to each other. And so for Wallerstein there are not the
many, but only one transition from feudalism to capitalism. This
occurs during the 'long 16th century' (Braudel) between 1450
and 1640 and coincides with the beginning of a comprehensive
'world capitalist system'.

It might appear from this brief and summary account that
Wallerstein is criticising the assumptions of the nineteenth-
century theoreticians and their later influences in twentieth-
century modernisation theory and social science (model character
of English-European-American development of capitalism and its
possibility for imitation by underdeveloped countries). But his
intentions as a historian are more serious and more critical. In
the historical concreteness of his analyses, in his
categorisation and the constructive sympathy with which
Wallerstein brings into his work his own experiences in the
'Third World' (as Africanist and sociologist of African Liberation
movements), he moves well beyond any attempt at a
modernisation theory.[19]

Wallerstein reveals the genesis of capitalism as a process,
which cannot be sufficiently explained in terms of either
immanent or endogamous factors. The dynamic of this
development may be released by the 'crisis of feudalism' and
represents a 'key prerequisite to a solution for the crisis of
feudalism'.[20] But it is not to be reduced to this impulsion.
Rather it drew strength at the very outset from specific
connections of an extra-regional division of labour and, by
contrast to the direct 'skimming off' of the feudal system, a new
indirect 'skimming off' through unequal exchange'. In this way,
mediated by the world market, two simultaneous processes were
set into motion and linked: the development of the core zones of
capitalist accumulation in northwest Europe on the one hand,
and on the other the exploitation and structural
underdevelopment of peripheral zones (Latin America, Eastern
Europe) as well as the pushing back of initial subcentres to the
'semi-periphery' (Spain, Portugal, Italy, and southern
Germany) (cf. the proximity of these theses to those of the
theoretician and historian of 'structural underdevelopment'
A.G. Frank[21], which Wallerstein readily admits).

The 'forcing house' for this development was extra-regional
trade, which, though sometimes conducted peacefully, more

often followed in the wake of war, piracy and the forcible appropriation of territory. The 'mother trade', founded primarily on the exchange of East European cereals for West European manufactured products and overseas imports (spices, gold and silver) and closely bound up with the Mediterranean-based economy, had been pursued with comparatively little aggression. But already by the sixteenth century, clustered around this relatively peaceable economy, there emerged a system of world trade and exchange in which West African slaves were as much commodities as were Hispano-American gold and silver.

The importance of Wallerstein's work in this context lies in his recognition of these already familiar trade and exchange relationships as both cause and consequence of the development of a structured and interdependent extra-regional division of labour. Within a single world economy, Wallerstein discovers a complementary divergence of the modes and relations of production: he sees the world economy as being divided into distinct and specialised geographical zones of production which are, at the same time, functionally interdependent and complementary. The *divergence* is manifested both in terms of produce (East European cereals/ West European manufactured goods) and of the relative intensity of 'work control': the amount of coercion applied to the labour force varied according to the structure of class relations within differing socio-economic formations. The *complementarity* of the modes of production, however, was ultimately determined by the universal desire to make the maximum profit on the world market. To this end 'coerced cash-crop labour' was used in the peripheral areas (on the feudal estates in the cereal-producing areas of Eastern Europe labour services were extracted after the introduction of the second serfdom, while slave labour was used on the Caribbean plantations and forced labour in the mines of the Latin-American *encomienda*). In the 'core zones', 'free labour' was the norm (small peasant craft producers and wage labourers), while in the 'semiperiphery' - above all in southern Europe - intermediate forms such as share-cropping (*mezzadria*) completed the system.

Considering the number of questions raised by Wallerstein, it would be wrong simply to condemn him for his being a neo-Marxian follower of Adam Smith, obsessed with the problems of exchange and circulation.[22] In facing up to the unresolved problems arising from the Dobb/Sweezy debate (the interaction of 'internal' and 'external' elements in emergent capitalism), he makes an important contribution, deserving of critical consideration and further research.

NOTES

1 I. Wallerstein, *The Modern World System: Capitalist Agriculture and the Origins of the European World Economy in the Sixteenth Century*, London 1974.
2 R. Brenner, 'Agrarian class structure and economic development in pre-industrial Europe', *Past and Present* 70, 1976, pp. 30–75.
3 R. Hilton, ed. and introd., *The Transition from Feudalism to Capitalism*, London 1976.
4 M. Dobb, *Studies in the Development of Capitalism*, London 1946 (paperback edn., London 1963), p. 32.
5 E. Hobsbawm, 'The Historian's Group of the Communist Party', in M. Cornforth, ed., *Rebels and their Causes: Essays in Honour of A.L. Morton*, London 1979, p. 23.
6 *Ibid.*, p. 37.
7 *Ibid.*
8 M. Dobb, 'From Feudalism to Capitalism', in Hilton, *op. cit.*, p. 167.
9 G. Bois, *Crise du Féodalisme. Économie rurale et demographie en Normandie Orientale du début du 14e siècle au milieu de 16e siècle*, Paris 1976; C. Lis and H. Soly, *Poverty and Capitalism in Pre-Industrial Europe*, Hassocks 1979.
10 Brenner, *op. cit.*, passim.
11 See especially R. Brenner, 'The origins of capitalist development: A critique of neo-Smithian Marxism', *New Left Review*, 104, 1977, pp. 25–92; and R. Brenner, 'Dobb on the transition from feudalism to capitalism', *Cambridge Journal of Economics*, 2, 1978, pp. 121–39.
12 Brenner, 'Agrarian class structure', p. 47.
13 *Ibid.*, p. 63.
14 *Ibid.*, pp. 68 ff.
15 *Ibid.*, p. 64.
16 J. de Vries, *The Dutch Rural Economy in the Gold Age 1500–1700*, New Haven 1974 and E. Hobsbawm, 'Capitalisme et agriculture: Les reformateurs écossais au 18e siècle', *Annales ESC*, 33, 1978, pp. 580–601.
17 H. Harnisch, 'Produktivkräfte und Produktionsverhältnisse in der Landwirtschaft der Magdeburger Börde von der Mitte des 18 Jhs. bis zum Beginn des Zuckerrübenanbaus in der Mitte der dreissiger Jahre des 19. Jhs.', in *Landwirtschaft und Kapitalismus: Zur Entwicklung der ökonomischen und sozialen Verhältnisse in der Magdeburger Börde vom Ausgang des 18. Jahrhunderts bis zum Ende des 1. Weltkrieges*, 1, ed. by H.J. Rach, Berlin 1978, pp. 67–173.
18 See Wallerstein, *op. cit.* and I. Wallerstein, *The Capitalist World Economy*, Cambridge 1978.
19 See 'Modernization: requiescat in pace', in Wallerstein, *The Capitalist World Economy*, pp. 132 ff.
20 Wallerstein, *The Modern World System*, p. 38.

21 A.G. Frank, *World Accumulation 1492-1789*, London 1978.
22 Brenner, 'The origins of capitalist development'.

16 PRIMITIVE ACCUMULATION REVISITED

Michael Ignatieff*

For Marx, there was no mystification more fundamental in classical political economy's account of the capitalist system than its silence about the violence, expropriation and forcible dispossession which accompanied its creation. Political economy simply took for granted a social order divided into capitalist and worker, landlord and landless agricultural labourer. It presented these as immemorial social categories and did so in order to portray the system as a natural one, requiring no justification. It could only do so, however, by consigning the real history of capitalist accumulation to oblivion. It could not ask how it was that peasants had been dispossessed of their land, artisans of their tools and looms, cottagers of their plots and gardens - yet this protracted expropriation, this primitive accumulation, had assembled the units of land and capital necessary for capitalist development and had forced labour into the fate of wage slavery. This primitive accumulation, achieved with the aid of the state's house of correction, its gibbet and its hangman, was the secret of capitalism's own making which the political economists could not admit.

The historical etymology of the idea of primitive accumulation before Marx has yet to be written, but we do know, from William Cobbett's historical writing, to take but one example, that the dynamics of dispossession were deeply understood in popular, radical consciousness two generations before *Capital*. We can now go further and ask whether primitive accumulation was even a secret for classical political economy. A recent article by Eric Hobsbawm has suggested that the idea, if not the term, primitive accumulation can be traced into the roots of political economy itself, in the writings of the Scottish

*Michael Ignatieff is an editor of *History Workshop Journal*; author of *A Just Measure of Pain* (a study of the eighteenth-century origins of the prison system) New York 1978; co-director of the King's College Cambridge project on *The Wealth of Nations and classical political economy*.

philosophers and improvers of the late eighteenth century. If
the full-blown political economy of Nassau Senior, MacCulloch
and Mill was studiously silent about the origins of capitalism, if
they had expunged history from the purposes of their science,
their Scottish forebears knew full well the part which
enclosure, eviction, and expropriation had played in the
creation of a capitalist social structure. Hobsbawm's article,
'Capitalism and Agriculture: The Scottish reformers of the 18th
century' (*Annales*, Summer 1978) interprets the Scottish
political economists, Smith, Anderson, Sinclair, Kames and
Hume, as theorists of development, as the first thinkers to set
out a model of the social preconditions of capitalist agriculture,
and the first to identify the social structure required if the
agricultural sector was going to be able to respond to the
demand stimulus of the urban manufacturing sector.

The Scottish theorists' interest in the mechanisms of
development emerged, Hobsbawm argues, out of their own
encounter with economic backwardness. After the Union, the
retarded character of lowlands farming became inescapably
evident, above all, in Scotland's failure, for forty years, to
exploit the new English markets for agricultural produce opened
up by the Union. The trauma of '15 and '45 also brought home
to lowland gentry society the necessity of 'civilising' the 'feudal'
and 'gothic' economy of the highlands, both to put an end to the
threat of the clans to lowland society and the Hanoverian
settlement, but also to open up highland fisheries, linen and
sheep farming to capitalist exploitation.

In Hobsbawm's argument, therefore, the *Wealth of Nations* is
to be read, first and foremost, as a 'manual of economic
development' written for a gentry elite of a provincial hinterland
seeking to catch up with the English metropolis and to
'civilise' the gothic backwardness at its borders. Crucial to both
of these goals, Hobsbawm maintains, was the conviction that it
was necessary to eliminate the small owner-occupier, the
communal tenantry of the run-rig system and the parcellisation
of land through sub-tenancies. In their place, the political
economists argued, must be substituted the classic social
structure of English farming - landlord, capitalist tenant farmer
and wage-labourer. This clear-sighted recognition of the
necessity of a 'primitive accumulation' makes the political
economists, in Hobsbawm's words, 'without doubt the first
example of a bourgeoisie being able to envisage its purposes
and role in precise terms.'

The legacy of this recognition, if such is the case, is heavy
with consequence. From the Scottish description of the process
of creating a capitalist agriculture, Marx' primitive accumulation
chapter draws his model of the social formation appropriate to
capitalist agriculture, and from this historically contingent
description, Lenin finds warrant for the 'historical necessity' of
forced collectivisation. That is to say, it is in 1775 that the
theoretical viability of a peasant road to modernity is

foreclosed, despite the evidence from France, Netherlands and Germany that industrial development can be sustained on the surpluses generated by peasant farming.

To this characteristically pungent thesis of Hobsbawm, we ought to ask, first of all, whether the social context of Scottish backwardness did constitute the *raison d'être* of the new political economy? Here we must distinguish, I think, between political economists like Hume and Smith, and agricultural 'improvers' like Sinclair and Anderson. While the 'high' theorists were unquestionably concerned with Scottish problems and while the 'improvers' were sophisticated theorists in their own right, the intellectual intentions of the two groups ought not to be conflated. Hume and Smith's intellectual project cannot be derived from their undoubted interest in the Scottish backwardness without jettisoning their moral philosophy, jurisprudence, history of civil society and theories of science and language. They insistently distinguished their essentially speculative project from the short-term political enthusiasms of projectors, and they self-consciously described their interests in metropolitan rather than parochial terms. Thus they were concerned with the Scottish context largely to the degree that it provided a mine of homely examples of the much larger process of the emergence of 'commercial society'. Book III of the *Wealth of Nations*, which has been mined by Brenner, Hobsbawm and others as a manual of economic development, is surely painted on a larger canvas. It is nothing less than an historical panorama of the emergence of commercial society in Europe since the fall of Rome. Calling the *Wealth of Nations* a manual of economic development is like calling *Capital*, volumes 1 through 3, an economics textbook – it is to take the part for the whole.

Making these points against Eric Hobsbawm is somewhat unfair, since his article is not intended as an interpretation of Scottish political economy, but as a contribution to 'the Brenner debate' about the social preconditions for capitalist development in agriculture. But others may be tempted to see his article as offering a new substitute for the shopworn conception of political economy as the ideology of the rising bourgeoisie, in this case, with a capitalist gentry elite standing in for the bourgeois leaven. This sociological explanation is inadequate, not because the problem of creating a capitalist agriculture within a backward society was not on the political economists' minds, but because they had so much more on their minds besides.

(Parenthetically, I would not speak for the 'relative autonomy' of theoretical reflection from sociological context in every case. Any general model of the sociology of knowledge must be altered, revised and thrown out if it doesn't work in specific historical instances. In some cases, for example the counter-revolutionary ideologists of the 1790s, Mrs Trimmer and Hannah More, were transparently and self-consciously the voices of their class, 'constructing' this voice in the process of

giving utterance to the platitudes of its social fear. The
political economists of Scotland, on the other hand, had the
institutional prestige of Scottish universities behind them and
were treated as leaders of polite society, indeed as the source
of their society's civic identity. Moreover, removed from the
parochial antinomies of British political debate, and living
through a post-'45 period of political stability, they could
develop a speculative discourse largely unconstrained by
polemical counter-pressure. From this position of relative social
autonomy and political detachment, their theorising, it seems to
me, could develop with a degree of speculative autonomy from
the prejudices, commonplaces and ideological exigencies of their
immediate social milieu.)

The second question about Eric Hobsbawm's argument is
whether the development economists, either the Scottish
agricultural reformers or of the classical economists, can be said
to insist on the legal forcible dispossession of the peasantry.
This is, after all, what primitive accumulation is all about. A
proper answer to this question would require an excursion into
the social history of Scottish agriculture as well as the enormous
output of 'improvement' literature in the eighteenth century. To
say the least, I am not qualified to speak on these subjects, but
I can at least express some doubts about the Hobsbawm
argument, based on my reading of the economic and social
history of Scottish farming. The first difficulty with the
Hobsbawm argument is that he doesn't specify what peasants
mean in their Scottish setting. As far as I can gather from T.C.
Smout and Ian White's work, by the end of the seventeenth
century there were few owner-occupier peasants, except the
'bonnet lairds' of the southwest in Galloway, and the small family
farms of Aberdeenshire and the northeast. Throughout the
seventeenth century there had been a very slow, uneven
shaking out of sub-tenants, and consolidation of tenancies,
resulting in the creation of a landlord, tenant, wage-labourer
social structure in many parts of the lowlands. The enclosure
acts of the 1690s both ratify a process underway for several
generations and encourage its extension. Thus, if the
transformation of Scottish agriculture is traced back into the
1660s, the emergence of an improvement literature in the 1740s
would then appear as an attempt to systematise and encapsulate
what had been going on, piecemeal, for some time. In the
Hobsbawm account, theories of development are seen as
ideological preparations of development; it is equally possible to
see them as ideological ratifications of a glacial process already
underway.

While the pace of agricultural change quickened after 1740,
both as a result of an emerging ideological consensus in favour
of improvement and in consequence of expanded market
opportunities, the actual emergence of a capitalist agriculture in
Scotland seems a markedly more peaceable transition than in the
southern counties of England. Apart from the 1724 uprising in

Galloway, there was relatively little collective resistance to the incremental shaking out of sub-tenancies, enclosing of pastures, and elimination of run-rig and other communal agricultural practices. The key victims of the process were the small sub-tenants, whose land was consolidated and re-leased on long terms to entrepreneurial tenants. As Tom Devine has shown, however, the smaller, mixed farms of lowland agriculture made more stable and continuous demand on labour than the highly seasonal wheat mining of southern English farming. As a consequence, Scottish lowland farmers did not 'casualize' their labour supply, preferring to board their farm servants or keep them in cottages to guarantee a steady year-round workforce. If the victims of Scottish 'primitive accumulation' were the sub-tenants, they did not descend into a casual labour pool, but into a stable employment relation which remained compatible with small-scale family cultivation of cottage plots.

The gradualist character of the Scottish transition is reflected in the development literature itself. Improvers like Sinclair were opposed to the casualisation of labour supply and argued that cottage labourers should always have 10-15 acre plots to supplement their cash incomes. Their accounts of setting up a capitalist farm focus on size of farm and length of lease, rather than on the legal dispossession of smallholders, for the very good reason that by the 1750s and 1760s, a social structure of peasant holders had ceased to exist.

Thus Smith's discussion of agricultural development simply took for granted the existence of a landlord-tenant-labourer social structure. He located its emergence, not in the immediate present, or in primitive accumulation of the discernible past, but much further back, in the emergence of luxury needs among the landlord class of medieval times. This taste for 'baubles and trinkets', awakened by contact with export goods traded by urban merchants, forced the feudal lords to convert a serf economy into one based on cash rentals. The mechanism of change in the conversion to capitalist agriculture was thus the emergence of new needs, aroused by contact with the urban market.

What Smith did not explain, as Robert Brenner has pointed out, is why landlords in England and Scotland should have gone on to initiate the shaking out of sub-tenants, the granting of long leases and investment in their own domain lands, instead of simply screwing down on their serfs and increasing their feudal revenues. Why, to use Brenner's useful distinction, did feudal landlords in Scotland, faced with new needs for money income, choose 'output maximization' as opposed to 'surplus maximization'? In Scotland, the extraordinary leverage over smallholders conferred by Scottish feudal law made a surplus maximisation strategy particularly easy. In fact, beginning sometime in the sixteenth and seventeenth century, lowland lords began to engage in an initially costly and unprofitable reorganization of social relations in order to increase output.

Market demand from the cities cannot explain this momentous
choice, for in Eastern Europe the pressure of market demand
from the Baltic grain trade was met by Polish landlords simply
by reimposing and increasing old feudal burdens. In Western
Europe, the landlord class appears to have chosen the route of
output maximization. If there were two equally 'rational' ways
for landlords to respond to new economic incentives, if indeed
one of these ways was counterintuitive (i.e., initially
unprofitable), we cannot 'derive' their response from the
incentive, without lapsing into economism. We must locate the
Scottish landlord's change of economic behaviour to some
broader transformation of their cultural outlook towards the
employment of land and labour. We must look for this shift in
mentalité, not in the 1750s, but much further back in the
sixteenth and seventeenth centuries, if we are to understand
the emergence of the agricultural surpluses which made
possible, not only Scotland's passage from backwardness, but
also the emergence of 'improvement' literature itself, and the
development of the secular science of society among the urban
elite.

FURTHER READING

Hobsbawm, E.H., 'Capitalisme et agriculture: les reformateurs
     écossais au XVIII siècle', *Annales*, Summer 1979.
Sinclair, John, *An Account of the System of Husbandry
     Adopted in the more improved districts of Scotland*,
     Edinburgh 1812.
Smith, Adam, *The Wealth of Nations*, Book III.
Smout, T.C., *A History of the Scottish People*, London 1972.
Whyte, E.N., *Agriculture and Society in 17th Century
     Scotland*, Edinburgh 1979.

Socialism

17 UTOPIAN SOCIALISM RECONSIDERED

Gareth Stedman Jones*

Utopian socialism has rarely been considered in its own right.
Its very title suggests a juxtaposition to a 'scientific' successor
and the general approach to the subject (see for example Cole
or Lichtheim) still bears the imprint first placed upon it in the
Communist Manifesto and *Anti-Dühring.*

Engels' interpretation of 'utopian socialism' in *Anti-Dühring*
is characterised by two features. (1) The highlighting of those
elements of the thought of St Simon, Fourier and Owen which
look forward to the positions of Marxist socialism. (2) The
definition of 'utopian socialism' from its inception as an ideology
corresponding to the aspirations of an immature class - the
proletariat. This line of approach has tended to be followed in most
general histories of socialism.

A reconsideration of 'utopian socialism' involves the removal
of the teleological and reductionist presuppositions that
characterised Engels's approach. Rather than pick out certain
elements of interest to a later quite different theorisation of
socialism, while relegating the rest to the individual
'eccentricity' or 'naiveté' of founding fathers (Fourier, Owen)
and rather than presuming its special affinity from the
beginning to the outlook of the working class, an attempt should
be made to re-establish the integrity of 'socialist' discourse in
its initial phase - without imposing anachronistically later
preoccupations upon it. (I use the word 'socialism' here for
convenience, the word only came into common parlance in the
1830s, when the theoretical work of St Simon, Owen and Fourier
was already virtually complete.)

I argue that despite manifest differences between the thought
of these theorists, there was by the late 1820s and early 1830s,
a sense of a common socialist platform, recognised both by
socialists themselves and by their opponents. The aim of the
rest of this chapter is to unearth the tacit and explicit
presuppositions that went together to make up this platform.
Most histories of socialism concentrate upon the differences
between particular socialist schools and their shifts from year to
year in strategy and tactics. I am interested in the reverse
problem - the underlying assumptions that distinguished
socialists from non-socialists, and what remained constant in

---

*Gareth Stedman Jones is university lecturer in history at
Cambridge and an editor of *History Workshop Journal.* Author
of *Outcast London,* London 1971; now working on a life of
Engels. The report of the discussion is by Hugh Cunningham.

these assumptions between the end of the Napoleonic Wars and the revolution of 1848. This continuity of shared assumption, I argue, is best located in the form of socialist reasoning rather than the changing content of particular schools of socialist thought.

I begin by comparing the first systematic works of the three founders – St Simon's *Letters from an Inhabitant of Genève* (1802), Fourier's *Theory of the Four Movements* (1808) and Owen's *New View* (1812–16), and show how they became the founding documents of the three major strands of a socialist movement in England and France up to the mid-1830s. I illustrate the difference between the theories by examining the disagreements between the adherents of the different tendencies when they began to enter into active competition with each other at the end of the 1820s. These disagreements did not cluster around rival analyses of the nature of capitalism, for it is an anachronism to assume that they were concerned with such an analysis; they focused, rather, around religious and philosophical issues (equality v hierarchy, human uniformity v differentiation of human types, the speed of social transformation, self-interest or 'devotion' (altruism) as the mainspring of human and socialist progress, the relationship between socialism and religion).

Beneath these disagreements, I try to uncover common presuppositions:
(1) All three theories start from the ambition to construct a new science of human nature.
(2) They focus on the moral/ideological sphere as the determining basis of all other aspects of human behaviour.
(3) The ambition is to make this sphere the object of an exact science which will resolve the problem of social harmony.
(4) Each identified pre-existing moral, religious and political *theory* (not class or state practices) as the principal obstacle to the actualisation of the newly discovered laws of harmony.
(5) No distinction is made between physical and social science, each had the ambition to be the Newton of the human/social sphere.

These similarities demarcate what is relatively constant in the many variants and hybrids of 'socialism' which sprang up between the 1820s and 1840s. They explain aspects of the political stance of socialism which looks aberrant, if interpreted as some reflex of a workers' movement, and they illuminate the extent of the gulf between pre-existing socialism and historical materialism as it developed from the mid-1840s.

I amplify this analysis by examining four major features of socialist analysis in the 1815–48 period.
(1) The consistent idealism of socialist conceptions of history.
(2) The absence of a specifically economic sphere of conflict in their diagnosis of the current situation.
(3) In the light of (1) and (2), their conception of the place of a working-class movement and class struggle.

(4) The peculiar intertwining between socialism and religion
which characterised the whole phenomenon of 'utopian socialism'.

1 *On history*
I emphasise the common tendency to model history on the
development of the individual human being - a tendency most
marked in St Simon whose new science of 'social physiology'
should be understood literally (e.g., the French Revolution as
the crisis of adolescence, force and exploitation as the gradual
diminution of childish aggression, etc.). I similarly show how an
idealism of scientific discovery dominates Owen's treatment of
the industrial revolution. In the case of Fourier, I emphasise
how it is the mode of love and amatory relations, rather than
production, which provides the determinant principle of each
historical phase.

2 *The lack of a specifically economic analysis*
My general point is that while nearly all socialist critiques were
agreed in defining competition or egoism as the essential feature
of the present, competition was seen as an ideological
phenomenon with economic effects, rather than an economic
phenomenon with ideological effects. Competition governed the
economy, but it does not arise from the economy, nor is it
confined to it. The social is a field of antagonism between man
and woman, rich and poor, Catholic and Protestant, nation and
nation, man and man. Competition is only the most striking
manifestation of how human potentiality in every sphere is
thwarted by institutions and ideologies which promote
individualism. Moreover, no variety of socialism in the period
questions the wage relation itself. Since there is an axiomatic
assumption of natural harmony between nature and human
nature, the problem of antagonism and evil is displaced away
from the sphere of production (the sphere of the interaction
between man and nature) into the spheres of circulation,
distribution, politics, force, ideology and morality (the spheres
of the interaction between man and man through the medium of
humanly created institutions). The socialist critique of political
economy precisely concentrated upon emphasising the
impossibility of isolating a distinct economic sphere.

3 (a) *On the working class*
The attitude of early theory towards the worker was distant and
paternalist. Both Owen and St Simon before the late 1820s focus
primarily upon their lack of education. It is the middle class
(when not the sovereign himself) as the enlightened section of
the population which is most likely to form the vanguard of
progress towards socialism (because of its educational level).
After 1830, the working class is seen in a more hopeful light.
Working-class enthusiasm for co-operation could show them to be
harbingers of a purer morality (in Owen's view); or more widely,
workers and women as the most oppressed groups were likely to

adopt the socialist cause, as slaves had led the movement towards Christianity. Since the coming of Christianity was the main allegorical model for the coming of socialism, however, a movement of the oppressed at the bottom of society did not exclude the possibility of its ultimate promulgation from the top (the emperor Constantine).

3 (b) *On class struggle*
This, by the whole character of socialist theory, was generally regarded in a negative light. Socialism was the cause of humanity, the general harmony between each and all. Class struggle was part of the phenomenon of competition, the striving for particular and individual material interests. There were those, after 1830, however, pulled by the weight of a working-class movement, to attribute a more positive significance to the workers' struggle. Such struggle could be positively evaluated in socialist terms if the material struggle was shown at a more profound level to have an ideal and universal (rather than particular) meaning. I analyse some of the writings of Leroux and the young Marx to illustrate this point.

The problem of knowing what significance to attribute to class struggle was closely connected with the problem of 'devotion' versus material self-interest as a trigger to action. I show how this problem was resolved in an ideal and universal direction by the Owenites (with the aid of phrenology), by the St Simonians (through their division of history into organic and critical epochs); and, finally, the creative disagreement it introduced into the first discussions of German socialists in the early 1840s - provoked by the argument of Lorenz von Stein (the first major source of information about French socialism in Germany in 1842) that communism depended not upon the power of its ideas, but the needs of the stomach. I show how this idea was treated by Marx, Engels and Hess in their early writings.

(4) *The problem of religion*
This problem is not satisfactorily solved in secondary sources. Most often, (a) religion is treated as an external embellishment to the real secular core of socialist thought (Stein, Engels, Cole, Lichtheim); or (b) it is seen as a colouration given to the socialism of the period by the still semi-secularised aspirations of its constituency - a sort of modernisation theory of utopian socialism (see the otherwise excellent studies of the Owenites by J.F.C. Harrison or the Cabetists by C. Johnson); or (c) socialism is treated as the last phase of a Christian millennial tradition which had surfaced with Thomas Münzer in the sixteenth century (Henri Desroches).

Against (a) I argue on the general grounds outlined above that one must attempt to analyse the socialist theory of the period as an integral whole and not arbitrarily dissolve it into forward-looking and redundant elements. Against (b) I argue that the religiosity of the socialism of the period cannot be satisfactorily explained in sociological terms. While a religious background may indeed illuminate the religious tone of the aspirations and language of many socialist supporters, it will not adequately explain the paradox of the founding theorists themselves - from free-thought backgrounds, cool and detached in their discussion of religious phenomena, yet also comparing their status to that of Christ and explicitly or implicitly claiming divine inspiration for their thought. I argue that religiosity was not extrinsic but inherent in the structure of early socialist thought. It was not personal megalomania or sociological predisposition that led to a religion of socialism but the very nature and object of the thought itself. Since socialism claimed to be a science of human nature, and to have solved the mystery of social harmony and universal happiness, it impinged directly upon the territory of pre-existing moral theory - *par excellence* the Christian church. Since the founders of socialism were deists and regarded the newly discovered laws of human nature as the laws of God, they could not but imply a privileged intimacy with the mechanics of the divine. Christ could then be seen as the ancestor of their science, disallowed by God the father, in Fourier's words, from expressing except in 'parabolic form' the true laws of human nature and thus the solution to human happiness which had to be the product of human free will. Against (c) therefore, I argue that utopian socialism was indeed a religious movement, but not in any meaningful sense a Christian one. It was a new humanist religion, whose gospel was the new science. Socialism possessed no critique of the state and no conception of a capitalist economy. It attacked not the practices of the state or the ruling class, but the false or ignorant or alienated theory, on which it presumed the practices were based. Its yardstick of judgment was its knowledge of the true nature of man, which excluded original sin and the laws and coercion based upon it. Its true enemy was the church which had distorted Christ's original message, and in practice as well, socialists fought their battles more consistently against the church than the state or a class of capitalists.

Once 'utopian socialism' is redefined as a new 'science' of man and by the same token a new religion of human emancipation, much that otherwise looks incoherent, inconsistent or irrelevant in the socialist story can be set back into place.

DISCUSSION

Utopian socialism and economic analysis
A number of speakers questioned Stedman Jones's emphasis on utopian socialism as an ideological phenomenon. Patricia Hollis argued that by the early 1830s Owenism was a bran tub from which many different things might be taken. The shift in

emphasis in thinking from pauperism to unemployment suggests a complex inter-relationship between economy and society in the development and thinking of the movement. Rosalind Delmar said that in Fourier there is a critique of commerce as leading to waste, over-production and economic crisis. Peter Sedgwick argued that, compared to Marx, there may be a lack of emphasis on an economic base, but if the starting point was French Revolutionary liberalism then one might be more struck by the extent of economic analysis within utopian socialism. Andrew Spooner suggested that another way of looking at the context of utopian socialism was to compare their utopia with the rival utopia of the classical political economists in which there was a vision of wealth widely distributed. Stedman Jones replied that the Owenites did indeed regard themselves as materialists, and in eighteenth-century terms they were. But they did not have a materialist conception of history, nor is there in utopian socialism any sense of an economic structure which is the basis for human society and behaviour.

The relationship between utopian and scientific socialism
John Brixton commented that the New Life socialism of the later nineteenth-century cast some doubt on the notion that there was a connection between the immaturity of the working class and the formation of utopian socialism. Denise Riley looked at the relationship between science and socialism, and in particular at the way in which an argument which could be described as 'scientific' acquired respectability. She noted how 'scientific' anthropology had had a marked impact on socialism. Bob Young was impressed by the continuities between utopian and scientific socialism, and noted how many writers on society, not only socialists but also conservatives, used physiological metaphors.

Theory and practice
Eddie Frow urged us to look at Owenism in practice, and at the context in which it flourished. In Manchester and Salford the first Owenist Hall was opened in 1835, followed in 1840 by the largest Owenite Hall in the country. Yet by the end of the decade Owenism had been destroyed. Many skilled artisans, he argued, took some of their ideas from Owen, but they also had other frameworks of reference.

Feminism and men
Delmar noted that much of the most ardent feminist argument came from men, for example Fourier and William Thompson. Barbara Taylor thought that part of the reason for this might lie in the pressure imposed on men by current notions of masculinity. Masculinity was indeed at the heart of the ideology of competition against which the utopian socialists pitted themselves.

Feminism and socialism
There was considerable interest in and speculation about the kinds of conditions in which feminists can be heard in socialist movements. Alex Hall suggested the need to compare different countries and movements. Ruth Frow noted that there was upsurge of feminism up to the 1840s but then a decline. She linked this with the 1842 strike in England; skilled artisan trade unionists played a leading role in this strike, and afterwards concentrated on the organisation of themselves as skilled unionists and ceased to accept feminism. Barbara Taylor noted that there were conflicts within utopian socialism about the role of women, for example within St Simonianism between proletarian women and civil servant leaders, and in Owenism about marriage. There was, however, little open confrontation on the issue except in the trade union movement where a tiny number of women took a very militant stand on women's rights to organise. Certainly within utopian socialism women played a full role, for example in education. This was recognised to be one of the most important themes opened up by the session.

Marriage
Miriam Steiner argued that the romanticisation of the early socialist movement presented dangers both to the working class and to women, for it could be used to subvert their needs. In some ways, she argued, a rigid market and contract model of marriage offered more egalitarian potential than utopian socialism. Anne Bamfield doubted this, and drew attention to the ambiguous remarks on the issue in the *Communist Manifesto* and to Mary Wollstonecraft's demonstration of the way legal contracts broke down.

FURTHER READING

Cole, G.D.H., *A History of Socialist Thought: The forerunners, 1789-1815*, London 1953.
Engels, Frederick, *Socialism, Utopian and Scientific*, in Marx-Engels, *Selected Works*, Moscow 1977.
Evans, David Owen, *Social Romanticism in France 1830-1848*, Oxford 1951.
Fourier, C., *La Théorie des Quatre Mouvements*, in *Ouvres de Charles Fourier*, Paris 1968.
Gustave d'Eichtal: a French sociologist looks at Britain . . . in 1828, Manchester 1977.
Harrison, J.F.C., *Robert Owen and the Owenites in Britain and America*, London 1969.
Iggers, G.C., trans. and ed., *Doctrine of Saint-Simon, an exposition, 1st year, 1828-9*, New York 1958.
Johnson, Christopher, *Utopian Communism in France, Cabet and the Icarians, 1839-1851*, Ithaca 1974.
Lichtheim, George, *The Origins of Socialism*, London 1969.

Ouvres de Saint-Simon, ed. by Olinde Rodrigues, Paris 1841.
Owen, Robert, *A New View of Society*, ed. by G.D.H. Cole,
    Everyman ed.
Owen, Robert, *Report to the County of Lanark*, ed. by V.
    Gattrell, Harmondsworth 1969.
Pankhurst, R.K.P., *The Saint Simoniens, Mill and Carlyle*,
    London 1957.

18 COMMUNIST PARTY HISTORY

Perry Anderson*

TYPES OF LITERATURE

Writing in communist parties is extensive, in any perspective.
The character and quality of the literature varies greatly, and
some indication of the main categories may be helpful to
introduce any discussion of current problems in the field. I
should say at the outset that I will confine myself to Europe,
not - obviously - because that's the only interesting or
important continent, but simply to set some sort of manageable
limit on the topic. The literature on European communism is not
only quite exceptionally large; it is also unusually varied both
in intellectual quality and political orientation - a variety that
stems directly from the centrality in our century of the
international communist movement as the focal point of conflicts
between capital and labour. So you get great interest focused
from the camp of revolution and from the camp of counter-
revolution, and histories of CPs vary accordingly.
    Approximately, five main types of work can be distinguished:
1 Memoirs - either in traditional autobiographical form, or more
recently, in collective taped form. These obviously give in
principle the greatest subjective feel of the communist
experience, but vary between the official-anecdotal
reminiscences of, say, Pollitt, Longo or Kuusinen, and more
carefully composed accounts of a life of militancy, like that under
way from Amendola. Gornick's recent book (*The Romance of*

---

*Perry Anderson is editor of *New Left Review*. Author of
Passages from Antiquity and *Lineages of the Absolutist State*,
London 1975; *Considerations on Western Marxism*, London 1976
and *Arguments within English Marxism*, London 1980.

American Communism) is a popular attempt at a collective
tapestry.
2 Official histories – either uncritical or semi-critical.
Klugmann's volumes on the British Communist Party are the
unambitious local example; Spriano's massive work on the Italian
Communist Party is unique in its documentation, coverage and
intellectual standard. So far this is a rare genre, although some
of the Eastern European parties are now starting to produce
interesting works of this type (e.g. the Polish Party history,
which uses undisclosed archival material).
3 Independent left histories – some by former communists, some
by unattached socialists or Marxists. Many of the most acute
works in the field we owe to this category. It includes
Macfarlane's book on the British Communist Party up to 1929,
Weber's work on the KPD in the 1920s, Kriegel's early work on
the French Communist Party, Broué's book on the 'German
Revolution', and – above all – Claudin's study of the
Comintern-Cominform epoch as a whole, the work of a former
leading functionary in the Spanish Communist Party.
4 Works of liberal scholarship (in the best sense) – in other
words, studies by professional historians without overt political
allegiances, produced in a conventional way within the academy.
These include two of the best single books in the whole
literature – Rothschild's great study of the Bulgarian Party
before the war, and Angress's book on the KPD in 1921–3.
Also notable is the huge work on the Czechoslovak Party in
1964–8 by Skilling, remarkable for its wealth of documentation.
Other samples of the genre, however, are often mediocre misses
at crucial subjects e.g. Brower on the French Communist Party
and the Popular Front.
5 Cold War monographs – far the most numerous genre, spawned
by the specialised institutions and grants for communism-
watching. Written in a frankly counter-revolutionary spirit for
the most part, their quality too is most uneven. None are
without interest, and some succeed rather well in their limited
objectives. Volumes that are poor by any standards would
include Dziewanowski (Polish Party), Kousalas (Greek),
Avakumovich (Yugoslav pre-Tito), Ionescu (Rumanian).
However, Zinner's study of the Czech Communist Party is a
solid piece of work, as is Tökes's book on the Hungarian
Commune. This category also include two brilliant and
fundamental studies – Borkenau's pre and post-war surveys of
European communism as a whole, which stand alone in their
combination of qualities to this day.
    Generally, then, if we restrict ourselves for reasons of space
to Europe, there is a wide, if various literature. Most of the
national sections of the former Third International have at least
one, and often much more, study devoted to them. The major
gaps to date appear to be the two parties most recently
emerged from the underground in the West (Spain and Portugal),
plus possibly the Hungarian Party in the East.

PROCEDURAL PROBLEMS

None of the works cited above, including even the best, really approximate to the full criteria one should pose for a Marxist history of any given communist party. Taking it for granted that attainment of these would be a kind of asymptotic limit, it is still useful to note the three basic requirements for adequate historical reconstruction of a given CP:

1 Internal political trajectory: in other words, an accurate account of the membership, organisation, leadership, tendencies and policies of the party, as a unit of analysis. Most of the existing literature starts off by looking at the composition of the party, its organisation, its leadership, its functional struggles, its programmes and policies, its changes of line, as a methodological base-line. Characteristically, such literature runs up against the problems of archives, since, except in the case of the official party histories, communist parties do not normally make their internal records freely available to researchers, particularly in the very sensitive period running from the formation of the Third International up to the morrow of the Second World War. This is still an acute problem today – one that becomes a virtually absolute barrier to detailed study of the history of the Comintern itself. The Comintern archives are centralised in Moscow, and even loyal historians from fraternal parties, not only in Western Europe but also in Eastern Europe, are not permitted to examine them freely by the Soviet authorities. What they can do at most is study those documents which set out the national side of the historical correspondence between, say, the Hungarian or Rumanian or Italian party, and the Comintern. But they cannot use the documents from the side of the international organisation itself. That remains a great fetter on modern historical research into this area. Within the national framework itself, on the other hand, this restriction does not prevail, and there is now one example, namely Spriano's, of a party history based on really thorough archival research. Curiously, however, the result in this case is a rather top-heavy historical approach, in which nearly all the attention is concentrated on the debate within a narrow group of party leaders. Admittedly, in Italy this is in itself a fascinating subject. We see the formation and development of the party, first under the leadership of Bordiga, then under Gramsci, then after the imprisonment of Gramsci under Togliatti. But the cost of Spriano's immensely detailed and meticulous tracking of the shifts and changing opinions and alliances at the top of the party is that the reader gets rather little sense of the social history of the rank and file of the Italian Communist Party over that period. That is less the case in the later volumes devoted to the Resistance but is a quite acute omission in the earlier ones.

2 National balance of forces: in other words, at once the relation of the CP concerned to the working class *as a whole*

(not just those enlisted in its ranks), as well as to other classes
and groups (intellectuals are often important as a sub-category),
and the relationship of bourgeois and other intermediate strata
to the Communist Party, and among themselves. The totality of
these relationships will be immersed in certain specific traits of
a national political culture, affecting all forces, very often.
None of these should be neglected.

Any decent history of a communist party must take seriously
a Gramscian maxim, that to write a history of a political party
is to write the history of the society of which it is a component
from a particular monographic standpoint. In other words, no
history of a communist party is finally intelligible unless it is
constantly related to the national balance of forces of which the
party is only one moment, and which forms the context in which
it must operate. This sense tends to be critically lacking in
much of the best existing literature. To take the example again
of Spriano's book, it tells one an enormous amount about the
Italian Communist Party in the period of its formation but does
not really explore the question in any depth whether there was
a genuine chance of an Italian socialist revolution after the First
World War. One might say it does not set the Italian Communist
Party in scientific proportion. All other political factors and
forces, whether they be social democracy, fascism, liberalism,
the army or the church appear in too fleeting and subsidiary
role within the main narrative to yield a satisfactory overall
result. Paradoxically, it can happen that books which are
inferior at the level of the internal history of a party are rather
better at providing at least some elements of the national
political context. In the case of the British Communist Party,
for instance, while MacFarlane's is much the better study in
most respects – more honest, more thorough, more insightful
about the early history of the British Communist Party – it is
also weaker than Klugmann's in its treatment of the relationship
of the British party either to the Labour Party or to the British
state. Klugmann's book has more of a real sense of what was
going on in national politics in the early 1920s which he did try
to integrate into his account of the early history of the British
party, where MacFarlane remains very sketchy.

Still on this plane, one of the besetting sins of a lot of
communist party historiography is a failure to take seriously, or
to weave into the picture adequately, what the non-communist
sections of the national working class are feeling and doing.
Nearly all sections of the Third International were formed by and
large as breakaways from prior organisations of the Second
International, or if they weren't, they were formed in rivalry
to existing sections of it, as in England. But normally speaking,
after the critical period of formation, their histories tend to be
compartmentalised unduly from what is going on in the
juxtaposed camp of social democracy. A glaring example is the
otherwise meritorious book by Broué on the German Communist
Party in the early 1920s (*La Révolution Allemande*). In general,

Weimar communism is incomprehensible unless understood in tandem with the *concurrent* development of the SPD, too often treated as a dead dog intellectually after 1918. Another characteristic failing of many communist party histories is that they tend to ignore large sections of the working class, which – particularly in the interwar period – were either a-political or apathetic or else formed part of the electoral constituency of bourgeois parties, whether liberal, conservative or catholic. Again, the relationship of any given communist party to the national intelligentsia is a further variable that remains little explored or understood. The forms of this relationship are subject to very wide variations. In Germany the Communist Party failed to connect with the very rich left culture of the Weimar period. In Britain, relatively large numbers of intellectuals rallied to the banner of the British Communist Party under the impact of the Depression and of fascism, producing a communist intelligentsia which was talented, active, often illustrious, but most of it fundamentally divorced from the major political life of the party itself, playing little or no role in the determination of policy, if anything, hived off as a specialised area of external prestige in the Popular Front period, and left rather underpoliticised. Much the same pattern seems to have occurred in France. It contrasts very strikingly with the record of the Italian Communist Party, where from the start the majority of the party leadership was itself recruited from the intelligentsia. There have been few purely working-class leaders, without higher education, in the history of the Italian party, down to the present day, when a trade union secretary in the CGIL (the left-wing Italian TUC) may be a university professor by background without any experience of the shop floor. A pattern of this kind – a socialist movement led by intellectuals rather than workers – is, of course, much more typical of underdeveloped countries. A classical case in point is Albania, the most backward society in Europe, where the successful revolutionary movement was led very largely by teachers in a country which had a very high rate of illiteracy. Why Italy should have reproduced something of this configuration down to the 1970s is not at all clear.

Finally, the difficult yet inescapable questions of national 'tradition' and 'culture' have to be confronted. The major pioneer here was certainly Borkenau, an ex-Comintern functionary with an unrivalled sense of national differentials. But the most fruitful thinker to have written on this subject in recent years is Hobsbawm, whose short essays on the particular temper of German, French, British and Spanish communism/anarchism in *Revolutionaries* are worth volumes.

INTERNATIONAL FRAMEWORK

The third essential level at which the history of any communist party must, of course, be studied, is international. The Comintern remains to date a sociologically unique phenomenon, as an organisation which commands an absolute loyalty, a disciplined fidelity, amongst its constituent national sections.

It was a condition of membership of the International that the policies determined by it were followed. Thus, each party in Europe lacked ultimate political autonomy in its major strategic orientations. That form of iron international discipline is in many ways an embarrassing memory for the communist parties of Western Europe today, which tend to advertise very strongly the merits of their own national road. Therefore some of the official histories have been tempted to play down massive interventions by the Soviet bloc in the early life of these parties. Eric Hobsbawm has criticised quite sharply James Klugmann's history of the British party for simply writing out, or affecting to ignore, the role of the Third International.

On the other hand, it is also necessary not to bend the stick too far in the other direction, that of the characteristic Cold War histories, which tend to present each national communist party as if it were just a puppet whose limbs were manipulated mechanically by strings pulled in Moscow. That was never the case. In a number of famous historical watersheds we can see a complex dialectic between the international and the national determinants of party policies, that have to be very delicately weighed against each other. The Third Period, when the communist parties in the late 1920s were rushing into battle against the social-democratic organisations in their own countries as the main enemy, as forms of social fascism, is a good example. This was generally a disastrous episode in the history of the international communist movement. Now it is perfectly true that the major theorists of the notion of social fascism were leaders of the Russian Communist Party (although with some precursors in the PCI), so it is quite easy to present it as if it was a purely Soviet confection. Yet in at least two cases, namely Britain and Germany, there were indigenous national dynamics leading very strongly in the same direction in the later 1920s. In Britain the bitter feelings of betrayal at the role of the TUC and Labour Party leaderships in the General Strike gave a certain plausible colour to the extreme radicalisation of the great left turn of 1928, which was also accelerated by generational shifts. The Young Communist League was one of the most important driving forces for the triumph of the Third Period line in the British Communist Party. So, too, in the case of the German party, it is necessary to remember that the slogan of social fascism was lent a sort of plausibility by the vivid national memories on the left of the assassination of Rosa Luxemburg and Karl Liebknecht by the Freikorps at the behest of a social democratic Minister of

War. Social Democrats had proved themselves capable of political murder and repression, while the dimensions of the Nazi threat were not yet so visible in 1928 - before the onset of the Depression. It is against that background that the enthusiasm of the German Communist Party for the Third Period should be seen. By contrast in France, where the SFIO (Socialist Party) had never been a governing party, it had very little national impetus behind it. Although there again elements in the youth tried to stoke up ultra-left attacks on other sections of the labour movement, as a line it never really got off the ground - thereby leading to a disastrous contradiction of the party.

The same sort of analytical problem recurs if we look at the quite opposite period of the Popular Front. It remains an interesting and moot question how far Popular Front policy originated in France itself in the period 1934-5, and if so who was really responsible for the sudden change in the attitude of the French Communist Party towards the SFIO, which paved the way for anti-fascist unity. In this case, there was a particularly able, intelligent and decisive Comintern delegate, Jeno Fried, a Czech communist later hanged as an imperialist spy in Czechoslovakia after the Second World War, who was advising, directing, and playing a central role behind the scenes in the affairs of the French Communist Party. There is a certain amount of evidence to suggest that the idea of the Popular Front, with its very strong national patriotic overtones, was actually the brainchild of this non-French militant. The French party is not very anxious to explore this sensitive question, for understandable reasons; the episode still awaits a real clarification. An analogous question, if with very different overtones, is the exact attitude of the Spanish Communist Party during the Civil War to the extremely repressive and divisive policies adopted towards the anarchist movement and POUM in Catalonia in 1937. Much controversy surrounds the question of whether or not the Spanish Political Bureau itself wanted to resist the worst aspects of the repression, which was certainly teleguided by the Russians, or to what extent it was itself responsible for it. The matter remains to be resolved.

At the bottom of the issues of the relationship between the international allegiances and national destinies of the European communist parties in the period running from the 1920s up to at least the mid-1960s, is the more general question - an enigmatic and unanswered one - of what is the nature of a Stalinist party in a society in which that party enjoys no form of police coercion, administrative power, or any other form of physical duress over its membership. The case of the term in ordinary political vocabulary suggests a direct equation between the CPSU, which commanded state power and exercised massive police repression both within its own ranks and against all other social forces by the 1930s, and mass communist parties in the West before or soon after the Second World War. Yet clearly these are quite different political structures. Why was it that parties which were manifestly and profoundly undemocratic in their internal organisation, and which remained associated with the Soviet Union over a long period when it was the object of a constant barrage of very effective bourgeois propaganda, much of it based on historical facts, nevertheless won and kept the freely consented allegiance of the vanguard sectors of their national working class?

THE TRANSFER OF ALLEGIANCES

That brings us to the final set of problems – the most tragic substantive issue posed by the history of the European communist parties. The first of these is the question of what might be called the general transfer of allegiances itself. The communist parties of the Third International were formed, in their great majority, as breakaways from the Second International. In a short period of time, running approximately from 1919 to, say, 1922 or 1923, something historically very rare occurred in many European countries; there was a transfer of loyalties within large sections of the working class from one political organisation and programme to another. That process is something that has later proved very difficult to repeat. We encounter here the phenomenon of the fixity of a social and political identification among large groups of working men and (if to a lesser extent) women. It is as if some short periods of historical time have a peculiar privilege, in forming aspirations, identities and loyalties, which can then endure, apparently regardless of external circumstances, for long periods thereafter, during which time other groups – of Marxists or socialists have often tried in vain to alter these orientations and allegiances once more. In the history of the international communist movement, there are two what I would call 'founding moments' in which a mass transfer of allegiances successfully operated. One runs from about 1919 up to 1922/3; it is in that period that the majority of the French Socialist Party voted to join the Third International, the majority of the Independent Social Democratic Party in Germany, an effective majority of Czech Social Democracy, and a significant minority of the Italian Socialist Party. The same process failed to 'take', of course, in the USA and Great Britain, where in each case much smaller communist parties emerged, which failed to gain anything like the mass influence of the major parties on the European continent. It is significant that the same sort of historical polemic has developed over those two national parties. In the USA the historian James Weinstein has blamed the whole attempt to create a communist party for the collapse of pre-war American socialism, which had been a fairly substantial movement, up to at least 1916, if not later. He argues that the intervention of the Third International in effect killed off an indigenous US socialism as a major force within the working class. In Britain Walter

Kendall's distinguished study of the British revolutionary movement between 1900 and 1920, an admirable book in many ways, nevertheless also sees Moscow gold as a corrupting force that spoiled the fair prospects of British socialism after the First World War. Neither case do I think particularly persuasive.

Turning to the structure of this first founding moment itself, its success in Europe was determined by two massive historical events. One of these was the First World War, a demonstration on a gigantic scale of the practical consequences of capitalism and imperialism, and of the complicity of the major social democratic parties with them. The result was a profound disillusionment and radicalisation among major sections of the more politicised workers after the First World War. At the same time the ranks of social democracy were typically also filled up from the reservoir of hitherto unpoliticised workers; so there was a dual movement in this period – social democratic parties and trade unions often grew very rapidly, even as large sections of former social democratic movements switched over to the communist movement. Of course, the second overdetermining force in this founding moment was the October Revolution itself – which was the positive demonstration of the possibilities of a socialist future. There was thus the combination of a deep discrediting of capitalism through the experience of 1914-18 and an inspiring contrast to it in the Russian Revolution of 1917. The impact of communism as an organised political doctrine – an entirely new sort of theory to the mass of the European labour movement – was to provide the ideological cement for the transfer of allegiance that had effectively occurred in 1917-21. All kinds of characteristic difficulties soon followed. Most of the European parties contracted in size in the late 1920s and early 1930s. In the last years before the war the French party was able to achieve a new breakthrough after having fallen back severely into a minority position in the French labour movement. The Spanish party, a hitherto insignificant force in Spain, registered a somewhat artificially rapid growth during the Civil War. But by and large few basic changes marked this period.

The second real founding moment occurs in the Second World War, from about 1942 to 1945, which witnessed a further great wave of communisation within popular and labour movements, especially in Central and Eastern Europe. This is the period in which the Yugoslav party, the Czechoslovakia party, the Albanian party and the Greek party, all suddenly grew from small or modest pre-war starting points to hegemonic national forces. It is also the period in which the Italian party is transformed from a cadre into a mass party for the first time, and in which the French party becomes the unquestionably leading organisation of the working class in France. Even the smaller parties, as James Hinton has pointed out in the case of the British party, acquired a scale and influence which they never possessed before. That second founding moment also comprised two components which were in some ways very similar to the first. One was the impact of German occupation and popular resistance to it – the impact of political domination and repression by a foreign army, which made the national motif so important for the whole colouration of this second wave of communism. The ordeal of Nazi conquest was then overdetermined by the central role in the liberation of Europe from it played by the Red Army. Stalingrad in 1942 performs the homologous function to Petrograd in 1917. Both the negative demonstration of Nazi rule and the positive demonstration of Soviet victories over it produced once again a big mass shift leftwards. The mechanisms of that change in popular allegiance remain vitally interesting for any socialist concerned with the stability of the pattern of allegiances within the European working class in the decades thereafter.

A second historical question of great moment is the role of the communist parties in Eastern Europe after the Second World War. This is often presented as a totally artificial growth, leading to a surrogate socialism imposed upon the region at the point of Red Army bayonets. Such an image is very misleading, partly because Eastern Europe is much more geographically and historically differentiated than is often assumed in Western Europe. In the four southernmost countries of Eastern Europe, the Balkan states proper – namely Yugoslavia, Albania, Greece and Bulgaria – there were genuine popular revolutions, defeated in the case of Greece only by massive outside intervention, and aided in the case of Bulgaria by rather less intervention. Even in the four northern countries, the communist parties emerged from the war much stronger than their social democratic counterparts (the exception is Hungary), approaching hegemony on the left even without the presence of Soviet troops, while capitalism was weak in the region as a whole. It is a very interesting question what purely endogenous balance of forces would have resulted here. In the event the whole political process was enormously complicated and compromised by the administrative and military presence of the Russian occupying forces. But even within the constraints of the onset of the Cold War, it is still necessary to adjudicate carefully the pressures within national politics as against the international pressures from the Soviet Union.

Finally, there is the classical issue of those junctures of major crisis where the policy adopted by a communist party appears to have been disastrous, mistaken or at least missed crucial opportunities. This area raises perhaps more sharply than any other for the historian the question which has been posed so eloquently by Edward Thompson, of historical agency, for political parties, are, by definition, organisations that cast themselves as historical actors in the full sense, in a way that neither states nor even churches customarily have done. In the twentieth century political parties present themselves as collective agents *par excellence* – endowed with a high degree of volition, intention and clearly articulated goals. Thus it is no surprise that there are a number of famous moments in the history of European communist parties, around which a large polemical literature has accrued, focussing on the question of whether the party should have adopted this or that policy. Was a German revolution possible in October 1923? Could the German Communist Party have avoided the triumph of Nazism, or even perhaps ushered in a socialist revolution in Germany at the beginning of the 1930s, by pursuing genuine unity with social democracy? Would even the unity of the two workers' parties in Germany in 1931-3 have been sufficient to stop Nazism? Were the French and Italian parties right to renounce any prospect of popular power in 1945-6; even if they were, could they have tried to win more advanced positions for the working class within capitalism after the war? Was a socialist revolution possible in France in May-June 1968, and if so what strategy should the French Communist Party have adopted to accomplish one? More recently still, how ought the role of the Portugese Communist Party in the summer of 1975 - when arguably the best single chance of a socialist revolution in Western Europe in this century was spectacularly missed - be judged?

These are some of the most burning questions of European communist party history: as can be seen, they take us right up to the present. The kind of historical imagination needed to tackle them is best evidenced in Claudin's book, which for all its distance from the texture of events, constantly tries to keep open a sense of realistic alternatives, at every major conjuncture in the development of the communist movement. It will also be noticed that every time a key turning-point is in view, it becomes obvious how essential an *overall* evaluation of the balance of forces, national and international, is to any materialist account of a given communist party. There can be no such thing as a satisfactory 'internal' party history.

FURTHER READING

Angress, Werner, *Stillborn Revolution: the Communist bid for power in Germany, 1921-1923*, London 1972.
Dziewanowski, Marian Kamid, *The Communist Party of Poland: An outline history*, Cambridge, Mass., 1959.
Galli, Giorgi, 'Italian Communism' in *Communism in Europe*, ed. by William E. Griffith, 1959.
Klugmann, James, *History of the Communist Party of Great Britain*, London 1968.
Kriegel, Annie, *Aux origines du communisme française*, Paris 1964, 2 vols.
Macfarlane, L.J., *The British Communist Party: its origin and development*, London 1966.
Kousalas, Dimitrios, *Revolution and Defeat: The story of the Greek Communist Party*, London 1965.

Skilling, Harold G., *Communism, Nationalism and
    Internationalism: Eastern Europe after Stalin*, Toronto 1964.
Spriano, Paolo, *Storia del partitide Communisto Italiano*, Turin
    1967.
Wood, Neal, *Communism and British Intellectuals*, London 1959.
Avakumovic, Ivan, *History of the Communist Party of
    Yugoslavia*, Aberdeen 1964.
Rothschild, Joseph, *The Communist Party of Bulgaria: Origins
    and development*, London 1959.
Tőkes, Rudolf, *Bela Kun and the Hungarian Soviet Republic*,
    New York 1957.
Ionescu, Ghita, *Communism in Rumania: 1944-1962*, London 1964.
Brower, Daniel R., *The New Jacobins: The French Communist
    Party and the Popular Front*, New York 1968.
Zinner, Paul E., *Communist Strategy and Tactics in
    Czechoslovakia, 1918-48*, London 1963.
Claudin, F., *The Communist Movement, from Comintern to
    Cominform*, Harmondsworth 1975.
Broué, P., *Revolution en Allemagne, 1917-23*, Paris 1977.

Feminism

19 SOCIALIST FEMINISM: UTOPIAN OR SCIENTIFIC?

Barbara Taylor*

Exactly a century ago Engels consigned the ideas and hopes of
the first British socialists, the Owenites, to a Utopian pre-
history of scientific socialism, a period of 'crude theories' and
'grand fantasies' which had to be superseded by historical
materialism before the communist struggle could be waged on a
sound, scientific basic. Here I want to suggest that it is time
this evaluation was re-assessed, and that an important
beginning point for this re-assessment is one aspect of Owenite
policy on which they sharply differed from their Marxist
successors: the issue of women's emancipation.

The Owenite commitment to feminism was part of the general
humanist outlook which Engels later identified as a key feature
of all utopian thought: the 'claim to emancipate . . . all
humanity at once' rather than 'a particular class to begin with'.
The goals were spelled out in detail: with the establishment of a
worldwide network of Communities of Mutual Association, all
institutional and ideological impediments to sexual equality would
disappear, including oppressive marriage laws, privatised
households, and private ownership of wealth. The nuclear family
(which was held to be responsible not only for the direct
subordination of women to men but also for the inculcation of
'competitive' ideology) would be abolished and replaced by
communal homes and collective child-rearing. This
transformation in living conditions would allow a new sexual
division of labour to be introduced: housework ('domestic
drudgery') would be performed on a rotational basis (either by
women or by children of both sexes) with 'the most scientific
methods available', leaving women to participate in all other
aspects of community life, from manufacturing and agricultural
labour to government office and educational and cultural
activities. With childcare collectivised and all economic pressures
removed, marriage would become a matter of 'romantic affection'
only, to be entered on mutual agreement and dissolved by
mutual choice. Or as one leading socialist-feminist told an
Owenite congress in 1841, 'when all should labour for each, and
each be expected to labour for the whole, then would woman
be placed in a position in which she would not sell her liberties
and her finest feelings.'

Alongside these revolutionary hopes went a whole series of
lesser reform proposals, including demands for immediate

---

*Barbara Taylor is an editor of *History Workshop Journal*,
completing a book on women in the Owenite movement.

changes in the marriage laws to allow civil marriage and divorce,
support for the female franchise (the Owenites frequently
criticised the Chartists for excluding women from their suffrage
demands), campaigns to extend education for women and girls.
Many of the women who agitated for these reforms were lower
middle class, but as the popular base of the movement
expanded they were joined by a small number of working-class
feminists, particularly during the general union phase of
Owenism in 1833-4 when a number of women's trade unions were
formed. These unions sometimes became centres of lively
feminist discussion, encouraged by the Owenite newspaper, *The
Pioneer*, which opened a 'Woman's Page' to carry letters from
female trade unionists on subjects like equal pay and the right
to equal employment. The problem of sex prejudice within the
radical working class itself was a common theme. 'The working
men complain that the masters exercise authority over them; and
they maintain their right to associate, and prescribe laws for
their own protection,' ran one 'Woman's Page' editorial at the
height of the trade union agitation, 'but speak of any project
which will diminish the authority of the male, or give him an
equal, where once he found an inferior, and then the spirit of
Toryism awakes.' When it comes to women, another woman wrote,
all men were aristocrats, whatever their class. 'Can it be right,
can it be just . . . that woman should be thus trampled on and
despised by those who style themselves the lords of creation?'
she demanded, going on to add that in her view

nothing short of a total revolution in all present modes of
acting and thinking among all mankind, will be productive of
the great change so loudly called for by [women's] miserable
state; and there is certainly no system so . . . likely . . .
as that proposed by the benevolent Owen, of community of
property and equality of persons, in which all are *free and
equal.* . . . Indeed, I am confident that if women really
understood the principles and practice of Socialism, there
would not be one who would not become a devoted Socialist.

These were indeed, as Engels later said of the Utopian
outlook as a whole, 'stupendously grand thoughts'; but were
they only that? Before going on to consider this question in
greater detail, it is worth reminding ourselves that what he and
later Marxists offered instead was a wholly different outcome of
gender/class relations, one in which sexism was reduced to a
bourgeois property relation and thereby evacuated from the
working-class struggle. The Owenite emphasis on the universal,
trans-class character of 'male supremacy' (their own term)
disappeared to be replaced with dogmatic assertions of sexual
equality within the proletariat, calls for sex unity in the face of
the common class enemy, and a repudiation of organised
feminism as bourgeois liberal deviationism. The vision of a
reorganised sexual and family existence which had been so
central to Owenite thinking was increasingly pushed to the far
side of a socialist agenda whose major focus became an economic

revolution which would automatically liberate the whole of the working class. This is something of a caricature, since so many staunch sexual egalitarians were to be found in the ranks of later Marxist organisations, but even the bravest of them rarely flouted an orthodoxy in which the Woman Question was subsumed under the Class Question. 'It is not women's petty interests of the moment that we should put in the foreground,' Clara Zetkin told a cheering audience of fellow Social Democrats in 1896, 'our task must be to enroll the modern proletarian woman in the class struggle.'

There was more separating these two ways of thinking about women's oppression than merely the alleged gap between an immature, voluntarist utopianism and a mature, scientific socialism. The movement from Owenism to Marxism meant the repudiation of an independent feminist platform within socialist politics. Why was the struggle against sexual oppression an integral part of the early socialist strategy?

For the Owenites, unlike later Marxist theorists, capitalism was not simply an economic order dominated by a single, class-based division, but an arena of multiple antagonisms and contradictions, each of them lived in the hearts and minds of women and men as well as in their material circumstances. The very term which they used to describe this society - 'the competitive system' - indicated the style of their critique, which moved freely between an economic analysis of workers' exploitation, a moral condemnation of selfish individualism, and a psychological account of the 'dissocial impulses' which were being bred not only in factories and workshops, but in schools, churches and - above all - in the home where, in the words of William Thompson,

the uniform injustice . . . practised by man towards woman, confounds all notions of right and wrong. . . . Every family is a centre of absolute despotism, where of course intelligence and persuasion are quite superfluous to him who has only to command to be obeyed: from these centres, in the midst of which all mankind are now trained, spreads the contagion of selfishness and the love of domination through all human transactions.

The psychological underpinnings of the competitive system, in other words, were habits of dominance and subordination formed within the most intimate areas of human life. The enslavement of women by men deformed human character and strangled human potential to the point where social hierarchy became generally accepted as both natural and inevitable. Having been trained to mastery within the family, men took this self-seeking mode into public life as well: *Homo oeconomicus*, the atomised, competitive individual at the centre of bourgeois culture, was the product of a patriarchal system of psycho-sexual relations.

Building an alternative to this crippling style of social existence would involve not merely the transfer of economic power from one class to another, but a wholesale transformation of personal life in which all 'artificial' divisions of wealth and power would be supplanted by the organic bonds of communal fellowship. Within each co-operative community women and men would learn new ways of living and loving together. This project, which seemed so 'phantastical' to later Marxists, was absolutely central to the early socialist strategy. For how could 'social sentiment' defeat the 'competitive spirit', unless competition was uprooted from the most intimate areas of life? 'Where does freedom begin, unless in the heart?' For the Owenites, like the earlier Puritan reformers and all the Romantics of the period, it was the establishment of a right order in sexual relations which was the key to general moral re-organisation. Communism found its first and foremost expression in the liberated male-female relation. Feminism was therefore not merely an ancillary feature of the socialist project, but one of its key motivating impulses.

Why did Owenism develop in this way? If, as I have suggested, later Marxist thinkers took a different view of the Woman Question, how and why did this difference arise?

Owenism developed in a period of rapid social transition, when both class and gender relations were being sharply transformed by new patterns of work and family life. Most early socialists were craftworkers or small tradespeople for whom the 1830s and 1840s represented a period of extended economic and social crisis: - the crisis which produced a modern working class. At the most general level, early socialism represented a systematic struggle against these critical developments, and an attempt to re-route them in a new, progressive direction. Unlike later socialist movements, in which working people organised as proletarians, the Owenites were organising against the process of proletarianisation, believing that through economic co-operation and the re-moulding of human character they could effectively short-circuit capitalist social relations.

But if in the 1830s plans to establish a new world outside the range of capitalist control still seemed a viable option, by the 1880s, when the second phase of British socialism began, there was far less 'outside' to go to, and working-class organisations which developed within the boundaries set by their proletarian status had their ability to see past those boundaries correspondingly reduced. The experience of living within capitalism wore down the socialist imagination, and the effects of this erosion were felt at the theoretical level as well. 'At any point after 1850,' Edward Thompson has written, 'Scientific Socialism had no more need for Utopias (and doctrinal authority for suspecting them). Speculation as to the society of the future was repressed, and displaced by attention to strategy' (Postscript to *William Morris*, London 1976, p. 787). The result for British revolutionary Marxists was a systematic denial of the necessary visionary element within socialist consciousness, ending all too often in what William Morris described as a 'sham,

Utilitarian Socialism' divested of any genuine libertarian aims, or
what his twentieth-century disciple (Thompson again) has
characterised as
> the whole problem of the subordination of the imaginative
> utopian faculties within the later Marxist tradition: its lack of
> a moral self-consciousness or even a vocabulary of desire, its
> inability to project any images of the future or even its
> tendency to fall back in lieu of these upon the utilitarian's
> earthly paradise - the maximisation of economic growth.

The decline of a genuine feminist vision within British
revolutionary movements was one measure of this loss. As the
older dream of emancipating 'all humanity at once' was displaced
by the economic struggle of a single class, so women and
women's interests were pushed to one side. This occurred in
two ways.

First, the strategic shift away from the struggle against
proletarianisation to the proletarian struggle meant the political
marginalisation of all those who were not, scientifically speaking,
proletarians. If the Owenites had cast their net too wide in
hoping to attract 'all classes of all nations' to the co-operative
cause, Marxism, with its insistence that there was only one
route to communism and only one group who would walk it -
organised productive workers - tightened the net to the point
where only a minority of women were drawn into it, even on a
class basis. When combined with a low level of female
employment in the most highly organised industrial sectors, this
made the fight for socialism seem pretty much a masculine affair.
Women Marxists who challenged this situation did so not on the
grounds that there was a separate women's cause to be fought
alongside and within the class movement, but that women (at
least working women) had a right to stand alongside their
menfolk in the common cause. The Woman Question which
displaced earlier socialist-feminism within late nineteenth-
century Marxism was concerned not with the question of how to
make a revolution which would free women as a sex, but how to
shape women for the class revolution. '. . . what do women
have to do?' Eleanor Marx demanded in 1892, 'we will organise
- not as "women" but as *proletarians* . . . for us there is
nothing but the working-class movement.'

Second, this contraction of the socialist struggle pushed a
whole range of issues beyond the boundaries of revolutionary
politics. Since it was no longer the total reformation of women
and men which was at stake, but simply the re-organisation of
productive relations, all questions connected to reproduction,
marriage or personal existence became converted from central
problems of strategy to merely private matters. 'I have been
told that at the meetings arranged for reading and discussing
with working women, sex and marriage problems come first,'
Lenin scolded Clara Zetkin in their famous dialogue, 'I could
not believe my ears when I heard that. *The first state of
proletarian dictatorship is battling with the counter-*

revolutionaries of the whole world . . . and active communist women are busy discussing sex problems.' Not all British revolutionaries, even Leninist ones, shared this attitude, but those who held out against it tended to be a beleaguered minority, particularly in this century. It is not surprising to find (then) that when socialist-feminists began to organise again in the 1970s, it was with the slogan 'the personal is political' that they mounted their first challenge to the male-dominated left. The issues had never disappeared; it was just that the voices which could raise them had been long suppressed.

The present must always condescend to the past, and from our vantage point there is indeed a great deal in the thinking of the pre-Marxian socialists which seems theoretically naive and strategically implausible. It is not necessary to deny this, however, in order to suggest that the wholesale dismissal of Utopian Socialism by later Marxist socialists revealed certain limitations in their own thinking as well: a narrowing of both means and ends which has had serious consequences for the libertarian cause in general and for the liberation of women in particular. Socialist-feminists look back to the Owenites, then, not out of nostalgia for a transition long past but as a way of tracing the beginnings of a democratic-communist project which is still very much our own and with which we are still struggling to redefine the ends of modern Marxist movements. For, after all, what count as Utopian answers depends on who is raising the questions.

FURTHER READING

Harrison, J.F.C., *Robert Owen and the Owenites*, London 1969.
Killham, John, *Tennyson and the Princess: Reflections of an Age*, London 1958.
Malmgreen, Gail, *Neither Bread nor Roses* (obtainable from J.L. Noyce, P.O. Box 450, Brighton).
Taylor, Barbara, 'The woman-power: Religious heresy and feminism in early English socialism', in *Tearing the Veil*, ed. by S. Lipshitz, London 1978.
Taylor, Barbara, 'The men are as bad as their masters . . .: socialism, feminism, and sexual antagonism in the London tailoring trade in the early 1830s', *Feminist Studies*, 5, no. 1, 1979.

20 GENDER DIVISIONS AND CLASS FORMATION IN THE BIRMINGHAM MIDDLE CLASS, 1780-1850

Catherine Hall*

The flowering of socialist historiography in the last fifteen years, of which the History Workshop is of course one very important instance, has seen an enormous development in working-class and people's history. This development has not been complemented by an equivalent amount of research going on into the dominant classes; the emphasis for socialist historians has been on cultures of opposition and resistance and on the mechanisms of control and subordination, rather than on the culture of the ruling class. The same point can be made about feminist history, which in England has been profoundly influenced by the particular way in which social history has developed. The vast majority of the work done so far has been on working-class women and the working-class family. This is entirely understandable, particularly in a period when the importance of our struggle has been stressed politically, as it has been, for example, in the women's movement. For most socialists it is clearly more attractive to work on material which offers some assertion and celebration of resistance rather than on material which documents the continuing power, albeit often challenged, of the bourgeoisie. This does leave us, however, with a somewhat unbalanced historiography. Any discussion on the 'making of the English middle class' for example, is infinitely less well documented and theorised than it is on the working class. John Foster's work on the bourgeoisie in his *Class Struggle and the Industrial Revolution* provides us with a starting point, but there is little else that is easily available.
    The work that is available on the 'making of the middle class' in the late eighteenth and early nineteenth centuries is not for the most part placed within a socialist framework (for example Briggs or McCord)[1] but it also faces us with a second problem - the absence of gender. The middle class is treated as male and the account of the formation of middle-class consciousness is

---

*Catherine Hall is researching on the construction of femininity in early nineteenth-century England. An active feminist and member of the Birmingham Feminist Historians collective. Associate editor of *History Workshop Journal*.

This paper is a brief introduction to some of the work which is being done by Leonore Davidoff and myself for an SSRC sponsored project at the University of Essex on Domesticity and the Middle Class.

structured around a series of public events in which women
played no part: the imposition of income tax, the reaction to the
Orders in Council, the Queen Caroline affair, the 1832 reform
agitation and the Anti-Corn Law League are usually seen as the
seminal moments in the emergence of the middle class as a
powerful and self-confident class. Yet when we come to
descriptions of the Victorian family much emphasis is placed on
the part which domesticity played in middle-class culture and
on the social importance of the home. That is to say the class
once formed is seen as sexually divided but that process of
division is taken as given. Since eighteenth-century middle-class
women did not, as far as we can tell, lead the sheltered and
domestically defined lives of their Victorian counterparts it
seems important to explore the relation between the process of
class formation and gender division. Was 'the separation of
spheres' and the division between the public and the private a
given or was it constructed as an integral part of middle-class
culture and self-identity? The development of the middle class
between 1780-1850 must be thought of as gendered; the ideals
of masculinity and femininity are important to the middle-class
sense of self and the ideology of separate spheres played a
crucial part in the construction of a specifically middle-class
culture - separating them off from both the aristocracy and
gentry above them and the working class below them.

Gender divisions appear also to have played an important
part in unifying the middle class. The class is significantly
divided, as Marx pointed out, between the bourgeoisie and the
petit bourgeoisie. Foster uses this division and helps to extend
its meaning as does R.J. Morris in his work.[2] The two groups
are divided economically, socially and politically, and much of
the political history of the period is concerned with the shifting
alliances between these two factions and other classes - as for
example in Birmingham over the reform agitation and the
movement into Chartism. But one of the ways in which the middle
class was held together, despite the many divisive factors, was
by their ideas about masculinity and femininity. Men came to
share a sense of what constituted masculinity and women a sense
of what constituted femininity. One central opposition was that
masculinity meant having dependants, femininity meant being
dependent. Clearly the available ideals were not always ones
which could be acted upon - petit-bourgeois men would often
need their wives to work in the business, but they would often
also aspire for that not to be so. Clearly, looking at gender
divisions as having a unifying theme within the middle class is
only one way of approaching the subject; it would be equally
possible to examine the way in which it unites men across
classes, or the way in which it creates contradictions within the
middle class which led to the emergence of bourgeois feminism in
the second half of the nineteenth century. For the moment it
seems important to stress the class-specific nature of masculinity
and femininity in this period; the idea of a universal womanhood

is weak in comparison with the idea of certain types of sexual differentiation being a necessary part of class identity. This may help to explain the relative absence and weakness of feminism in the first half of the nineteenth-century - *Jane Eyre*, for example, provides us with a very sensitive account of the limitations of middle-class femininity which leaves little space for the possibility of a cross-class alliance.

This general theme of the importance of a sharpened division between men and women, between the public and the private, and its relation to class formation can be illustrated by looking at the development of the Birmingham middle class between 1780-1850. The account that is being offered here is extremely sketchy, but can perhaps provide a framework for further discussion. Birmingham was a fast growing industrial town by the late eighteenth century - its population of only 40,000 in 1780 had grown to 250,000 by 1850. Its wealth was built on the metal industries and had been made possible by its strategic position in relation to coal and iron. The town has usually been taken, following Briggs, as one dominated by small masters with workshops but recent work, particularly that of Clive Behagg, has somewhat modified this view and suggested that factory production was better established by the 1830s and 1840s than has usually been thought. Although Birmingham had been gradually expanding since the seventeenth century the impression by the end of the eighteenth century is that the middle class within the town are only gradually coming to realise their potential strength and power. Consequently, Birmingham offers us a relatively uncomplicated account of the emergence of the middle class - uncomplicated by factors such as the struggle between the well-established merchant class of the eighteenth century and the new manufacturers, which took place in Leeds.

We can briefly examine the separation between the sexes as it took place in Birmingham in this period at three levels - that of the economic, the political and social, and the ideological. If we look first at the economic level it is important to stress from the beginning that the ideology of separate spheres has an economic effectivity. Clearly, the crucial problem which faces us is the question of what the relation is between the emergence of separate spheres and the development of industrial capitalism. Is there any relation at all? At this point it is only possible to say that women seem to be increasingly defined as economically dependent in our period, and that this economic dependence has important consequences for the ways in which industrial capitalism developed. That is to say, we cannot argue that industrial capitalism would not have developed without sexual divisions, but that the increasingly polarised form which sexual divisions took affected the forms of capitalist social relations and of capitalist accumulation.

The legal framework for this is provided by the centrality of the notion of dependence in marriage - Blackstone's famous dictum that the husband and wife are one person and that person is the husband. Married women's property passed automatically to their husbands unless a settlement had been made in the courts of equity. Married women had no right to sue or be sued or to make contracts. For working-class families the idea of the family wage came to encapsulate the idea of economic dependence – though we know that in reality few working-class families were in a position to afford to do without the earnings which a wife could bring in. For middle-class families there is no equivalent concept, since the men do not earn wages, but still the economic dependence of the wife and children was assumed. Amongst the aristocracy and gentry patrilineal rights to property had been established for a very long time, but although the middle class broke with their 'betters' at many other points the connection between masculinity and property rights was not broken. Two inter-related points need to be made here; first, the importance of marriage settlements in capital accumulation and second, the sexual specificity of inheritance practices. Neither of these are new developments – making an advantageous marriage had long been a crucial way of getting on in the world but whereas in the past the gentry and aristocracy had for the most part used money so acquired to enlarge their houses or consolidate their estates, small producers were now using it to build up their businesses. Archibald Kenrick, for example, a Birmingham buckle maker in the late 1780s who was caught up in the decline of the buckle trade, got married in 1790 and used his wife's marriage settlement to set up in business as an iron founder in 1791. Sometimes the capital would come from a mother rather than a wife, for amongst the wealthier bourgeoisie it was common practice to have a marriage settlement which protected the wife's property whereas amongst the petit bourgeoisie this would have been very unusual.[3] Richard and George Cadbury both inherited a substantial amount from their mother Candia Barrow at a time when the family business was doing rather badly and used the capital to re-organise and re-vitalise the business.[4] Marx noted that the bourgeoisie practised partible inheritance rather than primogeniture and widows and daughters were not disinherited, but the forms of female inheritance tended increasingly to be linked to dependence. In general boys would receive an education and training to enter a business or profession and then would be given either a share in the existing family business or capital to invest in another business. Thomas Southall, for example, who came to Birmingham in 1820 to set up in business as a chemist, had been educated and apprenticed by his father who had a mixed retailing business himself and set up each of his sons in one aspect – one as a draper, one as a vintner and one as a chemist.[5] Daughters, on the other hand, would either be given a lump sum as a marriage settlement (though it should be noted that as Freer has demonstrated they were sometimes not allowed to marry because of the impossibility of removing capital from the business) or

they would be left money in trust, usually under the aegis of a
male relative, to provide an income for them together with their
widowed mothers. The money in trust would then often be
available for the male relatives to invest as they pleased. It
should be pointed out, however, that widows amongst the petit
bourgeoisie often were left the business to manage - it might be
a shop, for example - and this different pattern of inheritance
marks an important division between the two groups in the
middle class. Right of dower were finally abolished in 1833 but
long before that it was accepted that men had a right to leave
their property as they liked. Life insurance developed in the
late eighteenth century as a way of providing for dependants,
and this provides another instance of the ways in which sexual
divisions structure the forms of capitalist development -
insurance companies became important sources of capital
accumulation which could not have existed without the notion of
dependants.

Meanwhile the kinds of businesses which women were running
seem to have altered. An examination of the Birmingham
Directories reveals women working in surprising trades
throughout our period; only in very small numbers it is true,
but still they survived. To take a few examples, there were
women brass founders at the end of the eighteenth century, a
bedscrew maker and a coach maker in 1803, several women
engaged in aspects of the gun trade in 1812, an engine cutter
and an iron and steel merchant in 1821, plumbers and painters
in the 1830s and 1840s, burnishers and brushmakers in the
1850s. There are certain trades in which women never seem to
appear as the owners - awl-blade making, for example, or iron
founders. But although the percentage of women to men engaged
in business goes up rather than down in the early nineteenth
century, at least according to the evidence provided by the
directories, there seems to be a significant shift towards the
concentration of women in certain trades. In the late eighteenth
century women were well represented among the button makers,
and button making was one of the staple trades of Birmingham.
Sketchley's Directory of 1767 described the button trade as

> very extensive and distinguished under the following heads
> viz. Gilt, Plated, Silvered, Lacquered, and Pinchback, the
> beautiful new Manufactures Platina, Inlaid, Glass, Horn,
> Ivory, and Pearl: Metal Buttons such as Bath, Hard and
> Soft White etc. there is likewise made Link Buttons in most
> of the above Metals, as well as of Paste, Stones, etc. in short
> the vast variety of sorts in both Branches is really amazing,
> and we may with Truth aver that this is the cheapest Market
> in the world for these Articles.

But by the 1830s and 1840s women were concentrated in what
became traditional women's trades - in dressmaking, millinery,
school teaching and the retail trade. Women were no longer
engaged as employers in the central productive trades of the
town in any number, they were marginalised into the servicing

sector, though, of course, it should be clear that many working-class women continued as employers in, for example, the metal trades. G.J. Holyoake, described in his own autobiography his mother's disappearance from business:

> In those days horn buttons were made in Birmingham, and my mother had a workshop attached to the house, in which she conducted a business herself, employing several hands. She had the business before her marriage. She received the orders; made the purchases of materials; superintended the making of the goods; made out the accounts; and received the money; besides taking care of her growing family. There were no 'Rights of Women' thought of in her day, but she was an entirely self-acting, managing mistress. . . . The button business died out while I was young, and from the remarks which came from merchants, I learned that my mother was the last maker of that kind of button in the town.[6]

It is worth remarking that his mother became a keen attender at Carr's Lane Chapel where, as we shall see, John Angell James taught the domestic subordination of women from the pulpit for fifty years. Women increasingly did not have the necessary forms of knowledge and expertise to enter many businesses – jobs were being redefined as managerial or skilled and, therefore, masculine. For instance, as Michael Ignatieff points out, women goalers were actually excluded by statute as not fitted to the job.[7] Women could manage the family and the household but not the workshop of the factory. Furthermore, a whole series of new financial institutions were being developed in this period which also specifically excluded women – trusts, for example, and forms of partnership. Ivy Pinchbeck has argued that women were gradually being excluded from a sphere which they had previously occupied; it appears that in addition they were never allowed into a whole new economic sphere.

The separation of work from home obviously played an important part in this process of demarcation between men's work and women's work. That separation has often been thought of as the material basis of separate spheres. But once the enormous variety of types of middle-class housing has been established that argument can no longer be maintained. Separating work from home was one way of concretising the division between the sexes, but since it was often not possible it cannot be seen as the crucial factor in establishing domesticity. The many other ways in which the division was established have to be remembered. For doctors there could often be no separation, whereas for ironfounders the separation was almost automatic. In some trades the question of scale was vital – in the Birmingham metal trades some workshops had houses attached but in many cases they were separated. Sometimes there is a house attached and yet the chief employee lived there rather than the family. James Luckcock, for example, a Birmingham jeweller, when he was just starting up in business on his own

not only lived next to his workshop but also used the labour of
his wife and children. As soon as he could afford it he moved
out, moved his manager into the house and his wife stopped
working in the business.[8] Shopkeepers moving out from their
premises and establishing a separate homes for their families
obviously lost the assistance of wives and daughters in the
shop – Mrs Cadbury and her daughters all helped in the shop
until the family moved out to Edgbaston.

So far I have tried to suggest that the economic basis for the
expansion of the middle class is underpinned by assumptions of
male superiority and female dependence. When we turn to the
level of the political and social we can see the construction in
our period of a whole new public world in which women have no
part. That world is built on the basis of those who are defined
as individuals – men with property. The Birmingham middle class
had developed very little in the way of institutions or
organisations by the mid-eighteenth century, but by the end of
the century a whole new range had appeared. In the voluntary
societies which sprang up in the town the male middle class
learnt the skills of local government and established their rights
to political leadership. These societies placed women on the
periphery, if they placed them at all. Dorothy Thompson has
argued in her piece on working-class women in radical politics
that as organisations became more formal so women were
increasingly marginalised. This process took place earlier for
the middle class since their formal organisations were being
established from the mid-eighteenth century. As in all other
towns and cities Birmingham societies covered an extraordinarily
wide range of activities through religion, philanthropy, trade,
finance and politics. The personnel of these societies were often
the same people who were finding their way onto the boards of
local banks, insurance companies and municipal trusts. In
Birmingham there were a series of political struggles between
the governing classes and the middle class in our period which
resulted in the formation of political organisations; to take one
example, the Chamber of Commerce first founded in 1785 was the
first attempt to bring manufacturers together to protect their
interests and had no place for women. The Birmingham Political
Union, the Complete Suffrage Union, the dissenting
organisations to fight the established church, the organisations
which worked for municipal incorporation and the Anti-Corn Law
League were all male bodies. It is interesting to note that the
BPU made provision for the wives of artisans in the Female
Political Union, but there was no equivalent provision for
middle-class ladies. Women were not defined by the middle class
as political – they could play a supportive role, for example
fund-raising for the Anti-Corn Law League, but that marked the
limit. The only political organisation where they did play an
important part was the Anti-Slavery movement where separate
ladies' auxiliary committees were set up after considerable
argument within the movement, but even here their real

contribution was seen as a moral one. Women were appealed to
as mothers to save their 'dusky sisters' from having their
children torn from them, but the activities which women could
engage in to achieve this end were strictly limited. It was often
the very weakness of women which was called upon - as God's
poorest creatures perhaps their prayers would be heard.
    Similarly the relationship of women to new social organisa-
tions and institutions was strictly limited. Thye could
not be full members of the libraries and reading rooms, or of
the literary and philosophical societies, even the concerts and
assemblies were organised by male committees. When we look at
the huge range of philanthropic societies again the pattern is
that men hold all the positions of power - more specifically the
bourgeoisie provide the governors and managing committees
while the petit bourgeoisie sit on the committees of the less
prestigious institutions and do much of the work of day-to-day
maintenance. Women are used by some societies as visitors, or
tract distributors, or collectors of money, but they are never,
formally at least, the decision-makers. Even in an institution
like the Protestant Dissenting Charity School which was a girls'
school in Birmingham, there was a ladies' committee involved
with the daily maintenance of the school, but any decision of
any importance had to be taken to the men's managing
committee and membership of the ladies' committee was achieved
by recommendation from the men. Ladies could be subscribers
to the charity but their subscriptions did not carry the same
rights as it did for the men - for example, ladies could only
sponsor girls to be taken into the school by proxy. The ladies'
committee had no formal status and relied on informal contact
with the men - often taking the form of a wife promising that
she would pass some point onto her husband who would then
raise it with the men. The constitution of most kinds of society,
whether political or cultural, usually either formally excluded
women from full membership by detailing the partial forms of
membership they could enjoy, or never even thought the
question worth discussing. Women never became officers, they
never spoke in large meetings, indeed they could not attend
most meetings either because they were formally excluded or
because the informal exclusion mechanisms were so powerful -
for example, having meetings which were centred around a
dinner in an hotel, a place where ladies were clearly not
expected to be. Nor did women sign the letters and petitions
which frequently appeared in the press.
    So far I hope that I have succeeded in establishing that at
both the economic and political level middle-class women were
increasingly being defined as subordinate and marginal;
anything to do with the public world was not their sphere. At
the same time a whole range of new activities was opening up
for men, and men had the freedom to move between the public
and the private. It is at the level of the ideological that we
find the articulation of separate spheres which informed many

of the developments we have looked at. The period 1780-1850 saw a constant stream of pamphlets and books - the best known authors of which are probably Hannah More and Mrs Ellis - telling middle-class women how to behave. But domesticity was a local issue as well as a national one, and the activities of the Birmingham clergy in our period give us plenty of evidence of the way in which congregations were left in no uncertain state as to the relative positions of men and women. John Angell James has already been referred to. He was the minister of the most important Independent church in the town from 1805-57 and was recognised as a great preacher and prolific writer. Carr's Lane had a large membership drawn from both the bourgeoisie and the petit bourgeoisie whilst several hundred working-class children attended the sunday schools. James' books sold extremely well and his series on the family - *Female Piety, The Young Man's Friend and Guide Through Life to Immortality* and *The Family Monitor, or a Help to Domestic Happiness* - were long-term best-sellers.[9] James believed that women were naturally subordinate to men - it was decreed in the Scriptures.

> Every family, when directed as it should be, has a sacred character, inasmuch as the head of it acts the part of both the prophet and the priest of his household, in instructing them in the knowledge, and leading them in the worship, of God; and, at the same time, he discharges the duty of a king, by supporting a system of order, subordination and discipline.

Furthermore home was the woman's proper sphere:

> In general, it is for the benefit of a family that a married woman should devote her time and attention almost exclusively to the ways of her household: her place is in the centre of domestic cares. What is gained by her in the shop is oftentimes lost in the house, for want of the judicious superintendence of a mother and a mistress. Comforts and order, as well as money, are domestic wealth; and can these be rationally expected in the absence of female management? The children always want a mother's eye and hand, and should always have them. Let the husband, then, have the care of providing for the necessities of the family, and the wife that of personally superintending it: for this is the rule both of reason and of revelation.[10]

James' ideas were not simply spoken from the pulpit; the domination of such ideas was reflected in the organisation of his church and in the way in which church societies were established. Nor were such ideas limited to the Independents. The Quakers and the Unitarians were both important groups in Birmingham - many of the most influential families in the town were in one of these two groups. Both Quakers and Unitarians inherited a fairly radical view of the relations between the sexes but the Quakers in the late eighteenth century were moving towards a more formal subordination of women, introducing, for example, separate seating for men and women. However, the

Quakers still offered women the opportunity to preach and thus guaranteed the maintenance of a spiritual significance for women. The Unitarians, though believing in some education for women, maintained strict lines of demarcation as has already been mentioned in connection with the Protestant Dissenting Charity School which was a Unitarian foundation. But it should not be thought that it was left to Nonconformists to lead the way on questions relating to the divisions between the sexes. Birmingham saw a considerable Evangelical revival from the late 1820s, associated with the influence of the Evangelical Bishop Ryder in Coventry and Lichfield. There is substantial evidence of the particular interest which Evangelicals took in the importance of a proper home and family life, and the belief they had in the centrality of the religious household in the struggle to reconstruct a properly Christian community. Christ Church, a large Anglican church in the town centre, was occupied by an enthusiastic Evangelical in the 1830s who inaugurated separate benches for men and women; this led to a popular rhyme –

The churches in general we everywhere find,
Are places where men to the women are joined;
But at *Christ Church*, it seems, they are more cruel hearted,
For men and their wives are brought here to be parted.[11]

The Rev. John Casebow Barrett, the Rector of St Mary's from the late 1830s and a much liked and admired preacher in the town maintained a similar stance from his pulpit as in his sermon in memory of Adelaide Queen Dowager in 1849 where he extolled her virtues as an ordinary wife and mother:

As a *wife*, her conduct was unexceptionable; and her devotedness, her untiring watchfulness to her royal consort during his last illness, stands forth as a bright model, which the wives of England will do well to imitate. Here, in her husband's sick chamber, by day and by night, she – then the Queen of this mighty Empire – proved herself the fond and loving wife, the meek and feeling woman, the careful and uncomplaining nurse. *Her* eye watched the royal sufferer: *her* hand administered the medicine and smoothed the pillow: *her* feet hastened to give relief by changing the position: *her* voice was heard in prayer, or in the reading of the words of eternal life. And the character she then exhibited won for her – which we believe in her estimation was more precious than the crown she wore – the deep respect, the high approval, the honest, truthful love of an entire nation, which, whatever its other faults may be, is not insensible to those charities and affections, which give a bright and transcendent charm to the circle of every home.[12]

Domesticity often seems to have an important religious component, but it was not always expressed in religious terms. The local papers often carried poems with a heavily idealised domestic content and the ideology of separate spheres seems to have gained very wide usage. James Luckcock, a Birmingham

jeweller who has already been mentioned, was deeply attached
to the domestic ideal. He was a political Radical, a great friend
of George Edmonds, and was very active in the Birmingham
Political Union. There seems to be no evidence that an
attachment to domesticity had anything to do with political
allegiances – it appears to have cut cleanly across party lines.
Luckcock loved the idea of both his home and garden –
particularly the home which he built for his wife and himself
for his retirement in leafy Edgbaston. His relationship with
his two sons seems in reality to have been fraught with tension
but he continued to celebrate poetically the joys of domestic
bliss. At one point when he was seriously ill and thought he
might die he composed a poem for his wife about himself; it was
entitled *My Husband* and catalogued his thoughtfulness and
caring qualities as a husband and father:

Who first inspir'd my virgin breast,
With tumults not to be express'd,
And gave to life unwonted zest?
                    My husband.
Who told me that his gains were small,
But that whatever might befal,
To me he'd gladly yield them all?
                    My husband.
Who shun'd the giddy town's turmoil,
To share with me the garden's toil,
And joy with labour reconcile?
                    My husband.
Whose arduous struggles long maintain'd
Adversity's cold hand restrain'd
And competence at length attain'd?
                    My husband's.[13]

Unfortunately we do not even know the name of James
Luckcock's wife, much less her reaction to this poem!

In this brief and introductory paper I have tried to suggest
how central gender divisions were to the middle class in the
period 1780-1850. Definitions of masculinity and femininity
played an important part in marking out the middle class,
separating it off from other classes and creating strong links
between disparate groups within that class – Nonconformists
and Anglicans, Radicals and conservatives, the richer
bourgeoisie and the petit bourgeoisie, The separation between
the sexes was marked out at every level within the society –
in manufacturing, the retail trades and the professions, in
public life of all kinds, in the churches, in the press and in
the home. The separation of spheres was one of the fundamental
organising characteristics of middle-class society in late
eighteenth and early nineteenth-century England.

NOTES

1 N. McCord, *The Anti-Corn Law League 1836-1848*, London 1958.
2 R.J. Morris, 'The making of the British middle class', unpublished paper delivered at the University of Birmingham Social History seminar 1979.
3 R.A. Church, *Kenricks in Hardware. A family business 1791-1966*, Newton Abbot 1969.
4 A.G. Gardiner, *Life of George Cadbury*, London 1923.
5 C. Southall, *Records of the Southall Family*, London, private circulation, 1932.
6 G.S. Holyoake, *Sixty Years of an Agitator's Life*, London 1900.
7 M. Ignatieff, *A Just Measure of Pain: The penitentiary in the industrial revolution 1750-1850*, London 1978.
8 J. Luckcock, *Sequel to Memoirs in Humble Life*, Birmingham 1825.
9 J.A. James, *Female Piety or the Young Woman's Friend and Guide Through Life to Immortality*, 5th edn, London 1856; *The Young Man's Friend and Guide Through Life to Immortality*, London 1851; *The Family Monitor, or a Help to Domestic Happiness*, London 1828.
10 J.A. James, *The Family Monitor* in *The Works of John Angell James*, ed. by T.F. James, Birmingham 1860, pp. 17 and 56.
11 W. Bates, *A Pictorial Guide to Birmingham*, Birmingham 1849, p. 46.
12 Rev. J.C. Barrett, *Sermon in Memory of Adelaide Queen Dowager*, Birmingham 1849, p. 11.
13 Luckcock, *op. cit.*, p. 49.

FURTHER READING

Behagg, C., 'Custom, class and change: The trade societies of Birmingham', *Social History*, 4, no. 3, Oct. 1979.
Briggs, A., *Victorian Cities*, London 1963.
Foster, J., *Class Struggle and the Industrial Revolution*, London 1974.
Hall, C., 'The early formation of Victorian domestic ideology' in *Fit Work for Women* ed. by S. Burman, London 1979.
Pinchbeck, I., *Women Workers and the Industrial Revolution 1750-1850*, London 1969.
Thompson, D., 'Women and nineteenth-century radical politics: A lost dimension' in *The Rights and Wrongs of Women* ed. by J. Mitchell and A. Oakley, Harmondsworth 1976.

21 FEMINISM AND LABOUR HISTORY

Anna Davin*

The term 'labour history' is potentially a fairly open one,
allowing a number of interpretations. It could involve history of
the conditions of labour, in both senses - work, and also the
working class. It could focus on the history of the labour
movement - of the working class in struggle. Or it could mean
history whose perspective was sympathetic to labour, socialist
or revolutionary history seeking to understand the experience
of labour as part of the history of capitalism, with the aim of
improving our understanding of capitalism so as to be better
equipped to fight it. None of these approaches need exclude
consideration of women, as workers, as members of the working
class, as militants and participants in struggle, as part of
capitalist society.

To some extent labour historians have indeed worked in all
these ways; nevertheless the main focus has been the second
one - the history of the working class in struggle, complemented
to some extent by the history of work. One explanation of this
is perhaps the way that since the term was first used other
specialisms (of approach or subject matter or method) have
developed, narrowing its boundaries by the definition of their
territories. Social history, economic history, oral history and
women's history all overlap with labour history, and have
probably contributed to, or at least reinforced, its narrow
identification with labour organisation and work. This
fragmentation is not in the interests of good history. But to the
narrow definition of labour history there has generally been
added a further restriction - that of male bias.

Such bias is not the result of conscious conspiracy; it is
nevertheless very pervasive and sadly weakens the usefulness
of labour history. It arises in part from the nature of the
sources: information about men is much easier to come by.
Records survive from organisations, regular well-paid workers
are more likely to be in organisations, women were rarely
regular or well-paid workers. Newspapers wrote up long
dramatic strikes, long strikes needed strike funds or outside
support, women's actions were more often spontaneous, brief,
and scarcely reported, especially at national level. Accounts of
work are to be found in autobiography (but for the working

---

*Anna Davin is a part-time teacher in adult education, an editor
of *History Workshop Journal* and a co-ordinator of the London
feminist history group. Researching on working girls in
nineteenth-century London.

class women's autobiographies are even rarer than men's), or in compilations of information such as parliamentary inquiries where the questions were asked by men, mostly of men, and mostly concerned men or problems from men's point of view. (So for instance women's low wages were undercutting men's, a threat, rather than inadequate wages for any person to live on.) And the bias of the sources is often matched by the unconscious bias of the historian, who has grown up with the assumptions of a male-dominated society and profession, and of a male-dominated left and labour movement. The values and attitudes of the skilled male workers of the nineteenth century - the backbone of most labour history - seem to creep in, from their heirs in the labour movement today perhaps (whose approval validates the work of the socialist historian guilty at being an academic), as well as from the minute-books and memoirs of the early labour movement.

Labour historians often say that the material for women's history simply doesn't exist. Often, when a woman is starting her research she will be told: 'Oh no, that's much too difficult, you'll find there is nothing at all about that.' It's hard for someone without confidence or experience to get past such initial discouragement. Yet those who do, often discover with indignation that material can be found, if you are asking the right questions, and coming with the right perceptions, and above all if you persevere. It is just less obvious and more scattered, and with even more filters (gender as well as class and authority distorting the information) than the evidence concerning men. Researchers' findings are always determined at least partly by what they are looking for and how hard they look, and labour historians have tended to be less interested in women. An important contributing factor here has been a limiting political analysis stressing work and struggle (with very narrow definitions) and ignoring other important areas of experience.

The sexual division of labour has tended somehow to be taken as a given ('Typically, it was the male who had to leave home every day to work for wages and the woman who did not'), and variants on this pattern, if they are even noticed, are assumed to be aberrations from the norm, 'special cases'. (Important exceptions to this generalisation are of course to be found, notably in the work of Alice Clark, Ivy Pinchbeck and Eileen Power, ignored for decades.) And at the same time only half the equation is seen as important - the male 'worked for wages', the woman did not. What she did instead does not need investigation; it was not work, or not work needing to be noticed because it was not waged. (Even there the assumption sometimes overrides the fact and married women's waged work is denied without proper investigation.) For most labour historians work has meant waged work, and preferably work done in mine or workshop or building site or dock or steelworks - not outwork or laundry or service, let alone unpaid domestic labour. And struggle has also been defined in a partial way, concentrating on issues relating to wage and employment, and excluding those relating to the quality of life, or taking place away from the point of production. (Here of course the exception as so often is E.P. Thompson.) The family is left to demographers and social historians, and to cover the omission students are directed to speculative and preliminary works like Edward Shorter's *Making of the Modern Family*, whose confident generalisations appear to fill the gap but are based on thin research and anachronistic assumptions.

But most serious has been the neglect of the sexual division of labour as both an object of study and a tool of analysis. Here the influence of feminist political experience has presented a real challenge, leading not only to the search for new sources, but the rereading of old ones and the posing of new questions. The contribution of feminist historians (by no means yet fully acknowledged by labour historians, who indeed seem often not to have read the relevant work) has been to argue that the sexual division of labour must itself be examined for shifts and variations both as to practice and ideology, because once understood it can be a key to the changing actuality of work, of daily life and of struggle, as well as for the analysis of how capitalism maintains itself. Because feminists are fighting the subjugation of women in contemporary society, they see the central importance of the sexual division of labour in allowing capitalism to divide the workforce and thus obtain lower wages and a reserve army of labour (one used particularly effectively to break down craft skills and power), while at the same time also gaining cheap maintenance and reproduction (physical and ideological) of the workforce. And they cannot accept as adequate any historical description or analysis which does not closely examine this area. It is not just that women are left out - as when the 1860s radical organisation for the extension of the franchise is acceptable labour history, while the women's struggle for the vote is relegated to women's history or treated as something of a joke; or as when the sole (and atypical) example of the matchgirls' strike is presented to illustrate the far more extensive and complex tradition of women's militancy; or the daily drudgery and double shift of many women's lives are ignored and discounted. It is that the questions which are dismissed or never asked because they fall outside the male-defined interests of labour history are in fact crucial for any proper analysis of the very subjects with which labour history should be concerned.

So the study of work should recognise the contribution and the inter-relation of all the different kinds of work, not accept the status awarded at the time to this or that skill as justifying attention or exclusion from research today, and not neglecting the unpaid work which kept the workers fed and clothed and enabled them to work. The study of the working class should recognise the existence of women and children, of young and

old, of families and relationships which determined so many
aspects of daily life, including work, and gave richness and
complexity to the class. The study of struggle should look for
where women did struggle, instead of denouncing them for
absence from male-dominated organisations. And the study of
capitalism should recognise how the sexual divisions have been
shaped and exploited as part of capitalist strategy.

Feminist history and labour history need not be such
separate disciplines: they share many interests and can
strengthen each other. There is, nevertheless, an important
distinction between them. Take any of the definitions of labour
history we started with - history of the conditions of labour,
work and also the working class, or history of the labour
movement, the working class in struggle, or history whose
perspective is sympathetic to labour - and add the definition
suggested in this discussion, of history which helps us to
understand the part that work plays in people's lives. In all of
these, though not so much in the last two, labour history is
basically being defined in terms of its subject matter. Now in my
view feminist history is not defined that way. Feminist history
is a question of that approach you bring to the work you're
doing. You can be a feminist historian without being concerned
largely with women, and that to me is the distinction between
feminist history and women's history. That means for instance
that I found it was relevant in my exploration of connections
between 'Imperialism and Motherhood' (see *History Workshop
Journal* 5, Spring 1977) to look at quite a large range of the
ideas that were current at the beginning of the century, and not
only as they directly affected women or the sexual division of
labour. It means that the work that I'm focusing on now is on
working-class childhood at the end of the nineteenth century.
Now it's true that I am centrally concerned with the differences
that there were in boys' and girls' experience of childhood -
both differences that were there and differences that were being
created - but I'm also looking at how the whole understanding
and experience of childhood was changing, particularly after the
introduction of compulsory education. The subject matter could
be categorised as educational history, labour history, women's
history, social history, or whatever, but the questions I ask
and the answers I formulate make it feminist history.

My interest in these areas of study relates very directly to
labour history, and that is why I'm so impatient with narrow
definitions of it. Early on in the feminist movement the
temptation was very much to look particularly for women who
would provide an example and an inspiration, who'd been
militant in whatever way; or (the other face of that) to see
women as victims. Both of these tendencies continue to recur,
and they are also present in much labour history: the victories
and the sufferings of workers, the awfulness of their oppression
and the struggle to end it. When I started my research I
decided that this dichotomy was misleading, especially perhaps

in relation to women. If women's lives in the late nineteenth-century working class (the focus of my interest) were really so atrocious, characterised by poverty, ill-health, cramped and insanitary and inconvenient housing, sometimes violence, and every kind of exploitation, then why weren't they getting up and revolting, why weren't they joining organisations or making their own, why was there not more resistance, more revolution? In terms of research, that involved exploring and redefining both aspects, and trying to go beyond them. The questions changed: I was now trying to see whether they were really as much victims as they appeared, and whether there were other forms of resistance to discover; but also I was asking what was there in their total life-experience which might be conditioning them to endure rather than to resist; how did they see their own lives; did they tolerate them because there seemed to be no alternative, or because they did not see them as intolerable? That's really how I came into looking at childhood and education, formation of consciousness and attitudes about class and about gender and all the rest of it.

But I think that these things need to be looked at just as much in terms of men as in terms of women. Women's work experience has to be seen in the light of their whole life-cycle if we are to understand the shifts between paid and unpaid labour, the balance between domestic responsibility and outside employment, their place in the labour force (whether national or local). But so does men's: their attitude to their work would also change in the course of their lives depending on how the rest of their life circumstances changed. The development of a family wage meant higher male wages but also greater responsibilities: it can be seen as a labour victory, or as one for capital, stabilising the workforce and reducing militancy, as well as securing cheaper and more efficient reproduction. At the very least its implications within and outside the family need critical examination. To argue different interests between members of a class is not seen as unacceptable or irrelevant when the groups involved are defined say by religion or ethnic origin, or conflicting commercial or industrial requirements, or identification with city and town: why should gender difference not also be permitted as a valid and useful area to explore? (Age too, but that's another whole question.)

The subject matter then of labour history in the enlarged definition which it should have, and the approach of feminist history, raising central questions about sexual division, class formation, consciousness, culture and economy, are not only not incompatible: they are indispensable to each other if historians are to further our understanding of the past and the present of class society. Of course different historians will have particular interests and areas; individual experience and political formation will lead to different questions and answers. But socialist historians, who include many labour and many feminist historians, cannot afford to reject each others' insights and analyses sight unseen, as sometimes seems to happen now: there is too much to do and it is too important. Comradely criticism and exchange will strengthen us all; fragmentation and resistance to new ideas only help the other side.

FURTHER READING

Alexander, Sally, 'Women's work in nineteenth-century London: A study of the years 1820-1850' in *The Rights and Wrongs of Women*, ed. by J. Mitchell and A. Oakley, Harmondsworth 1976.
Alexander, Sally and Davin, Anna, 'Feminist History' (editorial) *History Workshop Journal*, 1, Spring 1976.
Alexander, Sally, Davin, Anna and Hostettler, Eve, 'Labouring Women' *History Workshop Journal*, 8, Autumn 1979.
Clark, Alice, *Working Life of Women in the Seventeenth Century*, 1919.
Davidoff, Leonore, 'Class and gender in Victorian England: The diaries of Arthur J. Munby and Hannah Culwick' *Feminist Studies* 5, no. 1, Spring 1979; 'The separation of home and work? Landladies and lodgers in nineteenth- and twentieth-century England' in *Fit Work for Women*, ed. by S. Burman, London 1979.
Hall, Catherine, 'The early formation of Victorian domestic ideology' in *Fit Work for Women*, ed. by S. Burman, London 1979.
John, Angela, *By the Sweat of their Brow: Women Workers at Victorian Coal Mines*, London 1980.
Liddington, Jill and Norris, Jill, *One Hand Tied Behind Us*, London 1977.
Pinchbeck, Ivy, *Women Workers in the Industrial Revolution*, London 1977.
Neff, Wanda, *Victorian Working Women*, London 1966.
Summers, Anne, 'A home from home? Women's philanthropic work in the nineteenth century' in *Fit Work for Women*, ed. by S. Burman, London 1979.
Taylor, Barbara, 'The men are as bad as their masters: Socialism, feminism and sexual antagonism in the London tailoring trade in the early 1830s', *Feminist Studies*, 5, no. 1, Spring 1979.
Thompson, Dorothy, 'Women and nineteenth-century radical politics: A lost dimension' in *The Rights and Wrongs of Women*, ed. by J. Mitchell and A. Oakley, Harmondsworth 1976.
Tilly, Louise, and Scott, Joan, *Women, Work and the Family*, New York 1978.

22 WOMEN'S HISTORY IN THE USA

Ellen Ross*

It is hardly news, at a conference on People's History and
Socialist Theory, to point to the political inspiration for
historical analysis. The current generation of US women's
historians began not only as women wanting to clarify their own
historical identity, but as members of a feminist movement cut
off from its own past by the nearly five decades which had
intervened between the Suffrage era and the revival of
feminism in the 1960s. Movement women inside and outside the
universities devoured information about women's and feminist
history, and today women's history is accepted even in the
stuffiest circles as a sub-discipline in the historical profession.
Though under attack by an increasingly organised political
right, feminism even today remains a mass movement. Its
continued strength has been the political backdrop against
which the study of women's history in the USA has reached a
high level of empirical depth and methodological
sophistication.

In the ten or twelve years since its revival, women's history
in the USA has passed rapidly through a series of developmental
stages, beginning with the rediscovery of our famous
'foremothers' and 'compensatory' history ('What were the women
doing?'), to analyses of the historical sources of female
oppression, through re-evaluation of the canons of traditional
historiography (is 'the Renaissance' a term applicable to
women's history?), to still further stages. This paper tunes in
only at the more recent of these stages.[1] I want to discuss the
recent impact on historical work[2] of one important tendency in
US feminism - radical feminism. I will confine myself to laying it
out as a philosophical and political position, and then explaining
its impact on historical study.

Of the dozens of feminist strains in the USA, very few class
themselves as socialist. This is not surprising, since while there
is still a lively radical tradition in American culture and politics,
this tradition has very seldom been explicitly socialist, but
instead has drawn on libertarian, democratic and populist
strands. Most of the largest groups in the American left today,
for example, avoid openly defining themselves as socialist in
their organising work, and instead appeal to more 'native'
political traditions. Socialists are a small minority of feminists

*Ellen Ross teaches at Ramapo College, New York, researching
on family life in nineteenth-century Bethnal Green. An active
socialist and feminist.

also. More important numerically are so-called 'bourgeois feminists,' represented by such nationally based groups as the National Organisation of Women, and the National Women's Political Caucus. But radical feminists are perhaps equally important in feminist communities all over the country. By setting up alternative living arrangements and economic and political structures, many radical feminist 'separatists' are trying to live at a distance from male domination. Radical feminists are emphatic that the central social cleavage today is between men and women, that the system needing radical transformation is 'patriarchy.' Many consider heterosexuality one of the most oppressive cornerstones of current gender arrangements.

This feminist tendency has generated original and important social analysis. In the now classic *Sexual Politics*, published only ten years ago, Kate Millett outlined the structure of 'patriarchy', which she labelled a political system, that is, an arrangement in which power was allocated differently to men and women, old and young. Shulamith Firestone's *Dialectic of Sex* (also 1970) is still a valuable exploration of the implications of gender in the wider culture. More recently, anthropologist Gayle Rubin has tried to sketch out 'the sex/gender system' which she argues parallels and predates capitalism, appearing in the earliest organised human societies with the origins of marriage, i.e. the exchange of women between men.[3] Human beings in all societies are divided into two rigidly distinct groups, women and men, who are usually defined in terms of polarities like yin and yang, weakness and strength, etc. But this division is not a product of nature, which creates people with some biological differences by sex but with far vaster areas of commonality. 'Men' and 'women' as such are really social creations, products of societies' 'sex/gender systems.' Societies shape people who will feel physical attraction for members of the 'opposite' sex, who abhor incest, and who participate in the division of labour by sex. All three of these characteristics make us 'marriageable' (exchangeable between men): women need male skills to survive in most societies, and, besides, find them 'attractive'. Rubin sees kinship systems as the vehicles of sex/gender systems and the exchange of women, for nearly all societies worldwide, incorporate some degree of male dominance, taboos of incest and obligatory heterosexuality. Reading Freud through the eyes of Lacan, Rubin then argues that in the Oedipal crisis, young children, whose gender identity is as yet relatively neutral, grasp the details of kinship systems. They have to assimilate into their personalities assigned gender roles, heterosexuality (the hope in adulthood to marry someone like their parent of the opposite sex), and the acknowledgment of male privilege (the social advantages of having a penis). In Rubin's wonderful synthesis of Lévi-Strauss, Freud and Lacan, we can appreciate the power of the cultural forces that reproduce each generation as gendered beings, without succumbing to the notion that these arrangements are 'natural' or inevitable. We can also comprehend the ways in which capitalism becomes intertwined with sex and gender, while becoming clear that eliminating the former will not completely transform the sex/gender system whose roots are in kinship systems and individual psyches.

Radical feminist theories are inadequate in fully analysing women's situation in capitalist societies, but their value in calling attention to the centrality of gender in our social arrangements is enormous. They make amply clear that traditional socialist demands on behalf of women such as full and equal labour-force participation, or wages for housework, do not get at the root of female oppression. And they suggest how narrow a sphere of women's social life is encompassed in historical studies focusing only on women's work, whether in the home or in the labour market. Radical feminists are asking new questions about female subordination from which we can learn: How are gender and heterosexuality created in individuals and reproduced from generation to generation? What wider social structures perpetuate stratification by gender? How can women survive in male-dominated societies? How have they managed in the past? Given the gulf separating the experience of women and men, what is the nature of same-sex relationships? Can heterosexual intimacy really transcend this gulf, or does it also reflect or even perpetuate male domination?

Questions from radical feminism have begun to influence women's history with very fruitful results. Carroll Smith-Rosenberg's 1975 study, 'The Female World of Love and Ritual', explored the nature of middle-class women's ties with one another in early Victorian America. It pieces together a picture of the kind of world women made for themselves in the patriarchal and highly sex-segregated society of the early nineteenth-century middle class. Using hundreds of diaries and family papers dating from the late eighteenth to the mid-nineteenth centuries, Smith-Rosenberg showed how a shared, enclosed world of domestic life, church and charity organisations formed the basis for dense networks of deeply cherished ties between women friends and kin. Through such networks, women provided each other not only with help in difficult times, but a sense of being valued and appreciated not often available elsewhere. In this and other studies of nineteenth-century American women's shared lives, women cease to be simply objects of male oppression and patriarchal ideology, and their real experience and activity becomes more visible.[4] A second radical feminist agenda in these studies is to shed light on possibilities inherent in same-sex relationships. Those Smith-Rosenberg studied were openly physically demonstrative; the women exchanged letters that today are only written by people 'in love'. But the social classification 'lesbian' did not yet exist, and these women were quite unselfconscious about their physical intimacy and emotional tenderness. When

Eleanor Roosevelt's very similar friendship was uncovered this autumn by a biographer, her descendants, obviously embarrassed by Roosevelt's 'lesbian' feelings for her friend, were at pains to point out the prevalence of this style of relationship among women of her age and class.

As the female experience becomes more vivid, we are also learning more about areas of life where male and female life intersected: sexuality and sexual identity, and marriage. Studies of nineteenth-century 'women's culture', for example, show its richness diminishing toward the end of the century as marriage increased as an emotional focus. At about the same time, as Jeffrey Weeks documents for England, gender roles increased in rigidity, as love between women (or between men) became increasingly defined as deviant. Inspired by questions from radical feminism, historians are also exploring sexual attitudes and practices, and political movements that have grown up around sexual questions, like that for birth control in the USA, or to repeal the Contagious Diseases Acts in England. For if sexuality is defined as pivotal in our social system, we will be more likely to see sexual reformers as genuine radicals, and to notice the sexual imagery that clusters around other social divisions such as class, and which comes to the surface particularly during periods of intense class conflict.[5]

Through this work on 'women's culture' we are also beginning to gain some understanding of the cultures in which individual and group acts of female rebellion, or wider political movements, can originate. The Women's Christian Temperance Union, for example, emerging in the 1870s as a 'mass organisation of women unprecedented in scale and organisation', spoke to women as participants in 'women's culture' and propelled thousands for the first time into political activity. Many went on to emerge as agitators for women's rights, or as socialist leaders at the turn of the century. The consciousness of a shared female experience - of belonging to a particular social category, womanhood - was a prerequisite for the emergence of nineteenth-century feminism. As Elizabeth Cady Stanton wrote, 'Womanhood is the primal fact, wifehood and motherhood its incidents.'[6]

Our understanding of nineteenth-century American women's social life is sorely missing any attention to parallel networks among working-class women, and indeed to the class dimension of women's experience. This is partly due to the difficulty of grasping class relationships in areas and periods when subsistence farming was so prevalent. But it also reflects radical feminists' lack of interest in class. Yet there is ample evidence that poor and working-class women have formed networks structured not usually around friendship but around kinship or neighbourhood proximity. American anthropologist Carol Stack has described the networks of female kin which help black welfare recipients to survive today.[7] British sources for both the nineteenth and the twentieth centuries suggest

that important self-help networks of neighbours have exchanged
food, childcare, and substantial help during crises. Prostitutes
in Plymouth and Southampton, harassed under the Contagious
Diseases Acts in the 1860s and 1870s, established a subculture
providing companionship and mutual aid which connected closely
with female neighbours and kin who supplied financial help and
support in court proceedings.[8] Bread riots in eighteenth- and
nineteenth-century towns in England and the Continent are
likely to have been products of similar neighbourhood networks.
Certainly the 1905 Kosher Meat Riots in New York emerged out
of women's neighbourhood and religious connections.

For those of us who think of class as a central social division,
and want to chart a history of the working class in Britain,
accepting a second social cleavage based on gender adds untold
complications as well as richness to our picture of the historical
process. We have to integrate into our picture of working-class
life the sexual differences in living standards – within the same
households – documented in turn-of the century studies of
family budgets and analysed by feminist historians.[9] We need
to acknowledge that the relative indifference of the majority of
trades unions toward organising working women, as well as
their support for protective legislation, was based at least in
part on their assumptions about the prerogatives of *men*. We
further need to explore the significance of women's experience
and of neighbourhood life in shaping the varieties of working-
class culture. Gender was lived out differently in 'respectable'
and 'rough' neighbourhoods; in the former, for example, a
female presence on the streets and stoops, and in pubs, was
far less acceptable than in the poorest areas. Sources like
Round About a Pound a Week[10] show how networks of women
neighbours, through gossip, snooping and mutual aid systems
helped to form some of the central boundaries of working-class
culture: patterns of drinking, child-rearing, of cleanliness
and thrift. Incorporating radical feminist insights into the social
history of the working class is to rethink and to refine our
concept of class itself.

NOTES

1 These stages are well documented in the following excellent
  review essays: Barbara Sicherman, 'Review Essay: American
  History,' *Signs* 1, no. 2, Winter 1975; Carolyn Lougee,
  'Review Essay: Modern European History,' *Signs* 2, no. 3,
  Spring 1977; Gerda Lerner, 'Placing Women in History:
  Definitions and challenges,' *Feminist Studies* 3, nos 1/2,
  Fall 1975; Carroll Smith-Rosenberg, 'The New Woman and the
  New History,' *ibid.*; Natalie Davis, ' "Women's History" in
  Transition: The European case,' *Feminist Studies* 3, nos 3/4,
  Spring/Summer 1976.
2 I will be discussing American histories of women, though not

all specialise in US history.
3 Gayle Rubin, 'The Traffic in Women: Notes on the "political
   economy" of sex,' in *Toward an Anthropology of Women*, ed.
   by Rayna R. Reiter, London 1975.
4 Carroll Smith-Rosenberg's essay is in *Signs* 1, no. 1,
   Autumn 1975. Some examples of other studies of 'women's
   culture' as embodied in female networks are: Nancy Cott,
   The Bonds of Womanhood, New Haven 1977; Nancy Sahli,
   'Smashing: Women's Relationships before the fall,' *Chrysalis*,
   no. 8, Summer 1979; Mary P. Ryan, 'The Power of Women's
   Networks,' *Feminist Studies* 5, no. 1, Spring 1979; Susan
   Porter Benson, 'Business Heads and Sympathizing Hearts:
   The women of the Providence Employment Society,' *Journal
   of Social History* 12, no. 2, Winter 1978. The connection
   between feminism and women's culture is explicitly made in
   Blanche Hersh, *The Slavery of Sex: Feminist abolitionists
   in America*, Urbana 1979.
5 Two studies of movements in which sexuality was a central
   theme are: Linda Gordon, *Woman's Body, Woman's Right. A
   Social History of Birth Control in America*, New York 1976;
   and Judith Walkowitz, *Prostitution in Victorian England:
   Women, class, and the state*, London 1980. The sharpening
   of sexual identities toward the end of the nineteenth century
   is analysed in Jeffrey Weeks' 'Movements of affirmation:
   Sexual meanings and homosexual identities,' *Radical History
   Review*, Spring/Summer 1979. The intermingling of issues of
   class and gender is lucidly explored, in different ways, by
   Barbara Taylor, 'Socialism, feminism, and sexual
   antagonism in the London tailoring trade in the early 1830s',
   Feminist Studies 5, no. 1, Spring 1979, and by Leonore
   Davidoff, 'Class and gender in Victorian England: The
   diaries of Arthur J. Munby and Hannah Cullwick,' *ibid.*
6 Stanton is quoted in Cott, *op. cit.*, p. 206. The quotation on
   the WCTU is from Mary Jo Buhle's 'Women's Culture and
   Feminism,' *Feminist Studies*, forthcoming (1980). In her
   contribution to a symposium on 'Women's Culture and Women's
   Networks' prepared for *Feminist Studies* (which includes
   Buhle's article), Ellen Dubois warns against using women's
   culture as a static concept. Though they provided women
   with strength and satisfaction, these cultures were formed
   out of women's political and social weakness; thus it is
   important to maintain at the centre of our consciousness of
   women's past a sense of the importance of organised political
   groups fighting for social and sexual equality.
7 Carol Stack, *All Our Kin. Strategies for Survival in an
   Urban Black Community*, New York 1974.
8 Judith Walkowitz, 'The making of an outcast group,' in *A
   Widening Sphere*, ed. Martha Vicinus, Bloomington 1977.
9 Laura Oren, 'The welfare of women in labouring families:
   England, 1860-1950,' *Feminist Studies* 1, nos 3-4, Winter-
   Spring 1973.

10 Maud Pember Reeves, *Round About a Pound a Week*, introduction Sally Alexander, London 1977.

Fascism and anti-fascism

Paul Preston*

THE HISTORIOGRAPHICAL CATEGORIES

Broadly speaking, the historiography of the Spanish Civil War
and its origins has fallen into three categories: the work
produced by the defeated Republicans, whether anarchist,
socialist, communist or liberal; the out-pourings of writers in
Spain, in some way or other at the service of the Franco
regime; and lastly the work of ostensibly neutral foreigners,
whether academics or journalists. In the case of the first two
groups, their writing constituted a continuation of the civil war
by other means. In the case of the last group, despite claims
to objectivity, the large majority of the books were also
partisan. Since the death of Franco in 1975, there has emerged
another category – serious scholarship produced within Spain
itself.

Pro-Republican Works
As soon as the war was over, the exile produced a flood of
inquests on the defeat which still remain among the best writings
on the war. Much of it was in memoir form and should be
considered as a primary source: among the outstanding works
are the memoirs of the socialist Juan Siméon-Vidarte, those of
the anarchists Cipriano Mera and Juan García Oliver, the rather
embittered accounts of the renegade communists, Jesús
Hernández and Enrique Castro Delgado, and the remarkable
collected works of the Republican president Manuel Azaña.
Every bit as important as these personal accounts were a number
of interpretative works concerning the defeat of the Republic.
Among the anarchists, Diego Abad de Santillán's *?Porqué
perdimos la guerra?* was the most interesting, although José
Peirats' document-filled *La CNT en la revolución* remains
indispensable. The socialist Julián Zugazagoitia produced his
Historia de la guerra de España shortly before being handed
over by the Vichy regime to be shot by Franco. Arguably one
of the most important books on the war was written by a
Trotskyist, Grandizo Munis, *Jalones de derrota, promesa de
victoria.*

All the above works and many more like them were partisan
not only in that they were anti-Franco and pro-Republican, but
also in so far as they reflected the bitter divisions within the

---

*Paul Preston teaches history at Queen Mary College, London.
Author of *The Coming of the Spanish Civil War*, London 1979.

Republican side. The obvious broad division was between the
communists and the rest. The debate over the primacy of
revolution or victory in a conventional war had left anarchists
and POUMists as the enraged victims of communist policies.
Consequently, much of their writing reflects both the debate
and the resulting bitterness. By the time the Cold War was
under way, many Spanish anarchists, POUMists, socialists and
ex-communists were actually producing fiercely anti-communist
tracts. On the other side, the communists produced rigidly
partisan accounts of which the best example is probably the
PCE's official history of the war *Guerra y revolución en
España*.

Underlying the vicious internecine polemics was a crucial
debate. Since the Spanish war constituted a major blow for the
European working class in an era of successive defeats, the
inevitability of that defeat does not have to be taken for
granted. Post-war writing has reflected the sort of thinking
which permeated the Spanish left before the war and which went
some way to dictating its policies during the war. Both the
socialists and the communists were victims of a crude vulgar
Marxist analysis of Spain's development and their actions were
conditioned by the consequent belief that Spain had to pass
through a classic bourgeois revolution. We will return to this
point in the second section of this article. However, suffice it
to say that a rigid commitment to this view, strengthened by
the exigencies of Soviet foreign policy, ensured short shrift
for those groups which advocated more flexible revolutionary
policies. In this respect, Grandizo Munis's book, mentioned
above, is of the first importance, exposing the burden created
by this inflexibility.

Pro-Franco works
During and immediately after the war, the Franco regime tried
to justify its existence by an interpretation of the war which
portrayed it as a struggle between the godless hordes of the
proletariat and guardians of traditional Christian values. Much
of this work was done by policemen - like Eduardo Comín
Colomer and Angel Ruiz Ayucar, by soldiers, by government
propagandists and by priests. In terms of interpretation, this
body of work is less than illuminating, but it is useful as a
source on the activities of the right before the war and on the
politics of the Franco zone during it. The outstanding work is
that by Joaquín Arrarás, an extreme authoritarian monarchist,
who produced the four-volume *Historia de la segunda República
española* and the monumental thirty-six-volume *Historia de la
cruzada*, whose title alone gives away the author's ideological
commitment. Almost all the work which aimed at presenting the
civil war as a religious crusade was equally intent on obscuring
the war's class nature.

Francoist historiography was not totally inflexible; it
changed according to the political needs of the day. In the

immediate aftermath of the war when the executions of
Republican prisoners were still in full swing and the prisons
and work-camps overflowing, the tone was of hysterical
denunciation of alleged atrocities committed by the rabble such
as those by Tomás Borras, *Checas de Madrid*, *epopeya de los
caídos* and Aniceto de Castro Albarran's *La gran víctima: la
iglesia española mártir de la revolución roja*, or else of semi-
religious veneration of Falangist martyrs, like Francisco
Bravo's *José Antonio: el hombre, el jefe, el camarada*. However,
with the fall of Axis, the main need of the Franco dictatorship
was to ingratiate itself with the Western allies, and by the late
1940s the tendency of Spanish historical writing on the Civil
War was to present Franco as a clairvoyant pioneer in the war
against communism – the most extreme example being Luis
Galinsoga's *Centinela del occidente*. A more dramatic change
took place in the 1960s when a major operation to streamline
and modernise official historiography took place under the
direction of Ricardo de la Cierva. This was partly a response to
modernisation in Spanish society as a whole – higher standards
of education and the growth of a militant student body, which
travelled abroad, made the old propaganda untenable. But it
was also a reply to the impact of foreign work being smuggled
into the country. The greatest impact was created by Hugh
Thomas's *The Spanish Civil War* in its Spanish translation, but
the most devastating blow was delivered by what is now one of
the great classics of civil war historiography, Herbert R.
Southworth's *El mito de la cruzada de Franco*, a savage
exposure of the many distortions on which the Francoists had
built their history. La Cierva's many books moved away from
the religious tone of earlier work and dug in at the position
which maintained that the war was the result of left-wing
extremism driving moderate men reluctantly to take up arms in
self-defence.

   Perhaps more interesting from the Francoist side are the
many memoirs of which the most revealing are by far José
María Gil Robles' *No fue posible la paz* which inadvertently
reveals how the right provoked the war by making democracy
unworkable. Since Franco died, many of his erstwhile
supporters have produced memoirs which, in their differ-
end ways are illuminating and often hostile to Franco.
Outstanding are those by his brother-in-law and foreign
minister during the early 1940s, Ramón Serrano Súñer, and by
an ex-Minister of Education, the monarchist, Pedro Sainz
Rodríguez.

The work of foreigners
Much of the writing produced by volunteers of the International
Brigades and by some deeply committed right-wing journalists
in the Francoist zone might properly be placed in the previous
categories. Superb eyewitness accounts of the major battles
have been provided by British volunteers like Esmond Romilly,

Jason Guerney, Tom Wintringham and many others, and their point of view is broadly pro-Republican. Similarly, the books by the pro-Franco volunteer Peter Kemp and by the rightist journalists Harold Cardozo, William Foss and Cecil Gerahty are totally Francoist in their sympathies. These testimonial accounts aside, there was serious interpretative work produced from the beginning. Frank Jellinek's *The Civil War in Spain*, a pro-communist account, and Rudolf Rocker's *The Tragedy of Spain*, came out as early as 1938. On the Nationalist side, there were highly propagandistic essays such as Arnold Lunn's *Spanish Rehearsal* and Robert Sencourt's *Spain's Ordeal*. However, the great leap forward in historical interpretation came in 1943 with Gerald Brenan's *The Spanish Labyrinth*.

Brenan's work is now widely accepted as the starting point for research on the Spanish war. Even though parts of his work have been challenged by subsequent investigations, his interpretation is still highly valued. Although he did not start from any specific analytical model and indeed would probably have considered himself an objective liberal, his book was a major historiographical contribution as well as being an elegantly written essay by a man with close Bloomsbury connections. As a consequence of having lived in the Andalusian countryside since the end of the Great War, Brenan had two profound perceptions which remain as important now as they were when his book was first published. Whereas most contemporary writers on Spain took the great ideological battles of the 1930s - fascism versus communism, democracy versus totalitarianism - Brenan saw that the Spanish war was fundamentally a Spanish war. The two great perceptions were the sheer centrality of the agrarian question behind the war and the fact that the war could only be understood in terms of the previous hundred years of Spanish development.

A similar perspective illuminates an equally significant contribution to the historiography of the civil war, Raymond Carr's *Spain 1808-1939*. Carr's central theme is the failure of Spanish liberalism to wrest power from the old agrarian oligarchy and to make an industrial revolution and a corresponding bourgeois democratic political revolution. Unfortunately, the contributions of Carr and Brenan have tended to be overshadowed by the enormous popular success of Hugh Thomas's *The Spanish Civil War*. A highly colourful, blow-by-blow account of the Spanish war, it was hailed by a number of pundits - Cyril Connolly, Philip Toynbee, Michael Foot - who were not historians, but who had supported the Republic in the 1930s and had subsequently moved to the right. Thomas's liberal objective stance went so far in its search for BBC-style balance that it had no central position at all, merely attempting to find an equilibrium of favourable and hostile material about both sides. This inevitably led to a dominance of narrative over analysis, something which seems to have endeared

the book to a large audience. In the absence of an analytical
framework, the highly charged purple prose left the impression
that the civil war was fought because the Spaniards were of a
peculiarly violent nature. This tendency has been corrected
somewhat in subsequent editions.

The success of Hugh Thomas rather obscured two important
works which centred on the central 'war or revolution' dilemma
– Burnett Bolloten's *The Grand Camouflage* and Pierre Broué
and Emile Témime's *The Revolution and the Civil War in Spain*.
Gabriel Jackson's *The Spanish Republic and the Civil War*,
written from a left Republican standpoint fared better. The need
for a longer-term structural interpretation which had been
highlighted by the contributions of Brenan and Carr was taken
up again in 1970 by Edward E. Malefakis's *Agrarian Reform and
Peasant Revolution in Spain* which re-emphasised the crucial
importance of the agrarian problem. In 1978, my book *The
Coming of the Spanish Civil War* attempted to interpret the
breakdown of the Second Republic in terms of rural class
conflict. Then in mid-1979, a major breakthrough took place
with the appearance of Ronald Fraser's *Blood of Spain*, a work
of oral social history which emphasised the interplay of long-
term structural problems and the contemporary pressures of the
international problems of the Soviet Union.

The new wave in Spain
The disappearance of Francoist censorship has seen the
re-emergence of a healthy historical scholarship in Spain. The
main emphasis has been on the detailed history of the workers'
movement – of particular note are the works of Santos Juliá and
Marta Bizcarrondo on the socialist movement during the
Republic. On the Civil War itself, there has been little except
for the outstanding studies of the financing of the war and of
German aid by the economic historian Angel Viñas. Perhaps of
the greatest significance historiographically speaking, albeit
not immediately concerned with the war nor even with the
twentieth century, are the works of the two Catalan economic
historians, Jordi Nadal and Josep Fontana, on the failure of
industrial revolution and the way in which liberal energies were
diverted away from bourgeois revolution.

THE LAND QUESTION

In order to understand the nature of the Spanish Civil War it is
essential to understand the nature of Spanish capitalism. The
error of analysis of the Spanish left in the 1930s – and even in
the struggle against Franco, until the mid-1960s – and of many
sympathetic historians has been to assume that because Spain
suffered from a backward agriculture, the central issue in
modern history has been the need to make a bourgeois revolution

against feudal remnants. In fact, just because Spain's
agriculture was inefficient, it was no less capitalist. Spain's
development took, in rather less spectacular circumstances, the
Prussian path to modernisation.

The progressive political impulse of the Spanish bourgeoisie
was sufficiently weak throughout the nineteenth century to
preclude any major swing of social power. In the first two major
periods of pressure - 1833-43 and 1854-6 - the liberal
commercial bourgeoisie was virtually bought off by the sale of
church, aristocratic and common lands on the open market. This
process diverted much urban mercantile capital into the land and
the consolidation of the system of enormous latifundia estates.
The urban bourgeoisie and the landholding oligarchy were linked
further by inter-marriage and by the penetration of the financial
elite by aristocratic and ecclesiastical capital. The second two
periods of bourgeois revolutionary impulse - 1868-74 and 1916-18
- emphasised even further the weakness of the bourgeoisie. On
both occasions, the conjunction of worker and peasant agitation
was enough to induce the urban oligarchy to accentuate its ties
with the rural. The 1918 government of national coalition and,
in a different way, the dictatorship of Primo de Rivera,
illustrated the extent to which a reactionary coalition of land
and industry had been created, with the industrial elites in a
subordinate position.

The Second Republic was to constitute a massive challenge to
the balance of social and economic power built up in the previous
century. Various means were adopted to defend the threatened
structures ranging from legal obstruction of reform to violent
destabilisation of the Republican regime. Eventually, the
proletarian rising of 1934 and the electoral victory of the
Popular Front in February 1936 were a cumulative
demonstration of the fact that the old order could not be shored
up by the legal establishment of a corporative state. Thus, the
representatives of the oligarchy turned to the military. The
regime which emerged victorious from the war was essentially
an agrarian dictatorship which was only to be rendered obsolete
by the economic development of the late 1950s and 1960s.

This interpretation stresses the importance of an
examination of the century before the Civil War in order to
explain the creation of two entirely antagonistic social blocs. It
also sees agrarian conflict as the crucial issue behind the war.
This is not to ignore the other issues - industrial conflict,
regionalism, religious hatreds, etc. - which were part of the
breakdown of political co-existence in 1936. Nor is it to ignore
the extent to which the political representatives of both right
and left were profoundly influenced by contemporary events
abroad, and particularly by the rise of fascism. Nor is it to
suggest that, for all the long-term nature of the war's agrarian
origins, in the last resort, the war was profoundly conditioned
in its conduct and outcome by foreign intervention. After all, if
the Spanish Civil War was an agrarian war - and in its origins it

certainly was – then that agrarian war was quickly over. By the winter of 1936, the army, with the great Andalusian landlords in their wake, had established control over the great latifundia zones of rural proletarian militancy. Nevertheless, the definition of the war in agrarian terms remains important, not least with regard to the debate over the primacy of war effort or social revolution in the Republican camp. Even if the burden of the Republican war effort fell on the urban working class and their petit bourgeois allies, the enemy remained the landed oligarchy. Accordingly, there might well be a case for re-assessing the efficacy of revolutionary experiments which were not directed at the liberation of those areas which, before 1936, had contained the most militant, and worst organised, sectors of the Spanish rural proletariat.

24 THE SPANISH CIVIL WAR

Ronald Fraser*

The Spanish Civil War does not properly fit into the categories of fascism and anti-fascism. The long social crisis which led to the war might well, in an 'underdeveloped' capitalist country which, like Spain, had lost an empire, have found its resolution in fascism. But for a number of reasons it did not.

The inauguration of an advanced parliamentary democracy under the 1931 Republic – a stage in the ruling class crisis – was an attempt to arrive at new political forms of legitimising the domination of the possessing classes and their rate of accumulation. The necessary reforms would both 'modernise' capitalist relations of production and serve to incorporate a growing and increasingly militant proletariat into the new parliamentary democracy for the first time, thus warding off the threat of social revolution. The crisis was so deep, however, that the ruling classes were not fully in control of the transition. The threat of revolution remained constantly – and not always unjustifiably – before their eyes. None the less, they

---

*Ronald Fraser is a novelist turned historian, author of *Blood of Spain*, London 1979, an oral history of the Spanish Civil War, and of *Work, Twenty Personal Accounts*, 2 vols, Harmondsworth 1967. An associate editor of *History Workshop Journal*.

did not turn to the newly created fascist Falange; until
February 1936, and the Popular Front electoral victory, they
supported a parliamentary road to a Catholic corporative state,
via the CEDA (Confederación Española de Derechas Antónomas,
the mass Catholic party).

A number of hypotheses can be advanced for the Falange's
pre-war failure. (1) The absence of a large industrial petit
bourgeoisie deeply marked by the contradictions of capitalist
development. (2) In the areas where such a petit bourgeoisie
existed – Catalonia and the Basque Country – it generally
supported autonomist solutions which were directly threatened
by Falangist totalitarian centralism and territorial unity. (3)
The working class and its organisations, which had suffered no
serious defeat, were 'impermeable' to fascism as a 'solution' to
the class struggle. (4) The possessing classes, fearful of
revolution, had historically placed their trust in another force
to protect their interests: the army. This it had most recently
done in crushing the October 1934 rising in Asturias. By
comparison, the Falange was not a serious force. Moreover,
imperialist expansion – even at the rhetorical Falangist level –
may not have appeared a 'solution' to sectors of the possessing
classes who had seen the social and financial cost of the long
war to hold Spanish Morocco.

After the Popular Front elections, many disillusioned CEDA
supporters – especially the youth – joined the Falange. But the
latter, harassed by the new government, was still unable to
become an organised mass movement. Its leader, Primo de
Rivera, along with many of the other prominent Falangists,
was in gaol. Local organisations were closed down and its
members held under 'administrative' arrest. Primo de Rivera
was himself suspicious of a military rising and did not give
instructions to collaborate until close to the moment.

The Falange's street violence after February 1936
contributed to the conviction of the possessing classes that the
Republic could not contain the threatening revolution; but the
latter's eyes remained on the military to save the situation.

Indeed, it was the army which led the counter-revolutionary
rising of July 1936. The rising created a political vacuum (the
military having no clear political instrument) on the insurgent
side which the Falange filled in large part. But it was never
able to take over the state. Before the war it had 'leaders and
few members'; now it had 'members and few leaders'.[1] Despite
its mass membership, the Falange never became a mass party;
it lacked the leaders and the internal dynamic, in the view of a
leading Falangist of the time: 'It was a hierarchical party, much
more similar to an army than a mass party – and there's nothing
less like a mass party than an army.' Instead of taking over the
state, the Falange was taken over by Franco, who repressed
its populist 'revolutionary' elements and used its totalitarianism
to reinforce his own.

Franco's power was exercised with two fundamental aims.

(1) To crush once and for all the threat of social revolution and nationalist secession (the absence of a fascist project can be seen in the insurgents' attitude to the working masses in their zone: 'salvation' by firing squad rather than through incorporation into a national-syndicalist imperial 'revolution'). (2) To make good the old ruling classes' inability to legitimise their domination, as demonstrated under the Republic. This domination would now be exercised by Franco as an overt dictatorship, initially in the form of a totalitarian fascist administration, on behalf of the bourgeoisie. The form, however, did not accurately represent the real content.

On the Republican side, the masses who rose initially to crush the insurgents and inaugurate the revolution did not in general consider fascism their enemy. It was rather *reaction* – the military and behind them the old ruling classes and church which was the enemy. Their expropriations were not directed at fascists *per se*, but at their class enemy: landlords and factory owners.

The social revolution – ultra-leftist in many regards – failed. It failed, I would argue, because it was unable to create the necessary conditions for pressing the revolution forward *in order to* win the war – its *primordial* task. The major condition for this was to create out of fragmented local powers a revolutionary power that would overthrow the remains of the bourgeois state and mobilise the total energies of the populace in the task of fighting the war. The latter required a revolutionary fighting force under a single command. The disparate militias were not this. Their defeats (or, at best, their lack of success) after the first few weeks led to the need for a different concept of war if the enemy were to be defeated. The revolution's failure must lead to the establishment of a different power capable of organising the war effort.

It was this that the Spanish Communist Party, and to a less important extent the liberal republicans, argued for. The party, under Comintern guidance, had since 1935 considered fascism the main enemy; the task of completing the bourgeois democratic revolution in Spain had since then been overshadowed by the struggle of 'democracy against fascism'. The Spanish Communist Party's line at the national level, and the Soviet Union's policies at the international level, found an apparently perfect 'fit': anti-fascist alliances with bourgeois democratic nations and domestic parties.

The revolution's failure opened the political space for, and made necessary, the Spanish Communist Party's Popular Front option. The implementation of the Popular Front policies aligning the petit bourgeoisie nationally, and the bourgeois democracies internationally, precluded social revolution. Even more, it precluded revolutionary methods of fighting the war. Working-class alliance with anti-fascist sectors of the bourgeoisie was conflated into bourgeois (in mentality and politics, if not sociological) *leadership* of the struggle. The

bitter polemic over war and revolution was, in many senses, a
false one. It concerned not the vital question of revolutionary
war, but of political control of revolutionary conquests in the
rearguard. The Party waged a pitiless, sectarian and more than
once bloody struggle to win this control. In leaning towards the
reformist sectors of the socialists and liberal republicans, in
seeking to 'contain' the revolution, it rejected an alliance with
those sectors of the anarcho-syndicalist movement and left
socialists who understood (or were open to understanding) the
needs of the revolution in terms of the war (and thus isolating
the ultra-left sectors unable to assimilate this). In neglecting
this revolutionary potential, the Spanish Communist Party
reinforced the historical divisions of the Spanish working class
- divisions already in large part responsible for the revolution's
failure - instead of securing the unity of purpose so necessary
to winning the war. This, I would argue, was the major error
ascribable to the policy of an 'anti-fascist' war.

NOTE

1 Herbert Southworth, 'The Falange: An analysis of Spain's
 fascist heritage' in *Spain in Crisis*, ed. by Paul Preston,
 London 1976. Southworth's essay is a good introduction to
 the Falange.

25 'SUBVERSIVENESS' AND ANTI-FASCISM IN ITALY

Franco Andreucci*

In Italy, some time ago, I went to see a fairly good film. Its
title was *The Spider's Strategy* and the director was Bernardo
Bertolucci. The story was really quite simple; it was the
biography, more or less, of one Athos Magnani, an invented
hero who was the symbol of the rebellious anti-fascism and
subversiveness typical of vast zones in Italy, especially in the
area of the southern Po Valley.
 The climax of the film takes place during a holiday folkdance

---

*Franco Andreucci is director of the Ragioneri Institute,
Florence, teaches history at Florence University and is editor of
the *Biographical Dictionary of the Italian Labour Movement*.

in a large square in front of the homes of the peasants. Some of the couples are dancing, while others are sitting at tables chatting and listening to a small orchestra. Suddenly a group of fascist leaders arrive and order the orchestra to stop playing and begin *Giovinezza*, the official national fascist hymn. Here is where Athos Magnani, young, strong and courageous, intolerant of arrogance and injustice, makes his sensational move. He pulls up the most beautiful blonde in the group and begins to dance boldly and contemptuously to the fascist hymn as if it were a common foxtrot. Besides this poignant event, there are many other examples which constitute the film biography of this young rebel: the preparation of an impossible attempt on Mussolini's life, the secret reunion with other unlikely conspirators, all united by a passion for opera, food and wine.

These episodes bring to mind thousands of other analogous events, thousands of episodes which together formed a primitive opposition to fascism, an opposition which was often pre-political and even when it was political at times manifested such impotence that it bordered on farce.

In the region near Empoli, in Tuscany, there was an illegal communist federation which continued to exist during the whole period of fascism. It was extremely strong and had a large number of clandestine members who used to meet regularly at a corner tavern. There is a story which has come to light regarding this group. In the mid-1930s they had a plan to defeat fascism in the following manner; at a determined hour X each one of a group of 200 revolutionaries armed with a revolver would station himself near one of a pre-selected group of fascist leaders. If they all succeeded in killing their victim at this designated hour, fascism would fall.

An utterly ridiculous plan, in fact one might call it pure day-dreaming. However, the history of Italy under fascism is full of such dramatic impotencies; of projects and attempts which were planned and never carried out. It would be an error to think of Italy under fascism either as a solid building with a foundation constructed from a compact consensus, or as a country divided into two, with the fascists on one side and anti-fascist militants on the other. The reality is much more complex.

Let's try to illuminate the dreams and vendettas which may be said to define the rebellious tradition - 'preindustrial', 'preurban', according to the terminology used by Gramsci.[1] It's only recently that we have begun to take out each small piece of the mosaic in order to see every detail, in order to deal with the daily life, political attitudes and social conditions of the popular masses during the twenty years in which Italy was dominated by fascism. Old theories, both ideological and historiographical, are now discredited; theories such as those of Benedetto Croce in his formula that fascism in Italy was a 'sickness', an invasion of foreign bodies in the fabric of

Italian society. Other hypotheses which have also undergone
questioning are those which offer a Manichaean, moralistic or
sectarian conception, according to which on one side were the
martyrs (whom we must remember as symbols) and on the other
side fascism.[2]

Naturally, serious and documented attempts to reconstruct
the history of Italian fascism are not lacking, especially those
regarding the study of the institutions of the regime, its laws,
and the general lines of its home and foreign policy.[3] Serious
studies concerning movements of opposition to fascism are also
not lacking, in particular those dedicated to the Italian
Communist Party, the only organised political force which
conducted an uninterrupted underground fight.[4]

However, what does seem to be missing are studies of the
workers and peasants, their actions, their thoughts, their
feelings.

How was it possible that a strong labour movement, such as
Italy possessed before 1922, could be defeated in an exhausting
civil war? And, how could it come back again twenty years later
with renewed strength, giving rise to a victorious partisan war,
reconstructing its own image - through its parties and its labour
organisations - as a rich and meaningful expression of Italian
history? How did its militants live during the twenty years of
the dictatorship? Had they awaited, perhaps, in silence the end
of the venture, maintaining their forces intact in order to form
a sort of silent minority? Whoever goes on to analyse the
average age of the partisans or of the communist and socialist
militants after 1945, would see that the large majority of them
were extremely young, born during or after the First World
War. Therefore, how did they become anti-fascists? Some of the
questions are well posed by Togliatti's lectures on fascism which,
even though given in 1935, only became known at the beginning
of the 1970s. This interpretation has made the question of
'consensus' and its variants, both positive and negative, the
centre of attention.[5]

'Subversiveness' is one of the central aspects of this problem.
One could call it an old tradition in the history of the Italian
people, one which is difficult to define. It was an attitude, a
mood, which spread to the borders and even outside the borders
of the labour movement, in the strict sense of the word.
Subversiveness has always been something more than a simple
feeling of spontaneous rebellion against the state.

In wide sectors of the working class of Turin, as G. Sapelli
has demonstrated, among the artisans and workers of Florence
who were recently analysed by G. Santomassimo, as among the
dockers of Leghorn, on whom E. Mannari is working - that is
to say among social groups partly influenced by the Socialist
Party up until the period immediately following the First World
War - political militancy had always been expressed in daily
attitudes of defiance and independence. In fact we must
remember that in the Italian labour movement the relationship

of socialists with the anarchists was never one of complete and implacable opposition, as it was in other European countries.[6] But all this seemed to disappear, as snow in the sunshine, in front of the fascist conquest of power and the organisation of a totalitarian state from 1922 to 1926.

Yet still in those years, if we look closely at the column in *l'Unita* called 'Letters from Workers and Peasants', and analyse the information which accompanied news about political prisoners, one can see that the organisational breakdown of the Socialist Party was accompanied by a passage of militants and political traditions into the ranks of the Communist Party.[7]

But if until 1926 it's still possible to follow the problem on the basis of printed sources, after this date the subject matter becomes extremely complex. Who are the rebels after 1926? Did they maintain their isolated position or did they join organised anti-fascism? And how did this take place?

Oppressed by a reactionary dictatorship, by a police state which exercised extensive forms of control, the subversives did not leave direct testimony at the time, and their retrospective memoirs and autobiographies are strongly influenced by a political judgment, organised teleologically, which takes the place of personal recollection. The political parties of the Left, whether they were poorly or well organised, usually had their archives completely destroyed or else they produced documents which are more useful for studying their central organisation or general policy than for the situation of the country. Certainly, generalisations are impossible but some documentation survives: for example among the archives of the Italian Communist Party - which were saved by the fact that much of the internal documentation of the party was sent to Moscow - are numerous reports from clandestine 'inspectors' who give a vivid image of Italy at that time.

But there are other kinds of sources. Quite often the repressive institutions, the police and security forces of authoritarian regimes present to the historian a serious dilemma. He finds himself in front of an enormous quantity of documentation which often represents an absured, almost morbid curiosity - I would even say a 'total' curiosity - on the part of the police. The results, however, are often documents which are inexact, unfaithful representations, at times even complete inventions. In fact, one of the peculiar aspects of the work of the contemporary historian is the necessity to know how to make a critical reading of police sources.

Fascism introduced into the traditions of the Italian police a new, 'disorderly', efficiency, extending even further the system of information and repression which had grown in an extraordinary way during the First World War.

In the central archives of the Italian state, under the heading *Ministero dell'Interno, Direzione Generale Pubblica Sicurezza, Divisione Affari Generali e Riservati* (Ministry of the Interior, General Direction of Public Security, Division of General and

Reserved Affairs) there are miles and miles of documents kept
on the opposition to fascism. There are hundreds of thousands
of biographical files on revolutionaries, militants, rebels,
traitors, all of which represented a solid working basis for the
volume of the *Biographical Dictionary of the Italian Labour
Movement*[8] which I edited along with Tommaso Detti.

But there are also, divided according to place and year,
general and specific reports from the various police corps on
the situation and the tendencies of public opinion: reports on
rumours and jokes, but also on investigations concerning
organised anti-fascism.

I would just like to point out briefly here that for the study
of this phenomenon of 'subversiveness' there do exist police
sources which are fairly genuine and immediate. These are the
collections of anonymous letters - similar to those addressed to
the king during the First World War which R. Monteleone has
edited[9] - and the slogans written on walls, which were copied
down and filed by the police.

Looking at these, we receive a completely new image of Italy:
ferments, small rebellions, elementary expressions of protest,
which bear witness to the permanence of the myths and ideas of
the revolution with a richness and fascination of detail about
day-to-day life.

Lavatories are extremely 'talkative' public places, and the
Red Revolution, Lenin, Stalin, the Red Flag, the hammer-and-
sickle all filled Italian lavatories as positive symbols, while
the Duce and fascism receive epithets which are easy to imagine.
The same description applies to other public places: post
offices, waiting rooms, etc. Trains, too, carried written slogans
both inside and outside the compartments, especially if they
originated outside Italy.

Often, in the same handwriting we find in the same slogan
praise for Lenin, cycling and soccer heroes. The picture which
emerges is of a slow deterioration of fascism's internal hold in
the years leading up to the Second World War, a picture drawn
directly by the opposers to the regime. We find evidence of the
drawing together of the rebellious traditions and communist
political organisation, especially after the turn to the left which
took place in 1929. We even find evidence of the communist
policy of penetrating fascist organisations and working from the
inside, as in the case of a young man from a working-class
family, the son of an unemployed bricklayer from Castelmaggiore
in the province of Bologna, who had joined the Fascist Party in
1933 and was discovered the following June in the act of writing
on the walls of the cloakroom of the Fascist Party headquarters
the phrase 'Down with Mussolini - Long live Lenin'.

Interest in this type of problem - the study of which has
just begun - should be reinforced by two general final
observations: (1) This daily elementary opposition was a
demonstration of the continuing existence in Italy of opposition
to the state - among workers, peasants, artisans - and allows

us to correct the thesis of an undifferentiated 'consensus' which is reconstructed more on the basis of sociological categories than on that of empirical research.
(2) It allows us to bring into focus some of the manifestations of the relationship between the masses and the image of communism which later on would represent a nucleus of the Resistance and of the strength of the Italian Communist Party after the war. Both seem to me excellent reasons for dedicating even greater attention to the 'subversives' during fascism.

NOTES

1 A. Gramsci, *Quaderni del carcere*, vol. 1, Turin 1975, p. 323. See also the classic book by E.J. Hobsbawm, *Primitive Rebels*, Manchester 1958.
2 See G. Quazza, *Resistenza e storia d'Italia. Problemi e ipotesi di Ricerca*, Milan 1976, pp. 7–104.
3 G. Carocci, *La politica estera dell'Italia fascista*, Bari 1969; A. Aquarone, *L'organizzazione dello stato totalitario*, Turin 1965.
4 P. Spriano, *Storia del PCI*, 5 vols, Turin 1967–75.
5 See R. De Felice, *Mussolini il duce, I, Gli anni del consenso 1929-1936*, Turin 1974, and the criticism of C. Santomassimo, 'Il fascismo degli anni '30', in *Sudi Storici*, XVI, n. 1, Jan.-March 1975, pp. 102–25.
6 G. Sapelli, 'Macchina repressiva, Sovvertivismo e tradizione politica durante il fascismo', in *Mezzosecolo: Materiali di ricerca storica*, Turin 1978, pp. 107–60.
7 E. Ragionieri, 'Il partito della svolta e la politica di massa', in *La Terza Internazionale e il partito communista italiano*, ed. by E. Ragionieri, Turin 1978, pp. 283–314.
8 F. Andreucci and T. Detti, *Il movimento operaio italiano. Dizionario biografico*, 6 vols, Rome 1975–9.
9 R. Monteleone, *Lettere al re*, Rome 1972.

Supplementary note
For an English language discussion of some of these questions, Luisa Passerini, 'Work, Ideology and Consensus under Italian Fascism', *History Workshop Journal* 8, November 1979.

26 OPEN QUESTIONS ON NAZISM

Tim Mason*

I want to make some brief comments about the agenda of
unresolved problems in attempts to give a Marxist account of
fascism, in particular of national socialism in Germany. Max
Horkheimer, a Marxist German philosopher and sociologist, said
that whoever wishes to speak of fascism cannot remain silent
about capitalism. This is helpful, but it does not tell us exactly
what we have to say about the relationship. In the course of
what can be described as a small renaissance of Marxist work on
the problem of fascism, in the 1960s and 1970s, a great deal
has been said. There has been a lively theoretical discussion
attempting to clarify the categories and concepts of our
analysis: notions of *class* and *state* have been more thoroughly
discussed in respect of fascism than in respect of any other
form of political domination in advanced capitalist societies.
There has been a good deal of analytical, empirical history: on
the economic crisis of 1928 onwards which was so decisive in the
rise of national socialism; on the form of the Nazi state; on forms
of exploitation in Nazi Germany, and in occupied territories; and
on the working-class resistance to fascism; East German
historians of orthodox communist persuasion have written on the
structure and role of the various monopoly groups within the
German capitalist economy in the fascist period. These are not
isolated achievements; they have genuinely contributed to a
broader understanding of fascism and national socialism beyond
the ranks of socialist scholars. It is, to a considerable extent,
due to the work of Marxist writers that the concept of
totalitarianism is falling into disuse in the work of liberal and
conservative scholars.
   Nevertheless there are no grounds for complacency. There
remain a number of acute problems for research and
interpretation. I want to single out three, and to rehearse types
of Marxist explanation which seem to be inadequate. The first
concerns the person of Hitler, the leader of the party and leader
of the Third Reich. We do not yet have even the makings of a
Marxist account of the personal power of the fascist leader in
the inter-war years. We have a number of unsatisfactory or
partial suggestions. Many readers will have in their minds John
Heartfield's brilliant photo-montage from the November 1932
election campaign - Hitler making his fascist salute, and behind
him an enormous business man putting banknotes into his hand:
'Millions stand behind me'. That was both a true image and good

*Tim Mason is fellow of St Peter's College, Oxford and an editor
of *History Workshop Journal*.

propaganda. But how much did those banknotes matter? The image is inadequate and misleading as a suggestion of categories for historical analysis. (It still does suggest such categories to some simplistic Marxist writers.) In the light of what has been found out about the way in which the Third Reich was governed, Hitler as a puppet simply will not do. Only slightly less unsatisfactory is the notion of Hitler as the figurehead, as the drummer and the demagogue, the brilliant manipulator of popular opinion and moods, who could maintain popular support for policies and developments which were actually quite different from those for which he and the movement were supposed to stand. This was a vital component of Nazi rule, but again, an inspection of the way in which the Third Reich was actually governed shows that Hitler was something more than that. He personally took many important and open decisions.

Sohn-Rethel, whose analytical memoir has recently been translated by the Conference of Socialist Economists group, had from his first-hand experience of upper-class Berlin in the early 1930s a clear sense that Hitler mattered, was important in many different ways. He struggles with this problem throughout his text. He suggests, for example, that businessmen trusted Hitler absolutely at those junctures when they got lost in the maze of bureaucracies, political uncertainties and policy options which the regime generated; or that they turned with faith to Hitler personally when the global situation of Nazi Germany seemed insecure or uncontrollable. This is a fruitful idea, but neither its truth nor its importance can be demonstrated. Was this really one of the important links between the political leader and capital? Sohn-Rethel suggests on other occasions that Hitler was used by contemporaries and has been used by historians as a shorthand for certain institutions and interest groups who were really making policy: they had got or could claim Hitler's blanket approval for this or that line and were able to speak in his name in order to gain or assert their authority. There are occasions where it can be demonstrated that this did happen; that particular fractions of monopoly capital were able to get through to the one man who acted as though he were running the state and to get their interests translated into state policy. The Four Year Plan of 1936, which rested so heavily on the chemicals combine I.G. Farben, is a case in point. But there were many other critical occasions when there is no evidence that the politics of personal dictatorship worked in this manner. Many of the decisions for which Hitler himself was personally responsible – in the sense that he would have been called to account if disasters had followed – appear to be his decisions: that, for example, not to join a bourgeois coalition government and become the political chorus for a 'normal' autocracy in 1932, but to hold out for supreme power in the state; and then there are the decisions over the foreign policy which did not lead to war at Munich in 1938 and did lead to war over Poland in 1939.

One of the main grounds of Hitler's personal political power
within the system was his great popularity, and one way to get
at this question of the power of the leader is to look at the
reasons why he should have been so popular – reasons which
are located first in those who adored him, rather than in the
leader himself. This is a possible research task which could be
assimilated to a range of Marxist theories and insights. But I
am still not clear in my own mind how far the notion of the
charismatic political leader can be accommodated in Marxist
accounts of the modern forms of the capitalist state. Similar
sorts of difficulties arise with attempts to give accounts of
national socialist anti-semitism and genocide. I find it both
striking and disturbing that some Marxist writers have
practically nothing to say about this. Sohn-Rethel is frank
enough to admit in his conclusion that he does have very little
to say about it. Vajda's study, recently translated into English,
attempts to establish a sophisticated theory of fascism at a high
level of generality, but touches hardly at all on anti-semitism.
Silence will not do. It has sometimes been argued, in particular
by East German historians – though I think no longer – that the
persecution and extermination of the Jews was a form of
exemplary terror, that the intention was instrumental – to
terrorise the rest of the population of the German occupied
territories. This interpretation is utterly lacking in
foundation. Inadequate, rather than lacking in foundation, are
the suggestions by Marxist writers that we are dealing with the
deliberate implementation of scapegoating by a dictatorial regime
which needed to divert public attention from real political and
economic problems. The intention, it is argued, was to
establish a group of people as responsible for all past and
future disasters: the Jews. It is quite true that anti-semitic
propaganda was used in this manner and with this conscious
intention, but this insight cannot explain Auschwitz. This
manipulative propaganda represented a different kind of anti-
semitism from the paranoid biological doctrine which, once
institutionalised in the SS, progressively degraded the Jewish
people of Germany and occupied Europe to the status of
non-human, before actually exterminating them. Scapegoating
was but one aspect of this process.
    Nor do simple economic and social explanations of the
persecution of the Jews meet the facts. There is no doubt that
there *was* a very strong element of professional rivalry and
economic competition at all levels, petit bourgeois, middle-class
and monopoly capital, in the process of the degradation of
German Jews and their removal from economic life. There is also
no doubt that there was a lot of lower middle-class philistine
resentment at the cultural achievements of the Jewish
bourgeoisie. These too, however, were forms of prejudice which
did not necessarily lead to the 'final solution'. Further,
Auschwitz has to be seen as in a different category from what
might be described as normal imperial racism. The Nazi regime

practised that too, in a particularly barbaric way, especially
on the Slav peoples of Eastern Europe and Russia. One can
perhaps account for that in the same way as one can account for
the imposition and justification of domination, the repression of
resistance and the wholesale forcible removal of colonial peoples
in the empires of Great Britain, Belgium, France. But Nazi
anti-semitism constituted European-wide genocide; the deliberate
transfer of Jews from Salonika, Paris . . . to camps for
extermination. The evidence suggests that at least some leading
Nazis were driven by a vision of a new eugenic anti-utopia, by
world view of a biological materialism, which has an important
place in any account of the extermination of the Jews by this
regime. This is not the whole explanation, perhaps not even the
key to an understanding of Auschwitz; the machinery of
persecution and extermination developed its own momentum.
Still, the full implications of Auschwitz for a Marxist
understanding of the modern capitalist state have still to be
faced, and it cannot be considered as an excrescence upon the
regime's other policies which may be more amenable to analysis
in conventional Marxist terms.

Last, a problem with a slightly different shape, a problem in
which it is not so difficult to identify the relevant facts, but
where the explanation of these facts *is* difficult. This concerns
the question of the motivation of rank-and-file Nazis during
the period of the struggle for power (1928-33). A great deal of
detailed and valuable work has been done by professional
scholars on the identity of the rank-and-file activists of the
fascist movement in Germany: who they were, in social terms;
their age, location and the precise nature of their activities;
what immediate interests they had; how these were articulated in
political groups which were dominated by social interests rather
different from their own. The picture is now fairly clear. The
crucial political function of the Nazi rank-and-file movement is
also fairly clear: namely the annihilation of the organised
working class in March, April and May, 1933. This is
fundamentally what it had been there for, what it had been
practising for in the street fights before March 1933. And this
was its vital contribution to the erection of a full fascist
dictatorship by the end of 1933, a distinct contribution from
that of supportive elite groups in industry, the army, the
civil service.

But we are dealing with hundreds of thousands of people,
mostly men, many of whom went out, day in day out,
frequently at the risk of having the hell beaten out of them by
the organised working class in street fights, agitating and
propagandising for the Nazi movement. This involved for many a
substantial and sustained commitment of time, energy and - for
the propertied - of economic resources too; it involved a
willingness to risk life and limb, to make sacrifices, and it
generated its own perverse sense of righteousness. Many joined
for six months, stood on the sidelines and then left; but many

did not leave, and remained active for several years. Part of this activity can be explained by opportunism of the most multifarious kinds, but this is not a full answer; reference to the skilful propagandistic and organisational manipulation of Nazi activists by their own leaders is also, of course, essential in any account of this issue, but a core of consistent fanaticism remains unexplained.

The political motivation on the fascist right was quite different from that which existed, for example, in counter-revolutionary France 1848-51 or in 1871. It was not a bourgeois response to an immediate revolutionary threat. If anything, the organised left was in political retreat after 1930. There was a lot of deliberately alarmist talk of the threat of red revolution, but few signs which even good German burgers could read as evidence of its reality. Fascist mobilisation in Germany did not grow out of the white heat of violent and brutal rage in response to revolutionary insurgency. It involved a different structure of motivation. The work that we have to hand on the 'authoritarian personality', and on the relationship between authoritarian personality types and family structures characteristic of capitalist development, is not very helpful here. The *activist* Nazis were not on the whole particularly authoritarian in any aspect of their personality development or behaviour. They were for the most part young middle-class men in a state of partial but violent rebellion, and their movement was correspondingly inchoate and dynamic.

The three big problems outlined above have two things in common. First, they represent those issues in the interpretation of national socialism which are most emphasised and most thoroughly treated in the work of liberal and conservative historians. They comprise the main points in the non- or anti-marxist claim that the Third Reich can only be understood as a unique regime, defined by the pre-eminence of unique individuals and their utterly distinctive ideology. This claim cannot be accepted, but neither can the work in question simply be dismissed or ignored – it calls for a more thorough materialist critique than it has yet received. Second, the three problems have a substantive common denominator: bourgeois political attitudes and ideologies in the twentieth century. This represents a whole field of historical and political study which Marxists are only beginning to take seriously. Where, for the post-1914 world, are the scholarly and political partners of those who write with detailed literary knowledge and analytical sophistication about Puritanism, Moral Economy, the Liberalism of artisan elites? Some of the methodological difficulties in studying Nazism have been faced in this work on earlier centuries, but for many Marxists this century has become a century of working-class revolutions and capitalist economics, full-stop. The problem is perhaps not so much knowing how to do it, but deciding where to begin. In respect of the Third Reich (and not only of that movement/regime), nationalism may be one good starting point and social Darwinism a second. The diffusion and persistence of the latter mode of thought in the capitalist societies of the 1920s and 1930s urgently requires investigation. What presently passes for intellectual history should not be left to intellectual and political historians.

FURTHER READING

These comments are in good measure a criticism of my own work on Nazism and the Third Reich. The debate about the 'primacy of politics' concerned itself at best indirectly with genocide – see S.J. Woolf, ed., *The Nature of Fascism*, London 1968. My more recent effort to give a materialist account of the Nazi movement before 1933 is weak on the question of motivation: 'National socialism and the working class, 1925 – May 1933', *New German Critique* (Milwaukee), no. 11, Spring 1977. Much Marxist writing on the Third Reich falls back behind the synthetic ambition of one of the earliest studies: Franz Neumann, *Behemoth. The Structure and Practice of National Socialism*, first published in the UK by the Left Book Club in 1942; Harper Torchbooks, New York, has just allowed the extended paperback edition to go out of print. It remains the best single work and ought to be re-printed. The most imaginative recent study of fascist motivation is Klaus Theweleit, *Männerphantasien*, Frankfurt 1977/78, 2 vols; see the theoretically very important review essay by Lutz Niethammer, *History Workshop Journal*, no. 7, Spring 1979. The most helpful recent contribution on the bases of state power in fascism is Jane Caplan, 'Theories of fascism: Nicos Poulantzas as historian', *History Workshop Journal*, no. 3, Spring 1977. The works referred to in the text are Alfred Sohn-Rethel, *Economy and Class Structure of German Fascism*, London 1978, and Mihaly Vajda, *Fascism as a Mass Movement*, London 1976. I have made a first attempt at a critique of liberal interpretations of national socialism in a contribution in G. Hirschfeld and L. Kettenacker, eds, *The Führer-State: Myth and Reality*, Stuttgart 1980.

27 ANTI-FASCISM IN POST-WAR GERMANY

Lutz Niethammer*

The following short article tries to outline the role of anti-fascism as a tradition and as subject of historiography in postwar West Germany. In contrast to most European countries, where anti-fascism was amalgamated with a national resistance against the German occupier, the various resistance traditions in Germany lacked a unifying pattern.

ANTI-FASCISM AFTER FASCISM

While the German labour movement did not combine into an anti-fascist front before or during the rule of the Nazis, anti-fascism (or some variety thereof, i.e., anti-national socialism, anti-Hitlerism) loomed large in all parts of political and trade-union life which were built up after 1945. But the political rhetoric was not derived from an experience of combined anti-fascist struggle, and largely reflected a superficial convergence of anti-Hitler sentiment. In fact, the fascist experience left the German labour movement with no realistic perspective but a recourse to the lowest common denominator of pre-1933 socialist politics - by and large the social democratic conception of economic democracy of the 1920s. Attempts to enforce partial nationalisation of big business were blocked by the Western occupying powers; while the representatives of the left were drawn into the de-Nazified bureaucracy set up by the Western powers, where they could not work for an independent socialist programme.

In the early days after the liberation, there had been, in most cities, a popular movement of anti-fascist committees, grass roots organisations, that tried by spontaneous collective activity in the tradition of the labour movement to provide for the immediate needs of the working population, to reconstruct a basic public order and to fight whatever was left of the fascist heritage, be it persons, concepts or local power structures. The underlying idea of much of this activity was anti-fascist redistribution - but beyond that a positive and unified programme was absent, and was not given the chance to evolve, as all four occupying powers closed the committees

---

*Lutz Niethammer is professor of history at Essen University; author of studies of de-nazification and anti-fascism in post-1945 Germany, and engaged in comparative study of housing in France, Britain and Germany.

down. So anti-fascism was transposed to the level of trade union and political party leaders, who built up their organisations largely from the top down, relying in their struggle for mass support on the direct or indirect backing of their respective occupying power.

SELECTIVE PASTS FOR A DIVIDED COUNTRY

How little these leadership factions had taken root in a common movement came into the open when Germany became increasingly divided from 1946 onwards. Though all varieties of the left stressed national unity, socialism and anti-fascism, public debate adapted to the concepts of the two leading occupying powers. In the East, the new state built up a past that centred on the tradition of the communist party. In the West, the resistance tradition was appropriated by the conservatives, who tried to invoke the circles around the July 1944 Putsch as the central legitimising tradition of the Federal Republic by showing that there had been opposition to Nazism from the right, the conservative aristocracy and parts of the big bourgeoisie, who stood in the continuity of German conservativism and had opened their mind to the basic values of Western civilisation. Though the 20 July never became a state holiday, it was treated as a central political event by the more decent and enlightened conservatives in power.

West German historiography in the 1950s largely worked on three lines: to exalt the 20 July as *the* German resistance and to play down all other more anti-fascist types of resistance as either little documented or questionable in their legitimacy. Second, fascism was mostly interpreted as totalitarianism thus equating the foes of the Federal Republic in the present and those in its own earlier history. Third (and this was the only field where conservative apology and more critical enquiry met) historians engaged in a regressive analysis of the developments that led up to either 1933 or 1945.

Between these appropriations of a well-designed past by the dominant political forces in the East and West, the reality of anti-fascism was largely buried, and an autonomous socialist thinking was hardly heard in public or even in the labour movement, which gradually adapted to the basic paradigms of neo-capitalist growth.

GENERATIONAL CONFLICT AND THE REDISCOVERY OF A LEFTIST TRADITION

In the 1960s various factors contributed to broaden the political spectrum in West Germany, among them the politics of international detente, the end of the reconstruction boom, the remarkable electoral success of a neo-fascist party, and a search

for identity for West Germany, now again a medium-size power.
The most notable factor, however, was the link between the
youth culture of the 1960s, the politicisation of generational
conflicts in terms of fascism versus anti-fascism, and the
rediscovery of the theoretical and cultural heritage of the left.
Its backbone of authoritarian elements in contemporary
capitalism as remnants of identical structures in fascism.

Looking back, it may seem to be a bitter irony that the turn
by the younger generation of intellectuals towards the labour
movement was accompanied by an identification with that phase
of the German left that immediately preceded its utter defeat.
The intellectuals ignored a gap of forty years by engaging in
discussions about Reich and the Frankfurt School, about
Thalheimer, Trotsky and the Comintern with hardly a sense of
time, and their attempts to organise working-class parties, or
even to get in some social or cultural contact with real workers
of their own time, led an important part of their movement into
frustrating dead-ends, ranging from Maoism to careerism, from
terrorism to *Innerlichkeit*. By the early 1970s, the major
discourse about the theories of fascism and the possibilities of
resistance was dead.

APPROACHES TO REALITY WITHIN A BROADER SPECTRUM

The return of anti-fascist refugees took German intellectual life
out of the provincialism of the Cold War and, so to speak,
renormalised the spectrum of positions offered. The major
historiographical results may be identified as follows: first,
there was a major attempt to reconstruct ideologies,
organisations and movements that had hitherto been neglected,
in a positive way, including emigrant political groups, workers'
especially communist resistance, and the post-1945 anti-fascist
committees. A second result was a change in paradigm: social
and economic history were introduced into contemporary history
and looked at first as being something left *per se*. Within a
short time, of course, this leftish innovation rarely proved to
have leftish results. But it was so much of a success that the
former dominant approach (*Geistesgeschichte*, political history
proper) had to fight back from a minority position. A third
historiographical result was isolated creativity. The
confrontation of resurrected pre-1933 socialist theory with the
present life-experience of the historians, and the knowledge
gained from empirical research, produced, in a number of
research projects, work of real originality of which Klaus
Theweleit's psychological interpretation of proto-Nazi
autobiographies *Male Fantasies* may be the best example.
Another good example is the general change from ideological and
organisational concepts to a concern with *Alltag* - experience,
work place, family, culture.

But these researches tend to work back to the most heroic

phases of the German labour movement, whereas the research on
fascism accumulates without a common subject of debate.

Today, quite in contrast to the 1960s, the political life of the
Federal Republic stimulates little debate about fascism: the rise
of Franz-Josef Strauss to the leadership of the Christian
Democratic opposition serves to make people scared, and
stimulates in some quarters a sort of popular front agitation,
but hardly produces any theoretical debate on the actuality of
fascism. The fascination amongst some of the youth in schools,
and especially amongst the unemployed, with authoritarian
violence and Nazi symbols has alarmed educators and social
workers but only inspired research into analogous phenomena
in the Weimar republic, the Nazi movement then being one of
the youngest in average age that Germany ever had.

The lack of framework and orientation is not true only of the
intellectual left, but of many parts of German society as well.
The trade-union organisations, especially, seem to feel a need
for identity in a situation where the fight for wages is no longer
obviously the self-evident priority. The unions look for a
cultural tradition, they even invite intellectuals' advice, and
when they staged the first historical conference that German
trade unions ever undertook, they selected for the sessions the
two classic themes of historical debate in the student movement:
the revolution of 1918/19 and the defeat of the labour movement
in 1932/33. But there is as yet no real juncture between the
conceptualisation of fascism and the more traditional themes of
labour history.

Cultural studies

Peter Burke*

The idea of 'popular culture', as opposed to 'learned culture', is a late eighteenth-century one, first formulated by the German writer J.G. Herder. Antiquaries had, of course, described popular customs before this: Henry Bourne, for example, the curate of All Saints'. Newcastle, published a book on 'popular antiquities' in 1725, and Pepys had collected broadside ballads and chapbooks in the later seventeenth century. What was new in the approach of Herder and his friends and followers, among whom were the brothers Grimm, was the idea that songs and stories, plays and proverbs, customs and ceremonies were all part of a whole, expressing the 'spirit' of a particular people. Hence the rise of terms like *Volkslied* ('folksong'), which Herder was one of the first to use, or 'folklore', a word coined by William Thoms in 1846. These terms express what might be called the intellectuals' 'discovery' of popular culture. Most of these intellectuals came from the upper classes, to whom the people were a mysterious 'other', described in terms of everything their discoverers were not (or thought they were not); natural, simple, instinctive, irrational, and rooted in the local soil.

Why the upper classes (some of them at any rate) should have become interested in the attitudes, values and daily lives of ordinary people at this particular moment in history is an intriguing question, and I would not claim to have the whole answer to it. But there were clearly both aesthetic and political reasons for the discovery of the people and their culture in the late eighteenth and early nineteenth centuries.

The aesthetic reason was the revolt against classicism which began in the later eighteenth century and culminated in the Romantic movement. Folkplays, like Shakespeare, became objects of enthusiasm because they broke the 'rules' of Aristotle and his commentators, rules which had become orthodoxy in French and German and Italian drama. Folksongs were seen as works of nature rather than as works of art, just as peasants were seen as picturesque parts of the landscape. They were 'romanticised' in every sense.

---

*Peter Burke teaches at Emmanuel College, Cambridge. Author of *Popular Culture in Early Modern Europe*, London 1978; *Venice and Amsterdam: A study of seventeenth-century elites*, London 1974; *History and Sociology*, London 1980. An associate editor of *History Workshop Journal*.

The report of the discussion is by John Gillis.

The political reason for the discovery of popular culture was that it fitted into and legitimated the movements of national liberation which erupted all over Europe in the early nineteenth century, in Greece, Serbia, Belgium, etc. To collect Polish or Finnish or Italian folksongs became a subversive act, implying that Russian, Swedish or Austrian rule was alien to these nations. The discovery of the people was a 'nativistic' movement in the sense that it was an attempt by a number of European countries, many of which were under foreign domination, to revive their traditional cultures. It is no accident that this movement had more resonance in Brittany than in Paris, in Scotland than in England. In these movements of national liberation, intellectuals and peasants fought side by side, so that the ambiguities in the term 'people' were not as apparent as they later became. 'People' was a keyword in an ideology.

From this period of struggle we have inherited not only terms like 'popular culture', 'folksong' and 'folklore', but also some rather dangerous assumptions about them, including what may be called 'primitivism', 'purism' and 'communalism'.

By 'primitivism' I mean the assumption that the songs, stories, beliefs, customs, and artefacts which were discovered c.1800 had been handed down unchanged for thousands of years. It may well be the case that they (or some of them) had been handed down for a long time, that there had never been a sharp break in the tradition, but it does not follow that the songs, stories, etc. had not changed. We know all too little about the popular culture of the Middle Ages, but it is not difficult to show that in more recent times, between 1500 and 1800, European popular traditions had changed in all sorts of ways. During the Reformation and Counter Reformation, the clergy, Catholic and Protestant, made many attempts to change popular culture, with varying degrees of success (in parts of Switzerland and the Protestant South of France, the psalms drove out the traditional folksongs and took over their functions as dance-tunes and lullabies). Popular culture grows out of the local way of life, and necessarily changes with it. The spread of literacy, the growing power of the nation-state and the rise of commercial capitalism were bound to transform both the oral traditions and the material culture of different regions. Some of the 'primitive' traditions discovered by folklorists in the nineteenth century may not have gone back more than a generation or two.

'Purism' is a label for the assumption that 'the people' really means 'the peasants'. As Herder once put it, 'The mob in the streets, which never sings or composes but shrieks and mutilates, is not the people.' The peasants were seen as the true People because they lived close to Nature and because they were unspoiled by new or foreign ways. No doubt the European peasantry c.1800 did live a more traditional way of life than other groups, though they were beginning to discover the delights of printed cotton curtains and fire-shovels at much the same time as the intellectuals were waxing enthusiastic over homemade furniture and houses without chimneys. The peasants tended to be less literate than the townspeople, and unlike the townspeople they did not speak the language of their foreign conquerors (Castilian in Catalonia, German in Bohemia, Danish in Norway, etc.). However, if it is agreed that popular culture is always changing, we have no basis for excluding the inhabitants of the towns from 'the people' because their culture is less traditional. Townspeople, too, had their traditions, including oral traditions. Conversely, some of the peasants were literate. In rural Sweden in the eighteenth century, there was virtually 100 per cent adult literacy, in the sense of ability to read if not ability to write.

Even more dangerous is 'communalism', the assumption that the people creates collectively: '*Das Volk dichtet*', as the Grimm brothers put it. It is true that traditional ballads, for example, are collective products in the sense that a number of people have taken a hand in the making of each one. In an oral tradition, what does not meet with general approval is not passed on; in that sense, the audience acts as a censor. However, over the last fifty years or so research has shown that working within an oral tradition does not inhibit the development of an individual style. Avdo Mededović, an illiterate oral poet from Montenegro who died, full of years, in 1955, has become a celebrated example of individual creativity within a popular tradition.

A still more important distinction is hidden by the formula 'the People creates'. This is the distinction between the culture which comes *from* ordinary people (especially the most gifted of them, like Avdo), and the culture which is provided *for* ordinary people by someone else. Long before the Industrial Revolution, let alone the age of television, a considerable amount of popular culture came to people from outside rather than being homemade in the local community. Eighteenth-century villagers in France (say) or Sweden might buy an almanac or a painted grandfather clock at a fair, or listen to performances by itinerant actors or preachers. These artefacts and performances may be seen as so many messages, about which we need to ask, as Raymond Williams has done about contemporary forms of communication, 'who says what, how, to whom, with what effect and for what purpose?' It may be useful to explore these questions by means of a case-study, that of the so-called 'Blue Library' (*Bibliothèque Bleue*).

The *Bibliothèque Bleue* is the name for chapbooks in France, because they came in blue covers. They began to be printed in the seventeenth century, especially in Troyes. They were only a few pages long in many cases, often illustrated (though illustrations might be irrelevant to the text because it was cheaper to use the same woodcuts over and over again in different books), but relatively inexpensive (a book cost about the same as a loaf of bread). They were distributed at fairs and also by itinerant pedlars. A little is known about these pedlars in the early nineteenth century; they had fixed routes, worked in groups, and tended to come from the southwest. They were part-time farmers who sold chapbooks in the slack season.

What sort of books did they bring? A sample of 450 titles of the seventeenth and eighteenth centuries still preserved at Troyes reveals 120 works of piety, 67 fairy tales, about 30 romances of chivalry (*Ogier the Dane*, *The Four Sons of Aymon*, etc.), some almanacs, a few guides to letter-writing and good behaviour, and the lives of famous criminals such as the robber Cartouche and the smuggler Mandrin.

These chapbooks have been the object of intensive study by French historians over the last few years, but they have come up with some extremely divergent conclusions. For Robert Mandrou, the function of the *Bibliothèque Bleue* was to provide what the readers wanted, 'escapist literature' with the emphasis on the marvellous, the extraordinary and the supernatural. According to him it expressed popular values. For Robert Muchembled, on the other hand, the *Bibliothèque Bleue* was a form of propaganda, the opium of the people (he speaks of 'tranquillisers'), its diffusion part of a general movement of 'acculturation', in other words the imposition on the people of the ideals and values of the ruling class as an ideology which would enable them to be controlled more easily. Who is right, Mandrou or Muchembled? What evidence have we for deciding?

Who is speaking through these chapbooks? Most of them are anonymous. Some of the repertoire seems to echo the voice of the clergy. In the mid-seventeenth century, a synod of the clergy of Chalons suggested that the faithful should be encouraged to buy and read three devotional books and that these books should also be read aloud 'in the porch or at the entry to the church' on Sundays and feast-days. Part of the secular repertoire, notably the romances of chivalry, comes from medieval aristocratic culture. A good deal of translation, abridgement and simplification took place before these texts appeared in chapbook form, and we do not know who did this; it was probably organised by the publishers, some of whom (like the Oudot family of Troyes), specialised in this trade for generations. It is likely that the decision what to print in this format was made by the publishers on the basis of what had sold well in the past; market forces, rather than a policy imposed by church or state.

This last point is supported by the sheer heterogeneity of *what* was printed and sold. The choice of (say) the *Sermon des Cocus*, the *Histoire de Mandrin*, the *Prophéties Perpétuelles* and the *Règles de la Bienséance* does not look like the result of any coherent policy. The authorities did censor these booklets to ensure that nothing irreligious or subversive was put out, but they did not suppress the biographies of outlaws like Mandrin, who is, incidentally, presented in ambivalent terms; brave, attractive, yet a 'monster of ferocity', all within the pages of the same book. The inconsistency may reflect the 'something for everyone' approach of private enterprise.

To *whom* were these messages addressed? Mandrou suggested that the audience was primarily a peasant one, and the existence of a distribution network of country chapmen shows that there must be something in his suggestion. However, if the capacity to sign one's name is anything to go on, fewer than 30 per cent of French men (and far fewer women) were literate in 1700. In any case many peasants, especially in Brittany and the south, did not know French. Some Paris booksellers carried stocks of the *Bibliothèque Bleue* and it is plausible to suggest that books about letter-writing and good behaviour appealed more widely to urban readers than in the villages. Perhaps it would be safest to assume that the *Bibliothèque Bleue* was read primarily by (or to) the craftsmen and shopkeepers of the towns and their wives and daughters, together with the more prosperous peasants living northeast of a line running diagonally across France from St Malo to Geneva. It was no accident that Troyes (in Champagne, in the northeast) was the centre of the distribution network.

We are left with the most difficult questions, those of intentions and effects. Personally I do not believe it likely that the French government used the chapbook medium for propaganda. The government was certainly conscious of the need for a good public image, particularly in the time of Colbert, who functioned as a kind of minister of propaganda to Louis XIV in the 1660s and 1670s, erecting triumphal arches and statues of 'Louis the Great' and issuing medals to commemorate his victories. However, this propaganda was directed at the elite. The church was also interested in propaganda (in the original sense of the term, the 'propagation' of the faith), and in the northeast, in the diocese of Valenciennes for example, did promote literacy and Sunday schools in the seventeenth century. However, most bishops seem to have relied on the traditional oral medium of the pulpits rather than on chapbooks. There was no one quite like Hannah More, trying to drive out ungodly chapbooks with godly ones, in France in the seventeenth and eighteenth centuries. On the intentions of the publishers, no evidence seems to have survived.

What were the effects of the *Bibliothèque Bleue*? What did it mean to its urban and rural readers? We must not assume that it meant the same thing in the towns and in the countryside, or in different parts of the countryside, or even to different groups in the same village. My own hypothesis is that these booklets appealed particularly to the more prosperous peasant families within a given community, the 'brokers' between that community and the outside world (*laboureurs*, millers, etc.), who bought them as a status symbol and a means of reinforcing their position in the community with the prestige of print. We must not assume either that the different stories of the *Bibliothèque Bleue* meant the same thing to readers and

listeners. The problem is that from the texts alone we cannot
tell what Mandrin or the sons of Aymon signified, whether the
audience identified with their rebellion against authority or
rejoiced when Mandrin was brought to justice or the sons of
Aymon reconciled with Charlemagne. We need to know, but do
not know, how individuals reacted to these stories. To treat
the *Bibliothèque Bleue* as direct evidence of the attitudes and
values of the French craftsmen and peasants of the seventeenth
and eighteenth centuries is like treating TV shows and tabloid
newspapers as direct evidence of the attitudes of the British
working class today. It is at best only indirect evidence. That
the peasants went on buying the *Bibliothèque Bleue* is clear.
That they absorbed ideas from it is likely. What they selected,
and how they modified or 'negotiated' these ideas to make them
their own is unclear. It is probable that they saw the new
printed material through the spectacles or stereotypes of their
oral traditions (like Menocchio, the miller of sixteenth-century
Friuli, recently studied by Carlo Ginzburg). We need to
remember, too, that the *Bibliothèque Bleue* was only part of the
culture of even the most literate peasants. Its values may seem
conformist, but there were other ways of expressing protest,
from satirical verses and charivaris against tax-collectors to
full-scale revolt.

With so many gaps in our knowledge, a dogmatic conclusion
would be a mistake. However, the fragments of evidence we have
suggest that the *Bibliothèque Bleue* was not official propaganda
for church or state but the creation (out of existing material)
of entrepreneurs with an eye on the market. Some of the
booklets had a wide appeal, for they were frequently reprinted
and their publishers remained in business. These texts became
part of popular culture, at least among the better-off
craftsmen and peasants of the northeast. The values expressed
in these texts, however they were interpreted, were the values
of 'official' culture. The diffusion of these chapbooks is one of
many examples of the diffusion of a cultural model downwards
through society. As Gramsci once suggested, with reference to
a similar situation in Italy, this literature both reflected and
helped maintain the cultural hegemony of the ruling class. In
this somewhat imprecise sense, the French pedlars were the
carriers of an ideology.

DISCUSSION

It was clear from the discussion that followed that Peter Burke's
paper had opened a very wide range of questions both about
sources and the actual practice of research. Tony Frye
(Birmingham) initiated discussion by stressing the need for
content analysis in cases where texts were available. This kind
of research was likely to get at the themes of popular culture in
ways that market-oriented studies could not. Frye also raised

the question of whether the circulation of chapbooks may not have had the effect of extending literacy and thus subverting elite control. Alun Howkins (Sussex) was more sceptical about the study of a single source. Chapbooks could not be seen in isolation and the acceptance of the existence of separate oral and literate cultures was bound to lead to distortions. Books of all kinds were commonly read aloud and their subjects reached a much larger audience through subsequent 'telling'. Furthermore, reading was not a private, isolated event, but often a collective enterprise, involving an active exchange between those who were literate and those who were not. If we are to understand what reading meant we must know much more about the larger culture at every level.

Alun Howkins' comments led Hans Medick (Göttingen) to raise the crucial question of social and economic context. Too often popular culture had been abstracted from the people, a method which had distorted our understanding of its genesis, function and meaning. Medick attempted to suggest that the popular cultures of early modern Europe must be seen as an aspect of an evolving capitalist society, and not as survivals of peasant traditions or the interventions of literate elites. Many of the most visible and active popular cultures of this period were associated with communities already at an advanced state of rural industrialisation. Their unique forms of family economy, in which the family acted as both unit of production and unit of consumption, provided the material base for cultural creativity very different from that which existed among the peasantry and the urban elites. The popular cultures that developed were different from those of pre-existing lower classes, and not necessarily identical to the working-class cultures of later periods of urban industrial capitalism. The values were not so unambiguously 'plebeian' as Edward Thompson has suggested, yet popular cultures of this period were clearly not an extension of bourgeois hegemony. Rural industrialisation had altered the nature of the family by re-orienting both the relations between the sexes and the status of the young and the old. Consumption patterns had been transformed in such a way that defied the sumptuary restrictions imposed by the disapproving elites. Many of the popular forms - drinking, feasting, dancing and singing - were, in effect, 'displaced class conflict'. Thus, among this particular strata popular culture was clearly an arena of contest, even of subversion.

At this point, the discussion returned to the question of sources and Nick Rogers (London) expressed scepticism about the value of chapbooks in getting to deep levels of popular attitudes. Ballads and broadsides were a much more useful source. Many of these had found their way into government hands in the eighteenth century and these show the authors using 'paternalist' language as a vehicle of social protest. The instruments of authority were being turned against the ruling class in ways that beg further investigation. So much of the discussion had turned on the influence of town over the countryside, that Peter Christensen (Copenhagen) asked whether there was a city audience for chapbooks and what their reception had been. Peter Burke replied that indeed there was an urban market and that the town-country dichotomy might be a false one. He went on to take up the suggestion that content analysis would be a way of getting at changes of meaning that happened over time. The tale written in the early seventeenth century might be altered to fit eighteenth-century taste; and this was important evidence. A careful reading of the text was important, though he continued to insist that the distinction between an elite and plebeian culture worked well for France in the early modern period.

Many Ann Conant (London) was not so sure that English chapbooks were written by the elite for the common people. She cited the recent work of Margaret Spufford that showed that printers' apprentices may have written some of the early English versions. At this point Hans Medick intervened to suggest that an emphasis on literacy could be distorting, for this focus necessarily neglected so much, and obscured the fact that a great 'renaissance' of popular culture was occurring quite independent of what was happening within literate circles. In regions of rural industrialisation the family was itself the consumer and creator of culture. Women as well as men, the young together with their elders, gained access to the necessary time, resources and freedom to involve themselves in activities sanctioned by neither church nor state, and often in opposition to these institutions. Medick suggested that eighteenth-century efforts to inculcate an ethic of austerity and savings should be viewed not only as a means of capital accumulation, but as a means of subduing a culture threatening to elite interests.

The discussion returned again to the content of chapbooks when Cathérine Delaval (Paris) suggested that they might also offer a unique way of exploring the role of women. In response to a request for further explanation by Ellen Ross (New York), she explained that seventeenth-century French chapbooks show young women being quite free of restraint. References to nudity were common and many other inhibitions, sexual and social, were absent. By the eighteenth century, however, young women were portrayed as timid, reserved and, in the exercise of sexuality, coy. The next century's literature found them even more confined; the good woman becomes the homebody without access to the world outside. The chapbook images of women seem to confirm Foucault's thesis concerning the 'great confinement' of the early modern period, but also give it a special meaning with respect to women.

Peter Larsen (Denmark) was concerned that texts should not be taken at face value. The meaning of a narrative or tale depended to a large extent on the reader's own frame of reference, which in turn was defined by a larger culture. A similar point was made by Alun Howkins, who noted that there was much controversy over seventeenth-century English folksong as to whether its 'liberated' image of women's sexuality represented social reality or the pornographic fantasy of male singers. Apart from the work done by Vic Gammon, little was known of the actual singers and their audiences. Much research would be necessary before the genesis of the songs and the context of their performance was known sufficiently to resolve such questions. Susan Amusson (USA) thought the distinction between pornography and social practice to be a false one, but she too suggested that further investigation was necessary.

At this point the discussion turned in a new direction with the intervention of Dave Harker (Manchester), whose studies of the culture of the northeast in the eighteenth and nineteenth centuries had led him to a profound distrust of those approaches which treated culture 'as a thing', as something created and distributed by one group and consumed by another. By focusing on a single source, the chapbook, Peter Burke had perpetuated this error. Harker was emphatic in his rejection of the notion of culture as something that 'people accept'. We should be concerned with what 'people create', which is a *process* involving both mediation and struggle. According to Harker much more attention must be given to the mediators and creators within the working class. The very terminology employed by cultural historians - 'culture', 'tradition', 'peasantry' - tells us more about their preoccupations than it does about the nature of popular culture itself. Words such as these obscure the active, protean aspect of culture as lived experience by abstracting and alienating it from the actual lives of people.

Harker's comments were warmly received and Adrian Rifkin (Portsmouth) reinforced his point about the dangers of studying culture as an object, a practice which invariably placed emphasis on the elites. John Gillis (New Jersey) added that so-called cultural historians had tended to locate the creative forces within public institutions like the church, school and literary circle, leaving the impression of a popular culture principally male and adult. He believed Hans Medick was correct in thinking that the renaissance of popular culture in the eighteenth century had much to do with the family economy associated with rural industrialisation. While we are not accustomed to looking for creative forces within the family itself, studies of domestic culture would reveal the ways in which those who have not had access to public institutions, namely women and young people, were active in the cultural processes of the early modern period. The term 'popular culture' may have the tendency to homogenise and obscure the diverse sources of creativity. By starting with the family, it should be possible to 'unpack' the various age and sexual dimensions of this cultural renaissance.

By this time Carlo Ginzburg (Bologna) had arrived. Instead of giving a paper, he commented briefly on the foregoing

discussion and made some points of his own. He was much
concerned with the problem of evidence and the difficulty of
arriving at an accurate picture of what people actually thought
and did. He agreed with Dave Harker that much more must be
made of 'active mediations' that are as evident today as they
were in earlier periods. As an example, he cited studies of
television-watching that have shown that people do not
passively absorb what is fed to them. Instead they break it
down and reassemble it for their own purposes. Children mock
the ads they see; and there is a perpetual 'feedback' that may
have consequences unintended by the producers of the
television programmes. He was sceptical about Bahktin's work
because he had relied too much on literary sources. What was
needed Ginzburg argued was a 'disciplined' way to approach the
cultures of the past. The need is for 'new rules of evidence'
comparable to those which had been developed over the past
decade to deal with other areas of social history. The field is,
in effect, insufficiently developed and comparative work is
therefore difficult. Until it becomes more rigorous in both theory
and strategy of research it cannot answer the questions that
have been raised in this and other discussions.

Some of the problems of interpretation and evidence that
Ginzburg had alluded to were then nicely illustrated by Sandro
Portelli (Rome), who stressed that reading itself must be looked
at not as a passive process but as 'struggle' in which the reader
engages himself with the material in an active way. Often the
results are very different from those intended by the author,
especially when the reader is not of the same class background.
In the highland areas of Italy texts from classical literature
and poetry are often reworked by persons who might otherwise
be thought to be quite 'uncultured'. He knew personally of a
cowherd who had constructed his own version of the *Odyssey*
because he found the original too long to memorise. Portelli had
heard a peasant lecturing his fellows on the First Canto of the
Divine Comedy, interpreting Dante's poem in his own original
manner. According to the man's version, the wolf stood for the
rich and the First Canto became an allegory of the coming of
communism to Italy. But although the message might seem to be
revolutionary, the author of this original interpretation was not
himself socially or politically radical. Clearly the history of
popular culture was as contradictory as it was rich and
evocative.

It seemed appropriate that the session should end with the
concrete, indeed the impenetrable. Peter Burke's introduction
to the chapbook literature had been a useful point of
departure, even though the value of concentrating on a single
source had been challenged in the course of discussion. The
definition of popular culture had been broadened considerably,
although no one had been sufficiently bold to put forward a
definition. At times we seemed to be talking, as an
anthropologist would, of the whole way of life of a people; and

there was the danger that the subject itself might dissolve into
something quite unmanageable. However, there also seemed to
be consensus that an authentic history of popular culture was
possible and that it should begin not with the artefacts of elite
culture but with the various points of production and mediation
within the working classes themselves. Terms like 'hegemony'
seemed to conflate and obscure the vitality of culture as lived
experience.

Despite the notable efforts of Hans Medick to provide a
larger historical frame for the cultural renaissance of the period,
generalisation was not the order of the day. Diversity,
ambiguity and contradiction intruded at every point in the
discussion. As was the case with social history a decade ago,
there was so much unexplored territory that the provision of a
new set of maps seemed a very long way off. What was needed,
it seemed, were appropriately standardised tools for further
exploration, guidelines as well as rules of evidence which
would, in time, make theory possible.

FURTHER READING

On the discovery of the people, P. Burke, *Popular Culture in
Early Modern Europe*, London 1978, ch. 1. On oral poetry,
Ruth Finnegan, *Oral Poetry*, Cambridge 1977. On the French
chapbooks, R. Mandrou, *De la culture populaire aux 17e et
18e siècles*, Paris 1964, and G. Bollême, *La Bibliothèque Bleue*,
Paris 1971; c.f. R. Muchembled, *Culture populaire et culture
des élites*, Paris 1978, and H.-J. Lüsebrink, 'L'image de
Mandrin', *Revue de l'Histoire Moderne*, 26, 1979, pp. 345-64.
C. Ginzburg, 'Cheese and Worms', in *Religion and the People*,
ed. by J. Obelkevich, Chapel Hill 1979, deals with the
cosmology of a sixteenth-century miller who owned a few books.
V. Neuburg, *Popular Literature*, Harmondsworth 1977, is a
guide to English chapbooks; their distribution network has been
studied in a forthcoming book by Margaret Spufford. On
'ideology' and 'hegemony', R. Williams, *Marxism and Literature*,
London 1977.

29 NOTES ON DECONSTRUCTING 'THE POPULAR'

Stuart Hall*

First, I want to say something about periodisations in the study
of popular culture. Difficult problems are posed here by
periodisation – I don't offer it to you simply as a sort of gesture
to the historians. Are the major breaks largely descriptive? Do
they arise largely from within popular culture itself, or from
factors which are outside of but impinge on it? With what other
movements and periodisations is 'popular culture' most
revealingly linked? Then I want to tell you some of the
difficulties I have with the term 'popular'. I have almost as
many problems with 'popular' as I have with 'culture'. When you
put the two terms together, the difficulties can be pretty
horrendous.

Throughout the long transition into agrarian capitalism and then
in the formation and development of industrial capitalism, there
is a more or less continuous struggle over the culture of
working people, the labouring classes and the poor. This fact
must be the starting point for any study, both of the basis for,
and of the transformations of, popular culture. The changing
balance and relations of social forces throughout that history
reveal themselves, time and again, in struggles over the forms
of the culture, traditions and ways of life of the popular
classes. Capital had a stake in the culture of the popular
classes because the constitution of a whole new social order
around capital required a more or less continuous, if
intermittent, process of re-education, in the broadest sense.
And one of the principal sites of resistance to the forms through
which this 'reformation' of the people was pursued lay in
popular tradition. That is why popular culture is linked, for so
long, to questions of tradition, of traditional forms of life – and
why its 'traditionalism' has been so often misinterpreted as a
product of a merely conservative impulse, backward looking and
anachronistic. Struggle and resistance – but also, of course,
appropriation and *ex*-propriation. Time and again, what we are
really looking at is the active destruction of particular ways of
life, and their transformation into something new. 'Cultural
change' is a polite euphemism for the process by which some
cultural forms and practices are driven out of the centre of

---

*Stuart Hall, a founder editor of *New Left Review* and for many
years director of the Centre for Contemporary Cultural Studies
Birmingham, is now professor of sociology at the Open
University.

popular life, actively marginalised. Rather than simply 'falling
into disuse' through the Long March to modernisation, things
are actively pushed aside, so that something else can take their
place. The magistrate and the evangelical police have, or ought
to have, a more 'honoured' place in the history of popular
culture than they have usually been accorded. Even more
important than ban and proscription is that subtle and slippery
customer - 'reform' (with all the positive and unambiguous
overtones it carries today). One way or another, 'the people'
are frequently the object of 'reform': often, for their own good,
of course - 'in their best interests'. We understand struggle
and resistance, nowadays, rather better than we do reform and
transformation. Yet 'transformations' are at the heart of the
study of popular culture. I mean the active work on existing
traditions and activities, their active re-working, so that they
come out a different way: they appear to 'persist' - yet, from
one period to another, they come to stand in a different relation
to the ways working people live and the ways they define their
relations to each other, to 'the others' and to their conditions of
life. Transformation is the key to the long and protracted
process of the 'moralisation' of the labouring classes, and the
'demoralisation' of the poor, and the 're-education' of the
people. Popular culture is neither, in a 'pure' sense, the
popular traditions of resistance to these processes; nor is it the
forms which are superimposed on and over them. It is the
ground on which the transformations are worked.

In the study of popular culture, we should always start here:
with the double-stake in popular culture, the double movement
of containment and resistance, which is always inevitably inside
it.

The study of popular culture has tended to oscillate wildly
between the two alternative poles of that dialectic - containment/
resistance. We have had some striking and marvellous reversals.
Think of the really major revolution in historical understanding
which has followed as the history of 'polite society' and the Whig
aristocracy in eighteenth-century England has been upturned
by the addition of the history of the turbulent and ungovernable
people. The popular traditions of the eighteenth-century
labouring poor, the popular classes and the 'loose and
disorderly sort' often, now, appear as virtually independent
formations: tolerated in a state of permanently unstable
equilibrium in relatively peaceful and prosperous times; subject
to arbitrary excursions and expeditions in times of panic and
crisis. Yet, though formally these were the cultures of the
people 'outside the walls', beyond political society and the
triangle of power, they were never, in fact, outside of the
larger field of social forces and cultural relations. They not
only constantly pressed on 'society'; they were linked and
connected with it, by a multitude of traditions and practices.
Lines of 'alliance' as well as lines of cleavage. From these
cultural bases, often far removed from the dispositions of law,

power and authority, 'the people' threatened constantly to erupt: and, when they did so, they break on to the stage of patronage and power with a threatening din and clamour – with fife and drum, cockade and effigy, proclamation and ritual – and, often, with a striking, popular, ritual discipline. Yet never quite overturning the delicate strands of paternalism, deference and terror within which they were constantly if insecurely constrained. In the following century, where the 'labouring' and the 'dangerous' classes lived without benefit of that fine distinction the reformers were so anxious to draw (this was a *cultural* distinction as well as a moral and economic one: and a great deal of legislation and regulation was devised to operate directly on it), some areas preserved for long periods a virtually impenetrable enclave character. It took virtually the whole length of the century before the representatives of 'law and order' – the new police – could acquire anything like a regular and customary foothold within them. Yet, at the same time, the penetration of the cultures of the labouring masses and the urban poor was deeper, more continuous – and more continuously 'educative' and reformatory – in that period than at any time since.

One of the main difficulties standing in the way of a proper periodisation of popular culture is the profound transformation in the culture of the popular classes which occurs between the 1880s and the 1920s. There are whole histories yet to be written about this period. But, although there are probably many things not right about its detail, I do think Gareth Stedman Jones's article on the 'Re-making of the English working class' in this period has drawn our attention to something fundamental and qualitatively different and important about it. It was a period of deep structural change. The more we look at it, the more convinced we become that somewhere in this period lies the matrix of factors and problems from which *our* history – and our peculiar dilemmas – arise. Everything changes – not just a shift in the relations of forces but a reconstitution of the terrain of political struggle itself. It isn't just by chance that so many of the characteristic forms of what we now think of as 'traditional' popular culture either emerge from or emerge in their distinctive modern form, in that period. What has been done for the 1790s and for the 1840s, and is being done for the eighteenth century, now radically needs to be done for the period of what we might call the 'social imperialist' crisis.

The general point made earlier is true, without qualification, for this period, so far as popular culture is concerned. There is no separate, autonomous, 'authentic' layer of working-class culture to be found. Much of the most immediate forms of popular recreation, for example, are saturated by popular imperialism. Could we expect otherwise? How could we explain, and what would we *do* with the idea of, the culture of a dominated class which, despite its complex interior formations and differentiations, stood in a very particular relation to a major

restructuring of capital; which itself stood in a peculiar relation
to the rest of the world; a people bound by the most complex
ties to a changing set of material relations and conditions; who
managed somehow to construct 'a culture' which remained
untouched by the most powerful dominant ideology - popular
imperialism? Especially when that ideology - belying its name -
was directed as much at them as it was at Britain's changing
position in a world capitalist expansion?

Think, in relation to the question of popular imperialism, of
the history and relations between the people and one of the
major means of cultural expression: the press. To go back to
displacement and superimposition - we can see clearly how the
liberal middle-class press of the mid-nineteenth century was
constructed on the back of the active destruction and
marginalisation of the indigenous radical and working-class
press. But, on top of that process, something qualitatively new
occurs towards the end of the nineteenth century and the
beginning of the twentieth century in this area: the active, mass
insertion of a developed and mature working-class audience into
a new kind of *popular*, commercial press. This has had profound
cultural consequences: though it isn't in any narrow sense
exclusively a 'cultural' question at all. It required the whole
reorganisation of the capital basis and structure of the cultural
industry; a harnessing of new forms of technology and of
labour processes; the establishment of new types of distribution,
operating through the new cultural mass markets. But one of
its effects was indeed a reconstituting of the cultural and
political relations between the dominant and the dominated
classes: a change intimately connected with that containment of
popular democracy on which 'our democratic way of life' today,
appears to be so securely based. Its results are all too palpably
with us still, today: a popular press, the more strident and
virulent as it gradually shrinks; organised by capital 'for' the
working classes; with, nevertheless, deep and influential roots
in the culture and language of the 'underdog', of 'Us': with the
power to represent the class to itself in its most traditionalist
form. This is a slice of the history of 'popular culture' well
worth unravelling.

Of course, one could not begin to do so without talking about
many things which don't usually figure in the discussion of
'culture' at all. They have to do with the reconstruction of
capital and the rise of the collectivisms and the formation of a
new kind of 'educative' state as much as with recreation, dance
and popular song. As an area of serious historical work, the
study of popular culture is like the study of labour history and
its institutions. To declare an interest in it is to correct a major
imbalance, to mark a significant oversight. But, in the end, it
yields most when it is seen in relation to a more general, a
wider history.

I select this period - the 1880s-1920s - because it is one of
the real test cases for the revived interest in popular culture.

Without in any way casting aspersions on the important historical work which has been done and remains to do on earlier periods, I do believe that many of the real difficulties (theoretical as well as empirical) will only be confronted when we begin to examine closely popular culture in a period which begins to resemble our own, which poses the same kind of interpretive problems as our own, and which is informed by our own sense of contemporary questions. I am dubious about that kind of interest in 'popular culture' which comes to a sudden and unexpected halt at roughly the same point as the decline of Chartism. It isn't by chance that very few of us are working in popular culture in the 1930s. I suspect there is something peculiarly awkward, especially for socialists, in the non-appearance of a militant, radical mature culture of the working class in the 1930s when - to tell you the truth - most of us would have expected it to appear. From the viewpoint of a purely 'heroic' or 'autonomous' popular culture, the 1930s is a pretty barren period. This 'barrenness' - like the earlier unexpected richness and diversity - cannot be explained from *within* popular culture alone.

We have now, to begin to speak, not just about discontinuities and qualitative change, but about a very severe fracture, a deep rupture - especially in popular culture in the postwar period. Here it is not only a matter of a change in cultural relations between the classes, but of the changed relationship between the people and the concentration and expansion of the new cultural apparatuses themselves. But could one seriously now set out to write the history of popular culture without taking into account the monopolisation of the cultural industries, on the back of a profound technological revolution (it goes without saying that no 'profound technological revolution' is ever in any sense 'purely' technical)? To write a history of the culture of the popular classes exclusively from inside those classes, without understanding the ways in which they are constantly held in relation with the institutions of dominant cultural production, is not to live in the twentieth century. The point is clear about the twentieth century. I believe it holds good for the nineteenth and eighteenth centuries as well.

So much for 'some problems of periodisation'.

Next, I want to say something about 'popular'. The term can have a number of different meanings: not all of them useful. Take the most common-sense meaning: the things which are said to be 'popular' because masses of people listen to them, buy them, read them, consume them, and seem to enjoy them to the full. This is the 'market' or commercial definition of the term: the one which brings socialists out in spots. It is quite rightly associated with the manipulation and debasement of the culture of the people. In one sense, it is the direct opposite of the way I have been using the word earlier. I have, though, two reservations about entirely dispensing with this meaning, unsatisfactory as it is.

First, if it is true that, in the twentieth century, vast numbers of people *do* consume and even indeed enjoy the cultural products of our modern cultural industry, then it follows that very substantial numbers of working people must be included within the audiences for such products. Now, if the forms and relationships, on which participation in this sort of commercially provided 'culture' depend, are purely manipulative and debased, then the people who consume and enjoy them must either be themselves debased by these activities or else living in a permanent state of 'false consciousness'. They must be 'cultural dopes' who can't tell that what they are being fed is an up-dated form of the opium of the people. That judgment may make us feel right, decent and self-satisfied about our denunciations of the agents of mass manipulation and deception – the capitalist cultural industries: but I don't know that it is a view which can survive for long as an adequate account of cultural relationships; and even less as a socialist perspective on the culture and nature of the working class. Ultimately, the notion of the people as a purely *passive*, outline force is a deeply unsocialist perspective.

Second, then: can we get around this problem without dropping the inevitable and necessary attention to the manipulative aspect of a great deal of commercial popular culture? There are a number of strategies for doing so, adopted by radical critics and theorists of popular culture, which, I think, are highly dubious. One is to counterpose to it another, whole, 'alternative' culture – the authentic 'popular culture'; and to suggest that the 'real' working class (whatever that is) isn't taken in by the commercial substitutes. This is a heroic alternative; but not a very convincing one. Basically what is wrong with it is that it neglects the absolutely essential relations of cultural power – of domination and subordination – which is an intrinsic feature of cultural relations. I want to assert on the contrary that there is *no* whole, authentic, autonomous 'popular culture' which lies outside the field of force of the relations of cultural power and domination. Second, it greatly underestimates the power of cultural implantation. This is a tricky point to make, for, as soon as it *is* made, one opens oneself to the charge that one is subscribing to the thesis of cultural incorporation. The study of popular culture keeps shifting between these two, quite unacceptable, poles: pure 'autonomy' or total incapsulation.

Actually, I don't think it is necessary or right to subscribe to either. Since ordinary people are not cultural dopes, they are perfectly capable of recognising the way the realities of working-class life are reorganised, reconstructed and reshaped by the way they are represented (i.e. re-presented) in, say, *Coronation Street*. The cultural industries do have the power constantly to rework and reshape what they represent; and, by repetition and selection, to impose and implant such definitions of ourselves as fit more easily the descriptions of the dominant or preferred culture. That is what the concentration of cultural power – the means of culture-making in the heads of the few – actually means. These definitions don't have the power to occupy our minds; they don't function on us as if we are blank screens. But they do occupy and rework the interior contradictions of feeling and perception in the dominated classes; they *do* find or clear a space of recognition in those who respond to them. Cultural domination has real effects – even if these are neither all-powerful nor all-inclusive. If we were to argue that these imposed forms have no influence, it would be tantamount to arguing that the culture of the people can exist as a separate enclave, outside the distribution of cultural power and the relations of cultural force. I do not believe that. Rather, I think there is a continuous and necessarily uneven and unequal struggle, by the dominant culture, constantly to disorganise and reorganise popular culture; to enclose and confine its definitions and forms within a more inclusive range of dominant forms. There are points of resistance; there are also moments of supersession. This is the dialectic of cultural struggle. In our times, it goes on continuously, in the complex lines of resistance and acceptance, refusal and capitulation, which make the field of culture a sort of constant battlefield. A battlefield where no once-for-all victories are obtained but where there are always strategic positions to be won and lost.

This first definition, then, is not a useful one for our purposes; but it might force us to think more deeply about the complexity of cultural relations, about the reality of cultural power and about the nature of cultural implantation. If the forms of provided commercial popular culture are not purely manipulative, then it is because, alongside the false appeals, the foreshortenings, the trivialisation and shortcircuits, there are also elements of recognition and identification, something approaching a recreation of recognisable experiences and attitudes, to which people are responding. The danger arises because we tend to think of cultural forms as whole and coherent: either wholly corrupt or wholly authentic. Whereas, they are deeply contradictory; they play on contradictions, especially when they function in the domain of the 'popular'. The language of the *Daily Mirror* is neither a pure construction of Fleet Street 'newspeak' nor is it the language which its working-class readers actually speak. It is a highly complex species of linguistic *ventriloquism* in which the debased brutalism of popular journalism is skilfully combined and intricated with some elements of the directness and vivid particularity of working-class language. It cannot get by without preserving some element of its roots in a real vernacular – in 'the popular'. It wouldn't get very far unless it were capable of reshaping popular elements into a species of canned and neutralised demotic populism.

The second definition of 'popular' is easier to live with. This is the descriptive one. Popular culture is all those things that 'the people' do or have done. This is close to an 'anthropological' definition of the term: the culture, mores, customs and folkways of 'the people'. What defines their 'distinctive way of life'. I have two difficulties with this definition, too.

First, I am suspicious of it precisely because it is too descriptive. This is putting it mildly. Actually, it is based on an infinitely expanding inventory. Virtually *anything* which 'the people' have ever done can fall into the list. Pigeon-fancying and stamp-collecting, flying ducks on the wall and garden gnomes. The problem is how to distinguish this infinite list, in any but a descriptive way, from what popular culture is *not*.

But the second difficulty is more important – and relates to a point made earlier. We can't simply collect into one category all the things which 'the people' do, without observing that the real analytic distinction arises, not from the list itself – an inert category of things and activities – but from the key opposition: the people/not of the people. That is to say, the structuring principle of 'the popular' in this sense is the tensions and oppositions between what belongs to the central domain of elite or dominant culture, and the culture of the 'periphery'. It is this opposition which constantly structures the domain of culture into the 'popular' and the 'non-popular'. But you cannot construct these oppositions in a purely descriptive way. For, from period to period, the *contents* of each category changes. Popular forms become enhanced in cultural value, go up the cultural escalator – and find themselves on the opposite side. Others things cease to have high cultural value, and are appropriated into the popular, becoming transformed in the process. The structuring principle does not consist of the contents of each category – which, I insist, will alter from one period to another. Rather it consists of the forces and relations which sustain the distinction, the difference: roughly, between what, at any time, counts as an elite cultural activity or form, and what does not. These categories remain, though the inventories change. What is more, a whole set of institutions and institutional processes are required to sustain each – and to continually mark the difference between them. The school and the education system is one such institution – distinguishing the valued part of the culture, the cultural heritage, the history to be transmitted, from the 'valueless' part. The literary and scholarly apparatus is another – marking-off certain kinds of valued knowledge from others. The important fact, then, is not a mere descriptive inventory – which may have the negative effect of freezing popular culture into some timeless descriptive mould – but the relations of power which are constantly punctuating and dividing the domain of culture into its preferred and its residual categories.

So I settle for a third definition of 'popular', though it is a rather uneasy one. This looks, in any particular period, at those

forms and activities which have their roots in the social and
material conditions of particular classes; which have been
embodied in popular traditions and practices. In this sense,
it retains what is valuable in the descriptive definition. But it
goes on to insist that what is essential to the definition of
popular culture is the relations which define 'popular culture' in
a continuing tension (relationship, influence and antagonism)
to the dominant culture. It is a conception of culture which is
polarised around this cultural dialectic. It treats the domain of
cultural forms and activities as a constantly changing field.
Then it looks at the relations which constantly structure this
field into dominant and subordinate formations. It looks at the
process by which these relations of dominance and subordination
are articulated. It treats them as a process: the process by
means of which some things are actively preferred so that
others can be dethroned. It has at its centre the changing and
uneven relations of force which define the field of culture –
that is, the question of cultural struggle and its many forms.
Its main focus of attention is the relation between culture and
questions of hegemony.

What we have to be concerned with, in this definition, is not
the question of the 'authenticity' or organic wholeness of
popular culture. Actually, it recognises that almost *all* cultural
forms will be contradictory in this sense, composed of
antagonistic and unstable elements. The meaning of a cultural
form and its place or position in the cultural field is *not*
inscribed inside its form. Nor is its position fixed once and
forever. This year's radical symbol or slogan will be neutralised
into next year's fashion; the year after, it will be the object of
a profound cultural nostalgia. Today's rebel folksinger ends up,
tomorrow, on the cover of *The Observer* colour magazine. The
meaning of a cultural symbol is given in part by the social field
into which it is incorporated, the practices with which it
articulates and is made to resonate. What matters is *not* the
intrinsic or historically fixed objects of culture, but the state of
play in cultural relations: to put it bluntly and in an oversimplified form – what counts is the class struggle in and over
culture.

Almost every fixed inventory will betray us. Is the novel a
'bourgeois' form? The answer can only be historically
provisional: when? which novels? for whom? under what
conditions?

What that very great Marxist theoretician of language who
used the name Volosinov, once said about the sign – the key
element of all signifying practices – is true of cultural forms:

Class does not coincide with the sign community, i.e. with
. . . the totality of users of the same sets of signs for
ideological communication. Thus various different classes will
use one and the same language. As a result, differently
oriented accents intersect in every ideological sign. Sign
becomes an arena of class struggle. . . . By and large it is

thanks to this intersecting of accents that a sign maintains its
vitality and dynamism and the capacity for further
development. A sign that has been withdrawn from the
pressure of the social struggle – which so to speak crosses
beyond the pale of the social struggle – inevitably loses
force, degenerating into an allegory and becoming the object
not of live social intelligibility but of philosophical
comprehension. . . . The ruling class strives to impart a
supraclass, eternal character to the ideological sign, to
extinguish or drive inward the struggle between social value
judgements which occurs in it, to make the sign unaccentual.
In actual fact, each living ideological sign has two faces,
like Janus. Any current curse word can become a word of
praise, any current truth must inevitably sound to many
people as the greatest lie. This inner dialectic quality of the
sign comes out fully in the open only in times of social crisis
or revolutionary change.[1]
Cultural struggle, of course, takes many forms: incorporation,
distortion, resistance, negotiation, recuperation. Raymond
Williams has done us a great deal of service by outlining some of
these processes, with his distinction between emergent, residual
and incorporated moments. We need to expand and develop this
rudimentary schema. The important thing is to look at it
dynamically: as an historical process. Emergent forces reappear
in ancient historical disguise; emergent forces, pointing to the
future, lose their anticipatory power, and become merely
backward looking; today's cultural breaks can be recuperated
as a support to tomorrow's dominant system of values and
meanings. The struggle continues: but it is almost never in the
same place, over the same meaning or value. It seems to me that
the cultural process – cultural power – in our society depends,
in the first instance, on this drawing of the line, always in each
period in a different place, as to what is to be incorporated into
'the great tradition' and what is not. Educational and cultural
institutions, along with the many positive things they do, also
help to discipline and police this boundary.
   This should make us think again about that tricky term in
popular culture, 'tradition'. Tradition is a vital element in
culture; but it has little to do with the mere persistence of old
forms. It has much more to do with the way elements have been
linked together or articulated. These arrangements in a
national-popular culture have no fixed or inscribed position, and
certainly no meaning which is carried along, so to speak, in the
stream of historical tradition, unchanged. Not only can the
elements of 'tradition' be rearranged, so that they articulate
with different practices and positions, and take on a new meaning
and relevance. It is also often the case that cultural struggle
arises in its sharpest form just at the point where different,
opposed traditions meet, intersect. They seek to detach a
cultural form from its implantation in one tradition, and to give
it a new cultural resonance or accent. Traditions are not fixed

forever: certainly not in any universal position in relation to a
single class. Cultures, conceived not as separate 'ways of life'
but as 'ways of struggle' constantly intersect: the pertinent
cultural struggles arise at the points of intersection. Think of
the ways in the eighteenth century, in which a certain language
of legality, of constitutionalism and of 'rights' becomes a
battleground, at the point of intersection between two divergent
traditions: between the 'tradition' of gentry 'majesty and terror'
and the traditions of popular justice. Gramsci, providing a
tentative answer to his own question as to how a new 'collective
will' arises, and a national-popular culture is transformed,
observed that

> What matters is the criticism to which such an ideological
> complex is subjected by the first representatives of the new
> historical phase. This criticism makes possible a process of
> differentiation and change in the relative weight that the
> elements of old ideologies used to possess. What was
> previously secondary and subordinate, even incidental, is
> now taken to be primary – becomes the nucleus of a new
> ideological and theoretical complex. The old collective will
> dissolves into its contradictory elements since the
> subordinate ones develop socially.

This is the terrain of national-popular culture and tradition as
a battlefield.

This provides us with a warning against those self-enclosed
approaches to popular culture which, valuing 'tradition' for its
own sake, and treating it in an a-historical manner, analyse
popular cultural forms as if they contained within themselves,
from their moment of origin, some fixed and unchanging meaning
or value. The relationship between historical position and
aesthetic value is an important and difficult question in popular
culture. But the attempt to develop some universal popular
aesthetic, founded on the moment of origin of cultural forms and
practices, is almost certainly profoundly mistaken. What could
be more eclectic and random than that assemblage of dead
symbols and bric-a-brac, ransacked from yesterday's dressing-
up box, in which, just now, many young people have chosen
to adorn themselves? These symbols and bits and pieces are
profoundly ambiguous. A thousand lost cultural causes could be
summoned up through them. Every now and then, amongst the
other trinkets, we find that sign which, above all other signs,
ought to be fixed - solidified - in its cultural meaning and
connotation forever: the swastika. And yet there it dangles,
partly – but not entirely – cut loose from its profound cultural
reference in twentieth-century history. What does it mean? What
is it signifying? Its signification is rich, and richly ambiguous:
certainly unstable. This terrifying sign may delimit a range of
meanings but it carries no guarantee of a single meaning within
itself. The streets are full of kids who are not 'fascist' because
they may wear a swastika on a chain. On the other hand,
perhaps they *could* be. . . . What this sign means will ultimately

depend, in the politics of youth culture, less on the intrinsic
cultural symbolism of the thing in itself, and more on the
balance of forces between, say, the National Front and the
Anti-Nazi League, between White Rock and the Two Tone Sound.
Not only is there no intrinsic guarantee within the cultural
sign or form itself. There is no guarantee that, because at one
time it was linked with a pertinent struggle, that it will always
be the living expression of a class: so that every time you give
it an airing it will 'speak the language of socialism'. If cultural
expressions register for socialism, it is because they have been
linked as the practices, the forms and organisation of a living
struggle, which has succeeded in appropriating those symbols
and giving them a socialist connotation. Culture is not already
permanently inscribed with the conditions of a class before that
struggle begins. The struggle consists in the success or failure
to give 'the cultural' a socialist accent.

The term 'popular' has very complex relations to the term
'class'. We know this, but are often at pains to forget it. We
speak of particular forms of working-class culture; but we use
the more inclusive term, 'popular culture' to refer to the
general field of enquiry. It's perfectly clear that what I've been
saying would make little sense without reference to a class
perspective and to class struggle. But it is also clear that there
is no one-to-one relationship between a class and a particular
cultural form or practice. The terms 'class' and 'popular' are
deeply related but they are not absolutely interchangeable. The
reason for that is obvious. There are no wholly separate
'cultures' paradigmatically attached, in a relation of historical
fixity, to specific 'whole' classes - although there are clearly
distinct and variable class-cultural formations. Class cultures
tend to intersect and overlap in the same field of struggle. The
term 'popular' indicates this somewhat displaced relationship of
culture to classes. More accurately, it refers to that alliance of
classes and forces which constitute the 'popular classes'. The
culture of the oppressed, the excluded classes: this is the
area to which the term 'popular' refers us. And the opposite
side to that - the side with the cultural power to decide what
belongs and what does not - is, by definition, not another
'whole' class, but that other alliance of classes, strata and
social forces which constitute what is not 'the people' and not
the 'popular classes': the culture of the power-bloc.

The people versus the power-bloc: this, rather than 'class-
against-class', is the central line of contradiction around which
the terrain of culture is polarised. Popular culture, especially,
is organised around the contradiction: the popular forces versus
the power-bloc. This gives to the terrain of cultural struggle
its own kind of specificity. But the term 'popular', and even
more, the collective subject to which it must refer - 'the people'
- is highly problematic. It is made problematic by, say, the
ability of Mrs Thatcher to pronounce a sentence like, 'We have
to limit the power of the trade unions because that is what the

people want.' That suggests to me that, just as there is no
fixed content to the category of 'popular culture', so there is no
fixed subject to attach to it – 'the people'. 'The people' are not
always back there, where they have always been, their culture
untouched, their liberties and their instincts intact, still
struggling on against the Norman yoke or whatever: as if, if
only we can 'discover' them and bring them back on stage, they
will always stand up in the right, appointed place and be
counted. The capacity to *constitute* classes and individuals as a
popular force – that is the nature of political and cultural
struggle: to *make* the divided classes and the separated peoples
– divided and separated by culture as much as by other factors
– *into* a popular-democratic cultural force.

We can be certain that *other* forces also have a stake in
defining 'the people' as something else: 'the people' who need to
be disciplined more, ruled better, more effectively policed,
whose way of life needs to be protected from 'alien cultures',
and so on. There is some part of both those alternatives inside
each of us. Sometimes we can be constituted as a force against
the power-bloc: that is the historical opening in which it is
possible to construct a culture which is genuinely popular. But,
in our society, if we are not constituted like that, we will be
constituted into its opposite: an effective populist force, saying
'Yes' to power. Popular culture is one of the sites where this
struggle for and against a culture of the powerful is engaged:
it is also the stake to be won or lost *in* that struggle. It is the
arena of consent and resistance. It is partly where hegemony
arises, and where it is secured. It is not a sphere where
socialism, a socialist culture – already fully formed – might be
simply 'expressed'. But it is one of the places where socialism
might be constituted. That is why 'popular culture' matters.
Otherwise, to tell you the truth, I don't give a damn about it.

NOTE

1   A. Volosinov, *Marxism and the Philosophy of Language*,
New York 1977.

FURTHER READING

Bailey, Peter, *Leisure and Class in Victorian England
1830-1885*, London 1978.
Hall, Stuart and Whannel, A.D., *The Popular Arts*, London
1964.
Johnson, Richard, 'Three problematics: elements of a theory of
working-class culture' in *Working-Class Culture, Studies in
History and Theory*, ed. by John Clarke, Charles Chrichter
and Richard Johnson, London 1979.

Malcolmson, R.W., *Popular Recreation in English Society, 1700-1850*, Cambridge 1973.

Nowell-Smith, Geoffrey, 'Gramsci and the national-popular', *Screen Education*, Spring 1977.

Stedman Jones, Gareth, 'Working-Class culture and working class politics in London, 1870-1890', *Journal of Social History*, Summer 1974.

Thompson, E.P., 'Patrician society, plebeian culture', *Journal of Social History*, Summer 1974.

Williams, Raymond, 'Radical or popular' in *The Press We Deserve*, ed. by James Curran, London 1970.

Socialist history in Europe

Bob Scribner*

The German Peasant War of 1525 can be described as the most
important of the pre-modern European peasant revolts and as
the first of the great modern revolutions. It stands beside the
Revolution of November 1918 as one of the landmarks of German
revolutionary history. This paper examines the treatment of this
event by German socialist historians since the mid-nineteenth
century. The ways in which they dealt with the subject raise
important issues for the relationship between people's history
and socialist theory.

AN OUTLINE OF THE HISTORIOGRAPHY

The forerunners of a socialist interpretation of the German
Peasant War appeared in the years immediately following the
French Revolution. Several German liberal historians saw close
parallels between the revolution occurring in their own time and
that of 1525. Historians such as Karl Hammerdörfer (1793),
Georg Sartorius (1795) and Georg Theodor Strobel (1795)
rejected the dominant view of the early sixteenth century, which
saw it largely in terms of religious history and through the eyes
of Luther. They directed attention to the extensive social
conflicts of the period and restored to historical prominence the
major revolutionary figure of the Peasant War, Thomas Muntzer.
Hammerdörfer even set him up as one of the great heroes of the
struggle for freedom, alongside William Tell. In general these
historians had little desire to approve of or justify the peasant
rebellion, but they did see it as embodying one of the
predominant political lessons of their own day: that tyranny and
ignorance had provoked revolution in both cases, while reason
and enlightenment were the means towards progress and justice.[1]

Zimmermann
Their work inspired that of Wilhelm Zimmermann, *General History
of the Great Peasant War* (3 volumes, 1841-3), which became the
cornerstone of socialist interpretations and has been republished
as a classic work of radical history for over a century.[2]
Zimmermann was a left Hegelian and never became a socialist but
his book had three features which appealed to socialists:

---

*Bob Scribner teaches history at King's College London and
researches on Reformation Germany.

(i) His belief that the history of mankind was the history of the struggle for freedom, a struggle by and on behalf of 'the common man'. The German Peasant War was a major event in this history, 'the armed uprising of the common man'.[3]

(ii) He placed it within a tradition of oppositional movements and revolts in Germany dating from the ninth century.[4]

(iii) He saw it as an active intervention in the political struggles of his own day, a view confirmed by the fact that the first instalment was scarcely off the press (the first volume appeared in booklet-sized instalments) before it was banned in Bavaria and Württemberg.[5]

Thus Zimmermann was writing both people's history and revolutionary history, and using history as a weapon of political struggle.

Zimmermann's appeal was strengthened by his involvement in the Revolution of 1848, when he was elected to the Frankfurt Assembly, in which he belonged to the radical wing. Afterwards he was dismissed from his post as professor at the Karlsruhe Polytechnic and lived out the rest of his life as a parson in an impoverished parish near Stuttgart, a post provided only on a promise of his complete withdrawal from politics. This change of circumstances was reflected in the second edition of his book, published in 1856. He expunged many passages in which he expressed his radical commitment, characterising them as the work of headstrong youth, and he played down the parallels between the revolutionary events of the sixteenth century and those of his own age.[6]

Nonetheless, Zimmermann's work made such an impression on socialist readers that this retreat was regarded with indulgence. Engels based his own treatment of the Peasant War entirely on Zimmermann, using the first edition, and in 1870 he commented: 'The same revolutionary instinct, which everywhere makes him champion the oppressed classes, made him later one of the best of the extreme left in Frankfurt.' Only in 1875 did he add the qualifying comment: 'It is true that since then he is said to have aged somewhat.'[7]

A third version of the book was published in 1891, a 'popular edition' abridged by the socialist publicist Wilhelm Blos, who saw it as 'a democratic work in the best sense'. Its continuing popularity was attested by a new impression of this 1891 edition in 1921, and by another 'popular edition' issued in the German Democratic Republic in 1952. This was based on the Blos version, but restored some passages from Zimmermann's 1856 edition. This version has been reprinted several times in the GDR, most recently in 1977. Through sales there and in the Federal Republic of Germany, it continues to interest a new generation of socialist readers in the German Peasant War.[8] The book was highly regarded not only by socialists. Academic reviewers protested that the Blos edition was a mutilation of the work, and in 1939 a more 'scholarly' edition was published by the noted Reformation historian Hermann Barge. There was also an edition published in 1933, substantially the same as that of Blos, but reshaped into a Nazi edition by a racist introduction by Gottfried Falkner.[9]

It is worth commenting on the historical value of Zimmermann, for it has often been a cardinal criticism of socialist histories of the Peasant War that they drew on an unreliable source. In writing the book Zimmermann attempted to apply the best available rules of historical criticism. He sought to found his arguments on 'genuine documents and on the evidence of reliable witnesses'. Where possible he used manuscript sources, especially for south Germany, making particular use of the source regarded by present-day scholars as one of the most valuable for understanding the Peasant War, the documents in Stuttgart of the Swabian League, the south German alliance of princes and great towns which was instrumental in defeating the rebellion in the south. Where he had no access to manuscript sources, largely for Saxony, he used whatever printed sources were available and earlier historical works.[10]

The book appeared at almost the same time as the classic work on the Reformation by Leopold von Ranke, which was to establish the dominant conservative interpretation of the period for most of the nineteenth century. Zimmermann's book, however, remained the only comprehensive history of the Peasant War until that published by Gunther Franz in 1933. A recent critic has accused Zimmermann of distorting his evidence, misusing sources and of over-reliance on Strobel's 1795 life of Muntzer (all faults not uncommon among professional historians). Even this hostile critic, writing from the position of a firm anti-Marxist, had to concede that the work was 'in many respects . . . sound'.[11]

Engels

We can now place in perspective the most famous work of socialist history on this subject, Friedrich Engels' *The Peasant War in Germany*, written as articles for the *Neue Rheinische Zeitung* in 1850, and first published separately in 1870. Engels undertook no original research for his work, but based it entirely on Zimmermann, who provided, as Engels claimed in 1870, probably with full justification, 'the best array of the factual material'.[12] Engels' contribution was twofold. First, he supplied a new theoretical analysis of the Peasant War, using the materialist conception of history originated by himself and Marx. Second, he made out a more detailed case for the parallels between the events of the sixteenth century and those of the second half of the nineteenth.

In the first area, Engels attempted to show the connections between changes in the mode of production and social changes taking place in the early sixteenth century. He traced the beginnings of the capitalist mode in the development of new technology (navigation, printing, mining, military technology), and the expansion of mining and cloth production. There was an accompanying rise of trade and increasing agricultural production to supply an expanding economy. Guild-based industrial production in the towns began to replace more local feudal industries in the countryside. But German industrial production and trade still lagged behind other countries such as Italy, the Low Countries or England. Thus, there could be no fusing of interests across the whole of Germany to overcome the fragmentation produced by the feudal system.

Alongside this economic analysis Engels set an analysis of German society at the beginning of the sixteenth century. The sociological picture he drew was fairly sophisticated for the mid-nineteenth century. Among the representatives of feudalism, the nobility and the clergy, he discerned a polarisation into great princes gaining autonomous power and a lower nobility being forced into impoverishment, between the great prelates and a 'plebeian clergy' living on the margin in town and country. In the cities he saw a threefold division: an urban patriciate who acted little differently from the feudal nobility and clergy, a rising middle bourgeoisie, and a 'plebeian opposition' comprised of ruined townsmen and the rest of the disprivileged urban classes. All the urban groups outside the patriciate often united in a 'burgher opposition' to the ruling urban elite. At the very bottom of society stood the peasantry, 'the exploited bulk of the nation', whom Engels made no attempt to differentiate further.

Engels linked the two elements of his analysis through the notion that the religious ideas of the Reformation were an expression of these class oppositions. The various social groups of his analysis of society were represented by the various religious parties which appeared in the Reformation. Lutheran opposition to Catholicism, which Engels saw as the truest representation of feudal ideology, attracted into a broad opposition movement all the anti-feudal elements of society. Thomas Muntzer, with his chiliastic and revolutionary theology, provided a hope of revolutionary change, which the peasant revolt of 1525 attempted to implement. Under the cloak of theology, Muntzer provided an anticipation of revolutionary communism, while Muntzer himself became a prototype of the revolutionary communist agitator. However, the burgher classes took fright at such radical developments, abandoned the cause of the anti-feudal opposition and joined the princes to repress the revolution. This change of direction was carried through at the religious level by Luther's change of direction, who in 1525 turned against radical reform and upheld the princes against the peasants and plebeians. Although the revolution was seen by Engels as a middle-class revolution, the only truly radical groups had been the peasants and the plebeian opposition in the towns. The latter had failed the revolution because they were unformed as a class, the former out of 'provincial narrow-mindedness'.

Thus far Engels was attempting to bring socialist theory to

Zimmermann's 'people's history'. However, the political events of
his own day influenced the attempt in a very marked fashion.
Writing in 1850, Engels was preoccupied with the failure of the
1848 revolutions. The cause he saw in the betrayal of the
bourgeoisie, a judgment which certainly coloured his reading of
the sixteenth century. In 1525 a middle-class revolution had
also failed because of the weakness of the bourgeoisie. To be
sure, this was no crude case of history repeating itself, for he
saw the two terms of historical analogy. In both cases a victory
of the princes was brought about by lack of unity among the
opposition and revolutionary forces, and by the failure of the
middle classes to act in revolutionary manner. But Engels saw
clearly that the burgher classes and the 'plebeians' of the
sixteenth century were very different from the bourgeoisie and
proletariat of the nineteenth. Moreover, where the 1525
revolution was a 'domestic German event', that of 1848 was 'an
episode in a great European movement'. Yet his obsession with
the bourgeoisie in 1850 did lead him to think more about the
burgher classes of 1525, and to ignore any comparable analysis
of the peasantry to his sophisticated discussion of the urban
classes. More curiously, he chose to characterise the
sixteenth-century revolution as middle class, despite the
predominant role of the peasantry in it.

The Peasant question

Engels' *Peasant War in Germany* was largely an expression of
frustration at the failure of 1848, and a restatement of his belief
in the continuance of the revolutionary tradition in Germany.
Just as 1525 had not put an end to it, so 1848 would not do so.
The *ad hoc* character of his work is attested by the fact that it
was not published again for twenty years. The occasion was
then somewhat different. In the 1850s Marx and Engels had
opposed Ferdinand Lassalle's underestimation of the
revolutionary potential of the peasantry, and by 1869 the First
International made a conscious effort to tap that potential.
Engels' preface to the 1870 edition of his *Peasant War* summed up
socialist thinking on the question, arising from the realisation
that the success of any revolution was dependent on the
response of the peasantry.

Since 1848 the great bourgeoisie had been driven into the
arms of monarchy, nobility and bureaucracy by their fear of the
growing strength of the proletariat. The petit bourgeoisie,
artisans and shopkeepers, were unreliable allies. The only other
allies of the proletariat were the lumpenproletariat, whom Engels
believed to be as unreliable as the petit bourgeoisie, the small
peasants and the agricultural labourers. It was to the latter two
groups that the proletariat must turn to find allies whose class
interests also lay in the overturning of the revived feudal order
in Germany, an order embodied in the Prussian state.

The German peasantry could be seen as made up of several
groups. The large tenant was little different from the

landowner, who confronted his agricultural workers much as the capitalist confronted industrial workers. The small peasants were either feudal peasants whose only hope of freedom from the services owed to their lords lay with the working class, or tenant farmers, who were burdened with debt such that their property really belonged to capitalist moneylenders. It was these two groups who would benefit from a nationalisation of landownership, and to this end the First International had called in 1869 for the transformation of landed property into common, nationally owned property. Agricultural labourers, who were most numerous in areas with medium and large-size estates, were the 'most natural' allies of the workers.

Here socialists faced a double problem. Small peasants clung closely to 'their' small patches of land, ignoring that it was in reality owned by their creditors. They thus had to be convinced that nationally owned land represented a better deal than their existing situation. Agricultural labourers could be equally unaware of their class interests. They provided the bulk of princely armies, and were trapped by a false sense of loyalty to landlords or feudal lords, which led them under universal suffrage to vote these into parliament.[13]

The 1870 edition of Engels' *Peasant War* thus served a clear political purpose. It provided a model of peasant radicalism from the sixteenth century, which showed the way forward for an alliance of workers and peasants. It also spelled out the results of a failure to realise the coincidence of class interest of these two groups, for it was as much the narrow-mindedness of the peasantry as the weakness of the burgher classes which Engels saw as responsible for the failure of the revolution of 1525. The republication was apt, but it did not lead Engels to revise his rather offhand treatment of the peasantry as an undifferentiated mass.

Other works

Engels' book was popular enough for another edition to be issued in 1875, and it was thenceforth established as the classic socialist work on the Peasant War. However, Engels did not stand entirely alone as a socialist historian of the subject. In 1876 August Bebel also published his *The German Peasant War*, written without knowledge of Engels' work. He also relied on Zimmermann without any pretence of original research. Like Zimmermann, Bebel saw his history as an attempt to redress the neglect of people's history and revolutionary history in the prevailing conservative orthodoxy of history writing. Bebel had much in common with Engels in his treatment, stressing the role of the bourgeoisie and the need to understand the political events of the period through analysis of the social position of various classes. However, his sociological analysis was cruder, conceiving sixteenth-century classes in the image of those of the nineteenth. Thus the revolts of the urban lower classes were spoken of as though they were a proletarian movement. He also did not argue as precisely as Engels that the religious conflicts were the expression of social conflicts, nor attempt such a close alignment of religious and political groupings. Luther was not the representative of the moderate burgher party, as he was with Engels, although Bebel did stress the appeal of his ideas for 'our present bourgeoisie . . . who see in him their model and image'. He thus saw somewhat more perceptively than Engels that Luther was socially conservative from the very beginning, and very early had set his doctrines apart from social or political implications.[14]

After Bebel there were no separate histories of the Peasant War written by socialists, although the topic retained its interest and a number of new insights were added. In 1889 Karl Kautsky published a study of miners in the Peasant War, and in 1894 devoted attention to Muntzer in his *Forerunners of Socialism*. Kautsky's discussion of the Saxon mining industry pointed out the enormous wealth created by the expansion of mining production, overcoming an important inconsistency in Engels' work, whereby an expansion of the middle classes and a largely middle-class revolution had occurred at the time when the German economy was lagging. Kautsky, who was more interested in workers' movements than in the peasantry, also called attention to the support given Thomas Muntzer by the miners in central Germany.

It was above all in his investigation of Muntzer that Kautsky went further than Engels. Engels had probably not read any of Muntzer's works, but had relied on Zimmermann, who had done little original research on the Peasant War in Saxony. Kautsky, however, studied Muntzer's writings closely, and rejected much of Zimmermann's idealist interpretation which saw Muntzer as standing outside of, and ahead of, his time. For Kautsky Muntzer's significance was not found in any originality of revolutionary ideas or exceptional organising ability, but in his revolutionary vision and fervour. On the whole, Kautsky lacked Engels' broader interpretational sweep, and saw the Peasant War within a narrower context. However, he did stimulate Engels to new thoughts on the theme, and the latter projected a new history of the Peasant War which was never undertaken. All that survives are a few sketches and partial discussions in correspondence.[15]

The next significant stage of socialist interpretation was reached in 1921, with Ernst Bloch's *Thomas Muntzer as Theologian of Revolution*. Influenced largely by his own 'philosophy of hope', which emphasised the emancipatory role of utopian visions in history, Bloch brought out the significance of Muntzer's chiliasm. This was able to inspire both peasants and urban workers with a vision of a Kingdom of God on earth where equality and justice would prevail. It was this apocalyptic vision which spurred the oppressed classes to revolution in 1525.[16]

During the 1920s there was also a broader interest in the Peasant War, especially among the Communist Party of Germany

(KPD). This arose both in the wake of Lenin's views on the
importance of the agrarian question, and because of the united
front policy advocated by the Third International. The
Revolution of November 1918 also turned thoughts to the former
highpoint of Germany's revolutionary history, although it found
little expression in weightier works of history. The average
socialist reader was more likely to know about the Peasant War
through Engels or Zimmermann, or as occurred in the 1880s
and 1890s through popularisations in short novel form, such as
those by Robert Schweichel (1895 and 1899), or through plays
such as Friedrich Wolf's *Poor Conrad* of 1923.[17] This interest,
however, was clearly carried over into the post-1945 period,
when the socialist interpretation became identified with that
propounded by historians in the GDR. The peasant question,
which formed the background to continued interest in the
Peasant War, recurred here too, for the new socialist state saw
itself as a resolution of that question, as a workers' and
farmers' state. The central place of the Peasant War in the
historiography of the GDR was clearly the result of the desire
to legitimate itself in terms of Germany's peasant as well as
proletarian revolutionary past. There is no time to pursue the
GDR tradition of interpretation, but it is sufficient to say that
this was built largely on Engels as an authoritative and
exemplary model for the pursuit of the subject.[18]

SOCIALIST HISTORY AND SOCIALIST THEORY

All of the works we have considered so far represent history
written from an active concern with the present. In these,
socialist history was related to the present in three ways:
(1) It supplied *lessons for the present*, often through moralising
didacticism. There was a good deal of this in Engels' bitter
comments about the unreliability of the petit bourgeoisie in 1525
and 1850 and later. At his more reflective, Engels stressed the
importance of the proper analysis of historical analogy. Careful
comparative analysis of analogous historical situations would
reveal the nature of the historical process and so aid
understanding of the present. Like all social scientists, Engels
was interested in the predictive possibilities of analysis of
social processes.

Later socialist use of the 'lessons of the Peasant War' hovered
uncomfortably between these two positions. In 1925 Edwin
Hoernle wrote a short article in *Die Internationale*, the
theoretical journal of the German Communist Party, drawing the
lessons of the Peasant War for 'the proletariat of today'. The
sixteenth-century revolution had been a bourgeois revolution,
and all bourgeois revolutions occur at the expense of the
workers. The bourgeoisie were not to be trusted, nor were
bourgeois intellectuals, who had provided leadership but were
inclined to moderate compromises. The sixteenth century had

lacked discipline, organisation, and above all clear political aims. All this showed the modern proletariat both the necessity of the worker peasant alliance and the need for an organised and disciplined revolutionary party. As the party with a Leninist peasant policy, the German Communist Party could provide both.[19]

(2) History was *a form of propaganda*, in the more neutral sense of the term. That is, it educated the repressed classes by recalling past struggles. It raised morale by demonstrating that not all previous history had been a story of misery, but that there had been liberating moments of opposition to oppression. It also gave hope by supplying a revolutionary tradition which was to inspire future action. All of these reasons were given by Franz Mehring for the edition of Engels' *Peasant War* he produced in 1908, which was reprinted five times up to 1920:

This work today is a weapon of powerful propaganda, suited as nothing else to present the German Revolution to the modern proletariat as something living in the historical core of its being, not only widening their historical knowledge, but also sharpening their understanding of the problems which the current struggle for emancipation has to solve.[20]

(3) History was *part of an active class struggle*, understood not as an academic pursuit but as a form of politics taken directly to the people. The activities of the German Communist Party in the 1920s provide a good example. We mentioned that the party was pursuing a united front policy during the early 1920s, while at the same time it was engaged in internal struggles over the Leninist direction of the party. The policy of alliance with the peasantry met both points of policy, and the 400th anniversary of the Peasant War in 1925 was used both to stress the importance of the worker-peasant alliance and the correctness of Lenin's views. The party sponsored a new edition of Engels' book, edited by Hermann Duncker, and numerous articles appeared in various party journals, of which that by Edwin Hoernle cited above is an example. There was also a series of short pamphlets on the Peasant War, aimed at a rural readership and produced by the party press *Neues Dorf* (*New Village*).[21]

The party also went beyond mere literary activity, staging in spring 1925 a series of 'Rural Red Sundays' around Berlin, in Saxony and in Württemberg, where works on the history of the Peasant War were distributed alongside political agitation material. Usually linked to marches, these led up to gatherings commemorating the anniversary of the Peasant War in Thuringia and Saxony, attaining a peak attendance with the 15,000 who turned out at Eisleben on Whitsun 1925 to commemorate the death of Muntzer.

Earlier the German Communist Party had organised mass festivals in each of the years 1920-2 in Leipzig, based on the Workers' Choral and Gymnastic Society. These enacted scenes from the revolutionary highpoints of the past, with up to 3,000 participants. In 1921 the theme was the German Peasant War,

while the Spartacist Rising and the French Revolution formed
the themes of 1920 and 1922 respectively. With this kind of
activity, history was more than an academic subject; it was
something actively realised by the people. People's history was
conceived of as the political activity of the people.[22]

Shortcomings of socialist history
It would be impossible to ignore in this context the inadequacies
of socialist history, and many were quite apparent in the
nineteenth-century works.
(1) Socialist history suffered from preoccupation with theory at
the expense of basic research. The original aims of Engels' work
were admirable – to achieve a synthesis of socialist theory and
historical investigation. This desire informed his continuing
interest in the subject until his death, his attempts to
incorporate new findings such as those of Kautsky and to
modify his theoretical considerations accordingly. However, the
value of his work for the modern historian is circumscribed by
his lack of source studies. Mehring conceded in his 1920 preface
that 'it is only the historical method which gives this work its
distinctive value'.[23]
(2) Socialist historians were too preoccupied with the problems
of their own time, and this dulled their historical perception.
Bebel's tendency to see opposition movements in the sixteenth-
century towns as similar to modern workers' movements would
be too easy an example to choose, were it not that the same
mistake has been made by many modern historians. Although
Engels was more aware of the different social structure of
sixteenth-century Germany, his obsession with the nineteenth-
century bourgeoisie and their effect on revolutionary politics
led him to make fundamental errors. He ignored the
stratification of the sixteenth-century peasantry, even though
he was well aware of that of the nineteenth. This casualness
allied to his assumption that 1525, like 1848, was a bourgeois
revolution led him into the inconsistency of having a peasant
revolt which formed the main thrust of a middle-class revolution.
Again, his view of the nineteenth century led him to see
Catholic and Lutheran ideas too facilely as the ideological
expression of feudal and bourgeois class positions respectively.
A little investigation reveals the situation to be more complex.
As critics of socialist interpretations have continually pointed
out, these have remained central weaknesses.
(3) Because of these faults, the very dominance of Engels' work
is itself an inadequacy. There has been no lack of socialist
interest in the Peasant War, and no lack of variety in socialist
historians' treatments of it. Yet it is striking that two books
written so long ago as Engels and Zimmermann remain the
'standard' works. Whatever their considerable merit in their own
time, and it is merit which we can still recognise today and pay
tribute to, they are now completely out of date. It can only be
considered as a failure of socialist historiography that others

have not followed the lead given by Engels, who aimed continually at revision and recasting of his own work to produce a more adequate history. This is the more remarkable since there has been no similar dearth of socialist theory building on the foundations laid by socialist 'classics'.

Some problems of social theory and people's history
These arise naturally from what has been said above, and again a simple enumeration will suffice as a springboard for wider discussion.
(1) The interrelation between socialist theory and empirical research remains an area where solutions have yet to be found (as is indeed the case with any history with claims to be based on theoretical analysis). More successful socialist histories in other fields often appear to be so because of their absence of theory, or else they allow a minimal amount of theory to grow out of their empirical investigations. In studies on the early sixteenth century, most recent empirical studies implicitly challenge older theoretical assumptions about the nature and composition of classes, their relations to economic developments, and the nature of ideology and its formation. The situation of classes can be established as more confused and fragmented, feudalism was more resilient to change, the creation of nascent capitalism was more complex. All this seems to suggest a reshaping, or at least refinement, of socialist theory to take account of new knowledge.
(2) A further problem is that of relevance and immediacy, raised by the place of this paper in a session on peasants, while the tradition which it discusses has paid minimal attention to them. Given the active political involvement inherent in socialist history, how is any study of a pre-industrial peasantry relevant to the tasks confronting the historian in twentieth-century Europe? Even in the nineteenth century, where it had at least a tactical relevance, the question of the peasantry was subordinated to other more immediate concerns. How immediate is a socialist history of the peasantry to us today? Certainly, we may follow Zimmermann and Engels and see it as showing an alternative history and as restating a revolutionary history in danger of being obscured. This is clearly the purpose of some works which have appeared recently in the Federal Republic of Germany, but the political immediacy of the matter may well appear dubious.[24]
(3) In so far as socialist history is politically involved history, that is, that the historian is actively involved in politics, there is a problem of time and resources to carry out historical investigations with the necessary rigour. This is the major extenuating circumstance in the case of Engels and Bebel. Engels wrote in London in 1850, without any possibility of access to sources; Bebel wrote his work in prison while serving a sentence for *lèse majesté* in 1875. The higher his level of political involvement, the less time a historian is likely to have

for close research. This may suggest, in contradiction to the
historical tradition we have just discussed, that history as a
form of political activity invariably stands on the fringes of
political struggle.
(4) A response to the previous suggestion is to see socialist
history as a form of education, and so as a more relevant area
of political involvement. This is clearly the intention behind the
teaching pack on the Peasant War produced in 1979 by the
Künstlergruppe Jorg Ratgeb with lino-cuts by Nil Fricke.[25]
Where the history of the Peasant War is generally ignored in the
school curriculum, or presented in non-socialist form, such
history has both an educational and a political purpose. This
indicates, however, the need for a history which operates at
different levels from 'academic' history, for a history which is
genuinely popular and is integrated with the political needs and
activities of the people. Its relation to more 'academic' history
will pose new problems.
(5) Assuming the creation of a more genuine 'people's history',
will there be any need for the 'socialist historian'? Will he or
she any longer be required to 'give' the people their history?
Moreover the kinds of theoretical explanation that the 'academic'
historian is called upon to use may seem to have little relevance
to people as they make their own history. The author of a
recent book on punk and subcultures commented that the people
involved in the creation of punk subculture may not recognise
the theoretical description and analysis he gave of the
phenomenon, nor might they care particularly if they did.[26]
This may be taken as an argument against 'academic' history,
but it is clear from the case of the German Peasant War that
both kinds of history are required. We need the modern
equivalents of Zimmermann and Engels, for this will affect the
accuracy and soundness of any popular history that may
succeed them. We need also the kind of 'people's history'
developed by the German Communist Party in the 1920s. How
the two are to be related should be the major task of
contemporary socialist history.

NOTES

1 A. Friesen, *Reformation and Utopia. The Marxist
interpretation of the Reformation and its antecedents*,
Wiesbaden 1974, pp. 10-11. Allowing for its anti-Marxist bias
and occasionally quirky interpretations, this work contains
much valuable information on modern socialist historiography
of the German Peasant War. Chapter 3 is especially useful
on the development of the traditional religious
interpretations, which socialist interpretations sought to
correct. However, to appreciate Zimmermann one is better
advised to read the original, where one discovers a somewhat
different work from that depicted by Friesen.

2 W. Zimmermann, *Allgemeine Geschichte des grossen Bauernkrieges*, 3 vols, Stuttgart 1841, 1842, 1843.
3 *Ibid.*, vol. 1, p. 4: 'die bewaffnete Erhebung des gemeinen Mannes'.
4 *Ibid.*, vol. 2, pp. 10-102. This is the section most severely abridged in modern editions.
5 *Ibid.*, vol. 3, p. vii.
6 Friesen, *op. cit.*, pp. 109-10.
7 F. Engels, *The Peasant War in Germany*, Moscow 1956, p. 15.
8 W. Zimmermann, *Grosser Deutscher Bauernkrieg*, ed. by Wilhelm Blos, Stuttgart 1891; W. Zimmermann, *Der Grosse Deutsche Bauernkrieg*, Berlin 1952, which mentions in its preface the changes from Blos' edition.
9 W. Zimmermann, *Geschichte des grossen Bauernkrieges*, ed. by H. Barge, 2 vols, Naunhof and Leipzig 1939; W. Zimmermann, *Der deutsche Bauernkrieg*, revised by Gottfried Falkner, Berlin 1933, an edition overlooked by Friesen.
10 Zimmermann, *Allgemeine Geschichte*, vol. 3, pp. iv-v.
11 Friesen, *op. cit.*, p. 123. It is largely Zimmermann's left-wing interpretation which prejudices Friesen against him.
12 Engels, *op. cit.*, p. 15.
13 *Ibid.*, pp. 23-5.
14 A. Bebel, *Der deutsche Bauernkrieg mit Berücksichtigung der hauptsächlichsten sozialen Bewegungen des Mittelalters*, Braunschweig 1876, esp. p. 97 on Luther.
15 Friesen, *op. cit.*, pp. 170-7.
16 E. Bloch, *Thomas Münzer als Theologe der Revolution*, Baden-Baden 1972, first edn Munich 1921.
17 H. Bartel, 'Der deutsche Bauernkrieg in der Tradition der revolutionären Arbeiterbewegung', *Zeitschrift für Geschichtswissenschaft*, 23, 1975, pp. 137, 141; K. Kinner, 'Die frühbürgerliche Revolution in Deutschland im Geschichtsbild der KPD in den Jahren der revolutionären Nachkriegskrise', in G. Brendler and A. Laube, eds, *Der deutsche Bauernkrieg 1524/25*, Berlin 1977, pp. 393 ff., 401.
18 On the GDR interpretation and the role of Engels in it, see J. Bak, ed., *The German Peasant War of 1525*, London 1975, pp. 89-131; B. Scribner and G. Benecke, *The German Peasant War 1525 - New Viewpoints*, London 1979, ch. 1.
19 E. Hoernle, 'Der grosse Bauernkrieg vor 400 Jahren und das revolutionäre Proletariat von Heute', *Die Internationale. Zeitschrift für Praxis und Theorie des Marxismus*, 8, 1925, pp. 182-8.
20 F. Engels, *Der deutsche Bauernkrieg*, with introduction and notes by F. Mehring, Berlin 1920, fifth printing of 1908 edition, p. 7.
21 F. Engels, *Der deutsche Bauernkrieg*, ed. H. Duncker, Berlin 1925; D. Greiner, *Der grosse Bauernkrieg und Thomas Münzer*, Berlin 1925; E. Janisch, *Der Freiheitskampf der Bauern. Zum 400jährigen Gedächtnis des grossen*

Bauernkrieges, Berlin 1925.
22 Bartel, *op. cit.*, p. 143; Kinner, *op. cit.*, p. 145.
23 Engels, ed. Mehring, *op. cit.*, p. 7.
24 See, for example, *Die Schlacht unter dem Regenbogen. Frankenhausen, Ein Lehrstuck aus dem Bauernkrieg*, collected by Ludwig Fischer, Berlin 1975.
25 N.I.L. Fricke, Künstlergruppe Ratgeb, *Blätter zur deutschen Geschichte. I. Der Bauernkrieg*, Berlin 1979.
26 D. Hebdige, *Subculture: A study of style*, London 1979.

31 THROUGH THE UNDERGROWTH: CAPITALIST DEVELOPMENT AND SOCIAL FORMATION IN NINETEENTH-CENTURY FRANCE

Andrew Lincoln*

The preliminary remarks which follow try to convey the fruits of an attempt to come to terms with the landscape of post-war scholarship dealing with the development of capitalism and social formation in nineteenth-century France. They could be likened to the first landmarks picked out by a parachutist on his touching down. Isolated in its origins - unlike on the French Revolution, there is no established British tradition of work in nineteenth-century French social and economic history - this mission has since been characterised by considerable fraternisation with those encountered on the ground, some of whose oral testimonies have been incorporated into the text. Although it is not dealt with here directly, the more particular problem that lies behind this survey is why the predominant image of nineteenth-century Paris, the original crucible of a socialist politics and a critical reference point for Marxist theory, takes the form of a tired picture of 'artisans' living and working within a context of economic stasis more akin to petty commodity production than to capitalism, and largely abstracted from any sense of a relationship between classes. These bearings may serve more than a hermetic academic purpose if they allow the specificity of the tools with which we are working

*Andrew Lincoln is an editor of *History Workshop Journal* who has been researching for the past six years in the history of nineteenth-century Paris, and living and teaching there.

to become a little clearer.

Much of recent French historical scholarship has drawn its inspiration from the methodological positions developed by Marc Bloch and Lucien Febvre during the 1930s in the review that they had founded at Strasbourg in 1929, the *Annales d'histoire économique et sociale*. The latter's relationship to modern history, however, has been complex.[1] The first decade of the review's life is striking both for the attention given to contemporary history and the relative silence with regard to the nineteenth century. At least a third of the articles which appeared each year were on subjects close to, if not within, the domain of 'current affairs': in 1933, for instance, it carried a piece of research entitled 'In the United States. The Banking Crisis and the Great Depression'. This presence, quite foreign to the review of the 1970s, was the product of the founders' position on the relationship between present and past: 'Let us be trained to make a correct use of the manifest suggestive force that the precise knowledge of contemporary facts exercises on the spirit of historians, if they really wish to understand the past.'[2] The subsequent passage from the study of a contemporary problem to its history was seen as being a means to relativising the incidence of the former, the better to understand it.[3] But the nineteenth century was not the chosen ground of this exercise in historical relativity, as if it were too bound up by the form of political history, which reduces all history to that of the decisions and intentions of the actors on the official political scene, against which Febvre and Bloch stood, for it to be a possible field of reflection.

Post-war, this silence on the nineteenth century extended to the twentieth, the *Annales* drawing a *de facto* outer limit to the past at 1789. The breakdown of the 1930s model of the relationship between present and past, and the consequent elimination of 'precise knowledge of contemporary facts', have recently been acknowledged by a third generation of 'We, the Annales' ready to reintegrate modern history into the review. But the explanation for their having taken place, which turns largely on changing relationships between academic disciplines, seems to me inadequate, or only a part of the truth.[4] We are here also confronting an aspect of the effects of the Cold War upon the French academic community, and in particular on a section of it, which, during the 1930s, had belonged to 'the moderate left, lay, republic, open to socialist ideas, but also patriotic and attached to the French Colonial Empire'.[5] Whatever its mutations under the impact of the Resistance,[6] after the Second World War this was a world view which had difficulty in working outwards from the present. Significantly, members of the second generation (formed principally under Braudel, rather than Febvre, within the 6th Section (Social Sciences) of the Ecole pratique des hautes études, founded in 1948), such as Emmanuel Le Roy Ladurie, were to pass through the French Communist Party in this period as a means to obtaining a purchase on the world. But the particular form of disenchantment with Stalinism which followed, that for Le Roy Ladurie can be expressed in shorthand by the passage from Marx to Malthus, did not lend itself to the re-establishment of a clear line of reflection between present and past. Indeed, as Jacques Rancière points out, it tended to confine the nineteenth century in general, its social movements in particular, to the realm of the noisy, and relatively meaningless, epiphenomenon of a deeper history which stopped, conveniently, in 1789.[7]

But whatever the explanation adopted, the point to retain is that, for the fifteen years that followed the end of the war, the study of nineteenth- and twentieth-century France was to hinge almost entirely on the impulsion given by a single man, Ernest Labrousse. Possessed of a rare rhetorical talent, whose importance should not be underestimated in any explanation of his predominance over *all* research in the period - Pierre Chaunu has estimated that 'Labrousse by himself supervised during ten or fifteen years about as many theses as all his fellow historians at Paris or in the provinces, early modernists and modernists alike, put together'[8] - his intellectual preoccupations radiated out towards students of progressive sympathies from the two essential *loci* of the academic historical profession, the Sorbonne, the only university in Paris at the time, and the newly founded 6th Section, a largely research-oriented institute. His own research of the 1930s had been on Ancien Régime France, and was essentially concerned with the different effects of pre-capitalist crises of underproduction on varying sections of the eighteenth-century rural population as distinguished by their relationship to the basic commodity exchange of the period, that of corn: at its most simple this gave those with a surplus to sell on the market, those needing to buy and those who were self-sufficient.[9] The framework of his presentation of the subject was provided by long statistical series of corn prices and agricultural revenues; as such it represented the vital bridge with the earlier quantitative work on wages and prices of Francois Simiand, a socialist Durkheimian, the breadth of whose intellectual interests is perhaps best expressed by the neologism a 'socio-historical economist'.[10] Both Simiand[11] and Labrousse were favourably viewed by Bloch and Febvre - one is indeed here far from 'political history' as defined above - and Labrousse was himself briefly to be a member of the editorial committee of the review at the end of the 1930s.

But, symptomatically, he was not among the number of the editors after the war. By contrast with the general tendency of the *Annales*, his own research and teaching marched resolutely into the nineteenth century with a set of lectures entitled 'The Working Class Movement and Social Ideas in France from 1815 to the End of the Nineteenth Century',[12] which added a third dimension to those interests of the 1930s well-resuméd by the

title of his Festschrift 'Economic Conjuncture and Social
Structure'.[13] In these lectures Labrousse was excavating the
beginnings of a tradition to which he was attached in a way
that the founders of the *Annales* were not.[14] Formal ideologies
and the history of class organisation were here given *droit de
cité*, although the theoretical focus on, and the explanatory
power given to, economic conjuncture, always threatened to
reduce their weight in any more global account of a particular
period.[15] Seemingly it was Labrousse's socialism which allowed
him to maintain an explicit problematic of present and past and
which had prepared him for the cracking of the brittle shell in
which the nineteenth century had been left enclosed.[16]

What has been the nature of the work on the nineteenth
century inspired by exposure to Labrousse, of the first decade
after the war? Starting with the question of economic
conjuncture, there is an initial visible line of reflection on the
transition of France towards capitalism thought in terms of the
passage from crises of the 'old type' – agricultural
underproduction – to 'properly capitalist' crises of
overproduction.[17] Coupled to the magnificently sustained critical
positions on modern economic analysis and history achieved by
Pierre Vilar[18] and to a chance encounter of a then young
communist historian with the archives of one of France's leading
clearing banks (the Crédit Lyonnais)[19] this more economic
portion of the Labrousse heritage has flowered into a full-bred
Marxist economic history, which, from an examination of
banking capital, has been able to move forward to the relations
between banking capital and industrial capital – finance
capital – and its relationship to French imperialism.[20]

Labrousse's interest in class relations has undergone a less
happy development. Among his postwar preoccupations none was
perhaps more central than the desire to move history forward
from the study of massive economic infrastructural facts to that
of their social equivalents: it is this that structures his
impassioned call of 1955 for a systematic study of the
bourgeoisie.[21] The book which incarnates this imperative is
Adeline Daumard's *The Parisian Bourgeoisie from 1815 to 1848*,[22]
which then rapidly became the model for a more global approach
to nineteenth-century French social structure in the course of a
collective research project on Paris, Toulouse, Bordeaux and
Lille co-ordinated by Daumard herself.[23] Yet despite all its
merits, among which figures principally the first systematic use
of nineteenth-century probate material, the problems begin with
'The Parisian Bourgeoisie'. Firstly, it represents a rupture
between economic and social analysis: by means of a vulgar
materialism of the social, different fractions of the bourgeoisie
fall out too easily from the breaks in a column graph of levels of
fortune at death but the book conveys little on how those
fortunes were generated. There are, for instance, no figures by
trade leading back into the social relations of production of the
period; one is left with a formal topography of the bourgeoisie

ranging from the 'financial aristocracy' through to the 'popular
bourgeoisie'. And, as Pierre Vilar has remarked more generally,
'The problem is not how one is rich or poor. It is to know how
one becomes it. Accumulation, immiseration, these are the major
problems of social history. And one becomes rich or poor by the
way in which one participates in production. . . . It is the
mechanism of accumulation which constitutes the significant and
light-shedding social fact.'[24] This neglect of accumulation also
means that the bourgeoisie is thought of largely in a distorted
form, abstracted from a relationship between classes, and the
book gives no sense of how class relations evolved in the
workshop between 1815 and 1848, the critical experience, no
doubt, for the numerically most important category of the
bourgeoisie, those employing labour, whether productive or
unproductive. There is no whisper of the bourgeoisie's least
mediated of class organisations, the incipient employers'
association, and little attention to the underlay of its male
collective life in the Clubs which developed rapidly from 1830
onwards. Rather, and this constitutes the book's second major
vulnerability, the vulgar materialism of the social has a
symmetrical idealism to it: Daumard tries to reconstruct a
unified 'soul' of the bourgeoisie from its reactions to two
important events of the period, the return of Napoleon's ashes
and the 1840 Treaty with Great Britain, instead of building on
the formal complexity and divisions revealed by the first part
of her analysis, whatever their limitations, to achieve a
nuanced, conflict-ridden, piece of cultural analysis.

It is worth considering what distinguishes the relative
strength of what I have called a Marxist economic history from
the relative weakness of this approach to the social. The
achievements of the former have been the product of the
marriage of the Labroussian heritage with a more explicit use of
Marxist categories deriving from its practitioners' close
association, at some stage in their lives, with the French
Communist Party.[25] Marxism has here broken out from its
dominant mode in France, philosophical, to rebecome a living
historical materialism. But those taking up the call for a
systematic approach to the social, Daumard in particular, have
not effected the expansion of the Labroussean problematic
necessary to tackle the problems discerned by Labrousse
himself. Two areas of critical reflection are missing. The first
concerns the question of the transitions between the different
forms of the capitalist mode of production, most notably between
manufacture and modern industry or machinofacture. The
rupture between social and economic analysis has thereby
necessarily set in as the categories with which to think the 'way
in which one participates in production' have been left in
obscurity. This is a particularly crippling absence for French
social and economic history given the exceptionally long
drawn-out nature of this transition in France - usually wrapped
up in a quite inappropriate package labelled 'the survival of

small-scale industry' - and even more so in the case of Paris,
where, as with London, things are at their full metropolitan
complexity, simple averages on the size of establishments
representing the net result of contradictory movements of
geographical dispersion and concentration of production, linked
to changing levels of division of labour, mechanisation and
capital concentration.[26] The Marxist economic historians will no
doubt have to come back on their tracks and deal with the
relations between merchant capital, incipient industrial capital
and the organisation of work before the economic and the social
are sewed back together.

The second absence is any sustained thought about the
cultural dimensions of class.[27] Labrousse's work on the
eighteenth century provides an important point of
methodological reference for any treatment of 'class in itself' but
his propositions stop short of 'class for itself'. The severance
with the *Annales* is probably here at its most important: a
transposition of the preoccupations of Febvre in his *The Problem
of Disbelief in the Sixteenth Century*, and of those who have
subsequently taken up the history of mentalities, married to a
close knowledge of the everyday material realities underlying the
mental world of 'common sense', without being a panacea, would
have done much to advance the question. As it is, Daumard's
bourgeois, already disengaged from their daily exercise of
power in the workshop and from the texture of their family
lives, rest so many unthinking mannequins. It has taken Tim
Clark, a British historian burrowing down from art history, and
his efforts to knock down the partitions between 'high culture' or
'visual ideology' and culture more widely defined, to bring these
figures to life.[28]

These same two lacunae are no less evident in the work of
those who took up the third dimension of Labrousse's heritage,
working-class history. Michelle Perrot's 'Workers on Strike:
France 1871-1890' represents the most substantial piece of work
to have come out within this subject.[29] It starts with an
illuminating essay in conjuncture in which the economic (notably
the depression of the 1880s), the political (the passage from
the phoney monarchical Republic of the first years of the Third
Republic to the republican Republic), and the social (the
numbers of strikes and their participants, the demands raised)
conjunctures are delicately woven together. But in moving from
this diachronic approach to a more structural analysis, whole
sections of the everyday realities of workshop life progressively
reveal themselves as absent to the point that the meaning of the
strikes of the period is often seriously deformed: what appear
as wage demands, for instance, are almost always taken at face
value whereas they frequently resulted from changes in systems
of exploitation involving the intensification of work or a new
division of labour linked to a different level of mechanisation
and with an altered system of payment.[30] This absence is again a
function of the marginalisation of reflection on the couplet

valorisation - the organisation of work, which, when carried
through, leads into just such classic subjects of *Capital* as
differing wage systems and their logic, and beyond, to the
divisions internal to the working class. Rémi Gossez's work on
Parisian workers in the 1848 revolution has a much keener sense
of this type of issue.[31] Its syndicalist leanings, which, however,
tend to eliminate the complex interactions between working-class
culture and the Utopian and producer co-operative ideologies
of the working-class movement, make it sympathetic to the
resonance and meaning of the ten hour movement of the pre-
June Days. But for want of the explicit posing of the
manufacture-modern industry transition, it is left to the reader,
across Gossez's contorted prose, to piece together the dynamics
of the situation against which there was such striking collective
working-class resistance.

George Duveau's book *Working Class Life under the Second
Empire* and its relative lack of impact on research in the years
following its publication in 1946 is a final but crucial link in
our survey.[32] Duveau was not a historian by origin but a
sociologist: his training at the hands of Charles Bouglé,
Director of the Ecole normale supérieure at the end of the 1930s,
placed him in direct descent from Durkheim. His work in this
sense presents a fragile, because solitary, post-war link
between the study of nineteenth-century labour and an
important element of the intellectual conjuncture of the 1900s
from which Bloch and Febvre drew much of their inspiration.[33]
It is characterised precisely by a concern with the material life
of the working class and its culture, which are given an
autonomy in respect of more structured forms of class
organisation and ideology. Whatever the criticisms one can make
of his interpretation, Duveau was on fertile terrain. Without
going so far as to tackle the transition full on, his
preoccupation with getting at the material life of the workers of
the period led him to draw up what is effectively a typology of
the co-existing forms of production in Second Empire France,
whose industrial and geographical incidence is described with
precision. The book then moves out from this foundation to deal
with other areas of working-class existence. The deaf ears on
which these questions fell would seem to have been the product
of their foreignness to the Labroussian paradigm coupled to a
certain defensive reflex on the part of labour's organisations.
The autonomy ascribed to material life and culture was in itself
enough to throw up a screen on those subjects for those whose
point of departure towards labour history was their organisation,
whether party or trade-union, and its antecedents: the various
blends of hagiography and teleology often resulting from this
type of motivation made short work of the levels of experience
which might have rendered their full significance to the stories
they had to tell.[34] A new departure along these lines had to
await the context of the period following May 1968, in which the
certainties of the relationship between party and class were in

radical dissolution. The contribution which best represents what
is now again on the agenda is Alain Cottereau's long
introduction to the re-edition of an account of the lives of
Second Empire Paris's metal workers, written by an employer
of the period, Denis Poulot.[35] Cottereau extracts the
anthropological kernel from a book which, at first glance, is
only another version of the pathology of the working classes.
The almost contradictory, because literal, reading of the same
text made by Duveau is a measure of how the questions posed
have advanced. It remains to integrate the ideologies and
political practice of the working-class movement into this new
picture of working-class material, life and culture in all its
heterogeneity.

NOTES

1 French history is traditionally divided by the date of 1789.
   The period preceding it is known as modern history, what
   follows 1815 as contemporary history; the years in between
   lie in the limbo of the revolutionary and imperial period. In
   this article I use the term modern to denote the history of
   the nineteenth and twentieth centuries, and contemporary as
   a relative term referring to the history of events which are
   recent for their historian.
2 Lucien Febvre (1933), cited in A. Burguière, 'Histoire d'une
   histoire: la Naissance des Annales', *Annales E.S.C.*,
   November-December 1979, p. 1355.
3 This conception of the relationship between past and present
   needs to be distinguished from that which sees the past as
   containing the truth of the present by virtue either of the
   lessons of history or the explanation of the present by its
   origins in the past. Burguière also points out that another
   model of research reversing the traditional relationship
   between past and present was advanced by Febvre and Bloch
   but was to have little immediate effect: 'It consists in
   working out from a contemporary situation, for example the
   rural landscape, eating habits or a more complex
   phenomenon such as a map of voting patterns, and in
   working back up through time to reconstitute the genesis of
   this situation, or rather to distinguish the permanencies and
   the innovations, the different levels of temporality, the
   combinations of short and long periods which have shaped
   our present' (*ibid.*, p. 1355). This seems, however, to be
   close to what 'writing history in the present tense' means
   for Michel Foucault and those working with his concepts (see
   Jacques Donzelot, 'The Poverty of Political Culture',
   Ideology and Consciousness, Spring 1979, p. 78; Colin
   Gordon, 'Other Inquisitions', *Ideology and Consciousness*,
   Autumn 1979, p. 32).

4 Let us reread once again the Annales of the first years: the
   specialities of Marc Bloch and Lucien Febvre, the medieval
   and the early modern periods, are far from being
   predominant. The history of the present, by contrast,
   occupies a remarkable position. It has since almost
   completely disappeared from the review. The reasons for this
   gradual obliteration are complex. On the one hand the
   alliances of the early period came apart, at least partially; as
   with geography, for instance, which has not always
   experienced parallel developments with history in France; as
   with economic analysis, for a long period and contrary to all
   appearances. On the other, new links were created, with
   anthropology for example; but for a long time the latter
   refused to take an interest in social change, and when it
   turns towards 'developed' societies, it most readily addresses
   itself to a past that it is not far from considering as without
   a diachronic dimension. For the historians themselves, the
   choice of the 'long period' seemed to have to exclude the
   analysis of contemporary history, whereas it can,
   doubtlessly, allow for a reformulation of approaches to it.
   And then one must take into account the part played by
   already consolidated positions, by prudence: medieval and
   early modern history, more recently and more locally ancient
   history, are the domains where the renewal of research has
   been the most spectacular. It is not certain, however, that
   these successes should dictate the choices of to-day. Is a
   new history of the present possible? The Annales are ready
   to encourage it. ('Les Annales, 1929-1979', *Annales E.S.C.*,
   November-December 1979, p. 1345)
5 Burguière, *op. cit.*, p. 1358.
6 For a powerful evocation of Lucien Febvre's life during the
   war, see the very personal contribution by Braudel to the
   Mélanges for Febvre.
7 See below, p. 258.
8 *Histoire Quantitative, Histoire Sérielle*, Paris 1978, p. 167,
   note 21.
9 C.E. Labrousse, *Esquisse du mouvement des prix et des
   revenus en France au XVIIIe Siècle*, Paris 1933; *La Crise de
   l'économie francaise à la fin de l'Ancien Régime*, Paris 1944.
10 See *Le Salaire, l'évolution sociale et la monnaie*, Paris 1932.
   The intellectual affinities of Simiand and Labrousse were, of
   course, much deeper than a preoccupation with weighing
   social and economic processes, and turned upon common
   interest in a possible social history of the economic. On
   Simiand see J. Le Goff ed., *La Nouvelle histoire*, Paris 1978,
   pp. 513-15; J. Bouvier, Introduction to *L'Histoire économique
   et sociale de la France*, t. IV, vol. 1, Paris 1979.
11 See in particular Febvre's review of Simiand's *Cours
   d'économie politique au Conservatoire des Arts et Metiers*
   (duplicated, Paris 1930-1, 3 vols), 'Histoire, économie et
   statistique', *Annales d'histoire économique et sociale*, 1930.

As early as 1903, Simiand had been the author of a Durkheimian inspired attack on positivist history, which had asserted the need for a social science (singular) studying 'facts which repeat themselves' for which history would simply provide the diachronic element. 'Méthode historique et science sociale', *Revue de synthèse historique*, 1903, t. VI, pp. 1-22 and 129-57. The lineage between this text and the early *Annales* was relatively direct, and indeed the whole article was reprinted in the *Annales* in 1958 at Braudel's instigation. On this episode see J. Revel, 'Les Paradigmes des Annales', *Annales E.S.C.*, November-December 1979, pp. 1362-4.

12 *Le Mouvement ouvrier et les idées sociales en France de 1815 à la fin du XIXe Siècle*, Paris C.D.U. (i.e. the reproduction service for Sorbonne lectures) 1948.

13 *Conjoncture économique, structures sociales: hommage à Ernest Labrousse*, Paris 1974.

14 Born in 1895, Labrousse arrived in Paris sufficiently early to have personal contact with anarcho-syndicalist tendencies in the labour movement. He was an early member of the Communist Party, and briefly Parliamentary correspondent for *L'Humanité*, before opting in the mid-1920s for the socialism personified by Léon Blum.

15 Labrousse almost caricatures his own historical method in the article '1848, 1830, 1789: comment naissent les révolutions?' His answer: crises of agricultural underproduction.

16 His immediate post-war frame of mind best comes across in two articles, 'La montée du socialisme (1848-1945)', *Revue socialiste*, May 1945, which traces the inexorable rise of the left-wing vote in France, especially since the 1890s, and 'Geographie du socialisme (13 Mai 1849-2 Juin 1946)', *Revue socialiste*, June 1946.

17 See in particular J. Bouvier, 'Les crises économiques' in J. Le Goff and Pierre Nora, eds, *Faire de l'histoire*, Paris 1974, t. II, pp. 51-73. The Labroussian mantle has in many ways fallen on the shoulders of Jean Bouvier: he is, for instance, director of the institute founded by Labrousse, the Institut d'histoire économique et sociale, succeeding Pierre Vilar in this position, whose age and own field of specialisation, Spain, but by no means his intellectual qualities, made him a transitional figure.

18 Vilar's report to the First International Conference of Economic Historians at Stockholm in 1960, 'Croissance économique et analyse historique', is the key document for anybody battling their way out of the intellectual quagmire represented by the ideological complex of 'growth' and 'take-off'.

19 In the early 1950s, Jean Bouvier, then a prominent member of the Rhône Departmental Federation of the French Communist Party, was let into the warehouse containing the complete archives of the Crédit Lyonnais while hunting

around for sources for a thesis on the social and economic
history of nineteenth-century Lyon and its surroundings.
He worked there unbeknownst to the directors of the bank
for the next eight years, producing the seminal *Le Crédit
lyonnais de 1863 à 1882. Les années de formation d'une
banque de dépot*, Paris 1961, an irreplaceable foundation
stone in our knowledge of French capitalism and the
internal mechanisms of its functioning.

20 The book which best represents where this line of thinking
   has got to is Jacques Thobie, *Intérêts et impérialisme
   francaise dans l'Empire ottoman, 1895-1914*, Paris 1977.
21 'Voies nouvelles vers une histoire de la bourgeoisie
   occidentale aux XVIIIe et XIXe siècles. (1700-1850)', *X
   Congresso Internazionale di Scienze Storiche*, Relazioni,
   Roma 1955, t. IV, pp. 367-96.
22 *La Bourgeoisie parisienne de 1815 à 1848*, Paris 1963.
23 This research project resulted in the book A. Daumard,
   ed., *Les Fortunes francaises au XIXe siècle*, Paris 1973.
24 'Histoire sociale et philosophie de l'histoire', *Recherches et
   débats du Centre catholique des intellectuels francais*,
   cahier 47, 1964, p. 53.
25 Labrousse's own relation to Marxism is a subject of debate:
   Bouvier has characterised his work as being 'a sort of fusion
   of Marx and Simiand, enriched by the craft proper to the
   historian, which is to work on archives'; Guy Bois has
   chosen to stress his refusal of the concept of mode of
   production, leaving a work which has 'an "economistic" tone
   to it, half conjuncturalist, half malthusian' ('Tendances
   actuelles des recherches d'histoire économique et sociale en
   France', *Aujourd'hui l'histoire*, Paris 1974, p. 134; 'Marxisme
   et histoire nouvelle', in Le Goff, *op. cit.*, p. 379). Bouvier's
   overall assessment of the influence of Marxism is worth
   citing:
      It is as a method of analysis uniting economy and history
      (*and not as a political problematic*) that Marxism has
      influenced historical science in France during the
      twentieth century. Its impact has consequently been both
      wide and deep but indirect, marked by a degree of
      confusion. It is certain that the Marxist problematic has
      enriched social and economic history, but without one
      being able to say, far from it, that the majority of
      economic historians have *consciously* rallied to Marxism.
      In a way, many of them do work, without knowing it,
      which is Marxist to a greater or lesser extent. And those
      who proclaim themselves to be Marxists do not
      necessarily carry out the most Marxist research, nor the
      most successful. (Bouvier, *op. cit.*, p. 133)
   Bois's article gives a useful over-view of the interaction
   between Marxist and post-war *Annales* history.
26 This lacuna seems to me to be responsible for the banality of
   certain sections of the recent collective synthesis on the

period *Histoire économique et sociale de la France, t. III, L'avènement de l'ère industrielle (1789-années 1880)*, Paris 1976. See the excellent short review by Louis Bergeron, 'Le premier élan de la croissance industrielle', *Annales E.S.C.*, November–December 1979, pp. 1317-23.

27 Culture is used here in the sense defined by Richard Johnson: 'By culture is understood the common sense or way of life of a particular class, group or social category, the complex of ideologies that are actually *adopted* as moral preferences or principles of life' ('Three problematics: elements of a theory of working class culture' in John Clarke, Chas Critcher and Richard Johnson, eds, *Working Class Culture: Studies in History and Theory*, London 1979, p. 234). It is worth noting in passing that the Sartre of the *Critique of Dialectical Reason* had unfortunately among his listeners few historians able to realise in research terms the potential import of his work for this level of historical writing. Let us hope that his death at least succeeds in finally sundering the made-to-measure dustbin, 'humanism', of Althusserian design, to which his work of this period was too rapidly consigned.

28 T.J. Clark, *Image of the People*, London 1973, and more recently his article 'The Bar at the Folies-Bergère' in *The Wolf and the Lamb, Popular Culture in France*, ed. by Jacques Beauroy *et al.*, Stamford 1977. The work of Maurice Agulhon can be seen as an attempt to restore the cultural moment to class analysis but it has been largely at the expense of any treatment of the social relations of production. For Paris, see his *Le Cercle dans la France bourgeoisie, 1810-1848: étude d'une mutation de sociabilité*, Paris 1977.

29 *Les Ouvriers en grève. France 1871-1890*, Paris 1974.

30 Post-1968 preoccupations with deskilling and subsequent work on the labour process have finally imposed reflection on this subject, although the literature still reflects a break between economic (strategies of valorisation) and social (sociology of work) analysis. See Michelle Perrot's own 'Les ouvriers et les machines en France dans la première moitié du XIXe siècle' in Le Soldat du travail, *Recherches*, September 1978, 32-3, pp. 347-74. As she points out, prior to the 1970s, there had barely been any systematic work on the history of mechanisation and the labour process since the early 1920s.

31 *Les Ouvriers de Paris, Livre Ier, L'Organisation, 1848-1851*, La Roche-sur-Yon 1967.

32 *La Vie ouvrière sous le Second Empire*, Paris 1946.

33 On the two other components of this intellectual conjuncture, the French geographical school of Vidal de la Blache and the movement created by Henri Berr around the Revue de synthèse, see Burguière, *op. cit.*, pp. 1351-2.

34 See, by contrast, the long review of Duveau in *Socialisme*

ou barbarie, July-August 1949, 3, pp. 100-9.

35 Etude préalable to Denis Poulot, *Le Sublime ou le travailleur comme il est en 1870 et ce qu'il peut être*, Paris Maspero 1980, pp. 7-102.

32 'LE SOCIAL': THE LOST TRADITION IN FRENCH LABOUR HISTORY

Jacques Rancière*

A problem of central concern for French social historiography is that of the real, deep gap between social history[1] as an intellectual product and the organised working-class movements. The problem is how to explain that gap. Alain Cottereau's position appears to accuse academics of being ill-disposed, of wishing to remain detached from the real working-class movement. I believe the gap has deeper historical origins, and must be explained by the past of French historiography, which itself must be explained by the past of French social history.

We have to examine two main questions: who needs social history, or working-class history; and who does it? With regard to the first, it is not evident that a working class needs its own history. If we take the organised working-class movement in France, the socialists or more especially the Communist Party, as well as the Marxist historians in France, it is clear that none of them was much interested in French working-class history. For them, the main question was not working-class history, but revolution - the French Revolution of 1789. This presented them, especially the Communist Party, with a political problem of legitimation, not legitimation as a working-class party but as a national democratic party, the offspring and inheritor of the great French Revolution. Interest and research focused on the Revolution and dwelt on this question of who is the heir of the Revolution; is it the radical democratic movement, the socialists or the communists or the workers' movement? It was the same for the Communist Party as a whole and for the Marxist

*Jacques Rancière is an editor of *Révoltes Logiques*. An author (with Louis Althusser and Etienne Balibar) of *Lire le Capitale*, Paris 1966; engaged in both theoretical and empirical work on nineteenth- and twentieth-century labour and popular movements.

historians, whether or not they were members of the party.
There is also (in France) a tradition deriving from the *Histoire
Socialiste* of Jaurès, which attempts to prove that the
organisations of the working class are heirs of the French
Revolution. It also includes too the kind of research on the
Revolution that reveals germs of socialism already present in
the French Revolution. So it was the same for Marxists and
for non-Marxists like Jaurès, for communists and
anti-communists.

It was not only a matter of the party apparatuses repressing
the working-class history, for it is not evident that
working-class militants felt the need for their own history. On
this point I disagree with Alain Cottereau, who tells us that,
around the middle of the last century, enormous labour was
channelled by workers into researching their own history. I do
not know exactly what he means, but I doubt if this was the
case. For instance, there was an important literary movement
among French workers in the mid-nineteenth century, but they
wrote poetry rather than history. We may wonder why they did
so, but those are the facts.

There seem to be two main explanations. The first is that
perhaps we overestimate history as a form of memory leading to
self-possession and self-recognition. Those workers wanted to
gain their identity through other means than history or memory,
and even the history of their own struggles, working-class
struggles, did not serve their purpose. Very often even militant
leaders of the struggles and strikes in the nineteenth century
considered the sort of struggle they had been involved in as
something hard and rude; rather, if I may use Marxian
terminology, pre-history than history. So, in my opinion, that
kind of history was not their main concern.

I want to emphasise the fact that when there was
autobiographical material from workers, especially at the end of
the last century, it was more a political attempt to give
legitimacy to the Republic in the 1880s than a real record of the
working-class movement. The best-known of this type of book
is Martin Nadeau's *Mémoir de Léonard, Garçon Macon* – a memoir
of the Republic rather than the working class. What was the
main purpose of these autobiographies? I think it was to say
how hard life was before the Republic, how hard, coarse and
rude the workers themselves were, as described by one of their
own number and to show how a man could clamber out of this
rude, dull life and rise above it.

So this kind of writing had two aims; it was a call to the
upper and middle classes asking them to recognise the lower
classes, and in the other direction it was a call to the lower
classes to show them how to gain recognition. That kind of
recognition is an important issue for social history in France.

If it is not possible to demonstrate an impetus from below
towards social or working-class history, where did it come
from? I believe we can identify two main forces, the first of

which is a political need coming from the state itself. At the end
of the nineteenth century when the Republic was well-
established, social legislation was introduced including a law
which legalised trade unions and the French government created
a labour office whose task was to investigate the effects of this
legislation. Consequently there was a tradition of social
investigation created by the state itself; not the state in
general, but the radical democratic forces of the republican
state, whose aim was to effect a conciliation between the
Republic, the state and the working class. There was a great
deal of investigation into the trade unions and strikes and so
on. This Labour Office was an important factor in the
formation of social and working-class history.

The second important question is who did, who wrote, that
history? The fact is that the first investigators were not only
civil servants, they were veteran militants of the working-class
movement who had been dismissed and marginalised by the new
forces – socialist, collectivist, eventually anarchist. The first
books representing real research into the history of trades
unions and the working class were written by men who had
been defeated in their own attempts to reconcile the classes
when they were militants in the labour movement, but wanted
to take their revenge as civil servants, as investigators for
the state. This, I think, is important, because it creates a
discourse on working-class history which was a kind of dialogue
between unions or the working class generally and the state,
which encompassed an appeal to the workers for honourable
conduct and an appeal to the state or the middle class for
acknowledgment and understanding.

There also developed a new interest in the underlay of social
history, especially in the trade union movement considered as
the real working-class movement as opposed to the vociferous
socialist, collectivist and anarchist movements in France. The
lynchpin of that tradition was the idea of 'industrial democracy'
which held sway in France at the beginning of this century and
which provided the framework for the major research in social
history at that time. It was necessary to supply historical
legitimacy for the concept of industrial democracy and to oppose
it to the hubbub of the goings-on in the workings of the various
working-class organisations, the socialists, the anarcho-
syndicalists and so on.

There was a convergence between the demands of the state
and those of the representatives of the co-operative and
mutualist movement, the apolitical and anti-anarchist trade
unions. The new thrust was reflected on the academic scene,
where a history of the working-class movement began to be
created at the beginning of this century; but not, it should be
noted, by historians. Those who tried to reconstitute the story
of the unions, of trade, of the co-operative movement, and so
on, were not historians; they were generally sociologists,
because sociology was the official science of the new radical

Republic. It was the science of social solidarity and reciprocity, whose main concern was social relations, with a view to resolving the social questions through state intervention. Most of all, sociology was the science of social relations as production curves, of unions conceived as a force of negotiation, of discussion with the state rather than struggle.

The prevailing philosophy of that sociology was 'solidarism'. The leading research on social and working-class history was done within that tradition. At first it was a kind of radical reaction against the rise of socialism. Then, after 1914-18, when there was a break between the socialist and communist parties in France, it became the official ideology of the Socialist Party and of the national trade unions – there were two central trade unions, one communist and one socialist, and it became the official ideology of the socialist confederation. Most of the people who wrote that history worked in an institute linked to the CGT, which was the socialist, anti-communist trade union confederation, running courses for trade union militants. There was a very strong nexus between that historical research and that section of the working-class movement.

Besides trade union history, there was also a demand for a kind of ethnological study of the working class. A book which came out in 1920, *La Coûtume Ouvrière* by Maxim Leroy, is the bible of that tendency. Maxim Leroy was a socialist philosopher, a jurist, the person who asked Freud to interpret the dream of Descartes, but not exactly a social historian. He wrote a preface for his book in which he claimed for the anthropology or ethnology of the working class the same aim as that of the social historians, a kind of rapprochement between the official culture of the state and the upper classes and the people of the lower classes. This is another aspect of the same problem – how to understand the ways of life and the actions of lower class people, working-class civilisation, something like that. Trade unionism is conceived as a kind of moral reform and a kind of culture of the working class, to some extent as a culture and a civilisation of the future. These are the claims he makes through that book, for an ethnology of the people. The well-known book by Georges Duveau, *La vie ouvrière sous le Second Empire* (referred to in Andrew Lincoln's article) can be considered as an attempt to realise Leroy's aims. What Duveau set out to do, with a wealth of detail, was to show the roots of the working-class movement in the particular configurations of working-class sociability, indigenous cultures and geographical diversity and so on. But there are limits to this school also.

The importance of militant autobiography should also be emphasised, because that school, or tendency, represented the old conceptions of socialism as opposed to the conception of communism as the struggle of the rank and file, unskilled workers without culture. It emphasised the history of militants rather than of the masses.

The problem is that these tendencies crumbled in the last war because some of their proposals were too close to the direction taken by the corporate state of Pétain. There were ideological, and sometimes real, material confirmations of their propositions within Vichy France. After the war, at the time of the Cold War, there was no longer any place for that kind of historiography; there was no space for these tendencies of a divided working class. There was space for two positions only. Within the working-class movement there occurred a polarisation, the old tendencies towards co-operation between the working class and the state disappeared, as did its historiographical tradition. All those people who had written social history from the beginning up to the 1940s had archives, records, and we have lost most of them. Thus there was a kind of material disappearance, not only an ideological decomposition. Some institutional links between historical research, university work and the socialist working-class movement had disappeared.

So the gap between the academic scene and the working-class movement which Alain Cottereau refers to is also the result of that story, and not only of the historians' refusal to listen to workers or their desire to remain in their own milieu. With the disappearance of that old current of social history, with the Cold War and the important political divisions accompanying it, there was no space for that link between workers and the academic world.

There is one further point I would like to make. After the Cold War, instead of another attempt to use social history against the Communist Party, the organ of Stalinism in France, we saw the appearance of what Le Roy Ladurie called 'l'histoire immobile' - static history - a kind of comeback, not to a real working-class movement, but beyond it, to the Middle Ages or the eighteenth century. This was part of the same reaction against a certain kind of politics and against the Cold War. After the Cold War, in the 1950s, there were some historians in France, of whom Le Roy Ladurie is the most representative, who had been members of the French CP but who were disgusted by Stalinism and the Cold War, etc. The ideology and practice of 'static history' were for them a way of leaving the scene of politics, and of expressing disgust.

Its main ideological feature is to say that the story of the working-class movement, the story of strikes and congresses and struggles and all that, is only superstructural illusion, ideology. It attempts to be more Marxist than the Marxists, more materialist than the Marxists, by saying - and I quote Le Roy Ladurie - 'I agree with Marx that the main thing is to study the material conditions of history', that is to say, for instance, questions of climate, population, food, eating habits, death, birth, demographic equilibria, epidemics and so on. That is real history; that is the way the masses made history. But the history of struggle is only superstructure.

This tendency succeeded in taking the place of historical

materialism. It produced an ideology, approximately as I have outlined, denying any real change from below. There are long periods between changes, and during their course there exists a permanency and a regulation which are independent of the intentions and the will of the people, and especially of the will of the masses. Change may come at the end of a long period, but change is always brought about by the elite.

Here we have an ideology and a mythology which together relegate working-class history to a very poor position, because working-class history is seen as a story of illusions without real importance. What is important for them is basic demographic movement, the deep conditions of history, which can be traced up to the French Revolution; beyond this point, in their terms, it seems we have only a story of ideological and superficial movements, of no real importance.

So social history, working-class history, has become very much underestimated; this is clearly true in the French universities. If you write social history, you are taken to be a militant, interested in that kind of history because of your political involvement. Real history is supposed not to be that kind of history.

NOTE

1   The term 'social history' has a double meaning in French. Recently its most common usage has been the same as in English but ever since the 'social question' of the antagonistic co-existence of labour and capital had first been posed in the nineteenth century it has also had another resonance to it. The 'social movement' was a current term for all those popular forces fighting to resolve the 'social question'; 'social history' was the history of that struggle, in other words something much more akin to the term 'labour history'. Indeed the principal labour history publication in France is called 'The Social Movement' (*Le Mouvement social*), which in addition was the title of an important anarcho-syndicalist review of the 1900s. In Rancière's paper it is this latter meaning which is predominant.

33 FROM GRAMSCI TO 'WORKERISM': NOTES ON ITALIAN WORKING-CLASS HISTORY

Sandra Pescarolo*

If we compare the historical knowledge available on the Italian working class with the total production of English historiography the most obvious difference is the relative backwardness of Italian studies on the life of workers outside the factory - or in general, on that which, today, is termed working-class culture. The Anglo-Saxon tradition of Marxist scholarship, which Richard Johnson has called 'culturalism' (E.P. Thompson, Genovese, oral history groups, History Workshop and some strands of women's history) has only recently begun to be debated in Italy, and the question remains, primarily, at a methodological level, for there is, as yet, very little detailed research. At a recent conference of the Fondazione Basso in Rome, it was rightly said that

for decades Italian workers, under the eyes of those who study them, have been regarded as orphans: they are workers without fathers or mothers, brothers or kin who pass from the factory to the resistance leagues (entering the tavern to get drunk but not to socialise); at the most, objects of meagre statistics on the family budget from which they drew, perhaps, a meagre subsistence but certainly no hot meals or affective relationships and support.

Although theoretical perspectives have been changing since 1975, historical research on the working class has focused on political, economic and organisational questions while totally ignoring the conditions of day-to-day existence; neither factory conditions nor socialist activity have been analysed in the context of the workers' daily lives. Until now, research has taken two directions - the Gramscian (since 1949) and the 'workerist' (from 1962) - I will seek to summarise these lines and their internal differences.

Marxist theory, in Italy as elsewhere, has always insisted on the primary importance of the working class. At the same time - following a line originally elaborated by one of the founders of Italian communism, Antonio Gramsci - there has always been a preoccupation with national tradition, and with relating working-class struggle to a socialist redefinition of national identity. During the years 1943-4, when the Communist Party

*Sandra Pescarolo researches at the Fondazione Basso, Rome. Her article was translated and worked out in close association with Miranda Chaytor, Glynis Cousin and Susan Amusson, to whom the author and the editor give their thanks.

had emerged as the undisputed leader of the anti-fascist resistance, and when there was a vast influx of new members into the party, the working class had indeed taken on that role which Gramsci had always assigned to it - that of the 'national' class, the bearer of national regeneration. But with the advent of the Cold War, the communists came under increasing attack. The political defeat of the Communist-Socialist alliance in the general election of 1948 was a symptom of a right turn among the middle class, sections of whom had participated in the anti-fascist Resistance, and of the deep ideological penetration of Christian Democracy - the Catholic party - in the countryside. Thereafter the strategic aim of the Italian Communist Party under the leadership of Togliatti became the consolidation and organisational growth of the party based on its solid nucleus, the working class.

At the same time, the old Gramscian preoccupation with the working class as a potential national and 'hegemonic' class, as the modernising class representing the interests of all other social strata in the struggle against a national bourgeoisie locked in its own contradictions, and against a stagnant capitalism incapable of self-reform, or of ending the uneven development between north and south, was retained and even emphasised. This is very apparent in the work of the socialist and communist historians, centred around the Feltrinelli Institute and the journal *Movimento Operaio*, the Gramsci Institute and the Edizioni Rinascita. In the years from 1949 to 1956, these historians made great inroads into local working-class and peasant history, reconstituting particular moments and at the same time interpreting them within a broadly Gramscian perspective. Manacorda's book, *La storia del movimento operaio-italiano attraverso i suoi congressi* (1953) is a good example. Here, the development of the nineteenth-century workers' movement is seen as the history of an encounter - as felicitous as it is historically necessary - between a popular democratic workers' movement (which was itself economistic and syndicalist) and the socialist ideas produced in other countries whose industrial development was more advanced. Manacorda challenged the notion that the history of socialism could be written as a history of ideas or of national movements alone. He called for a recognition of the contribution of lesser known figures and unknown militants who had participated in the construction of the socialist movement. Thus Manacorda dates his history not from the foundation of the Italian Socialist Party (1892) but from the constitution of 'cellular elements of the party', the workers' societies and friendly societies, which, with their co-operative and benevolent elements, carried within themselves the seeds of an inevitable and necessary development (although their founders did not intend or foresee this).

In the same way, Ragionieri in his *Un comune socialista: Sesto Fiorentino* (1953) not only assesses local history as a provocative contrast to 'national history' but also uses it as a

point of departure for the discovery of 'a national history of a
different kind, whose central moment of greatest importance is
found in the activity of the men [sic - translators' note] who
constitute the whole of civil society' (p. 11). Thus both
Ragionieri and Manacorda seek to re-write national history along
Gramscian lines from the standpoint of the groups which they
perceive as emerging.

After the crisis in world communism in 1956, associated with
the Twentieth Congress of the Soviet Communist Party,
Krushchev's secret speech, and Togliatti's affirmation of
polycentrism (i.e., of an 'Italian' road to socialism), Marxist
historians distanced themselves from this type of 'history from
below'. In the context of an increased participation of the
Communist Party in national political life, with the formulation
of the strategy of 'structural reform', and the first steps along
the road to the 'historic compromise' with Christian democracy,
communist intellectuals turned their attention to the
examination of the structures and functions of the economy as a
whole, while historians focused on the development of Marxist
theory and economic history. A symptom of this passage was the
closing down in 1956 of the historical journal *Movimento operaio*
which had published many studies of both local worker and
peasant history and the history of social struggles.

This turn away from the working class was reversed in the
1960s, with the rise in 'spontaneous' working-class struggles,
and the growth of both political and trade union support for the
Communist Party. The rise in working-class militancy brought
the factory back to the centre of discussion, in history as it did
in Italian political life. At the same time, intellectually, there
was a sharp break within the Communist Party with those
Crocean and idealist versions of Marxism which had made
historians hostile to the social sciences, and to the empirical
study of class formation. In this context, the possibility of a
development of a historiography 'from below' inserted in the
Gramscian tradition was taken up by Procacci. He was the first
to develop a clear and convincing analysis of the conditions of
the Italian proletariat during the first phase of industrialisation
by using precise quantitative data. He describes Italy in 1900
as a country with few factory workers and a large number of
marginal agricultural and industrial workers who alternated
between manufacturing and work in the fields and with relative
material privileges in wages and hours for skilled workers based
on the organisation of the old crafts. Procacci's analysis of this
data formed the basis of an explanation of the peculiar character
of the nascent Italian workers' movement, and of its anarchic
elements which are, for Procacci, both 'its weakness and
strength'.

Thus Procacci's work stresses not only the process of
political organisation but also that of industrialisation. He shares
with the traditional Gramscian historiography, however, an
assumption which distinguishes Italian writers from those

historians in England who refer to Gramsci, particularly
E.P. Thompson. For the Italian historians, the working class
becomes the working class only by liberating itself completely
from the heritage of values and beliefs of the co-operative
manufacturing period of the peasant world. Only the cultural
forms which the development of capitalism selects and renders
victorious are seen as 'real' working-class culture. The price
paid by the protagonists of that development doesn't count.
Working-class culture becomes valid by liberating itself from
that which helps neither party-building nor the political
struggle.

'Workers' centrality' was most radically stressed by the
workerist groups of 1961-7 and particularly by Tronti and
Panzieri. They elaborated a global anti-capitalist strategy and
an optimistic theory of the imminence of revolution in the West.
At the centre of this theory was the idea that the factory and
labour organisation were the material seats and nerve centres
of the organisation of capitalist power and therefore the places
in which the construction of workers' counter-power posed an
immediate revolutionary political challenge greater than that of
the reformist programmes of parties and trade unions. On this
basis, the workers' spontaneous struggles, the processes of
industrial re-organisation - as well as the transformations of
the productive processes derived therefrom - came to be seen
as totally political phenomena and indeed became the central
moment for the interpretation of historic change.

This line of thought was to influence the majority of
historians on the new left, but it also gained currency in the
1970s, among Italian party intellectuals. France '68 and Italy '69
seemed to confirm this view. With the radicalisation of the
political situation and the rise in worker-militancy which
climaxed in the 'Hot Autumn' of 1969, there was a sharpening of
differences between the new, far left, spontaneist and
extremist groups, such as Lotta Continua and Potere Operaio,
and the Communist Party. Theoretically (and historically) it
was expressed in two increasingly opposed versions of
working-class struggle: the one, Leninist and Gramscian, laying
emphasis on the national, organised and co-ordinated nature of
class politics, the other exalting the molecular and
spontaneous. Associated with this far left tendency, was the
leftist historiography represented by such journals as *Primo
Maggio* and *Classe*. A strand of 'militant' anti-academic,
anti-institutional, 'workerist' history was developed which -
whatever one might think of its political perspectives - had the
great merit, historically speaking, of producing a close focus on
industrial and material conditions. Thus Stefano Merli and the
group around the journal *Classe*, studied in great detail
working hours, factory regulations and labour organisation at
the level of the individual plant; Revelli studied the dynamics
of wage struggles over long periods of time - something which,
in a historiography long suspicious of empiricism, was a real

innovation, however commonplace it may be for British labour
historians. Another main focus of attention was on the character
of economic and political crises and the ways in which, under
the pressure of intense class struggle, the capitalist class set
about attempting to restructure the labour force as a way of
undermining workers' solidarity and collectivity. This is one of
the themes explored in Majone's *Bienno Rosso, 1919-1920* (1975)
- a study of the period of the workers' councils in Italy and of
the revolutionary upsurge which followed the First World War.
It was also central to Tronti and Panzieri's thesis about
capitalism and class struggle in contemporary Italy. Another
historical study arising out of the same tendency is that of
Lay, Marucco and Pesante on the period 1880-1920, in which a
great deal of stress is laid on the autonomy of workers'
struggles, and their relation to the economic cycle rather than
to the political organisations of the left. All of these studies,
both in the past and in the present, tend to stress the
sectional and uneven character of workers' struggles, and the
difficulty of co-ordinating them in a unified national and
political struggle. These studies raised, in sharp form, the
possible gap between spontaneous workers' demands and the
programmes and perspectives of the political organisations of
the working class. But the point of reference was to
exclusively economic needs, and to the conditions of life and
work in the factory. Whereas in the Gramscian perspective,
struggles in the factory were emancipatory and linked to a
forward movement in the society as a whole, here the workers'
movement was treated as very largely self-contained, engaged
in a fixed antagonism to capital, but in purely negative,
defensive terms.

It is only recently then that historians have studied working-
class life and popular culture and perceived them as decisive
sources of social change. It is impossible to define the reasons
for this because we lack a relationship with the past, a historic
memory of these changes. Basic areas such as the history of
the family, popular religion, education and women are still
insufficiently studied. Any comparison between the times and
forms of change in these fields in Italy and other Western
societies is still impossible. As so often happens in Italy, sudden
changes in orientation tend to become fashionable and to be
consumed before they produce actual historical work.

FURTHER READING

Carria, Renzo del, *Proletari senza rivoluzione: storia della classi
    subalterne italiane dal 1860 al 1950*, 2 vols, Milan 1970.
Ley, Marucco and Pesante, 'Classe operaie e scioperi: ipotesi
    per il periodo 1880-1923', *Quaderni Storici* 1973.
Majone, Guiseppe, *Bienno Rossa*, Bologna 1975.
Manacorda, Gastone, *La storia del movimento operaio italiano*

attraverso i suoi congressi, Rome 1953.
Merli, Stefano, *Proletariato di fabrica e capitalismo industriale*,
    Florence 1972.
Proccacci, Giuliano, *Le lotte di classe in Italia a l'inizio del 20
    siecolo*, Florence 1962.
Ragioneri, Ernesto, *Une commune socialista: sesto Fiorentino*,
    Rome 1953.
Revelli, Mario, 'Fascismo come rivoluzione del alto', Primo
    Maggio 1975.
An English translation of essays by Tronti and Panzieti, which
will indicate their general standpoint, has been published by
the Conference of Socialist Economists.

34 'TO BE OR NOT TO BE': SOCIALIST HISTORIANS IN DENMARK

Niels Finn Christiansen and Jens Rahbek Rasmussen*

The large number of Danish participants in the Ruskin History
Workshop 13 have at least one thing in common: they are all
working, as teachers or students, in the socialist academic
community which has been created during the last ten or twelve
years. Since the mid-1960s we have gone through a phase of
intensive political and theoretical development without parallel
or precedent in Denmark. Traditionally the universities (or
rather, until fifty years ago, *the* university) have been almost
hermetically closed institutions with no links either to the
agrarian people's movements in the nineteenth century, or to
the labour movement in the twentieth century.

   The agrarian popular movement on its own resources was
capable of developing a dynamic and autonomous ideology, and
an awareness of the social and historical roots of the movement;
also it established a widely ramified net of institutions (e.g.,
the *folkehøjskoler*, where rural middle-class youth spent a
year or two before returning to their native village),
communicating the ideology to large sections of the agrarian
classes. The norms of these classes, and the way they perceived
their own role, imbued the outlook of other classes and groups

---

*Niels Finn Christiansen and Jens Rahbek Rasmussen teach at
the Copenhagen University and work with *Kritiske Historike*,
a Marxist history journal.

to a considerable degree. The labour movement, on the other hand, did not succeed in creating a comparable historical consciousness of the life, the struggles, and the class *identity* of the working class. From the beginning, the Danish labour movement was deeply reformist, a-theoretical and anti-academic. Subordinated to the bourgeois and petit-bourgeois understanding of history, they failed to recognise the need to develop an autonomous class *identity*; the tradition of social history which in Britain ran parallel with the growth of the labour movement had no Danish counterpart. The material causes of this cannot be discussed here; suffice it to stress the economic, political and ideological hegemony of the Danish petit bourgeoisie (especially its agrarian sector) up to the 1950s.

The frail attempts made in the 1880s to introduce Marxism into the Danish labour movement were discontinued in the 1890s, as unionisation and struggle against employers became the principal tasks. No stratum of academics or working-class intellectuals joined the movement. Significantly, the most important work in the field of theory before 1914 was due *not* to a collective effort of the movement, but to a single individual, the historian Gustav Bang (1871-1915). From around 1900, Bang tried to give the Danish Social Democratic Party a Marxist theoretical basis comparable to that of the 'Centrists' in the Second International. Writing extensively on theory in leaflets, books, and articles in the social democratic press, he attempted to build up a Marxist view of society in the working class, though politically he remained strictly loyal to the party, and never questioned its reformist practice. His forceful analysis of the total life-experience and the struggles of the working class were to remain unique, however; no circle formed around him, nor had he any successors.

Bang, as an historian, covered a wide variety of subjects. In his academic writings he was not ashamed to adopt the empiricist orthodoxy of bourgeois historiography. His popular works (published in large editions) were, in contrast, broad narratives reflecting his strong socialist commitment. Unable to bridge this gap between empiricism and socialist people's history, he did not succeed in creating a genuinely scientific *and* socialist history - bequeathing to us a dilemma that has still not been overcome. With his premature death, all attempts to create an autonomous Marxist theory and a socialist historiography came to an abrupt halt.

The lack of revolutionary tendencies of any importance in the Danish working class meant that the inter-war split between social democrats and communists had only the slightest repercussions in Denmark. The reformist Social Democracy was still the predominant political labour organisation, while the attempts of the Danish Communist Party to establish a revolutionary alternative met with failure as far as the vast majority of workers were concerned. During the 1920s, the

Danish Communist Party suffered from a series of internal
schisms, becoming consolidated only in the 1930s. Though it
was to remain a minor party, it did represent a major
breakthrough in the relationship between the labour movement
and the intellectuals, who in comparatively large numbers
either joined the party or became closely associated with it and
its socio-cultural organisations and activities. For the first time
in Denmark, there was formed a community (if not quite a
stratum) of revolutionary intellectuals, especially artists,
writers and doctors who saw it as their principal political task to
build an alliance with the proletariat, using their scientific and
artistic talents to give theoretical as well as practical support
to the revolutionary tendencies. From the present point of view,
however, the crucial point is that no historians or social
scientists (with the exception of a few economists) joined this
community. The writing of history that took place under the
party's auspices was quantitatively rather modest, and had as
its main purpose to justify the party line. None of the party
historians had any association with university historiography
(still completely dominated by idealism and empiricism).
Furthermore, the Communist Party historiography was limited to
the 'grand' political questions and the internal fighting in the
party. No attempt was being made to treat the total life-
experience of the working class, let alone to help the class itself
develop its own historical consciousness - an important theme in
the 1930s was the anti-fascist movement, where the communists
co-operated with those new intellectual strata who joined the
Social Democracy during the inter-war period.

Where revolutionary socialist historians feared to tread,
bourgeois historiography rushed in. The 1930s saw a fair amount
of research in the social and organisational history of the
working class. Most of it, however, consisted of a deliberately
de-politicised collection of data which were eventually pieced
together in bulky monographs. The building of an autonomous
understanding of history in the working class was no concern of
this line of research; remaining strictly within the academic
bounds, it lacked any advanced theory or method, and was
strongly though indirectly influenced by the ideology of class
collaboration which in those years permeated both the Social
Democracy, the bourgeoisie and the petit bourgeoisie. This is
not to deny, however, that a substantial amount of source
material relating to the living and working conditions of the
working class, and to its organisations, were uncovered; or that
this research, in spite of all its limitations, has constituted an
important empirical point of departure for the last decade's
efforts to establish an alternative historiography for and about
the working class and the labour movement.

During the two post-war decades, the academic community
was extremely conservative, and in history dullness and tedium
prevailed. The empiricist tradition, never very impressive even
at its best, had by now thoroughly exhausted its explanatory

potential, and was capable only of blocking thematic and methodological innovations. The analyses of economic and social history produced by the steadily degenerating bourgeois historiography were characterised by excessive detail and vulgar atomisation. There were no attempts to synthesise, or to analyse the interconnections between the economic, political and ideological levels. The research conducted before the war in the social history of the rural and the urban working classes was discontinued. Collective historical factors and the history of classes were ignored. In so far as questions of methodology were taken up at all, the discussion never transgressed the framework of an increasingly anaemic positivism.

The object of painting this sombre picture of the past has not been to imply that all is now well. Traditional bourgeois norms still determine success or failure in academic life, including history. Still, from the mid-1960s certain radical changes began to take place in the universities. The new departures associated with the dates 1956 and 1968 affected the left and the universities all over the Western world, and were strongly influential in Denmark as well. The measure of radicalisation in Denmark was due to the fact that here a relatively strong revolutionary, non-communist left wing emerged for the first time, and with the universities as one of its most important strongholds, at least in the initial phase. A direct link was forged between the anti-imperialist activities, the increasingly militant working class, and the student movement. The 1960s saw an explosion in the number of students (and of university teachers); and, an albeit moderate democratisation of the students' social background, thus made the relationship between universities and society a question of immediate relevance. The pressure from students and junior teachers resulted in a comparatively democratic reorganisation of university government, giving these groups considerable influence on the choice of subjects and methods. The most notable results were achieved in the social and behavioural sciences (sociology, psychology) and in the arts and humanities, where the legitimate subject matter of each discipline was substantially extended and the limits of each subject redefined. Current class contradictions in society became for many of us the point of departure for the topics and problems we wanted to take on.

The lack of a socialist tradition in almost all subjects led initially to heavy concentration on the attempts to establish a Marxist theory. Indeed, until the mid-1970s theoretical work was the overriding concern of the student movement. Reading Marx became a crucial part of both individual and collective study. More recent sources of inspiration included French structuralism (Althusser, Poulantzas) and the perhaps more influential German 'school of reconstruction', whose approach was known in Denmark as *kapitallogik* (literally, 'capital logic'). The latter tried to bypass, as it were, the development of Marxist theory

since Marx, and to substitute for it a 'true' and 'original'
Marxism, based primarily on a close reading of *Capital*.
Innumerable books and journals of theory have been published
during the last decade, accompanied by heated theoretical
debates and militant criticism of the positivism, empiricism and
lack of theory typical of the university establishment. This
debate took place in most of the social sciences, and many of
the humanities, but significantly reached history only later
and in a weakened form. The methodological demands of
empiricism are still so firmly rooted, and so central in the
training of historians as practised today that socialist students
of history in Denmark (as no doubt in most other countries)
must pursue two lines of study simultaneously: the official
university curriculum on the one hand, and (collective)
self-study of Marxist theory on the other.

Due to the tremendous upsurge in theoretical studies, a
fairly large number of students and teachers are well trained in
the critique of political economy. An unfortunate consequence
has been the inability to connect the increasingly sophisticated
theory with the writing of solidly researched narratives
informed by historical materialism. Therefore, we are now
trying to work out a more satisfactory relationship between
theoretical and empirical work, attempting at the same time to
transgress the academic limitations of purely theoretical studies.
An increasingly important objective is to connect our academic
work with the class-based movements which figure so
conspicuously in today's crisis-ridden Danish society. Though
we still have a long way to go before we achieve the level of
consciousness and the broad foundations represented by
History Workshop, several groups have at least set out,
inspired and encouraged by the 'historical practice' of your
activities.

In view of the steady widening of the subjects studied, the
following remarks only serve to indicate some of the current
trends and topics in Danish socialist history.

As was the case in many other countries, *the history of the
labour movement* played an important role in the initial phase –
partly because the subject had been largely 'forgotten' by
bourgeois historiography, partly because of a desire to correct
the self-justifying tendencies of the existing historiography of
parties and organisations. Trying to explain the hegemony of
reformism in the Danish working-class and labour movement has
been a central concern, though the focus is now less on the
study of ideology and organisations than on a materialist
explanation of the total life experience of the working class and
its relations to other classes, especially the petit bourgeoisie.
The progress has been particularly rapid, and the
methodological innovations have been particularly sophisticated
in such areas as *women's history* and *the history of the family*.
There is an increasing awareness that a full understanding

of the working class and its organisations presupposes an analysis of Danish (and to a certain degree international) capitalism. An important field of study today is *the history of capitalist crises*, with special attention being paid to the crises of the 1930s. Another indispensable condition for understanding the Danish social formation is an insight into the particular *transition from feudalism to capitalism* that Denmark experienced, and which produced an agrarian petit bourgeoisie with considerable numerical and political strength. This problem, and the particularities of Danish feudalism, have been the object of several analyses. Here we have been able to draw on the extensive international discussion of the transition which has also generated a number of *periodisation debates* of a more general nature.

Another subject in which Danish Marxists have shown great interest is (international) fascism. This may seem surprising, considering the marginal role which fascism played in Danish history, but may be at least partially explained by the fact that corporative political and ideological views have appeared on the Danish political scene during the last five or six years, influencing even the liberals and the social democrats. Still another subject of great interest has been *the history of historiography* which has contributed to understanding the reigning orthodoxy, and helped us to define more clearly the demarcation line and the differences between 'us' and 'them'.

The degree and the form of organisation have varied greatly from one milieu (discipline, university) to another. A common aspiration in recent years has been to establish an interdisciplinary co-operation. In this process, history has had an important (though often indirect) part to play through the marked trend towards increasing 'historicisation' of other subjects. This has especially been true in literary studies, and indeed the largest historical project in progress today is a multi-volume Marxist *History of Danish Literature* which not only includes the 'low' literature hitherto ignored by academic literary historians, but also harbours ambitions of giving a truly dialectical survey of the relations between literature and society.

Finally, mention should be made of the plethora of journals providing a forum for publishing and debating the findings of critical research, and the quite amazing number - considering the limited effective demand on the left - of socialist publishers putting out scores of books every year.

The above survey has been able to give only the barest outline of Danish socialist historiography. Reasons of space have compelled us to leave out many important and interesting activities. We hope that you have at least gained an impression of our work; certainly we hope and expect that the work and example of the comrades participating in the History Workshop will inspire us to improve our historical practice.

African history

Alessandro Triulzi*

What are the original characteristics of African historiography?
Simplifying, it might be possible to speak of three.
The first concerns its extremely contemporary nature. I am
not here referring so much to the obvious contemporary interest
of a continent that from the 1960s onwards has never ceased to
be a focus of world attention and whose struggles - from the
first moves towards economic development to the struggles for
liberation - have involved us all. I refer rather to its more
properly historiographical impact, which has imposed a revision
of ethnocentric conceptual and classificatory schemes. A
reflection on contemporary Africa confirms the inadequacy of
traditional chronological divisions, poorly adapted to the
progress of extra-European historical development, and
demonstrates the extraordinary continuity between the
pre-colonial past and post-colonial present that is the keystone
of the current African debate. The classical studies of
pre-colonial African society (such as Vancosina or Manacorda)
are a testimony not only to the breadth of this particularly rich
and innovatory debate, but also to their necessity for an
understanding of the problems of contemporary African history,
above all today when the strategies chosen for economic and
social development are more and more tied to the structures of
traditional societies. At the same time, the variety of the new
political, social and economic formations in contemporary Africa
calls for a reconsideration of 'traditional' societies whose
complexity and human density ranges far beyond the simple
designation of 'pre-capitalist society'.
The second characteristic, linked to the first, concerns the
specific nature of African history as a discipline born, and in a
certain sense grown up, in the margins between history and the
other social sciences. After an initial phase of neglect, this has
placed African historiography in an interdisciplinary setting
with its own methods and means of development.
The scarcity of written sources which was seen by the
traditional historians as the major obstacle to placing African
historiography amongst the historical sciences has forced
African historians to use the methods and results of the social
sciences, thus developing an interdisciplinary practice which

---

*Alessandro Triulzi teaches anthropology at the University of
Naples. He has lived and worked in Ethiopia, and is currently
writing a book on its late-eighteenth- and early-nineteenth-
century history.

has influenced not only African historiography but historical
science and methodology in its entirety. One thinks of the
extraordinary development of oral sources in which African
historians, following from the studies of Jan Vansina, have made
first-class methodological and disciplinary contributions. These
contributions, from the foundation of the growth of interest in
oral history, are important not only for the study of the
so-called non-literate societies of Africa but for the peasant
and worker societies of the industrialised West.

In addition one thinks of the development of collateral
disciplines such as anthropology, linguistics or archaeology to
which African history has brought innovatory approaches and
methods. Thus enriching the discussion of an interdisciplinary
method of research, which no longer consists of random
combinations and the juxtaposition of diverse results but of
contributions of an organic nature as underlined in the work of
Benedetto Manacorda. It is certainly due to this collaboration
with other social sciences, particularly those, like anthropology,
concerned with the study of structures and the definition of
general laws and processes, that African historiography, above
all in recent years, has left the narrow confines of
'événementielle' history to embrace a knowledge of the great
themes and processes of historical evolution.

A third characteristic concerns the relevance and indeed
urgency of an understanding of African history for the
questions of the present day. The vitality of current debate
arises from its constant interaction with the social and political
practice of the countries of Africa, between theoretical
interpretation and normative characteristics, between history
and society. That is, it arises from the fact that in Africa,
through the fusion of the intellectual and managerial classes
and the objective drama of the decisions forced daily on its
governments, rarely can studies be abstracted from the
surrounding social reality; there are fewer temptations and less
possibility to confine such studies to the restrictions of
academic circles and university institutes. In Africa, more than
elsewhere, science is never abstract and neutral but feeds on
the socio-political context in which it grows and develops and,
perhaps more so than in Europe, correspondingly influences
and helps to articulate that context. This encounter between
historiographical debate and social practice, a constant
characteristic of the discipline is relevant not only for the
historian, but even more pressingly, for its contribution
towards determining social and cultural choices.

African history was born in the wake of a past closely linked
with the colonial period and its own official historiography,
with prejudices acquired and diffused even on an academic level,
and with eurocentric assumptions and disciplinary certainty.
The resources of the first historians dedicated to the scientific
study of Africa were very meagre: reports of the travels of
explorers and missionaries, memoirs and diaries of colonial

functionaries which contained only rare digressions into the
field of history, and a number of ethnographical and
ethnological studies of good quality though often these were
linked to the administrative needs of the colonialists. Until this
period – 1950s – African history was for the most part the
history of Europeans in Africa, a part of the historical progress
and development of Western Europe and an appendix of the
national history of the metropolis. It was said at the time that
Africa had no history because history begins with writing and
thus with the arrival of the Europeans. Therefore, their
presence in the continent came to be justified, among other
things, by their ability to place Africa in the 'path of history'.
That the genuine path was only the European was an assumption
which few seemed to doubt, and this reflected the arrogant
certainty of the colonial period.

A new African historiography was born in the wake of the
post-war nationalist movements. It derived its strength both
from an indigenous political movement, and from an external
intellectual culture – that of European socialism. Its first
practitioners – the generation of the 1950s – were independent
or dissident spirits on the European left, such as Thomas
Hodgkin and Basil Davidson, who had cut their teeth in armed
conflicts – Davidson having fought with the Yugoslav partisans,
Hodgkin having sided, before the war, with the Palestinian
resistance and later with the Algerian movement for
independence – and who were militantly anti-colonial. They were
joined by a small group of African researchers and some
Afro-Americans in exile. This group took an active part in
educational, cultural and political work in the post-colonial
societies – as, for instance, in Nkrumah's Ghana, so that
research was joined from the start to a degree of active
participation in the reshaping of African reality. This practice
of working on the ground has been a distinguishing feature of
the African historian – 'historiens de plein air' as they were
later to be called by Hubert Deschampes.

It has been said that this first phase has had an essentially
'demonstrative' character (Ranger): it was necessary to
demonstrate that African history could have been written
without recourse to colonial archives, that it was a subject with
full academic dignity and that local documentary sources existed
(oral and written) that were able to make up for the absence of
traditional written or archival sources. A rediscovery of
pre-colonial history was necessary to bring the old civilisation
to light, to place new value on African culture and art, and to
reveal the blanket of European prejudice. To accomplish this it
was therefore thought sufficient to excavate the surface, find
the data and accumulate the facts, events and news that would
allow history to write itself.

It was a period of both great enthusiasm and naivity. With
the supply of the first results and discoveries African history
seemed to gain a legitimacy that the first years of decolonisation

helped to confirm. The first important contributions to the new
African historiography began; those of the Nigerian historian
K. Onwuka Dikee (*Trade and Politics in the Niger Delta*, 1956),
soon followed by the works of Basil Davidson, Ivor Wilks, and
Thomas Hodgkin in Great Britain, Jean Suret-Canale and
Georges Balandier in France, followed in turn by other scholars
in Europe, the United States and in Africa where the school of
Legon in Ghana or that of Dar-es-Salaam in Tanzania began to
produce their first collective work. It was the golden age of
African history. The *Journal of African History* in London and
the *Cahiers d'études africaines* in Paris, both founded in 1960,
represented the manifesto and show-case of the first pioneers of
the new discipline.

The nationalist history of the 1950s and 1960s gave
preference to the themes of African history considered useful
to the development of new state structures, and therefore to
breathe historical life into the model of the Nation-State that was
the legacy of the colonial period. The main themes of the first
African historiographers were therefore the history of the
precolonial states; their bureaucratic and institutional
apparatus, their political events and programmes of expansion,
the history of states, wars, famous personalities, cultural
heroes and local dynasties that proclaimed themselves national
and thus nationalist.

Born in fact in the same period, and concomitant with the
independence of African countries, the 'sociology of
development' had an even greater certainty and naivety;
economic well-being and the 'take-off' seemed to be promised, it
was enough to follow the route indicated by the Western
democracies and knowledgeably delineated by the economist
W.W. Rostow in *The Stages of Economic Development* (1960) a
work then considered as the 'Bible of development' capable of
carrying the Third World to the radiant dawn of 'consumerism'.

'Modernisation' theory had its counterpart in a liberal
historiography which interpreted the whole of African history in
a developmental perspective. According to this view,
independence through decolonisation was the result of
'collaboration' between Europe and Africa, the independence
movements were not therefore born of revolt and resistance to
colonialism but in collaboration with it. Thus the 'resistors'
were for the most part 'reactionary romantics' (Robinson and
Gallagher); they lost because they did not collaborate with
colonialism. On the other hand the 'collaborators' were the
'fortunate' (Oliver and Atmore), they were progressive because
they looked to the future. Colonial resistance was defined as
'primitive', and 'irrational', the inheritance of the first African
nationalism was collaboration rather than struggle. The rebellion
of the Mau Mau in Kenya, bloodily repressed by the English,
was a typical testimony; it was an irrational and bloody form of
protest which displayed none of the anticipated forms of action
of the liberation movements, not because it might be criticised

for the absence of political analysis beyond an explosion of
anger and violence, but because this explosion in some way was
opposed to the 'soft face' of African nationalism and the process
of decolonisation then in progress, which was, and desired to
be, peaceful, urbane and above all non-violent.

Liberal historiography and modernisation theory was
everywhere in the ascendant in the middle 1960s, favouring an
ordered decolonisation, through agreement rather than armed
struggle. Thus in South African historiography, in the
encounter between liberals and Marxists, the liberal thesis
prevailed in favour of a gradual development and peaceful
integration of the different racial groups in South Africa.
According to such a thesis, from the end of the Anglo-Boer
conflict of 1899, South African society has seen the progressive
factor (mining and later industrial capital sustained by England)
prevail over the reactionary factor (agricultural capital)
represented by the Boer 'Trekkers', in whom the kindling of
the flame of nationalism had brought about the system of
apartheid, a deviation and abnormal by-product of a
fundamentally sane economic system. Thus the extraordinary
economic development of South Africa came to be seen as a
spontaneous process, abstracted from the social context, in
which the enterprise of the (white) South African *homo
oeconomicus* has prevailed over the passivity and isolation of
traditional society, unable to adapt to the modern world. The
political consequences of such a so-called liberal thesis are
known; the more the capitalist system in South Africa
developed the more the racial question - seen as the principal
factor in apartheid - came to be put in second place.

In the late 1960s, both the liberal and the nationalist versions
of African history came under attack. As before, there was a
close link between theory and practice, historical work and the
changing contours of political reality. By this time the countries
'granted' their independence by the imperialist powers began to
reveal both their structural fragility, and their close ties to the
preceding colonial regime. The end of the 1960s saw, in fact, a
bankruptcy of the political experiences of the newly
independent African states. The 'decade of development'
officially decreed by the United Nations, in the vision of an
international effort towards economic and social progress in the
Third World, was exhausted in a multiplicity of development
programmes based on the presuppositions of neoliberal
economics, of which all or most failed miserably. Africa was
troubled by continual crises of political instability and economic
depressions, in the main resolved by military coups and an
accentuated tendency towards authoritarianism, bureaucratic
centralism and a rigid re-enforcement of the executive and its
capacity for repression.

At the same time growing doubts began to spread of the
ability of the capitalist system to guarantee self-development,
and of its capacity to be transferred into a society of such

different historical and cultural interlinking. The critical
re-examination of nationalist historiography and its basic
presuppositions was united with the criticism of the same
development proposals that were principally inspired by the
West. A deliberate parallel came to be drawn, as underlined in
agreement, though from different visual angles, by Manacorda,
Hopkins, Ranger or Gentili, between the growing disaffection
of the African masses no longer feeling represented by the
'elites' of the 1960s and the birth of a radical historiography
which no longer looked to the liberal or nationalist faiths for
the resolution of new problems brought by independence.

The doubts raised by African political and economic
development were sharply reflected in a new and more
questioning mood among the historians. African historiography,
it was seen, had taken up the cause of anti-colonialism and the
legitimation of the newly independent nation states at the cost
of a falsification of the past, replacing the 'savage' and
primitive Africa of the colonialist historians with a no less
simplified picture of an intrinsically egalitarian and socially
compact 'traditional' society, an 'Africa felix' to be contrasted
to the dark ages and savagery of colonialism. The colonial phase
was not the 'true' history of Africa but only a distracting and
artificial interlude which had momentarily interrupted, but not
broken, the bond of continuity linking the precolonial states to
those of post-independence.

On one hand it was widely recognised that the
historiographical debate had made many advances during the
1960s, whilst on the other it was criticised for accompanying the
growth and potential of cultural nationalism too closely, instead
of considering the real and functional divisions of society, it
had ratified the hegemony of the managerial classes who came to
power after independence (Atieno Odhiambo) and thus served
to support the new consensus.

The acritical adoption of such a view by some of the African
historians necessarily led, as has been said, to a 'purely
nationalistic vision' of the past. A past that too often is required
to ratify the present and has thus been objectively transformed
into 'a legitimising document of the regimes in power' (Ranger).
In this sense, the view of a mythical pre-colonial Africa without
conflict - the 'Africa felix' of the 1960s, was not only the
application of ideology to a vision of the past but established a
bond of continuity between this past and its direct descendants;
the 'new man' of independence. The nationalist historiography
thus served the politicians rather more than the historians.

Connected with this fundamental criticism, new and more
embarrassing questions were put to the African historians and
entered the core of the debate. What impact had historiography
made on the life of the people, on the problems of
underdevelopment, on the poverty or economic backwardness of
African society? What weight had the historians' careful
enquiries had on the pre-colonial states and their glories

compared with the social and political formation of the new
states? Tradition and modernity - were they really so separate?
And what sense had words like modernisation, progress or
development if only applied to limited sectors of society, if the
continent as a whole made no progress and the division between
elites and masses was visibly growing? These and similar
questions had a definite bearing on the development of the
historiographical debate because they raised the question of the
relevance of the historical disciplines in the so-called
transitional society.

A second critical line in African historiography was opened
up by the challenge to modernisation theory, and by the
application to Third World studies of Marxist theories of uneven
development. I am referring here to the impact of such studies
as those of Andre Gundar Frank (*Capitalism and
Underdevelopment in Latin America*), Arghiri Emmanuel
(*Unequal Exchange: A Study of the Imperialism of Trade*), and
Samir Amin (*Imperialism and Unequal Development*). These
works argued for a precise relationship between the economic
development of the centre (the metropolis or ex-metropolis)
and the underdevelopment of the countryside (the first colonies,
now 'independent' states), the latter being a direct function of
the high rate of development of the former.

The theory of dependence or 'development of
underdevelopment', giving a rational explanation in economic
terms of the 'necessity' for underdevelopment in the Third
World, had an easy success among those in this period who were
convinced of the contradictions of the capitalist system and its
true bearing on the problems of hunger and economic
backwardness. It was to many a persuasive reply to the
question of development and transition. In terms of the
historiographical debate, the theory of dependence seemed to
offer, and in reality offered, a key to understanding the
central-peripheral colonial relationship and the Euro-African
system of relations and conditioning. However, it soon became
clear, as underlined by the historians and anthropologists of
Africa, that such a theory, acritically assumed and unduly
generalised, risked becoming a simple tautology, since it
undervalued the forces of reaction and internal dynamic of
African society by reducing these to a passive role as in the
analysis of the old colonial historiography.

The debate on the post-colonial state and its internal and
external limits, of the first decolonisation and its failures, was
thus reopened, analysing the processes and mechanism of
interaction between the structural roots of underdevelopment
and the external dominion, it was not only the forms and
methods of control of this dominion that were tracked down,
but also the basis that confined it to a 'contractual' relationship
(Mafeje) between the dominant and dominated. This opened the
debate on the role of the bourgeois African 'auxiliaries' (Leys)
or 'intermediaries' (Fanon) for external imperialism. The African

political economy was no longer studied as a disconnected
subject acquired and abstracted from its social or international
context. It was revalued with the full weight of tradition, of
the pre-colonial past and the conditioning of the colonial period,
the role of ideology and the transition to socialism (Bénot).
    History quickly assumed fundamental importance in the
discussion of 'underdevelopment', both for its practical
dimensions (the nature and origins of underdevelopment seen as
the key to the choices of economic development) and for its
theoretical implications (the debate on pre-capitalist society and
its stages of growth). Again history is found at the centre of
the debate as the point of balance for research for the correct
analysis of African society and for a fuller understanding of
its structural mechanisms. The studies of sociology, politics
and economics had demonstrated the inadequacy of
modernisation theory. To understand the problems of
underdevelopment required investigation into the causes and
not only the outward manifestations; it is necessary to turn to
the past to understand the present better and to be able to
intervene in it. The concepts of relevance and functionality
were thus taken up again and applied to the study of the past,
but this time with a different significance. History, particularly
economic and social history, is no longer required to legitimate
the post-colonial state but to investigate the roots of
underdevelopment afflicting most African countries. As Anthony
G. Hopkins has recently written, the historians now ally
themselves with the other social scientists in the search for
the mysterious 'black box' capable of explaining why the
aeroplane of the theory of W.W. Rostow has crashed to the
ground.
    A third line of critical historical enquiry was opened up by
French Marxist structuralism and the discussion - initiated in
the first place by the French Marxist anthropologists - on the
notion of there being an 'African' mode of production. The
discussion was launched, in the first place, at the level of
theory and on the basis of ethnographic data, but since it was
concerned, essentially, with pre-capitalist modes of production,
it inevitably carried an implicit historical dimension. The debate
was anticipated in the work of the French sociologist Balandier
in his *Anthropologie Politique* (1967), and it was developed
above all by the French school of economic anthropologists -
Meillasoux, Rey, Terray, Godelier. Amongst the Marxists, the
debate was launched by a series of articles in the theoretical
journal *La Pensée*, and it served as a kind of rallying point for
some of the critical and open spirits in or close to the French
Communist Party, questioning well-established Marxist
orthodoxies in an attempt to bring theoretical discussion into
line with their own research. The debate was important not only
for a more profound understanding of the nature of traditional
societies but moreover for its theoretical implications and the
immediate link they offer to the comprehension of the roots and

contradictions of underdevelopment. It is interesting to note
that this debate was initially stimulated, not by the historians,
but the anthropologists and economists; that is the workers in
the field of analysis and interpretation of contemporary Africa.
They contributed to a growth of awareness, and knowledge, of
the elements of current events in the historiographical debate
with influential results on many levels. The young radical
African historiography (Atieno, Adhiambo, Depelchin) quickly
allied itself to these studies, in the defence of history as a
social science *par excellence* and as such 'an essential
instrument for the explanation of the temporal dynamic of actual
phenomena and problems and for the formulation of criteria for
intervention' (Manacorda). The basic hypothesis of this school
and principal element of the new debate was the restitution of a
dimension of time to the analysis of economic phenomena, and
their examination not through means of abstract theories but in
the context of a totality of social relations, as used in the
determination of history.

From the contributions and corrections brought from the
school of economic anthropology of Marxist inspiration,
indications for research were born adapted for the examination
of the extreme complexity and internal dynamism of social
structures. An analysis no longer on a purely ethnographical
level but in a wider dimension that gave a new breath of
historiographical life to the discussion of pre-colonial society.
In particular, the analysis of economic structure puts the
substantivist dichotomy between the so-called market and
non-market societies back into discussion, broadening the
analysis on the circulation and distribution of goods to that
more pregnant of the production and reproduction of the
material conditions of existence. The discussion of methods of
production, which appeared limited to a mechanistic analysis
derived from the a-critical adoption of Marxist models, was
likewise enriched to reveal on the one hand their limited
application to the African situation and on the other their
interpretative values if not their terminological and conceptual
differentiation. It is above all in the emphasis placed on
traditional societies' principal structures that the mechanisms
of social control and the inequalities of traditional society, not
least that between the sexes, have been made explicit.
Structures such as those of land tenure and kinship were no
longer seen as in classical ethnology as a-historical factors but
as the principal fulcrum of material culture, the social relations
of production, and historical change.

The debate, which is still an open one on pre-capitalist modes
of production, has already brought notable contributions on
both method and historical interpretation. Above all it has
stimulated a critical re-reading of Marxist analytic categories on
a less ethnocentric basis. European-derived 'laws of
development' are no longer arbitrarily imposed on phenomena
which require to be understood in their specificity, and Marxism

- in the hands of the French economic anthropologists - is seen
as a method rather than as providing an all-purpose and
ready-made explanatory scheme. The inductive method of social
analysis has been shown to be absolutely indispensable: general
formulations can only be made after a rigorous and careful
examination of the concrete. Finally, so far as African history
is concerned, peoples and societies that were denied a history,
in the hey-day of structural-functionalism (represented, in
Britain, by the anthropology of Malinowski and Radcliffe-
Brown), and which were the subject of enthnographic and
anthropological study alone - like Evans-Pritchard's timeless
Nuer - have had history given back to them. The way to a
fuller, more historical understanding of these societies has
been opened up.

The debate on pre-colonial society, from the point of view of
its contents, has both stimulated a critical revision of many
themes dear to the first African historiography and opened up
new ones. Thus the nationalist writings of the anticolonial
resistance have been enriched by analysis on the formation of
class in resistance movements (Depelchin), on the role effected
by the subaltern classes in such movements (Isaacman), and on
the anti-oppressive and anti-authoritarian character, apart
from nationalist, of such movements (Thornton). The analysis
of the minority white regimes in southern Africa became likewise
detached from both the liberal position and from the thesis of
'internal colonialism' which saw South Africa as a 'colony' (the
Africans) dominated by the 'metropolis' (the white minority)
against whom the black population would inevitably revolt.

The debate on the state and on the transition was rekindled
in a particular way following the liberation of the ex-Portuguese
colonies. The form and objectives of this struggle led to a wide
discussion centred on the meaning and political weight of what
was termed 'the second independence' of Africa. The
contemporary interest and relevance of this debate is derived
less from an external interest in the immediate history, than
from the deliberate re-evaluation of history carried out by the
major leaders of the liberation movement. They contributed to
a demystification of the a-critical vision of the past, and based
their claims for independence on a reconstruction of the
relations of production and pre-colonialist social structures
linked to an analysis of the socio-economic conditions within
which and against which the liberation struggles were active.

African history was born and grew up in a climate of action
and movement in which the meeting of theory and practice was
an actual and essential element in the debate itself, and not an
external fact. This is still very true to-day, when there is a
general attempt to conceptualise the original features of African
societies as a whole. In one line, discussion is moving from a
chronological reconstruction and territorial limitations in favour
of a thematic and comparative approach, as in the discussion of
African 'modes of production'; in another, historical enquiry

is subverting the whole notion of 'traditional' society. African historians take sides, but they do not refuse to take a critical position in face of the changing political and social events of their time, but rather find in them a stimulus to self-questioning and a more intensive search for greater historical truth. The debate is still in progress on the themes discussed in this paper, with theoretical and conceptual questions inseparably linked to the empirical work of research. Marxist historians of Africa refuse to impose elaborate theoretical schemes derived from elsewhere to the historically very different situations which they were called upon to explain. At the same time, they are not afraid to enter into dialogue with other disciplines - such as that of economic anthropology - or to discuss their work in relation to the wider questions of social theory.

FURTHER READING

This paper is based on my Introduction to a recent volume of essays in African History: A. Triulzi, ed., *Storia dell'Africa a sud del Sahara*, Part I, *Il Mondo Contemporaneo*, vol. IV, *La Nuova Italia*, Florence 1979. A few authors' names which appear in brackets in the text (B. Manacorda, T.O. Ranger, A.G. Hopkins, A.M. Gentili, Y. Bénot, L. Passerini) refer to their respective essays in the volume. References have also been made to the following works:

Ajayi, J.F.A., 'Colonialism: An Episode in African History', in T.O. Ranger, ed., *Emerging Themes in African History*, London 1968.

Atieno-Odhiambo, E.S., *The Paradox of Collaboration and Other Essays*, Nairobi 1974.

Cliffe, L., 'Decolonizzazione e neocolonialismo', in A. Triulzi, ed., *Storia dell'Africa a sud del Sahara*, Florence 1979.

Davidson, B., *Alle radici dell'Africa nuova*, Intervista di A. Bronda, Rome 1979.

Depelchin, J., 'Toward a Problematic History of Africa', in *Tanzania Zamani*, Dar es-Salaam, 1 January 1976.

First, R., 'Regimi coloniali dell'Africa australe', in A. Triulzi, ed., *Storia dell'Africa a sud del Sahara*, Florence 1979.

Gentili, A.M., *Elites e regimi politici in Africa occidentale*, Bologna 1974.

Hodgkin, T., 'Where the Paths Begin', in C. Fyfe, ed., *African Studies since 1945: A Tribute to B. Davidson*, London 1976.

Hopkins, A.G., 'Clio Antics: A Horoscope for African Economic History', in C. Fyfe, ed., *African Studies since 1945: A Tribute to B. Davidson*, London 1976.

Isaacman, A., 'Resistance and Collaboration in Southern and Central Africa', *International Journal of African Historical Studies*, 1, 1977.

Leys, C., *Underdevelopment in Kenya: The Political Economy of Neo-Colonialism, 1964-1971*, London 1975.

Mafeje, A., 'Neo-Colonialism, State Capitalism or Revolution?',
    in P.C.W. Gutkind and P. Waterman, eds, *African Social
    Studies. A Radical Reader*, London 1977.
Oliver, R. and Atmore, A., *Africa since 1800*, Cambridge 1967.
Passerini, L., 'Il dibattito sulla storia dell'Africa portoghese:
    recenti contributi', in *Rivista di Storia Contemporanea*, 3,
    1972.
Ranger, T.O., 'Towards a Usable African Past', in C. Fyfe,
    ed., *African Studies since 1945: A Tribute to B. Davidson*,
    London 1976.
Robinson, R. and Gallagher, J., *Africa and the Victorians.
    The Official Mind of Imperialism*, London 1961.
Thornton, J., 'The State of African Historiography', in
    Ufahamu, 2, 1973.
Wolpe, H., 'The Theory of Internal Colonialism: The South
    African Case', in I. Oxaal, T. Barnett and D. Booth, eds,
    Beyond the Sociology of Development, London 1975.

36 TOWARDS A PEOPLE'S HISTORY OF SOUTH AFRICA?
RECENT DEVELOPMENTS IN THE HISTORIOGRAPHY OF SOUTH AFRICA

Shula Marks*

Any attempt to write a position paper on the current state of
South African historiography can only be described as either
foolhardy or arrogant - or both. My only excuse is the

*Shula Marks teaches at the School of Oriental and African
Studies, London.

temptation of sharing some of our preoccupations with the
Ruskin History Workshop. The rich variety of work in progress
at the moment on South Africa, the differing emphases and the
fact that much of it is still in the pipeline and that our ideas
are in a state of constant development, make this attempt a far
more difficult one than it would have been even three or four
years ago. The last eight or ten years have witnessed a
burgeoning of historical research by young scholars, largely
but not wholly based in this country, who have questioned many
of the basic assumptions of the earlier writing in South Africa's
past. Quite how recent these developments have been can be
witnessed both from the nature of the two-volume *Oxford
History of South Africa*, published between 1968 and 1971, as
the definitive synthesis on South African history, and the
reviews which greeted it. In 1972, for example, Richard Gray's
was simply one of many voices deploring 'the extraordinary
degree [to which] South African historical research has fallen
behind that of other African countries, let alone that of other
modern industrial countries.'

To appreciate the nature of the change, it is necessary to
return - briefly - to the situation in the 1960s, and how it had
come about. While the 1950s and 1960s witnessed a general
outpouring of books and university courses on Africa, by and
large South Africa was left out, whether because of an
unconscious boycott, a deliberate decision by scholars not to
work in the Republic, or because of the feeling (not entirely
ill-founded) that its problems were different from those of newly
independent African states. What Eric Stokes called the 'African
historiographical revolution' - with all its limitations - stopped
short on South Africa's northern borders.

In large measure this is, of course, explicable in political
terms. As has often been remarked, the end of colonialism was a
major reason for the attempts in the 1950s and 1960s to reclaim
Africa's precolonial past. 'The wind of change' did not,
however, bring the end of colonialism or its equivalent for
blacks in South Africa. While elsewhere in Africa the transfer
of political power to local elites led historians to look for the
continuities before and after the colonial era (now seen as a
'mere episode' in the long history of human society in Africa),
and to explore the origins of 'nationalism' and its roots in
'primary resistance', all this tended to avert eyes from South
Africa. And on the whole white South Africans within the
Republic were not going to focus their attention on these issues
either.

With a social climate in which intellectual enquiry is not
exactly encouraged and a regime in power whose legitimating
ideology is based on a view of history as the unveiling of the
manifest destiny of the white man (and especially of the Volk -
the Afrikaner people), it is perhaps hardly surprising that the
vast majority of South Africans, already excluded from the body
politic, should also be denied their history. For average white

South Africans, then as now, the history of South Africa is the history of the triumphant progress of their pioneering ancestors who overcame both nature and black savagery in the interests of 'Christian civilisation'.

At a slightly more sophisticated level, South African historiography - again not surprisingly - has reflected the intense and bitter 'racial' and political divisions in the country. Afrikaans-speaking South Africans are almost obsessively absorbed in their own exclusive national past; their historiography centres on the evolution of the Afrikaner 'nation' and the triumph of Afrikaner nationalism. The highly romanticised episodes in this saga have become elements in what has been termed a 'secular religion'. The spirit of much of this history can be summed up in the title of a pamphlet written during the Anglo-Boer War: *A Century of Wrong*. Afrikaner 'nationalist' historians have had their counterpart amongst certain English-speaking historians, whose main concern seems to have been to defend the actions of white settlers, whether English- or Afrikaans-speaking.

Probably more important still in imposing a kind of straitjacket on South African historiography were two further factors: the absence of any major thrust into this historiography from below, from the Africans themselves - itself in large measure an outcome of the grotesquely unequal access to education for different sectors of the population in South Africa and the tight state control over even the history syllabus for blacks; and the intellectual hegemony of the liberal tradition over scholars attempting to present an alternative. Although there was both a black and a radical tradition of history, they remained virtually unheard. The problem with the 'liberal tradition' was not that it lacked concern for the contemporary issues confronting the people of South Africa; nor indeed that it did not produce a formidable body of empirically useful work: work which still has to be taken seriously. Essentially, however, the intellectual foundations of this liberal tradition were laid nearly fifty years ago; and its assumptions were those of classical liberalism. Deeply concerned as these scholars were with the tension and conflict which they saw around them as they witnessed the effects of South Africa's industrial revolution, they explained these as arising essentially from the irrational heritage of the past: much as neo-classical economists, both in South Africa and elsewhere, attribute the failure of capitalism to achieve perfect equilibrium, perfect competition, to extraneous non-economic - broadly speaking 'political' - 'factors'.

Thus the origins of racism were sought, for example, particularly in the wake of I.D. McCrone's influential *Race Attitudes in South Africa*[1] in the formative influence of the 'frontier' on Afrikaner society in the seventeenth and eighteenth centuries, and attention was averted from the way in which forms of racism developed within the capitalist economy, and were intrinsically related to the specific form capitalism took in South Africa. Significantly McCrone's book, which is largely devoted to race-attitude testing amongst students in the 1930s, stops its 'historical introduction' in 1806 - when the Cape Colony was taken over by Britain. And while undoubtedly the major liberal historians were deeply concerned with the impact of the British on Cape society, by and large they have taken the ideology of imperial humanitarianism at face value. It is a view powerfully transmitted by the media in this country, which persist in attributing the present situation in South Africa to the peculiar vices of the Afrikaner. The result has been to ignore the essential collusion between settler colonialism and British imperialism in the subjection and exploitation of African societies and to ignore the role of imperialism in the creation of contemporary South Africa.

At another level, although liberal historians were concerned with the position of the black man in South African history, it was still largely with his role as the object of the policies and practices of white South Africans; and although the *Oxford History of South Africa*[2] opens with the stirring declaration that it was 'planned and written in the belief that the central theme of South African history is the interaction between peoples of diverse origins, languages, technologies, ideologies and social systems meeting on South African soil', significantly even here the pre-colonial history of the black man has been relegated to an anthropologist, and is handled in wholly static, a-historical terms. The result has been to portray African societies as both unchanging and isolated - and this in turn has led to misconceptions which reverberate through the account of the complex relationships later on of black and white societies and the way in which capitalist and pre-capitalist modes of production articulated in the nineteenth century. In this, and many other ways, the *Oxford History* can be seen as the apogee of the liberal tradition.

I have singled this work out because in a sense its publication marked a kind of watershed. In many ways it was an attempt to do for South Africa what had been happening to African history in the 1960s - but it was an African history poorly served at that stage by the ancillary evidence from archaeology, oral tradition and historical linguistics, and it was grafted on to a strong English-speaking academic liberal tradition, which led to a concentration on the processes of 'interaction', 'collaboration' between white and black, rather than on an appreciation of the independent development of very different social formations in the interior until the mineral discoveries, on the uneven penetration of capitalism and colonialism, and the resultant subordination of Africans, class formation and class conflict. And it was in part being forced to think of the inadequacies of the *Oxford History* in the new context of the early 1970s which acted as a spur to the younger historians of South Africa. On the one hand there was a widely felt dissatisfaction with the conception of the volumes at a general organisational and intellectual level. In the *Oxford History* eminent practitioners in the disciplines of archaeology, anthropology, economics and political science were called on to make their contributions, while the historians were left to 'tell the story'. On the other hand at a more profound level, perhaps, it was the nature of the questions which were not asked which was more worrying at a time when, to the north of the Limpopo, the first flush of enthusiasm for the nationalist revolution had swung into some disillusion with the realities of African poverty and neo-colonialism. This led a number of scholars, many of whom had left South Africa for political reasons during the previous decade, to start asking new kinds of questions. Here there was a decided resonance with what was also beginning to develop north of the Limpopo, with the increasing awareness that independence in the political sphere had in many African countries resolved relatively few problems, and had not relieved either economic inequalities or - despite the euphoria of the 1960s - the problems of development. With this change of focus the South African example in turn became acutely relevant elsewhere, as one of the few peripheral countries to have successfully industrialised - albeit at the expense of the majority of its inhabitants.

It would be wrong, though, to focus only on the connections between what was happening in South African historiography and developments to the north. Clearly of equal or even greater importance was the fact that there was now a body of South African historians studying outside the Republic and coming into contact with a far more varied intellectual diet: the *Annales* school; British social and socialist history; American writing on slavery and race; French Marxist traditions - primarily from Althusser, Poulantzas and the Marxist anthropologists; and the Latin American underdevelopment debate.

What then have been the new developments over the past few years? How does one encapsulate the present 'position'?

Probably at the centre of the contemporary debate is a shift away from 'explaining' contemporary South African society in terms of race and race attitudes which have somehow been carried over as McCrone seemed to suggest from the eighteenth-century frontier, to an examination of social process and a recognition that racism cannot simply be explained in its own terms, whatever the relative autonomy of ideology, but has to be related to the material base of society. (Indeed the recent work may have gone a little too far in this direction, and failed to give sufficient thought to the nature of symbolism and the intellectual history of racism.) However, by forcing the historians to go back to basic questions, whether about the nature of society at the Cape in the seventeenth and eighteenth century, or the shape of the social formations in the interior in the nineteenth, this has been most salutary.

If the frontier (or the Afrikaner in a simplistic sense, or Calvinism) can no longer be seen as the origin of South African race attitudes this opens up a number of questions both in relation to the seventeenth and eighteenth centuries and to the more recent past. If race attitudes are not attributable – in an almost mysterious, or at least a geographical sense – to the 'influence of the frontier', what about the archetypal attitudes supposedly first carried north by the Voortrekkers who, again according to the liberal interpretation, left the Cape because of the attempt of an alien government, the British, to impose its notions of law and order, and in particular its supposedly more 'liberal' notions of 'master-and-servant' relations on the frontier? Here again, detailed research, as much inspired by an attempt to look at the history of African people and understand the experience for blacks of the coming of the trekkers to the Transvaal as by a desire to unravel the nature of trekker society and its mode of production, suggests that settler society in the interior of South Africa was never as monolithic in its attitudes to people of colour as the stereotyped textbooks imply.

This fresh look at the nature of European domination at the Cape and settler states in the interior has also led to an appreciation of how *weak* colonial power was in these areas – and not how strong. And with the new appreciation of the African side of South African history, this weakness of white power takes on a new significance and opens again the question – at what point, and why and by whom and in whose interest was white supremacy ultimately imposed? This in turn takes us back to my earlier remarks about the collusion between Afrikaner and British settler colonialism and imperialism: we need very different terms of reference to those used by the liberal historians, and slowly these are coming clearer.

Through a more careful, but as yet far from complete, examination of the nature of black and white societies in South Africa before the era of the mineral discoveries, at least in the interior, what is striking is the uneasy co-existence of social formations whose power is relatively evenly matched. In this situation the British intervened not – as both liberal, pro-settler and Afrikaner interpretations would have it – on the side of Africans, but ineluctably to tip the balance in favour of the capitalist transformation of South Africa in which the settlers (or most of the settlers) were the main beneficiaries. The conquest of most of the major African societies and the restructuring of social relations in others was very largely the result of the intervention of British soldiers, missionaries and traders. Indeed, outside the Cape, most of these conquests can be directly related to the era of mineral discoveries and the heightened British intervention in South Africa which these occasioned.

This leads directly into the area where much of the debate has centred over the past few years: South Africa's industrial revolution which followed in the wake of the discovery of diamonds at Kimberley in 1868 and gold on the Witwatersrand in 1886. It is in the interpretation of the meaning and effects of this industrial revolution that the 'revisionist' interpretation differs most dramatically from that of the liberals. Here the 'conventional wisdom', which was accepted almost without question and interestingly as much by the 'left' as by liberals in the 1950s and most of the 1960s, held that the process of capitalist development in South Africa demanded a rationalisation of colour attitudes, and that the forces of 'economic growth' would in and by themselves break down *apartheid*: a view which accords well with the interests of those who call for increased overseas investment in South Africa. This model drew on the liberal picture of what was supposed to have happened during the British industrial revolution: a Whig interpretation if ever there was one, in which the British ruling class benevolently expanded the franchise to include the working class and increased their wages, virtually out of the goodness of their hearts. By breaking with the notion that racism is simply an atavistic carry-over from the eighteenth century, and by recognising the complex paths which different societies have followed to industrialisation, this comforting model as applied to South Africa has been pretty well exploded.

Much of the first stage of the 'revisionist' history concentrated on the particular role of the gold-mining industry, with its huge demand for labour and its vast sums of international investment, in the transformation of South African society in the late nineteenth century. It was in the policies of the Chamber of Mines with their drive to cut labour costs that the origins of many of the critical constituents of contemporary *apartheid* were found: the migrant labour system based on pass laws and compounds; the policy of setting aside 'reserves' in which the African population could reproduce itself and thus cut down on the welfare costs to be borne by the industry; the division of the working class into white skilled and highly paid labour, and black unskilled and super-exploited labour - and so on.

From this, attention moved to the nature of the white state and capital accumulation in twentieth-century South Africa, and to an examination both of the role of Afrikaner nationalism and the ideology of English-speaking South Africans, especially in manufacturing industry. Even in this area a large number of issues remain to be addressed and indeed to be raised, though there is neither the space nor the occasion to explore these at length here. It is, however, significant that many of the radical attempts to look at South Africa's twentieth-century history have come from political scientists and sociologists, heavily influenced by Poulantzas: it has been far more concerned with struggles between 'fractions of capital' than the struggles of Africans: where the working class has entered the arena, it has, by and large, been the white working class. The silence of much of the debate on the nature of African struggles and

African consciousness - not necessarily class consciousness - is I think not accidental; nor is it simply a function of the greater intractability of the sources. It is in large measure a reflection of the continued absence of an African contribution to this historiography; and this is deplorable, not because I believe in any simple sense that only blacks can write black history - but because until they do a crucial dimension is going to be missing from our historiography.

By its emphasis on the structure of the white state and the processes of proletarianisation and impoverishment, there is much in the recent debate which stresses the crucial role of international and settler agencies in the control of African destiny and powerlessness; to ignore these determinants in the South African context would be to ignore some of the most fundamental aspects of its historical and contemporary predicament. To write social or socialist history without an analysis of these determinants is to imagine you can have flowers without roots or trunk. Nevertheless, in order to understand the ways in which white rule has operated and the struggles which have given it its peculiar shape and form, it is crucial to be constantly aware of the African side of the story. One of the areas in which South Africa lagged behind the rest of Africa in the 1960s was in its attempt to come to terms with the pre-colonial past. In South Africa what we need is both an understanding of the pre-colonial and of the immediate pre-industrial past. To some extent historians have begun this task, but it is still far from complete.

There are, of course, problems in establishing this, and the attempts which were made in the rest of Africa in reconstructing African history from archaeological evidence, ethnography, oral tradition and historical linguistics has not always been particularly convincing. Nevertheless, by missing out on this phase of African historiography, there is a sense in which South Africans missed out on something vital and important. One should not exaggerate: in archaeology particularly, there has been a good deal of catching up, and some very important work in the past few years - work which has both radically revised our time-scale for African settlement in South Africa, and begun to illuminate the nature of pre-capitalist social formations.

Archaeological evidence has its own pitfalls. Even more than history, archaeology tends to be the record of the successful and of the material. There are limits to what mud floors and bits of bone and pot can tell us about social relations of production, political power and exploitation - let alone man's hopes and dreams and fears. But it does give us some handle on the long centuries before we have any written record. Nor is an interest in South Africa's pre-colonial past simply the preserve of the ivory-towered academic. It may well require a leap of the imagination, yet I would argue that our ignorance of the pre-colonial past bedevils our understanding of the more immediate past and of the nature of the colonial experience.

As Maurice Godelier has pointed out:
> As Marx and Engels have endlessly repeated, it is impossible
> to analyse and understand the forms and routes taken by the
> transition from one mode of production and social life to
> another without taking fully into consideration the 'premises'
> from which this transition develops. Far from their
> disappearing from the scene of history at a stroke, it is
> these earlier relations of production and the other social
> relations which transform themselves, and we must start
> from them in order to understand the *forms* which the
> effects of the new conditions of material life will take and the
> *places* where they will manifest themselves within the
> previous social structures.[3]

The importance of the pre-colonial past is something which
FRELIMO and the People's Republic of Mozambique are well
aware of, as the high priority which has been given to
archaeological research since independence, and the
fascinating series of 'peoples' histories' produced and widely
circulated through the newspapers reveal: it is perhaps not as
widely appreciated by expatriate white radical scholars from
South Africa. Yet we still know far too little about such broad
questions as the modes of production in pre-industrial societies
(and I use the term in the loose sense castigated by Hindess
and Hirst), the precise nature of the relationship between
hunter-gatherer, herder and farming communities in South
Africa before the advent of colonialism, the extent and nature
of surplus production, and expropriation, the internal
stratification of pre-colonial societies and their increasing
linkage with the world economy from the seventeenth century
onwards. Until we have a clearer picture of all of this, we will
be unable to interpret aright the impact of the Dutch at the
Cape, the Voortrekkers in the interior, or the mining capitalists
on the Rand, and the social formations they created.

Perhaps this can be most clearly seen through a more recent
example. Until recently it has been held that labour migration
from south Mozambique to the goldfields of South Africa in the
late nineteenth century (when they constituted between a fifth
and a third of all mine labour) was solely to be attributed to
the Portuguese conquest of the territory and its labour
policies, and to the activities of the recruiting agency of the
Transvaal Chamber of Mines. Yet it would appear that
Mozambiquans, especially the Tsonga people, were migrating to
South Africa in search of work from the 1850s, long before there
was any effective Portuguese administrative presence in the
area. It is only now that we are beginning to learn more of the
social and political organisation of the Tsonga, the ecology of
the region, the impact of nineteenth-century invasions from
Zululand, the extent to which by the nineteenth century this
was already an area linked into the world economy and whose
social relations had already been transformed by that linkage,
that we can provide some insights into an explanation of the

phenomenon.

Or, to take an example even more germane to the nature of contemporary South African society - the differential experience of proletarianisation for Africans and Afrikaners in this century. Generally 'explained' in the liberal historiography as the product of 'racism' and purely at the level of ideology (Afrikaners became 'poor whites' because they had an aversion to manual labour, known as 'kaffir-work'; they were saved from the consequences of their idleness and ignorance by their access to the franchise because they were white; Africans have remained unskilled and poor because of the 'racism of the white working class' which blocked upward mobility for blacks, and so on), it is now increasingly clear that one of the crucial reasons for the differences lay in the very different division of labour within the families of black and white precapitalist farmers. The fact that in African society it was the women who did the agricultural work in the main meant that when the men were forced into town to earn money for taxes, they left their families behind in the countryside; when Afrikaners were displaced from the land as a result of the expansion of capitalist farming in this century, the women were amongst the first to move to the towns, for it was the able-bodied young men who were wanted for farm-work. The outright expropriation of Afrikaners compared to the continued access which Africans were to have - under the migrant labour system - to a diminishing amount of land was to have the profoundest consequences for class struggles and consciousness in twentieth-century South Africa.

This paper started by suggesting that the past few years had seen a major transformation in the nature and amount of historical research being done on South Africa. Needless to say, much remains to be done. In many ways the greatest challenges still remain. We now have a far better picture of the political economy of South Africa in the nineteenth and twentieth century, and of the world the mine-magnates made. By exploring the connections between this political economy and African culture and consciousness, we should be able now both to demolish the *apartheid* myth that there is no such thing as an African urban culture or an African working class, simply a migrant whose true consciousness lies in some mythical traditional past, rooted in some tribal homeland; and on the other, that the experience of capitalist development, apartheid and white power have been so brutal and traumatic that Africans have been totally helpless victims in the face of it, and could exercise no choices in the face of their powerlessness.

NOTES

1   I.D. MacCrone, *Race Attitudes in South Africa*, London 1937.
2   *Oxford History of South Africa*, ed. by M. Wilson and

L. Thompson, 2 vols, Oxford 1969 and 1971.
3 Maurice Godelier, 'The object and method of economic
   anthropology' in *Relations of Production*, ed. by D. Seddon,
   London 1978, p. 107.

FURTHER READING

It is impossible to do justice in a short bibliography to all the
topics touched upon above, but the following should provide
some introduction to the growing debate on South African
history.

Much of the early debate was reproduced in the *Collected
Papers of the Seminar on the Societies of South Africa in the
Nineteenth and Twentieth Centuries*, produced annually by the
Institute of Commonwealth Studies, London. A selection of the
nineteenth-century papers together with additional articles,
especially on the pre-capitalist social formations of South Africa
are included in S. Marks and A. Atmore, eds, *Economy and
Society in Pre-industrial South Africa*, London 1980.

Other influential articles on the nature of South Africa's
industrialisation were S. Trapido, 'South Africa in a
comparative study of industrialization', *Journal of Development
Studies*, 1972; H. Wolpe, 'Capitalism and cheap labour power
in South Africa: From segregation to apartheid', *Economy and
Society*, 1972; and a number of articles by Martin Legassick,
including 'The frontier tradition in South African
historiography' in S. Marks and A. Atmore, *Economy and
Society in Pre-industrial South Africa*, London 1980; 'South
Africa: capital accumulation and violence', *Economy and Society*,
1974; and 'Legislation, ideology and economy in post-1948
South Africa', *Journal of Southern African Studies*, 1974.

A key work analysing the relationship of class and race in
the mining industry on the Witwatersrand was F.A. Johnstone,
*Class, Race and Gold: A Study of Class Relations and Racial
Discrimination in South Africa*, London 1976. Some of the themes
in this have been taken up, refined and elaborated in Robert
H. Davies, *Capital, State and White Labour in South Africa,
1900-1960. An Historical Materialist Analysis of Class Formation
and Class Relations*, Brighton 1979, the first of the
Poulantzian-influenced Sussex work to be published. Much of
this deals with the nature of the South African state.

The capitalist transformation of the countryside has been
tackled by Colin Bundy in his pioneering work on the African
peasantry, *The Rise and Fall of the South African Peasantry*,
London 1979. This is being pursued further by a number of
scholars, some of whose work is included in the special agrarian
issue of the *Journal of Southern African Studies*, 1, 1978 (see
especially S. Trapido, 'Landlord and tenant in a colonial
economy: The Transvaal, 1880-1910' and the review article by
Terence Ranger). For the transformation of white agriculture,

see also M. Morris, 'The development of capitalism in southern African agriculture: class struggle in the countryside', *Economy and Society*, 1976.

Although it deals with the mines of Southern Rhodesia, Charles van Onselen's *Chibaro: African Mine Labour in Southern Rhodesia 1900-1933*, London 1976, was a milestone in the study of material conditions and worker consciousness in southern Africa. His more recent work is on a two-volume social history of Johannesburg to be published by Macmillan: it represents probably the most original social history being written in and about South Africa. Two readily accessible pieces from this collection are his 'Randlords and Rotgut, 1886-1903: an essay on the role of alcohol in the development of European imperialism and southern African capitalism', *History Workshop, Journal*, Autumn, 1976; and ' "The regiment of the hills": South Africa's lumpenproletarian army, 1890-1920', *Past and Present*, August 1978.

For attempts to look at the class forces underpinning Afrikaner and African nationalism, see two crucial articles (drawn from his PhD thesis, to be published soon), by Dan O'Meara, 'The Afrikaner Broederbond 1927-1948: class vanguard of Afrikaner nationalism', *Journal of Southern African Studies*, 1977, and 'Analysing Afrikaner Nationalism: The "Christian National" assault on white trade unionism in South Africa, 1934-48', *African Affairs*, 1978; and B. Willan, 'Sol Plaatje, de Beers and an old tramshed: class relations and social control in a South African town, 1918-19', *Journal of Southern African Studies*, 1978.

On the conquest of African societies and the role of imperialism, Shula Marks and Stanley Trapido, 'Milner and the South African State', *History Workshop Journal*, Autumn 1979; A. Atmore and Shula Marks, 'The imperial factor in South African history: Towards a reassessment', *Journal for Commonwealth and Imperial Studies*, 1974; and an important new book by Jeff Guy, *The Destruction of the Zulu kingdom*, London 1979.

37 SLAVERY IN PRE-COLONIAL AFRICA

Richard Rathbone*

The limp exchanges of a few, a very few, historians of Africa
on the subject of whether there was or was not slavery in
Africa independent of the Atlantic slave trade hardly deserves
the description of debate. For the most part its protagonists
have been either apologetic or polemical and the amount of
original research on the subject remains depressingly limited.
It is indeed a depressing subject, but ignoring it does not make
it go away and a better understanding of it would be of
assistance in understanding the complexity of pre-capitalist
social formations in Africa. Part of the understandable reticence
by historians has been occasioned by a hesitation to be
thought of as part of the tradition of Western apologists who
claim that the Atlantic trade merely latched on to an already
thriving local trade. A further inhibition has been more
intellectually reputable. The very terminology of 'slavery' and
'freedom' is unmistakeably part of the Western tradition. For
this reason the heavily juridical definitional approach of Hindess
and Hirst, and Miers and Kopytoff, with an insistence on
concepts like 'rights' which may not be appropriate in the
special circumstances of Africa,[1] make scholars edgy. When the
documents talk of 'slaves', do they really mean slaves or are
they describing very different sorts of relationships? It is for
this reason that the exhaustive recent work of John Fage, for
example,[2] ranging through all the extant European sources
which describe West African society before the nineteenth
century needs to be constantly questioned.
   The much more exciting exchanges between French
anthropologists,[3] and particularly the work of Claude
Meillassoux[4] can be used to provide historians with a framework
and, implicitly, something close to a definition of slavery which
works in the variety of African contexts. Such work is, of
course, highly schematic, and provides us with models and not
descriptions of reality. We can with such insights approach the
sources asking rather different sorts of questions and hopefully
we can emerge with greater knowledge of pre-capitalist political
economy.
   The starting point is the ideal type of the African self-
subsistent society. There is much debate over the appropriate
delimitation of the 'lineage' of the 'African' mode of production
but its basic qualities are clear enough. Normatively we are

*Richard Rathbone teaches at the School of Oriental and African
Studies, London.

talking about social formations in which fundamental needs are appropriated from nature in a very direct fashion. In terms of process the technology is far from complex, and the hoe, rather than the plough and animal draught, is dominant. Such a social formation can produce only as much as can be generated by the maximisation of styles and co-operation. And as muscle power is the primary force of production, the quantity and quality of labour is crucial to levels of production. As Meillassoux points out these are not social formations which are innocent of exchange or the division of labour, but such as are governed by relations of a reciprocal kind rather than factors of market exchange. Market exchange remains, normatively, marginal for such social formations in terms of internal relations and, perhaps less plausibly, in terms of external transactions.

Despite the palpable variety of such formations the African evidence is vocal on two points, one of which the scholarship follows, and the other which it does not. First, they are organised along complex and varied kinship principles. Second, they are organised along lines of sexual demarcation and division of labour. And because of the nature of such social formations it is clear that 'growth' is possible only through population increase in absolute terms.

In an ideal world the labourer would appropriate his product. But in such social formations at least some of the surplus is 'controlled' by senior members of the lineage – the elders and chiefs – whilst the young men and the women bend their backs. Again there is a lively debate as to whether this constitutes 'exploitation'. This is not the place to echo the thrust of *Padre, Padrone* (or to deny it) but Meillassoux favours an alternative view. The surplus is 'administered' and not accumulated by the 'elders'. The direct producers therefore can expect to reappropriate it as they move on, and hence, up the lineage with age. Moreover the surplus is used, to some extent, in a redistributive fashion. It provides younger males with wives for example through the payment of 'bride-wealth'. The contract with the young is that they in time will be able to enjoy access to the surplus generated by their own children. Women's share in this process is shadowy in the extreme.

Given that the ancients will want to accumulate, how can they go about it? They can do so only by direct exploitation and that can only emerge when part of the social formation is denied room on the upward escalator of the kinship system whilst still performing the role of producers. Meillassoux points out that the most convenient way of achieving this end would be to prevent in-marriage. Through the denial of a wife the coterminous and parallel cycles of production and reproduction would be ripped apart. Whilst such treatment can be meted out to some parts of the social collectivity – to those deemed deviant, for example – such practice on any wide scale would amount to social suicide. If the kinship structure is to survive then there are clear limits to the extent to which the elders can so act.

The elders need have no such inhibitions about outsiders, of course. In this area Meillassoux sees the intrusion of slavery as a totally understandable mode of exploitation. In order to explain an apparent regularity in much of the African material he sees this as a doubly exploitative relationship. First, and reasonably obviously, it is exploitative in that the slave himself or herself is exploited. That is, his or her labour is unrewarded because of his or her exclusion from the lineage structure. The slaves' surplus labour feeds very directly into the lineage but being a slave implicitly means that the surplus generated by his or her children belongs to the 'master' and not to him. Lineage authority is denied the slave. As Meillassoux says their 'outsider' quality excludes them from the cycle of reproduction, but uses them solely in the cycle of production.

But the second area of exploitation is less obvious. It has some explanatory force in enabling us to understand better the frequency of observed absorption into society of slave-born after a lapse of time, in Africa. The first-generation slave in the manner of his transfer (capture for the most part) is a stolen object - stolen from a social formation that has invested much in his/her upbringing. And all that social labour embodied in the capacity of any human being to perform human tasks is transferred as social wealth into the social formation that enslaves him or her.

It follows, of course, that the reproduction costs of any second-generation slaves cannot be so evaded by the enslaving society. They must be communally borne if the slave-child is to be kept alive and socialised, and such costs are probably identical to those involved in bringing a free child to adolescence. Consequently a slave child can only be exploited or be an object of exploitation in the first fashion. From the point of view of the free lineage, the exploiters, they constitute a markedly less valuable addition to the total community. This might go some way towards explaining the frequently observed improvement in the position of the second and third generation of second-generation slaves, which has tended to be accounted for by arguments about either the superior humanity of Africa or a mechanistic response to demographic sparseness.

But such also implies that there is a positive bar to the internal reproduction of slave relations within such 'auto-subsistent' social formations. Only by recourse to continual new slave acquisition can such relations be perpetuated. Meillassoux argues that the emergence over time of formations that are notable for slave appropriation and formations that are condemned to producing slaves confirms this judgment.

There are many unresolved problems in such analysis. The failure to integrate the significance of the sexual division of labour has already been mentioned and remains a research priority in all periods of African history. This lacuna is one that Meillassoux is acutely aware of. Similarly, there is a tendency in such analysis to gloss the powerful differences between social and biological reproduction of slave populations. It may also be felt that the analysis sets up an unnecessary tension when it is forced to confront the undoubted existence of slave formations in Africa that are 'self-reproducing'. Lastly, but not exhaustively finally, there is scant attention to the problematic of the articulation of slave formations with modes of production that are not usefully translated as 'lineage' or 'African' modes. Nonetheless, it is an analysis that is at worst suggestive and controversial, and at best suggests new ways of looking at a very difficult area of pre-capitalist Africa.

NOTES

1   Barry Hindess and Paul Hirst, *Pre-capitalist Modes of Production*, London 1975. Especially their chapter on the 'Slave mode of production'. Suzanne Miers and Igor Kopytoff, *Slavery in Africa*, Wisconsin 1977. Especially the editors' introduction.
2   Unpublished paper given to the African History Seminar, School of Oriental and African Studies, October 1979.
3   The wealth of this material is considerable. For the purposes of this note the most useful and accessible are: E. Terray, *Marxism and Primitive Societies*, London 1972; C. Meillassoux, 'The political economy of the hunting band' in *French Perspectives in African Studies*, ed. by P. Alexandre, London 1973; C. Meillassoux, 'From reproduction to production', *Economy and Society*, 1, no. 1, Feb. 1972; C. Meillassoux, 'The social organisation of the peasantry: The economic basis of kinship', *Journal of Peasant Studies*, 1, no. 1, Oct. 1973; C. Coquery-Vidrovitch, 'The political economy of the African peasantry and modes of production' in *The Political Economy of Contemporary Africa*, ed. by P. Gutkind and I. Wallerstein, New York 1977; G. Dupre and P.-P. Rey, 'Reflections on the pertinence of a theory of the history of exchange', *Economy and Society*, 2, no. 2, 1973; P.-P. Rey, 'The lineage mode of production', *Critique of Anthropology*, 3, Spring 1973; B. Bradby, 'The destruction of natural economy', *Economy and Society*, 4, no. 2, May 1975; A. Foster-Carter, 'The modes of production controversy', *New Left Review*, 107, Jan./Feb. 1978; and E. Terray, 'Long distance exchange and the formation of the state', *Economy and Society*, 3, no. 3, August 1974.
4   And now his exciting reflections in *Dialectiques*, 21, 1978.

FURTHER READING

Bloch, M. (ed.), *Marxist Analyses and Social Anthropology*, Oxford 1975.

Bradby, B., 'The destruction of natural economy', *Economy
   and Society*, 4, no. 2, May 1975.
Godelier, M., 'Structure and contradiction in capital', *The
   Socialist Register*, 1967.
Godelier, M., *Rationality and Irrationality in Economics*, London,
   1972.
Seddon, D. (ed.), *Relationships of Production: Marxist
   approaches to economic anthropology*, London 1978.

38 HOW NOT TO BE A MARXIST HISTORIAN: THE ALTHUSSERIAN THREAT TO AFRICAN HISTORY

Robin Law*

In a recent review article, published in the *Journal of African
History* (vol. 19, 1978), I suggested that it was possible to
discern a growing (or perhaps impending) wave of Marxist
influence in the study of the history of sub-Saharan Africa
during the pre-colonial period. Further portents of this wave
have since accumulated: for example, a programmatic statement
of the supposed character of a Marxist history of Africa and its
relationship to existing historiography published in the
methodological journal *History in Africa*[1] and, more concretely,
an analysis of the 'mode of production' of the Central African
Lozi kingdom (classified as feudal, more or less) published in
the *Journal of African History*.[2]
   Historians of Africa, whether calling themselves Marxists or
not, ought to welcome this growth of Marxist influence, since it
helps to focus attention on a crucial but so far inadequately
studied set of issues, relating to the relationship between
technology, social structure, political institutions and ideology
in the indigenous societies of pre-colonial Africa – though it is
as well to remember that important contributions to discussion
of these issues have been made by scholars not classifiable as
Marxists (for example, Goody and Hopkins). There is, however,
cause for concern in that there are signs that 'Marxism' is being
imported into pre-colonial African history predominantly in a
form derived from the work of Louis Althusser. The
programmatic article by Bernstein and Depelchin, for example,
adopts an explicitly and indeed aggressively Althusserian

*Robin Law teaches at Stirling University, Scotland.

posture. More generally, it appears that historians of Africa interested in the application of Marxist theory to their subject are turning primarily (naturally enough) to the principal published attempt at a comprehensive treatment of Marxist thought on pre-capitalist societies, that by Hindess and Hirst:[3] this is, for example, the only work of Marxist theory directly cited in Clarence-Smith's study of the Lozi kingdom. And Hindess and Hirst also, despite differences from Althusser, adopt an essentially Althusserian approach to the study of history.

Althusser's version of Marxism presents a number of severe problems of application for the historian, as has been demonstrated in the recently published polemic against it by Thompson[4] – a work which ought to be compulsory reading for all aspirant Marxist historians of Africa. The point is not the degree to which Althusser revises or departs from the thought of Marx himself: as John Peel has recently observed 'whether a historian inspired by but developing Marx's thought remains properly Marxist' is 'a question of no serious intellectual importance whatsoever'.[5] The real threat of Althusserian Marxism is represented by its particular conception of the relationship between Marxist theory and the analysis of historical data, which necessarily involves dogmatism and bibliolatry.

Althusser, faithfully followed by Hindess and Hirst and by Bernstein and Depelchin, insists on the primacy of theory. They polemicise against 'empiricism', rejecting the idea that there are any 'facts' given independently of theorisation. Marxism has a distinctive theoretical framework, or 'problematic' – defined by Althusser as 'a systematically interrelated set of concepts'.[6] These concepts are not, as one might suppose, constructed by abstraction from empirical data; they are in some sense prior to empirical data. 'Facts' can only be apprehended through the mediation of concepts, and it is the problematic which determines the content and significance of the 'facts'. 'Facts' are therefore not *given* independently of theorisation, but *produced* by it. Althusser and Bernstein and Depelchin believe that it is meaningful to apply the Marxist problematic to the study of history, though in ways not very clearly specified or illustrated; Hindess and Hirst, however, carry Althusser's anti-empiricism to its logical conclusion and separate Marxist theory from history altogether – 'The field of application of these concepts is not history. We reject the notion of history as a coherent and worthwhile object of study'.[7] These statements should be taken seriously: historians of Africa need to confront the implications of these theoretical postures if they wish to apply Althusserian Marxism in their own work.

Bernstein and Depelchin declare, on p. 1 of their article, that historical method 'necessarily starts with the correct posing of questions'. But which are the correct questions? Althusserian Marxism necessarily involves the assumption that these are given in the texts of Marx, or at least those of them judged acceptable. As is explicitly stated in the translator's glossary to Althusser's works (endorsed by Althusser himself): 'The problems of Marxist theory (or of any other theory) can only be solved by learning to read the texts correctly.' This immediately raises the further question of which is the 'correct' reading of Marx's texts, a problem which is compounded by Althusser's explicit acknowledgment that his 'symptomatic' reading involves not merely accepting what Marx actually said, but reconstructing what he ought to have said – going beyond the text to the 'discourse of the silence' behind it.[8] But in any case, how do we know that what Marx said (or what Althusser says he really meant, although he didn't quite say it) is 'correct'? It might be supposed that Marxist theory is correct because (or as far as) it helps to make sense of the data. This was the view, for example, of Lenin, in one of his rare moments of theoretical lucidity: Marxism was 'scientifically proven', or at least more satisfactory than any alternative theory on offer, because of its success (in Marx's *Capital*) in 'introducing order into the "pertinent facts" ' (*What the 'Friends of the People' are and How They Fight the Social Democrats*). But this view is explicitly rejected by Althusser: according to him, Marx's theory is not 'true' because it can be successfully applied, but can be successfully applied because it is 'true'.[9] Bernstein and Depelchin likewise pour scorn on the procedure of 'counterfactualisation', that is the appeal to facts as the test of the validity of a theory. And Hindess and Hirst assert that their accounts of the Marxist concepts appropriate to pre-capitalist modes of production 'cannot be refuted by any empiricist recourse to the supposed "facts" of history'.[10] Yet no other criterion is offered in place of 'counterfactualisation': Marxism is presented as self-confirming, it is true because it says it is.

Related to this is the assertion that a 'problematic' is self-contained, and that discussion between people applying different problematics is effectively impossible. Since it is the problematic which produces its own 'facts', each problematic has its own different facts, and there is no common ground between them. Indeed, different problematics are not studying the same subjects at all (despite appearances), since each constitutes its own object of study. Marx and Weber, for example, 'do not provide different interpretations of the same process, the rise of capitalism': they used different problematic and therefore study different objects.[11]

Althusserian Marxism thus produces a version of Marxism which replicates all the dogmatic features conventionally ascribed to it by anti-Marxists: the veneration of texts, the repudiation of disconfirmatory facts, and the insistence that one must accept Marxist theory before being able to discuss it. Is this really the sort of Marxism which will advance historical studies in Africa?

The only way out of the Althusserian impasse is to

rehabilitate the notion of the historical 'fact'. It is quite true
that, as the Althusserians insist, 'facts' do not exist
independently of theory; but equally, as the Althusserians are
unwilling to acknowledge, theory does not originate
independently of the 'facts'. The relationship between the two
is, to use the approved jargon, dialectical; historical study
involves, as Thompson stresses, a *dialogue* between theory and
fact, between concept and evidence. And within this dialectic
primacy must belong to the facts. What is claimed for the facts,
it should be stressed, is not any 'absolute givenness' (such as
the Althusserians in effect claim for theory), but rather a
'relative independence'.[12] It is this relative independence of
the facts which makes it possible (as experience demonstrates,
in spite of its theoretical impossibility according to Althusserian
precept) for historians operating within different 'problematics'
to achieve in practice an often considerable degree of
agreement on 'the facts', if not on their interpretation: it is
this which makes possible a measure of meaningful argument (if
not of agreement) between, for example, Marxist and non-
Marxist historians. And it is this relative independence of the
facts which accounts for the possibility (again, frequently
observed in practice) of a historian modifying or even
abandoning a theory in the face of awkward data. Marxist
theory, like any other, is 'correct' only in so far as it makes
sense of the evidence, and must be modified or abandoned in so
far as it does not.

These points apply to all fields of history, but they are
perhaps especially crucial for the history of Africa. Marxist
theory was devised with reference to the capitalist societies of
Western Europe; even if they are regarded as wholly
satisfactory for the analysis of these societies, it cannot follow
that they will be equally appropriate in the analysis of others.
Too often Marxist writers on Africa, even those not entangled
within the Althusserian epistemological maze, proceed by
assuming what is in fact at issue, namely the validity of Marxist
theory. Thus Terray defines the task of Marxist
anthropologists as 'bringing the field so far reserved for social
anthropology within the ambit of historical materialism, and thus
demonstrating the universal validity of the concepts and methods
developed by the latter':[13] why not rather *finding out whether*
these concepts and methods will work in non-capitalist societies?
Marxists dispute each other's analyses regularly in terms of
orthodoxy rather than of plausibility: thus, Terray condemns
Coquery-Vidrovitch's attempt to delineate an 'African mode of
production' in which the ruling group's position depends upon
the control of long-distance trade on the grounds that we know
(from volume III of *Capital*) that relations of distribution are
secondary and relations of production primary;[14] while Hindess
and Hirst condemn Terray and Meillassoux for allegedly taking
the productive forces as the determinant element in a mode of
production, whereas we know (from Althusser's reading of

Marx) that the relations of production are dominant. This is all, surely, quite irrelevant: what matters is not how faithfully historians cleave to Marx's position (supposing we could agree on what that was), but how far their analyses are convincing.

It is clear, in any case, that Marx's texts do not in fact provide aspirant Marxist historians with a clear conceptual framework for the analysis of African societies. If, as is often asserted, the fundamental concept of Marxist theory is that of 'mode of production', then Marxist theory is built upon a very ill-defined and perhaps incoherent foundation (as Hindess and Hirst perhaps recognise by abandoning the concept of 'mode of production' altogether in their *Auto-critique*[15] – a publication apparently unnoticed by Clarence-Smith and others who continue to draw upon the earlier work of Hindess and Hirst without comment). The 'mode of production', it is generally agreed, comprises some sort of combination of the 'forces of production' and the 'relations of production'. The Althusserians claim to know that the relations of production are the dominant element in this combination, but this is difficult to square with Marx's conception of 'social revolution' as arising through the conflict between developing forces of production and existing relations of production, and an interpretation of Marx as arguing the primacy of the productive forces is equally if not more convincing, as two recent publications have shown.[16] But even if we could resolve this, there is considerable doubt about what the concepts 'forces' and 'relations of production' in fact designate. We can distinguish the material elements involved in production, the material or technical relations of production (or work relations), and the social relations of production (comprising both relations of control or ownership, and the mode of appropriation of the surplus product): but where do the material relations of production belong – with the productive forces (according to the Althusserians) or with the relations of production (as argued by Shaw) or with neither (as argued by Cohen)? The debate cannot be settled, as the Althusserians suggest, by 'reading the texts'; and even supposing it could, this would not get us very far, for there remains the problem of whether the concepts will 'work' in practice. If it is true, for example, that Meillassoux's analysis of Guro society suggests 'an arbitrary and contingent variation' of the relations of production relative to the forces of production,[17] this may perhaps be because Meillassoux has not understood Marx's theory; but it may also be because Marx's theory does not 'work' in the case of (i.e. it does not satisfactorily account for the nature of) Guro society. Engels claimed that the proofs of Marxist theory had been found in the study of history (*Ludwig Feuerbach and the End of Classical German Philosophy*); if we are to avoid an arid dogmatism, we must at least acknowledge the possibility that the disproofs may be found there also.

NOTES

1 H. Bernstein and J. Depelchin, 'The object of African
  history: A materialist perspective', *History in Africa*, 5,
  1978, pp. 1–19 and 6, 1979, pp. 17–43.
2 W.G. Clarence-Smith, 'Slaves, commoners and landlords in
  Bulozi, c. 1875 to 1906', *Journal of African History*, 20,
  1979, pp. 219–34.
3 B. Hindess and P.Q. Hirst, *Pre-capitalist Modes of
  Production*, London 1975.
4 E.P. Thompson, *The Poverty of Theory*, London 1979.
5 J.D.Y. Peel, 'Two cheers for empiricism', *Sociology*, 12,
  no. 2, 1978, pp. 347–58.
6 L. Althusser, *For Marx*, London 1977 edn, originally
  published in 1969.
7 Hindess and Hirst, *op. cit.*
8 L. Althusser, *Reading Capital*, London 1970.
9 *Ibid.*
10 Hindess and Hirst, *op. cit.*
11 Bernstein and Depelchin, *op. cit.*, p. 10.
12 Peel, *op. cit.*, p. 354.
13 E. Terray, *Marxism and 'Primitive' Societies*, London 1972,
  p. 184.
14 E. Terray, 'Long-distance exchange and the formation of
  the state: The case of the Abron kingdom of Gyaman',
  Economy and Society, 3, no. 3, 1974, p. 340.
15 B. Hindess and P.Q. Hirst, *Mode of Production and Social
  Formation: An Auto-critique*, London 1977.
16 W.H. Shaw, *Marx's Theory of History*, London 1978, and
  G.A. Cohen, *Karl Marx's Theory of History*, Oxford 1978.
17 Hindess and Hirst, *Pre-capitalist Modes of Production*, p. 12.

FURTHER READING

Althusser, Louis, *For Marx*, London 1977 edn.
Althusser, Louis, *Reading Capital*, London 1970.
Bernstein, Henry and Depelchin, Jacques, 'The object of
  African history: A materialist perspective', *History in
  Africa*, 2 parts, vols 5, 1978, pp. 1–19, and 6, 1979,
  pp. 17–43.
Clarence-Smith, W.G., 'Slaves, commoners and landlords in
  Bulozi, c.1875 to 1906', *Journal of African History*, 20,
  1979, pp. 219–34.
Cohen, G.A., *Karl Marx's Theory of History*, Oxford 1978.
Goody, Jack, *Technology, Tradition and the State in Africa*,
  International African Institute, 1971.
Goody, Jack, *Production and Reproduction*, Cambridge 1976.
Hindess, Barry, and Hirst, Paul Q., *Pre-Capitalist Modes of
  Production*, London 1975.
Hindess, Barry and Hirst, Paul Q., *Mode of Production and*

Social Formation: An Auto-critique, London 1977.
Hopkins, A.G., *An Economic History of West Africa*, London 1973.
Law, Robin, 'In search of a Marxist perspective on pre-colonial tropical Africa', *Journal of African History*, 19, 1978, pp. 441-52.
Peel, J.D.Y., 'Two cheers for empiricism', *Sociology*, 12, no. 2, 1978, pp. 347-58.
Shaw, William H., *Marx's Theory of History*, London 1978.
Terray, Emmanuel, *Marxism and 'Primitive' Societies*, London 1972.
Terray, Emmanuel, 'Long-distance exchange and the formation of the state: the case of the Abron kingdom of Gyaman', *Economy and Society*, 3, no. 3, 1974, pp. 315-45.
Thompson, E.P., *The Poverty of Theory*, London 1979.

Labour history

Royden Harrison*

Both Beatrice and Sidney Webb held high public office. However, their importance lies, on the one hand, in their achievement as founders of long-lasting institutions (the Fabian Society, the LSE, the re-constructed Labour Party, the *New Statesman* and the *Political Quarterly*) and on the other, as writers and publicists. They wrote literally hundreds of books and major articles, separately or together. Among them the classic *History of English Local Government*, the *History of Trade Unionism* and *Industrial Democracy*.

The Webbs were the founders of British Labour Historiography. Until their publications of the 1890s British labour history had been left to foreign observers (Engels, Comte de Paris, Brentano) or else to chroniclers, sometimes quite astute, of specific moments, movements or institutions.

Why did they embark on their work? Beatrice was studying co-operation and was alarmed by its rivalries and conflicts with trade-unionism. Sidney was deeply impressed by the Great Dock Strike of 1889 which suggested to him a relevance for socialism which he had hitherto not suspected. From these starting points the Webbs sought to bring socialism and trade unionism into new relationships with each other both in theory and in practice: they were active in the Labour Movement while they were engaged in their literary work. By shaping a view of the past they intended to help transform the future. Of course they intended to do this 'scientifically', i.e. their own preferences and recommendations were to be made to emerge as the necessary outcome of 'Experience' - whether they did or could is the great question. The Webbs aspired to be the chroniclers or clerks or advisers of working people whether they were *writing* their history or whether they were trying to *make* it as in *To Your Tents O Israel*, or when drafting for Tom Mann the *Report from the Whole Trade Union Minority on the Royal Commission on Labour*.

How did they try to write history? What *techniques* did they use distinct from *methods*? Beatrice saw herself as the inspirer

---

*Royden Harrison is director of the Centre for Social History, Warwick University. Co-editor of the *Bulletin* of the Society for the Study of Labour History. Author of *Before the Socialists*, London 1965, he has been engaged for many years on a life of the Webbs.

The report of the discussion is by Barbara Caine.

who began their books and Sidney as the workhorse who
finished them.

Their *method* was *not* to start from the basic economic and
demographic facts. Rather they preferred their own organising
insights into Man as an animal who shapes and is shaped by
institutions. This gave them their definition of a trade union
and their chronology. They exclude ad hoc if not hermit crab
unionism. As for the chronology it was structured around the
inter-related themes of trade unions and government and the
government of trade unions. Little or nothing before the 'Age
of Repression': then the 'Years of Revolutionary Expectations',
then the 'New Model' and, finally, the 'Advent of the New
Unionism'.

How this was supposed to be related to 'theory' and to policy
was only fully disclosed in their *Industrial Democracy*. They
used that term in three distinct but inter-related senses. It
was, first of all, a homage to proletarian culture, a culture
which was on the point of making – with the help of Sidney
and Beatrice – certain important discoveries about itself and
about its possible and desirable futures. Within their
pre-eminently political conceptual framework the Webbs made an
advance on all the hitherto existing literature on the role of
'Civil Servants'. They anticipated (and improved upon) the
conclusions of Italian sociology, respecting the cruel irony of
the labour leader. They offered a conception of what a labour
leader should be which broke the dichotomy between the notions
of a 'representative' and a 'delegate'. They simultaneously
stimulated and armed Bernstein and Lenin.

What are the main lines of criticism of the Webbs and how are
these criticisms to be evaluated?

(i) Their organising insight was the wrong one. (Perhaps, but
was anything else possible in England at the time? Anyway was
it unrewarding?)

(ii) Their spirit was patronising. (Consistently so? Critics from
this stable are sometimes tainted with ouvrièrism and
romanticism.)

(iii) Their chronology was defective. They started too late:
made too many concessions to Carlyle's interpretation of history
(over-estimating great men like Francis Place). They neglected
continuities and were responsible for the 'myth' of the New
Model Unionism. (Perhaps, but some of these critics are not
very critical. Some of the findings of recent research
strengthens the Webbs and shows that the revisionists
themselves need to be revised.)

(iv) They made lots of mistakes in detail. (Why yes! But not
nearly as many mistakes as might have been expected given the
pioneering nature of their undertaking.)

DISCUSSION

The first session in the Labour History section of the Workshop
was an interesting and stimulating one – despite its
uncomfortable setting in the chilly, dilapidated and somewhat
forbidding interior of St Paul's. Royden Harrison's paper was
amusing and informative and the discussion that followed was
wide-ranging and spirited.

In his paper Royden Harrison interpreted the 'making' of the
History in a very broad sense and discussed the Webbs'
marriage and relationship, their working habits and their use of
research assistants rather than the detailed work which went
into this particular book. He stressed the importance of the
notion of committees in the Webbs' *History of Trade Unionism*,
and in their life and work generally and pointed to their
marriage as the ultimate committee involving, especially from
Sydney, the kind of renunciation and dedication to collective
work and decision-making which was so fundamental to his
social thought. The central concern of the paper was to capture
the life and work of the Webbs in its entirety and in the
context of their time. Royden Harrison acknowledged the
limitations of their treatment of trade unions, especially their
overemphasis on institutions, but insisted on the recognition of
their merits and their contribution to contemporary
understanding of political and social processes. Their discovery
of the role of the Civil Service, as influencing and even making
policy, rather than just carrying out, was important here as
was their understanding of the nature and the problems of
labour leadership. It was the Webbs who first pointed to the
cruel irony in the position of the labour leader who, while
engaged in acquiring the necessary skills and contacts to carry
on his job, loses his links with the movement he represents. At
a theoretical level, they also made a major contribution by
breaking through the existing dichotomy between delegates and
representatives. They pointed to the labour leader as someone
who was neither simply a delegate putting forward the views of
his members nor a representative in Burke's sense, but as one
who, on the one hand put forward the views of his members
and, on the other, was a genuine leader engaged in discussions
with and persuasion of those members. In his concluding
remarks, Royden Harrison looked at the various criticisms made
of the Webbs and stressed the importance of keeping criticism
in proportion and of tempering it with the respect due to a
'great ruin'.

Despite this, criticism of the Webbs was the dominant note
in the discussion and Royden Harrison, while pointing to the
problems faced by a biographer who does not wish to be an
apologist, was largely engaged in defending the Webbs against
the familiar charges of elitism, authoritarianism and an
overemphasis on the role of experts.

The most interesting issue raised related to the Webbs' ideas

on leadership. Stuart Hall introduced this by pointing to the
different ways in which it had been taken up. For Lenin, who
was possibly influenced by the Webbs here, the need to
supersede the opposition between the delegate and the
representative involved making the central point in leadership
an educative relationship between delegates and the masses.
This was a key point in class formation. But in capitalist states
there was a quite different development. Here delegates and
representatives were superseded by the use of experts and
their relationship with the masses was a disciplinary rather
than an educative one. Hall argued that the Webbs themselves
had been very ambiguous as to which of these alternatives they
actually favoured and it was this which made them such
controversial figures within socialist thought. Logie Barrow
extended this by pointing to the crisis in trade union
leadership in the 1880s and 1890s, especially within the
engineering union. The hostility to union leaders and officials
evident amongst rank and file was echoed in socialist groups
and publications like the *Clarion* which denounced
representatives and praised delegates. He had the impression
from this that there was no coherent conception of leadership
amongst rank and file and no clear idea as to how to form a
more satisfactory organisation. He and other speakers pointed
to the inadequacy of the Webbs' analysis of the relationship
between leaders and rank and file. Royden Harrison accepted
that this was a problem within the Webbs' thought – and
insisted that it still needed much research and clarification. He
agreed that the Webbs overestimated the role and ability of
leaders and underestimated that of the rank and file, but
insisted that for the Webbs the relationship between the two
was a dynamic one in which leaders learnt from rank and file.
     The actual making of the *History* was illuminated in the
discussion in response to comments from Bill Pritchard and
Stirling Smith about the Webbs' elitism. Royden Harrison
argued that the Webbs were not as authoritarian or as elitist as
is usually thought. They were very interested in proletarian
culture but were unable, in the context of the 1880s, to get in
touch with the whole of the working class. David Goodway
supported this view and pointed to the differences between the
manuscript of the *History of Trade Unionism* and the final
version. In the manuscript, there is much information about
rank and file gathered through interviews, discussions and
detailed questionnaires which the Webbs had sent to officials
of small trade clubs seeking information about the lives of their
members. He argued that it was not possible to use this
information in the 1890s as there was no coherent framework for
it. Moreover, it was an institutional history that was needed
then. But here as elsewhere the defence of the Webbs was
queried. Jonathan Zeitlin argued that one had to see the
Webbs' selection of material as an interpretation and a judgment
– a fairly good judgment, but one which represented the

Webbs' view.

The importance for the Webbs of the intellectual and social developments of the 1880s and 1890s received considerable attention. The influence on the Webbs of Comte and Spencer, the relationship between their approach and the general shift in interest from economics to sociology in the late Victorian period were all mentioned. The importance for the Webbs of the upsurge in trade union activity in the late 1880s was emphasised – indeed it was this which first made Sydney see trade unions as worthy of serious attention. Here, as in his paper, Royden Harrison emphasised the fact that the Webbs were the only socialists who offered a viable relationship between socialism and trade unions and, moreover, that they alone saw an important role for unions in a future socialist state.

In the final moments of the discussion attention returned to the marital and domestic life of the Webbs. Alice Kessler Harris raised the question of how the Webbs came to decide on 'books instead of babies' and whether there was any tension in their lives as a result of this. Royden Harrison saw this as Beatrice's decision accepted by the 'selfless' Sydney. He commented on Beatrice's complete incapacity for domestic life and the conflicts she faced as a woman trying to live the life of a man in late Victorian society. He agreed that her ideas on this, as on feminism in general, were very complex – as one would expect from one who was so very much a 'divided self'.

One felt at the end that the critics of the Webbs had not really been convinced, but that the whole session demonstrated the degree of interest that currently exists in them and in their work.

40 RUHR MINERS AND THEIR HISTORIANS

Franz-Josef Brüggemeier*

The history of the Ruhr miners offers all the characteristics labour historians usually dream of: huge strike movements in

---

*Franz-Josef Brüggemeier was born and bred in the Ruhr and is now researching at Essen University.

The report of the discussion has been written by John Field.

1889, 1905, 1912 and 1918-19, the latter culminating in a four-week long strike with more than 300,000 miners taking part and demanding that the mines should be socialised and run by a *Räte-System* (soviet-system). As a consequence of the reactionary *Kapp-Putsch* in 1920, a 'red army' came into existence, which virtually controlled the Ruhr area, though it was later on defeated by the *Reichswehr* and the 'free corps'. Furthermore, the area experienced an enormous growth; from 1880 to 1910 the number of miners alone rose from 80,000 to 345,000, and there were places like Hamborn, which had a population of just over 4,000 in 1890 but more than 100,000 in 1910. The new inhabitants had migrated over long distances, approximately half came from the eastern Prussian provinces, a considerable number being Polish. In addition, there were many workers from the Netherlands, Austria, Hungary, Italy and Russia. Their mobility didn't stop after arriving at the Ruhr district; in 1904, for example, when there were some 275,000 miners in the Ruhr, the mining companies registered 150,000 people taking up work and 133,000 leaving it.

Contemporaries found these developments alarming. They were afraid of the great number of miners, the high proportion of foreign workers (the Poles, for example, though they were Prussian citizens); the solidarity and strength they showed in their strikes, their high mobility, which seemed to allow them to escape political and social control. These fears generated an impressive number of articles, books and investigations on the plight of the miners. The writers complained of the harsh treatment in the mines, the low wages, and the miserable housing conditions. The two most impressive books on the miners, covering their history from the Middle Ages onwards, were written by the leader of the socialist and of the Christian trade union O. Hue (1910) and C. Imbusch (1908) respectively. From the beginning, the employers had their point of view published, but they couldn't prevent themselves being regarded as villains.

This picture changed in the Weimar period. The strikes in 1918-19 and especially the red army in 1920 were seen as a threat to the young republic, all the more so, since the Communist Party attracted a large local following. In a typical mining community like Bottrop, both the Communist and the Catholic Party received about 40 per cent of the vote each, with the SPD rarely exceeding 10 per cent. H. Spethmann's book of 1928, a philippic against the workers, found a sympathetic readership. It stressed the role played by the employers in defending the state against the assaults of the miners, a task, which, as the employers saw it, had never been fully appreciated, but which was to bring them honour and influence in the Third Reich.

The relation between the miners and the unions and the political parties had never been an easy one. In 1889, when some 90,000 of them (approx. 85-90 per cent of all miners and

almost 98 per cent of the ones working underground) went on
strike, there existed no union; by 1905, when 220,000 took part
in the strike, there existed three unions: a socialist, a Catholic,
and a Polish union, and in addition to these a rather small
liberal one. All of them originally opposed the strike and
agitated against it as they regarded their own organisation as
being too weak. Only after the strike had broken out and
rapidly spread, did they give it support. The demands to
socialise the mines and the ensuing strike in 1919 were also
bitterly opposed by the unions, which antagonised a part of the
miners to the extent that the socialist union and especially the
SPD, which was blamed for defeating the movement, lost heavily
in influence to the communists. Even the communists, though,
despite the support they gained in the Ruhr, complained of not
being able to establish party discipline among their followers.

Generally, the miners are blamed for these uneasy
relationships. It is argued that their high mobility, the
difficulties they experienced in having to adjust to industrial
life, the harsh treatment in the mines and their overall
unsatisfactory living conditions made them explode once in a
while, without them being able to show the discipline and
self-control necessary for a powerful union. This argument
seems to fit the facts so well and it is so persuasive that it had
been generally accepted by historians; what has changed over
the last twenty-five years is the political evaluation of the
miners' movements. In 1958 Peter Oertzen published an article
arguing that the socialisation of the mines - if extended to other
industries - would have offered a 'third way', which would have
altered the power structure of the Weimar system thereby
giving it a more viable basis.

With regard to living and working conditions, however, he
accepted the conventional picture of social disorganisation. The
same holds true for the post-1968 historians of the 'other'
working class (K.H. Roth, E. Brockhaus) who are very much
influenced by the Italian 'workerist' historians S. Bologna and
M. Cacciceri. Adopting a very crude materialism, they describe
an even more sinister picture of the living conditions only to
let the miners rise later on like a phoenix out of the ashes into
the more glamourous sphere of revolutionary action, claiming to
have found the long-lost revolutionary subject at last.
Conservative interpretations, on the other hand, stress that
workers living under such bad conditions are not likely to form
the basis of a politically conscious movement, and they therefore
deny that the miners' movements of 1919 had any far-reaching
political implications.

This basically political discussion could have continued
unresolved for a long time, if two important books had not been
published over the last three years. The first one, by K.
Tenfelde, analyses in great detail the social conditions of the
Ruhr miners from approximately 1800-90 and develops an
argumentation similar to the one put forward in R. Harrison's

The Independent Collier, though there are, of course, differences in tradition, developments and tendencies. He argues that the miners had some definite notion of having experienced a better time before the unimpeded capitalist exploitation set in after the 1850s and 1860s. For a long time, this notion made them direct their complaints to the Prussian king, who had been the head of a corporatively (*ständisch*) organised mining industry until the 1850s. They soon learned that they needed to have a new orientation, a process, which culminated in the strike of 1889 and the foundation of a union. In this process they derived great strength, self-respect and discipline from their memory of bygone times. This argumentation - impressively as it is put forward - has one major setback: it is difficult to explain how the memory of better times could be so powerful as to shape the thinking and behaviour of miners, who in 1889 had not experienced these times themselves. This holds true even more so for all the immigrants who went on strike in 1905 and in 1918-19. K. Tenfelde seems to see the problem himself: for him, the 'learning-process' (*Lern-Prozess*), which culminated in the foundation of a union in 1889 is not continued in the following years. Instead, the growing number of immigrants, their high mobility, their expectations and their background are seen as 'disrupting factors' (*Störfaktoren*), which prevented the development of an ever stronger and more powerful union.

The other important book has been written by Erhard Lucas, who could be regarded as a representative of the New Left in West Germany with his very critical evaluation of the unions and the political parties and his anti-establishment orientation. His book gives an extremely informative insight into the everyday life of miners in a mining village (Hamborn). With great sympathy he describes their housing conditions, their leisure activities, the shortage of women in a male-dominated industrial region, etc. In the second part of his study, he analyses the developments of 1918-19 and sees the Hamborn miners as protagonists of a revolutionary movement, who ultimately were lacking a proper strategy and leadership and who were too isolated to win the day. Unfortunately, to my mind, he is not able to combine the two parts of his book. Sympathetically as it is written, the picture he gives of the living conditions is very much similar to the one mentioned above. He doesn't really explain, why, out of all the oppressed and expropriated workers, it was the miners who showed such a degree of autonomous action, self-confidence and solidarity. Most important, he largely neglects their working conditions.

Lucas's book was published in 1976, in a period of dis- and reorientation of the left in Germany. He was the first one to radically break away from the very theoretical and abstract discussion, which is still very influential on the left. Of all the factors which may account for his approach, I would like to mention only one: since the early 1970s there have existed a great number of *Bürger-Initiativen* (civic initiatives) among the miners, who want to defend the existence of their houses, and the so-called 'colonies', against attempts to demolish them and to replace them by high-rise buildings. So far they have been rather successful and their 'initiatives' are about the only ones whose membership is not entirely made up of middle-class people and students.

The initiatives definitely had an impact on the group of historians at Essen University, and they most certainly influenced me. When I took up my research on the history of the miners, I felt dissatisfied with the published works in two ways: (a) intellectually, as outlined above, and (b) emotionally. I felt very uneasy with an argument which basically regards three generations of miners as being unadjusted, undisciplined and immature, thereby writing off a very active and not - as is commonly done - a silent majority of workers. This emotional dissatisfaction was enhanced by interviews with old miners, whose life-stories and experiences evoked an enormous respect and some curiosity. Above all, the interviews provided new view points and allowed me to ask different questions. These were followed up in archival studies and I summarise briefly, some of the findings here.

The immigrants from the eastern provinces mostly settled in the northern, only very sparsely populated part of the Ruhr, where the new mines with a workforce of several thousand sprang up. In this region there hardly existed any infrastructure at all, which could have made it easier for the new inhabitants to settle down. There was a massive deficit of roads, schools, hospitals, pubs, houses, etc. The villages whose population increased from a couple of thousand to as much as 100,000 (e.g. Hamborn) did not have either the resources or the will to finance the necessary expenditures and, most important, almost all aspects of urban life were largely missing.

The Prussian state refused these villages city rights (*Stadtrechte*), i.e. an autonomous local administration, as it was afraid that the workers might dominate the city council; the consequence was that communities with as many as 100,000 inhabitants kept the status of villages. The tax-paying middle classes were very small; the tax-income therefore was very low, although the local rate of taxation was about twice as high as in other places of the same size; i.e. structural deficits in local finance remained, some of them until today. The housing stock was restricted as there were not enough people who had the resources required to build houses; the companies had to compensate for it by building 'colonies', in the hope of better controlling their workers this way. An urban working-class culture (usually based upon small tradesmen and craftsmen) was largely missing and with it debating societies, political parties and unions. These factors help to explain why political organisations did not seem to be a promising solution to the pressing problems and why they remained weak.

In the Ruhr area - as well as elsewhere in Germany - there existed a family structure, which might best be called a semi-open one. Up to 20 per cent of all households had lodgers, and the number of families which have accommodated a lodger at one time or the other was even higher; very often lodgers were only taken in to overcome difficult financial situations in the life-cycle of a family: loss of income through illness, accident or death of one of the parents, unforeseen expenditure of any kind and - above all - the rearing of children who not only cost money, but at the same time did not allow the wives to go out to work. The lodgers were usually single men, who could not afford a flat and appreciated the advantages of living-in with a family: personal contacts, sharing of family life, and services such as mending of clothes, etc. This was of particular importance, as very many of them were immigrants, who had to settle down in a new and sometimes alien surrounding. Being a lodger made it much easier to change the workplace and to move around. Though there are no exact numbers, it has been estimated that in 1914 80,000 out of approximately 400,000 miners were lodgers. In the mining 'colonies' statistically there was one lodger for every two families. If the single miners changed their workplace more frequently than their married colleagues, this was not because they were not integrated. Rather, it was due to their greater independence, and the possibility of easily finding a new 'home' wherever they went. There are different ways for lodgers to choose their families (and vice versa); they might have been related, have come from the same village, or have had common acquaintances. Others got into contact at the workplace knowing thereby who and what to expect.

With regard to working conditions, findings are very similar to the ones described by Carter Goodrich and Dave Douglass. The miners at the coal face worked very independently and autonomously. They worked in small units known as 'comradeships', who had to organise their work and to train newcomers themselves, i.e. they were still independent colliers. In fact, one can see the harsh disciplinary measures of the employers as an attempt to regain the control which had largely been lost; to the miners, these methods must have been arbitrary and they stood in stark contrast to their largely autonomous working conditions. This discrepancy, I would argue, lies at the heart of their frequent strikes.

The portrait of the miners as a group of 'insufficiently integrated' workers, who felt completely lost, seems to be a superficial one. Rather, the semi-open family structure and their work experience provided them with an orientation and the opportunity to exercise control over their living and working conditions. Both these mechanisms were operating below the level of public life, i.e. on a private and/or semi-public level, while public collective organisations remained of secondary importance. This is not to deny that the miners

were living under very bad conditions; rather, it should be
argued that there existed informal structures or even an
informal sector, that allowed even the unskilled immigrant to
develop strength, solidarity and self-respect. The demand to
socialise the mines, therefore, should be seen as the logical
consequence of their autonomous work-experience, a demand
that could be put forward after the political and social
control-mechanisms of the *Kaiserreich* had collapsed. In the case
of the Ruhr miners, the mechanisms and institutions which are
usually seen as having had a decisive importance for the
workers and which almost exclusively command the interest of
historians did not play an important part: political/trade union
organisation, state interference, the capitalist market. For the
Ruhr miners, informal structures and mechanisms were much
more important.

FURTHER READING

In German
Brockhaus, Eckhard, *Zusammensetzung und Neustrukturierung
    der Arbeiterklasse vor dem 1.Weltkrieg*, Munich 1975.
Hue, Otto, *Die Bergarbeiter*, 2 vols, Stuttgart 1910/13.
Imbusch, Heinrich, *Arbeitsverhältnis und Arbeiterorganisation
    im deutschen Bergbau*, Essen 1908.
Lucas, Erhard, *Zwei Formen von Radikalismus in der deutschen
    Arbeiterbewegung*, Frankfurt 1976.
Oertzen, Peter von, *Betriebsräte in der Novemberrevolution*,
    Düsseldorf 1963.
Roth, Karl Heinz, *Die 'andere' Arbeiterbewegung und die
    Entwicklung der kapitalistischen Repression von 1880 bis zur
    Gegenwart*, Munich 1974.
Spethmann, Hans, *12 Jahre Ruhrbergbau*, Berlin 1928.
Tenfelde, Klaus, *Sozialgeschichte der Bergarbeiterschaft an der
    Ruhr im 19. Jahrhundert (1815-1889)*, Bonn-Bad Godesberg
    1977.

In English
Goodrich, Carter, *The Miners' Freedom*, 1921.
Douglass, Dave, 'Pit Life in County Durham' in *Miners,
    Quarrymen and Saltworkers*, ed. by R. Samuel, London 1977.
Harrison, Royden, ed., *The Independent Collier*, Brighton 1977.

DISCUSSION ON MINERS' HISTORY

The most famous venue of this Workshop, St Paul's Church, was
also its greatest curse. Shivering in a musty hall, frowned at
by stained walls and chipped memorials, might have been all
right for Morris's comrades; but these days, socialists prefer
their meetings in places where politics is washed down in ale

and warmth; if these aren't available, then toilets and a coffee
machine might retain the most committed. Lacking even these,
aggrieved labour historians started to retreat to Walton Hall
even before the discussion of the Webbs had ended. The session
on Work in Progress was abandoned with little reluctance by a
ragged band of convenors and note-takers. Perhaps, we
thought, it would be better after lunch.

The discussion of miners was much more civilised. The few
square yards needed for the forty or fifty participants was
shifted from the raised podium at the end of the church to its
right-hand side, which meant that we could hear each other
over the echoes. Someone had found two great big heaters that
blasted enormous gouts of warmth over the congregation, and
at least meant that the place no longer echoed to the rhythm of
chattering teeth. Dave Douglass, the only man wearing a suit
as usual, arrived late and interrupted the earlier pattern of
questioning on the German paper. From this stage, interest
focused upon the causes of miners' militancy, and the place of
women in the communities. A third, subsidiary, concern was
the part played by mine-workers outside the coal industry –
the tinners, ironstone miners, or quarrymen – who in contrast
were usually fairly moderate characters, occasionally used to
break strikes. Finally, a number of people wanted to know
where the customary militancy of the coalfields was going: not
just the direction it might be taking, but also what happened
as mining declined and the workforce transferred to new jobs
with different conditions.

Because of familiarity, people tended to speak more about
the British than the German miners. 'Familiarity' – but most of
us have trouble making sense of the divergencies within British
mining to come to terms with trans-national comparisons. As
Kevin Devanney, an ex-Yorkshire miner, asked Dave Douglass,
why is it that traditions like folksongs differ so greatly between
coalfields? The Doncaster area, said Dave, had no traditions
of its own; the pits were too new and its traditions were those
of the Geordies and Welshmen who provided the labour force;
the militants around Doncaster were all Scots; by contrast,
Northumberland and Durham were puzzlingly backward
(although it must be added that Durham's vote for the National
Coal Board's 1979 pay offer was much closer than Dave
predicted). One speaker reckoned that regional variations in
wages were the root of these differences, in conjunction with
the quality of coal and the nature of the market. Perhaps;
Dave's view was that regional wage differentials changed over
time, and anyway employers would deliberately take it in turns
to attack workers in their different regions.

Briefly the discussion returned to the German miners. Had
any part been played by the outbreak of disease in 1893-94? It
had. Was not a great deal of what is said about miners a
mythology, including that which was really only about

coalminers (metal-miners lacked a history too often)? How do we
analyse the rich oral material presented by Dave Douglass, and
was there anything similar in Germany? There was not anything
similar in Germany. British coalminers' histories are woefully
inadequate: Page Arnot volumes are mainly concerned with
bureaucratic structures. The traditions are not to be found
here. Rod Pritchard, a Ford worker from Llanelly, South Wales,
reminded us that these traditions had not been confined to a
single trade: in his region, these elements fused; when times
were hard in South Wales, quarrymen went and worked in North
Wales. Today, these traditions were being sold and their
bearers brainwashed, by people like Fords in Swansea. Again,
this was missing from most history.

It was at this stage that we started to think about the part
played by women in the coalfields. The missing dimension in
formal history, Anna Davin said, was people – not just ordinary
miners or miners other than coalminers, but also the rest of the
community, including the families. This was even absent in
Dave Douglass's account, for many of the stories told to
children about the past came from the mothers. Dave accepted
this criticism, immediately incurring the accusation of evasion:
who, asked Ann Phillips, serviced the miners? The criticism
was of the attitude to women which doesn't include those
experiences, of providing services to industrial labour, as
valid. The need to study organised labour was defended by
Kevin Devanney, who instanced *The World on Our Backs* as a
book which did genuinely sum up the miners' experiences of the
1972 strike; the National Union of Miners represented workers
who had been organised for a long time, who were a force, and
who had to be understood. The impression you get at your
parents' knees is one of defeat and depression; Pitt's book
gives the consciousness of being able to change things, and he
hoped the lead of the Kent National Union of Miners in
sponsoring the book would be followed. Women, it was agreed,
were active as pickets, and often goaded the enemy forces much
as they seemed to in Northern Ireland. Had they worked in the
Ruhr, asked Dave Middlemass? This was difficult to establish;
there is no oral tradition in this period, as there was the
enormous disruption of the 1920s, then fascism, then the
post-war upheaval; the result is that you get nowhere from
talking to people, and the remaining archives tend to be partial.

Even with the people's backing, how do we communicate
history to a wider audience? Joyce Marlowe was struck by the
dangers of, on the one hand, making one's history too dry –
because you recognised all the complexity – and on the other,
over-romanticising the past by trying to bring it to life. She
had come from a cotton background, and learnt about the past
at home; she now wrote novels, which allowed her to control
the characters involved, to finance her history. Roger Thomas
disagreed that the dimension now lacking in formal histories was
appropriate to fictional forms; the transcripts in the South Wales

Miners' Library are direct and convey the experiences; the
SSRC has withdrawn funds from the Library, and the only
person collecting photographic materials is an amateur. American
universities will probably buy the lot. Gwyn David, also paying
tribute to the Miners' Library, thought the problem was also
created by Welsh national historiography, which saw South
Wales as a 'huge blot'.

More cold water was thrown upon any lingering romanticism
by Lutz Niethammer, who asked whether the shift in German
miners' class consciousness following the war was paralleled in
Britain. The Ruhr had seen a new wave of immigrants from
inside Germany, largely middle class. Essen, once a coal and
steel town, is now a service centre. The mineworkers are the
highest-paid group in German industry, entitled to privileged
social welfare, and have the most right-wing union in the
right-wing German labour movement. Co-determination was first
instituted in the mines; they went bankrupt in the 1950s, the
union persuading the state to nationalise them and continue
(after some redundancies) on a high-wage basis. A recent
phase of growth had brought in some temporary workers from
Turkey, who were quite isolated. It is romantic to try and keep
up older traditions, especially as hardly any of the area's
population now works in the mines. Dave Douglass took up this
theme, of the dying mining villages and their traditions; but
he dated the decline in traditions from before the actual
run-down of the industry. In the past, mining communities
were very in-grown places. The National Coal Board
seemed to be recruiting a few people from non-mining
backgrounds, and he was worried what effect that might have.
It was hard to put your finger on the root causes of militancy,
though: when he first started research he had found some
self-consciously militant and revolutionary communities along
the Tyne, and had thought it possible that the explanation
was their cosmopolitan background. Then he found some isolated
villages with traditions going back to the Chartists. On this
note of healthy uncertainty, and increasingly drowned by the
whispering of a migrant audience wondering where Sheila
Rowbotham was, the convenor closed the session.

This session was less intense - and less tense - than the rest
of the weekend. Perhaps that reflects a position of strength:
we can afford to feel fairly secure about our recent studies of
the mine-worker: just look at Royden Harrison's *Independent
Collier*, or Jim MacFarlane's *Essays from the Yorkshire Coalfield*,
or the representation of the MFGB in John Saville's *Dictionary
of Labour Biography*. Other areas are weaker, and for political
reasons. Logie Barrow and Anna Davin argued, quite
compellingly, that it was largely through the challenges of
feminist historians that the two terms of the Workshop -
People's History/Socialist Theory - were being brought together.
The lesson drawn for this session might be that mining ought to
be studied in tandem with the conditions for its reproduction -

the families, housing, transport, even the increasingly
neglected (by socialists) mine-owners. And that lesson is not
limited to mining!

SOME RECENT MINERS' HISTORIES

Campbell, A.B., *The Lanarkshire Miners, a social history of
their Trade Union, 1775-1874*, Edinburgh 1979.
Douglass, Dave, *Pit Life in County Durham* and *Pit Talk in
County Durham*, History Workshop Pamphlets, nos 5 and 12,
reprinted in *Miners, Quarrymen and Saltworkers*, ed. by
Raphael Samuel, London 1977. The first of these studies –
which combined a study of union records with personal
experience and oral testimony – is concerned with 'job
control' – the second with language, culture and song.
Francis, Hywel and Smith, David, *The Fed. A History of the
South Wales Miners in the Twentieth Century*, London 1980.
Newly-published history which does honour to its subject
by drawing on oral history and archives created in the
course of research, as well as on a mass of printed and MSS
sources. A work of scholarship informed by a strong sense
of both politics and place, and written in close association
with the establishment of the Miners' Library and archive at
Swansea.
Harrison, Royden, ed., *The Independent Collier: the Miner as
Archetypal Proletarian*, Hassocks 1977. A series of studies
produced by the centre for social history at the University
of Warwick, the book includes a valuable study of the
'free miners' of the Forest of Dean, an example of the kind
of independent working group which preceded the
establishment of the big mining companies.
Pitt, Malcolm, *The World on Our Backs*, London 1979. A history
and chronicle of the Kent miners written by one of them. The
book focuses on the 1972 miners' strike, but is firmly set in
the 'underground world' of work. Like other books by
miner-historians it is independent-minded, notably
well-written and extremely perceptive about both politics and
trade unionism.

41 THE CLASS STRUGGLE AT RENAULT

Patrick Fridenson*

Introducing his talk, Patrick Fridenson pointed out that there
had been virtually nothing written about the history of Renault
car workers until 1971, when the French Communist Party
published an oral history of militants. This pioneering work
contained a number of important silences: nothing on women; no
treatment of either the period of revolutionary syndicalism
before the First World War or the events of the war itself. Most
importantly, while contributing to the image of Renault-
Billancourt as the centre of class struggle in France, the
interviews confined themselves to the period 1912–44; i.e. they
stopped at just that moment when Renault became the *fortresse
ouvrière* for which it became famous, thus avoiding any analysis
of the role of the Communist Party unions themselves in the
post-Second-World-War development of the factory. It was in
part to redress this balance, to put developments at Renault
into perspective in relation to the rest of French labour and
social history, that Patrick was addressing himself.

Why did the myth of Renault come into being and what part
did it play in French political life? What role did labour play in
the development of managerial strategy within the enterprise?
How effective were workers' struggles? What was the role of the
state? These were the main questions raised in the talk. Patrick
argued that labour was always in the background of managerial
strategies, but moved into the foreground at certain moments –
e.g. during the First World War (absenteeism) and the Second
World War (Communist Party-led restriction of output as part
of the Resistance) – at these points management was compelled
to adapt its strategies, though not to change the rule of the
game as such. On the effectiveness of workers' struggles, the
key memory both for activists and for the nation as a whole is
that of the 1936 sit-down strikes. After the war, union
militants tended to view the record as one of progress,
especially in the direction of increasing union liberties; in the
long term, however, one can be less sanguine about the
effectiveness of union organisations on management's freedom of
action.

On the role of the state: Of course, at Renault as elsewhere,

*Patrick Fridenson is an editor of *Mouvement Social*, the French
labour history journal, teaches and researches at the Sórbonne.
Author of a history of Renault.

This report has been written by Jonathan Zeitlin.

the French state can be seen as a regulator of class struggle, but it was also used as a weapon of the working class against management: the key moments were 1917-18 when the state was used to bring in shop stewards against the will of management, and in 1906, when Sunday work was abolished under similar circumstances.

Finally, on the place of Renault in French social history: the cliche has it that 'when Renault workers sneeze, France catches cold'. This hides a significant change in the character of class struggle during the twentieth century, from a disciplined struggle led by highly politicised (communist) skilled workers to a fluctuating one led by largely unorganised unskilled workers (since 1945). The date and circumstances when this concept of Renault passed into popular memory have also been largely forgotten: it was during the 1917-18 strikes of women munition workers – the 'munitionettes' – rather than through the struggles of the male skilled workers.

DISCUSSION

The discussion centred above all on the role of the state in industrial relations. Some participants were dubious about a positive role for the state in promoting unionisation: Steve Tolliday suggested that wartime is an 'exceptional' period in which the demand for labour makes the state more responsive to workers than normally; similarly Len Haldon argued that in relation to the British car industry (specifically Vauxhall) the state played no positive role until the war itself. Others placed more emphasis on the circumstances in which the state could indeed play a positive role of this kind: Niels Christiansen argued that in Scandinavia, during periods of crisis, it had been possible for the working class to put pressure on the state to restrain management's initiatives – currently in the shipbuilding industry and also during the 1930s; this explains the strong support there for labour governments, even minority ones. Jonathan Zeitlin argued that the unionisation of the car industry in Britain and especially in the USA required state support. Without the Wagner Act and the support of the Roosevelt administration, there is little reason to think that the waves of organisation in the mass production industries during the 1930s would ultimately have been more successful than the 1919 steel strike; similarly in Britain, Bevin's Essential Work Order during the war played a central role – along with tight labour markets – in winning recognition for unions and in many cases for shop stewards from reluctant employers. Mariuccia Salvati, speaking about Italy, argued that there was a need for periodisation in the role of the state. Before 1939, there was a power struggle between workers and entrepreneurs for control of the internal organisation of the factory, in which workers tried to use the state to further their ends. After the war,

the entry of the left parties into the government undermined the
political opposition of workers; one could argue that the same
thing happened at Renault.

In replying, Patrick argued that the exceptional element of
wartime is above all full employment; wartime must be treated as
part and parcel of workers' total experience. For example, the
sit-down strikes of the popular front period were led by a new
generation of communist militants whose first experience of
industrial conflict was in the mass strikes of 1917-18; similarly,
the restriction of output campaign during the Second World War
represented a crucial demonstration of communist strength,
which was recognised by the state and which gave confidence to
activists. In the USA, the idea of long-term collective
bargaining was forged by the head of General Motors during the
Second World War.

On the abolition of Sunday work: it was the result of
nationwide strikes, behind which was workers' reaction to
employers' pressure for increased productivity through changes
in the organisation of work. In response to a question on the
relationship between political activism and union weakness,
Patrick pointed out that the turn towards politics was confined
to skilled workers (the best organised); after the Second World
War, as in the 1920s, the majority of the unskilled were
immigrants, who remained excluded from national politics.

On the post-war role of the state: after the war, the French
state was concerned with two problems: (1) the viciousness of
pre-war managerial policies towards labour, especially in the car
industry; (2) the rise of mass unionism. Therefore, the state
sought to create a 'pilot' firm out of the nationalised Renault
works as regards social and labour policy, hoping thereby to
cut off the Communist Party from its mass base. The working
class at Renault was accordingly given a privileged status in
many respects - including the institutionalisation of unionism -
denied in private firms. The party had no counter-strategy -
in fact it saw organisational advantages in the management's
plans - and therefore failed to respond to the tendencies to
deskilling and the decentralisation of plants which were
undermining the position of the skilled workers at Billancourt.
One way of seeing this is to look at the 1947-8 strikes at
Renault - according to the Communist Party, these were
launched by extreme leftists (Trotskyists, anarchists), but
they couldn't have happened without the real discontent of the
unskilled who followed them. Initially there were clashes
between the strikers and the party; after ten days of
opposition, the party suddenly swung behind the strike to try
to contain and control it, and in so doing got their ministers
expelled from the government.

Debates

Political economy

Michael Ignatieff*

I have heard it said by socialist economists whom I respect that
the best history of political economy remains Marx's *Theories of
Surplus Value*. Since the message of this paper is that we have
more to fear intellectually from the orthodoxies of our friends
than we do from the blandishments of our political and
intellectual enemies, I must say that filio-piety towards Marx as
a historian of economic thought is perhaps the most considerable
obstacle to a socialist understanding of political economy. It can
even be said that Marx in fact was not a historian of economic
thought at all, if by that we mean someone attempting to
reconstitute past projects of speculation in the full integrity of
their thinkers' milieu and intentions. In writing *Theories of
Surplus Value*, Marx was working as an economic theorist, not
as a historian, as the protean fashioner of the new, rather than
as an archaeologist of the old. He had no intention of
reconstituting old theory. His purpose was to ransack a rubbish
tip of old encounters with a problem in order to bring back
home the bricks, the glass and the window frames for a new
house of theory. We are all the better for the fact that Marx's
encounter with his intellectual inheritance in political economy
did not take the form of an antiquarianism of the McCulloch
variety – but we emphatically cannot model our historical
practice on his own, that is, if we wish to understand how and
why, in their own terms, Smith, Hume, Quesnay and Steuart
were able to create, from within the old disciplines of
jurisprudence and moral philosophy, a science of man capable of
providing systematic understanding of 'commercial society'.
   At this point, I ought to make a distinction between the
encounters with political economy which are appropriate to an
economic theorist, and those which are appropriate to a
historian. I am addressing myself only to historians, not for
example to those who have sought to reinvigorate Marxian
economic theory by an immersion in the Ricardian transformation
problem. I cannot tell whether this encounter will produce
anything more than a politically unusable scholasticism, but
from a methodological viewpoint, a historian cannot raise valid
objection. Because the purposes and intentions of the reading of

*Michael Ignatieff is an editor of *History Workshop Journal*;
author of *A Just Measure of Pain* (a study of the eighteenth-
century origins of the prison system), New York 1978;
co-director, King's College Cambridge project on *The Wealth of
Nations and classical political economy*.

the classical texts are to sharpen and refine contemporary
understanding of the philosophical and economic meaning of
'value'. It is not to explicate the conditions, social and
intellectual, which made possible the historical creation of this
discourse on value. That is the historians' as opposed to the
theorists' job.

Yet it must be said that socialist economic theorists' manner
of using the classical texts does tend to preclude one potential
source of renewal for Marxist economics. By assuming, for
example, that the *Wealth of Nations* is within the same boundary
field as modern economics, some Marxist economists forego the
pleasure of actually discovering that Smith's boundaries for
'economics' were vastly broader than our own. For Smith, and
indeed for all the Scottish philosophers, political economy was
not simply a model of the laws of market equilibrium, but also a
history of civil society, a historical sociology of the growth
process ('the progress of arts and manufactures'), a theory of
government in its relation to the laws of civil society, and a
theory of fiscal and economy policy. In modern parlance,
political economy sought to express the inter-relationship of
polity, economy and society, an inter-relationship which we
now seek to grasp in the divided camps of sociology,
economics, psychology and history which have emerged as the
balkanised fragments produced in the dissolution of the
original eighteenth-century project as a science of society.
Those 'radical' economics faculties in the USA which are
beginning to rename themselves political economy departments
are evidently seeking to reconstitute that vanished unity of
politics and economics as disciplines, and by doing so, to break
down the idea that the market is an autonomous sphere,
intruded upon by contingent political interventions. One
wonders whether they, and we, will go further and include
social psychology and moral philosophy (the other elements of the
eighteenth-century project) into a political economy capable,
in its interdisciplinary articulation, of comprehending the
interrelatedness of historical change.

The implication of this is that an encounter with the
eighteenth-century science of society is a constant experience
of the narrowness and the fragmented incoherence of the social
sciences which claim them as their forefathers. From this
perspective the historical problem in thinking about political
economy is to explain the progressive disaggregation of the
initial theoretical project. This is work that lies before us all,
but even an initial reconnoitre suggests that in two
generations after Smith's death, the history of civil society had
been jettisoned, leaving an economics ever-more precariously
resting on a natural psychology of a-historical propensities to
labour and self-improvement. For reasons which we do not
understand yet, the Ricardian elaboration of the market model
seems to have required the hiving off from economics proper of
that comparative and historical sense of the interconnection

between manners, modes of subsistence, politics and human
propensities which characterised Smith's social science. At the
same time, a psychology and ethics, which in Smith's hands had
been made the *locus* of a profound enquiry into the moral and
motivational basis of economic behaviour returned to the
traditional epistemological tasks of moral philosophy. The history
which had interconnected systems of authority and economic
systems split into Morgan's anthropology, Spencer's sociology,
and Macaulay's political history. This process of fragmentation
and differentiation is *terra incognita* for me, at least, despite
Burrow's pioneering and penetrating efforts to figure it out.
But one initial assumption ought to be cleared away, before
we can get down to the history of the process. That assumption,
a kind of tacit Parsonianism, is that the increasingly more
self-conscious and rigorous definition of boundaries between
disciplines helped to improve the conceptual efficiency and
scientific grounding, in methodological terms, of their
conclusions. We simply cannot approach the history of the
human sciences in terms of this functionalist assumption that
things have been getting better, and more efficient, since the
eighteenth century. The protean character of the eighteenth-
century project is to be dismissed as an amateurish first
approximation only at the cost of real complacency towards the
walls which bar our attempts to speak together as historians,
sociologists, psychologists and economists.

Perhaps an example of eighteenth-century theoretical
practice would help to illustrate the impoverishment which has
followed from the fragmentation of contemporary social science.
It has become a major theoretical struggle in recent years,
especially evident in the women's movement, to re-apprehend
sexuality as a political, social and economic authority relation,
that is, to work out from a narrowly psychological conception of
sex as impulse, to understand sex as a social relationship whose
social history is inscribed within the history of modes of
production, systems of authority and cultural images of power
and desire. The struggle to achieve this systemic understanding
has required hauling ourselves over the walls that have isolated
psychoanalysis from history, sociology and economics.

Given the immense effort it has cost us to reach this
understanding, it may come as a surprise to return to the
Scottish political economy of the 1770s and to discover in, for
example, John Millar's *Origin of Ranks* an economic history of
sexual relations which tried to investigate the intertwining of
sexual and accumulative desire and the corruption of sexual
need by acquisitive individualism in commercial societies. Within
the Marxist history of social science Millar has been seen,
especially by Professor Meek, as a prescient bearer of the
economic interpretation of history. In this faintly patronising
practice of handing out prizes to our theoretical ancestors,
Marxist historiography faithfully reproduces the most unhelpful
teleological readings to be found, say, in Schumpeter's history

of economic thought. Meek's reading is unhelpful because it has actively increased our difficulty in noticing those passages in which Millar emphasises the political determination of the economic, and the contingent but decisive role of charismatic leadership, national character and manners in deflecting economic development from its 'natural' course.

Millar was a symptomatic rather than an original thinker, but even an encounter with his work raises the question of how the elements of an interdisciplinary understanding of human desire was fragmented over the next two centuries into compartments which we now must struggle against in our own minds. Teleological readings, whether of a Marxist or Schumpeterian cast, effectively foreclose on the use of past theory as a vantage point from which to criticise and renew present orthodoxy. And the history of political economy, like the history of any social science, is pointless, if beguiling antiquarianism if its reconstruction of the vanished terrains of debate does not help us to become self-conscious about the intellectual boundaries which subliminally constrain our analytical imaginations.

I must say I do not know what interpretation should be substituted in place of these false teleologies, and I would not wish to speak for a reading of the story in terms of a unilinear fall from eighteenth-century grace. Indeed the key question may be why eighteenth-century social science germinated the seed of its own disaggregation. It has often been argued, most famously by Halévy, that the fissiparous establishment of politics, economics and sociology as separate terrains must be traced back to the Scottish political economists' assertion of the relative autonomy of the laws of the market and of civil society from politics. It is maintained that 'the discovery of the self-equilibrating mechanisms of the market' proved fatal for the later understanding of the inter-relation of polity, economy and society. But we still have to determine, in fact, what Smith, Hume, Millar and Ferguson actually asserted about the articulation between polity and economy.

A true understanding of Marx's theory of politics may turn on understanding the same articulation. A recent essay by a French socialist trade unionist, Pierre Rosainvallon, has argued that Marx inherited from political economy the Utopia of a civil society able to function without political intervention, and that his post-revolutionary society, beyond class antagonism, would be beyond politics. With no conflicts of a collective nature to adjudicate, politics would become the administration of things. Rosainvallon argues that the Marxist Utopia is in fact a mirror of the capitalist Utopia of a self-regulation, self-subsisting market, sustained by a political superstructure confining itself to the administration of justice and the maintenance of order. Both Utopias fatally foreclose on politics, on the sometimes squalid necessities of a mechanism for expressing and conciliating conflicts arising within civil society.

The question of Marx's theory of politics is a matter of some real importance, as Lenin and Stalin's post-revolutionary behaviour towards political and social opposition may, in fact, have found an ideological warrant in the texts of the master. That is not a question I am competent to discuss. But it is worth observing, as far as political economy's conception of the political is concerned, that the Rosainvallon argument confuses Smith with Godwin and Paine. It is in the political theory of Jacobinism, and in Godwin's *Political Justice*, not in the *Wealth of Nations*, that one finds the argument that civil society could subsist without the state. While both Godwin and Paine drew upon Smith, they did not pay heed to those passages of his history of civil society in which the establishment of 'regular government' is made the crucial condition for the creation of markets and the improvement of manners. Nor did they attend to the passages in Book V which by giving government warrant to intervene to protect the populace against the 'moral' effects of the division of labour effectively sanction the whole apparatus of the liberal interventionist state. In his discussion of monopoly, moreover, Smith puts his finger on precisely those conflicts between private interest and public good which a state would have to resolve in civil society. While there does not seem to be an argument for the autonomy of the economic from the political in the *Wealth of Nations*, there is a fairly powerful epistemological argument about the inability of any sovereign authority to command the social knowledge necessary for authoritative direction of civil society. That there was a public good, Smith's belief in principles of natural law would not allow him to doubt. But that any body of men or form of political authority could obtain a monopoly on the knowledge of the public good he insistently denied. The only passably adequate guarantee of effective political leadership was competition within the market for political office, sustained by a rapid circulation of wealth. In James Steuart and in Dugald Stewart one also finds the argument that the activities of government ought to be constrained by knowledge of the 'laws of political economy'.

This already simplified account of Scottish doctrine suggests that formulae like the economic determination of politics, or the autonomy of civil society will not adequately describe a theory which insisted on the role of government as enforcer of the rules of justice in market society, but which simultaneously maintained that government lacked the epistemological basis for socially planned concertation of individual market action. I do not know what to call the subtle articulation of polity and economy which resulted, but Rosainvallon's model of a market beyond politics will not do.

It ought to be said here that the articulation of the relation between society, polity and economy was the primary theoretical objective of Scottish political economy. Were it not for the relentless reduction of political economy to 'economics' by historians of the discipline, it would not be necessary to insist

on this point. There already existed, in the work of the late
seventeenth-century political arithmeticians and 'later
mercantilists' a clear understanding of the operation of markets
in money and international trade. The task of Scottish political
economy was to integrate the market models into a
comprehensive social theory which would provide a critical
anatomy of the emerging 'commercial society'. And in this
project the most difficult question was redefining the purpose
of politics in the light of an historical understanding of the law
of unintended consequences, i.e., that commercial society had
taken shape without concerted, collective action, but from the
glacier-like movement of uncoordinated individual wills bent on
improving themselves. Again, I cannot say I fully understand
the relation between their theory of politics and their histories
of civil society, but I do know that the relation must be
understood, endogenously, that is, within its own theoretical
terms, rather than exogenously, as a cobbling together of
intellectual spare parts for the service of a rising class. The
history of political economy cannot be written, in other words,
as the history of bourgeois ideology. The tendency to do so,
most recently in Therborn's work, has proceeded in part at
least from a confusion between the question of the intentions of
theorists and the uses to which theory is put.

On the question of use, there is no doubt that the doctrines
of political economy, in particular the wages fund theory, and
the more general idea that market equilibrium naturally brings
about distributive justice between producer and consumer,
were used in egregiously interested fashion by employers,
politicians and intellectuals in the post-1815 period to conciliate
working-class opinion and to still qualms within the owning
class itself as to the consequences of their own handiwork.
Nineteenth-century bourgeois ideology is historically distinctive
as a form of legitimising power precisely because it based its
claim on the supposed objectivity of the laws which rule the
distribution of wealth. While its claim to rule was made on a
plethora of claims, moral, historical, psychological, the element
of novelty in its post-1815 intellectual armour was the claim
that its social conception was 'scientific'. In the work of several
later Scottish political economists, notably Dugald Stewart,
there is a frank awareness of the social utility of a 'science of
society' as a kind of shared consensual ground for the
adjudication of competing social claims within the forum of
public opinion, and as the knowledge-basis for the practice of
government. Dugald Stewart, the teacher of James Mill and the
Edinburgh Review generation, was perhaps most forward in
looking to the diffusion of the true principles of political
economy as a means of pacifying and calming the turbulence of
the multitude. Not all of this is egregiously class-interested
argument. In part, Stewart was addressing the problem of
substituting secular forms of consensus for religious or
paternal legitimisations of authority. And yet in his intentions,

one can already see stalking the worthy figures of Hannah
More, Mrs Trimmer and Harriet Martineau.

Yet, admitting all of this to be true, it cannot be said that
the makers of political economy intended their social theory to
provide 'good reasons' either for the rulers of their own times,
or less plausibly still, for those to come after. By intentions, I
do not mean what, e.g., Smith or Hume said they were trying
to do. Autobiographical or methodological statements of intent
from either of them are quite sparse. I mean rather what
purposes their social theory can be reasonably said to have
been supposed to accomplish when we look at its ensemble. While
individual portions of their work can be said to be addressed to
discrete problems, for example, finding the best strategy for
developing the backward economy of Scotland, their overall
theoretical ambition was to develop a new language of secular
analysis capable of comprehending 'commercial society', as an
economic, cultural, social and political phenomenon. The
emphasis was always emphatically on understanding rather than
advocacy, as their sceptical detachment both from the
enthusiasms of eighteenth-century factional politics, or from the
moralising jeremiads about modernity, ought to make clear.

Of course there is advocacy in the sections of the *Wealth of
Nations* devoted to commercial policy, but Smith's endorsement
of private enterprise owed more to a negative conviction of the
futility of available interventionist strategies of economic
growth, than to a larger moral endorsement of competitive
individualism as a social process. In the eighteenth century
political economists still assumed that a moral assessment of the
impact of commerce upon our daily behaviour as parents,
citizens, employers, workers, was a necessary project for any
science of society. The ultimately enfeebling distinction between
fact and value had not begun to work a split between 'hard
sciences', like economics, and humane studies, like moral
philosophy. When one draws together the Scottish assessment of
modern individualism, one discovers a powerful critique.
Marxist historians of economic thought have been too busy
explaining why there is not an exploitation analysis of
production in Scottish economics to notice the older vernacular
of moral opprorium, but it is there. As producers of wealth,
commercial peoples were inconceivably more efficient, and
modern society's capacity to satisfy the needs of ordinary
labourers for shoes, clothing and food was the sole basis for
according it moral approval. Yet as citizens, modern people were
less virtuous, as husbands and wives less devoted, as friends
less loyal. They were more assertive of their rights, but less
willing to sacrifice themselves for others. This ambivalent,
sometimes damning assessment of commercial society's impact
upon human manners cannot be tortured into an anticipatory
endorsement of capitalist modernity, or into an armoury of
arguments for anyone.

I do not know what happens to the space accorded moral

evaluation in the political economy which follows Smith's death. Certainly Ricardian economics accords it little place in its conception of the discipline's boundaries. Perhaps it is this cold-blooded rigour which attracts modern Marxian theorists in search of scientific renewal. But the moral assessment of individualism does not disappear. In the 'Stable State' chapter of Mill's *Principles* we encounter a denunciation of the self-deceiving adulation for wealth which one finds in the last, sombre edition of Smith's *Theory of Moral Sentiments*. We cannot solve the problem of reconciling political economy's critique of individualism, with its use as an armoury of arguments in the class war, by conceiving the moralism as a kind of vestigial trace gradually expunged by triumphant science. Political economy remained the bearer of a critique of capitalism throughout its life.

Yet a critique of modernity was not the aim of political economy, even if it was a result. The purpose of the new science was 'understanding'; was the creation of a vocabulary capable of generating a systemic conception of social, political and economic variables. This may seem anodyne, or self-evident, only if we take it for granted that the elements of such a vocabulary lay at hand. Yet if we go back to Smith's beginnings as a professor of jurisprudence, it becomes apparent that the available language of social analysis treated social relations in terms of juridical rights and duties. The family was analysed in terms of the natural and positive law of marriage; the market was understood in terms of the law of contrast; and as John Dunn has argued, the theory of political obligation was still understood as a branch of applied theology. The creation of social theory required the forging of a vocabulary of social science, free of juridical and theological association. We still do not know how a discernibly 'modern' language of social science took shape in their hands between 1750 and 1775, but it is clear, at least in the case of jurisprudence, that Smith conceived his first task to be, not so much describing the market itself, but in emancipating that description from the juristic framework of the law of contract, and in showing that the market obeyed laws dependent upon, but autonomous of, those of the state.

I want to point to this problem of 'language' because the Marxist tradition of intellectual history places so much emphasis on the sociological milieu as the origin of ideas that it either takes for granted or assumes away the problem of generating language adequate to one's conception of social reality. The origin of political economy must be understood as a problem in the transmutation of the available languages of theology, jurisprudence, natural law, and only secondarily as a problem in the sociology of knowledge. It is as makers of the linguistic coinage of our everyday lives that Smith, Hume and the Scots must be studied. The sociological and the linguistic study of their achievement are interdependent, but the former will not

'give' us the latter. Our reflexive, unthinking tendency to
assume that the past speaks the same language as our own has
led us, quite wrongly, to assume that as 'commercial society'
takes shape, in their daily experience and in their reading, a
language of 'markets', 'classes', and 'social relations' is there
at hand to guide them cognitively. It was not, and that fact is
the measure of their achievement, and the major challenge for
our interpretation.

FURTHER READING

Burrow, J.W., *Evolution and Society: A study in Victorian social theory*, London 1966.
Dunn, John, *The political thought of John Locke*, Cambridge 1969.
Halevy, Elie, *The growth of philosophic radicalism*, London 1946
McCulloch, J.R., *Principles of political economy*, London 1825.
Meek, Ronald L., *Social science and the ignoble savage*, Cambridge 1976.
Meek, Ronald L., 'The Scottish contribution to Marxist sociology', in *Economics and Ideology*, London 1967.
Mill, John Stuart, *Principles of political economy*, London 1847.
Millar, John, *The origin of the distinction of Ranks...*, 4th ed., Edinburgh 1806.
Rosanvillon, Pierre, *Le Capitalisme utopique: critique de l'ideologie economique*, Paris 1979.
Schumpeter, Joseph A., *History of economic analysis*, 6th ed, London 1967.
Sraffa, P., Introduction to David Ricardo, *Works and correspondenc* Cambridge 1951, 1, pp. xiii-lxii.
Steuart, James, *An inquiry into the principles of political economy*, 2 vols, London 1767.
Stewart, Dugald, 'Lectures on political economy' in *Collected Works*, ed. Sir William Hamilton, Edinburgh 1855, VIII.
Therborn, G., *Science, class and society*, London 1976.

Religion

43 METHODISM AND THE COMMON PEOPLE

John Walsh*

John Walsh addressed a full-to-standing Workshop beneath the faded print of a reaper and against the traffic noise of Walton Street. A brilliant-white screen behind the speakers' table seemed to define 'the chair' with the authority of print, and somewhere at the back a man lurked with microphone and tape. Walsh, having first to recover from his introduction as 'the outstanding religious historian in England', saw his job as laying the foundations of a debate.

After praising recent regional Methodist histories, and statistical work ('tightening the parameters of debate' but often 'more attractive in appearance than reality'), Walsh quickly focused his paper on two great theses of Methodist historiography: Edward Thompson's theories of displacement and work discipline, and Elie Halévy's theory that Methodism prevented political revolution in England. Halévy's was first presented in 1913, and Walsh reckoned that it had 'smouldered like a firecracker' ever since, forever moving the debate onto new ground, ground which Thompson's *The Making of the English Working Class* had dominated since 1963.

Did Methodism prevent revolution? Was it 'the psychic component of counter-revolution or a friend to working people'? Before looking at Walsh's presentation of the issues it might be helpful to remind readers of Halévy's first thrust. Halévy was not, it will be noticed, just talking tightly of Methodism, or more loosely of polity, or even generally, of ideas; rather he was addressing *England itself*, a total entity and historical process. And as if this was not ambitious enough, Halévy compared this process, and lack of it, with European experiences:

> Why was it that of all the countries of Europe England has been the most free from revolutions, violent crises, and sudden changes? We have sought in vain to find the explanation by an analysis of her political institutions and economic organization. Her political institutions were such that society might easily have lapsed into anarchy had there existed in England a bourgeoisie animated by the spirit of

---

*John Walsh is fellow and tutor in modern history at Jesus College, Oxford; brought up in a Methodist family 'much influenced by the teachings of R.H. Tawney'; engaged for many years in the study of eighteenth-century Wesleyan history.

This report has been written by Robert Colls.

revolution. And a system of economic production that was in
fact totally without organization of any kind would have
plunged the kingdom into violent revolution had the working
classes found in the middle class leaders to provide it with a
definite ideal, a creed, a practical programme. But the elite
of the working class, the hard-working and capable
bourgeois, had been imbued by the evangelical movement
with a spirit from which the established order had nothing
to fear.

No doubt the English Nonconformists continued to oppose
any movement towards bureaucracy. Without freedom of
association they could not exist. But for all their freedom of
theological difference the sects agreed among themselves and
with the national authorities to impose on the nation a
rigorous conformity and at least an outward respect for
Christian social order. With their passion for liberty they
united a devotion to order, and in the last resort the latter
predominated. Hence freedom of association proved in the
end the restriction of individual freedom and the authority
of custom replaced and almost superseded the authority of
law. And this is modern England.[1]

Much of this is contentious and some of it is confusing but
Halévy's thesis nevertheless attracted interest in Methodist
history on new and exciting levels. From the left it was polished
by the Hammonds (*The Village Labourer*, 1917) and refined by
E.P. Thompson and now, in spite of criticism and conten-
tion, it stands as People's History - Socialist Theory on the
grand scale. A rough diamond perhaps, but still a dazzling
contribution.

It remained for Walsh to split the diamond. This he did with
neatness and precision. From within he identified three angles
of attack, and from without, four possible lines of counter-
attack. First, the History-Theory as a model of 'the
displacement of energy'. Methodism, it is argued here,
'pre-empted' the time, talent, and money of potentially
revolutionary sources. By attributing suffering to the hand of
Providence, and by preaching spiritual regeneration as the
ultimate answer, the Methodist intellect emphasised the next-
world rather than this, moral reform rather than politics, and
individual salvation rather than class struggle. On week-nights
the chapel stood as a 'total community absorbing the energy of
its members', displacing the ambition of a working-class and
artisan elite who might otherwise have been more gainfully
employed. On Sunday evenings the displacement might be more
raw - revivals being a self-manipulated form of psychic release
from all that was oppressive without the chapel and all that
was repressive within it.

Second, the History-Theory's criticisms of Methodist practice
as ideology. Here, it is suggested that Methodist ideology was
tactically useful for a developing industrial capitalism: as an
emotional canalisation of working-class frustration; as a

propagandist, along Weberian lines, of 'a pitiless ideology of
work'; and as a destroyer of community and tradition,
'recasting the pre-industrial personality into a new industrial
mould'. Hard work as a religious duty was performed through
ideologically individualistic notions of self-help and self-
discipline. These notions were useful for proletarian
'incorporation' into the system. That resulting high-Victorian
conceit, 'respectability', divided working-class consciousness
against itself.

Third, the stress of Methodism as politically reactionary.
Under the Conference, the circuits adhered to a formal
neutrality, but in practice 'the no-politics rule operated one-
way only' - 'no politics meant no Radical politics'.

Against these criticisms Walsh traced four lines of reply.
First, that it was questionable whether there were enough
Methodists to matter. In 1811 there were about 150,000 of all
sects against a national population of 10 million; by 1851
worshipping Methodists only accounted for about 4 per cent of
the population. Whereas Halévy thought 'it would be difficult
to overestimate the part played by the Wesleyan revival', it
could be that he and others (including Methodists) had
seriously overrated the Methodist presence in national life.

Second, there was a research problem. Walsh pointed out
that much early nineteenth-century evidence stems from
'official, elite sources'. It could be that such sources had
refracted the historians' view of the movement 'on the ground'.
The professional ministry was too small to impose a Conference
absolutism, and its itinerancy suggests a looser grip on
members' hearts and minds than the Bunting-ites would have
cared to admit. Even then, the difference between a minister's
public oration (made perhaps to deflect the disapprobation of a
repressive Establishment) and private admissions (the
republicanism of the prescient Rev. Dr Clarke for example) must
also be borne in mind. The expulsion of radicals from Wesleyan
circuits often meant their subsequent reappearance in other
Methodist offshoots. This leads on to the third line of reply.

The *Primitive* Methodist contribution to working-class
movements was rich and durable. Movements copied its
organisational forms, benefited from the experience of its lay-
government, and absorbed its strictures on dignity, worth and
self-respect. The cadre role of Primitive Methodists in trade
union and Lib-Lab activity is acknowledged, and if 'Methodism'
can be blamed for pre-empting a radical elite it cannot
simultaneously be blamed for making one. Primitive activists
could be seen as re-educators of their class away from anarchic
pre-industrial forms and into disciplined, organised, 'modern'
forms of class struggle.

Lastly, Walsh drew attention to the over-concentration of
research on Methodism as an urban phenomenon, particularly
with reference to Manchester and its hinterland. He thought
this trend was to the detriment of that 'hegemony of Methodist

culture' in rural parts. In Lincolnshire the rural chapel had a
potentially radical dimension as the creator of a social and legal
space for criticism, or shunning, of church and squirearchy.
The debate was opened by Bill Luckin who wondered whether
John Wesley had inherited any of the work of the Anglican
Society for the Reformation of Manners, especially the Society's
work in re-phrasing the notion of manners to mean social
behaviour. Walsh attributed this and other voluntary efforts of
the 1690s to Anglican unease about its established position and
the apparent erosion of church controls. Hugh Cunningham
matched Methodist concern for Sabbath laws with a late-
seventeenth-century concern, and Francoise Decominck
believed Methodism might have 'filled the gap' left by a society
increasingly ineffective by the 1730s. Walsh was not sure about
such detailed connections between church silence and extra
mural revival but commended it as a worthwhile area of
investigation.

Bill Pritchard asked about the chapel and the formation of an
'aristocracy of labour' in the middle of the nineteenth century.
Walsh passed this question to Robert Colls who thought that
traditional Marxist understandings of the aristocracy of labour
were now in disarray and contended that any appreciation of
Methodism which started with 'Its' effect on the people was
misconceived. In an era of explosive growth the starting-point
must be the peoples' effect on 'It'. Here, Walsh drew attention
to the interaction of Methodist and Welsh cultures to produce a
distinctive folk-style of preaching and story-telling.

Colls hoped that the workshop would not build too rigid a
concept of 'cultures', where Methodist, Welsh-folk, industrial,
and pre-industrial 'cultures' were perceived as lumbering
around each other like fully formed cultural blocks. He wanted
to check this conceptalisation for a more immediate approach to
historical choice and experience. Working-class mothers, for
instance, encountered the miscarriage or still-birth of their
children with a frequency difficult for us to appreciate. People
did not go to worship in 'a culture' but rather responded to
catastrophes and crises such as this. It was the interaction of
such responses with the Methodist economy which the historian
had to note. Paul Stigant had found evidence of the deliberate
use of death and fear of death for the 'political' displacement of
working-class energies. Alun Howkins looked to the 1840s and
after. In rural communities Methodist revival tended to break
at times of social crisis, offering a vigorous democratic hope
for those in trouble. He believed that what was being said about
'cultures' was that there were many Methodisms in many places
and times. Walsh agreed. Moreover, he stressed that revivals
must not only be seen in terms of unbottled emotion. A revival
might be an attempt by a single chapel to bring those on its
periphery into its organisation, or to heal schisms within the
existing membership. The 1905 revivals were often the lay
members' way of redressing the power of the ministerial elite.

Thompson's concept of the 'chiliasm of despair', to do with the timing of the revival, he thought not proven one way or the other. David Vincent wanted to correct any over-emphasis on 'hope'. Working-class autobiography also records the Sunday-school inculcation of guilt. Vincent wondered whether social historians could learn from child psychologists about the sorts of tension extremes of guilt and hope, rationality and emotion, might produce. Joyce Marlow objected to any portrayal of Methodism as a cult of death. She queried the feasibility of this in a century of falling death-rates. She was sure that Methodism, above all else, gave working people hope.

Walsh ended provocatively by challenging the received view of John Wesley as a reactionary Tory. He recalled Wesley's aim to reorganise Methodist goods and property on the collective paradigms of Acts II, 44-7. He also teased a 'proletarian chauvinism' out of Wesley's conviction that all great spiritual movement surged from the Poor, but lost their force by the time of their steep upward gravitation to the perches of the Rich. Wesley scorned that theology which referred to amassed wealth as a sign of grace, and drew no distinction between a deserving and undeserving poor. On this high, but unchallenged note, the workshop scraped chairs and went forth to the fresh air beyond the door:

Blest be the dear uniting love
    That will not let us part;
Our bodies may far off remove -
    We still are one in heart.

The debate was disappointing. That is to say, it was better than many in so far as it was *a debate* with threads of continuity and exchange, but in terms of the power of the issues it fell far short. There seems to have been two reasons for this, both easy to behold but both difficult to resolve: one to do with the nature of the 'workshops', and the other more profound reason to do with the History Workshop project generally.

There was insufficient time, too many participants and too uneven a level of information between them. For Walsh, this was a preacher's problem: the problem of pitching the issues in a way that involved most of the congregation for most of the time. Walsh did this admirably. His exposition was lucid, his theory clear-headed, and he spoke in the English language. He took no refuge in the mystifications of casuistry, nor did he resort to the pseudo-precision of a jargon derived from too many books and too many 'points' (why do socialists invariably round-off their 'points' by saying 'and so on, and so on'?) Walsh's theory was embedded in an historical event; his 'hegemony' was in red-brick Lincolnshire chapels, his 'ideology' was in the words and actions of black-coated Lib-Lab preachers, there was an opening-out of historical problems rather than an exegetic consideration of them in the light of an assumed knowledge. Thankfully, the historian's problems were not construed in the precocious vocabulary of 'problematics' and 'double dialectics', or of understanding 'the consciousness of external realities out of individual experiences', or of theorising their mediated experiences by us theorising our experiences in such a way as to help us all understand where we actually stand, basically, in relationship to the mode of production, and so on. . . . Of course, for those who know these songs there was an irreversible tendency in a whole range of workshops to contribute in the style of all good folk-clubs. Four from the floor consecutively stand up to deliver their 'piece'. Each 'piece' connected more by opportunity than debate. At another workshop these contributions reached such a point that one woman who had asked a straight question three pieces before was moved to protest: each must sing her own song – you in your small corner and me in mine.

Where the songs were not known debates could degenerate from the folk-club style (at least collective) into cabarets. Here, either because participant information was low, or was felt to be low against the master at the front, the debate became more a question and answer session. I am all for the power of knowledge but sensed a surprising degree of deference from democrats and Jacobins. The Methodist debate was neither folk-club nor cabaret, but only just. Not that this was anyone's fault. The weekend was packed with crucial themes, participants entered and left workshops as they wished, there was a feeling of informality and fraternity. I like this and understand History Workshop's reasons for doing it, but it may be that the price one pays for celebration is critique. The Thompson thesis on Methodism is at once complicated and shifting. At times it speaks boldly, at other times it is softer and more qualified. Occasionally, the two manners contradict each other. As a unity, it enjoyed an uncomfortable twinning with Halévy's thesis. Walsh probably skirted over the detail of textual criticism and comparison in order to accommodate an audience who were never going to be so intimately involved. This was obviously to the detriment of any serious engagement. If History Workshop wanted critical debate on Methodism it would need to adopt a Methodist discipline: smaller, prepared groups, willing to talk at length, and publish a joint report with room for disagreement, and exact location of where this disagreement lay. This would diminish the celebration – although not necessarily the fraternity – but the debate might mean something. As it is, fairs are pleasurable but chapels might be where things get done.

Walsh was let off lightly. The debate was benignly academic and none of the debaters drove to the heart of the History-Theory. Walsh's apologia has probably received rougher rides at the high table of Jesus College than it did here. The hard problems were not confronted – how does socialist theory approach the deep religious commitments of history? When can

this commitment be called 'ideology' and when 'religion', and
how can it be both? Do socialists who are historians 'first' (in
the morning, behind their desk?) respect Methodist worthies for
their labours in a way in which they do not respect them when
they are historians who are socialists 'first' (in the evening, at
a meeting)? How does one avoid an historical quasi-functionalism
as a part answer to these problems? John Walsh is a Christian.
Presumably he believes in a place for God in history. This must
imply an approach to spiritual experiences quite different from
those who are Marxists. At the same time, Edward Thompson's
bald distinction between spiritual experiences which are
'genuine' and not genuine is, at best, unhelpful. For History
Workshoppers of one strain there is no question that religious
idealism could ever, in an adequate sense, be in Walsh's words,
'a friend to working people'; for History Workshoppers of
another sort the question is open. There is a current of this
beneath the footnotes in the recent argument between Yeo and
Harrison in the *History Workshop Journal*, nos 4-7. The massive
eclecticism of the workshops, drawing as they do on a multitude
of provenances and constituencies tenuously held together as
being in some sense about 'Socialist History' is not in a
position to probe at this level.

History Workshop stands as a forum for those who are, in
the main, academics. It has also assumed the vigour of a
movement - a surrogate politics for those depressed by the
dismal political options of a country which no longer has a
radical movement worthy of the name. As political 'movement'
and academic 'forum', History Workshop exists for 'socialist
historians'. The problem with its debates is that in seeking to
be both, one stance weakens the other. On the one hand the
fraternity of a movement constrains the liberty of critique. On
the other hand the liberty of critique could appear to weaken
the coherence of the movement. The temptation is to call for a
'minimum programme' of shared intellectual positions if
coherence is to be achieved. However, to do this would diminish
the existing forum-aspect and probably drive the Workshop
even deeper into epistemological categories, categories which
already seem to have made the gap between academics and the
working class as wide as it could be. Ironically, such an
attempt to brace History Workshop as a 'movement' might only
serve to reproduce it as a 'forum', a forum less significant,
innovative, participatory and enjoyable than it is now.

On the Saturday morning Ken Worpole quoted Jack Common
to the effect that 'Socialism will not be built book by book. . . .'
Perhaps one difficulty has been that History Workshoppers have
taken the conflation, 'socialist-historians', too literally. There is
an implication here that there is a natural harmony between
socialism and history, that one resolves the other. Now to those
who are socialists (of whatever ilk) and historians, there is
clearly a visceral relationship between both commitments. This is
indisputable. However, for a movement rather than individuals

the conflation is confusing. It divides the identity of History
Workshop between movement and forum, fraternity and critique
- shown in the limpness of some debates; and it beguiles its
power to menace its enemies - they tend to withdraw from its
academic challenge because it is written off as 'ideological' and
tainted.

Moreover, a belief that we as socialist historians are
collectively involved in writing something called 'socialist
history' as opposed to other interpretations of history will only
serve to isolate our position. 'Socialist history' could become
an intellectual assembly point, taking us out of the battle and
disarming our challenge.

No doubt this suggestion will upset those who have a more
immaculate conception of history, but it seems to me that
socialism involves a commitment and participation at quite
another plane, a plane accessible to all men and women and
about moral choices concerning the way in which they live
together. How history addresses this plane will be the ground
on which socialists who are also historians can fight, but the
fight is not alone nor is it the only fight. If this clarification
was made it might be that workshop debates could become less
constrained from within, as a forum, and more combative with
the outside world, as a movement.

NOTE

1 E. Halévy, *A History of the English People in the
   Nineteenth Century*, vol. 1, *England in 1815*, first published
   in French in 1913, in English in 1924.

FURTHER READING

Carwardine, Richard, *Transatlantic revivalism*, Westport, Conn.
   1979.
Colls, Robert, *The colliers' rant*, London 1977.
Everitt, Alan, *The patterns of rural dissent in the nineteenth
   century*, Leicester 1972.
Gilbert, A.D., *Religion and society in industrial England*, London
   1976.
Gowland, A.D., *Methodist secessions: the origins of Free Methodism
   in three Lancashire towns*, Manchester 1979.
Kendall, H.B., *The origins and history of Primitive Methodism*,
   2 vols, London n.d.
Moore, Robert, *Pitmen, preachers and politics*, Cambridge 1974.
Obelkevich, James, *Religion and rural society: south Lindsey
   1825-1875*, Oxford 1976.
Semmel, Bernard, *The Methodist revolution*, New York 1973.
Shaw, Thomas, *A history of Cornish Methodism*, Truro 1962.
Thompson, E.P., *The making of the English working class*, London
   1963, pp. 250-374.

Ward, W.R., *Religion and society in England, 1790-1850*, London 1972.

Warner, W.J., *The Wesleyan movement in the industrial revolution*, London 1930.

Sexual politics

44 THE TROUBLE WITH 'PATRIARCHY'

Sheila Rowbotham*

When contemporary feminists began to examine the world from a new perspective, bringing their own experience to bear on their understanding of history and modern society, they found it was necessary to distinguish women's subordination as a sex from class oppression. Inequality between men and women was not just a creation of capitalism: it was a feature of all societies for which we had reliable evidence. It was a separate phenomenon, which needed to be observed in connection with, rather than simply as a response to, changes that occurred in the organisation and control of production. So the term 'patriarchy' was pressed into service - as an analytical tool which might help to describe this vital distinction.

The term has been used in a great variety of ways. 'Patriarchy' has been discussed as an ideology which arose out of men's power to exchange women between kinship groups; as a symbolic male principle; and as the power of the father (its literal meaning). It has been used to express men's control over women's sexuality and fertility; and to describe the institutional structure of male domination. Recently the phrase 'capitalist patriarchy' has suggested a form peculiar to capitalism. Zilla Eisenstein, who has edited an anthology of writings under that heading, defines patriarchy as providing 'the sexual hierarchical ordering of society for political control'.[1]

There was felt to be a need (not confined to feminists) for a wider understanding of power relationships and hierarchy than was offered by current Marxist ideas. And with that came the realisation that we needed to resist not only the outer folds of power structures but their inner coils. For their hold over our lives through symbol, myth and archetype would not dissolve automatically with the other bondages, even in the fierce heat of revolution. There had to be an inner psychological and spiritual contest, along with the confrontation and transformation of external power.

---

*Sheila Rowbotham, who has been speaking at History Workshops since 1967, is author of *Women, Resistance and Revolution*, Harmondsworth 1974; *Women's Consciousness, Man's World*, Harmondsworth 1973, and (with Lynne Segal and Hilary Wainwright) *Beyond the Fragments*, London 1979. Teaches in adult education and lives in Hackney, East London. An associate editor of *History Workshop Journal*. This article first appeared in *The New Statesman*, December 1979, and is reproduced, like the reply, by permission.

However, the word 'patriarchy' presents problems of its own. It implies a universal and historical form of oppression which returns us to biology - and thus it obscures the need to recognise not only biological differences, but also the multiplicity of ways in which societies have defined gender. By focusing upon the bearing and rearing of children ('patriarchy' = the power of the father) it suggests there is a single determining cause of women's subordination. This either produces a kind of feminist base-superstructure model to contend with the more blinkered versions of Marxism, or it rushes us off on the misty quest for the original moment of male supremacy. Moreover, the world leaves us with two separate systems in which a new male/female split is implied. We have patriarchy oppressing women and capitalism oppressing male workers. We have biological reproduction on the one hand and work on the other. We have the ideology of 'patriarchy' opposed to the mode of production, which is seen as a purely economic matter.

'Patriarchy' implies a structure which is fixed, rather than the kaleidoscope of forms within which women and men have encountered one another. It does not carry any notion of how women might act to transform their situation as a sex. Nor does it even convey a sense of how women have resolutely manoeuvred for a better position within the general context of subordination - by shifting for themselves, turning the tables, ruling the roost, wearing the trousers, hen-pecking, gossiping, hustling, or (in the words of a woman I once overheard) just 'going drip, drip at him'. 'Patriarchy' suggests a fatalistic submission which allows no space for the complexities of women's defiance.
    It is worth remembering every time we use words like 'class' and 'gender' that they are only being labelled as structures for our convenience, because human relationships move with such complexity and speed that our descriptions freeze them at the point of understanding. Nancy Hartstock[2] recalls Marx's insistence that we should regard 'every historically developed social form as in fluid movement'; thus we must take into account its 'transient nature not less than its momentary existence'. Within Marxism there is at least a possibility of a dialectical unity of transience and moment. But it seems to me that the concept of 'patriarchy' offers no such prospect. We have stretched its meaning in umpteen different ways, but there is no transience in it at all. It simply refuses to budge.
    A word which fails to convey movement is not much help when it comes to examining the differences between the subordination of women, and class. The capitalist is defined by his or her ownership of capital. This is not the same kettle of fish at all as a biological male person. Despite the protestations of employers, their activities could be organised quite differently and, in this sense, the working class carries the possibility of doing without

the capitalist and thus of abolishing the hierarchies of class. But a biological male person is a more delicate matter altogether and is not to be abolished (by socialist feminists at least).

It is not sexual difference which is the problem, but the social inequalities of gender – the different kinds of power societies have given to sexual differences, and the hierarchical forms these have imposed on human relationships. Some aspects of male-female relationships are evidently not simply oppressive, but include varying degrees of mutual aid. The concept of 'patriarchy' has no room for such subtleties, however.

Unless we have a sense of these reciprocities and the ways they have changed among different classes, along with the inequalities between men and women, we cannot explain why women have perceived different aspects of their relationship to men to be oppressive at different times. We cannot explain why genuine feelings of love and friendship are possible between men and women, and boys and girls, or why people have acted together in popular movements. In times of revolution (such as the Paris Commune, the early days of Russian communism, or more recent liberation struggles in developing countries), women's public political action has often challenged not only the ruling class, the invader or the coloniser, but also the men's idea of women's role. Less dramatically in everyday life, men's dependence on women in the family, in the community and at work, is as evident as women's subordination – and the two often seem to be inextricably bound together. Some feminists regard this as an elaborate trick, but I think it is precisely within these shifting interstices that women have manoeuvred and resisted. We thus need an approach which can encompass both the conflict and the complementary association between the sexes.

If we could develop an historical concept of sex-gender relationships, this would encompass changing patterns of male control and its congruence or incongruence with various aspects of women's power. It would enable us to delineate the specific shapes of sex-gender relationships within different social relationships, without submerging the experiences of women in those of men, or vice versa. If we stopped viewing patriarchy and capitalism as two separate interlocking systems, and looked instead at how sex-gender as well as class and race relations have developed historically, we could avoid a simple category 'woman' – who must either be a matriarchal stereotype or a hopelessly downtrodden victim, and whose fortunes rise and fall at the same time as all her sisters. We could begin to see women and men born into relationships within families which are not of their making. We could see how their ideas of themselves and other people, their work, habits and sexuality, their participation in organisation, their responses to authority, religion and the state, and the expression of their creativity in art and culture – how all these things are affected by relations in the family as well as by class and race. But sex-gender relationships are clearly not confined to the family (we are not just sex-beings in the family and class-beings in the community, the state and at work): like class relations, they permeate all aspects of life.

Equally, we inherit the historical actions and experience of people in the past through institutions and culture - and the balance of sex-gender relations is as much a part of this inheritance as is class. The changes which men and women make within these prevailing limitations need not be regarded simply as a response to the reorganisation of production, not even as a reflection of class struggle. Indeed, we could see these shifts in sex-gender relationships as *contributing* historically towards the creation of suitable conditions for people to make things differently and perceive the world in new ways.

Rosalind Petchesky has argued that
    if we understand that patriarchal kinship relations are not
    static, but like class relations, are characterised by
    antagonism and struggle, then we begin to speculate that
    women's consciousness and their periodic attempts to resist
    or change the dominant kinship structures will themselves
    affect class relations.[3]
Relations between men and women are also characterised by certain reciprocities, so we cannot assume the antagonism is a constant factor. There are times when class or race solidarity are much stronger than sex-gender conflict and times when relations within the family are a source of mutual resistance to class power. Nonetheless, the approach suggested by Petchesky opens up an exciting way of thinking about women's and men's position in the past, through which we can locate sex-gender relations in the family and see how they are present within all other relationships between men and women in society.

However, we need to be cautious about the assumptions we bring to the past. For instance, women have seen the defining features of oppression very differently at different times. Large numbers of children, for example, could be regarded as a sign of value and status, whereas most Western women now would insist on their right to restrict the numbers of children they have, or to remain childless. Feminist anthropologists are particularly aware of the dangers of imposing the values of Western capitalism on women of other cultures. But we can colonise women in the past, too, by imposing modern values.

We also need to be clear about which groups we are comparing in any given society, and to search for a sense of movement within each period. For instance, the possibilities for women among the richer peasantry in the Middle Ages were clearly quite different from those of poor peasants without land. And presumably these were not the same before and after the Black Death. Change - whether for better or worse - does not necessarily go all one way between the classes, nor even between their various sub-strata, and the same is true of changes which varying modes of production have brought to sex-gender relationships. The growth of domestic industry, for example, is usually associated with the control of the father over the family. But it could also alter the domestic division of labour, because women's particular work skills were vital to the family economy at certain times in the production process. This might have made it easier for women in domestic industry to question sexual hierarchy than for peasant women.

Similarly, nineteenth-century capitalism exploited poor women's labour in the factories, isolated middle-class women in the home, and forced a growing body of impecunious gentlewomen on to the labour market. Yet at the same time it brought working-class women into large-scale popular movements at work and in the community, in the course of which some of them demanded their rights as a sex while resisting class oppression. Out of domestic isolation, the extreme control of middle-class men over their wives and daughters, and the impoverished dependence of unmarried women, came the first movement of feminists.

An historical approach to sex-gender relations could help us to understand why women, radicalised by contemporary feminism, have found the present division of domestic labour and men's continued hold over women's bodies and minds to be particularly oppressive. These were not really the emphases of nineteenth-century feminism. What then are the specific antagonisms we have encountered within sex-gender relationships? And what possibilities do they imply for change?

It has often been said that as women we have come to know that the personal is 'political' because we have been isolated in the personal sphere. I think this is only half the story. We *were* isolated in the personal sphere, but some of us were hurtled dramatically out of it by the expansion of education and the growth of administrative and welfare work, while some (working-class and black women) were never so luxuriously confined. What is more, modern capitalism has created forms of political control and social care, and has produced new technologies and methods of mass communication, which have disturbed and shifted the early nineteenth-century division of private and public spheres. As a result, the direct and immediate forms through which men have controlled women have been *both* reinforced *and* undermined. Kinship relations have increasingly become the province of the state (we have to obey certain rules about the way we arrange our private lives in order to qualify for welfare benefits, for example). Contraceptive technology has enabled women to separate sexual pleasure from procreation. And the scope for sexual objectification has grown apace with the development of the visual media. Men are being sold more strenuously than ever the fantasy of controlling the ultimate feminine, just as their hold

over real women is being resisted. Women are meanwhile being
delivered from the possibility of acting out male-defined fantasy
of ultimate femininity in order to compete with other women for
men. All the oppressive features of male culture have been
thrown into relief and have served to radicalise women: who
does the housework, unequal pay and access to jobs, violence
in the home, rape, the denial of abortion rights, prostitution,
lack of nursery provision, and male-dominated and exclusively
heterosexual attitudes towards sex and love.

This convoluted state of affairs has created a new kind of
political consciousness in socialist feminism. In tussling with the
specifics of sex-gender relations in modern capitalism, feminists
have challenged the way we see our identities and experience
our bodies, the way we organise work and childcare, and the
way we express love and develop thoughts. In other words,
they have challenged the basic components of hierarchy to
create a vision of society in which sexual difference does not
imply subordination and oppression.

Just as the abolition of class power would release people
outside the working class, and thus requires their support and
involvement, so the movement against hierarchy which is carried
in feminism goes beyond the liberation of a sex. It contains the
possibility of equal relations not only between women and men,
but also between men and men, and women and women, and
even between adults and children.

NOTES

1 For critical accounts of how the word 'patriarchy' has been
   used see: Paul Atkinson, 'The problem with patriarchy',
   Achilles' Heel, 2, 1979; Zilla Eisenstein and Heidi Hartman,
   Capitalist Patriarchy and the Case for Socialist Feminism,
   London 1978; Linda Gordon and Allen Hunter, 'Sexual
   Politics and the New Right', *Radical America*, Nov. 1977
   and Feb. 1978; Olivia Harris and Kate Young, 'The Subordination of women in cross-cultural perspective', *Patriarchy Papers*, London 1976: Roisin McDonough and Rachel
   Harrison, 'Patriarchy and relations of production', in *Feminism and Materialism*, ed. A. Kuhn and A.M. Wolpe, London
   1978; Gayle Rubin, 'The traffic in women', in *Towards an
   Anthropology of Women*, ed. Rayna Reiter, London 1975;
   Veronica Beechey, 'On patriarchy', *Feminist Review*, 3,
   1979.
2 See Eisenstein and Hartman, *op. cit.*
3 See *ibid.*

45 IN DEFENCE OF 'PATRIARCHY'

Sally Alexander and Barbara Taylor*

The major problem with the theory of patriarchy, Sheila
Rowbotham claims, is that it ascribes women's subordination and
men's domination to their respective biological roles – a
politically dangerous position which can only lead to a call for
the abolition of all 'biological male persons'. Feminists must
realise, she says, that 'it is not sexual difference which is the
problem, but the social inequalities of gender': it is not men we
want to eliminate, but male power.
    Like Sheila, we are socialist feminists. But we believe that
sexual difference *is* the problem, or at least a fundamental part
of it. Does that mean that we are busy training for a final day
of sexual Armageddon, when all 'biological male persons' will
receive their just deserts (castration or annihilation, as we
choose at the time)? No doubt every woman has had moments
when such a vision seemed attractive, but what we have in mind
is (to use Sheila's words) 'a more delicate matter altogether'.
    Throughout her article Sheila assumes that sexual difference
is a biological given, linked to reproduction. Clearly if it is
defined in this way, it is hard to see how it can be changed.
However, one of the most important breakthroughs in feminist
theory occurred when women began to question this
commonsense definition of sex, pushing past all the old
assumptions about 'natural' womanhood and manhood to examine
how deep the roots of women's oppression really lay. What was
needed then, was a theory of gender itself, a new way of
thinking about reproduction and sexuality. The search drew
some of us towards structural anthropology and psychoanalysis.
From a feminist reading of anthropology we learned that the
social meaning of maleness and femaleness is constructed
through kinship rules which prescribe patterns of sexual

Thanks to Rosalind Delmar for her excellent advice on the first
draft; and to Gareth Stedman Jones, Maureen Mackintosh,
Carole Furnivall and Jane Caplan.

*Sally Alexander is an editor of *History Workshop Journal* and
teaches in adult education. Student at Ruskin College, 1968–70.
Active in the women's movement and Pimlico Labour Party.
Researching on the political economy of women in nineteenth-
and twentieth-century London.

*Barbara Taylor is an editor of *History Workshop Journal*,
completing a book on women in the Owenite movement.

dominance and subordination. From psychoanalysis we learned how these kinship rules become inscribed on the unconscious psyche of the female child via the traumatic re-orientation of sexual desire within the Oedipal phase away from the mother and towards the father ('the law of the father'). The two arguments combined, as in Juliet Mitchell's highly influential *Psychoanalysis and Feminism*, provide a powerful account of the 'generation of a patriarchal system that must by definition oppress women'.

This account remains controversial within the women's movement, but it has greatly expanded our theoretical and political horizons. For if the mechanisms by which women's subordination are reproduced are also those which reproduce family structure and gendered individuals, then a revolution to eliminate such subordination would have to extend very widely indeed. It would need to be, as Juliet says, a 'cultural revolution' which not only eliminated social inequalities based on sexual difference, but transformed the meaning of sexuality itself. We would need to learn new ways of being women and men. It is this project, not the annihilation of 'biological male persons', which the theory of patriarchy points towards.

Constructing a theory of patriarchal relations is hazardous, not least because it analyses gender in terms wholly different from those of class. But without a theory of gender relations, any attempt to 'marry' the concepts of sex and class will simply do for theories of sex what marriage usually does for women: dissolve them into the stronger side of the partnership. It was precisely because a Marxist theory of class conflict, however elaborated, could not answer all our questions about sexual conflict that we tried to develop an alternative. If we need to keep the two areas of analysis apart for a time, so be it. Theories are not made all at once.

However, Sheila's own anxiety about this theoretical dualism conceals a greater anxiety about the whole attempt to construct a theory of sexual antagonism. She seems to view any such theory as an iron grid of abstractions placed over the flow of direct experience; and, as an alternative, she appeals to history to answer questions about female subordination which the 'fixed' and 'rigid' categories of theory cannot answer.

As feminist historians, we share Sheila's desire for more research into women's lives and experience. But this is no substitute for a theory of women's oppression. History only answers questions which are put to it: without a framework for these questions we shall founder in a welter of dissociated and contradictory 'facts'. Nor can women's own testimony about their relations with men be taken as unproblematic. Women have dwelt within their oppression at all times, but it is only occasionally that some have become sharply aware of it. Our analysis of women's consciousness must (as Sheila says) explain the periods of quiescence, as well as the times of anger. Simply recording how women behaved or what they said cannot give us this analysis, any more than recording what workers do gives us a theory of class: it is the underlying reality which must be examined.

Finally, Sheila is unhappy with the concept of patriarchy because it seems to discount all the good things which happen between men and women. She reminds us that women love men, that men need women, and that both sexes often find real support in each other, especially in moments of class confrontation – all true (at least of heterosexual women). But does all this loving and needing and solidarising prove there is no general structure of sexual antagonism, only bad times and good times? Does it mean that loving men is unproblematic for women, something to be gratefully accepted rather than critically investigated? Surely not. Learning to love men sexually is a social process, not a natural one, and in a patriarchal society it involves at least as much pain as joy, as much struggle as mutual support. Again, it is the analysis of kinship rules and unconscious mental life – not the study of biology – which helps us to understand how this channelling of desire towards reproductive heterosexuality occurs, and also what some of its costs have been: not only in terms of the systematic repression of homosexual love and lovers in most cultures, but also in terms of 'normal' feminine sexuality. Did not Freud help us to understand that in learning to love men we learn also to subordinate ourselves to them? The ropes which bind women are the hardest to cut, because they are woven with so many of our own desires.

The concept of patriarchy points to a strategy which will eliminate not men, but masculinity, and transform the whole web of psycho-social relations in which masculinity and femininity are formed. It is a position from which we can begin to reclaim for political change precisely those areas of life which are usually deemed biological or natural. It allows us to confront not only the day-to-day social practices through which men exercise power over women, but also mechanisms through which patterns of authority and submission become part of the sexed personality itself – 'the father in our heads', so to speak. It has helped us to think about sexual division – which cannot be understood simply as a by-product of economic class relations or of biology, but which has an independent dynamic that will only be overcome by an independent feminist politics. Finally, it has allowed us to look past our immediate experiences as women to the processes underlying and shaping that experience. For like class, sexual antagonism is not something which can be understood simply by living it: it needs to be analysed with concepts forged for that purpose. The theories which have developed around 'patriarchy' have been the first systematic attempts to provide them.

FURTHER READING

As our text indicates, we regard Juliet Mitchell's
Psychoanalysis and Feminism, Harmondsworth 1975 – a feminist
reading of Freud – as a fundamental contribution to the issue
of this debate. *Patriarchy Papers*, London 1976, contains some
of the most accessible British contributions to the discussion.
We would also refer readers to 'The unhappy marriage of
Marxism and feminism: Towards a more progressive union', by
Heidi I. Hartman, *Capital and Class*, Summer 1979. As well as
the articles cited by Sheila we would recommend – though they
are not written from our position – Kate Millet, *Sexual Politics*,
London 1980; and Shulamith Firestone, *The Dialectics of Sex*,
London 1979. Firestone gives a biological reading of social-
sexual relations without resorting to a theory of patriarchy.

Culturalism

debates around *The Poverty of Theory*

Raphael Samuel

This debate, which provided a kind of centrepiece for History Workshop 13, has two immediate provocations. First, a critique of British Marxist historiography prepared by a group at the Birmingham Centre for Contemporary Cultural Studies. This was published in mimeographed form in Spring 1979 and a section of it was then reproduced, in printed form, under the title of 'Thompson, Genovese and Socialist Humanist History' under the name of one of the authors, Richard Johnson, in *History Workshop Journal* No. 6 (Autumn 1978). The editors invited replies to Johnson's article which were published in the subsequent issue of the *History Workshop Journal*. Second, there was the publication of Thompson's *Poverty of Theory* in November 1978, a wholesale attack both on French Marxist structuralism and on its various English followers. A third, and longer term basis for the debate was the political and intellectual division in the English New Left which opened up in the mid-1960s, and which can be followed in Thompson's 'Peculiarities of the English' (reprinted as a chapter in *The Poverty of Theory*) and the radical revision of English history by Perry Anderson and Tom Nairn, published in various articles in *New Left Review*, to which it was a riposte. A still earlier division to which reference is made in the texts which follow, was that which helped to splinter the New Left of the early 1960s.

The texts are reprinted here partly for their historical interest to anyone who would like to know more about the development of socialist history and theory, and partly because of the substantive importance of the issues raised, in particular the centrality of the concept of 'experience' in current historical work. But the arguments are not self-sufficient, and the reader who feels him or herself baffled by some of the references, should go back to E.P. Thompson's book, to the exchanges between Richard Johnson and his critics, which appeared in *History Workshop Journal*, issues 6-10, and to Perry Anderson's *Arguments Within English Marxism* (London 1980) which offers both a lucid polemic with *The Poverty of Theory*, and a historical account of the positions taken up against Thompson by the post-1962 editors of *New Left Review*.

One context which cannot be re-created, but which seems relevant to a reading of these texts, is that of the evening itself. Against the intentions of the organisers, it resolved itself into something resembling a gladiatoral combat, and many of the contributions from the floor were concerned to protest at this style of debate. The following is an extract from the report on the Workshop which appeared in *New Society*:

Over the years, there have been some odd venues for workshop discussions, but the oddest of all was the one chosen for the central attempt to grapple with the theory problem on Saturday night.

St Paul's church is a crumbling neo-classical ruin near the Oxford University Press which looks down into the streets of the Jericho district of the town. (This is the part of 'Christminster' where Jude came to life.) For years, St Paul's has been closed, boarded up and overgrown, a shelter to Oxford's dossers. Recently, though, it has been reclaimed and is now being redeveloped as an arts centre.

Earlier on Saturday scarved and gloved historians clustered shivering amid the dust and the peeling paintwork of this cavernous church discussing the work of Sidney and Beatrice Webb. Almost every word spoken was wafted to the ceiling in a blurred echo. 'People must speak more slowly: it will be more democratic,' pleaded one man.

By the evening, things were different. Crammed with an audience of hundreds, the temperature boosted by the biggest blow heater imaginable, with a public address system installed, the conference settled down to its main task. Bright spotlights increased the sense that a theatrical performance was demanded, not a closely-knit discussion. From the chair, Stephen Yeo of the University of Sussex called for a high level of 'cooperative discourse' - a very History Workshop phrase, that. But in the circumstances, such a thing was unimaginable.

The object of the session was to discuss E.P. Thompson's attack on the Althusserian school of history in *The Poverty of Theory*. Stuart Hall (now Professor of Sociology at the Open University) commended Thompson for trouncing the 'thoeretical terrorism' of the 'Althusserian tank' - a pregnant phrase. But, he argued, the decline of theoreticism actually predates *The Poverty of Theory*. The elitism of the endless search for correctness - 'stumbling forward from correctness to correctness' - was already being discredited as 'a deformation of serious marxist work,' Hall said. And he drew attention to weaknesses in Thompson's approach. It was too polemical. It elevated History in a mystical manner. It failed to acknowledge that 'experience' remains a difficult problem in spite of Althusser's 'absurd' dismissal of it. Attacking the dangers of the view that 'in the end history speaks for itself' - a view to which Thompson and the History Workshop fall victim - Hall ended with a plea for 'the necessity of theory to put beside the poverty of theoreticism.'

Stuart Hall is a compelling speaker. Thompson's main antagonist of the evening, Richard Johnson (of the Centre for Contemporary Cultural Studies at Birmingham), is not; his insistence that 'theories and categories express real social problems' - which is the central point in his critique - is more compellingly expressed in his written work.

But Thompson himself *is* a great speaker - or at least a great polemicist. He now proceeded on a demolition job on his critics which caused evident personal pain and discomfort to many of those present. At one point he dismissed the theoreticists for performing 'a psycho-drama within the enclosed ghetto of the theoretical left,' for 'entrapping' generations of socialists into internal disputes, for offering 'ideological justifications of stalinism.' The Althusserians, he said, had captured philosophy, and art criticism, had invaded literary criticism and were now 'massing on the frontiers of history itself.'

All this was delivered with maximum theatrical force. The result was that subsequent discussion was almost impossible. The aftermath of the Saturday night's fusillade hung like a pall of smoke over the rest of the conference.

47 IN DEFENCE OF THEORY

Stuart Hall*

Edward Thompson's *Poverty of Theory* has proved to be a remarkable political and intellectual event. It has dominated intellectual debate on the left for more than a year. Part of its impact is undoubtedly due to Thompson's stature as an historian of the first rank. His *Making of the English Working Class* quickly and justly became a classic, inaugurating a new phase in social history and providing a source of political inspiration well outside the ranks of professional historians (History Workshop, for example, is unthinkable without it). Many of his qualities are to be seen to advantage in the essays reprinted in *The Poverty of Theory* - especially 'The Peculiarities Of The English',

*Stuart Hall, a founder editor of *New Left Review* and for many years director of the Centre for Contemporary Cultural Studies Birmingham, now professor of Sociology at the Open University.

a brilliant sketch of English historical development first published, as a polemic against Perry Anderson, in *The Socialist Register*. But the greater immediate impact must be assigned to the name-essay, 'The Poverty of Theory', which appears here for the first time. It is this essay which students are clutching to their hearts and which has raised the dust in intellectual circles. It develops the attack (first signalled at the end of *Whigs and Hunters*) into a sustained onslaught against Marxist Structuralism in general, and the influence of the dreaded Althusser and British 'Althusserians' in particular. For some time 'Althusserianism' has been the leading tendency within British Marxist theory. Thompson regards it as an idealist deviation, a form of intellectual 'Stalinism', which has exerted a baleful influence on political and theoretical work. 'The Poverty of Theory' is dedicated, not simply to taking this tendency apart, intellectually, but to stopping 'Althusserianism' dead in its tracks. It is this 'taking of positions' within a current theoretical struggle for intellectual hegemony within the British left which has given the book its immediate political resonance - as well as its distinctive whiff of cordite.

In fact, *The Poverty of Theory* appeared when Althusserianism, as a unified theoretical tendency, had already begun to fall apart, and theoreticism already exhausted. Althusser provided his own 'self-criticism'. But, before that, many of those who had been influenced by him had mounted a sustained critique - 'from the inside', so to speak. Others, who regarded his work as important, but always refused to adopt a religious inclination before it, had sustained a critical engagement with many of his positions. More important, the climate of the times has proved increasingly inhospitable to the abstract, theoreticist tenor of his writing. In the face of Thatcherism, monetarism and the ascendancy of the right, many have turned to more concrete, historically informed kinds of analysis - a wholly welcome development. This return to more conjunctural and concrete kinds of writing has, of course, attempted to build on some of the theoretical insights of the preceding phase. One question, indeed, is whether *The Poverty of Theory* doesn't provide a warrant for a sort of mindless 'anti-theory', taking us back behind positions laboriously won in the last few years. However this is assessed, the fact is that, though the book did not inaugurate the retreat from 'theoreticism', it is certainly well placed - and aspires - to provide the *coup de grâce*.

Althusserianism - in the sense of gospel and doctrine - is a vulnerable tendency and Thompson scores a number of palpable hits. The highly formalist, logical and rationalist framework for analysing social formations, embodied in Althusser's theory of 'structuralist causality', concealed an entrenched idealism, which Thompson rightly (but also Hirst, Hindess and indeed Althusser himself, and others, before Thompson) recognised as

a self-generating theoreticist 'machine'. A similar excessive
rationalism (and more than a due measure of intellectual elitism)
disfigured his privileging of 'Big' Theory, with a capital T, as
the only judge and guarantor of Marxist intellectual and
political practice. Especially when Theory only operated at the
most rarefied levels of abstraction, and was represented as
wholly autonomous of other practices. Much of this was
exercised in the context of a series of attacks on various
'theoretical errors' - also graced with grand capitals
(Empiricism, Humanism, Lukácsianism, etc.), and wheeled about
on the theoretical stage like heavy armoury. The conflation of
the (genuine) problem of 'empiricism' with an attack on any and
every piece of empirical, concrete analysis (because it was
Empiricist) was wholly damaging. It led Althusserians of an
orthodox hue into totally absurd positions about the necessarily
empiricist character of all historical writing (coupled with the
equally absurd argument that a theory could be 'correct' even
if all its propositions proved to be empirically unfounded) which
fully deserved Thompson's scorn. It also licensed a species of
intellectual terrorism - in which, despite claims of 'scientific
openness', the theoretical guillotine was wielded to despatch
any concept which had the temerity to stray from its appointed
epistemological path. I know of good graduate students unable
to commit a single sentence to paper for fear of being impaled
on one or other prong of the 'either/or' theoretical scissors.
This was 'vulgar Althusserianism'. It existed: and, while it did,
it did much to disfigure and degrade Marxist intellectual debate.
Its abject and supine dependency on anything, provided it was
written in French, continues: it says much about the low
temperature and failure of nerve of 'English ideas'. Thompson
- social historian and socialist humanist - has been smarting for
long from this irresponsible intellectual vandalism. Here, he
offers the Althusserian *epigoni* their come-uppance.
    Nevertheless, there is a question as to whether this is *all*
that 'the moment of Althusser' represents. Thompson's polemical
caricature of it is an excellent basis for intellectual knock-about.
It is less than adequate, either as an historical analysis of a
complex intellectual phase, or for that definitive 'placing' of it
to which *The Poverty* aspires. I declare a personal interest
here. I regard 'the Althusserian moment' as a highly significant
one. Certain positions - for example, precisely, a certain naive
'humanism' to which I myself subscribed - were subject to a
searching critique. He established the terms of a set of debates
within and about Marxism, some of which are seriously
inadequate or wrong, some of which are absolutely bang on
target. His intervention thus provides one of the terms of
reference - though by no means necessarily the correct
solutions - to what he has, rightly, seen as the 'crisis'/potential
for fruitful development of Marxist theory. The debates do not
have to take his positions: but they must register his
starting-points. 'Contradiction and over-determination' seems to

me, by any standards, a seminal essay in Marxist theory on the critical issue of how to think the problem of determinacy in a non-reductionist way. *Reading Capital* I regarded, from the outset, as deeply flawed by its structuralism, formalism, etc. The influential 'Ideological State Apparatuses' essay says important things, in a murky zone of Marxist theorising: but its functionalism stands out a mile; and its second half is a study in sustained ambiguity. Since I am not religious, I have never regarded 'working through' Althusser as a matter of belief, doubt or 'conversion'. I know that I am not alone in insisting, publicly, on a serious but critical engagement with these positions. Recent essays by my colleague, Richard Johnson, a social historian *formed* by Thompson's work, who has had to take the pressure of some parts of the structuralist critique, have been courageous enough to try to do this 'thinking through' in public in a serious way – and been personally savaged for their pains. I cannot find any trace of recognition of this side of 'Althusserianism' (sic) in Thompson's reductive caricatures.

This brings us to the strengths and limitations of the polemical mode, more generally. Thompson is indeed a master of polemic. But, as a mode, it has distinct weaknesses. In its search for the telling condensation, it woefully simplifies complex positions and arguments. It erects, against the Althusserian galaxy, its own equally composite hate-figures. This is to replace one form of intellectual brutalism with another. It does not provide that delicacy and sense of complexity which serious intellectual matters always require – something which Thompson, writing, say, about intellectual movements in the 1790s, would instantly acknowledge (indeed, polemically insists on). The polemic forces Thompson's hand. He is obliged to overshoot and short-circuit real issues. This leaves us uncertain as to the status of his own discourse. When the polemical dust settles, isn't there, after all, a problem about 'empiricism' – especially the unconscious empiricism of a good deal of English historiography? Aren't there, in Marxism, real difficulties about the relation of 'theory' and 'practice'? Or between the 'logic of argument' and the ' "logic" of history'? Thompson perfectly well knows these questions exist. By failing to do justice to his adversary, Thompson ends up by not doing justice to himself.

For example, polemic has the effect of obscuring certain real underlying convergences with Althusser. Both, after all, are concerned to rebut the real tendencies to reductionism and economism in orthodox Marxism. Both are concerned with the real specificity of different practices. The attempt to recognise this, while also holding to some notion of a 'complex totality', is brought together, by Althusser, under the concept of 'relative autonomy'. Anyone familiar with Thompson's historical work knows that, for him too, 'relative autonomy' is the name of the game – his problematic, to give it the fancy Althusserian title.

They both recognise the importance of Engels's contribution, at
the end of his life, in raising, in his *Letters*, the problem of
'economism' in Marxism. They both acknowledge that, though
Engels correctly put this problem on the agenda, he did not
succeed in offering an adequate theoretical solution. Yet,
because 'relative autonomy' is identified with Althusser's
influence, Thompson is driven by his polemic to play fast and
loose with the concept: now assigning it to some ninth circle of
damned concepts ('a kind of oratorical sauce to season our
researches with'), now offering it a last-minute reprieve ('a
helpful talisman against reductionism'). This produces real
theoretical fluctuations and incoherences in *The Poverty* - not
recouped by such disingenuous concessions in the form of
'Yes, yes, and perhaps all this is so' - which makes a mockery
of serious intellectual argument.

The Poverty of Theory, however, stands or falls, not only on
the brilliance of its polemic, but on the cogency of its theoretical
and political alternatives. On this score, too, there are serious
questions which must be posed, even at the risk of finding
oneself caricatured into place in the direct line of fire.

The Althusserians got themselves into an indefensible
position about History. All the same, there are real problems
with Thompson's defence of that 'dialogue between model and
evidence' which, for him, constitutes the basis of the historical
method. Whence do the 'models' arise? They cannot arise from
the evidence itself, since this is what they are tested against.
Either they are heuristic constructions - like Weber's ideal
types: or the question must be faced as to how concepts are
constructed, and the necessity to any form of theorising,
Thompson's included, of modes of abstraction. And there we
are, once again, with the problem of 'theory' and 'practice'.
Althusser took this too far in his propositions about the
autonomy of 'theoretical practice'. But he wasn't idiotic to
recognise that a problem exists. As Marx himself says, chemists
have reagents and botanists microscopes: the historian of
society has only one 'instrument' - the procedure of abstraction.
Thompson cannot acknowledge this, except half heartedly. To
him, since history presents itself as a complex 'lived' whole,
any conceptualisation of it must be a reduction of the 'evidence'.
But this is tantamount to saying that 'the evidence' speaks its
meaning transitively, without the mediation of concepts: it
provides its own 'models'. Like it or not, this represents,
theoretically, a conflation of 'thought' and 'the real'. It entails
an 'empiricist' theory of knowledge - in the proper, not simply
the 'theoreticist', sense. Thompson does acknowledge that
historical facts cannot speak for themselves. But, elsewhere, he
frequently advances history as its own author: historical
'experience' as the test of its authenticity. He is thus driven to
declare every part of Marx's *Capital* which is not 'historical' as a
form of 'Hegelianism' trapped in the abstractions of logical
deduction. Whatever concessions are made, this in fact dissolves

the real problem of abstraction - and Marx's *Capital* is organised
in terms of a complex set of types of abstraction of a more
'abstract' and more concretely determinate character - in an
empiricist manner.

This problem is compounded, in *The Poverty of Theory*, by
two other related ones: the status of history as such; and the
problem of 'experience'. In *The Poverty* Thompson's History is
counterposed to Althusser's Theory. Thompson speaks of a
unified, 'historical method' which unites all historians: an odd,
'professionalised' construction for a Marxist historian who has
polemicised vigorously against many professional colleagues. His
'History', like Althusser's 'Theory' is erected into an absolute.
He criticises Althusser, correctly, for applying to specific
historical cases an abstract, formal framework based on the
clear separation of their different aspects into 'instances'. Less
convincingly, he says this leads Althusser into ascribing some
practices - for example, the law - simply and unproblematically
to 'the superstructures'. His own work on eighteenth-century
law and crime, he argues, shows that sometimes the law was
'superstructural', securing the dominance of a ruling class;
sometimes directly intricated with the economy: sometimes
'running free' of all determination. Still, Marxists cannot be
satisfied with this positing of an endless series of contingent
'particularities' - even if they also have to be intensely careful
about how cases are generalised from. For then there would be
no 'general theoretical framework' at all, which might provide
insights into the (same or different) position of the law in other
societies or at other conjunctures (for example, today). This
would have the theoretical effect of establishing history as final
arbiter and judge: since only 'History' could say, in any
instance, whether the law was determined, relatively determined,
running free or standing on its head. This certainly saves
history: but it dissolves Marxism into it. This question is quite
inadequately dealt with in Thompson's book.

It is related to the problem about 'experience'. Thompson has
made himself the undisputed master of a history which
recaptures and recovers the lived historical experience of
classes which official History banished from the record. This
work stands as a permanent rebuke to those Althusserians who
read their Master as saying that experience was *purely*
ideological and unconscious and that a truly theoretical history
was one which treated classes as mere 'bearers' of the historical
process, without agency: and historical process itself as a
process 'without a subject'. But, there is no way in which the
category of 'experience' can be an unproblematic one for
Marxism. All experience is penetrated by cultural and ideological
categories. This does not render it 'false consciousness'. But it
must undermine the notion that 'experience' can simply be read
for its meaning, rather than being interrogated for its complex
interweaving of real and ideological elements. Reductive Marxism
treated class consciousness as paradigmatic with the economic

position. It tempted the analyst to 'read off' the former from the latter. The new social history, led by Thompson, has gone very far in correcting against this deformation, restoring the centrality of culture and consciousness to any account of historical transitions. Still, for Marxism, the problem remains: how to combine, in any analysis, the structural and the historical elements of a Marxist explanation. To absorb or elevate structural 'conditions' into the level of 'experience' is to dissolve the dialectic at the heart of the theory. Thompson constantly evokes the classical Marxist dialectic between 'being' and 'consciousness'. But he does, *sometimes* treat the former 'experientially' - reading social formations from the perspective of 'experience'. Whilst militantly refusing any criticism of his work from this viewpoint, he now acknowledges that his category of 'experience' is not an adequate one, precisely because it conflates things which, of course, 'in reality' (lived experience) occur together, but which have, analytically, to be distinguished. His attempt to overcome this by speaking of *two* 'experiences' - experience I (conditions) and experience II (how these are appropriated in consciousness) - is, however, still theoretically quite unsatisfactory. You do not facilitate the difficult process of thinking the relation *between* two terms by naming them with *the same* concept. This simply blurs distinctions which have to be kept conceptually separate.

This is a theoretical argument: but it has quite immediate political consequences. If class consciousness is itself an historical process, and cannot be simply derived from the economic position of class agents (a really non-reductive Marxism), then the whole problem of Marxist politics is caught in the related, but not necessarily corresponding connections between class-in-itself and class-for-itself. To resolve both into the catch-all category of 'experience' is to imply - despite all the complexities of any particular analysis - that 'the class' is always *really* in its place, at the ready, and can be summoned up 'for socialism'. Something very like this is often inscribed in, for example, History Workshop's notion of 'people's history' - as if, simply to tell the story of past oppressions and struggles is to find the promise of socialism already there, fully constituted, only waiting to 'speak out'. It is also, often, implied in Thompson's eloquent invocations of the traditions of the 'free-born Englishmen' and of 'the common people', which live on in popular tradition if only they can be free from their bourgeois constituents. But the whole record of socialism, up to and especially in the present moment, is against this too-simple 'populism'. A non-reductive Marxist theory must entail facing up to all that is involved in saying that socialism has to be constructed by a real political practice, not merely 'rediscovered' in a recuperative historical reflection. The latter can deeply inform, but not replace the former. This may seem a paradoxical point to put to an historical practice which has, correctly, stressed agency and struggle over structure and position. But 'theory', despite its 'poverty', lays funny, unexpected traps for all of us. Somewhere in there is a real difference between the hard road towards the building up, today, of different sites of struggle into a broad popular and democratic movement in the direction of a non-statist socialism; and what I think of as a sometimes too-easy invocation of an existing and unsullied radical 'populism', which can be a heartening thought in dark times, but may not prove to be as available a force, ready and waiting in the wings, as is sometimes supposed.

In general, I think *The Poverty of Theory*, despite its magisterial polemic, its correct engagement with 'vulgar Althusserianism', its socialist passion and the rich historical imagination on which it draws, does, in the end, evade these difficult issues, both of theory *and* politics, today. Humanism and the 'agenda of 1956' requires defence against their idiotic detractors: but they cannot simply be moved back into place. Between them and us, so far as the left is concerned, lies that complex moment of '1968' - a contradictory inheritance which has neither to be simply revived or simply denigrated but reckoned with. It has, after all, inflected every element - popular and socialist - out of which a popular democratic socialist politics has to be constructed today. Thompson's commitment to '1956' and his brutal dismissal of everything that has happened, politically and theoretically since - the 'lumpen-intelligentsia' busy 'doing its own thing' - is a striking blindness in so sophisticated and subtle a historian. The attempt to bury and obliterate, not only the worst excesses of 'vulgar Althusserianism', but also the real theoretical gains made in the interval, arises from the same, over-hasty and ill-tempered reaction. It does not do the current struggle much service. It leaves us with a set of matching sectarianisms - the theoretical absolutism of Althusser's Theory, the implicit absolutism of Thompson's 'Poverty'. Against both, we need Gramsci's 'pessimism of the intellect, optimism of the will' - but Gramsci knew better than to equate 'pessimism' - a realistic appraisal of the real situation before us, using every available intellectual and political resource we could muster - with theoretical impoverishment.

48 AGAINST ABSOLUTISM

Richard Johnson*

I want to argue a case against certain intellectual habits and certain political reflexes which are present in E.P. Thompson's *Poverty of Theory*, but which have a wider currency. I call them 'absolutist'. By this I mean the tendency to construe disagreements as wholesale oppositions: one whole position opposed to another whole position. And more than that: the tendency also to inhabit one side or other of this divide in a spirit of absolute partisanship. We are therefore offered – if we accept these terms of debate – equally absolute choices: follow me or follow her!

To pose this problem is not to reduce all issues to questions of 'style', though we do need to think about the form as well as the content of arguments. It is to pose, rather, questions about politics today: most broadly about the forms and processes of cultural struggle, more specifically about how new political forces are born and how people are 'won' to new positions, deeply moved thither with all the conviction of a patient and hard-learned commitment. More immediately, or at the same time in the self-same process, we have to learn how disagreements can be worked out among those who are, in some essential matters, on the same side.

The more I think about the dominant absolutist style the more the problems multiply. Intellectually it tends to a conservatism. It preserves the dichotomies between which we continue to bounce like some helpless ping-pong ball. All that changes is that we are invited to come down on a different side: the actual field of choices is not transformed. We must choose a sociology of structure or a sociology of struggle, become enmeshed in the machinery of 'function' or minimise conditions in favour of human praxis, construct logical and empty categories or fall back on the familiar method of hypothesis and 'fact'. No-one says 'but that is not quite the choice'. Pedagogically, absolutist modes reduce those not immediately participating to relative passivity. We may cheer the palpable hits, or be rocked in the aisles, or sympathise with participants afterwards, but do we actually *learn* anything? The dynamics of the boxing match, of the competitive spectacle take over. Nor am I sure that absolutism works politically – in fact I am sure it

*Richard Johnson is an historian working at the Centre for Contemporary Cultural Studies, Birmingham. Author (with John Clarke and Charles Chrichter) of *Working Class Culture, Studies in History and Theory*, London 1979.

does not. The stress is on drawing lines, on exclusion/
inclusion, on those who count as friends and allies and those
who don't, on the real historians and the not-historians-at-all
Is this really the best way to woo people to new positions, to
work on the contradictions of their lives? After all if socialist or
feminist positions are so difficult to achieve what chance for
ordinary un-Calvinistic people to move that way?

This argument is readily misunderstood, so it is important to
anticipate some objections. I am not arguing over elementary
political choices, the necessity of taking sides. Taking the
standpoint of the working class, of women and of all oppressed
social groups is the necessary and elementary move that
founds any socialist and feminist politics. The difficult problems,
intellectually, arise thereafter. What does this standpoint imply
for historical work? How far does it in fact provide a talisman
for the adoption of theoretical positions? What does it mean for
the styles of historical work and, a matter too seldom addressed,
the social relations of history production and readership? These
questions are complicated, which is not to say that only
'intellectuals' have the answers. They are complicated, not least,
because the various popular standpoints - on the side of women,
of blacks and of the working class - may involve contradictory
elements, demanding at the very least self-conscious
negotiations. The relation between 'politics' (in the elementary
sense of taking sides) and the precise theoretical position taken
is likewise complex. These questions and many others seem to
me to have *haunted* History Workshop 13, to have hovered
eerily round the rafters and the scaffolding, but never to have
been quite put. Perhaps this is because they are not easily
resolved polemically, or rather *too* easily, superficially and
formally, as in 'Debates'. Perhaps they require a degree of
self-conscious reflection which escapes the more objective
political modes. Certainly it helps to recognise that *none* of us
are immune from the structural determinations of history-
writing, not least from the micro-politics of the practice itself -
the being 'an historian'.

By using the term 'absolutist' I don't mean to dissolve real
differences of thought and politics. There are different ways of
being absolutist in different contexts. Lenin's polemic, for
instance, was thoroughly absolutist. It targeted the theoretical
mountings of the opponents of Bolshevism and pulverised them!
Yet that repertoire of crushing epithets, improvised to meet
the needs of a revolution-in-the-making, has long-since
ossified into slogan-forms and may be successfully parodied in
political cartoons and TV situation comedies (remember *Citizen
Smith,* the Tooting Popular Front and 'Power to the People').
Modern socialism, indeed, requires not only a programme but a
whole new style and vocabulary too.

Of course, we do need *clarity* and accuracy in the analysis
of existing differences. The question is - do we need absolute
partisanship in the inhabiting of them? Are there not

accumulative modes of critique (and even maybe of polemic)
that preserve some useful features of that which is criticised?
And don't we need a much more transformative and synthetic
practice? Isn't Raymond Williams right to say, in his own
criticism of 'young Marxist anti-realists' - 'this culture is rotten
with criticism'? And could we not extend that comment more
broadly? And isn't the fragmentation of theoretical positions
(the multiplicity of Marxisms) a product certainly of underlying
crisis, but also of inherently non-accumulative practices? It
does not help one jot that many positions claim the same
paternity in Marx, except to show perhaps how multi-faceted
that father figure was!

Finally, the criticism of certain styles is not meant to apply
exclusively to Edward Thompson's essay 'The Poverty of
Theory'. Nor is there any attempt here to absolve 'the other
side', or indeed oneself. This way of arguing has been a
general feature of socialist intellectual culture. This style may
persist long after the articulation with authority (in the form of
Stalinism) has been challenged. The form is all too familiar in
the (sometimes well-aimed) 'bourgeois' criticism of 'dogma'. It
is absolutely true (if you'll allow an absolutism) that
'structuralism' was a notable aggressor here. Its form of
absolutism was systematic and 'rigorous' and incorporated a
whole method of critique. This rested on the idea of a
'problematic', the organising concepts of any science or text,
and on the procedure of 'symptomatic reading', reading for
'silences', for what can *not* be spoken within the framework
adopted. This was allied to a very sharp distinction indeed
between 'science' and 'ideology' so that 'problematics' that were
held to be flawed were readily assigned to the ideological
(i.e. false) side. It is important to identify exactly what was
wrong about this mode of critique, and exactly what is worth
preserving from it. We might preserve the notion (not unique
to Althusser) that all intellectual productions have their own
theoretical and epistemological premises. They involve premises
about the nature of knowledge and about the general character
of 'society' or of social relations. In histories these premises
are often deeply implicit. It is useful to dig them out as one
aspect of historical debates. The absolutist excess comes in
when this partial description of how an account is organised
warrants a wholesale dismissal. The account is reduced to some
formal propositions. These are judged not to match up to the
conception of 'science' or of Marxism that informs the position
of the critic. The whole work is consigned to the scrapheap of
ideologies or of superseded problematics. Though the canons of
criticism may be rational enough, there is a radical
simplification built into the procedure which is especially gross
if applied to works of great density of detail - to most histories
in fact. Similarly, it is an accurate point against all formalist
criticism (those that stress the internal properties of a text)
that the historical conditions of intellectual work are neglected.

At its worst the method may produce judgments of astonishing arrogance and naiveté. The historical placing or reading of a text, however, is not necessarily incompatible with the more abstract theoretical approach. Similarly, while critical categories like 'humanism' or 'empiricism' *may* be used unthinkingly as labels they are not necessarily null if the arguments that established them in the first place are re-established in each case. It would be a characteristically absolutist move to ditch what we have learned from Althusserian and other formalisms in the interests of a return to 'history'. The problem here as elsewhere is to take the valuable elements from each tradition in a new and coherent combination which is appropriate to our politics and our times.

The criticism of absolutism, then, was not directed exclusively at *The Poverty of Theory*. But *The Poverty of Theory* is a thoroughly absolutist text. The choices could hardly be starker or presented in a more commanding manner. We are absolutely called upon to choose between the wholly mechanical, wholly irrational, wholly elitist, wholly idealist and wholly Stalinist Althusser and a tradition of historical research which is the true inheritor of historical materialism, without the Althusser-like elements which are present in Marx's *Capital*. Politically, we are asked to return to the themes of 1956, to the libertarian break from the Communist Party and to the pages of the *New Reasoner*. We are urged to carry through 'the agenda of 1956' to the bitter end, eradicating every aspect of 'the Stalinist legacy'.

These arguments are important and have been listened to. They have an immediate relevance today when the critique of what Thompson calls 'Stalinism' is being pushed through to a criticism of Leninist foundations. Similarly, the characterisations of 'Althusserianism' must cause discomfort to anyone who has occupied these modes, however unstereotypically. Yet there is a kind of extremism about the argument which is held to be justified by the creativity of 'polemic'. Post-1956 political forms, for instance, are seen in terms of duplicity (Eurocommunism) or of failure (of 'the alternative, libertarian tradition') or, most commonly in this text, of 'freakishness'. There is a disgust indeed (I do not think the word too strong) for much that demarcates 1968 and 1956, as if the political world turned and Thompson found everything quite changed. Althusserianism produced its own 'progeny' within the 'bourgeois lumpen intelligentsia', a mindless, histrionic and rather repulsive set of folk, unseasoned in a genuine politics, locked up in 'psycho-dramas', reproducing elitist language and attitudes. A kind of cross between hippiedom and the would-be mandarin! (At this point I look nervously over my shoulder and then in the mirror. Who *is* he talking about?) True, there comes a more sober note - 'I may sound more bitter than I am' - but the disgust continues to pop through in the image of '*Capital* navel-scrutiny groups',

in the later parodying of 'brotherly and sisterly' and more
generally in the irrepressible (and profoundly 'psychic')
metaphors. Even if you are carried along by the sheer
virtuosity of expression and by the stabbing good sense of so
much of the argument the exasperated question still escapes:
'Has there been nothing worth retrieving, then, from the
1960s and 1970s?'

Self-criticism is by contrast minimal. There is a section in
The Poverty which flirts jokingly with 'autocritique'. It turns
out to consist mainly of the sharpest rebukes to the left and the
most ringing recalls of 1956. In any case self-criticism has to be
posed from inside the problematic, or from some ally or friend.
It must not be admitted as part of the enemy case. Here again
a characteristic figure: the complete identification of intellectual
with political positions and the assumption, therefore, that
those who disagree are gullible ('taken for a ride') or naive
(lack political experience) or think sloppily (as lumpen
intellectuals are wont to do) or are simply on the other side. It
becomes difficult to argue in the end because each polemical bite
makes a return to the fray too painful to repeat.

It is important to stress all this, to suggest that polemic may
be as unyielding as more abstract and less literary modes. The
appeal for a conduct of struggles that is 'careful and
considerate – and in this sense brotherly and sisterly' is not
just a question of personalities. It is not just an appeal to be
nice. It has its own more general foundations in, to borrow a
term, 'experience'. It depends politically on considerations
which I understand to have been raised by the Women's
Movement, especially the recognition of the difficulty of
speaking, of speaking at all, when speech is a masterly
performance. This one leading insight alone promises a
deepening of democratic practices which can hardly be dismissed
as 'freakish'. From the point of view of the production of
knowledge it depends on the idea that 'problematics' are not
homogeneous but internally complex, contradictory and often
only loosely held together by the speaker. It is therefore
possible to take elements from different positions and combine
them in new ways. The very elements are thus transformed.
This often involves working through dichotomies rather than
assuming them to be necessary. These insights have already
been developed 'theoretically' in different places, notably by
Raymond Williams (a specialist in the transformation of
categories) and, more formally by Ernesto Laclau. At his best,
as in the profound practical transformation of orthodox Marxist
and Lukacsian notions of 'class consciousness', Thompson has
achieved this effect too. But we have scarcely started to think
about the wider political implications of this alternative practice,
especially outside the privileged spaces of small collectives.

But there is a more specifically historical reason for asking
for a transformation of particular polemical modes. It is a pity
that *The Poverty* does not recognise continuities between '1956'

and the new political forms. (Also missing, though I cannot pursue the heresy here, is the *common* ground between two different anti-Stalinisms: the anti-Stalinism of the British break and the anti-Stalinism of, yes, Althusser!) For the old New Left and Campaign for Nuclear Disarmament did prefigure the 'new' politics of the 1960s. The theme of the personal as political is announced on CND portfolios and is then central for movements among students, black people and women. Thompson's own project of bringing 'values' and moral judgments back into Marxism similarly resonates through these decades, which is why, of course, he was read so avidly by lumpen intellectuals in the mid-1960s and continues to be read today. We know what he meant by 'the education of desire'. It is hard to understand (and I mean this candidly not polemically) why these continuities are unrecognised. For we have tried to deepen and extend the original insights: the stress on the experiential, cultural and subjective dimensions of struggles, the re-definition of politics to take in the moral, the everyday and the personal and a heightened concern with political *forms* – organisation, language, political media. Of course, some of us have taken the 'structuralist' detour, Marx's own detour, in fact, through the ensembles of social relations, guided sometimes by Althusser, sometimes by Gramsci. And we think that that, too, has taught us something. It is true that a predominantly 'intellectual' radicalism, whose social base has been mainly college-going, has not found a more 'organic' connection with the popular classes or the Labour Movement, though there have been many relevant practices which *The Poverty of Theory* simply overlooks. But did the old New Left really solve that problem either? It certainly did not refound a popular socialist tradition in the way that was hoped. To that extent it is also implicated in the situation which *The Poverty of Theory* discovers as a feature of a later phase. I do think Thompson exaggerates, then, when he writes 'in the last two decades, a mountain of thought has not yet given birth to one political mouse'.

If we have really lived a progression and not some freakish retrogression, it makes sense to refer, as my original position paper did, to 'an exploration of differences within some broad notion of unity/solidarity'. And I insist once more that it is relevant to examine the relation between two 'moments' in this history which I called 'the Moment of Culture' and 'the Moment of Theory'. The first moment belongs to the period from the mid-1950s to the early 1960s. Politically this includes the break from the Communist Party, the history of the old New Left, the point of exit from the frustrations, contradictions and oppressions of the 1950s, the battle over 'the Bomb', within and outside the Labour Party, and the political experiments around *The New Reasoner*, the early *New Left Review* and, latterly, the *May Day Manifesto*. Intellectually it may variously be described as the birth of 'cultural studies', of 'New Left history'

and of the characteristically 'social' historiographies of this
period. If movements within a Marxist historiography, with
roots in the history of the CP History Group were paradigmatic
of the shifts, similar movements can be discerned outside
history and Marxism - the break with Leavis and with elitist
conceptions of 'culture' in a 'literary sociology', the
rediscovery of 'class' by an empirical social-democratic
sociology and the breaks with positivism and theoretical
functionalism in the new sociologies of the 1960s. The key texts
of this period include *The Making of the English Working Class*,
but also R. Hoggart's *Uses of Literacy* and Raymond Williams's
early work.

I admit that I am interested in all this from a particular
perspective - the founding of our working definitions of culture
and of cultural struggle. The chief features here included an
insistence on the centrality of lived experience whether through
the elaboration of 'culture' (Williams) or through a reworking,
in the light of 'culture' of the older Marxist category of 'class
consciousness' (Thompson). This was associated with a
commitment to concrete studies, usually in the form of histories
whether of social movements (especially of oppressed classes) or
of cultural forms and words. I still believe that this was
associated with a suspicion of theory and of abstraction, of
hard and fast analytical distinctions, of *a prioristic* reasonings,
of 'impositions' on experience. The preferred method itself was
experiential, witness Hoggart's memories, Williams's
autobiographical mode and Thompson's personalised polemic. All
this went in tandem with a popular democratic, anti-elitist and
incipiently anti-Leninist politics whose continuities I have
already noted. I still believe, however, that this was a simple
populism, most effective in its modes of address, but failing in
an analysis of the constituents of the popular, the different
positions and needs of *sections* of the people. This was
associated, I believe, with the overwhelming concern with the
cultural and with conscious active struggle and a neglect of
more structural and especially economic categories such as
might have made the postwar transformations of capitalist
societies and the re-structuring of the working class more
comprehensible. The weight of the stress on 'experience' made
the development of such categories especially difficult.

If I treat this as a predominantly intellectual rather than a
political moment this is because it reaches us mainly in this
form. Its most enduring products were books, not political
forces. *The Making* has endured as a statement long after the
dissipation of the direct political impetus of the old New Left.
We know Thompson as the author of that text rather than as
the Communist militant - though we now know him, too, as the
political writer of Wick Episcopi. Of course political urgency
has, all along, fuelled that articulacy but judged by its political
effects on the terrain of popular movements 'the Moment of
Culture' prefigured rather than solved the problems of the

1970s. The most creative breaks *were* intellectual: the political
implications were, it seems to me, contained. What the traditions
of this period *did* achieve was to help create a broader radical
social stratum but one placed in a not dissimilar dilemma as the
original New Left. The problem has been and remains the
inorganicity (or non-popularity) of new ways of thinking about
society and about history whose political realisation has been
slow and partial. What else underlies the anger and the
frustration of *The Poverty of Theory*, an anger often displaced,
however, with a massive load of 'guilt' onto a later generation?
Again what underlies this contradiction are structural and
historical conditions. We need to understand, in a properly
researched postwar history, why a radicalisation of sections of
intellectuals (from different social origins) has been
accompanied by the erosion of popular socialism, a marked
feature of the history of left parties since the 1940s. The rise of
a right-wing, authoritarian populism which exploits lived
divisions within the working class and divides the popular
classes makes this long-delayed historical analysis all the more
urgent. I doubt if the problematics of culture and of class
consciousness as they were developed in the key texts of the
earlier period are adequate, on their own, to this task.

   This takes us to our second moment, 'the Moment of Theory'.
I understand this as a development of the late 1960s to the
mid-1970s. There is a sense in which we have already passed
through it in its purer forms so that *The Poverty of Theory* is
more important as a recapitulation of past excesses than as a
programmatic statement for today. The political configurations
of this period are still very difficult to discern and the relation
between political and intellectual developments still more opaque.
But the image of diversity and fragmentation seems more
accurate than that of wholesale political nullity, continued
fragmentation along the older lines of parties and organised left
tendencies, the necessary and proper fragmentation of the
political autonomies of black people and of women, the pull
between the more 'academic' sides of movements concerned with
the development of theory and analysis and the popular activist
sides in their more workerist or 'community-based' forms. At the
same time the growth of new political forms has been
accompanied by the crisis of the old, witness the contemporary
history of the Communist Party and the profound crisis of
labourism and the whole social-democratic repertoire. The
period is full of strange and inconsistent encounters if judged
by older political criteria.

   One feature, intellectually, has been the internationalisation
of Marxist debate through agencies like the newer *New Left
Review*. This has transformed the field of debate in Britain
though unevenly between different sectors: massively in
sociology, in philosophy and political economy, minimally in
history. There have been many different strands in the
importations and they have been more or less assimilable to older

British traditions. The least digestible strands have been
various kinds of structuralism. This structuralist presence is
diverse and, by now, thoroughly indigenous. It includes the
attempt of the French communist philosopher Louis Althusser to
synthesise various elements of traditional French philosophy,
structuralist anthropology, and psychoanalysis with a particular
philosophical reading of *Capital*. But it also includes post-
Saussurean linguistics and 'semiology' (the structuralist science
of signs), much formalistic literary and filmic criticism and the
work of the French structuralist historian Michel Foucault.
Again at the cost of overgeneralisation we might list some key
structuralist features. One marked feature has been the
tendency to abstract and formal discussions, especially the
concern with general theoretical or epistemological questions:
the nature of science, or myth, or ideology, or language, or
societies *in general*. (Before we dismiss these preoccupations
as 'historians' we might note that general categories - e.g.
Marx's 'consciousness' or 'labour process' - do have a proper
place in concrete analysis.) A characteristic structuralist
abstraction is that of ideological, symbolic or linguistic systems
which are then understood in terms of their internal logics and
processes. Much structuralist ideology-analysis takes this form:
the concern is with the way in which a given structure of
writing or of discourse 'positions' the reader, or structures its
subjects. The typical empirical moment is, in one sense,
profoundly literary since it hinges on the close analysis of
'texts' of different kinds. Again, the questions are very
important ones: what is at issue is how we are implicated as
'readers' of 'texts' (using reader and text in the widest senses)
and on how this 'reading' forms or does not form human
subjectivities. There is a persistent and unresolved problem in
most structuralist analyses around the relation between practice
and structure, agency and determination, struggle and
conditions, but again, before we dismiss all structuralisms as
mechanical or functionalist, we need to recall that this is an old
problem within Marxism and one which has been a regular
preoccupation within other sociologies. Again, however, the
solutions lie in the direction of combining insights. In particular
we need a way of understanding the subjective moment of
politics which accepts the force of the argument that real
concrete human beings are constructed and fragmented in the
relations in which they are actively implicated and yet may be
involved in conscious and integral struggles to transform them.
Finally, I don't deny that, especially when transported from one
intellectual culture to another, structuralist discourse itself has
often assumed an intellectualistic and non-popular character,
including super-intellectualistic modes of address and writing.
It has contributed to the segregation of intellectual debates
from more popular located and common-sense understandings.
But because it is so centrally concerned with questions of
language, representation and signification, it also promises an

understanding of how such differences arise in the first place. I believe that these understandings will be increasingly important politically as part of an already perceptible drive to study the *relation* between what Gramsci called 'philosophy' and 'common sense' and what we may term, drawing on the two traditions, 'ideology' and 'culture'.

I have tried to argue, then, that in theoretical substance there are complementarities between 'structuralist' and 'culturalist' traditions as well as oppositions. I do not have space here to argue this case fully through just as it proved impossible to do this within the context of the workshop itself. Our subject, anyway, was a more limited one: the significance, intellectual and political, of Thompson's intervention in *The Poverty of Theory*. But I hope it is now clearer *why* 'I see *The Poverty of Theory* as mainly mischievous in its effects.' For it contributes to the preservation of the very oppositions which we have to work through: between theory (understood not as expectation or hypothesis but as developed categories which allow us to grasp the structural features of situations) and history, between history and other disciplines, between structure or determinations and human practice, and between culture and ideology (understood as structured representations not as false consciousness), between Marx as political economist and Marx as 'historian'. I should add perhaps that I do not subsume all of the key questions into the culturalist/ structuralist relation. This is partly because there are shared absences and problems in both traditions. Both are neglectful, for instance, of Marx's analysis of capitalism as a mode of the production of material life. The Marxist-structuralist representation of *Capital* is outrageously simplified and formal, while works like *The Making* and much subsequent social history presuppose an account of the socio-economic dynamics of capitalism rather than contribute to its theoretical clarification and development. The vigorous growth of different schools of Marxist political economy is testimony to this need in a period of the exhaustion of orthodox economics and the evident nullity of capitalist solutions to crisis. In saying this I hope I won't be attacked for returning to an older economic determinism. The problem, once again, is to work at the complementarity and mutual dependence of our different forms of analysis - of the economic, political *and* cultural conditions of a socialist transformation. There is no question, however, of a simple return to Marx. There are whole areas, especially the social sites of new political forms, about which an untransformed Marxism has very little to tell us. The transformative work of the feminist critique in particular has only just begun. It raises questions as important for matters of theoretical and historical substance as for the modes and styles of politics. And even the best work in structuralist theory and culturalist history is far from immune from its impact. If we look at all this, indeed, from the perspective of the practice of history, it is not merely Althusserianism (an early comer) that is 'massing on the borders of history' but a whole host of new perspectives and influences. In the course of these encounters 'a whole tradition of Marxist historical practice' will not simply disappear, since many will continue to appropriate and rework the newer influences from a standpoint within it. It will, however, be subject to similar transformations as those that marked the writing (and the reading) of *The Making of the English Working Class*.

If we hold hard to political essentials, neglect none of our newly won resources and find better ways of conducting our differences what is there to fear in that?

49 THE POLITICS OF THEORY

E.P. Thompson*

I have not contributed a position paper to this book, since *The Poverty of Theory* is that.† And it remains that. I have followed and am following the discussion which is going on, in *History Workshop Journal* and elsewhere, and am learning from it. But I have not changed my positions at any central point. However, the articles of Richard Johnson and Stuart Hall raise points which require a comment.

First, I simply want to place on this table certain refusals. Of which the most substantial is this: I reject without reservation the identification of the Marxist tradition of historiography of which I have been taken as one representative of 'culturalism'. The term is of Richard Johnson's invention. He comes before us, in his article, reproving everyone except himself for 'theoretical absolutism'. This results, he argues, in an inflation of issues, 'a whole massive . . . investment in one particular set of differences.' I am told that my polemic 'hardens up differences . . . reproduces really unhelpful polarities.' Yet it is, of course, the specious opposition between

*E.P. Thompson is author of *The Making of the English Working Class*, London 1963 and, most recently, *Writing by Candlelight*, London 1980. Formerly an editor of *The New Reasoner* and of *New Left Review*. Editorial board member, *Past and Present*.
†This is a corrected and expanded version of an intervention at the History Workshop, 1 December 1979.

his invented category, 'culturalism', and a supposedly authentic
Marxism (which, however, has no representative historical
works which he can point to . . . as yet) which is a theoretical
absolutism, and which does all these things.

This category of culturalism is constructed from some sloppy
and impressionistic history. Examine Johnson's description of
'the Moment of Culture'. 'Roughly mid-1950s - early 1960s.'
'Key texts: Raymond Williams's early work: EPT's *Making*:
Hoggart's *Uses*.' This gives us a mish-mash, a 'culturalist' blur.
What puzzles me is that Richard Johnson, who has worked
across a corridor from Stuart Hall for several years, could read
the history like that. In the mid-1950s Richard Hoggart's
attitude to Marxism was one of explicit hostility, Raymond
Williams's was one of active critique, Stuart Hall's (I would
surmise) was one of sceptical ambivalence, whereas, from
1956 onwards, the *Reasoner* group, with which was associated,
closely or loosely, a number of Marxist historians - among them
John Saville, Dorothy Thompson, myself, Ralph Miliband,
Michael Barratt Brown, Peter Worsley (an anthropologist, but
we will allow him in), Ronald Meek, Royden Harrison, and, less
closely, Christopher Hill and Rodney Hilton, and (as a friendly
but politically distanced critic) Eric Hobsbawm - this group was
attempting to defend, re-examine and extend the Marxist
tradition at a time of political and theoretical disaster.

I am not saying that we were right, and that Hoggart or
Raymond Williams or Stuart Hall were wrong. I am not trying to
fight out old fraternal battles or differences over again. It may
well be that we old Marxists at that time had got into ruts, and
that Hoggart, Williams or Hall, running free on the surrounding
terrain, helped to tow us out. What I am objecting to is this
mish-mash, coming from the Centre for Contemporary Cultural
Studies. After all, not only MI5 keeps files: some of *us* have
files as well. And there were some fierce polemics in those days
- for example, on the question of the Pilkington Report -
which turned precisely on the question of 'cultural studies'.

What I am struggling with is the irony that we Marxists then
were subjected to an unremitting critique from positions of an
explicit and articulated culturalism; yet today some of those
critics have turned full circle, and are accusing us, from
positions which are claimed as authentically Marxist, of those
culturalist sins - that 'Moment of Culture' - which was,
precisely, their own. It is not a question of the theoretical
rights or wrongs of the issues: the critique, then or now, may
have force. It is simply a question of getting the history
straight, which as historians we ought to do.

Let me give one illustration. Richard Johnson tells us that
this 'Moment of Culture' produced powerful paradigms of the
study of the cultural: for example, the 'centrality of lived
experience - culture as a whole way of life.' When Raymond
Williams's *The Long Revolution* came out, Stuart Hall, as
editor of *New Left Review*, commissioned me to write a review

article upon it. After reading the book I asked to be relieved of
the task, since I found my theoretical differences with Williams
to be so sharp that, to express them fully, would endanger the
political relations of the New Left. (I mention this anecdote
because it may illustrate the dangers of theoretical opportunism,
or the covert suppression of differences - without any Stalinist
or Leninist intervention - when one is engaged in an active,
urgent and fraternal common political movement.)

Stuart Hall, who was not then, and who is not now (I think)
a Stalinist, rejected my refusal and encouraged me to write out
my critique fully and without inhibition. My article, which
appeared in two numbers of *New Left Review* (Nos 9 and 10,
May-June and July-August 1961) - in fact in three, since a
page was inadvertently dropped and appeared subsequently on
the line like a single sock (September-October, 1961) - was
precisely a critique of Williams's claims for 'cultural history', as
the history of 'a whole way of life', and a critique in terms of
Marxist categories and the Marxist tradition, which offered the
counter-proposal of 'a whole way of struggle', that is, class
struggle. I argued in this piece:

> Any theory of culture must include the concept of the
> dialectical interaction between culture and something that is
> not culture. We must suppose the raw material of life-
> experience to be at one pole, and all the infinitely-complex
> human disciplines and systems, articulate and inarticulate,
> formalised in institutions or dispersed in the least formal
> ways, which 'handle', transmit, or distort this raw material
> to be at the other. It is the active *process* - which is at the
> same time *the process through which men make their history*
> - that I am insisting upon.

And I argued, explicitly, that we could not grasp the one pole
without the concept of the 'mode of production' nor the other
pole without the concept of 'ideology'. I proposed directly that
there was a theoretical gap, in the formative New Left, between
Williams's 'cultural history' and the Marxist tradition, and
discussed ways in which this might be bridged, or exchanges
between the traditions might be most fruitful.

Any reader going back to that exchange from today's more
theoretically conscious world will find my defence of the
Marxist tradition to be not only lacking in confidence but also
innocent. We Marxist dissidents, in the years 1956 to 1962,
were beset not only by radical inner doubts and self-criticism,
but also by a total climate of scepticism or active resistance to
Marxism in any form. This climate permeated the New Left also,
at its origin, and many comrades then shared the general view
that Marxism, in its association with the Soviet state and with
indefensible communist apologetics, was a liability which should
be dumped, while new theories were improvised from less
contaminated sources. My defence of the Marxist tradition then,
against culturalism, has none of the robust confidence which
characterises 'the Moment of Theory'. When I brought *Capital*

forward to challenge one of Williams's propositions, I felt it
obligatory to cover my quotation with an apology:
> Oh, *that* book! Do we really have to go over all that old
> nineteenth-century stuff again? We have all felt this
> response: Marx has become not only an embarrassment but a
> bore. But *The Long Revolution* has convinced me, finally,
> that go over it again we must.

In the past fifteen years - 'the Moment of Theory' - this
going-over has been done, even to the point of obsession.
There have been some strange reversals of position in the same
period. Williams has submitted some of his own culturalist
positions to a self-critique far more thoroughgoing than any
that I offered in 1961. Williams and, certainly, Stuart Hall have
shown increasing respect and confidence in the notion of a
Marxism as a total and systematic theory, and, to the same
degree, my own confidence in such systematisation has become
less. So . . . let me make clear, once again, what I am arguing
about. I am *not* proposing that, in 1961, I was right and that
Hoggart, Williams or Stuart Hall were then wrong. I admire all
these writers, for many things; the dialogue of the early New
Left was a fruitful one, from which both traditions gained; and
today I am very close indeed to Raymond Williams on critical
points of theory.

My point is that my critique of what Johnson calls culturalism
appeared in 1961: that is, *exactly* when I was in mid-flow in
writing the *Making of the English Working Class*. And that the
Making was written, not only during a period of polemics against
Stalinism and positivist economic history, but also during a
conscious and open-running critique of 'culturalism'. And it is
very easy to establish this point, without resort to nuanced
private histories or files.

What Richard Johnson is not interested in - what scarcely
seems to enter the door of the Birmingham Centre for Cultural
Studies - is any consideration of the *politics* of his 'moments'.
His notion of 'theory' is abstracted from any analysis of the
generative political context, and what he is interested in - and
how could he write this phrase without feeling a chill somewhere
in his epistemological organs? - is 'the production of really
useful knowledge'. Which knowledge, however, must not be
tainted by empiricism, must be at a high level of abstraction,
and must point towards a Utopia when total history will at last
be written. Some rather important 'texts' of that 'Moment of
Culture' are altogether overlooked: Khrushchev's secret speech
(a text which still requires close and symptomatic reading); the
speeches of John Foster Dulles; the crisis of British imperialism
at Suez; the debates at the 8th Plenum of the Polish Communist
Party, the poems of Wazyk, the stories of Tibor Dery, and on
and on.

What brought that jumble-sale of theoretical elements
together in the first New Left was not a moment of culture at all,
but a common sense of political crisis. It was the *politics* of that

moment which directed all of us, from different traditions, to certain common problems, which included those of class, of popular culture and of communications. Examine that moment - situate yourself for a Marxist historical or cultural analysis - and you must commence, not within theory, but within the political world. Marx would have started that way; for what concerned Marx most closely was not 'economics' nor even (dare I say it?) epistemology but *power*. It was to understand *power* in society that he entered that lifelong detour into economic theory.

We thought, in the late 1950s, watching the flames arise above Budapest, the traditional working-class movement erode around us, while nuclear war seemed imminent, that we had to enter different detours in pursuit of the same questions. Social being had made a convulsive and overdue entry upon social consciousness, including Marxist consciousness, and the times set us not only certain questions but indications as to how these must be pursued. This, and not culturalism, proposed the questions addressed in the *Making*. It is altogether right that readers today are dissatisfied with the book, or, if not dissatisfied, are looking for different books. Today is proposing, urgently, different questions.

But what is all this theory, or even 'socialist history', about if it is so ecumenical that power and politics scarcely matter at all? Richard Johnson will not have us inflating differences: our discourse must be 'careful and respectful' and be conducted in a 'sisterly and brotherly way'. It is easy to be respectful, sisterly and brotherly, if one's theory can never do so much as bend a pin in the real political world: if one never has to be called to account for one's theories, since the gap between theory and actuality is so rarely crossed: or if theory is reduced (in part by external determinations, in part by our own inward-turning mentalities) into little more than a psycho-drama within the enclosed ghetto of the theoretical left.

It is, I agree, improper to get heated about Stalinism in an academic seminar. It is certainly wrong for elderly teachers to bully or indoctrinate the young. But is it possible to carry over the proper procedures of academic discussion into the political world just like that? For there *is* another political world, to which *The Poverty of Theory* was addressed. And it is a world which, like it or not, is less than sisterly or brotherly, in which we must acknowledge solidarities, and discriminate between theoretical kin.

I was going to leave it at that. But I have recently received this criticism from many quarters - 'fighting old battles' and the like - and something more must be said. There is, first, the matter of aggression. *The Poverty of Theory* is sometimes presented as an unseemly act of aggression, breaking in upon and disorganising a constructive, 'careful and respectful' discourse of the theoretical left. But, from the position of my tradition, the matter of aggression can be seen very differently.

For a full decade a theoreticist and structuralist campaign had
been directed at our positions, for their supposed 'empiricism',
'humanism', 'moralism', 'historicism', theoretical vacuity, etc.
This campaign had almost overwhelmed the older Marxist
tradition in sociology, rooted itself deeply in the criticisms of
film, art and literature, and was massing on the borders of
history. What seemed to be at risk, then, was not this or that
book of mine or of Genovese's - and I don't at all wish to protect
our work from criticism - but a whole tradition of Marxist
historical practice, which had never been theoretically vacant,
and whose very continuity seemed to be under threat. In this
sense, *The Poverty of Theory* was not an act of aggression but
a counter-attack against a decade of Althusserian dismissal.

Second, I really don't think that Richard Johnson himself
understands the way in which a certain kind of appeal for an
absence of polemic, for 'careful and respectful' discussion in
'brotherly and sisterly' ways, can be a stratagem for doing
two things: first, removing socialist theory from a political to an
academic context and procedure, and, second, pre-empting the
terrain on which alone discussion is permissible. I have shown
that he has removed his supposed 'Moment of Culture' from any
political context, and he also insists that 'the Moment of Theory'
must be removed from context also. To point out, as I have
done, that this Moment originates in the work of Althusser, in a
very particular context of polemic (as well as organisational
measures, expulsions, controls, etc.) within the French
Communist Party against libertarian and humanist critics within
the French Marxist and socialist movement is to introduce
improper (untheoretical) considerations.

But this is pre-emption with a vengeance. It is to say that
discussion must be on the ground which he has indicated and on
no other. It is to say, also, that considerations of ideology,
while no doubt proper when we are examining racism, sexism,
empiricism, humanism and the rest, are quite improper - even
inconceivable - when considering the communist or Marxist
movement, where all arises in a medium of pure theory. Richard
Johnson declares, in his position paper, in his careful and
respectful way, that 'I see *The Poverty of Theory* as mainly
mischievous in its effects.' I have been trying to explain why I
find his new absolutist category of 'culturalism' to be
mischievous also. It is a category which he has shown, not only
into national but also into international discourse, and, if
uncontested, it would lead to serious misrecognitions, and
threaten to close off or eject a large and still-creative tradition
of open-ended Marxist or *marxisant* historical practice. But to
contest that ejection it is not adequate to enter meekly upon the
ground which he has declared to be legitimate, and then argue
respectfully that this or that formulation is incorrect. It is
necessary to refuse his ground and his terms.

In doing this, voices sometimes get raised. And I am chided
for this by Gareth Stedman Jones, a comrade and historian whom

I greatly respect. He says, in *History Workshop Journal* 8,
'Since *Pre-Capitalist Modes of Production* and *The Poverty of
Theory*, the tone of debate has fallen to the worst standards of
the Cold War. . . . We are enjoined to think in manichean
terms'. Now this also seems to me to be pre-emption - again,
perhaps, unconscious - of a different kind. I must remind you
where *The Poverty of Theory* came from. It came from the
socialist and Marxist tradition, in particular from the tradition
of the *Reasoner*. All of the comrades associated with that
tradition lived through the worst years of the ideological Cold
War, and we were at the receiving end of it. When our own
crisis came, in 1956 or thereabouts, not one person in that
tradition of Marxist historiography ran to *Encounter*, lamented
that our God had failed, or called for the wholesale rejection of
the Marxist tradition. Nor did we quit the socialist movement:
there are at least four members of the board of the old *New
Reasoner* (John Saville, Dorothy Thompson, Peter Worsley and
myself) at this workshop today. I mention these points because
I think they argue an entitlement in us - when we confront what
appear to be over-familiar idealist deformations, as well as large
and guilty silences, in what passes as a Marxism - to argue the
points, within the left, sharply and with force. *The Poverty of
Theory* was a political intervention, coming from a socialist
publishing house and addressed to the left.

We cannot discuss Marxist theory today, carefully and
respectfully, while holding the hand over the fact that in huge
territories of the world power is endorsed by a state-orthodoxy
called Marxism, which is profoundly authoritarian and hostile to
libertarian values. Those who ask us not to mention such matters
too loudly, in the name of solidarity on the 'left', are simply
asking to be left in the possession of the field - to define what
the 'left' is - and using solidarity as a gag. They are also
reassuring us, without permitting an inspection, that there
could not possibly be any *theoretical* component in the disasters
of real socialist history.

Now I find this very strange. Because the same theorists are
very sensitive, and sometimes enlightening, in showing us the
way in which capitalist, racist or sexist ideologies reproduce
themselves by theoretical means. But for some reason 'Marxism'
is proclaimed as utterly exempt from similar 'protocols': it is
improper even to suggest that Stalinist ideology, or
authoritarian, elitist, inhumane and philistine attitudes could
reproduce themselves within Marxism by theoretical means. A
very special privilege, an immunity from ideology, is claimed.
Well, I have argued otherwise in *The Poverty of Theory*: I have
argued that 'the Moment of Theory' had ideological origins, that
structuralism has enabled vast areas of guilty silence to be kept
as to Stalinist practice, and I have even argued, more carefully
than some critics suppose, the difference between Stalinism as a
historical eventuation and Stalinism as an existing ideological
tradition. I have been trying to establish libertarian positions,

not just on a basis of moralism or utopian aspiration, but at a
level of theory: and such a splitting-apart of authoritarian and
libertarian elements within a common theoretical tradition cannot
be effected without a polemic which must, on occasion, appear
'manichean'.

I will agree, however, that the indiscriminate hurling around
of accusations of 'Stalinism' is no more helpful to thought or
practice than any other sort of indiscriminate boo word: racism,
empiricism, sexism or humanism. Discrimination is what matters.
What matters is to explore those large and guilty areas of
silence which Althusserianism walled off with its own boo words
and its own specious appeals to a solidarity of the 'left' which
left its practitioners in command of every wall. If Gareth
Stedman Jones means that 'Stalinism' is a term so heavy with
emotion that it cannot be used for discrimination, then - if he
will also agree that the other walls must be pulled down which
have for too long protected that historical and theoretical object
from analysis - I will attend to his objection with care and
respect.

Some more refusals, very much more briefly. They chiefly
concern Stuart Hall's article. What puzzles me about this is that
it carries a whole set of assertions as to my positions which are
not founded upon any careful attention to my text. Of course I
see a problem in empiricism. I certainly do not reject filiations
between law and class rule in the twentieth-century - although
I do not always see these as he does, I have argued the
complexity of these, and I have certainly not argued '*contra* the
left, *tout court*'. I certainly do not reject concepts of structure:
I am at pains to distinguish such valid conceptual and heuristic
organisations from structural*ism*. I am astonished to find that
ideology is an 'absent category' from my work.

I am also astonished to find that I present values and norms
as 'transcendental human values *outside* of real historical
conditions', a point which also appears in Simon Clarke's
generous and historically informed critique 'Abstract and
Ahistorical Moralism', *History Workshop Journal* 8, p. 154.
This seems to me to indicate a serious closure or refusal which
still marks the Marxist tradition. For what I actually say about
this - 'A materialist examination of values must situate itself,
not by idealist propositions, but in the face of culture's material
abode: the people's way of life, and, above all, their productive
and familial relationships' (*Poverty of Theory*, p. 368) - allows
no warrant for this dismissal. This continues to be, as in my
revised *William Morris*, and my ongoing work on eighteenth-
century customs, a central piece of my own historical *and
theoretical* engagement: neither abstract, nor a-historical, nor
transcendental, but contextual and materialist.

I am surprised to find that, in my attempts to define the
historical discipline, with its own logic or discourse of the proof,
I have given the impression that all 'History' is somehow immune
from ideological intrusion and may stand above other disciplines

as a 'judge'. And, finally, I am surprised to find that readers
still think that I have proposed some 'culturalist' theory of
class, in which people float free of economic determinations and
discover themselves in terms of some immaterial consciousness.
(I have written about this, to different effect, repeatedly: most
recently in *Social History*, Vol. 3, no. 2: but see also the
excellent study by R.W. Connell, 'A Critique of the Althusserian
Approach to Class', *Theory and Society*, 8, 1979.)

I am not attempting to refuse all criticism. I am refusing the
category of 'culturalism' (which I see as one more wall of
silence), and inaccurate criticism. As for the general debate in
HWJ I have found much in it that is constructive, and clearly
find many points made by McLelland, Tim Mason, Clarke,
Williams and Stedman Jones to be helpful. The clarification of
concepts in *Capital* and respecting the Marxist notation of the
capitalist mode of production is very certainly helpful; and I
am more than willing to accept (and welcome) correction and
clarification in economy theory, where my work has obvious
weaknesses.

There are still certain difficulties in this exchange. That is,
it is not helpful to criticise me or Genovese for not having
written out different versions of *Capital*, when our objects of
study and our particular skills were not those of Marx! We have
both been working in a Marxist tradition of historiography,
supported by the skills of colleagues in adjacent disciplines, and
chastised or enlightened by their criticism. When writing the
Making, whose central object of study was a moment of class
formation, I compensated for my own weakness in economic
theory by borrowing heavily from that tradition (Marx or Dobb)
or by exchanges with colleagues (John Saville, Hobsbawm and
others). I am sure that weaknesses remain, which merit
criticism. But I am distinctly unhappy – *especially in relation to
Marxist historiography* – at this tendency towards a cult of the
methodological individual, whose themes, objects of study and
characteristic weaknesses (or even strengths) must be
prematurely defined as identifying an absolutist position. It is
not only that this puts upon one individual's work more than it
can bear (unless one is a Marx, which none of us are), thereby
distracting attention from equally significant adjacent work
within a common tradition. It is also that it erects walls *within*
a tradition, which need not be there. In fact, in the British
Marxist tradition of historiography these walls just have not
existed: colleagues of a much harder – even 'economistic' –
emphasis have argued with me, and I have argued back, and we
have both learned from the exchange, just as the very different
traditions of the Society for the Study of Labour History, *Past
and Present*, *Social History*, *New Left Review* and the History
Workshop engage in fruitful exchanges today. If I have resisted
structuralism so vigorously – and refuse with vigour the
attempt to label a whole ongoing tradition of work as 'culturalism'
– it is exactly because we should not allow these absolutist walls

to be built and to interrupt our exchanges.

The other difficulty in the exchange is that some of the contributors, while making valuable criticisms, appear to wish to reconstruct Marxism-as-system (Tim Mason of course is a warm exception) - and sometimes (as Gareth Stedman Jones suggests, *HWJ* 8) a system reconstructed in their own image. This is a difficult distance to argue across, but I hope that we can continue to do so. A characteristic of this notion of Marxism-as-system is an insistent attribution of heuristic priority, not only in an epochal sense, but in every detail of method, to the mode of production: the notion persists that, once this can be really theorised and put together with all the bits (including aesthetics and the common law) in the right places, all problems of explanation are ended; indeed, one might then not have to research history at all, because the theory would anticipate the results. I have explained, and I hope with some care, in *The Poverty of Theory*, why I reject this notion of 'theory' - in explaining everything, in one complex gulp, it leaves the actual history unexplained.

This is not, of course, a question of whether we need *theory* or not. Do I need to say that the title of my book did not invoke the jettisoning of all theory, any more than Marx, in writing *The Poverty of Philosophy*, intended to jettison all philosophy? My critique was of Theory, of the notion that it could all, somehow, be put together, as a system, by theoretical means. In every moment of our work we certainly need theory - whether in defining problems of the mode of production, or micro-economics, or the family, or culture or the state - and we need research which is both empirically and theoretically informed, and the theorised interrogation of what this research finds.

Two self-critical points. The first arises generally, but particularly in Gavin Kitching's position paper. What surprised me in Kitching was his assertion that I collapse exploitation into the *experience* of exploitation, reject material causes going on 'behind the back' of consciousness, suppose consciousness to be in some way 'autonomous' of any material determinations, and suppose that class arises in such ways. This is to repeat a similar line of critique in Johnson's original article.[1] This stands so much against the whole tenor of my work (and that of the older Marxist tradition of historiography) that I must suppose that the reading arises from a lack of clarity in my own definitions.

Some part of the fault lies with my critics. They persistently refuse to examine seriously the discriminations which Raymond Williams and I have made as to determination in its sense of 'setting limits' and 'exerting pressures', and which I have made as to 'junction-concepts'. But the other part may lie in my own use of 'experience'. For experience is exactly what makes the junction between culture and not-culture, lying half within social being, half within social consciousness. We might perhaps call these experience I - lived experience - and II - perceived experience.

Many contemporary epistemologists and sociologists, when they hear the word 'experience', immediately reach for experience II. That is, they move directly to what Marx called social consciousness. They then go on to show that experience II is a very imperfect and falsifying medium, corrupted by ideological intrusions, and so on. They even read us little epistemological lessons, to show that different persons experience the same thing differently, that experience is organised according to presuppositions and within ideologically-formed categories, etc. Which is all so. But this is exactly why I was so heavy about the distinctive discipline, the discourse of the proof, of the historian. Historians within the Marxist tradition - as well as many without - have for so long been using the term 'experience' in a different way that I had come to assume this usage so deeply myself that in *The Poverty of Theory* I did not adequately explain it.

What we see - and study - in our work are repeated events within 'social being' - such events being indeed often consequent upon material causes which go on behind the back of consciousness or intention - which inevitably do and must give rise to lived experience, experience I, which do not instantly break through as 'reflections' into experience II, but whose pressure upon the whole field of consciousness cannot be indefinitely diverted, postponed, falsified or suppressed by ideology. I gestured in *The Poverty of Theory* (pp. 200-1) to the kind of collective experience, within social being, which I mean:

> Experience walks in without knocking at the door, and announces deaths, crises of subsistence, trench warfare, unemployment, inflation, genocide. People starve: their survivors think in new ways about the market. People are imprisoned: in prison they meditate in new ways about the law.

And I argued:

> changes take place within social being, which give rise to changed *experience*: and this experience is *determining*, in the sense that it exerts pressures upon existent social consciousness, proposes new questions, and affords much of the material which the more elaborated intellectual exercises are about.

How else can a materialist explain historical change with any rationality at all? How else, at a time like our own, are we to suppose that there can ever be any human remedy to the hegemonic domination of the mind, the false descriptions of reality reproduced daily by the media? Experience I is in eternal friction with imposed consciousness, and, as it breaks through, we, who fight in all the intricate vocabularies and disciplines of experience II, are given moments of openness and opportunity before the mould of ideology is imposed once more.

The second self-criticism is too complex to work out, except
with pain and at length. I doubt whether I am competent to
attempt it. When he had read *Poverty of Theory* Hans Medick
wrote to me to argue that, when I offered to establish the
objectivity both of the historical discipline and of its object –
the finished historical process, with its pattern of (ultimately
unknowable) causation – I had lurched towards that positivism
which, at other points, I attempt to confront. I had put Popper
out at the front door, and then sneaked him in again at the
back. In short, by placing fact here and value there, I had
opened my argument to serious error.

I sent a grumpy answer to Hans Medick, but on reflection I
think that he is right, or partially right. The fact is – and
David Selborne in his paper makes this point[2] – we are all
making ferocious or lofty epistemological faces, but most of us,
especially in Britain, are the merest novices in philosophy. A
training by way of Althusser (who himself makes gross logical
blunders) or by way of a critique of Althusser is not an
adequate substitute for a more rigorous preparation. In my
present view, the distinction offered in *The Poverty of Theory*
remains valid, in the sense that the historical discipline (its
'discourse of the proof') presupposes that an encounter with
objective evidence is what is at issue: and particular techniques
and a particular disciplinary logic have been devised to that
end. But I concede also that the historian, in every moment of
his or her work, is a value-formed being, who cannot, when
proposing problems or interrogating evidence, in fact operate
in this value-free way. Medick considers that Habermas has
disclosed the nature of this problem and that we should attend
more carefully to his writing. I hope that Medick will write
further and assist us through this difficult point.

Finally, what, oh what, are we to do with our good friend
Philip Corrigan? Does he *know* what he has written? Philip
Corrigan, the enemy of theoretical 'terrorism' – how on earth
did his typewriter encompass that sentence, the most defeatist
and terrorist of all? 'It seems to me time, to be honest, to
recognise that History is a cultural form engaged in practices
of regulation just like Law – it is one of the ways in which the
subordinated are encouraged to agree to their own confinement.'
That *is* what he has written. Not that History can *sometimes* be
that: not that this is an ideological deformation or 'capture' of
History, which may go on, in certain academic circles, or in
school curricula, or even as popular myth. This point should
certainly be taken. But that History is . . . just that. Hindess
and Hirst come back! All is forgiven! No blow you ever struck
was as unkind as this!

No intellectual discipline or art is a cultural form engaged
only in practices of regulation, not even law. As Corrigan, of
course, well knows. History is a form within which we fight,
and many have fought before us. Nor are we alone when we
fight there. For the past is not just dead, inert, confining; it

carries signs and evidences also of creative resources which can
sustain the present and prefigure possibility.

NOTES

1   See Richard Johnson, 'Thompson, Genovese and socialist-
    humanist history', *History Workshop Journal*, 6, Autumn
    1978, and subsequent discussions in issues 7, 8 and 9.
2   See David Selbourne, 'On the methods of the History
    Workshop', *History Workshop Journal*, 8, Spring 1980.

Afterword

Raphael Samuel

History Workshop has existed for some thirteen years as a loose coalition of worker-historians and full-time socialist researchers. It started in 1966, at Ruskin College, Oxford, as an attack on the examination system, and the humiliations which it imposed on adult students. It was an attempt to create, within a very limited compass, an alternative educational practice, to encourage Ruskin students - working men and women, drawn from the labour and trade union movement - to engage in research, and to construct their own history as a way of giving them an independent critical vantage point in their reading. It was our argument that adult students, so far from being educationally underprivileged - the working definition adopted by the College authorities - were peculiarly well-placed to write about many facets of industrial and working-class history.

The Workshop began life as an informal seminar on 'The English Countryside in the 19th Century', and it was nearly closed down, after a few weeks of existence, because of the then Principal's anxiety that the students were listening to each other's talks, instead of to a lecture; he was also dismayed that they were attending to questions remote from the examination syllabus and over the following years the attempt to encourage more research-based methods of work met with bitter, if somewhat uneven, opposition.

A good deal of our early work was clandestine - i.e., discussed in tutorials ostensibly devoted to weekly essays - since at Ruskin then the very activity of primary research was a forbidden luxury, reserved for those who had been given the accolade of a university degree. The 13 Workshop Pamphlets (published between 1970 and 1974) were intended to break new ground in history; but all of them began life as unofficial student projects. In part, at least, they were pedagogical exercises, intended to demystify the processes of research, and to initiate students into the work of writing. All were by first-time historians, some of them plunged into research within weeks of arriving at College. The Workshop's predilection for local and workplace studies may partly be attributed to these straitened circumstances. Projects had to be undertaken in time snatched off, in vacation, from family obligations, or else, during term, filched from tutorial requirements; they had to be sufficiently circumscribed to make completion possible in a relatively short space of time and to allow for research which, for the most part, could only be undertaken in the student's home territory.

The Workshop placed great emphasis from the start on the use of primary sources, but we certainly never believed in

letting 'the facts' speak for themselves and I don't think the
early Workshop participants (among them six members of the
present editorial collective) were under any illusion that they
could do so. The socialism of the Workshop was from the
start quite explicit, and its theoretical perspectives, however
hesitant and ill-formed, certainly shaped the direction of its
work. Within labour history - our main early preoccupation -
the Workshop attempted to inscribe the labour process - the
class struggle 'at the point of production' - at the centre of the
enquiry rather than on the neglected peripheries; and it was no
less determinedly concerned, from the start, with the cultural
dimensions of politics. That is to say, it was an attempt to
challenge the dominant institutional bias which had shaped the
development of labour history in Britain.

So far as history generally was concerned, the Workshop's
enemy was that 'abstracted empiricism' which dominated (and
arguably still dominates) historical teaching and research - i.e.
an academic mode in which the historical subject was subsumed
in the methodological preoccupations of the historian; an
economic history which insisted on the primacy of the statistical,
irrespective of the significance of what was being measured, and
treated every other kind of historical representation as 'literary'
and 'impressionistic'; writing which left no space for political or
moral commitment; research topics which seemed to be
undertaken more for the purpose of 'filling in gaps' than for
their potential contribution to wider historical understanding.
More generally, the Workshop was concerned to create a space
for the discussion of themes which had remained 'hidden from
history' not because there was no documentation available to
study them but because they were at odds with the dominant
modes of historical publication and research.

Politically, the Workshop was shaped by - and to some extent
anticipated - a series of left-wing stirrings, common to Britain
and Europe in the later 1960s, even though it was some time
before they revealed their potential. As a trade union college,
largely recruited from young workers, Ruskin was peculiarly
sensitive to that rise in worker-militancy which in Britain might
be traced back, perhaps, to the time of the seamen's strike in
1966. It was also - for reasons of its own - very responsive to
the student revolt of 1968, and in fact the College was out on
strike some days before the May events in Paris. In other places
these two movements were quite separate: at Ruskin they came
together. Another, slightly later, political influence on the
Workshop was the women's movement. The first women's national
conference was held at Ruskin. It was first mooted by a women's
caucus who had come together at the November 1968 History
Workshop and was originally planned as a Workshop on women's
history.

Workshop meetings in these years were marked by a powerful,
if undenominational, libertarian undercurrent. The Workshop
took its stand, from the start, on the side of self-management.

In the sphere of education it was strongly opposed to the examination system, and it was also, from the circumstances of Ruskin students, many of whom had experienced education as an oppression, a natural ally of children's rights, even if it did not adopt the watchword of de-schooling. In labour history its main focus of attention was on rank and file movements, and the more spontaneous forms of working-class action, such as local insurrections and strikes. Retrospectively the Workshop appears at this time to have been somewhat ahead of events. It was engaged in battle with the College authorities two years before the events of May 1968 made such struggles general. The Workshop on 'Workers' Control in Nineteenth-Century England', a celebration of direct action, and an analysis of its workplace settings was held some four months before the workers' occupation of Upper Clyde Shipbuilders and the tremendous upsurge of trade union protest against the Industrial Relations Bill. *Pit Life in County Durham* - a part-autobiographical, part-historical attempt to explain the roots of miners' militancy - was prepared in the 18 months which preceded the national miners' strike of 1972, and the preface was datelined from the miners' picket at Didcot Power Station. In another sphere Dave Marson's *Children's Strikes of 1911* was published in the very month when thousands of working-class children took to the London streets to march against their schooling.

The Workshop's central early preoccupation with movements of popular resistance is clearly related to these political events; though it may be that our historical studies in some sense prepared us to anticipate them, and to welcome them when they came. Later, perhaps because of the Workshop's growing - if tense - association with the women's movement, there was a shift in research attention from the reservoirs of revolt to the structures of social dominance, and a new attention to the role of ideology. The first Workshop which was held under feminist influence - 'Childhood in History' - was a fairly simple extension of Workshop researches into modes of popular resistance, but the later ones - notably that on 'Family, Work and Home' - entered the more difficult terrain represented by Anna Davin's 'Imperialism and Motherhood' (*History Workshop Journal* 5) and Tim Mason's 'Women in Nazi Germany' (*Journal 1* and *2*), two of the papers which were produced for it. We did not, however, abandon one theme for another, but tried, rather, to inform our work with a sense of both, as in Dave Marson's *Children's Strikes in 1911* which focuses both on the exuberance of the children's action, and on the strike-breaking role of mothers, a clash which in his stage play about the strike (*Fall in and Follow Me*, *History Workshop Pamphlet* no 13) he makes the dialectical pivot of the drama; or in Frank McKenna's 'Victorian Railwaymen' (*History Workshop Journal 1*), a late product of the 1970 Workshop - which is a study both of the railwaymen's nineteenth-century servitude, and of their eventual revolt against it.

The central place which History Workshop has often given to 'real life experience', both as a subject for historical inquiry, and as a litmus to test the abstract against the particular, may conjecturally be ascribed to a succession of different influences. In part it comes from our original constituency of mainly worker-writers, and the high claims we were making for historical work to which the writer was bringing the fruits not only of research, but also of personal life history. Then, from a very different source, there was the then radicalising influence of the micro-sociology popularised in the middle 1960s by the early 'deviancy' theorists, with their emphasis on informal modes of resistance in such captive institutions as prisons. A more substantial influence at this time, was that of social and cultural anthropology, with its method of participant observation, it local and familial focus, and its attempt to give a theoretical and cultural dimension to the transactions of everyday life. The rise of the women's movement, and of what Sheila Rowbotham, in a seminal pamphlet, published in 1969, called *Women's Liberation and the New Politics* - a politics based on 'consciousness raising' and personal liberation as well as (in Britain) socialist commitment - powerfully reinforced these tendencies and invested them with political urgency. Finally and perhaps more recently, one might instance a radical dissatisfaction with the existing Marxist discussion of ideology and consciousness.

The Workshop could now perhaps be seen as being associated with, and to some extent anticipating, a whole series of democratic stirrings on the extra-curricular edges of higher education and research. One might instance, in historical work, the post-war renaissance of English local history, much of it in the hands of enthusiasts and part-timers; the rapid growth in the 1960s of industrial archaeology, and the enthusiasm, a little later, for the retrieval and publication of old photographs; the founding in 1971 of the Oral History society in which the Workshop has always played a part. More generally one might point to the folk-song revival of the 1950s and 1960s, with its emphasis on industrial folk-song, and the recovery of lost tradition. It is easy to sneer at such manifestations as 'populist'; but cumulatively they may be said to represent a sense of cultural loss which in recent years in Britain has been a major response to the fruits of post-war social change; a socialist politics which merely ignores this as 'backward-looking' does so at its peril, as one can see, in recent years, from the appeal of such protofascist movements as the National Front.

Marxist theory was not one of the original preoccupations of the Workshop, however much it may have entered the political and intellectual formation of workshop participants. But Marxist categories certainly provided us with our basic starting point, above all in the centrality we gave to class struggle, while more generally one might say that Marxism, like a commitment to the labour movement generally, was one of the common bonds between us. Although we did not problematise Marxism - in 1966 there was rather little explicit Marxism in this country - I think that what we were attempting to do, like others, was to re-establish contact between Marxist thought and the reality it purported to address. Like other Marxist historians at this time, we had tacitly abandoned focus on overall 'laws of development', and instead of taking the whole of human history for our province, confined ourselves to a relatively limited terrain - that of nineteenth- and twentieth-century capitalism. Even within this limited compass, we were anxious to situate our enquiries in as local a setting as possible. We remained, however, militant materialists. We stuck rather closely to industrial and economic questions, and a great deal of our effort went to anchoring labour history in production - both the material conditions of production in the workplace, and the social relations through which it was organised.

The relationship of the Workshop to the universities is complex. We grew up in the shadow of respected seniors - Hill, Hobsbawm and Thompson in particular - who by the mid-1960s were firmly implanted in British academic life, while in a more general way, the Workshop owed (and owes) a certain allegiance to *Past and Present*, a journal which began life in 1952 as a Marxist and neo-Marxist publication, and won its place as a centre of high scholarship. 'Back to the sources' - one of the Workshop's early watchwords, and the very centre of its early practice - was not one likely to alienate us from research historians, and indeed we leaned heavily on them in the struggle for survival at Ruskin: Christopher Hill and Joan Thirsk were among those who chaired the sessions at early Workshops, Thompson and Hobsbawm were among the early speakers. In Oxford, the Workshop ran in tandem with a weekly social history group of (syndicalist and Marxist hue) at St Antony's College, and the workshops themselves attracted a wide attendance from young, dissatisfied researchers in other parts. In short, the Workshop's association with the academy, though oppositional, was quite close.

At the same time, the Workshop did mark a break from more orthodox modes of historiography in a number of clearly defined ways. In the first place, the workshops themselves, the main forum at which our work was presented, were a deliberate attempt to escape from the conventions and the coldness of the research seminar. That is why they were called workshops.*

---

*The name was adapted from Ewan MacColl and Joan Littlewood's experimental 'Theatre Workshop' of the 1940s and 1950s. So far as I know, nobody else in Britain was using the term when we adopted it. Within three years, with the rise of the Women's Liberation Workshops, it became quite general and since then has been used as a kind of token for meetings which break down the barrier between speaker and audience. The point of this note is not to claim paternity, but to draw attention to a minor curiosity of contemporary history which is of some importance in the organisation of socialist cultural life.

They drew their attendance from far outside the walls of the
university and set up discussion in crowded smoke-filled halls.
The crowding and physical discomfort certainly helped to
generate a degree of informality, while the impromptu living
conditions (people who come to workshops often have to sleep
on floors) imparted a sense of urgency to the proceedings.
Folksong - an early component of the workshops - helped to
raise the emotional temperature, and the early workshops also
engaged in a species of action research e.g. a walk round
Jude's Oxford (after Thomas Hardy's tragic autodidact, *Jude
the Obscure*) in the case of the workshop on 'proletarian
Oxfordshire'.

In the second place, the workshop stood for the
democratisation of historical practice. We tried to avoid
sectarian academic controversy. We also attempted, from the
start, to enlarge the constituency of historical writers and
researchers, to demonstrate in practice that the career
historian had no monopoly of writing and research. Many of the
most effective workshop presentations have come from first-time
historians, sharing the platform with more experienced
researchers. All of our pamphlets came from that source.
Worker-writers have been less in evidence in the pages of
History Workshop Journal, but we have continued to draw
largely on the work of first-time historians and of those who
have received their formation outside the history schools. Our
point of address has remained consistently extra-mural - i.e.
never taking a particular set of references for granted,
explaining our terms, and attempting to create more open and
accessible forms of historical dialogue. This central democratic
thrust was directed, in the early days of the workshop,
primarily against the dominant bourgeois mode of historiography;
but it has gained additional if unexpected relevance in recent
years from the appearance in Britain of a university-based
Marxism which makes little attempt to translate its work into a
language which might be accessible to a larger socialist public,
and which seems at times positively to rejoice in the
incommunicability of its concepts, and the opacity of its prose.

Third, and in opposition to the whole tradition of historical
neutrality and 'value free' social science, the workshop has
asserted that truth was partisan. So far from attempting to
bury our beliefs, or to claim that they did not exist, we have
preferred openly to proclaim them, and to link our work,
wherever that was possible, to the labour movement, to
feminism and to fraternal socialist groups. The workshop, in
short, inhabits a political as well as a historiographical
territory, and, although it is certainly not one which we
attempt to impose on our readers, it is a principal source of the
workshop's energy and strength. History workshops are highly
political occasions. Those who come to them are often restless
and dissatisfied, impatient of anything resembling authority,

whether on the part of the speakers, the organisers or the
chair. The atmosphere was and is sometimes electric, but when
tempers flare (as they sometimes do in the closing session) it is
more likely to be for reasons of political disagreement than on
grounds of academic pique.

Finally History Workshop has tried to make historians more
present-minded and to revise the notion of the historical in such
a way that it can comprise the perception of contemporary
realities. The Workshop - more perhaps by its meetings than by
its publications - has implicitly challenged that Chinese wall
between past and present which is one of the chief legacies of
the Rankean revolution in historical scholarship, and which has
been powerfully re-inforced, in more recent times, by the
widespread rejection of evolutionary explanations of change.
This division, in our view, impoverishes the study of the past
as well as limiting the critical understanding of the present. It
encourages historians to exaggerate the importance of their
findings and to put forward interpretations which would never
pass muster if they had been tested for their explanatory force
outside a chosen period. It also effectively insulates historians
from those wider questions of social and ideological formation
which a more comparative view - or indeed common observation
and experience - might suggest. It deprives them, in brief, of
the precious advantage of hindsight. History Workshop has
often tried to make its starting point the present, adopting that
'regressive' method of enquiry - working backwards from the
known to the unknown - which Marc Bloch recommended to
historians many years ago, but which it seems they have been
frightened of following lest they find themselves in alien
territory. We have drawn extensively on the living memory of
the past as a way of interpreting its documentary remains; and
we have also tried more tentatively (as in History Workshop 12,
'In Our Time') to historicise understanding of the present.
Within its own limited field, History Workshop 13 could be seen
as a kindred endeavour - an attempt to make socialist historians
more aware of their own historicity, to see the ways in which
their own working practice is existentially limited and defined,
and to follow the invisible lines which connect their themes
to the work of their predecessors.

The Workshopp has outlived the original circumstances of its
formation, and now has to make its way in a colder political
climate. The *Journal* was founded in 1975 at a time of retreat in
the labour movement, of cuts in education and library provision
and at a time, when - as it now appears - many younger
Marxists were beginning to turn in on themselves and to engage
in increasingly esoteric discussion. The *Journal* resisted these
tendencies. It maintained a hopeful stance where others were
retreating into pessimism or abstraction. We did not see the
academic and the non-academic, the Marxist and the non-Marxist,
the scholarly and the political as being alternatives. Our
socialism, though by British standards extreme, is also

determinedly non-sectarian and we don't see a strong politics as being compatible with painstaking archive work. Starting the journal made us much more aware of the long tradition and exceptional strength of socialist historical work in Britain. It has also brought us into contact with our comrades and fellow workers in Europe. Paradoxically in a period of retreat by the left, the constituency of socialist historians seems to be growing.

If, from a socialist point of view, the main danger facing Marxist historical work in the 1960s was that it would become 'fat' and 'Norman' - i.e., comfortably incorporated into academic routines - today it is possibly that of fragmentation into entirely separate discourses. History Workshop 13 was an attempt to bring some of the different kinds of work into dialogue with each other. But there is a clear need for more frequent, and more informal modes of exchange. For this reason we are setting up a Federation of History Workshops to offer support to the part-time or isolated historian, and to encourage the formation of smaller working groups.